The Politics of Energy

The Politics of Energy:
The Development and Implementation
of the NEP

G. Bruce Doern
Glen Toner

⋔ METHUEN

Toronto   New York   London   Sydney   Auckland

Copyright © 1985 by Methuen Publications
(A division of The Carswell Company Limited)

Canadian Cataloguing in Publication Data

Doern, G. Bruce, 1942–
  The politics of energy

Bibliography: p.
Includes index.
ISBN 0-458-98920-7

1. Energy policy - Canada. 2. Gas industry -
Canada. 3. Petroleum industry and trade - Canada.
4. National Energy Program (Canada). I. Toner,
Glen B. II. Title.

HD9502.C32D63 1984   333.79'0971   C84-099466-4

Excerpts and tables from *Proceedings on the National Energy Program* and *Policy and Expenditure Management System: Envelope Procedures and Rules* reproduced by permission of the Minister of Supply and Services Canada.

Excerpt from *Pipeline* by W. Kilbourn © 1970 by Clarke, Irwin & Company Limited. Used by permission of Irwin Publishing Inc.

Excerpts from *Fuels and the National Policy* by John N. McDougall reproduced by permission of Butterworth and Co. (Canada) Ltd. Copyright © 1982.

Excerpts from *Discipline of Power* by Jeffrey Simpson (Toronto: Personal Library, 1980) reprinted by permission of Macmillan of Canada, A Division of Gage Publishing Ltd.

Cover design: Don Fernley

Printed and bound in Canada

1 2 3 4   85   89 88 87 86

CONTENTS

CONTENTS IN DETAIL

PREFACE

The focus of this book is on federal energy politics and policy in the oil and gas sector. Intergovernmental issues are examined in detail, but we do not examine the intraprovincial politics and the development of provincial policy except to the extent that they impinge on the larger issues examined. We have built our analysis partly on the work of others, but have been motivated strongly by the need to provide an integrative and historical look at energy politics in the oil and gas sector, which no existing book fully provides. We think Canadian energy policy makers, the energy industry, and other interested Canadians can learn more about themselves through the kind of approach used in this book.

For the academic reader, we have tried to provide an analysis that more explicitly bridges the study of Canadian politics and the study of public policy. Within the study of public policy per se we sought to do what few books do, namely, analyse the development and the implementation of policy over a significant period of time, from 1973 to 1984, including the National Energy Program itself, arguably one of the most significant and controversial policies ever adopted in Canada.

The analysis is based not only on the published sources that are cited, but also on an extensive review of speeches, unpublished government and industry reports and documents, as well as over 300 interviews conducted over the past four years. These interviews were conducted on a not-for-individual-attribution basis with senior officials and experts in all the relevant sectors: business (both the oil and gas and related financial and investment sectors), government (federal, provincial and territorial, U.S. and international agencies) and political parties (ministers, opposition critics, and key political advisors).

An analytical enterprise such as this produces many debts of gratitude and appreciation. These include the many persons interviewed who kindly gave us their time, several on more than one occasion. Several persons read all or parts of the manuscript, and improved it greatly through their comments and insights. These included Mike Whittington, Glen Williams, Allan Maslove, Bill Stevenson, John McDougall, Ian Smythe, François Bregha, Peter Eglington, Ken Norrie, Bertrand Paquet, and Vic Humphries. Other officials who read the manuscript remain anonymous at their own request; we thank them as well. The work also profited greatly from the discussions held over the past four years with graduate students at the School of Public Administration at Carleton University. A special debt is owed to our research assistants during this period, Ian Curry, Micheline McKay, Ben Cornick, Richard Gresser, Mike Kilpatrick and Courtney Tower. Special thanks are also owed to Jim Desveaux at the University of California at Berkeley, who was concurrently conducting research on the Department of Energy, Mines and Resources as an organization and who shared his insights with us. Though all of these persons have improved the final product, we alone are responsible for any remaining weaknesses or errors in the book.

The preparation and editing of the manuscript through the magic of word processors depended on the cheerful professionalism and cooperation of Jane Tallim, Bev Riley, Vi Tansley, and Margaret Johnston at the School of Public Administration at Carleton University.

We also gratefully acknowledge the research grant support that the authors received from the Humanities and Social Sciences Research Council of Canada, Imperial Oil Limited, and the Department of Energy, Mines and Resources, as well as the research cooperation provided by the Economic Council of Canada, which was concurrently carrying out a study on energy policy.

Bruce Doern
Glen Toner
Ottawa, October 1984

INTRODUCTION

This book critically examines the National Energy Program (NEP) and the politics of energy in Canada by focussing on the period from 1973 to 1984. It presents a systematic examination of the links between politics and public policy in Canada's oil and gas industry over the entire post-World War II period. Such a historical perspective is vital if one hopes to assess the NEP in a meaningful way.

Three overall themes pervade our analysis. First, we argue that the NEP, along with other events and decisions, has resulted, in the period since the early 1970s, in a greater balance of power among the key public and private interests involved in energy decisions. We raise questions about whether the new balance in evidence in the early 1980s can be sustained over the foreseeable future across all its dimensions. Second, we show that the NEP, though clearly a major policy initiative of historic importance, is not a radical policy when looked at in relation to either its objectives or its effects. Third, and more specifically, we give the NEP itself a mixed report card. It is neither as bad a policy as its critics believe, nor as good as its main political and bureaucratic sponsors say it is. There are some successes, some failures, and some areas of the policy where one cannot gauge effects in the short term, or perhaps at all. We are interested in the NEP as both a political phenomenon and as a public policy, and the analytical journey on which we take the reader is intended to deal with both these dimensions.

The book is organized into five parts. Part I presents an analytical approach and analyses in detail the origins of the NEP decision itself. Part II provides an overall historical account, and then re-examines key pre-NEP events with a detailed focus on energy politics per se. There is some necessary repetition in our account of these events in this section, because the government–industry and intergovernmental relationships of power are the dual focus of concern. Part III examines the same relationships of power in the post-NEP period from 1980 to 1984. In Part IV, energy policy and the implementation of the NEP are the focus. This is, however, not a realm where politics cease to exist. If anything, they intensify. Finally, in Part V we offer our concluding observations on energy politics and on the NEP as a policy initiative.

The Politics of Energy

PART I

THE FORGING
OF THE NEP

CHAPTER 1

ENERGY POLITICS AND THE NEP

The Trudeau government's 1980 National Energy Program (NEP) was first and foremost a political act intended simultaneously to change the structure of power between Ottawa and the provinces and between Ottawa and the oil industry. Like most significant national political decisions, it did not result in nor was it primarily intended to produce good economics. Economic issues were a part of the policy concern; but the nature of politics more often than not is that it must embrace a range of ideas beyond those of economic efficiency alone, particularly since even efficiency can be judged in either a short- or long-term time frame. Thus, to analyze the NEP only as economic policy is fundamentally to misunderstand its origins and nature.

This reality is evident when one recognizes the complexity of the issues facing those who govern Canada. By the time the NEP occupied centre stage in the fall of 1980, energy issues had long since ceased to be a matter of pure energy policy. They had acquired much of the political baggage inherent in Canadian politics. Energy policy was a summation of the Canadian body politic, embracing issues of nationalism, regionalism, foreign ownership of the economy, partisan conflict, theories and beliefs about Canada's resource heritage, bureaucratic growth and state intervention, and the realities of international dependence and Canada–United States relations.

The NEP and energy politics belie the myth of dull, gray, pragmatic Canadian politics. In energy politics, ideas are central and personalities, egos and reputations are rampant. Powerful governmental and private sector interests marshal the full range of political weapons, including ploy and counterploy, threats and olive branches, as well as periodic mixtures of sweet reason and harmonious agreement in pursuit of their material and other objectives.

Few issues, including constitutional reform and Québec, have stimulated and maintained as high a level of political controversy in Canada throughout the 1970s and 1980s as energy issues have. Indeed, energy-related events have been among the most important issues on the global stage since 1973. In part, this is because energy, unlike other internationally traded commodities, "is an essential element of economic development and social progress in all countries. Without adequate, secure supplies of energy the objectives of economic and social development are unlikely to be met, thus straining the political cohesiveness of our societies."[1] Clearly, Canada has not escaped the impact of dramatically higher oil prices and uncertain supplies. Canadians live in an intemperate climate, are separated by vast distances, and consequently require and use a lot of energy—more per capita, in fact, than any other nation in the world. It is not surprising, then, that the politics of energy, perhaps more than any other aspect of Canadian politics, expose the potentially conflicting constitutional, regional, partisan, intergovernmental, and government–industry relationships of power that underlie Canadian political and economic life.

Since the 1973 OPEC-induced energy crisis and the high-profile confrontation which followed in its wake, energy politics in Canada have been marked by conflict and controversy. In fact, Canada is unique among its western allies in the degree to which its governments and regions epitomize, within one country, the interests that, on the global stage, divide energy consumer and producer nations. October 1980 signalled a major escalation in this conflict, with the introduction of what has been referred to as a "radical" federal initiative, the National Energy Program. It must be stressed, however, that the conflict surrounding the 1980 Liberal budget and energy program was not new. Rather, it was a legacy of many years of confrontation over energy issues. Conflicts over specific energy policies, which each level of government has pursued since 1973, and generally conflicting objectives with respect to energy pricing, revenue sharing and resource management have at times provoked acrimonious confrontation, and indeed threatened the very foundation of Confederation. Moreover, it is not inconceivable that energy issues could become even more important in the last half of the 1980s, as energy developments move even closer to the heart of national and regional economic and political development in Canada.

Goals of the NEP
The official goals of the NEP announced on October 28, 1980 were:

To establish the basis for Canadians to seize control of their own energy future through *security* of supply and ultimate independence from the world market;

To offer to Canadians, all Canadians, the real *opportunity* to participate in the energy industry in general and the petroleum industry in particular, and

To share in the benefits of industry expansion; to establish a petroleum pricing and revenue-sharing regime that recognizes the requirement of *fairness* to all Canadians no matter where they live.[2]

All three of these stated NEP objectives—security (self-sufficiency in oil by 1990), opportunity (50 percent Canadian ownership and control by 1990), and fairness (made-in-Canada prices and a greater share of oil and gas revenues for the federal government) were separately desirable, but also partially in conflict with each other. The goal of **security** was to be achieved by both reducing the demand for oil and by increasing supply. On the demand side, "the centre-piece of the NEP was a drive to reduce oil consumption, through conservation efforts and the use of more plentiful fuels in place of oil."[3] More specifically, a massive new series of grants-based oil substitution and conservation initiatives, and increased incentives for the use of renewable sources were introduced. On the supply side, a generous grants-based petroleum exploration incentives program was designed to target oil exploration to the Canada Lands and the frontiers where, it was assumed, "major" new discoveries, which could have a significant impact on Canada's supply–demand equation, were more likely to be made. Security was also to be pursued by expanding the domestic energy distribution system with a natural gas pipeline through Québec to Atlantic Canada. In addition, a more rigorous exploration program was to be demanded of land holders on the Canada Lands.

The goal of **opportunity** was to be pursued by instituting an exploration and development incentive program skewed to favour firms with high Canadian Ownership Rate (COR) and Canadian Control Status (CCS) levels; by forcing foreign operators to take on Canadian partners to the level of 50 percent before production licences would be granted for projects on the Canada Lands; and by providing for the growth of Petro-Canada through takeovers of foreign firms paid for by a special levy on consumers known as the Canadian Ownership Charge.

Fairness to consumers was to be achieved by restraining the pace and level of price increases and by redistributing the burdens and benefits among Canadians. Fairness was to be promoted by increasing the federal share of oil and gas revenues via several new taxes and by reserving for the federal government a 25 percent interest in all existing and future petroleum rights on the Canada Lands. For producing provinces, fairness would be secured by increasing the price paid for their oil and gas.

1979-80 Energy Politics: A Capsule View

One need only recall the immediate period leading to the introduction of the NEP. The decade of the 1980s arrived with Canada in the midst of a heated election campaign. Not surprisingly, with the baleful stare of the Ayatollah bearing down on Canadians nightly from their television sets, energy was the centre of attention. As one reporter observed, noting the importance of energy in partisan politics: "The basic differences in philosophy and approach of the three major political parties are reflected nowhere more clearly than in the energy policies they are presenting to the electorate in this campaign."[4]

In fact, the 1980 election is often referred to as the "energy" election or the "eighteen cent" election, in reference to the eighteen cents per gallon increase in the excise tax on gasoline that was a key feature of the December 11, 1979 budget of Joseph Clark's Conservative government. Despite having an Albertan for Prime Minister and an energy minister from Saskatchewan, the federal Conservatives failed to negotiate a new pricing and revenue-sharing arrangement with their Conservative counterparts in Alberta. Moreover, by the time the budget was defeated and they found themselves in another election race, the Tories had seriously misjudged the public mood over the Petro-Canada issue as well.[5] These realities quickly outweighed, in political terms, some of the otherwise favourably viewed parts of the Conservative budget.

The Trudeau Liberals returned to power by recapturing most of twenty-three Ontario "swing" seats they had lost in the 1979 election, when Liberal support in Ontario had fallen from fifty-five to thirty-two seats. In 1980 they captured fifty-two seats. Together with their victory in seventy-four of seventy-five Québec seats, the Liberals returned to power with 86 percent of their parliamentary support in central Canada. The sudden defeat of a Conservative government with strong western Canadian representation, in effect by Toronto area voters on energy issues, only added to the historic build-up of western resentment and regional alienation. In their April 14, 1980 Throne Speech, the Liberals reiterated their election campaign promises about strengthening Petro-Canada, adopting as a specific goal at least 50 percent Canadian ownership by 1990 and generally strengthening the stake of Canadians in their own economic destiny.

In 1979–80, in the midst of the Iranian revolution and the doubling of the world price for oil, and renewed worldwide concern about energy supply and security, Alberta was experiencing a major exploration and construction boom. As a result of the major West Pembina oil and gas find in 1977 and the rather disappointing drilling results on the frontier, industry attention had been drawn back to Alberta in the late 1970s. In 1974 there were about 300 oil and gas companies in Calgary. By 1979 there were over 700. Many of the new ones were small operations headed by persons who had left the larger firms to go it alone. They had been willingly financed by the banks which had established themselves in Calgary in a major way. Debt funding was the norm for these smaller firms. Psychologically and ideologically, there was a contagious and invigorating spirit of free enterprise. Like all booms, it could not last, and the later fall was all the more deeply felt.

Thanks to the Ayatollah Khomeini and the Iranian revolution, the Canadian petroleum industry saw the international commodity value of its oil and gas assets double over night. Consequently, it redoubled its efforts to get much higher prices for its products. The industry thought it had finally achieved a large measure of success when the federal Tories agreed to peg Canadian prices to 85 percent of world price. It was not, however, pleased with the Conservatives' windfall tax of 50 percent on increases over $2 per barrel or thirty cents per thousand cubic feet. Canadian energy issues were not dissimilar in this context from U.S. issues. For example, in the United States the industry had also garnered large profit increases at precisely the same time when there were gasoline and heating fuel shortages and consumer outrage. This lent political support for the Carter Administration's passage of an energy windfall profits tax bill.

Yet, throughout the post-1973 period the oil and gas industry had experienced spectacular growth. The oil and gas index vastly outpaced the growth of all other industries represented by the Toronto Stock Exchange 300 Composite Index. The 1980 Petroleum Monitoring Agency (PMA) Monitoring Survey provides a comparison:

> . . . the 1970s was obviously a decade of outstanding growth. In 1972, the petroleum industry earned $18 in net income for every $100 earned by the aggregate of all other non-financial industries (excluding petroleum). (The comparable figures for 1975 and 1980 were $24 and $42.) For the petroleum industry, the rates of return on shareholders' equity rose from 10 percent in 1972, which mirrored the average for all non-financial industries at that time, to over 21 percent in 1980. The 21 percent rate of return in 1980 was well above the 15 percent average for other non-financial industries in that year.[6]

The petroleum industry recorded year-over-year increases in after-tax profits in 1979 and 1980 of 53.8 percent and 31.0 percent, respectively. Calgary was experiencing a construction boom of major proportions, and the entire Alberta economy was at the point of overheating. The federal and Alberta governments realized that huge economic rents could be generated by the single stroke of a pen, simply by moving the Canadian price closer to the then prevailing $32–34 (U.S.) world price. Virtually everyone was assuming in 1979–80 that oil prices would continue to rise throughout the 1980s, and the federal Conservative and Liberal governments realized that maintenance of the existing revenue sharing scheme would result in a massive shift of revenues to the industry and to the Alberta treasury. It would also challenge federal economic management power and, in the process, confound the intricate formulas for federal–provincial equalization payments. In the face of this, the Liberals decided to take on the industry and the producing provinces over pricing and revenue sharing when they returned to power. Marc Lalonde, the new Minister of Energy, and Prime Minister Trudeau found senior EMR officials were also anxious for substantial change, as a result of their frustration, even under the federal Conservatives, of being unable to negotiate an energy agreement with the Conservative government of Alberta.

It was in this context that on October 28, 1980 the Liberal government introduced the NEP in conjunction with their first post-election budget. The NEP unilaterally imposed a new four-year pricing regime for oil and gas; established a new revenue sharing scheme which would increase Ottawa's share of petroleum revenues by levying several new taxes including a new tax on natural gas sold in Canada or exported; launched a massive oil substitution program to reduce oil imports; and created a program to increase Canadian ownership in the petroleum industry, in part by changing the exploration and production incentive program from a tax-based to a grant-based system, and in part through direct acquisitions.

The reaction from the producing provinces and many elements of the industry was strong and hostile. Some elements of the western Canadian populace, who were already angry about Ontario's abandonment of the Clark Conservatives in the 1980 election, became even angrier; for a period of time, some flirted with the various nascent western separatist movements.

But these were only the most visible and immediate elements and events. A larger setting must be portrayed and examined briefly. The short-term perceptions that escalated into a concern for energy security in 1979 seemed real enough. Spot market prices more than doubled within a matter of weeks, and supply seemed threatened. But what would be the medium- and longer-term state of world oil prices and world supply and demand? Politics turn on both perception and reality; decisions are based on a future that is either uncertain to start with, or is made so by the lack of capacity to predict how interests will behave. Thus the overall context in which the NEP was forged requires some understanding of what had happened to the world oil market since 1973, a series of events now more readily understood with the advantage of hindsight.[7]

World Oil Markets: Perceptions, Realities and Uncertainty

Certain bald realities now stand out.[8] First, during the period from 1965–1973 real oil prices in OECD countries fell at an annual rate of about 2.5 percent, while Gross Domestic Product increased by close to 5 percent per year. This stands in sharp contrast to the 1974–1981 period, when real oil prices grew by 18 percent per annum and economic growth rates fell to 3.2 percent annually. Increased energy prices adversely affected economic output through effects on the terms of trade, through restrictive stabilization policies introduced to combat energy-induced inflation, through relative price changes and through declining exports. Second, energy consumption patterns also changed markedly. Energy consumed per unit of output declined on average about 2.5 percent per annum in the 1974–1981 period. This was caused by changes in both absolute and relative prices and by conservation and oil substitution policies introduced by governments, which gradually worked their way through the intricate processes that characterize a modern western economy.

As is now clear, however, there was in reality no serious shortage of supply in 1980 in terms of the overall global pattern of oil supply and demand. Spot prices reflected short-term supply–demand relationships, but the underlying condition did not justify the price increases that were then in place and forecast to continue for the rest of the decade. However, only a few voices in the analytical wilderness were saying this in the midst of the 1979–1980 period. As we show in greater detail in Chapters 2 and 8, a herd instinct overtook the forecasters, urged on by those with a vested interest in higher prices and by the not unreal short-term security concerns rekindled by the Iranian revolution. At the time, however, there was a veritable hallelujah chorus that prices were on a steady upward path.

Outside the Communist bloc and the OPEC nations, however, total oil consumption in the early 1980s was about the same as it had been in 1970, that is about 40 million barrels per day. Moreover, new non-OPEC sources of supply had entered the world market. Thus by 1983 the respected economist M.A. Adelman was able to assert that even the lowered 1983 prices could not be ascribed to competitive supply and demand. "What explains the evolution of the 1970s is the cartel of the OPEC nations...."[9] Adelman's view of what constituted the reality of the price-setting process is worth quoting at length:

In 1973, as in 1978, the sequence of price increases was clear. First, although the *boycott* of the United States was a failure—the target country fared better than the "friendly, preferred" British and French—the two *production* cuts were highly effective. Yet these cuts only amounted to at most 10 per cent of the world's consumption, and could have been absorbed by normal commercial inventories.

Second, the production cuts unleashed panic. The loss inflicted by shutting down a refinery, or an electric power plant— or a taxi, or a truck—for lack of feedstock or fuel, is so great, that extravagant prices will be paid to avoid it. So spot prices spurted.

Soon the needy were joined by the greedy. The hope of a quick speculative profit drew in much more buying, which drove prices still higher.

The OPEC nations were quick "to follow the market," which their Arab members had contrived, and raised the price from $2 per barrel in October to something over $7 per barrel, on December 31, 1973, by setting that as their tax.

The third stage was equally important. Almost from the start of 1974, there was an oil glut. But far from following spot prices down, the Persian Gulf price continued to increase several times, from $7 per barrel to $10.50 per barrel by October 1974. Saudi Arabia was the leader; the Shah of Iran talked a big game, but was content to follow.

There followed three more years of glut, but the price continued to increase, to $12.50 per barrel by 1977. Unfortunately for the OPEC nations, the increases were all speedily cancelled by inflation. We need to recall, however, how water persistently ran uphill, and prices increased in the face of over supply.

The year 1978 saw continued glut, *and* once again preparations for a new price increase. The Iranian Revolution provided an unexpected occasion.

As in 1973, the loss of output was so small it could have been covered from commercial stocks—had there been any assurance of continued supply. This should have been no problem, because there was considerable excess capacity. But any hope of stability vanished when Saudi Arabia cut production in January 1979. By the end of March, spot prices had stabilized, then began to weaken. A glut again seemed imminent, so the Saudis cut production once more, and spot prices erupted again.

There was continuing speculation about the Saudis' goals. At any moment, they could have lowered the price to any level they wished by the simple announcement that they would sell at that price, to the limits of their capacity. But the Saudis had no wish for lower prices; on the contrary, their production policy pushed prices higher.

In June 1979, Sheik Yamani told a grateful Tokyo summit that Saudi Arabia would "never" allow a price as high as $20 per barrel. I do not think this was duplicity. The Saudis were temporizing, acting like sensible cautious monopolists, feeling their way into what the traffic would bear.

As in 1973, official prices kept climbing long after spot prices had collapsed and the glut had become severe. The last increase was in October 1981, from $32 to $34 per barrel.

In both 1973 and in 1979, the power of the cartel was shown
less in its ability to create and use a price explosion, than its ability
to hold the line during the glut that followed very soon thereafter.
Its best offense has been a remarkable defense.[10]

Whether perception or reality, the immediate events of 1979–80
did produce the high price assumptions and crisis environment in
which the NEP was forged, and brought with it not only the short-term
politics of "energy security" but also other attributes of the politics of
"energy markets." These included arguments about whether the rising
prices were "market" prices and therefore to be followed automatically, or whether they were politically contrived cartel prices and hence
to be met by our own administered price regime. Because Canada
contained these global producer–consumer conflicts of interest *within*
its own political boundaries, the international perceptions and
assumptions about price, security, and overall supply and demand
exacerbated an already difficult domestic situation.

The politics and economics of future prices remain a decidedly
uncertain business several years after the NEP as well. Our concern in
this chapter is simply to locate the immediate 1979–80 events in the
context of world oil markets. We return several times to the later issues
involved in the politics of forecasting as the NEP unfolded, as well as to
analogous problems earlier in the 1970s.

However interesting the immediate 1979–1980 events may be,
however, neither the preceding decades nor subsequent events can be
very well understood without a frame of reference to examine the
evolution of energy politics.

Understanding Energy Politics: A Framework for Analysis

In general terms, about half this book focusses on the politics of energy,
that is, on the fundamental relationships of power, while the other half
focusses on energy policy, that is, on the degree to which the NEP's
policy objectives were implemented, adjusted and challenged over
time. Beyond a certain point, however, distinctions between politics
and policy pass the point of analytical and practical utility. Politics
help produce policy but policy, in turn, in intended and unintended
ways, profoundly affects the structure of power. These interconnec-

tions are evident throughout this book, and they are inherent in the general framework set out below.[11]

When we speak of energy politics we refer to the relationships among key interests. The key interests are influenced by a number of important material/physical and normative factors. The interests are also profoundly shaped by key institutions. Chart 1.1 portrays the key features of our energy politics framework.

At the centre of our analysis is the concept of *interests*. Interests are those economic and political actors that have the capacity to exercise power, that is, the capacity to act in order to achieve their objectives and to exercise their will. Interests are not synonymous with such familiar words as "government," "business," or "interest groups." As Chart 1.2 indicates, we treat the governments of Canada, Ontario, and Alberta as separate interests in energy politics. Similarly in the private sector, the term "interests" refers to the multinationals, the Canadian majors, the second-line Canadian firms and the Canadian juniors, to give only four of the more obvious examples. Interests can be distinguished from interest groups such as the Canadian Petroleum Association or the Independent Petroleum Association of Canada in that the latter, being collections of companies, have a capacity primarily to assert and advocate positions but do not usually possess a capacity to act in significant, concrete ways. By actions we mean the kinds of investment or other decisions indicated on the right side of Chart 1.1.

Moving from the centre to the left of Chart 1.1, we must appreciate that the reason these interests have the capacity to exercise power is the existence in Canada of three core **institutions**, namely, capitalism, federalism and Cabinet–parliamentary government. Capitalism enshrines the exercise of private power and the freedom within limits to invest or not invest and to take other kinds of decisions. It is central to the idea of efficiency, since it implies the capacity of the owners of capital to mobilize capital, land, labour, and knowledge to earn the best return possible. Federalism dictates that, in energy matters, there is a constitutional division of powers which provides for strong federal and provincial powers, while at the same time containing controversial areas of both overlapping and unclear jurisdiction. Cabinet–parliamentary government, in combination with political party discipline and partisanship, instills strong capacities for executive action which is

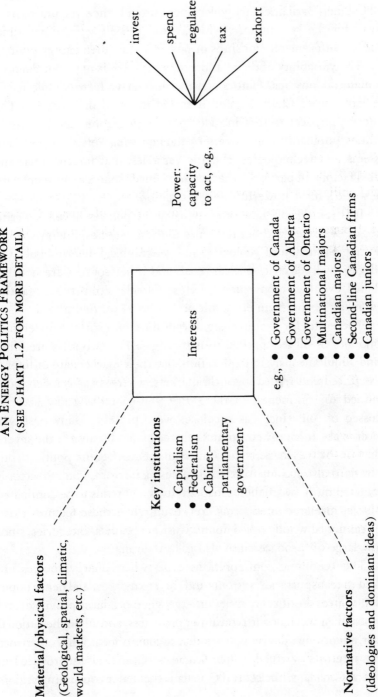

CHART 1.1
AN ENERGY POLITICS FRAMEWORK
(SEE CHART 1.2 FOR MORE DETAIL)

Material/physical factors
(Geological, spatial, climatic, world markets, etc.)

Key institutions
• Capitalism
• Federalism
• Cabinet–parliamentary government

Interests

Normative factors
(Ideologies and dominant ideas)

Power: capacity to act, e.g.,

invest
spend
regulate
tax
exhort

e.g., • Government of Canada
• Government of Alberta
• Government of Ontario
• Multinational majors
• Canadian majors
• Second-line Canadian firms
• Canadian juniors

only partially restrained by legislative bodies. Capitalism, federalism, and Cabinet–parliamentary government provide the structural basis of power for the key interests which, through their actions over time, produce different relationships of power in Canadian energy politics.

The variability of the relationships of power is in turn influenced by **material/physical factors** and the **normative factors** indicated at the left side of Chart 1.1 and itemized in detail in Chart 1.2. The material/physical factors include spatial, geographic and geological realities, population concentrations and hence markets, transportation systems and technologies, climatic variables, and international and global factors, in particular the fact that Canada shares a continent with the world's most powerful capitalist nation.

It is remarkable how often past energy policies have been criticized or evaluated without reference to these realities. Energy sources are first a function of geological and geographical determinants. Oil and gas, hydroelectric, nuclear, coal, and other sources are not distributed evenly or conveniently across Canada. From these realities flow many of the main economic and political configurations.

There are, for example, significant differences in the underlying economics of oil as opposed to natural gas. The two fuels are often found simultaneously in exploration, but their markets are different: oil is priced and traded in world markets, whereas gas is much more confined to continental markets. Pre-NEP concerns about security focussed on oil, since gas surpluses were present. Many post-NEP concerns about energy economics centred on gas because of the severe reduction of U.S. markets for Canadian gas. Different political configurations also accompany the oil versus gas sectors. The gas sector is populated more by smaller Canadian firms. Oil tends to be dominated by large, foreign-owned firms. Yet, even while these features exist, they cannot be wholly relied upon as distinct political categories, since many large oil producers are also gas producers.

The economic configurations arise when energy sources are linked to transportation systems and then to markets and hence population centres. Political realities emerge when producer provinces and regions must interact with consumer provinces, and when the national government must devise policies that favour, oppose, and/or balance these interests. Virtually all of Canada's oil and gas is produced in western Canada, while central Canada is the major consuming region.

CHART 1.2
DETAILED PORTRAIT OF THE ENERGY
POLITICS FRAMEWORK COMPONENTS

Material/physical factors	Normative factors	Institutions	Interests
Spatial/geographic realities	**Ideologies:**	Capitalism	Foreign owned majors
Geological realities	Liberalism	Federalism	Canadian majors
Proximity to markets	Conservativism	Cabinet–parliamentary government	Second-line Canadian companies
Transportation/ distribution systems	Socialism		Canadian juniors
Climatic conditions			Federal government
Canada's location in the global economy	**Ideas I:**		Provincial governments
Canada's location vis-à-vis the U.S.	Efficiency		United States government
	Individual liberty		Banks and financial intermediaries
	Stability		Particular companies, e.g., Dome, Nova, Petro-Canada, Imperial Oil, Gulf
	Equity		Political parties
	Redistribution and equality		
	National identity and integration		
	Regionalism and regional sensitivity		
	Ideas II:		
	Profits and fair return		
	Right to be consulted		
	Centralization and decentralization		
	Responsible and representative government		

Atlantic Canada is dependent on oil imports. Approximately 40 percent of the oil and gas Canadians consume flows through pipelines which pass through the United States. Well over 60 percent of the industry is foreign, primarily U.S. owned. Historically, the percentage has been much higher.[12]

The existence of world and continental energy markets is therefore a reality of the first order. Though Canada is resource rich, it is essential to stress that Canadians have in the past been dependent in selected ways on world supplies, and are likely to remain so. In short, there are finite limits to the quest for energy security, not only if sources of supply are defined as *national* sources, but also in relation to the absolute and relative costs of such supply given other demands on the public and private purse.

The normative factors include both general ideologies and more particular dominant ideas. Broad ideologies such as liberalism, socialism and conservatism do not in themselves determine energy politics or policy in a uniform way, but they are present as part of the general debate about the degree and form of state intervention, and they are a factor in the partisan contest both among the main political parties and, equally important, *within* them. Normative factors also include key dominant ideas of two kinds.

The first kind is the presence and persistence of dominant ideas such as efficiency, individual liberty, stability, equity, redistribution and equality, national identity, and regional sensitivity.[13] They are a central fact of life in Canadian energy politics (and energy policy). Indeed, the conflicts among these ideas as embodied in the actions of key interests are the very stuff of politics. The partial incompatibility between these ideas makes the development of policy, and its sustained implementation over time, an elusive affair.

The second category of ideas is that which resides at the heart of the core institutions. Thus capitalism generates both a defence of profits and demands for "consultation" of various kinds. Federalism generates and tests politics and public policy against ideas such as centralization and decentralization. Cabinet–parliamentary government demands both responsible and representative government simultaneously.

It is a mistake of the highest order to regard these normative factors as being some kind of symbolic trapping for otherwise unbridled self-interest. Interests may well utilize such ideas for rhetorical purposes from time to time, but ideologies and the dominant ideas are also central to the very definition of both the *ends* and the *means* of energy politics. Both the ends and the means are valued and hence are normative. Their persistence over time is an inescapable factor in understanding energy politics.

There are several ways in which these individually listed elements of our framework could be viewed. For example, in an overall sense, they alert us to the existence of at least five main relationships of power: the intergovernmental, government–industry, Canadian–American, interregional, and partisan relationships. Each relationship comprises interests which have the capacity to exercise some power to affect the outcome of an energy issue or development. This does not mean, however, that, for example, Ottawa and Edmonton, government and industry, or Alberta and Ontario are constantly in conflict over energy issues. There is a continuum of relations within each relationship, with consensus marking one end of the continuum and open conflict the other. Over the history of postwar energy politics, we show how each of the relationships experiences the full range of the continuum. There have been times when both interests in a relationship have calculated that an energy project or a pricing, taxation, or export arrangement, as examples, were acceptable to them, and as a result, there was consensus. Conversely, there have been times when the interests have been so far apart on issues that one or the other interest has employed its power to take some sort of unilateral action that resulted in the relationship's moving to a position of open conflict. Occasionally there are disputes between interests that fall short of open conflict; and at other times, grumpy agreements exist which fall short of total consensus.

It is not necessary in any absolute way to rank the various relationships, because their importance relative to one another changes with the energy issue being analyzed. For example, on the issue of oil and gas pricing the governments of Canada and Alberta are the key interests, and negotiate price arrangements between themselves. In certain instances, such as project-related pricing where the price of the product is being negotiated as one feature of an overall package, the industry proponents, via their power to cancel the project if they do not get an acceptable deal, become a direct interest. In the case where oil and gas prices become an election issue, such as in 1980, the federal parties become key interests. On the issue of oil and gas exports, the federal government, the producing provincial government, the industry and, because of its control over oil and gas imports, the U.S. government are all key interests. On northern energy issues, provincial jurisdiction does not apply, so arrangements are hammered out between Ottawa and the industry exploration firms. If production from federally controlled lands were to be exported to the United States, then the U.S. government would once again be a powerful interest. One could go on, but the point to be made is simply that the relative importance of the relationships varies with the energy issue being analysed.

One can confidently argue that the world of energy politics in Canada is complex. Regardless of the issue—determining a price for oil and gas in Canada; carving up the shares of oil and gas revenues; determining the incentive programs necessary to promote exploration in the hostile Canadian frontiers; or arriving at a taxation and pricing package necessary to bring on production of synthetic oil from exotic sources like the oil sands—a number of powerful interests are sure to be involved and pressing hard for a solution which satisfies their needs. Given the nature and power of the interests we are dealing with here— national and provincial governments, some of the largest companies in Canada, some of which are subsidiaries of a number of the world's largest private corporations—it is not surprising that it is often difficult to determine who caused what to happen, and for whose benefit and at whose expense. There are no shrinking violets among any of the interests, though there are clearly times when one or the other interest in a relationship appears, for a combination of reasons, to dominate or overpower the other. But all of these interests are relevant and part of the framework, because they have exhibited at various points throughout the postwar period that they have power and that, under certain conditions, they will attempt to exercise it.

Governmental and industry interests have obviously been among the pivotal interests in Canadian energy politics. Such factors as provincial ownership of natural resources within their boundaries and their right to collect a royalty on the sale of these resources; federal ownership of resources outside of provincial jurisdiction, coupled with Ottawa's extensive taxation powers and authority over all aspects of interprovincial and international trade, including pricing; and the fact that the industry has been almost entirely developed under private ownership, including very high percentages of foreign ownership, have all contributed to making provincial governments, the federal government, and the industry among the key interests in Canadian energy politics. Within these intergovernmental and government–industry relationships we focus on the following interests: the provincial governments of Alberta and Ontario, and the government of Canada; and within the industry, the multinational majors, the Canadian majors, the second-line Canadian firms, and the Canadian juniors.[14] Other interests listed in Chart 1.2 are also examined, but are not the focus of our attention.

In order to say anything meaningful about energy politics, we must assess evidence over a broad period of time. That is, only by tracing events over a broad time frame can one assess the relative strengths of various interests vis-à-vis others. The NEP in particular must be lodged in a broader context. In addition, one must examine several kinds of evidence including general policy decisions, decisions on major projects, and decisions not to act.[15]

It is also essential to look for evidence of shifts in power in Canadian energy politics caused by important world developments. Crises in the international energy system can have the effect of increasing or decreasing the relative strength of various interests in Canadian energy politics, and in motivating the various interests to exert pressure to affect the outcome of issues. The 1973 and 1979 world price shocks galvanized the governments of Alberta and the other producing provinces to press for substantially higher prices for, and a higher percentage of the revenues from, their depleting, non-renewable supplies of oil and natural gas. At the same time, the supply scares which accompanied the 1973 and 1979 crises motivated the federal government to pursue policies of self-sufficiency to remove Canada from the international oil market as soon as possible. Both of these developments had important ramifications for the balance of power among domestic energy interests in Canada.

There are other major analytical aspects to this book, namely, those dealing with public policy and implementation, and with evaluating the NEP as a policy initiative in more specific terms. We leave these primarily to Part IV. These aspects focus on the role of **ideas** as set out above, and their relationships to more specific policy structures and processes. The **structures** include departments and agencies such as Energy, Mines and Resources (EMR), the Department of Finance, Petro-Canada, the National Energy Board (NEB), the Canada Oil and Gas Lands Administration (COGLA), as well as the bureaucracies and organizations of the private sector. Each of these is in general bounded by the larger institutions and interests, but each also exerts an independent influence of its own. As to the **processes** of energy policy formulation, we examine the processes and dynamics inherent in, and revealed by, prices and taxes, energy expenditures and energy regulation. In all three of these domains the role of Crown corporations is also present. The term "process" in addition refers to uncertainty, and therefore to risk and perceptions of risk taking. All policies involve uncertainty—all are, in a sense, hypotheses waiting to be tested, except that key interests do not always want to co-operate in the experiment.

Evaluating the NEP: Official and Unofficial Goals

It is vital at the outset to appreciate the evaluative dilemmas inherent in the official and unofficial goals of the NEP and in what we refer to as the "shifting sands" of the NEP evaluation game. As noted earlier, the official goals of the NEP are to foster energy security, including self-sufficiency by 1990, to promote fairness among Canadians, and to generate increased opportunities for Canadians to participate in the development of the energy industry. The unofficial goals which emerge when one takes into account the politics of the NEP include: the restructuring of political power between Ottawa, and both the industry and the producing provinces, especially Alberta; the reassertion of federal powers over the economy and of Ottawa's visibility and presence in the eyes and hearts of Canadians; the acquisition of greater revenues for the federal treasury; and the preservation of the Liberal Party as chief political party that speaks for Canada.

The official goals of the NEP are not wholly compatible. While some actions may for a time achieve all three of the goals simultaneously, there quickly comes a point when actions intended to promote one goal may harm another. The excessive pursuit of energy security (does one spend $1, 2 or 10 billion?) eventually conflicts with a capacity to be fair in that less money (or other kinds of resource) is available to assist disadvantaged regional consumers or low-income persons. Canadianization, in the sense of either takeovers of foreign firms or special incentives for smaller Canadian firms, may first involve measures which conflict with energy security in that funds are spent in the short run which do not yield a single barrel of new oil and, second, because those small firms that are *unable* to take advantage of the incentives will regard the policy as unfair.

The trio of official NEP objectives are not at all unusual for those having to live with full or partial contradictions. These goals are in a very real and persistent way surrogates for, and verbal expressions of, the key underlying ideas inherent in governing Canada. Table 1.1 portrays their relation to energy policy. Security embraces a concern for both stability and national integration simultaneously. Fairness is a

TABLE 1.1
ENERGY POLICY: IDEAS AND POLICY COMPONENTS

Stability	Efficiency	Equity
• Frontier exploration incentives • Stable fiscal regimes • Export controls	• Let U.S. markets subsidize construction costs • Exports • Conservation	• Blended national price • National oil policy • Treating foreign and Canadian investment equally • NEB procedural fairness

Redistribution	Regional sensitivity	National unity and integration
• Energy pricing and regressive effects • Energy tax credits for low-income Canadians	• Producer provinces versus consumer provinces • Different energy sources of provinces • Offshore resource management • Resource control • Provincial industrial benefits	• Pipeline construction and extension • Canadian ownership and PIP grants • Equalization payments and resource rents • Petro-Canada • Canadian industrial benefits

code word that captures the ideas of equity, redistribution, and region-alism in the same rhetorical breath. Canadianization implies not just nationalism but also individual initiative and the entrepreneurial drive of medium and small Canadian firms. Among the less official but equally real goals of the NEP there are similar partial contradictions, e.g., political power may be demonstrated in the short or medium term, but only at the possible cost of later co-operation at a time when such co-operation may be even more essential.

Moreover, viewing the NEP through the above panoply of goals and ideas is not the only way in which it might be assessed or evaluated by different interests or by individual Canadians. No such comprehensive policy can ever be considered to embody or be viewed as a single flow of thought or action. Almost by definition, there are many rivulets and tributaries with different interests seeing different things in the same policy package. Thus some are more inclined to judge it in relation to the degree to which it adopted or ignored a conservation ethic. Others view it in social policy terms, expressing concern over the impact of the program on low-income Canadians. For example, the NEP was compared unfavourably to the Crosbie energy budget, which contained an energy tax credit for low-income Canadians. It hardly needs saying that the NEP was also viewed through the prism of regional policy, not only in the obvious context of western Canada, but also in the very different energy situation in Atlantic Canada.

As if the evaluation of the NEP were not an elusive enough beast, one is obliged to stress several other elements of the shifting sands of the NEP evaluation game. What is the time period in which the NEP is to be judged? Self-sufficiency and 50 percent Canadianization are goals to be achieved by 1990. Revenue shares are to show effects immediately. The visible spending of PIP grants earns short-term political credit, but later when PIP expenditures increase rapidly in the midst of a recession and a huge federal deficit, visibility becomes a liability.

The time frame of evaluation is also linked to the question of whether the NEP is a radical policy change or only an important one. Judged in the context of the 1979–1980 logjam it may seem to be radical. When juxtaposed against the broader events of the 1970s and when assessed against the actions of other governments (especially those other than the U.S. government) it is far less radical than it at first appears. While the major oil and gas interests professed their agreement with the goals of the NEP, many did not like the means, namely, the takeovers, the new front-end production taxes, the shift from taxes to grants, and the new regulatory regime. This focus on the means only confirms a well-established principle of public policy and democratic politics, namely that the means are not a matter of mere technique. They are the object of intense political dispute precisely because they are themselves valued, and because they deal with who holds or shares real decision-making power.

The array of "means–ends" disputes is also a function of the different interests involved. Some smaller Canadian firms who were the intended beneficiaries of the new NEP incentives saw indeed that they and their shareholders could benefit from the new regime. What they had to overcome was their own quite deep-seated ideological opposition to the interventionist package as a whole and their intense dislike of the Trudeau government. They also had to figure out how to get from A (the pre-NEP fiscal regime) to B (the new regime as later adjusted by the Canada–Alberta agreement) with their corporate balance sheets in some kind of order and to fight off the ravages of a deep recession as well. Other interests, such as the drilling and oil field service sectors in Alberta, were genuinely harmed by the NEP, or at least faced much agonizing uncertainty. In these cases their ideological opposition was in chorus with their reduced financial and material state.

These various evaluative states of affairs were also bedevilled by the intrusion into one's evaluative glasses (whether dark or rose coloured) of other events and factors. Chief among these was the massive recession of 1981 and 1982 and the high interest rates that both helped cause it and that certainly accompanied it. Events rarely stand still while a major policy is routinely implemented. This was even more the case with the NEP, in that it was not only an extremely complex program but coincided with a virtual depression. Cause and effect connections become all the more tenuous and therefore debatable, as both public and private interests jockey to allocate both credit and blame, especially the latter.

The chain of causality is also muddied by a failure to distinguish just who is making what decisions. For example, the NEP and government decision makers are blamed for the large outflow of capital that left the country to pay for the rash of Canadian takeovers of foreign oil and gas firms. There can be little doubt that partial responsibility undoubtedly resides there. But most of these decisions were taken by private oil and banking industry decision makers, allegedly the hard-nosed realists of corporate folklore.

Finally, it is essential to appreciate the numerous arenas in which these various modes of NEP evaluation took place on a continuous basis. One was certainly in the House of Commons, where the underlying partisan and ideological differences among the Liberals, the Progressive Conservatives, and the New Democrats held sway. In this arena the NEP, including its legislative introduction as an omnibus bill, came to symbolize many things, not the least of which was the Tories' portrayal of it as Liberal parliamentary arrogance. For the NDP, the NEP was on the one hand ideologically appealing but, on the other, regionally disturbing, especially to prairie NDP members. In the media the financial press in particular was almost uniformly opposed to the NEP. Other formal evaluations of all or parts of the NEP were published, many of which we refer to in greater detail in Chapters 9 and 10.

Finally, it should be noted that the nature of the NEP evaluation game is itself but the tip of the iceberg in giving some indication of the highly political nature of the implementation process that followed the introduction of the NEP. The implementation of public policy increasingly involves both public and private behaviour. It is not just a function of what public officials do, but also of how private decision makers—corporations, consumers, citizens—respond to and/or attempt to escape the consequences of the policy itself, or particular parts of the policy.

Notes

1. Ulf Lantzke, *World Energy Outlook* (Paris: International Energy Agency, 1982), p. 7.
2. Government of Canada, *The National Energy Program* (Ottawa: Supply and Services, 1980), p. 2.
3. *Ibid.*, p. 99.
4. James Rusk, *Globe and Mail,* January 14, 1980, p. 7. While energy issues were the focus in the media, it is not clear that voters saw it as a clear-cut "energy election." See Harold C. Clarke, J. Jenson, L. LeDuc and J.H. Pammett, *Absent Mandate* (Toronto: Gage, 1984), pp. 168–171.
5. See Jeffrey Simpson, *Discipline of Power* (Toronto: Personal Library, 1980), chapters 12 and 13.
6. Petroleum Monitoring Agency, *Canadian Petroleum Industry: 1980 Monitoring Survey* (Ottawa: Supply and Services, 1981), p. 2.
7. For overall assessments see John M. Blair, *The Control of Oil* (New York: Vintage, 1978); Peter R. Odell, *Oil and World Power*, seventh edition (London: Penguin, 1983).
8. See Larry J. Murphy, "Adapting Canadian Energy Policy to Changing World Energy Trends," *Canadian Business Review* (Spring, 1983), pp. 32–39 and M.A. Adelman, "The International Context," in Edward A. Carmichael and C. Herrera, eds., *Canada's Energy Policy: 1985 and Beyond* (Toronto: C.D. Howe Institute, 1984), pp. 17–37.
9. Adelman, *op. cit,* p. 5. See also George Horwich and David Weimer, "The Next Oil Shock—Giving the Market a Chance?" *Regulation* (March and April 1984), pp. 16–24.
10. Adelman, *op. cit.*, pp. 23–24.
11. On the concept of interests, see Glen Toner, "The Politics of Energy and the NEP: A Framework and Analysis," Ph.D. Dissertation, Carleton University, 1984; and, on the relationship among ideas, structure and process, see G. Bruce Doern and Richard W. Phidd, *Canadian Public Policy: Ideas, Structure, Process* (Toronto: Methuen, 1983). These two works review other literature on which our approach is based, and to which we are indebted.
12. It is useful to be aware at the outset of the many different measures of foreign ownership used by various groups inside and outside the government:

   1) **Ownership versus Control**
      The term "Canadian ownership" refers to the proportion of the value of all shares (or other forms of ownership) owned by Canadians. It is calculated by taking each individual company's level of Canadian ownership and multiplying it by its relative size. Therefore, a 25% Canadian ownership level of a company which has 10% of the market would contribute 2.5% to the overall industry Canadian ownership. A simple addition of all individual company numbers gives the industry

Canadian ownership. Percentage "Canadian control," on the other hand, describes the percentage of the industry which is *controlled* by Canadians. If the above noted 25% Canadian owned company were foreign controlled, it would contribute its full value (10% of the industry) to the foreign controlled column, with zero going to the Canadian controlled column.

2) **Revenues versus Assets**
Traditionally, assets have been used as the measuring tool in the calculation of industry ownership or control. However, there are difficulties with the use of assets, some of which are particularly significant in the oil and gas industry. These difficulties tend to overstate the true amount of Canadian ownership.

3) **Industry Revenues versus Upstream Revenues**
EMR publications often give both total industry revenues and upstream revenues. Total industry revenues tend to show higher levels of foreign investment than upstream production revenues, because of the relative strength of foreign-owned companies in the downstream. For purposes of measurement, the National Energy Program (NEP) chose upstream revenues, as they are more directly related to the policy thrusts of the program. Therefore, the 50% Canadianization objective for 1990 is measured in terms of upstream production revenues.

The distribution of revenues between foreign and Canadian owners shows declining foreign ownership in the early and mid-1970s, followed by slight increases in 1979 and 1980. These increases in foreign ownership would have been even greater if it had not been for Petro-Canada's acquisition of foreign-owned Pacific Petroleums in 1978. After the introduction of the NEP, foreign ownership declined dramatically, principally because of the acquisition wave of 1981.

13. For a detailed analysis of the persistence of these ideas, see Doern and Phidd, *op. cit.*, chapters 1 and 2.

14. Tables 1.2 and 1.3 convey some of the more basic divisions in the first three industry interests, distinguishing between them on the basis of oil and natural gas production. Thus in oil, the multinationals hold eight of the top ten positions, and in gas, six of the top ten. The Canadian majors include Petro-Canada and Dome as well as Nova (whose inclusion in this group is explained in Chapter 6). The group that we call the second-line firms include companies such as Pan Canadian, Canterra, Husky, Norcen, and Hiram Walker Resources (including Home Oil).

15. General *policy* decisions are one such kind of evidence, since they reflect an enunciated set of ideas and show whose positions prevailed at a particular time. Major energy *projects* provide another kind of evidence. The politics of projects tend to differ from those of single policy items

in that a whole range of related policies converge in a decision to invest millions of dollars to build an energy project. Unlike one-time policy decisions, episodic phenomena such as the determination of pricing policy provide evidence of the outcome of bargaining among interests over time.

The high-powered politics surrounding a key policy like the NEP or a major project like Syncrude or the Alaska Highway Pipeline provide evidence for determining the relative power of various key interests at specific points in time, as well as evidence for tracing shifts in power over time. Because one cannot rely solely on one-shot policies or projects for all the evidence, it is also necessary to follow an issue—such as the negotia-

TABLE 1.2

CANADA'S TOP OIL AND GAS LIQUIDS PRODUCERS

	Position 1983	1983 Gross crude oil and gas liquids (m³/d)
Esso Resources	1	24 800
Texaco Canada	2	23 400
Gulf Canada	3	18 800
Dome Petroleum	4	17 060
Chevron Canada	5	14 560
Petro-Canada	6	13 800
Mobil Oil Canada	7	13 300
Amoco Canada Petroleum	8	11 320
Shell Canada	9	10 100
Suncor	10	9 800
PanCanadian Petroleum	11	9 380
Husky Oil	12	6 100
Canterra Energy	13	5 000
Norcen Energy Resources	14	4 910
Canadian Superior Oil	15	4 760
Home Oil	16	4 100
TCPL Resources	17	3 850
Union Oil of Canada	18	3 080
BP Canada	19	2 760
Saskoil	20	2 050
Total production		202 930

Source: *Oilweek*, June 18, 1984, p. 4. Reproduced by permission.

tions to determine the price of Canadian oil and gas between 1973–1979—over a number of years to determine whose interests were best served and why. It is also important to consider the evidence of why some proposed project, such as the Mackenzie Valley Pipeline, was not built, or why Canadian prices have not reached the world level since 1973 despite great pressure by the industry and the producing provinces. Explanations of why certain things did not happen contribute further evidence to an analysis of which interests have and have not exercised power.

TABLE 1.3
CANADA'S TOP NATURAL GAS PRODUCERS

	Position 1983	1983 Gross natural gas (10^6 m^3/d)
Shell Canada	1	15.20
Dome Petroleum	2	13.07
Petro-Canada	3	10.00
Amoco Canada Petroleum	4	9.60
PanCanadian Petroleum	5	8.34
Gulf Canada Resources	6	7.40
Esso Resources Canada	7	6.90
Mobil Oil Canada	8	6.40
Alberta Energy	9	6.30
Chevron Canada	10	5.57
Canterra Energy	11	4.80
Canadian Superior Oil	12	4.32
Norcen Energy Resources	13	3.40
Texaco Canada Resources	14	3.20
Canadian Hunter	15	3.16
Home Oil	16	2.73
BP Canada	17	2.64
Ocelot Industries	18	2.63
Sulpetro	19	2.61
Canadian Occidental	20	2.33
Total Production		**120.60**

Source: *Oilweek*, June 18, 1984, p. 1. Reproduced by permission.

CHAPTER 2

THE NEP: ANATOMY OF A DECISION

The National Energy Program (NEP) was announced as the centre-piece of the ressurected Trudeau Liberals' first budget speech on October 28, 1980. It was a burst of political aggressiveness initially attributable to Ottawa's perceived need to break the bitter deadlock with the Alberta Lougheed Government. At the same time the NEP represented the convergence of even broader political, economic and geological forces and determinants. To trace the anatomy of the NEP decision, one must look at both these short- and longer-term factors.

Political factors were centred on Ottawa's determination to reassert federal power vis-à-vis both the oil and gas industry and the provinces, not only in energy matters but also in matters of constitutional change and economic management. Economic factors were reflected in the impact of rising energy prices on the federal budget, in the massive interregional transfer of wealth from consumer to producer provinces, in the need to respond to the increased outflow of funds to the energy multinationals, and in the need both to protect Canadian industry from excessive energy price increases while at the same time inducing and requiring it to modernize to compete with its more energy-efficient competitors in international trade. Geological factors were present in the long-held view that the western sedimentary basin was no longer an adequate source of conventional oil supply, and that exploration and development had to shift north and east to the Canada Lands.

To dissect the NEP decision itself, we must avoid the all too easy, glib assertion that the "bureaucrats did it" and recognize instead that the NEP became in a sense a summary of many of the major conflicts and ideas inherent in Canadian politics and in the governing of Canada.[1] This chapter analyses the NEP decision in this context. We first explore the larger Liberal view of national priorities as the Trudeau government saw them in 1980. This is followed by an examination of the foreign policy dimensions of the NEP decision, and an initial look at the relations between ministers and senior bureaucrats. In the ministerial–bureaucratic context, we examine key provisions of the NEP and the reasons certain alternatives were rejected.

The Trudeau Liberals and Priorities for the 1980s

The sudden and surprising return to power of the Trudeau Liberals following the defeat of the Crosbie budget and the electoral defeat of the Clark government brought with it a view of national priorities that was remarkably coherent primarily because it was so narrowly based. The Liberals used the rhetorical question, "Who speaks for Canada?" as their anchor for an aggressive federal visibility strategy on national priorities.[2] Their intent was to take whatever initiative they could in taxing, spending, and regulatory decisions to increase the federal government's (and therefore the Liberals') direct contact with individual Canadians and with interests and interest groups. The strategy was explicitly based on a desire to skirt the provinces and to increase the visibility of national institutions and of Ottawa's policies.

This domestic form of anti-provincial nationalism was reflected in two specific major policy initiatives and in the overall scope and intensity with which the Liberal view was pursued. It was a central feature behind the constitutional initiatives of 1980, particularly the Charter of Rights which Ottawa portrayed as a measure that gave power to individuals and took it from governments, both federal and provincial. It was a major element of the Liberal's defence of Petro-Canada both before and during the 1980 election. Its importance in the energy sphere was reinforced in the NEP itself by the proposed package of takeovers of unspecified foreign companies, and by the fundamental shift in oil and gas industry incentives from the tax system to a system of direct grants which favoured Canadian firms. The NEP grants were intended, in political terms, to show visibly and persistently how the energy industry was beholden to Ottawa rather than just to Alberta and other producer-province patrons.

The visibility strategy was also reflected in other major policies initially planned by the Liberals but which did not enjoy the initial heady success that the constitutional and NEP policies seemed to enjoy. These included the Liberals' promised national industrial policy (later to emerge as a broader statement on economic development), a special western Canada initiative under the aegus of a Western Development Fund, and new social policy proposals under the Established Programs Financing Act (EPF). These initiatives are discussed below.

In focussing on this overall view of Liberal priorities, one should note that particular policy initiatives were not motivated *solely* by

visibility concerns. There are other specific determinants and deadlines which drive public policy and politics. Nor does our focus imply
that the strategy was successful. Indeed the sheer scope of the plan—
metaphorically the equivalent of a five-front war—when combined
with the narrow anti-provincialism which helped propel it, and the
rapidly deteriorating economy which accompanied it, contained the
seeds of its own demise as a long-term approach. But the strategy must
be understood nonetheless, both as a strategy and in terms of several
currents of thought and political mood that generated it in the first
place.

A specific catalyst was the determination of Prime Minister
Pierre Trudeau and Energy Minister Marc Lalonde to use what they
both seemed to regard as their final—and unexpected—term of power
to leave an indelible mark on Canadian history. Lalonde in particular
candidly remarked in more than one press interview following the
1980 election how struck he was by the initial post-mortems which
emerged on the Trudeau era immediately following the announcement
in 1979 that Trudeau would step down as the leader of the Liberal
Party. While Trudeau was clearly given credit for language policy and
enhancing the power and influence of French Canadians in Ottawa, the
rest of the instant verdicts seemed to portray the Trudeau years,
especially in the 1970s, as a time of overall malaise and few accom-
plishments. Even among his partisans, the verdict was that Trudeau
had presided over the decline of the Liberal Party. In 1970 there had
been four provincial Liberal governments. By 1980 there were none,
and in several provinces the party was not even a serious contender as
the official opposition.

Thus with the unexpected chance to repair the historical record,
both Trudeau and Lalonde—and following their lead, other senior
ministers—returned to office in an aggressive mood. This mood was
reinforced by their amazement at the self-destructive capabilities of
the Clark Tories, which only confirmed the Liberal belief in their own
inherent superiority as the natural governing party. Senior Liberals
were also genuinely opposed to the Clark Tories' view of Canada as a
decentralized "community of communities," a concept that Trudeau
scornfully called the "Canada as a confederation of shopping centres"
view of nationhood.

But there were longer-term forces at work as well. On their return to power the Liberals, including the now feisty Liberal caucus, became increasingly fed up with what they perceived as the tendency in the 1970s on the part of the media and the provinces—the latter now wholly in opposition party hands—to portray Ottawa as a deficit-ridden, mismanaged and aloof seat of power. The provinces meanwhile were portrayed as aggressive, competent governments that were closely in touch with their people. The federal government and bureaucracy were also viewed to be growing and out of control, even though in fact provincial governments had expanded much more rapidly than had the federal government in the 1970s.

The political issue of Ottawa's deficits and deteriorating fiscal condition was not only a problem of perception and mood, it was also a real problem in several important respects. The capturing of the cata-pulting resource rents occasioned by the 1979 Iranian revolution, the fourfold increase to over $4 billion of the federal Oil Import Compensation Fund, and other fiscal issues were central features of the Ottawa–Alberta negotiating stalemate inherited by the Liberals in 1980.

The successful fight by the federalist forces, including key Québec Liberals, in the Québec referendum on sovereignty association for Québec also contributed greatly to the political hawkishness of the Liberals in 1980. It led directly to the renewed sense of urgency to break the decades-old constitutional deadlock. The referendum fight energized the Trudeau government and whetted their appetite for other battles in which the question "Who speaks for Canada?" could equally be the clarion call. Of vital importance was the fact that in 1980 and 1981, constitutional negotiations were underway simultaneously with the energy negotiations. This simultaneity produced a doubly complicated and heated agenda and environment.

A second immediate impact of the Québec referendum success was that it allowed key Liberal advisors such as Jim Coutts, Tom Axworthy and Keith Davey, in concert with key ministers, the time to turn their attention to devising a strategy for western Canada. Also engaged in this task were persons such as Lloyd Axworthy, elected in 1979 in Winnipeg South, and Senators Hazen Argue and Bud Olsen, the latter in charge of the Ministry of State for Economic Development in the Trudeau Cabinet. Western Canada had become a wasteland for the Liberal Party. There had been many attempts to construct strategies to win the west, including the elaborate Western Economic Opportunities Conference of 1973, but none produced electorally satisfying results. It was hoped that this time things would be different.

There were several strings to the Liberals' bow in western Canada. The first was the establishment of a Cabinet Committee on Western Affairs chaired by Lloyd Axworthy, then Minister of Employment and Immigration and a major advocate of the need for such a committee. That there should be a perceived need for such a committee was in itself an admission of political weakness in a Cabinet where one could count the number of elected western ministers on one's thumb. The committee, moreover, would be advisory only. It would have no direct custody over program budgets, including the newly established Western Development Fund.

The Western Fund was established because it was known by the early autumn of 1980 that the fiscal effect of the forthcoming NEP budget would inevitably be such that Ottawa would be seen to be taking several billions of dollars from the west. It was deemed essential, therefore, that several (but fewer) billions be funnelled back, and be seen to be recycled, in the west. In a similar way, as Chapter 10 shows, a special energy envelope of funds was established to help reinforce the view that the new NEP taxes and revenues were being used for *energy* purposes and not as a "revenue grab" or to bail out the federal deficit. Indeed, the desire to show a balance between the revenue "take" and the overall expenditure "give" was so strong that it resulted in pressure to add expenditure programs even where officials knew there was limited justification for the items themselves.

The Western Fund and the NEP are thus politically interwoven. The initial designers of the Western Fund had a quite different view of how it ought to be used to win the west from how it in fact was used. By far the largest part of the fund was actually spent on resolving the century-old Crows Nest grain transportation issues, and thus was quite a sensible use of funds. The original intent, however, was that it should be liberally sprinkled in numerous small or medium-sized projects across the west, preferably in winnable electoral constituencies. This was linked to the "skirt the provinces" strategy in that it was hoped the Liberals could build direct new bridges to indigenous western groups and institutions and thus construct a new coalition of political support. The western strategy was also informed by a view that the best way to do this was to appeal to the left-of-centre NDP voter. A manifestation of this strategy was already under way in the summer of 1980. Senator Hazen Argue, the former CCF prairie socialist, was engaged in active discussions with some of the prairie co-operatives. The co-ops were precisely the kind of indigenous western institutions with which, in the view of key Liberals, bridges could be built. Argue's political legwork led directly to later energy investment initiatives in which Ottawa provided about $100 million to enable a new co-operative enterprise to become involved in energy exploration. We conclude in Chapter 10 that the "co-ops project" was part sense and part boondoggle, but it was quite reflective of the Liberal western strategy as it was emerging in 1980.

Thus it can be seen that on the domestic front, the NEP was forged in the crucible of several interconnected policy fields, regional pressures, partisan considerations and historical and personal leadership legacies. It is these which shape, but at the same time are influenced by, the pure energy considerations inherent in the NEP and in the pre-NEP legacy traced in Chapter 3 and examined in greater detail in Chapters 4 and 5.

Foreign Policy, Canada–United States Relations and the NEP

With the exception of the importance given to OPEC and the Iranian revolution and their impact on world energy prices and supply, we have not in the above analysis focussed on foreign policy dimensions of the anatomy of the NEP decision. This may seem surprising in view of what we now know about U.S. reaction to the NEP. In general, though, it can still be said that the domestic factors outlined above had more to do with the NEP than did Canada–U.S. relations per se. If nationalism were present in the NEP—and it certainly was—it was far more anti-provincial nationalism than anti-U.S. nationalism. One is distinguishing here, of course, between overall intent as opposed to the effects and perceptions of the NEP as seen by U.S. political leaders.[4]

We will have more to say about foreign policy effects in later chapters, but in terms of the genesis of the NEP, one must keep in mind several relevant factors. First, it must be stressed that the NEP was developed with the Carter administration still in power in the United States. Canada–U.S. relations were in a somewhat euphoric state following Canada's assistance in the escape from Iran of several American embassy officials. The Carter administration was itself engaged in promulgating a reasonably aggressive (judged even by U.S. standards of government intervention) energy policy, including an excess profits tax on the oil industry. There was little inkling that the United States would react as vociferously as it later did to Canada's energy initiatives. To be sure, it is quite reasonable to argue that the NEP was forged without much involvement by External Affairs officials who might have helped avoid some later pitfalls. But given that the NEP was directed at the domestic balance of power vis-à-vis the industry and *among* the foreign-owned segment of the industry as well as the emerging Canadian firms, it is difficult to imagine how greater consultation would ultimately soothe what were fundamentally opposing interests. These interests were later expressed through the U.S. government, which later became the aggressive free-enterprise government led by President Reagan. The Reagan administration, moreover, linked the NEP to its broader criticism of Ottawa's vague plans to strengthen the Foreign Investment Review Agency (FIRA), plans contained in the first Liberal Throne Speech.[5]

To the extent that energy policy and foreign investment are linked, there certainly were some Canada–U.S. factors at work. At a substantive level, many but not all federal energy policy makers were concerned about the increased outflow of multinational oil company profits and/or the increased investment by such enterprises in other resource sectors such as uranium and coal. On the one hand such firms *should be* entitled to repatriate profits to their owners, given that their investments were made in good faith and were historically encouraged by previous Canadian policy. On the other hand, it is a moot point as to the degree to which the rapidly increasing profits were due to market forces and good corporate management, as opposed to non-market international political forces that were increasing severalfold the value of already discovered oil. A related issue concerns contending judgements and beliefs about "evidence," that is, about how fast Canadian ownership and control of the industry was proceeding in the 1970s and how rapidly it would proceed in the 1980s, with or without different governmental incentives. Some felt that the higher prices would so increase the value of the multinationals' assets that future attempts to repatriate ownership would be even more expensive, indeed perhaps prohibitive. Ottawa's overall view was that things were going to get worse and not better, and the time for action was now.

Canada–U.S. relations were clearly worsened, if one defines worsening relations as an increased level of short-term verbal conflict. On the other hand conflict may be viewed as a criterion of success, especially over the longer term, if occasional aggressive actions serve notice that certain interests of the two countries are not synonymous. Moreover, nothing in these relations stays constant for very long. For example, immediately before the NEP, Canada had agreed to proceed with the pre-build portion of the Alaska pipeline. Following the NEP, U.S. reaction to the NEP was exacerbated by the pattern of actual and attempted takeovers by Canadian firms of U.S. firms in the United States rather than in Canada. This behaviour of Canadian firms can in part be attributed to the NEP and the climate it created. But in large measure, as we see in Chapter 9, these were decisions taken by private decision makers and hard-nosed businessmen.

In general, then, it cannot be said that Canada–U.S. relations were not an important factor in the genesis of the NEP, but they did seem to be subordinate in the overall flow of forces.

Ministers, Bureaucrats and the Genesis of the NEP

What then of the bureaucrats, the original villains of the NEP in the eyes and hearts of many businessmen in the oil patch, as well as in the view of the Lougheed government and such authors as Peter Foster. There is no doubt that senior public servants in the Department of Energy, Mines and Resources, Finance, and Petro-Canada influenced energy policy and the NEP. Our analysis suggests, however, that the relative balance of power between ministers and bureaucrats was a much more even affair than was conventionally accorded in the early verdicts on the NEP. To appreciate this conclusion one must look at the issue of ministers and bureaucrats in at least three contexts:

- the general nature of the relationship between ministers and officials;

- the specific processes used to shape the NEP in general; and

- the actual content of key measures contained within the NEP

Each of these dimensions is examined in a preliminary way regarding the genesis of the NEP. They are also, however, an essential backdrop to our analysis in Chapters 8, 9, 10, and 11, when we focus on post-NEP policy developments.

Ministers and Bureaucrats: The General Relationship

Three features of the general relationship between ministers and bureaucrats need to be kept in mind: the links between the power to decide and the influence that flows from the power and the duty to advise; the need to distinguish "the bureaucracy" as a monolithic structure from its component parts; and the ultimate mutual dependence between minister and bureaucrat which evolves out of mutual need.[6]

There can be little doubt that the proper democratic principle is that elected ministers should make policy, and that public servants should carry it out as efficiently and effectively as possible. But there is also a democratic and constitutional obligation on the part of senior public servants to tender the best advice they can and to uphold current laws. It is at the nexus of these two desirable democratic ideas that judgements differ as to how much bureaucratic power there is and ought to be. Such judgements are dependent in part on one's overall ideological beliefs about the role of government. Such generalized views were certainly present in energy politics as we have already seen, and as we will see in more detail in Chapters 5 and 6. They are also coloured by one's views of particular decisions. A decision favourable to one's interests is made by a "public servant"; an unfavourable one is a decision imposed by a "bureaucrat." The NEP and energy policy in general involve both these dimensions, and we are required to examine both.

In the overall context of the debate about ministerial versus bureaucratic power in energy policy, it is necessary to confront the view presented in Peter Foster's book regarding the role of EMR's officials as "EMR" advisors versus their role as advisors to the government as a whole. Foster argues strongly for what might be called a "water-tight compartment" view of the role of officials.[7] The presumption is that if energy officials alone had stuck to energy items, as in the earlier days of EMR when it was composed of technical personnel and commodity specialists, all would be well—or at least "better"—in the world of

democratic politics. While this view has its adherents, it is fundamentally an unsupportable one when one takes into account two overriding factors. First, in general, public servants are not merely advisors
to their minister but are in fact advisors to a government, and hence
must take into account the government's problems and the limits it
faces in governing. This is not a function in the final analysis of
whether an official is a recent graduate of the finance department, but
rather is a constitutional imperative rooted in the very role of a public
servant under a system of Cabinet-responsible government. Second, in
the specific context of energy policy, it would have been naive in the
extreme to think in the 1970s that energy was merely an industrial
sector to be served faithfully by "its" line department. Energy had
moved to the centre of the political stage, and was accordingly now far
more than a matter of energy policy only. On both counts, the Foster
position is untenable.

There is also a larger notion of bureaucracy inherent in the NEP,
namely the issue of the degree to which the NEP "bureaucratizes" the
energy and related economic policy processes and thus results in a loss
of policy flexibility precisely when the energy world is volatile. The
term "bureaucratization" is used here to refer to the increasing reliance
on rules, each intended to make relationships and behaviour more
predictable. This point is best located in the second of our general
points, namely the "bureaucracy as monolith" question. To say that
"the bureaucracy" did this or that is to imply that the bureaucracy
speaks with one voice. We show below that this is not the case with the
NEP. The various key departments and agencies and components
within them tendered different kinds of advice, not only about the NEP
as a whole but also in respect to particular elements of it. Senior
officials in EMR, Finance, and Petro-Canada—interacting with their
ministers and reflecting their legal mandates, interests and constraints—did not all sing from the same hymn sheet.

With respect to the question that the NEP has excessively bureaucratized the policy process, there can be no doubt that concern about
this happening was a major issue in the genesis of the NEP within the
bureaucracy. Whether to retain or work towards an energy policy that
used the price mechanism as its chief engine, or to generate a policy
mixture composed of the price system superimposed on an elaborate
system of regulatory and incentive programs, was a key element of the

internal debate among bureaucrats and between ministers and bureaucrats. This is shown below in our discussion of the specific elements of the NEP.

In short, the relationship between ministers and bureaucrats is one of strong mutual dependence. Key ministers such as Prime Minister Trudeau and Marc Lalonde, in close alliance with Allan MacEachen, politically defined the scope, intensity, and even some of the details of the NEP. The senior bureaucracy supplied different kinds of data and strategic advice as well as a mixture of values and ideas. Both faced the need to make judgements in the face of much uncertainty and in the face of powerful opposition from interests armed and advised by "their" bureaucrats, public and private.

Formulating the NEP

To understand the dynamics involved in the formulation of the NEP itself, one must examine its genesis within the Liberal Party in its brief opposition days; the nature and composition of the NEP ministerial–bureaucratic team; and the immediate pre-NEP views that emerged both in the Clark and Trudeau negotiations with Alberta.

Within the Liberal Party apparatus, two items are of particular importance. First, the appointment of Marc Lalonde as energy critic for the opposition Liberals was a key ingredient. The sojourn in opposition, away from the detailed paperflow that inundates ministers, gave Lalonde the time, and in an important sense, the energy, to view energy policy in a more reflective light. His views were also steeled by what he saw before him in the House of Commons, where the Tories were clearly revealing their incapacity to get their energy act together. The perceived urgency of the Iranian-induced oil shortages and the inability to strike a deal with Alberta also contributed to Lalonde's developing energy commitment. In particular, it was Lalonde who forced the emphasis on security of supply, defined as "self-sufficiency," and set the pricing and revenue targets given to the NEP team, when the Liberals returned to power. Many EMR officials viewed this goal as being unrealistic, particularly because it cannot be totally separated from U.S. security and supply concerns.

In the extra-parliamentary setting of Liberal politics, there was also time for other kinds of input that do not readily occur when a party is in power. In this instance the input came from an ad hoc committee of Liberal policy activists assembled to advise on energy policy and on electoral strategy. Headed by Lalonde, the committee essentially devised many of the key elements of Liberal energy policy that found their way into Pierre Trudeau's Halifax speech in the midst of the 1980 election. It is important to note that, although there was some energy expertise on the committee, and although the committee built on past Liberal positions (including the December 1973 Trudeau commitments), the committee itself did not see its task as being one of energy policy only. Its lone researcher, Barbara Sulzenko, was not experienced in energy matters either.[8] Rather, the committee felt compelled to embrace a range of concerns. This should not be surprising, since what was to become the NEP had clearly become a surrogate for many issues and ideas in Canadian politics.

Far from being a bureaucratic imposition on unwilling ministers, the NEP was very much a ministerial political act. The Halifax speech gave an early warning of things to come. When the Liberals took office, Marc Lalonde brought with him the basic features of the NEP. The reaction of "the bureaucracy" to these ideas requires first an understanding of the NEP team established after the Liberals returned to power.

The existence of a large Cabinet notwithstanding, the reality of Cabinet government is that the truly crucial decisions are made by a small handful of ministers, advised by an equally small handful of senior public servants. This was certainly the case with the NEP. While such a concentration of power is normal on critical issues, there were two additional factors which dictated a concentration of power. First, the negotiations with Alberta then in progress dictated the need for a small, cohesive team. Second, when it was finally decided that the NEP would be part of a budget, then the dictates of budget secrecy also reinforced the need to concentrate power. Although he initially preferred that the NEP be announced as a separate package, Lalonde finally agreed that it had to be a budget, since it contained so many tax changes.

Quite predictably, this initial concentration of power led to later resentment by other ministers. Such resentment did not surface immediately, since an initial euphoria accompanied the early popularity of the NEP among voters. Within a year, however, other ministers increasingly resented the situation, not only because of the deteriorating economy of 1981–1982 but also because the mushrooming energy expenditures were crowding out other ministerial initiatives.

Within the Ottawa machinery, the NEP was formulated by a group which became known as ENFIN, an acronym for "energy-finance." ENFIN was in fact created by the Clark government. Under the Liberals at the ministerial level it involved Trudeau, Lalonde, and Minister of Finance Allan MacEachen, who was the least influential of the three. At the senior official level the equivalent portfolios were present in the persons of Michael Pitfield (later often represented by Bob Rabinovitch, a deputy secretary in the Privy Council Office (PCO)), Mickey Cohen, and Ian Stewart. Stewart had been Deputy Minister of the Energy Department during the Clark regime but was now Deputy Minister of Finance, and Cohen was a long-term Finance official with extensive tax expertise who was now Deputy Minister of EMR. Supporting this ENFIN group was a small band of advisors drawn together in EMR under Cohen. Chief among the latter was Ed Clark, to whom the label, "socialist bureaucrat with a Ph.D." was later frequently applied, and to whom much influence was attributed, and George Tough. Both Clark and Tough were also Finance graduates who came to EMR.

There is little doubt that Ed Clark, the senior Assistant Deputy Minister for policy in EMR, was a central catalyst and bureaucratic entrepreneur in the development of the NEP. His analytical and organizational skills as the operating head of the team that was given its marching orders by Marc Lalonde in the spring of 1980 were a major impetus in putting the full NEP package together. He was clearly an advocate of increased intervention, particularly vis-à-vis the use of Petro-Canada and the toughening of the regulatory regime in the Canada Lands. On pricing issues his views were more traditional. As we stress below, there was an inclination to favour a simple world price mechanism, but this was an option that key ministers insisted was not viable. Pricing was politically determined.

The role of EMR's deputy minister, Mickey Cohen, can partly be understood in relation to his position between his minister, Marc Lalonde, and Ed Clark, his assistant deputy minister. Marc Lalonde, unlike most ministers, was "his own DM." He actually read and criticized the Cabinet papers and others sent to him. Having the ear of Prime Minister Trudeau and sharing the latter's renewed determination to assert a new historical record, Lalonde commanded respect, deference and even fear from intellectuals and hard-nosed politicos alike.

Given the powerhouse above him, in the person of Marc Lalonde, and an analytical whirlwind below him, in the person of Ed Clark, one might be tempted to conclude that Cohen could not help but play the role of intermediary and facilitator. While this was sometimes the case, Cohen's overall role was hardly that of the docile middleman. For example, Clark and others in EMR opposed the TQM pipeline on economic grounds, but Cohen saw that it was included because Lalonde and MacEachen viewed it as essential to demonstrate the national benefits of the NEP to all regions. Of far greater importance, however, was Cohen's tactical role. With Finance Department experiences and memories dating back to earlier federal concessions to Alberta in the mid-1970s, Cohen advocated a tough approach to Alberta, so as not to repeat what were perceived as past tactical mistakes. He was also instrumental in promoting the strategy of downplaying any potential adverse U.S. reaction in 1980. Later, he also pressed hard to ensure that Dome would face a stringent regime under the 1982 rescue package devised by Ottawa and the banks. It was, however, the web of relationships between Lalonde, Cohen and Clark, in many ways a unique configuration, that contributed to the content and power tactics of the NEP.

Other EMR officials were also actively influential in the formulation of the NEP. George Tough wrote major sections of the NEP document. In conjunction with the prevailing mood in Ottawa in the late summer and early fall of 1980, he was among those who wanted to challenge the Alberta government and its bureaucrats, believing that there were serious national problems that simply had to be addressed. Other senior officials at EMR such as Digby Hunt, Roland Priddle, and David Scrim had more extensive industry experience and exposure, and argued for alternative policies either in whole or in part. It is worth mentioning that all of the above-named EMR officials were involved in advising on the Conservatives' energy policy in 1979. The key officials supported the Tories' preference for world prices and a simple price system, but some did resist the Tory plans for Petro-Canada.

There were other vignettes of influence in the total NEP package that lie outside its main thrust but are nonetheless worthy of note. For example, the creation of Petro-Canada International, as a tool of both energy and international development policy, can probably be attributed as much as anything to the fact that three members of the NEP team had experience earlier in their careers in developing countries. Similarly, the establishment of Canertech was inserted in the NEP package at the urging of Lalonde's executive assistant, Michael Phelps, in concert with officials from the Prime Minister's Office who were anxious to locate the agency in Winnipeg.

Operating outside the ENFIN network, but with direct access to Lalonde and Trudeau, were senior Petro-Canada officials Bill Hopper and Joel Bell. They (especially Bell) were involved, not only because of their rapport with key ministers, but also because Petro-Canada was independently preparing its medium- and long-term development plans. The Liberals' stout and popular defence of Petro-Canada during the election campaign obviously created an extremely favourable climate for the national oil company to make its financial demands on the government. Petro-Canada was also a source of considerable hands-on energy expertise.

At the bureaucratic level there can be little doubt that EMR's senior players, and senior Finance officials as well, were exasperated at the continuing deadlock with Alberta. This deadlock had already lasted well over a year and thus, given the deteriorating federal financial position on energy matters, some kind of decisive action was necessary. There was therefore a pervasive climate of bureaucratic receptivity to take aggressive action to break the stalemate. In this important sense, the NEP and its unilateral nature was viewed as much as a bargaining ploy as it was a radical package. That is, decisive action could be taken, and then flexibility and concessions offered later. This is where it is essential to appreciate the convergence of longer-term forces with short-term factors. Both involve the exercise of political power, but the exercise of that power is a product of somewhat more of a balance of ministerial–bureaucratic influence. The influence of bureaucrats also cannot be assessed without relating events to the power of Alberta and energy industry interests.

The 1980 Pre-NEP Alberta–Federal Government Discussions
The strengths, principles, strategies, and miscalculations of the Alberta Lougheed government in the specific pre-NEP discussions are

also integral to the formulation of the NEP and thus to the relations of power between ministers and bureaucrats. While we examine different aspects of the dynamics of both the 1980 and 1981 negotiations in Chapters 5 and 8, it is important to have an initial view of the political flavour of these discussions. We have already portrayed the feisty mood that key federal Liberals were in, and have indicated something of the intense disappointment and disillusionment that key Alberta ministers and officials felt about both the 1979 negotiations with the Clark Conservatives and their defeat at the hands of Toronto and Ontario voters.

Nevertheless, Alberta's key politicians and officials were in an aggressive, self-confident mood of their own. Several factors contributed to their bullish mood. First, the key Cold Lake and Alsands projects were ready to proceed. Therefore, Alberta's power brokers felt they held the upper hand vis-à-vis Ottawa in the supply equation, because the Liberals wanted self-sufficiency. Second, the rapidly growing Heritage Fund had given Alberta fiscal leverage and a capacity to build new intergovernmental alliances. Loans from the fund to Maritime provincial governments were appreciated by these governments. Third, Alberta thought that the Liberals would not have the political will to be too tough, and that they would soon be preoccupied with many issues other than energy. Fourth, key officials had grown used to working with several federal energy ministers whose clout in the federal Cabinet was not great. The Conservatives' Ray Hnatyshyn, the Liberals' Allastair Gillespie, and even Donald Macdonald, in the mid 1970s, were perceived in Alberta as being neither wholly dependable in their power to strike deals nor knowledgeable about the industry. Alberta's key decision makers were ill prepared for the carte-blanche power that Marc Lalonde was given.

A further central aspect of the interpersonal political equation was the firm belief by Premier Peter Lougheed that he was much more knowledgeable about the energy industry and energy policy than Prime Minister Trudeau. Underlying this was a firm confidence that in the final analysis he and Trudeau were the only real power brokers, standing head and shoulders above the other premiers, including Ontario's Bill Davis, and that, in the crunch, they would "do a deal." This kind of confidence affected the conduct of the 1980 pre-NEP discussions in a critical way, because there was a different relationship of power between Lougheed and his energy minister, Merv Leitch, and Trudeau and his energy minister, Marc Lalonde.

Leitch was given a much shorter leash than Lalonde, both in 1980 and later in the negotiations prior to the September 1981 Canada–Alberta Agreement. This was in part because Prime Minister Trudeau was far more interested in the Constitutional initiatives then being forged than in energy, and in part because Lalonde had power and political skill in his own right. Merv Leitch, who had been Alberta's Treasurer, was hardly a wilting flower either, but his personality differs from Lalonde's. Extremely loyal to Lougheed, he is a quiet but thoughtful politician—given neither to bluster nor bombast. During discussions he listened more than he talked. He was also much more interested in the details of energy agreements than in the big geopolitics and power games behind them. Like Lougheed himself, he was particularly interested in preserving the key principles of provincial resource ownership, and therefore of federalism, that the Lougheed Conservatives had defended. This was demonstrated at the final pre-NEP meeting between federal and Alberta negotiators held in Edmonton early in October 1980. Leitch was at his toughest here in asserting the inviolate nature of the principle of having no federal export tax on gas.

The October meeting was the last formal meeting but it had been preceded by three others, each of which cumulatively fueled the mutual perception that neither side was prepared to negotiate. This view was especially strong in the case of Alberta's judgement of Ottawa. It was by and large an accurate view.

Although Lalonde had paid a courtesy call on Leitch in Edmonton in April 1980, the first substantive meeting they had was in Ottawa in June 1980. Lalonde, who barely knew Leitch, was, in the view of some, overbearing and did most of the talking. Key EMR officials reinforced this view by being aggressive themselves. Some pricing proposals were suggested, but the meeting went nowhere. Then, at a meeting at Meach Lake in July 1980, it became conclusive that the two governments were on different wavelengths. This meeting involved Lougheed and Trudeau, but each was there for different reasons. Lougheed talked energy and Trudeau talked about the Constitution.

There were some vague inklings from Trudeau about the then germinating Western Development Fund, but the meeting was in the final analysis a totally non-productive one.

During this period the relations between and among bureaucrats at the intergovernmental level, and between ministers and officials within the Alberta government, were not uniform. For example, some senior Alberta officials did argue that Alberta ministers had been too tough on the Clark Conservatives in 1979, and urged moderation in the new round. The two respective energy deputy ministers, Mickey Cohen and Barry Mellon, had some contacts. But gradually the Alberta officials' suspicions, originally developed in 1978 and 1979, of the EMR bureaucrats as impractical interventionists, were confirmed by the tenor and content of the discussions over the three meetings that were held. By the end of the summer, they knew Ottawa did not want to bargain. They, along with their ministers, were content to see what Ottawa would announce, still more than confident that they held most of the bargaining chips that mattered, in the energy domain that they knew best.

Key NEP Provisions and the Ministerial–Bureaucratic Equation

The finer interdependencies between ministerial and bureaucratic power in the genesis of the NEP can be appreciated by looking at several of the key provisions of the NEP and, in the process, some of the alternatives not selected. These are best expressed as questions:

- Why was the world price mechanism rejected?
- Why were oil and gas incentives shifted from primarily a tax-based system to a system of direct grants?
- Why was the blended price and the Canadian Compensation Charge adopted?
- Why was the Canadian Ownership Account and the commitment to take over some foreign-owned companies adopted?
- Why was the 25 percent Crown interest provision established?

Each question is examined separately below and then is followed by an overall look at the art and politics of forecasting and analysis that underpinned the NEP. We analyse further aspects of these same questions in later chapters, as well as important items such as the demand-side "off-oil" incentives, the Canada Lands regulatory regime, and the role of Petro-Canada itself.

In classic economic terms, the best way to allocate energy resources is to allow the price mechanism to do its job. By moving rapidly to world prices one would in theory obtain an efficient allocation of resources. Any effects judged to be politically adverse on particular regions, sectors or income groups—the distributive effects— could be ameliorated by special subsidies. In the Canadian energy policy milieu of 1980 there was, of course, no absolutely pure notion of energy policy secured through the price mechanism *only*. This was because whatever was done in the NEP would be layered on top of the status quo, which by definition already contained some administered price components as well as an array of non-price policy instruments. At the same time the choices to be made in 1980 about the degree to which the NEP would rely on price mechanisms, as opposed to a greater reliance on administered prices below the world price, coupled with an array of even more complex programs, were critical.

As we noted above, this general issue was a source of dispute among key public servants. Outside of the issue of Petro-Canada, it must be noted that senior bureaucrats in both EMR and Finance in both the brief Clark government and in the early months of the refurbished Trudeau government, instinctively preferred in a general way the use of the price mechanism. These instincts were partly a product of the fact that virtually all the key advisors were economists whose training contains built-in preferences for market mechanisms. Even the early views of the mandate of Petro-Canada could be partly construed in this way, since it was envisioned as a company that would be engaged in the frontier areas where most private firms were reluctant to operate.

In the brief tenure of the Clark government, the pro-world-price instincts of the senior EMR and Finance officials were perhaps less noticeable, given the vigorous debate then in progress between EMR and key Clark advisors such as Jim Gillies. The latter was ardently anti-Petro-Canada. But this does not alter the fact that, on the larger issues, world prices were often expressed as the preferred route. It must be remembered that in the two years prior to 1979 the domestic and world prices were quite close. Indeed, federal policy was to move to world prices in stages.

Even when the Liberals returned to office after world prices had doubled in the wake of the Iranian revolution, senior officials in the two key agencies again questioned their ministers as to how firmly they were wedded to non-world-price scenarios. The reply was emphatically that the Liberals' commitment to a blended "made in Canada" price was an unalterable one. The blended price concept was thus primarily a choice made by elected ministers. In opting for a blended price, the key ministers rejected alternatives such as a single world price plus a windfall profits tax, the model adopted in the United States, and the approach that more closely mirrored that of the Clark Conservatives (at least as revealed in the Crosbie budget). Electoral and partisan factors as well as ideas about regionalism and equity were present in this choice. The Liberals believed they had to differentiate their position from that of the Clark Tories. That was what the election of 1980, decided in the political trenches of about twenty Toronto-area ridings, was all about. It was also the preferred position of the Ontario government headed by Bill Davis, whose support would be essential in the Constitutional negotiations, the strategy for which was being hatched at the same time as the NEP.

The blended price also reflected the need to build in some differential treatment of old versus new oil. If old oil, already discovered, were granted the world price, windfall profits would accrue to the oil industry. One could either tax such profits or create a two-price system. The latter was eventually chosen, especially in the September 1981 Canada–Alberta agreement. Contained within this choice are other interesting elements of the relative balance of power between ministers and bureaucrats. These are also tied to the broader decision in the NEP not to use the tax system as the main instrument for delivering incentives to the oil and gas industry.

The aversion to using the tax system either to tax excess profits or to provide further incentives to explore in the north was a product of several factors. At a general level, there emerged in the Finance department a view that the tax system was becoming overloaded with such incentives. The overload had reached such a state that the tax system was losing its capacity to perform its other essential functions, namely redistributing income and helping to foster a more efficient economy.[9] With respect to the oil industry in general and the multinationals in particular there was growing concern, as we show in greater detail in Chapter 3, that the effective tax rate on the industry was so much lower than for other industries. This of course was itself partly owing to previous tax-based public policies.

It is in this climate that one must relate the more specific elements of the NEP and the politics inherent in using taxes versus grants. In addition to the anti-tax expenditure climate stressed above, there were legal obstacles to using the tax system to discriminate in favour of Canadian-owned firms. Canada–U.S. tax treaties in particular made it virtually impossible. The only major way in which one could give greater support to Canadian firms was through direct grants, where international rules and conventions were less strict. The federal government wanted to favour Canadian firms because it feared that foreign ownership would otherwise increase, not decrease. The pre-NEP fiscal regime also had the effect of discriminating *against* smaller Canadian firms, simply because to take advantage of such incentives one had to have a sufficient cash flow and be in a taxpaying position. The need to use grants also coincided with, and mutually reinforced, the larger Liberal visibility strategy. The tax provisions were politically invisible. The new Petroleum Incentive Payments, the PIP grants, along with other grant programs, would be visible and therefore very political. The public would be aware of the industry's favoured treatment and would question it. Canadianization was a better justification. Later, as Chapter 10 shows, the PIPs became perhaps too visible when costs escalated.

The shift from taxes to grants was also congruent with the desire to demonstrate openly to the oil industry that a new balance of power had to be struck in the political triad composed of Ottawa, Alberta, and the industry. Visible grants would show that the industry could no longer take Ottawa for granted. They would also serve notice that, as the geological time clock propelled more activity in the north and off-shore and away from Alberta, there would be a new era in the fiscal regime and in the structure of ownership.

As well, the impetus to use grants was a direct result of the earlier 1979 debate within the Conservative government over the Tories' proposed Energy Bank, the investment device favoured by the Clark government to recycle petro dollars. Some Clark advisors insisted that this would have to include a significant grants component in addition to the "banking" role. Here too the concern was to demonstrate a national, federal government-run development role. The use of grants

was thus on the agenda at the time of the NEP. Indeed, somewhat para-
doxically in view of the later debate, the PIP grants were presented as
being a less interventionist instrument than the "bank" idea, since the
grants were based on general formulas rather than on numerous
discrete loan-grant decisions that would have to be made by the Energy
Bank officials, had the bank been created. Some Canadian benefits
regulations analogous to those found in the COGLA mandate would also
have been contained in the Tory energy bank proposal. PIPs were also
seen as being a less costly incentive in the north than the continuation
of the super-depletion tax breaks in place until October 1980 and
ostensibly in existence to benefit Dome Petroleum. To some EMR and
Finance officials, the depletion allowance was a form of "tax pornog-
raphy." Alberta's energy experts also viewed the super-depletion as
outrageously generous.

In the taxes-to-grants element of the NEP, the ministerial–
bureaucratic issue is therefore a decidedly mixed one. On the one hand
there was a sense in which the decision was almost automatic, in that
tax treaties prevented discrimination. On the other hand, there was a
bureaucratic aversion to using the tax system as the primary device for
conferring incentives on the oil industry. This aversion was not a
uniform one because, as Chapter 9 shows, when the tax system was
thought of as a "revenue producer" as opposed to a "policy instrument," the NEP planners were quite content to add several new taxes
onto the energy tax system, all in aid of the revenue goals of the NEP.
And there was a strong desire among key ministers to exercise power
vis-à-vis the industry through grants. Thus on this aspect of the NEP
the pattern of influence seemed fairly balanced between ministers and
bureaucrats.

What can one say then about the issue of the 25 percent Crown
interest contained in the NEP? This provision reserved for the federal
government a 25 percent interest in any oil and gas discovered in the
Canada Lands including pre-NEP discoveries. The foreign-owned
sector of the industry in particular, the U.S. government and the Tory
opposition angrily characterized this provision as being discriminatory
and unfair. Virtually all the industry saw it as a confiscation of
property, an act which easily assumed the appearance of socialism both
to the right-wing Tories in the Clark caucus and to the staunch free-
enterprisers of the Reagan administration. A more careful review of

the issues suggests, not surprisingly, that the motives and forces leading to this provision are more complex than this.

Underlying the 25 percent Crown interest was a view by key ministers and officials that no matter what kind of exploration incentive regime was put in place—that is, one that was tax-based as before or grant-based as was now contemplated—the federal government would be paying 90 to 100 percent of the costs (through foregone revenue or direct grants) but without any direct return for this public investment. The 25 percent Crown interest provision would provide such a return at the development stage. This general proposition was also linked to the then existing regulatory regime on the Canada Lands. It was governed by the 1961 Canada Oil and Gas Lands regulations (COGL).[10] The COGL provided for a system of long-term exploration permits and production leases. The exploration permits were available for a nominal sum and were generally issued on a first come, first served basis. The permits were for a definite term (usually nine to twelve years) but were for **exploration** rights only. These permits could be renewed but at the sole discretion of, and on terms set by, Ottawa. Any subsequent **production** arrangements under COGL were provided through separately negotiated leases. The COGL system stands in direct contrast to the U.S. system. In the United States, exploration rights on federal land are auctioned for large amounts of money, but they confer on the successful bidder ownership of any subsequent production.

Under the COGL, the federal government had automatically obtained a minimum 50 percent interest in the acreage of any area slated for production. Ottawa's acreage was allocated under a "modified checkerboard" formula to assure equity both to the Crown and the developer. Thus in defence of its NEP provisions, Ottawa argued that the NEP's 25 percent share was supported by the precedent of the previous COGL regime. It was also supported by the 1977 Petro-Canada precedent. The Crown corporation, under the renewal terms of some COGL exploration permits which had expired and which had proven to be barren until then, was given the right to acquire a 25 percent working interest subject to the level of Canadian ownership. Under this "back in" scheme, Petro-Canada did not have to pay its 25 percent of historical exploration expenses. The Hibernia discovery was partially the result of such an arrangement before the NEP. A similar arrangement allowed Petro-Canada access to lands previously held by Esso in the Beaufort Sea area.

In addition to these precedents, a more specific impetus for the 25 percent interest was the case involving Sable Island gas exploration in 1979. Petro-Canada's exploration partner, Mobil Oil, had pulled its rigs out of the area in search of more lucrative prospects elsewhere in the world. Petro-Canada farmed-in. After six dry holes, its drilling resulted in a significant discovery. This incident made a major impression on key bureaucrats and ministers alike, and was fresh on their minds in 1980. The moral of the story, in their view, was that just as Petro-Canada was a "window on the industry" as a whole, so also was there a need for a presence on every major project.

With respect to Canada–U.S. relations, the 25 percent Crown interest provision was undoubtedly the political equivalent of waving a red flag in front of a bull. The Americans regarded it as a form of confiscation because it was retroactive and did not involve payment of market value. Whether intended or not, this provision may in retrospect have been useful strategically in that it partly deflected the primary attention of American criticism away from the PIP grants and onto the 25 percent back-in. As to the merits of the confiscation charge, Ottawa's defence was as follows. Confiscation could not be a valid criticism because COGL permits issued and outstanding do not confer any production rights. One could therefore not confiscate a right that had not been conferred in the first place. Moreover, outstanding production leases were exempt from the Crown share provision in the NEP legislation through the grandfather clause. Ottawa would also pay for its working interest, that is 25 percent of the development and production costs. It would also pay, on an ex gratia basis, monies to oil and gas firms in relation to certain past exploration and development expenditures made by the companies. These involved discoveries made before December 31, 1982, if the discovery wells were initiated before December 31, 1981. It must be stressed, however, that the ex gratia payments were inserted only after U.S. pressure, as a conciliatory gesture to ease Canada–U.S. relations. This partially undermined Ottawa's defence of this provision.

While all the multinationals objected to this provision of the NEP, Mobil Oil, which had the key interest in the Hibernia and Venture developments in the east coast offshore area, was its strongest critic.

Mobil cited the fact that it had been in the risky offshore area since 1965 and had spent over $600 million without initially finding anything. It regarded the ex gratia payments as insufficient, since they only covered prior expenditures and did not include the inherent market value of the reserves taken by the Crown. Moreover, there were no negotiations to reach a settlement. Mobil's testimony on Bill C-48 went on to specify its objections:

> The Honourable Minister of Energy, Mines and Resources and other members of the government argue that the back-in provision is simply payment for taxes foregone as a result of earlier tax incentives. But where is the logic in an argument that used a system of tax incentives, which was introduced with the specific intent of encouraging high-risk and high-cost exploration, to justify subsequent retroactive measures? Furthermore, this reasoning ignores the fact that once commercial production is established, the government realizes its share of the proceeds automatically through royalty and tax payments.
>
> It was also asserted by the Minister in his May 14 appearance before the Natural Resources and Public Works Committee of the House of Commons that the back-in provision is needed to capture so-called economic rents. However, fiscal mechanisms are already included in Bill C-48 which are used for this purpose, namely, the basic ten per cent royalty and the Progressive Incremental Royalty. It is also worth noting that the "economic rent argument" is fundamentally different from the "tax incentive argument" which was originally used to defend the retroactive back-in. In this regard, it would be helpful for purposes of public discussion if the government could make up its mind on the rationale for the retroactive back-in.
>
> The proposed 25 per cent back-in provision is particularly difficult for Mobil to accept because in cases such as Hibernia it is an addition to the 25 per cent interest already acquired by Petro-Canada. Under the 1977 amendments to the Canada Oil and Gas Land Regulations, Petro-Canada obtained a 25 per cent interest in Hibernia in 1978 when applications were made for Special Renewal Permits. However, with the passage of Bill C-48 this right of Petro-Canada will be abrogated and replaced by the 25 per cent retroactive Crown share (Section 27). Furthermore, Section 62(5) of Bill C-48 states in effect where, under the 1977 amendments to the present regulations, Petro-Canada has acquired a 25 per cent interest after April 30, 1980, the back-in provision of Section 27 will not apply. These clauses were included to avoid

"double dipping" by the Crown during the transitional period. Yet in cases such as Hibernia, where Petro-Canada had obtained its interest prior to April 30, 1980, "double dipping" does occur. We believe this to be inequitable treatment and Section 62(5) should be amended to cover cases such as Hibernia.

The 25 per cent back-in, together with the prior interest obtained by Petro-Canada, would increase the Crown share in cases such as Hibernia to almost 44 per cent which severely limits and, indeed, effectively pre-empts the possibility of increasing private sector Canadian ownership. Mobil has indicated its willingness to move toward 50 per cent Canadian participation in production licenses on Canada Lands. However, we would prefer to accomplish this objective through commercial negotiations with Canadian private sector interests where compensation for divested interests would approach fair market value.

The government often compares Bill C-48 with oil and gas legislation in the U.K. and Norway. Such comparisons among different fiscal and regulatory regimes are difficult because specific items may be taken out of context. In this regard, it should be noted that the British National Oil Corporation does not lay claim to a share of producing fields, but only has preferred access at market value to a certain percentage of produced crude for purposes of distribution and marketing. In Norway, there is government participation and ownership but the Norwegian government has at no time resorted to confiscatory measures nor has it imposed retroactive provisions on existing licenses.[11]

Once again there was a mixture of bureaucratic and ministerial influence involved in the insertion of the 25 percent Crown interest provision in the NEP. It was probably the most heatedly debated item in the NEP, and a decision on it was not taken until quite late in the game. The final choice belonged to Marc Lalonde, who made it explicitly and willingly, urged on by senior Petro-Canada officials as well as some EMR officials. At the same time it followed major COGL precedents and principles under regulations initiated by the Conservative government of John Diefenbaker.

Last but certainly not least among the key provisions was the Canadian Ownership Account and the proposed takeover of one or more multinational oil companies. The genesis of this decision flows directly from the intensity of the 1980 election campaign and the partisan divisions that arose over the role of Petro-Canada. Lalonde and Trudeau were determined to show an expanded support for the company and for this central dimension of the larger Canadianization objectives of the NEP. While the accompanying Canadian Ownership Charge and the Ownership Account implied in principle possible take-overs by other federal instruments, it is clear that Petro-Canada was the key. The Ownership Charge became a "charge" on consumers primarily because if it had been a tax it would, along with other NEP provisions, have quickly sent the total Liberal package well beyond the less than 18 cent election pledge of the Liberals. They had promised that their energy proposals would cost the taxpayer less than the Tories' 18 cent tax contained in the Crosbie budget.

The notion of a separate visible "account" in the NEP package has more tenuous origins. In the mid 1970s, Saskatchewan Premier Allan Blakeney had proposed a national development account to be used to channel recycled petro-dollars into economic development projects, presumably managed in some suitable federal–provincial way. In the 1979 Ottawa–Alberta negotiations the Clark Tories had proposed an Energy Bank with not dissimilar purposes.[12] Neither of these earlier ideas had envisioned an account devoted solely to increasing Canadian ownership. As we have already noted, the Liberals tried to advertise the recycling of new energy revenues in other ways as well, by establishing a separate energy envelope and a Western Development Fund. In general terms, it is possible to infer a somewhat greater bureaucratic influence on the ownership account-takeover provisions in that Petro-Canada itself was a key influence.

There were other important components to the NEP that we have not fully examined in this chapter but which will be analysed in some detail later in the book. The non-price regulatory regime centred in COGLA has roots that go well beyond specific ministerial–bureaucratic "to-ing and fro-ing." They are a product of contentious views throughout the 1970s and even earlier about both energy and economic development as well as environmental policy, and are the subject of Chapter 11. Similarly, the demand-side "off-oil" programs of the NEP, programs which were not a central feature of any previous federal energy policy and which have followed their own track to the Cabinet table, are examined in Chapter 10. They were a major part of the security of supply strategy.

In general our review of several of the main provisions in the NEP suggests that the genesis of the NEP was much more a mixture of ministerial and bureaucratic factors rather than an assault by uncontrolled bureaucrats. This conclusion becomes all the more persuasive when one locates the NEP in the larger political and economic context presented here and in Chapter 3, and when one considers the art of forecasting and analysis that underpinned the NEP.

The Art of Forecasting and the NEP

An understanding of the energy forecasting processes, results and dilemmas inherent in the forging of the NEP begins with the effort in the late 1970s to strengthen EMR's economic and policy analysis capabilities. Former Finance and Treasury Board planning branch officials, mainly economists, were organized under Ed Clark. One of the branches under the overall Economic and Policy Analysis sector (EPAS) was concerned with modelling the macroeconomic impacts of energy policy. This included modelling the probable effects of different energy pricing scenarios on inflation, output and growth, and on different industrial sectors, regions and households. Much of this was done without fanfare in the inner EMR circles, but was viewed as an inappropriate activity for EMR by the finance department, which had the overall macroeconomic policy mandate.

EMR did not construct its own model per se but rather used models then in existence at both the Conference Board and at Informetrica, a private forecasting firm. These modelling efforts, like any modelling exercises, had widely varying links to the later energy policies of both the Clark and Trudeau governments. For example, the modelling influenced the Tory energy tax credit provision in the Crosbie budget. The modelling of households showed that low-income households were more affected by home heating fuel costs than transportation fuel costs, since the poor used public transit to a far greater extent. A tax on transport fuels was therefore fairer to this income group than one on home heating fuels. The Tories' tax on transportation fuels was also a decision based on the view that Alberta saw such a tax as more appropriate since it did not smack of anything that could be construed as a wellhead tax. The Tories also added the energy tax credit to alleviate further the burden of both higher prices and the transportation tax on the poor.

Other examples of the role of forecasting and the subsequent policies adopted are usually far less clear than the one cited above and are chock-full of diverse political influences. Each dispute, moreover, deals with different features being forecasted or modelled. For example, on the key issue of the probable inflationary impacts of swift heavy price increases versus gradual price increases, the views of economists within and outside of EMR varied. EMR's actual modelling of the several price scenarios was not seriously disputed. But there was dispute over how great the inflation impact would be. Advocates of the "hit the consumer fast and hard" school asserted that consumers would basically absorb the increased costs and not try to recoup most of these losses in renewed high wage demands. Others strongly doubted this view. Moreover, the implication of this view, namely that one should proceed swiftly to world price, utterly ignored the absolutely critical bargaining realities inherent in the Ottawa–Alberta political situation. If Ottawa conceded world price at the outset, there would be much less leverage to deal with the other features of the energy stalemate, such as the recycling of energy revenues. That forecasts and analysis have to meet both political and economic tests of relevance seems an elementary proposition, but it is often forgotten.

There were also different forecasting disputes over the issue of recycling petro-dollars and their economic effects. An Alberta-sponsored Hudson Institute study, a Shell-sponsored Informetrica study and a Texaco-sponsored Data Resources Inc. study all reached different conclusions about how best to get the most economic bang from the recycled petro-dollars, and varied widely as to how explicit they were about the assumptions and causal links in the complicated recycling chain. Thus Alberta's study argued that Alberta could produce nationally beneficial recycling effects even if it acted primarily only as a financier of other provinces' developments. The Texaco forecast showed, among other things, that leaving the dollars with the industry would produce the best effects. The Shell study was more explicit about its assumptions but nonetheless opted for primarily a private sector recycling/reinvestment path. While in part these conclusions seem to confirm the "hired gun" or "we'll give you what you want to hear" school of forecasting and analysis, it is necessary to put all of this in the far larger political and economic context that we have already traced. There is no easy causal link between analysis and policy.[13]

But if this is so, what does one make of the central issue of forecasts of higher oil prices which underpinned the NEP and whose failure to materialize adversely affected the policy and the later Canada–Alberta Agreement? There was no attempt to model world oil prices per se. Ottawa, along with Alberta and industry forecasters, strongly believed that these prices were essentially a function of OPEC's decisions. Early in 1981 the macroeconomic modelling clearly showed world economic growth declining sharply owing to the 1979 price increases, and thus it was known that the demand for oil would decline and thus affect prices. The capturing of the larger cumulative "conservation effects" produced by conservation and oil substitution programs put in place in Western industrialized countries since 1973 was not as easily discerned. This was because all such models have difficulty handling "institutional" factors and the lags inherent in the processes through which the new conservation measures worked their way through the economy. Only later, in the 1981–83 period, did it become more evident that for oil importing countries, which buy oil in U.S. dollars, the real price of oil did not drop with the oil price decline in 1982–83 because of the strength of the U.S. dollar. This in turn was a product of the U.S. policy of high interest rates.

Thus there were genuine forecasting problems in a game that is inherently more art than science, even under normal circumstances. But this still leaves the issue of whether, in the first nine months of 1981 when the Ottawa–Alberta agreement was being negotiated, there were not clear enough forecasting and other judgemental factors in evidence that would have suggested the need for caution about the pricing forecasts. With hindsight it is now possible to see that in 1981 there was sufficient evidence from the declining world economy alone to call into question the assumed 2 percent per annum real growth in prices over the 1980s. It is at this point, however, that the intense political negotiations with Alberta drove the forecasting rather than vice versa. (The dynamics of this process are analysed in Chapter 8.) There was too much momentum and extraordinary pressure on the two governments to reach an agreement, and the hoped-for large revenue dollars were too enticing. This extremely heavy pressure on the two governments to strike a deal came especially from the oil and gas industry and from other industrial sectors. Indeed, forecasts which produced a bigger overall pie were induced by design, since the bigger the pie that could be shown, the easier it would be to strike a deal on its division.

There is, however, evidence that less buoyant oil price forecasts were being circulated within the federal government in the spring of 1981. A document prepared by the Ministry of State for Economic Development (MSED) called the Medium Term Track report helped underpin the later November 1981 federal paper on "Economic Development for Canada in the 1980s." Though the MSED forecast dealt with *all* resource prices and helped encourage Ottawa to adopt its economic strategy of resources-led mega-projects, we cite it here in the context of what it said about future *oil* prices only. Less than seven months after the bouyant NEP forecasts and several months before the Alberta agreement, it cautiously concluded that

> the room for differences of view in the trend of real energy prices is wide but at currently and reasonably anticipated price levels, the scope for bringing on additional supplies as well as the ability to substitute other forms of energy and the incentives for conserva- tion are all significant. Thus while significant increases in real price are not impossible, it is more likely that if there is to be an increase at all, it will be small. . . . Thus while there may be some scope for modest fluctuations in the real price of energy, a reason- able assumption seems to be that it will remain constant or slightly increase.[14]

This is in sharp contrast to the assumptions about price contained in the Canada–Alberta Agreement. It must be remembered, however, that MSED was not a major player in the negotiations. During this same period its minister, Alberta Senator Bud Olson, was attempting to find his and MSED's own limited involvement in the post-NEP policy process partly through devices such as the Alberta Technical Advisory Committee, examined in Chapters 3 and 8.

Forecasting on the energy **supply** side within EMR was inherently more difficult and ad hoc than on the price and macroeconomic items noted above. In contrast to the apparent confidence in forecasting prices that the NEP planners demonstrated, there was much more caution in specifying which of the possible future sources of supply— oil sands, Beaufort, Hibernia or high Arctic, would, should or could come onstream first. The internal views varied, and were based on different kinds of variables and experience. For example, some of the traditional geological experts with long experience in EMR argued that the wisest strategy was to keep working the Western Sedimentary Basin, gradually working northwards to link up to Norman Wells and on to the Beaufort over the years. Others saw the oil sands in a similar way, because there was greater confidence that one could predict future costs of such projects, particularly if one built them gradually in moderately scaled proportions, improving the technology as experience was gained.

Both of these scenarios, however, were Alberta based in focus, and were gradualist strategies. They did not appeal to those in EMR who were driven more by the desire to find "Middle-East sized" discoveries, nor did they accord with the geo-politics of the NEP which saw Ottawa wanting the Canada Lands which *it* controlled as the focal point for future development. Ottawa also was under pressure from Dome, Petro-Canada and Imperial Oil, which had major stakes in the Canada Lands.

Given that each possible source of new supply had its own list of pros and cons, the NEP itself was cautious about saying which was the most probable. There was, however, a general belief that southern Alberta-based conventional supplies were declining and that new sources of supply were needed, but at that point specifics gave way to generalities. This is a further reason why the search to delineate further supply possibilities through the scatter-gun "come and explore and we'll give you grants" approach in the PIP program was initiated.

There are of course other dimensions to the risky art and politics of forecasting supply that we have not treated here. The debate over the adequacy of Canada's reserves for domestic versus export purposes are central to energy politics. We return to this point in Chapter 8 when we analyse the negotiations that led to the 1981 Canada–Alberta Agreement, and in Chapter 11 when we review energy regulation and the National Energy Board. In this brief analysis we have focussed on the forecasting dilemmas in the immediate context of the NEP itself and in the 1981–82 period.

Summary

The focus of this chapter has been on the genesis of the NEP (with some reference also to the later September 1981 Canada–Alberta agreement) rather than on its effects. We have much more to say in Parts III, IV and V about its effects politically and as a policy initiative. We also return to the key provisions surveyed above in a preliminary way. We have by no means exhausted the analysis of the origins of the NEP either. For example, one needs to understand briefly how the NEP legislation itself was passed and amended as key interests tried to adjust and/or recover from the Ottawa juggernaut. Chapter 3 surveys these other events and later chapters examine them in even greater detail.

What we have stressed here is that the NEP must first be seen as an act of political aggressiveness, an "act first—talk later" approach. It concerned far more than just energy policy; rather, it embraced and collided with competing views of Canada held by powerful political leaders on both ideological and regional grounds, and displayed the full context of powerful governmental, partisan, industrial and foreign interests in a world that was growing increasingly cantankerous, fearful and unpredictable. There were, of course, important energy issues of supply, price, and ownership at stake that the federal government had to address. But one cannot understand energy politics or the NEP unless one begins at the beginning and traces its roots in the broadest possible context. Politics rarely obeys the boundaries set by the definitions of single policy fields.

Notes

1. The arch advocate of a simplistic "the bureaucrats did it" thesis is Peter Foster, whose work we comment on later in this chapter. See Peter Foster, *The Sorcerer's Apprentices: Canada's Super Bureaucrats and the Energy Mess* (Toronto: Collins, 1982).
2. See G. Bruce Doern, ed., *How Ottawa Spends 1982 (*and *1983)* (Toronto: Lorimer, 1982 and 1983), chapter 1.
3. For data on this point see David K. Foot, ed., *Public Employment and Compensation in Canada: Myths and Realities* (Toronto: Butterworths, 1978).

4. See Glen Toner, "Oil, Gas and Integration: A Review of Five Major Energy Decisions," in J. Pammett and B. Tomlin, *The Integration Question: Political Economy and Public Policy in Canada and North America* (Toronto: Addison-Wesley, 1984).

5. See Stephen Clarkson, *Canada and the Reagan Challenge* (Toronto: Lorimer, 1982).

6. See V.S. Wilson, *Canadian Public Policy and Administration: Theory and Environment* (Toronto: McGraw Hill-Ryerson, 1981), chapters 7 to 11; Colin Campbell, *Governments Under Stress* (Toronto: University of Toronto Press, 1983); G. Bruce Doern and Richard W. Phidd, *Canadian Public Policy: Ideas, Structure, Process* (Toronto: Methuen, 1983), chapter 9. These books review other literature on the ministerial-bureaucratic power issues.

7. See Foster, *op. cit.*, especially chapter 10.

8. Foster's account of this phase of the NEP's development is both interesting and accurate. So is his discussion of the power of Marc Lalonde. Surprisingly, however, he does not relate these to his overall thesis. Lalonde is powerful, but it is the bureaucrats who "did it."

9. This was at the heart of the "tax expenditure" debate of the late 1970s and was resurrected again when Allan MacEachen's 1981 budget tried to close some such "loopholes," as they were now referred to by critics. See Allan Maslove, "The Other Side of Public Spending: Tax Expenditures in Canada," in G. Bruce Doern and Allan M. Maslove, eds., *The Public Evaluation of Government Spending* (Montreal: Institute for Research on Public Policy, 1979), pp. 149–168.

10. See Energy, Mines and Resources, "Canada Lands and the Crown Interest," paper dated November 3, 1981.

11. See Mobil Oil Canada Ltd., *Submission to the Senate Banking, Trade and Commerce Committee Studying Bill C-48* (November 4, 1981), pp. 4–6.

12. See Jeffrey Simpson, *Discipline of Power* (Toronto: Personal Library, 1980), chapter 6.

13. See Doern and Phidd, *op. cit.*, chapters 13 and 18.

14. Minister of State for Economic Development, "Sectoral and Regional Economic Development in the Medium Term Perspective and Outlook," Ottawa, pp. 34–36. This report is dated November 1981, but was circulated in draft form as early as the spring of 1981. See also G. Bruce Doern, "The Mega-project Episode and the Formulation of Canadian Economic Development Policy," *Canadian Public Administration*, vol. 26, no. 2 (Summer 1983), pp. 219–238.

PART II

CANADIAN ENERGY HISTORY AND THE PRE-NEP LEGACY

CHAPTER 3

THE HISTORY OF CANADIAN ENERGY POLITICS AND POLICY

History always matters. Both politicians and citizens have memories. Ideas and interests are forged in, and reinforced by, the passage of time. Some interests evaluate the justice and fairness of the NEP from a deep, historically entrenched perspective. Others see it as a short-term aberration. In either case, we need a historical perspective to gauge the contending political claims. This chapter therefore provides a chronology of key policies and events in Canada's energy history. The intention is to highlight historical events in a straightforward way on a decade-by-decade basis, with the focus on the post-World War II era in general and on the post-1973 period in particular. A historical perspective is necessary to appreciate the more detailed analysis in Parts II and III, especially since we revisit many of the key events, first to look at the relationship between government and industry and then at the inter-governmental relationships of power. Appendix I provides a list of key events to help guide the way. It is also essential to stress that our chronology focusses on the oil and gas elements of energy policy, since they have clearly been the dominant fuels in the last two decades. Other fuels are not ignored but are noted primarily in the context of their particular regional importance. Each region of Canada is endowed with a different energy-resource configuration and thus coal, hydroelectric and nuclear energy are important in the total national setting.[1]

The chapter is organized into four sections. The first provides a brief profile of the pre-1945 energy policy legacy. The next three sections examine the 1945–1973, 1973–1980 and 1980–1984 periods, respectively.

A Profile of the Pre-1945 Legacy

Canadian energy events must first be located in the context of the broad pre-1945 legacy of the Canadian political economy. Several of the main features of that legacy are summarily noted in this section without further comment. The necessary brevity of our discussion should not lull the reader into a false sense that what is past is past. The pre-1945 legacy has had a remarkable and persistent staying power and underpins the modern era.

The first legacy is Prime Minister John A. Macdonald's National Policy. It was an act of intervention that combined tariff policy, immigration policy, and transportation policy to support the central Canadian industrial heartland and to build a nation.[2] It was an act of political defiance against the economic efficiency of the north-south axis. It is also the ultimate precursor to the continued importance of state intervention in Canada. Such intervention took on more precise energy-related forms in later pre-1945 decades. For example, hydro electric power in Ontario was nationalized in 1906, the result of pressure brought to bear by the business community.[3] Later an atomic energy industry was fostered under state auspices through Atomic Energy of Canada and Eldorado Nuclear, albeit through the additional impetus supplied by World War II.[4]

The National Policy, though it forged a nation-state could not, and did not, override all the underlying realities of Canada's internal regional centrifugal forces nor the external dependencies created by continental trade and economics. Thus the National Policy also generated a significant counterreaction from those regions and economic classes that were not its primary beneficiaries. Successive bursts of prairie populism and western Canadian alienation against central Canada and central Canadian financial and industrial interests occurred. The cumulative impact of these historical grievances was revealed again in the decades after World War II.

One particular manifestation of the strength of regional views was the initial Constitutional arrangements regarding jurisdiction over natural resources.[5] Only after strong provincial pressure were the western provinces given primary control of resources in 1930. Sections 109, 92(2), 92(5), and 92(13) of the British North America Act provide the basis of provincial authority. The ownership of offshore resources is the object of major dispute particularly between Ottawa and Newfoundland. Resource management is also affected by the fact that much of the land under which oil and gas exploration is conducted is Crown owned, especially in Alberta and British Columbia, but also in the north in what are now labelled the Canada Lands. Since the 1930s, producer provinces have fought hard to secure greater constitutional protection of resource rights because the federal government, through its many indirect ways of controlling resources (e.g., its powers of taxation, interprovincial trade, and foreign policy) has increasingly exercised such powers for fiscal and other political reasons. These provincial concerns led to the achievement of additional protections in the Constitution Act of 1982. Section 50 of the Act, which adds section 92A to the 1867 Act, provides these protections. Thus, although property rights over resources became a deservedly important issue to the western provinces in particular, it is nonetheless a fact that overall energy policy involves shared constitutional powers between the two levels of government.

As to the continental pull of energy realities, the pre-1945 legacy contains useful reminders of the existence of larger energy markets. From the outset there have been continental energy supply issues that are a direct result of nature's physical assignment of resources and their geographic proximity to population centres. Thus coal has been imported into Ontario, electricity has been exported to the northern United States, and for much of the early oil era until 1950, Canada was heavily dependent upon oil imports from the United States. Indeed, during much of the pre-1973 period, Canadian oil supply and prices were benignly "managed" by the Texas Railway Commission, an arrangement thought to be politically quite secure.[6]

Finally, it is essential to mention the legacy left by the forging of the post-war reconstruction policies which emerged out of the 1944 White Paper on Employment and Income. They ushered in the Keynesian era and the welfare state.[7] They can also be said to have helped shift political attention to the issues of macroeconomic policy. Energy issues much like other industrial policy matters seemed thereafter to fall into the residual crevices of the new distinctions being made between macro- and microeconomics. Energy came to be viewed as an industry much like any other. Indeed, one did not even refer to energy policy or the energy industry as such. If anything, one spoke only of oil policy or the coal industry.

The 1947 Leduc and 1948 Redwater oil discoveries marked the birth of the modern Canadian oil industry. Although there had been significant discoveries made earlier in the century at Turner Valley, Alberta (1914) and Norman Wells, N.W.T. (1921), for example, neither of these had been followed up by a series of other major strikes. Leduc and Redwater accounted, by 1960, for 75 percent of the 30.8 billion barrels of oil and 56 percent of the natural gas discovered in Alberta since 1946.[8] Field names such as Steelman, Judy Creek, Pembina, Swan Hills, and Weyburn had become part of the lexicon of life on the Canadian prairies.

The 1950s form a component of the earliest of the three periods of Canadian energy events into which this chronology is divided. The 1950s really include the period from the 1947 Leduc strike to the promulgation of the National Oil Policy (NOP) in 1961. As shown below, the NOP was really a product of the major energy debates and conflicts of the 1950s and thus must be seen as more representative of the spirit of the '50s than that of the '60s (1962–1972). Before reviewing the major developments between 1947 and 1973, it is useful to characterize briefly the two component periods of this era, as well as the larger period itself.

The overall period between 1947 and 1973 was marked by a reasonable consensus of values between the federal and provincial governments over the management of Canada's growing oil and gas reserves. The overriding objective of energy policy was to encourage oil and gas production and to stimulate the growth of the domestic petroleum industry. This objective was achieved through the construction of major oil and natural gas pipelines from the producing prairie provinces to consuming regions in both Canada and the United States, the creation of a favourable tax climate to spur investment and an aggressive export policy. Within this policy framework, the oil and gas industry was given a wide latitude in the development of Canada's oil and gas reserves. The 1947–1973 period was characterized by much less government interference in the interplay of market forces than exists now; the assumption of abundance; price stability; the objective of promoting growth; and a consensus of values and objectives among the major private and governmental interests. As such, this period stands in relative contrast to the post-1973 period, in which increased state intervention, the assumption of scarcity, dramatic price increases and rapid inflation, the objective of promoting conservation, and government–industry and inter-governmental political conflict became much more prevalent. Within the 1947–1973 period, the '50s can be characterized as a time of dramatic start-up growth, and the '60s as a time of even more impressive production growth, but also quiet, consensus-based regulatory consolidation.

The 1950s: The Transformation to Oil

The 1950s marked the transformation of Canada from a coal- to an oil-based economy. Oil production increased from about 30 million barrels in 1950 to about 190 million in 1960. Natural gas production went from about 70 million cubic feet to over 500 million cubic feet in this same period.[9] By 1955 Canada was exporting about 50 000 barrels per day, a significant figure but still well below Canada's level of oil imports. While the oil and gas industry, as a whole, was experiencing prolific growth, the large, primarily foreign-owned firms were strengthening their control of the industry via the takeover of many smaller, Canadian-owned firms in both the upstream and downstream sides of the industry. The other major structural phenomenon of the 1950s was the veritable explosion in pipeline construction as the oil and gas lines, which served most of Canada's needs, were built. Accordingly, energy issues in this period revolved around questions of jurisdictional authority, pipeline routes, transmission costs, exports, and foreign ownership.

Jurisdictional Growth

The realization in the late 1940s of the size of the Alberta oil fields precipitated another of the intermittent rounds of constitutional jockeying for authority over the control and management of natural resources which have historically characterized federal–provincial relations. John Richards and Larry Pratt have characterized the political sentiment in Alberta which helped motivate the Social Credit government's expansion of its authority over oil and gas during this period:

> Social Credit, like the CCF in Saskatchewan, was eager to diversify Alberta's economic base out of its heavy dependence on agricultural commodities. Memories of the recent depression were still intense, and before Imperial's discovery of oil at Leduc in February 1947, the province's economic prospects were not particularly bright. ... Alberta's future, it seemed in 1946, would largely revolve around the wheat farm, the ranching and livestock industry, and

mixed farming: . . . many anticipated a gradual long-run decline in both the rural and the total provincial population. Oil promised growth and the prospect of diversification; it also held out hope that Alberta's public debt burdens could be eliminated without increasing personal taxation.[10]

Alberta's fear of outside corporate control under federal jurisdiction and the desire to ensure the primary access of Albertans to provincial gas supplies led the Alberta government to enact the **Gas Resources Preservation Act** in 1949. It acted in the same year to strengthen its constitutional jurisdiction over the regulation of the removal of gas from the province by establishing the Petroleum and Natural Gas Conservation Board (later changed to the Energy Resources Conservation Board).

In 1949 the federal government passed the **Pipe Line Act.** This legislation provided for federal control of interprovincial and international oil and gas pipelines. It required the incorporation by an act of Parliament of companies proposing to transmit Canadian oil and gas to markets outside the producing province. Following incorporation, the companies had to submit for approval by the Board of Transport Commissioners the details of the project, such as the route to be followed.

In 1954 Alberta created Alberta Gas Trunk Line (AGTL) to act as a single gas gathering system. AGTL would act as a common carrier inside Alberta and distribute pooled gas to export companies at the provincial border. Richards and Pratt sum up the logic behind its creation:

> On constitutional grounds the Manning government had long worried that federally incorporated pipelines could, by extending their gathering lines across Alberta's borders into its major gas fields, thereby also extend Ottawa's jurisdiction into the province and give the federal authorities well head control over Alberta's gas; this in turn could be used by the Dominion to undermine Alberta's emphasis on local priority in regard to supply and price and to provide consumers in eastern Canada or the United States with cheap western Canadian gas.[11]

The government chose a mixed private and public ownership structure for AGTL. In so doing they rejected the alternatives of a crown corporation, on ideological grounds, and a wholly privately owned firm, on the grounds that it could fall into the hands of outside (i.e. non-Alberta) interests.

Throughout the early 1950s the federal Parliament experienced a number of heated sessions associated with various pipeline incorporations. In 1956, however, Parliament was racked by an unusually acrimonious debate over the federal government's handling of the Trans-Canada Pipeline. The intensity of the debate over both the parliamentary behaviour and energy policy aspects of the pipeline debate contributed to the defeat of the St. Laurent Liberals by the Diefenbaker-led Conservatives.[12] In 1957 a Royal Commission on Energy was established. Following its report, the federal government created the National Energy Board in 1959 and established a National Oil Policy in 1961.

Pipeline Routes, Transmission Costs, Foreign Ownership, and Exports

The geographical fact that Canadian reserves and Canadian markets are separated by vast distances and natural barriers such as the Rocky Mountains and the Canadian Shield has conferred special importance on the issue of oil and gas transportation. Questions of pipeline routes, the inclusion of exports, the price of exports, and the cost of transmitting Canadian fuels to Canadian markets have been the focus of much acrimonious debate.

For example, concern about national integration and self-sufficiency in fuels was reflected in the objective of preserving exclusive Canadian jurisdiction over transmission systems by ensuring that they were built entirely within Canada. "All-Canadian" routes had the advantage of being free from U.S. interference in the delivery of Canadian oil and gas to Canadian markets across U.S. territory and second, would not be subject to pressure for excessive exports to the United States. This concern with exclusive jurisdiction, however, often clashed with the equally important concept of economic efficiency, which in this case was reflected in the objective of reducing the cost of transmitting Canadian fuels to Canadian markets and thereby improving the competitive position of Canadian fuels in Canadian markets. It was argued that the unit cost of transmitting Canadian fuels to Canadian markets could be lowered by building in an "export component" to take advantage of economies of scale achieved through increased throughput volumes. John McDougall, in his excellent history of Canadian fuel policies, characterizes the spirit of this debate and its outcome:

> . . . (given) the fact that pipelines routed through the U.S. were likely to market a portion of their throughput in the United States, it is not surprising that numerous debates in Canada over the construction of pipelines pitted nationalists who felt that Canadian markets should be served entirely with Canadian fuels and delivered by means of pipelines built exclusively within Canada, against "free marketers," who felt that Canadian markets should be served by Canadian sources only if necessary and then only by means of pipelines built along the cheapest possible routes. The former would maximize interprovincial trade at the expense of international trade, while the latter would do the reverse. The decisions actually taken and the transmission systems actually built resembled neither the nationalist nor the free-market, continentalist extreme. Viewed as a network of oil and gas transportation systems, the Canadian pipeline projects approved between 1949 and 1961 form what could be called either a quasi-national or a semi-continental pattern of fuel transportation and distribution. . . .[13]

Five major transmission systems were incorporated and given federal approval prior to 1960. Interprovincial and Trans-Canada were to supply central Canada with Alberta oil and gas respectively. Transmountain and Westcoast were to do the same for the west coast. All four employed the "joint service" concept. That is, they were designed to serve export as well as domestic markets and, in fact, depended on exports to be viable. In the most extreme case, Westcoast, in order to achieve export markets, entered into an arrangement whereby it sold gas to U.S. distributors at a price considerably lower than the prices charged Canadian consumers. The fifth line, Canada-Montana, was built at the request of the U.S. military and the Canadian Department of Defence to meet the gas needs of the Anaconda Copper smelter in northern Montana, which was producing war materials for the Korean War effort. In a chronological review of this kind, however, it is the Trans-Canada Pipeline which is most illustrative of the issues. Before presenting a brief portrait of the Trans-Canada debate, we must look at a major energy policy statement made by C.D. Howe on behalf of the St. Laurent government on March 13, 1953.

In a prescient nod to future conflicts, Howe acknowledged the constitutional provision respecting provincial resource ownership while also stressing Ottawa's power over international and interprovincial trade. Of central importance in this statement are the very different attitudes the government exhibited toward oil and gas. The major concern with oil was to move it "from the source of production to refineries within economic distance in the cheapest possible way," and "to arrange for markets for that portion of Canadian output that cannot be economically used in Canadian refineries in the market that offers the highest return to the producer."[14] The logic of this attitude is reflected in both the Interprovincial and Transmountain pipelines. In fact, Interprovincial was built south of the Great Lakes through the United States in order to serve markets in both the midwestern United States and central Canada.

For natural gas, on the other hand, Howe applied the logic which governed policy respecting the other premium energy source, electricity. It was government policy, Howe claimed, to refuse permits to move natural gas by pipeline across the border until the government was convinced "there can be no economic use present or future for that gas within Canada." Westcoast and Canadian-Montana were to be the only exceptions. So while Howe appeared to reject the idea of a nation-wide market for Canadian oil because of the high transportation costs to central Canada, he insisted that "the only reliable supply of natural gas for the provinces of Ontario and Québec must be from western Canada by means of an all-Canadian pipeline." The means would be the Trans-Canada Pipeline.

The Trans-Canada Pipeline

The Trans-Canada pipeline was lauded by its supporters as a classic example of nation building in action. Indeed, Howe was fond of comparing it to that other great transportation project—the building of the CPR railway, the project so central to John A. MacDonald's National Policy. Howe argued that the building of the natural gas pipeline was as crucial for the building of an east-west continental nation in the twentieth century as the building of the Canadian Pacific Railway had been in the nineteenth. It would carry Canadian resources from the west to Canadian consumers and manufacturers in central Canada, and do so entirely on Canadian soil. So commendable were its objectives that the lone voice of concern raised in Parliament during its original bill of incorporation was that of a member from Cape Breton, who was concerned that the proposal to market Alberta natural gas as far east as Montreal would threaten the market for Nova Scotia coal. Moreover, the initial proposal included no reference to exports. In fact, the pipeline was extolled as a means to reduce Canada's dependence on American supplies of coal and oil. Yet, before it was finished this project would tie Canada even more tightly into a continental energy market, bring down a national government and, as historian William Kilbourn put it, "raise most of the classic issues in Canada's survival as a nation."

> American economic influence and the nature of Canadian-American relations; the debate between north-south continentalism and east-west nationalism, the questions of transportation and national unity, of energy and national growth, of control over natural resources and their exploitation; the latent conflict between western producer and eastern consumer; dominion–provincial relations; the problem of public versus private enterprise and the compromise of the crown corporation; the connections between business and politics, and the role of regulatory bodies between them; the rights of Parliament; and the place of popular feelings, pressure groups and the press in the difficult matter of making decisions on complex issues of great national importance.[15]

The idea of the Trans-Canada was conceived by a U.S. entrepreneur in opposition to projects proposing a continental gas swap, in which Alberta gas would be exported to the western United States, and central Canada would be supplied from Texas by an extension of existing mid-western U.S. pipelines. During the development of the project, the Trans-Canada proposal was combined with the Western Pipe Lines proposal, which included an export component (at Emerson, Manitoba) to make it financially feasible. Initially, the Canadian owners of the Western project intended to build the line to central Canada south of the Great Lakes through the United States.

In 1954, Trans-Canada was in financial difficulty and had secured few supply or market contracts for gas. The following year Trans-Canada approached Howe, requesting government bond guarantees. Howe and the government agreed to provide financial support which could have resulted in government equity ownership in Trans-Canada. Gulf Corporation of Pittsburgh, whose Canadian subsidiary (now called Gulf Canada Ltd. but then known as British American Oil Ltd.) was to supply roughly 40 percent of Trans-Canada's gas needs, had established a policy of refusing to sell to a company controlled by government, or which could be controlled by government through the exercise of rights. Accordingly, Gulf refused to let Gulf Canada sign contracts with Trans-Canada. In their haste to get the project completed before the expected 1957 election and underway before the winter non-construction season, the government chose not to challenge Gulf. Rather, it chose another tack and created a Crown corporation to finance and operate the most expensive and difficult northern Ontario section of the all-Canadian route. Trans-Canada had by this time acquired an option on steel pipe and needed further support to ease its financial difficulties. The St. Laurent government agreed to a temporary arrangement whereby 51 percent ownership would reside with U.S. interests. Even though the company was then majority U.S.-owned, Howe still agreed to provide further loan guarantees and furthermore to use closure to force the Trans-Canada legislation through the frenzied House of Commons.

The Trans-Canada debate was particularly furious because of the opposition's anger at the government's readiness to grant loan guarantees to a U.S.-controlled firm and over the Liberals' treatment of Parliament. The controversy generated by the Pipeline debate both highlighted the importance of energy policy and contributed to the defeat of the Liberals after twenty-two years in power. One of the first acts of the new Diefenbaker government in 1957 was to appoint Toronto industrialist Henry Borden to head a Royal Commission on Energy. The Borden Commission achieved three things in particular: it helped depoliticize the volatile energy issue; it assessed the need for an independent agency to supervise the activities of the petroleum industry; and it settled the question of whether or not the oil pipeline system should be extended to Montreal in order that the refineries there could use Canadian crude oil rather than off-shore imports from Venezuela and elsewhere. The legacy of the Borden Commission was the creation of the National Energy Board in 1959, and the adoption of the National Oil Policy in 1961. Before reviewing these developments, we must note briefly the final report of yet another Royal Commission.

The Gordon Commission

One of the key issues addressed by the Royal Commission on Canada's Economic Prospects led by Walter Gordon was the impact of foreign direct investment on Canada's economic growth. With respect to the oil and gas industry, the Report was optimistic about its growth prospects, but pessimistic about it reducing its high level (roughly 80 percent) of foreign ownership. The Commission concluded that the foreign-owned subsidiaries—in large part owing to their access to parent company financial resources—had the size to finance large-scale capital investments, to engage in competitive bidding for land for exploration and development, to generate revenues at many or most stages of the integrated industry, and perhaps most importantly, to satisfy most of their expansion capital needs from retained earnings, thereby decreasing the need to involve Canadian equity ownership.

The Commission also noted a number of other advantages that foreign-owned subsidiaries had which resulted in decreasing the degree of decision making in the hands of the Canadian-owned sector and which in other ways worked to Canada's disadvantage. For instance, United States government tax incentives encouraged U.S. firms to go abroad to explore for oil and gas. Via inter-company transfers, foreign-controlled firms tended to charge their parent companies too little for raw materials and to overpay them for things they acquired from them such as imported oil, management and research, and development services. Subsidiaries also tended to use equipment and supplies from traditional parent company sources in the United States or elsewhere rather than to seek out Canadian supplies.

The Gordon Commission made a number of recommendations, including greater reliance on foreign capital in the form of bonds or mortgages; a minimum 20–25 percent Canadian ownership of companies operating in Canada; the appointment of more Canadians to senior management positions; the appointment of independent Canadians to the subsidiaries' board of directors; greater use by foreign-owned firms of Canadian engineering, professional, and service personnel; more Canadian sourcing of supplies, materials, and equipment; and the requirement of Canadian participation in future oil and gas exploration permits and leases.[16] These recommendations had little impact on the politicians and officials in Ottawa and the producing provinces, and it would be another twenty-three years before these issues would be addressed more directly in the 1980 NEP.

The Borden Commission, Natural Gas Exports, and the Alberta-to-Montreal Pipeline

John McDougall has argued that the vague generalities in which the terms of reference for the Borden Commission were phrased suggested that the new Diefenbaker government had not determined the substance of a new national energy policy. "The job of the commission would not simply be to recommend 'the policies that will serve the national interest' but in fact to define the national interest."[17] McDougall observed further that "the key question here is: whose interests were eventually to be taken by the commission to constitute the national interest?" The Commission's ultimate decision on export volumes and the Alberta-to-Montreal Pipeline, at least in part, answers this question.

The debate surrounding natural gas exports in the '50s was multi-faceted, despite the St. Laurent government's straightforward 1953 statement. The producing provinces, the cities of Edmonton and Calgary, and the major consuming provinces were in agreement that Canadian market requirements for natural gas should be met at the lowest possible price and that supplies should be reserved for a number of years in the future before exports were allowed. In other words, long term availability at stable prices was the objective. From the industry's perspective, however, it was availability that was the main concern. McDougall characterized the industry's argument as follows:

> The Canadian Petroleum Association (CPA), Westcoast Transmission, Shell Canada and others continuously stressed the importance of export markets in encouraging the development of reserves. The dynamics of the interdependence between markets and reserve development argued by these parties was that the enlarged demand caused by exports would raise prices and that in turn, higher revenues to producers would stimulate increased exploration and development. . . . There is a circularity to this reasoning which has persisted in export policy ever since. It is born of the producer's argument that the best protection with regard to

future supply is the export of gas. The circularity consists in the fact that the volumes of gas that are counted upon to justify the export of gas (that is, the volumes of gas necessary to protect the future increase in demand in the Canadian market) are allowed to depend upon the export of gas for their development. Whether the rate of discovery and development of reserves has, in fact, any relationship whatsoever to the rate of export of gas is a question open to empirical investigation. But a problem can arise even if new discoveries are so generated. The gas to be exported and the gas whose expected development is supposed to justify exports are, of course, different lots of gas; the latter may only become available at higher cost and in more inaccessible locations than the exported gas it is counted on to replace. Hence, it is possible that by making exports allowable on the basis of trends in discovery, proven reserves at current prices will be exported, while the protection of Canadian requirements will depend upon future reserves at higher prices.[18]

In its conclusions regarding gas exports, the Commission rejected the position of the cities and provincial governments and stated that "in the administration of export policy it would be unfair to producers of natural gas to require, at this time, that proven reserves be set aside for all long-term future needs in Canada."[19] McDougall thus concluded "that policies recommended as being in the Canadian national interest necessarily entail fairness to producers of natural gas is an assumption which may or may not be valid, but it is one that the Commission did not bother to justify."[20]

The Borden Commission's rejection of the Alberta to Montreal Pipeline also involved different dynamics in defining "the national interest." On the one hand, as a result of falling world oil prices, the Canadian oil industry in the late 1950s was encountering increasing difficulty in competing against imports of cheaper foreign oil. Because the price of Canadian-produced oil was established by the majors and based on the Chicago gate price, Alberta oil prices were considerably higher. Consequently, Alberta production was running at less than 50 percent capacity. On the other hand there was the problem of the U.S. government's 1959 decision, taken as a result of pressure from the independent U.S. producers, to establish a mandatory oil imports program. While Canada and Mexico were granted an "overland exemption" for reasons of U.S. security of supply, imports were still limited.

The Canadian independents, in particular, needed cash flow to finance their growth and were anxious to find new markets. The Canadian-owned Home Oil Company, supported by a group of other independents, proposed constructing a thirty-inch diameter oil pipeline from Edmonton to Montreal to deliver 200 000 barrels per day in 1960 and 320 000 barrels per day in 1965. Such a line would have the advantages of supplying Alberta crude oil producers with a guaranteed market; increasing Canadian national security by eliminating the dependence of Montreal refineries on imported oil; creating major industrial benefits across Canada; ending the $350 million per year outflow of foreign exchange to pay for imported oil; and by ensuring access to all three of Canada's major oil markets, create a major stimulus for new exploration and production in western Canada. The catch was that in order to make the pipeline a financial success, the Montreal refineries owned by the oil majors would have to sign long term agreements to use the full capacity of the line. Long term contracts themselves were not unusual, as most of the refineries had signed them with their foreign parent companies for offshore oil. Yet, the multinationals were unanimous in their opposition to Home Oil's proposal. The majors, led by Imperial Oil, phrased their opposition in terms of both increased costs and opposition to greater government involvement in the industry. It was argued that Alberta oil delivered to Montreal would be more expensive than offshore oil, and that alternative market opportunities for Canadian crude existed in the Pacific and north central United States. The multinationals argued that government protection of the Montreal market would be mandatory if the pipeline went ahead and governmental interference in the crude oil market was generally opposed.

In his interpretation of this period, J.G. Debanné points to two other related reasons for the multinationals' position. The oil imported into Eastern Canada from the Middle East and Venezuela was very profitable. The Venezuelan government was demanding an increasing share of revenue, and therefore the multinationals were anxious to produce their Venezuelan oil as soon as possible while conditions were favourable. Since the oil was higher priced than Middle East oil, both at the source and at the North American ports of entry, the multinationals preferred to route as much Venezuelan oil as possible to eastern Canada, where they were able to maintain higher prices than in comparable regions of the United States, such as New England.[21] The U.S. government, which had just imposed its own restrictions on imported oil, was concerned for political reasons that Venezuelan oil not be displaced in eastern Canada by western Canadian crude. They felt that the guaranteed market for the Venezuelan oil in eastern Canada would strengthen the Venezuelan economy and thereby enhance the stability of the Venezuelan government.

The second reason is related to the ownership of imported oil relative to the prorationed production from Alberta. As Debanné pointed out, the system allowed the Jersey- or Shell-controlled refineries in Montreal to be supplied exclusively from Jersey- or Shell-controlled oil fields respectively, and to have much of this oil transported in company-owned tankers. In other words, more Jersey or Shell oil was sold for every barrel of oil imported by Imperial and Shell refineries in Montreal than if this oil originated from "prorated" production in Alberta. This was because Shell and Imperial production in Alberta was diluted by the proration formula which allocated "production allowables" to all Alberta producers.[22]

In opposition to the Alberta–Montreal line many of the major companies, not surprisingly, expressed a preference for natural continental patterns of supply in which Canadian and U.S. crudes would be freely used in the most economical markets. What this meant in practice was that the Montreal market was to be reserved for overseas sources of supply, while Canadian production was to grow by expanding in markets in Ontario and lower mainland British Columbia, and by increasing penetration of accessible U.S. markets. Such a scheme would in fact emerge within a couple of years in the form of the 1961 NOP.

In addition to Debanné's account, other analysts have provided different interpretations of the outcome of the Borden Commission's decision to reject the Home Oil proposal. David Crane, for example, interpreted the same events even more starkly as a significant sacrifice of the national interest to the interests of the majors:

> . . . In this confrontation between the oil majors and the Canadian independents, the majors won. The Royal Commission came down clearly on the side of the majors. . . . Yet though the independents had lost this battle, there was a heightened awareness among Canadians of the ways in which the majors' power could override the national interest. Evidently there were two sets of rules: The

United States, at the urging of its oil industry, could establish quotas as well as a tariff on oil imports, but the Canadian subsidiaries of the same companies could argue that these things would be bad for Canada. The majors' preferred supply patterns were simply aggravating a reduced-production predicament in Alberta that increased the likelihood of more takeovers of cash and credit-poor Canadian independents.[23]

On the other hand, McDougall interpreted the same decision in terms that come much closer to saying that the general national interest was not badly served:

Still it is hard to sustain the argument that the Montreal pipeline issue pitted the Canadian interest or Canadian nationalism against the power of the American government and American firms. While these factors were unquestionably present, there is little evidence of Canadian interest in the scheme except on the part of the Canadian independent firms, and even then only if reliable American markets could not be obtained. Little support for the policy emanated from central Canada: Ontario already received Alberta oil, and no representatives from Quebec even addressed the issue in Parliament. This lack of support for the idea in Quebec was probably a reflection of the fact that Alberta oil would be more costly than Venezuelan oil delivered to Montreal. No one seemed impressed with the security advantages of self-sufficiency for Canada, despite the Suez crisis only two years before. In sum, the only Canadians with a strong interest in the movement of Alberta oil to Montreal were the independent Canadian oil producers, and even they had more to gain from seeking a reduction in the American restrictions against imports from Canada.[24]

The National Oil Policy
The Borden Commission was undoubtedly influenced by the economic rationality of a continental as opposed to a purely national approach to the problems of oil production and marketing. In rejecting the idea of import restrictions for the Montreal market, the commission declared that such a decision "if made before the potentialities of the United States markets were fully exploited, would, among other things, seriously impair Canada's position vis-à-vis existing United States import restrictions and might jeopardize the development of a continental energy policy."[25] Just over a year after the Borden Commission recommended it, the Diefenbaker government announced its National Oil Policy in 1961. Having rejected a line to serve Montreal markets

with Canadian oil, the Borden or Ottawa Valley Line and the NOP reflected a consensus that satisfied the established practice of the multinationals, that provided a protected national market for Alberta crude in Ontario and the rest of the country west of the line, and gave eastern Canadian consumers east of the line lower priced offshore oil. The Borden Commission also offered the following view about the value of future continental flexibility:

> We mention the possibility of a continental policy not because we believe it can be developed in the immediate future, but because we feel that care should be taken to ensure that Canada, by its actions and commitments now, does not jeopardize the subsequent possible development of such a policy.[26]

The Diefenbaker Tory government supported the mixed continentalist and gradual national market expansion line of argument and augmented it by stating that they would try to help the independent Canadian producers by seizing every opportunity to increase access to the U.S. market for Canadian oil. The Lester Pearson-led Liberals explicitly endorsed the overall NOP approach to resource sharing, arguing that "if defense is to be considered on a continental basis, then resources and materials for continental defense must also be based on a continental basis."[27] Thus, both major parties approved of the essential features of the NOP.

The NOP decision was therefore surprisingly non-controversial, in part at least because it reflected a delicate balance between the needs of a number of interests. Moreover, it was not a statutory policy, and thus could be interpreted to have been arrived at in a quasi-voluntary way. Markets were being regulated but not in an imposed, draconian way. There is no question that the NOP satisfied the multinationals and the U.S. government and served to enhance continental integration of the Canadian and U.S. oil markets—even though it could not achieve the status of a full continental energy policy because of the U.S. import restrictions. However, it is also important to note that this decision of the Canadian government also won the support of the Canadian provinces affected.

Specifically, western Canadian oil was ensured its "natural" market for expansion, the midwestern United States, and was safeguarded against competition from cheaper oil where such competition could have hurt, namely, in the Ontario market. This satisfied Ottawa, the producing provinces, and the industry as it ensured that the industry would continue to grow in the west. Québec and the Maritimes enjoyed somewhat lower prices than would have been possible had they been supplied by western Canadian oil. The Canadian government benefited in the balance of payments by importing "cheap oil" east of the Borden line and exporting "expensive oil" west of it.

The only Canadians who could be said to have been hurt financially by the NOP were the consumers in Ontario who had to pay for the marginally higher priced western Canadian oil. J.G. Debanné argues, however, that the Ontario government accepted the NOP and the higher retail prices it entailed in exchange for the concentration and expansion of a large refining and petrochemical industry in the province.[28] There is continuing dispute as to how harmful the NOP was to the smaller independents. In the early 1960s they were very marginal importers of foreign oil into Ontario. They became more involved in 1968, when the gap between Montreal and Toronto prices increased.

The 1960s: Production, Expansion and Regulatory Consolidation

Compared to the 1950s, the 1970s, and the 1980s, the 1960s—actually 1962–1972—must rank as a time of rapid production and expansion coupled with quiet regulatory consolidation. In many respects it was the calm before the storm. With the main oil and gas pipelines in place, a National Energy Board established to oversee the administration of energy policy, and the National Oil Policy protecting the domestic oil industry, no major new policy initiatives were launched until the early 1970s.

The early 1960s also saw the consolidation of ownership and control by the major oil companies as the Canadian-controlled oil industry experienced the largest takeover activity in its history. "The eight major internationals by 1962 (had) some 60 percent of oil production and about 95 percent of refining capacity; in Alberta the fourteen top companies held 63 percent of the oil and gas lands."[29] Virtually the only response to the issue of foreign ownership was the Diefenbaker government's 1961 policy that established land regulations in the north and offshore. Under the terms of the **Canadian Oil and Gas Lands Regulations**, this policy restricted the granting of production licences to Canadian-owned firms or foreign-controlled companies in which Canadians would have a chance to invest. In practice this meant very little, however, as there were few restrictions on who could hold exploration permits. On the frontiers, both in the 1960s and for many years to come, it was the exploration, and not the production stage that was important.

The other, albeit unsuccessful, attempt to deal with the issue of foreign ownership was taken by Walter Gordon in his first budget as finance minister in the newly elected 1963 Pearson Liberal government. Gordon proposed a series of tax amendments which were intended to curb foreign takeovers and to increase Canadian ownership in foreign-controlled companies. He introduced a tax of 30 percent on the value of Canadian corporations taken over by non-residents and a regulation which restricted the benefit from accelerated depreciation under Canadian tax laws to companies which had a degree of Canadian ownership, that is, above 25 percent. He also proposed that petroleum companies with 25 percent or more Canadian ownership could reduce the withholding tax on dividends to foreign stockholders from the usual 15 percent to 10 percent while the same tax for other companies would be increased to 20 percent. These provisions were withdrawn in the face of massive opposition from the multinationals, the opposition Conservative Party, and the Canadian business and investment community.

One of the key objectives of creating the NEB was to depoliticize the energy issue by shifting decision making responsibility with respect to pipeline construction and export volumes and prices from the high profile partisan Cabinet–Parliamentary arena of the 1950s to the low-profile business-like forum of a quasi-independent and expert regulatory agency. This objective was clearly achieved. Cabinet decisions to approve NEB actions do not automatically come before Parliament, and it would appear that much of the potential opposition was lulled by the "symbolic reassurance" of the NEB's independence and expertise. In fact, the consensus is that during the decade of the '60s the NEB decided energy issues almost exclusively in response to the representations of the provincial governments and private companies which participated in its proceedings. The central objective of Canadian energy policy throughout the 1960s was to expand production partly through the export of greater volumes of oil and natural gas to the United States. The lack of any significant public opposition to the decisions taken in promotion of this objective must be understood in the context of a decade that was dominated by cheap and apparently reliable supplies of foreign oil, and by increasing Canadian oil and gas reserves. Simply put, there seemed to be little reason to fear that a rising rate of exports was in conflict with national needs and priorities.

The NEB's decisions respecting pipeline construction and export volume and price determination reveal a set of issues that are, for the most part, still relevant today. More specifically, in order to licence exports the NEB had to determine the extent and adequacy of Canadian reserves. This presented two problems. The first was that numerous geographical, geological, economic, and political factors interacted in the determination of demand and supply forecasts and in the estimation of reserves. This forecasting of the future is still much more of an art than a science. As McDougall put it:

> The rate at which Canada exported gas to the United States, therefore, depended essentially on the apparently technical matter of how the NEB operationalized the basic formula: exportable surplus equals established reserves minus Canadian requirements (ES = ER − CR). There is no question that in its detailed procedures this was a technical matter, but it is also true that the board's use of data, methods, and formulae in arriving at such estimates was, and indeed had to be, also a matter of political judgement.[30]

The second factor relates to the issue of trust and dependence. While the NEB had some expertise, it was primarily dependent on the oil and gas industry for both the numbers and the expertise to interpret them. These structural and informational issues were of no minor consequence, as a large estimate of reserves could lead to a larger exportable surplus.

To the extent that there was any conflict or controversy during this period, it focussed on the dispute between producers and consumers—particularly the large gas distribution companies in Canada—as to whether the board should be more liberal or more conservative in its determination of exportable surplus. Increased gas exports would lead directly to greater competition among transmission companies for gas supplies, and thereby to higher well head prices. Producers would welcome this prospect, consumers would not.

Throughout this period the NEB pursued a generally liberal or export oriented approach, altering their rules throughout the period to accommodate this liberalization.[31] The liberalization culminated in the Board's August 1970 decision to approve for export the largest single volume of gas exports in Canadian history. Exports also, of course, affect the rate of new discoveries, and thus are an engine of development at the same time that they may reduce longer-term total supply for domestic needs.

In promoting a strong export-oriented policy for Canadian oil and gas, the Board was following the position espoused by the Borden Commission and strongly articulated by the Liberal government. The Liberals' commitment was in evidence in statements made by J.J. Greene, the Minister of Energy, Mines and Resources. In 1969, Greene encouraged Washington to share his idea of continental energy arrangements so that "people will benefit, and both countries will benefit, irrespective of where the imaginary border goes."[32] Even more grandly, in 1971 Greene tried to convince Americans to import more Canadian oil and gas "because Canada had 923 years of oil and 392 years of natural gas in the ground."[33] These statements reflect not only the effervescent buoyancy of the late '60s and early '70s, but also Ottawa's heavy reliance on industry-supplied information. Within three years the industry would be telling Ottawa that Canada was running out of oil and gas. Throughout the 1960s Ottawa was becoming increasingly aware of its dependence on industry for information and on its own limited policy instruments in this field. To that end, in 1966 the Department of Energy, Mines and Resources was created, and Ottawa purchased 45 percent, and controlling interest, of Panarctic Oils. Panarctic's task was to undertake risky oil and gas exploration in the high Arctic and thus was one of the earliest links between energy and northern development policy.[34]

Thus, it can be seen that while the 1950s had been a period of rapid start-up growth, the 1960s had been a period of even greater production and expansion but coupled with quiet regulatory consolidation. Canadian oil and gas consumption grew steadily, prices were stable and the country's hydrocarbon potential appeared unlimited. This politically less eventful decade made the adjustment to the energy crisis of the early 1970s all the more traumatic.

While the above chronological account focusses on oil and gas, it is essential to stress the role of other energy sources, their regional importance, and the political issues they generated. Table 3.1 shows that coal was the dominant primary fuel in the Canadian economy in 1950 but was well behind petroleum five years later. This had a significant regional impact. The Nova Scotia coal industry had declined so precipitously that in 1963 the federal government established the Cape Breton Development Corporation (DEVCO) to wind down the industry and to find alternative employment and development opportunities for the affected local communities. DEVCO was presented not as an energy policy issue but rather as part of a progressive regional economic policy by the Pearson Liberals.[35]

TABLE 3.1
SOURCES OF CANADIAN PRIMARY ENERGY CONSUMPTION
(percentages)
1950–1970

	1950	1955	1960	1965	1970
Petroleum	29.8	45.7	48.6	49.4	48.1
Natural gas	2.5	3.9	9.0	13.1	16.5
Coal and coke	47.6	27.7	14.7	13.0	10.7
Hydroelectricity	20.1	22.7	27.7	24.5	24.6
Nuclear electricity	—	—	—	—	—
Total BTUs (10^{12})	2 493	3 188	3 671	4 814	6 328

Natural gas: 1 000 000 BTUs/mcf
Hydro and nuclear electricity: 10 000 BTUs/kilowatt-hour
Source: EMR, *Energy Futures for Canadians*, Ottawa, 1978, p. 303. Reproduced by permission.

Table 3.2 shows that Canada, in the midst of the relative decline of coal, remained nonetheless a net importer of coal, primarily to Ontario. The Ontario dependence on coal to fire its electrical generating capacity was also propelling Ontario Hydro into nuclear power. Ontario Hydro was an active partner with Atomic Energy of Canada in developing the CANDU reactor, whose efficiency was proven in the early 1970s after the first years of operation of the Pickering reactors. Two decades of federal research and developmental money had forged the CANDU from its World War II crucible. An intimate Ontario–Ottawa state-sustained link to nuclear energy was also present in the uranium industry. Ontario possessed the main reserves and Ottawa helped sustain the strategic mineral initially through stockpiling in the 1960s and in the early 1970s through its orchestration of a uranium cartel.[36] Both actions were judged by Ottawa to be necessary to sustain prices caused by U.S. policies which prohibited imports to the United States. It was also in the 1970s that Ottawa sought to induce the use of CANDUs by other provincial utilities through offers of loan assistance, a policy which helped persuade New Brunswick to go nuclear and which involved Hydro-Québec in a limited way as well. Nuclear policy and "forced growth" regional policies were also linked through the construction of the ill-fated heavy water plant in Nova Scotia as a joint Ottawa–Nova Scotia venture.[37]

TABLE 3.2
COAL SUPPLY AND DEMAND
(MILLIONS OF SHORT TONS)
1960–1975

	1960	1965	1970	1975
Canadian production	10.0	11.5	16.6	27.9
Imports[1]	12.7	16.7	19.8	17.5
Domestic demand	22.5	25.8	28.3	28.4
Exports[1]	1.0	1.3	4.7	12.7
Net exports (imports	(11.7)	(15.4)	(15.1)	(4.8)

[1]Includes coke
Source: EMR, *Energy Futures for Canadians*, Ottawa, 1978, p. 307. Reproduced by permission.

The economics underlying the historical evolution of electrical utilities must also be appreciated. From the early part of the century to the mid-1940s electrical utilities evolved from decreasing cost, local monopolies into provincial electrical grids. Decreasing costs continued for a time but certainly, from about 1970 on, it became more debatable as to whether these utilities had become *increasing* cost economic entities. They had certainly become giant enterprises with increasing amounts of political power in their provincial settings.[38]

It is also essential to stress that electrical energy remained a regional affair. The costs and technologies were such that national power grids were not possible. Some interprovincial power arrangements and exports to neighbouring U.S. states emerged, but electricity was not an overt matter of national energy policy as oil and gas had become. Even in oil and gas matters, however, it is useful to recall that they too were once largely regional matters. Only after the building of the major pipelines in the 1950s did interprovincial trade in oil and gas begin to dominate. With this increase came an increased role for the federal government.

Further nationalization of provincial hydro utilities also occurred in this period. These were invariably linked to "province-building" and economic development efforts by provincial premiers, and to the need to capture export markets in the United States. B.C. Hydro and Hydro-Québec clearly fell into this category. Hydro-Québec is particularly important because it became a state corporate symbol of the Quiet Revolution and Québec nationalism, and was arguably Québec's chief instrument of economic development policy. The Hydro-Québec development of the giant James Bay project launched in 1970 sealed the fate of more than one Québec government. Hydro-Québec's 1969 contract with the Churchill Falls (Labrador) Corporation (initially a private firm but later two-thirds owned by the Government of New-foundland) also produced a later bitter dispute between Québec and Newfoundland. Because Hydro-Québec put up the risk capital, Québec obtained the entire output of the Churchill Falls project on a long-term contract until 2041 at the now ridiculously low rate of three mills a kilowatt hour. Newfoundland protested against what it later viewed to be an unwarranted windfall gain for Québec.

It need not be reiterated that in all of the above coal-electricity-nuclear nexus, direct state involvement was a paramount fact of life. The various developments were also invariably laced with the partisan and party controversies and visions of Canada and her constituent regions.

1973-1980: The Broadening Politicization of Energy

The oil price and supply shocks of 1973 are usually cited as the major turning point in the politics of energy both domestically and internationally.[39] And indeed they were. Yet, on both the domestic and international fronts, the 1973 shocks were preceded by unilateral actions on behalf of key governments which broke with traditional patterns of behaviour in fundamental ways, and in so doing, ultimately contributed in a significant fashion to the restructuring of relationships which took place in the post-1973 period.

OPEC was founded in 1960, but until 1970–71 had remained relatively ineffectual. Within a year of the 1969 overthrow of King Idris of Libya by the junta led by then Captain Khaddafi, the new Libyan regime had successfully imposed new operating terms on the independents and majors producing in Libya. The new terms included higher posted prices and higher tax rates. Libya's success precipitated OPEC-wide action of a similar nature. TheOPEC meetings in Caracas in 1970 and Tehran in 1971 resulted in new agreements with the international industry regarding increased prices and taxes and greater government participation. In addition, OPEC members agreed, for the first time, to employ concerted and simultaneous action to force compliance by the industry. By late 1973, however, the OPEC countries had become dissatisfied with the 1971 Tehran Agreements. This was in large part because repeated devaluations of the U.S. dollar and rising inflation in the western world had reduced much of OPEC's anticipated gain. OPEC's position as a supplier also assumed even greater importance after 1970 because U.S. sources of supply began to decline thus reducing the strategic role of the Texas Railway Commission in the "management of markets." On October 8, 1973 negotiations commenced with the companies to revise the 1971 Agreements. Two days earlier, war had broken out in the Middle East. Within weeks, oil had assumed a new status as a political weapon, and the resulting supply concerns among consumer nations and the militancy of some of the Arab members had presented new opportunities for OPEC with respect to oil pricing and state involvement.

Meanwhile, as these world events unfolded, there were significant domestic political changes as well. The Conservative party led by Peter Lougheed campaigned successfully in the 1971 Alberta provincial election on a platform promoting the use of the province's oil and gas wealth to diversify the provincial economy, thus resurrecting a historic and persistent theme in western Canadian politics.[40] The Conservative victory ended thirty-one years of Social Credit rule. The new government discovered in its attempt to increase the province's share of the economic rents generated by Alberta's depleting oil reserves that its hands were tied by a set of decisions taken by the Social Credit government in the late 1940s. In 1948 Social Credit agreed to insert in petroleum and natural gas leases a specific provision that the maximum royalty rate which would be payable by producers under the leases would be limited to 16⅔ percent of gross production. Social Credit even went so far as to provide statutory confirmation of these maximum royalty provisions in the 1949 **Mines and Minerals Act**. The new Conservative government argued that these arrangements were, in the seller's market of the early 1970s, generating unnecessarily large profits for Alberta producers.

In response to this situation, the Alberta government introduced in 1972 a Natural Resource Revenue Plan to boost royalties from the fixed maximum 16.7 percent level without actually breaking contractual arrangements with the industry. After extensive negotiations with the industry, the government proposed to superimpose on the royalty structure a tax on remaining oil reserves. This would have had the same effect as raising the maximum royalty rate to 23 percent. A few months later, in the face of federal government initiatives such as an oil price freeze and an oil export tax, Alberta moved unilaterally— eschewing the traditional practice of prior consultation with the industry—by withdrawing its proposed new royalty scheme and announcing that, in the future, royalties would rise with oil price increases.

For the industry, this was a major departure from past practice. This was virtually the first indication the industry had that the government of Alberta perceived that it had a set of interests related to oil and gas that were distinct from those of the industry. The fact that it was done by an avowedly conservative and free enterprise-oriented government was of little consolation to the industry. Yet, rather than acknowledge that conditions had changed materially since the late 1940s and that the royalty system was due for an overhaul, thereby garnering some political goodwill, the industry clung to "principled" arguments about the sanctity of contract while at the same time exploiting the advantageous terms of the 1949 clause. In retrospect, it is clear that the unilateral action of the Alberta government did in fact mark a major turning point in the relationship between the Alberta government and the industry. Within a year, Alberta and the neighbouring province of Saskatchewan moved to introduce new legislative initiatives designed to strengthen their constitutional control over the production, pricing, marketing, and regulation of their resources.

The OPEC Crisis and Producer-Consumer Relations

Canada, and indeed most of the industrialized world, was completely unprepared to cope with the consequences of the fourfold increase in international oil prices and the partial oil embargo imposed by the Arab members of OPEC in the wake of the 1973 Middle East war. The reasons for Canada's unreadiness were simple. First, the government had no direct access to information on which it could base its policy. In 1974, the Minister of Energy, Mines and Resources, Donald Macdonald, admitted that "one of the difficulties facing the Canadian government is that it is virtually dependent on major international companies for its sources of information."[41] Second, the government had only an embryonic policy-making ability. According to Bill Hopper, Petro-Canada's president, "you could (have) put the people in Energy, Mines and Resources who knew anything about oil and gas in one corner of Imperial's corporate economic department."[42]

With no means to gather information independently, and in any event, only limited means to digest it, the government predictably reeled from crisis to crisis in 1973 and 1974. Thus, in quick succession, the government imposed oil export controls, similar controls over the export of refined products, announced the extension of the Interprovincial oil pipeline to Montreal, froze domestic oil prices, levied an export tax on crude oil, developed an oil import compensation scheme to protect consumers dependent on imported oil, considered and rejected acquiring a subsidiary of one of the major multinational oil companies, and contemplated the imposition of oil rationing.[43]

An additional response by the minority Liberal government to the events of the fall of 1973, was the decision announced in December 1973 to establish a national oil company, Petro-Canada. Contributing factors to this decision were Ottawa's concern about the vulnerability of Québec and Atlantic Canada to interruption in world markets; Ottawa's growing frustration with its lack of control over security of supplies; the growing popularity among the producing nations of state-to-state contracts; Ottawa's recently recognized lack of solid information with respect to Canada's indigenous supplies and reserves and the growing apprehension of being dependent on the foreign-owned industry for this information. Two additional political factors which combined with the others to ensure Petro-Canada's creation were the growing acceptance among the bureaucrats in the Department of Energy, Mines and Resources that a state oil company could extend their control over the energy sector and expand their departmental influence, and the fact that the minority Liberal government was dependent for its parliamentary life on the support of the NDP, who advocated the creation of a state oil company. It is important to stress in this context, however, that Petro-Canada's creation was viewed as an alternative to nationalization, rather than an instrument of nationalization.

A number of Ottawa's initiatives in the 1973-74 period led to forceful provincial reaction.[44] In March 1973, Ottawa moved to control the export of oil when a rapid jump in shipments to the United States threatened to disrupt domestic supplies. In September 1973, Ottawa ended the essentially market-based price setting mechanism by freezing the domestic price of oil for six months and imposing an export tax on oil shipped to the United States.

The decision to freeze prices was taken quickly and followed the action of Imperial Oil (the acknowledged price setter) to increase prices. Of equal importance, the freeze decision was viewed by Alberta to be one of the first instances of small creeping unilateral acts by Ottawa, which were to escalate over the rest of the decade in a series of mutual acts of "political aggression" reflecting the different national and regional interests involved and the different political parties in power.

The proceeds from the export tax were used to help subsidize eastern Canadians dependent on oil imports. The Oil Import Compensation Program (OICP) was the result. Provoked by what they saw as federal intrusions into traditionally provincial areas of responsibility, the provinces retaliated through new legislation, to secure further their constitutional control over the production, regulation, marketing, and pricing of oil within the province. Because royalties were tax deductible, however, the federal government soon became concerned that, as oil prices rose, and with them royalty payments to the provinces, its own revenues would decline and its ability therefore to manage the inflationary and distributive effects of oil price increases would be reduced.

Accordingly, in the budget of May 6, 1974, Finance Minister John Turner proposed to amend the Income Tax Act to disallow the deductibility of provincial royalties for the purposes of calculating federal corporate income tax. This action angered the producing provinces even more. Meanwhile, the oil industry in the wake of the post-1973 economic downturn felt itself to be further squeezed by the two levels of government in the latter's attempt to capture a larger share of resource revenues. Faced with a widespread slowdown in exploration caused by both the economic downturn and by a desire by the industry to put pressure on the government, Alberta reduced the revenues it was collecting.

Later, in 1975, Ottawa passed the **Petroleum Administration Act** to provide itself with broad powers over the pricing of oil and gas in Canada. This showed Ottawa's determination to set prices itself if federal–provincial negotiations failed to produce a consensus. H.V. Nelles had concluded about this volatile 1973–75 period that

> the net effect of this vigorous federal intervention was to hold Canadian energy prices well below world levels, but thereby to internalize in the form of sharp federal–provincial conflict, the struggle raging internationally between oil importing and exporting countries.[45]

Yet, it is essential to recall that between 1973 and 1978, the price of oil and natural gas in Canada did rise quickly through Ottawa–producing provinces' agreements, albeit without reaching world levels.[46] After resisting Alberta's call for world prices, the federal government eventually agreed to let Canadian prices move towards that level. By mid-1978, Canadian prices were 80 percent of world price with the gap between domestic and international prices being less than $3 per barrel. In the wake of the 1979 Iranian revolution, world prices doubled, and the federal government renounced its policy of linking domestic prices to world prices. This not only left Canadian prices far below international ones, but also cooled the already difficult relations between Alberta and the federal government.

Generally speaking, federal policy initiatives throughout the '70s were motivated by the following objectives: to cushion the impact of rapidly escalating international petroleum prices on Canada's industrial sector, and in doing so, to provide a comparative advantage to Canadian export manufacturers; to protect all Canadian consumers from OPEC-set world prices and to subsidize those Canadians who are dependent on offshore crude; to slow the interregional transfer of income from oil-importing provinces to the western producing provinces; to dampen the inflationary impact of rising energy prices on the Canadian economy; to protect the federal tax base and federal revenues and to limit the size of equalization payments. At the same time, it sought to encourage the development of new supplies; to encourage conservation; and to ensure that the producing provinces, as owners of the resource, received an adequate price for their depleting resource. The "adequacy" of this price was of course central to the dispute and was not viewed in the same way in Ottawa and Edmonton.

Throughout most of the '70s the primary focus of the Ottawa-producing provinces conflict was not so much pricing as revenue sharing. Pricing, of course, had implicit and explicit revenue sharing effects, and so was not a minor matter. Ottawa saw the demands on its revenues increase directly as a result of rising prices—the Oil Import Compensation Program and equalization payments being the most obvious. Furthermore, the federal government argued that its tax base was being restricted through the provinces' new royalty schemes, and consequently it was not obtaining its fair share of natural resource revenues. The two most inflamatory federal legislative initiatives, the export tax and royalty deductibility disallowance, were specifically designed to increase the federal share of resource revenues.

Pricing, however, has been a particularly thorny issue in Western Canadian–Ontario relations, as the producing provinces wanted higher prices while Ontario argued that prices should increase slowly. Québec was also a large consumer, but chose as a matter of principle to side with the producing provinces and support unfettered provincial control over natural resources. Ontario feared that rapidly escalating petroleum prices would have severe repercussions for its industries' competitive position internationally and would increase unemployment. Ontario argued that it was economically unwise for Canada to follow blindly the monopoly price set by OPEC—a price which was not related to the cost of producing conventional supplies of Canadian oil and gas. Furthermore, Ontario charged, the price increases of the late '70s were not necessary to encourage the development of new energy supplies, but were simply the result of the competing appetites of the federal and provincial treasuries.

Perhaps the best example of how the Alberta–Ontario energy conflict reflected the larger clash of competing visions of the development of the Canadian economy, is found in the petrochemical industry. Alberta's plans for economic development are centred partly around making the province a world-scale petrochemical producer based on the local supply of feedstocks. Such a development would compete directly with Ontario's petrochemical industry. Alberta was particularly upset by the decision in 1974 to proceed with the Petrosar development in Ontario. Ontario feared that rising national prices and Alberta's control over its own prices, combined with the possibility of restricted availability of Alberta's supplies, would harm the Ontario industry's competitive position in the United States. Consequently, Ontario demanded some assurance of future energy supply; federal guarantees that supply commitments would be met; and the redistribution of resource revenues for use by consumers and for energy adaptation and conservation.

It is quite clear that throughout the post-1973 period, the major governments exhibited not only diverging interests and objectives with respect to the control of energy developments, but also differing perspectives regarding the constitutional powers over resources.

The Taxation of the Resource Industry

It is also essential to relate energy policy developments in the late 1970s to the overall debate about the comparative level of effective taxes paid by the resource industry as it evolved in the early and mid-1970s. These taxes are usually gathered in statistical data under the general title of the mining industry, but the category includes oil and gas. The Carter Royal Commission on Taxation questioned the generosity of the tax provisions.[47] Table 3.3 compares the effective tax rates on book profits (that is, before income tax but after all mining taxes and royalties) of the mining versus the manufacturing sector from 1969 to 1975. The resource sector has enjoyed a consistent advantage. The tax advantage has narrowed, however, from about 25 percentage points in the pre-Carter tax reform period to 7 points in 1975. The narrowing of the gap reflected both increases in the mining sector and reductions in the manufacturing sector. These data predate the existence of incentives such as the super-depletion allowances. It should also be noted that in the mid-1970s the entire sector provided only about 1.2 percent of provincial revenues and 0.5 percent of federal revenues.

TABLE 3.3
PROFIT RATE ON SHAREHOLDERS' EQUITY AND EFFECTIVE INCOME TAX RATES, MINING AND MANUFACTURING

	Mining			Manufacturing		
	Profit rate on shareholders' equity[1]		Effective tax rate[3]	Profit rate on shareholders' equity[1]		Effective tax rate
Years	Before income taxes %	After income taxes[2] %	%	Before income tax %	After income tax[2] %	%
1969	11.8	10.0	15.3	17.3	10.6	38.7
1970	14.9	12.5	16.1	12.4	7.3	41.1
1971	9.5	8.4	11.6	14.9	9.4	36.9
1972	6.8	5.7	16.2	16.9	10.8	36.1
1973	19.8	17.2	13.1	23.2	16.4	29.3
1974	21.4	16.3	23.8	26.7	18.7	39.0
1975	13.0	9.7	25.4	21.2	14.3	32.5

[1]The before-tax profit rate is after the subtractions of all provincial mining taxes and royalties. The after-tax profit rate is then obtained by subtracting federal and provincial income taxes. These income taxes are before reassessments.

[2]Income taxes subtracted to arrive at the after-tax profit rate are federal and provincial income taxes.

[3]Effective tax rate is the ratio of federal and provincial income taxes to the before-tax profit rate.

Source: Department of Finance, *Federal–Provincial Resource Taxation Review* (Ottawa, 1978), p. 29.

Table 3.4 provides another glimpse of the pattern of resource taxation in the 1969 to 1975 period. It shows the total of income taxes and other levies paid to governments as a percentage of book profits before any such payments. It again shows that effective tax rates on the resource sector increased, but shows that the provincial governments accounted for over 16 percentage points of the increase while the federal government accounted for only about 4.4 percentage points. The data also indicate that effective rates were lower except in 1974 and 1975 when mining taxes increased and manufacturing rates were reduced.

While the more detailed issues of resource taxation are examined in various contexts in Chapters 2, 5 and 9 it is important to understand the central basis of the tax advantages that the resource industries

TABLE 3.4

EFFECTIVE TAX AND ROYALTY RATES ON MINING AND MANUFACTURING[1]
1969 TO 1975

Year	Manufacturing			Mining					
	Federal income taxes	Provincial income taxes	Total	Federal income taxes	Income tax	Provincial Mining taxes and royalties	Total	Territorial mining taxes	Total
1969	29.9	8.7	38.6	10.0	2.7	7.7	10.4	0.3	20.7
1970	31.7	9.5	41.2	11.4	3.1	7.0	10.2	0.2	21.7
1971	28.2	8.8	37.0	8.4	2.5	7.5	9.9	0.2	18.5
1972	27.2	9.0	36.0	11.5	3.5	10.2	13.7	0.2	25.4
1973	21.3	8.0	29.3	9.4	2.6	7.4	10.0	0.2	19.5
1974	21.9	8.2	30.1	14.8	5.1	16.4	21.5	0.4	36.7
1975	23.6	8.9	32.5	14.4	5.5	21.1	26.6	0.8	4.18

[1]The effective tax and royalty rate is on book profits before the deduction of income taxes and provincial mining taxes and royalties. The effective income tax rate on mining differs from that shown in Table 9 because of the addition of provincial mining taxes and royalties to the base.

Source: Department of Finance, *Federal–Provincial Resource Taxation Review* (Ottawa, 1978), p. 31.

enjoyed. One key provision was their ability to write off expenditures on exploration and development immediately. Rather than allowing ordinary depreciation, this gave a tax advantage to the firm since the present value of tax payments is reduced by virtue of their being postponed. In addition, resource industries were able to deduct an earned depletion allowance. This is inherently a much less defensible tax break, since as an allowance for the using up of a depreciable asset, the costs of acquiring the asset (e.g., the exploration and development expenses) have already been written off.

A variety of reasons and rationales have been advocated by the resource industry for these special provisions. These include arguments that the risks are greater, that Canadian incentives cannot be out of line with U.S. tax regimes, and that other sectors are subsidized with tariffs and other incentives. Some tax economists argue that the advantages enjoyed by the resource industry cannot be justified on economic grounds. The existence of the advantages reflects partly the political skills of the industry and the central political role of resource ownership in the politics of federalism.

On this latter point, neither of the tables adequately captures the sensitive role of provincial royalties as a rent accruing to the owners of the resource, especially a depleting resource. A 1978 federal–provincial report on resource taxation expressed the issues in an understated language that stands in sharp contrast to the heated language and passion of the debate on this question in the post NEP-period. It cautioned the reader of taxation tables that

> considerable care must be exercised in using and interpreting such information. Mining taxes and royalties are in part payments to the provinces in their capacities as owners of the resources. If these resources were privately owned, there would obviously be some charge for their use and this payment would be considered a normal cost of production to the companies. Information on the ratio of total revenues of government from mining to book profit cannot therefore be treated in the same fashion as is information on the effective income tax rates given above. As well, interpretation of comparisons between sectors must proceed with caution given that payments by other sectors for society's scarce resources are costs of production and not taxes in these statistics.

Nevertheless, royalties and mining tax payments are subject to the discretion of governments just as are income taxes and do represent an actual cash flow from the mining sector to governments. Given governmental control in setting these charges, they are lumped in with income taxes in the debate about the treatment of the industry. In light of the difficulty of determining what proportion of provincial levies represents a reasonable payment for the use of resources, and what proportion constitutes a tax as such, this debate is not subject to easy resolution.[48]

As the value of resource revenues increased several fold in the late 1970s the issue of the appropriate share of revenues among all the key interests escalated quickly, as did the issue of ownership and control of resources. So also did the debate about the relative wealth of the oil and gas industry versus other industries, and the larger tax reform debates that these comparisons inevitably rekindled.

State Enterprises and the Expansion of Petro-Canada

Direct government intervention in the oil and gas industry increased significantly throughout the 1970s. Alberta and Saskatchewan created the Alberta Energy Corporation and Sask-Oil respectively. The governments of Canada, Alberta and Ontario invested equity in the Syncrude Tarsands project in 1975 to keep it from collapsing after a private firm had withdrawn. In 1978, the federal government created the Petroleum Monitoring Agency to monitor the financial performance of the oil and gas industry and thus overcome another of the government's perceived weaknesses in strategic policy information.

Petro-Canada came into existence in July 1975, and grew rapidly throughout the remainder of the 1970s.[49] In April and May 1976, the federal government transferred to Petro-Canada its 45 percent share of Pan-Arctic Oils Ltd. and its 15 percent share of the Syncrude project. In August 1976, Petro-Canada purchased Atlantic Richfield Canada and in 1978–79, Pacific Petroleum. The latter acquisition launched Petro-Canada into the full range of industry activity, including the downstream functions of refining and marketing. Petro-Canada became an active explorer in both the Arctic and the eastern offshore, and within five years of its birth was Canada's sixth largest producer of oil and gas with assets in excess of $4 billion.

In 1979, Petro-Canada became, for a short time, the object of privatization initiatives by the newly elected Conservative government of Joe Clark. In the face of strong public support for Petro-

Canada, the Tories puzzled over how to achieve privatization throughout their brief period in office. Their final proposal, unveiled during the 1979–80 election campaign, would have retained for the government a 30 percent controlling interest. The electoral defeat of the Conservatives in 1980 by a Liberal party committed to a strong and growing Petro-Canada ended the uncertainty about Petro-Canada's existence.

The Alaska Highway Pipeline Debate

Another key energy issue of the 1970s revolved around the choice of a northern pipeline system to deliver Alaskan natural gas to the mainland United States.[50] The Canadian government had been promoting a land based transmission system to the U.S. government since the mid-'60s, and in support of this idea established, in the late 1960s, an interdepartmental task force on northern energy development. By the early '70s a consortium had been formed to build a line from Alaska across the northern Yukon to the Mackenzie Delta and up the Mackenzie Valley through Alberta into the United States. This consortium was called the Canadian Arctic Gas Pipeline and was dominated by the major multinational oil companies. In 1974, Justice Thomas Berger was appointed to head the Mackenzie Valley Pipeline inquiry into the social and environmental impacts of such a development. In the mid-'70s, AGTL (now Nova, an Alberta Corporation) dropped out of the CAGPL consortium and sponsored an alternative project to build the northern pipeline down the Alaska Highway. In 1977, the Berger Inquiry suggested that a moratorium of ten years be placed on the Arctic Gas Proposal.[51] The National Energy Board, and ultimately the government, rejected the Arctic Gas proposal in favour of the newer Alaska Highway proposal.[52] Its Canadian ownership and commitment to a strong Canadian procurement policy as well as the fact that it crossed less environmentally and politically sensitive areas were all important contributing factors in these decisions. In an attempt to provide some impetus to the project as a whole, the federal government approved, in July 1980, the prebuilding of the southern section of the line from Alberta gas fields to U.S. markets. Ottawa also approved new exports of natural gas through the prebuilt section.

The Alberta Heritage Fund

Another key event in the pre-NEP era was the establishment by the Lougheed Conservative government of the Alberta Heritage Savings Trust Fund.[53] Created in 1976, the Heritage Fund was central to the principles continuously supported in the 1970s by the Alberta Conservatives and which we examine in detail in Chapters 6 and 8. The fund was to accumulate, contain, and build up a pool of capital in order that a portion of the revenues from non-renewable resources would be utilized to benefit future generations of Albertans. This central idea of intergenerational equity is simultaneously an appeal to longer term efficiency. It was intricately linked to the Lougheed government's commitment to diversify the Alberta economy and thus to break it away from its historic experience with the boom and bust cycles of a resource dependent economy. Some of the fund would also be utilized to improve the quality of life of Albertans that could not otherwise be afforded. It could also help to provide an alternative governmental revenue source in the future if one were needed. Though this fund was initiated by the Lougheed Conservatives, it is worth stressing that the federal government, through then Finance Minister John Turner, strongly urged Alberta to establish such a fund so that the revenues would not distort the equalization of revenue formulas that governed intergovernmental finances.

It must be stressed that only about 30 percent of the non-renewable resource revenue went into the fund. The rest went into the general coffers of the Alberta government. Such general revenues amounted to over 50 percent of Alberta's revenues and thus contributed to Alberta's capacity to have lower tax rates than other provinces, including no sales tax. The fund grew sixfold, increasing from $2.2 billion in 1977 to $13.1 billion in 1982. Though the fund did not initially attract great national attention, it quickly became the focal point for political and economic controversy at the national level and within Alberta. At the national level, despite the recognition that the concepts behind the fund were sensible and valid, the fund became a symbol of the westward transfer of wealth. This was especially the case in 1979 and 1980 when projections began to appear which showed the fund reaching the level of over $150 billion by the early 1990s. Alberta viewed the growing fund as the just desserts of its long historic wait to shed its dependence on central Canada. The federal government saw it as a demonstration that something was wrong with the national distribution of wealth, a view easily reinforced by the partisan elements of the conflict, by the federal government's growing deficits, and by the projected growth of the fund. Thus fundamental interests clashed, since both the federal and Alberta governments saw the same pool of petro-dollars as a potential tool of economic development. The notion of what "economic development" actually meant, however, was left to further debate. Within Alberta, despite massive political support for the overall purposes of the Heritage Fund, there was growing criticism about whether the fund was really being used for diversification or rather for relatively safe investments. Later, in the midst of the 1982 recession, it came under pressure in a different way in that criticism centred on why the fund was not being used to help those Albertans who were hit hard by the recession. In 1982 funds were, in fact, used for such purposes, and the proportion of revenues that went into the Heritage account was reduced to 15 percent for a two-year period.

There are many features of the Heritage Fund which are not dealt with in this book. It is essential, however, to stress the degree to which it encapsulated the debate which surrounded proposals for other funds whose purpose was to recycle petro-dollars. These included the dispute over the Clark Conservatives' Energy Bank and the Liberals' Owner-ship Account and Western Canada Fund examined in Chapters 2 and 10.

The Clark Government and the Domestic Effects of the Second OPEC Crisis

The 1970s (as we have referred to the 1973–79 period) went out with a roar just as they came in. Indeed, 1979 was, like 1973, a traumatic year for energy politics. 1979 included what is commonly referred to as the second OPEC crisis. While oil prices had actually declined 5 percent in real terms between 1974 and 1978, the 1979 Iranian revolution and the consequent removal of 2.5 million barrels a day from the world oil market, the subsequent fears of oil shortages and the resultant panic buying on the spot market caused the world oil price to double. The 1979 Tokyo Summit of the seven major industrialized nations was dominated by the energy issue. In Canada, energy taxes, oil and gas prices and the future of Petro-Canada dominated domestic politics, first in the Crosbie Conservative budget in December 1979 and in the subsequent election campaign which resulted in the return to power of the Trudeau Liberals in February 1980.

It is important to stress that despite the fact that the revolution continued in Iran, energy was not a key issue in the May 1979 Canadian election, which gave political power to the Progressive Conservatives under Joe Clark for the first time in sixteen years.[54] During their time in opposition the Conservatives' energy policy had been shaped by the members holding the key shadow Cabinet positions, who tended to represent that element of the Conservative party which deeply distrusted government intervention in the economy. At its core the Conservatives' policy consisted of the general objective of achieving self-sufficiency in oil by 1990, a general concept of promoting Canadianization through tax and investment incentives and an election promise to privatize Petro-Canada. One of the major themes of the Conservatives' 1979 campaign was that they could better manage the fractious and volatile federal–provincial relationship than could the Liberals. Clark felt that he could achieve more congenial federal–provincial relations by embracing a less centralist "community of communities" image of Canada, and second, by sharing the same partisan colours as the majority of provincial premiers.

Although the Clark government was unable to achieve a new pricing and revenue-sharing agreement with the Lougheed government during the summer and fall of 1979, they were nevertheless obligated to devise a framework for a pricing and fiscal regime in order to construct their December 11, 1979 budget. Energy measures comprised the main and most controversial features of John Crosbie's "short-term pain for long-term gain" budget, the defeat of which brought down the Clark minority government. The following quotation from a confidential memo from John Crosbie to the Conservative caucus is worth quoting at length, since it outlines how Crosbie explained the energy features of his budget to the Tory caucus:

> Tonight, I fulfill our election promise by providing detailed projections of our revenues, expenditures and deficits out to 1983–84. I am also releasing a paper which sets out and describes the economic assumptions on which the fiscal projections are based . . . I now refer to a series of major new measures in the

energy field to achieve our goal of self-sufficiency in oil by the 1990s.

Let me make the situation as clear as I can. The revenue and expenditure figures relating to 1980–81 and the following fiscal years are based on the assumption that we still conclude an agreement with the oil and gas producing provinces on our new energy policy and on oil and gas pricing. The agreement involves oil and natural gas price increases over the years 1980–84 so that prices rise at a measured pace toward 85 percent of the lesser of U.S. levels at Chicago or the international price.

The Government of Canada intends, in connection with any increase in oil and natural gas prices, to ensure that excess profits are not made by the industry as a result of accelerating prices but that the industry has an adequate rate of return and retains the necessary revenues for continuing exploration and development of new energy sources.

We intend to ensure, through our new energy tax, that the Government of Canada obtains roughly half of the returns from oil and gas price increases that exceed $2 per barrel and thirty cents per thousand cubic feet per year.

On this basis, the Government of Canada will have sufficient revenues from the increases in oil and gas prices to carry into effect energy programs, conservation programs, and offset programs to assist the regions and people of Canada.

The exact form of our energy tax has not yet been fully worked out, but it will be a tax sufficient to give the Government of Canada the revenues we have indicated we need from oil and gas price increases to carry out the programs we have indicated are necessary. I have every confidence that the agreements now reached will go forward and that a new energy tax will be in place before July, 1980.

Because of the absolute necessity of further encouraging our people to use fewer oil products, to conserve oil products now having to be imported in ever larger quantities and at ever greater prices as our own domestic supplies dwindle, and in order to raise badly needed revenues for the Government of Canada in a manner that also serves another vital national purpose, an excise tax of twenty-five cents per gallon is imposed on gasoline, diesel, and other transportation fuels effective tonight.

This tax will apply to all users of transportation fuels and will replace the current tax of seven cents a gallon on gasoline which applied only to non-commercial users. Thus the increase is eighteen cents a gallon for those using gasoline for personal use only. Farming, commercial fishing, and urban public transit systems will be entitled to a rebate of ten cents per gallon and so will be taxed effectively at fifteen cents.

All federal proceeds from the new energy tax and a substantial part of the proceeds from the excise tax will be returned to the economy in the form of direct measures to assist in developing alternate energy sources, conservation methods, and to assist regions and people in Canada in absorbing these higher costs. . . .

I am announcing tonight an income-tested, refundable, energy tax credit of $80 per adult and $30 per child per year, phased in over two years, for the benefit of lower- and middle-income Canadians. The cost of this measure when in full effect will be $1 billion each year. . . .

The super depletion allowance for frontier drilling will be extended at a reduced rate to the end of 1980 and then replaced. The write-off for Canadian oil and gas property, including land bonus payments, will be reduced from 30 percent to 10 percent. . . .

The Budget Papers also outline the energy package. The main thrust of this program is to give us self-sufficiency in all energy sources by the end of the century, including oil. I would recommend that you read the Budget Papers on energy which set out clearly our energy position and potential. It is estimated that the exports of gas the National Energy Board has approved will help our balance of payments in a major way. The reason we can allow ourselves this badly needed relief on our balance of payments is that our supply potential has increased. The exports we have approved are above and beyond the supplies needed to use for substitution for oil. Therefore, it is incorrect for anyone to say that we are jeopardizing our self-sufficiency plans by exporting at this time. . . .

The modification of the super depletion allowance was necessary in order to ensure that high income investments did not receive tax savings in excess of their investments. Also higher revenues will now be available to oil producing companies, because of increased prices. The allowance, as you know, is aimed at increasing capital available for exploration and development.[55]

Thus, though weakened by the absence of an agreement with Alberta, the Crosbie budget revealed components of an energy policy that were not present in the Conservatives' pre-1979 election platform. An excess-profits tax and an energy tax credit as well as the 18 cent increase in transportation fuel taxes were a recognition of the broader energy issues of the 1970s.

The defeat of the Crosbie budget and the later defeat of the Clark Conservatives in the February 1980 election provided the Trudeau

Liberals with their opportunity to introduce the NEP. Since the genesis of the NEP has already been explored in Chapter 2, we merely note it at this point in the historical chronology. The later analysis of the NEP, however, does depend on the reader's having a basic familiarity with the sequence of key post-NEP events in the 1980–1984 period.

1980–1984: A Portrait of Key Post-NEP Events

The Overall Reaction to the NEP

Despite the strong indications provided by the Trudeau Halifax speech that a major new policy which would stress Canadianization, a larger revenue share for the federal government, and a made-in-Canada price was forthcoming, much of the industry, the producing provinces, and the U.S. government reacted with surprise and anger at all or some aspects of the NEP. The Alberta government, charging that Ottawa had "without negotiation, without agreement, simply walked into our home and occupied the living room,"[56] unveiled a three-pronged retaliation to the NEP. It would challenge the legality of Ottawa's proposed tax on natural gas, delay the approval of new tarsands and heavy oil projects, and gradually reduce oil shipments to eastern Canada over a period of nine months. The Social Credit government of British Columbia, which was enraged by the new tax on natural gas (B.C. produces virtually all gas and very little oil), accused Ottawa of perpetrating a barefaced money grab and decided to withhold the revenue generated by the federal government's new natural gas tax. Ontario's Conservative government responded to Alberta's reduction of oil shipments to the east by accusing the Alberta government of greed and callousness, for "responding to a continued and prolonged disagreement by imposing deep economic penalties on the working men and women, the pensioners, the businessman, the people of Canada."[57] These varying responses of provincial governments are examined in detail in Chapter 8.

The new Reagan administration, which was elected a week after the unveiling of the NEP, reacted to it in a number of ways. Partly as a result of their opposition to the Canadianization aspects of the NEP on ideological grounds and partly as a result of the pressure applied on them by U.S. oil companies, the Reagan administration developed throughout 1981 a two-front bilateral and multilateral campaign (at

GATT, OECD, and the IEA) against the NEP. The Americans focussed their criticism on the features of the NEP which discriminated in favour of Canadian firms, and on the 25 percent Crown interest provision which applied equally to Canadian and foreign firms. After years of taking over Canadian oil companies, U.S. industry reacted angrily to a few high-profile takeovers or attempted takeovers of U.S. companies by Canadian firms.[58]

Elements of the Canadian industry, particularly the large Canadian-owned firms, while criticizing some features of the NEP reacted somewhat more positively but quietly to other aspects of it. Some big and medium-sized Canadian firms both in and outside of the oil industry saw the NEP as an opportunity to expand or enter the booming oil and gas business, and they participated in the above-mentioned takeovers or attempted takeovers of oil companies in both Canada and the United States. In this regard they were strongly supported by the willingness of Canadian banks to lend them the necessary money. The foreign-owned sector reacted with varying shades of anger to the NEP's plans to ensure that the industry would be 50 percent Canadian owned by 1990. The larger foreign-owned firms reacted by significantly slashing exploration budgets for the coming year, while their parent companies exerted pressure on the U.S., British, and Dutch governments to pressure Canada to change aspects of the NEP. Somewhat to Ottawa's surprise, many of the smaller Canadian-owned firms also reacted negatively to the NEP—in part on ideological grounds to the evident increase in government intervention, in part in opposition to the new NEP taxes which would in their view adversely affect their cashflow, and in part because the new incentive program encouraged exploration on the Canada Lands where few small firms were equipped or anxious to move. This element of the industry reacted by significantly curtailing drilling programs and by shifting a percentage of their exploration activity to the United States, where the Reagan administration had announced the complete deregulation of oil and the intention of deregulating gas prices. These diverse responses by industry interests are analysed in detail in Chapters 7 and 10.

The general public response to the NEP was extremely positive. Even the Canadian Petroleum Association's own confidential poll indicated that 84 percent of Canadians supported the move to make the oil and gas industry at least 50 percent Canadian owned.[59] A December

1981 Gallup poll showed that 64 percent of Canadians would favour even more rapid Canadianization, specifically 75 percent Canadian ownership by 1985.[60] This included a plurality of Canadians from all regions and age groups and both sexes. The same December 1981 poll asked respondents if they favoured or opposed the expansion of Petro-Canada into Canada's largest oil company, by buying one of the four major foreign-owned oil companies—Imperial, Gulf, Shell, or Texaco. Fifty-five percent favoured the proposal and 28 percent opposed, once again with a plurality in favour across all categories. Even as adamant an opponent of the NEP as the federal Tory energy critic, Harvey André, admitted that "the NEP is a successful policy. The people like it."[61]

Ottawa responded by asking if Alberta's planned retaliation did not "beg a fundamental question about our economic union: Should provinces interfere in the free movement of goods—especially strategic goods such as oil—within Canada?"[62] To the industry's threat to transfer a number of drilling rigs to the United States, Ottawa responded that little new oil had been discovered in Alberta anyhow in the last couple of years despite extensive drilling, and there was no need for new gas discoveries.[63] This reaction was based on the assumption (which not everyone shared) that Canada already had a large natural gas surplus and that *large* new oil discoveries would be needed to meet future Canadian oil demand. It was thought to be more likely that such discoveries would be made on the frontiers rather than in the already well-explored Western Sedimentary Basin. In March 1981, Ottawa instituted special increases in oil product prices, referred to unofficially as the "Lougheed levy," to pay for the additional imported oil needed to replace the cut-back Alberta production.

Other Important Post-NEP Developments

While some of Ottawa's energy planners revelled in the euphoria of the NEP initiatives, other ministers and bureaucrats became immediately concerned that Ottawa's reach had exceeded its grasp and that some bridge-building with the industry—or at least parts of it—had better begin. One manifestation of this concern was the establishment in November 1980 of the Alberta Technical Advisory Committee whose acronym, ATAC, was yet another example of Ottawa's creative nomenclature.

ATAC was the initiative of Senator Bud Olson, both in his political capacity as the only Alberta minister (albeit unelected) in the Trudeau Cabinet and in his role as the Minister of State for Economic Development which in theory (but as we show in Chapters 8 and 10, not in practice) was supposed to have control of the huge energy expenditure envelope.

We examine ATAC in greater detail in Chapter 8. The point to stress in this brief chronological account is that some channel of communication with the industry had to be found. The ground rules for the establishment of ATAC were that the basic principles and features of the NEP were not to be discussed. Only the fine-tuning of the NEP was to be allowed, hence the title "technical." ATAC was composed of about 15 senior oil and gas executives drawn from about 10 Canadian firms such as Nova, Dome, Home Oil, Husky, Voyageur, and Westcoast Petroleum, in short, some of the presumed beneficiaries of the NEP. An official of the Canadian Petroleum Association was also present, thus being the only indirect link to the multinationals whose firms dominate the CPA. It met frequently in Calgary from early November 1980 to the early spring of 1981, and had some influence on the content of the NEP legislation. The ATAC deliberations also reveal interesting features of the importance of different energy interests even among these firms, features we focus on in our analysis in Chapter 8 on the implementation of the NEP.

In November and December 1980, the federal government introduced the initial regulations regarding Canadian ownership rate determination and the Petroleum Incentives Program. In December Ottawa introduced Bill C-48, the **Canada Oil and Gas Act**. This act established new rules and regulations for exploration and production on the Canada Lands, and provided for the 25 percent Crown interest in every development right on the Canada Lands. The Canada Oil and Gas Lands Administration (COGLA) was established to administer the act and to renegotiate stricter exploration agreements on existing leases. COGLA became fully operational in 1982 and is examined in Chapter 11. In January 1981 the government introduced Bill C-57, **An Act to Amend the Excise Tax Act** and the **Excise Act**, to provide the enabling legislation for the petroleum and gas revenue tax (PGRT) and the natural gas and gas liquids tax (NGGLT).

In February 1981 Petro-Canada acquired Petrofina, an integrated,

Belgian-owned oil company for 1.46 billion dollars. In April, Ottawa announced that beginning May 1, 1981 it would implement the special Canadian Ownership Charge provided for in the NEP on sales of petroleum products and natural gas to cover the costs of Petro-Canada's purchase of Petrofina. Later in 1981, the partially federal government-owned Canadian Development Corporation acquired Elf Aquitaine, a French company, for $1.6 billion. Critics of these purchases argued that while they increased the level of Canadian ownership and control, the expenditures of vast sums of money were uneconomic, did not produce any additional oil or gas, and thereby did not contribute to greater security of supply for Canada. Thus, as stressed above, the opponents of the NEP used one NEP objective to criticize another. NEP supporters also resorted to this practice of selective evaluation.

In May 1981, the federal government announced the inauguration of the Canadian Oil Substitution Program (COSP), a major off-oil initiative of the NEP. It was to be operated by the Department of Energy, Mines and Resources and by utilities in the provinces, and was intended for the conversion from oil to natural gas or electricity or to other energy sources. Throughout the following few months, additional oil substitution programs were put in place in pursuit of NEP objectives.

In June 1981, the Major Projects Task Force submitted its Report.[64] The Task Force, which was set up in 1978, constituted a bipartite group of eighty senior labour and business leaders under co-chairperson Shirley Carr, executive vice-president of the Canadian Labour Congress, and Robert Blair, president of Nova, an Alberta Corporation, formerly AGTL. This Task Force identified some $440 billion worth of potential investment in mega-projects by the year 2000, 90 percent of which could be spent on energy production and distribution and hydrocarbon processing. The Task Force concluded that, based on historical practice, the participation of foreign-owned firms in key decision-making positions of these mega-projects would likely decrease the benefits to Canada. It went on to make no less than fifty-one recommendations for improving the benefits to the Canadian economy from the construction of major projects. The main recommendation was that Canadian-owned firms be chosen to play key roles in the management, engineering, procurement, and construction of future mega-projects so that industrial and regional benefits from these projects would be maximized.

At the height of the industry campaign against the new energy taxes, the Petro-Canada purchase of Petrofina, and other aspects of the NEP, the Federal government released in March 1981 **The State of Competition in the Canadian Petroleum Industry,**[65] the report of the Director of Investigation and Research, prepared under the authority of the **Combines Investigation Act.** This report charged that the major integrated firms had, as a result of following uncompetitive practices such as overpaying parent companies for imported oil and operating an inefficient gasoline distribution system, overcharged Canadians by $12 billion for petroleum products between 1958 and 1973. The report also listed other practices employed by the majors which had acted to restrict competition in the industry. Based on the evidence provided in the report, The Restrictive Trade Practices Commission began an investigation complete with hearings across Canada. The release of the report in March, when the government had had the report in its possession much earlier, reveals some of the tactical political manoeuvring that was being engaged in by the various interests. The report had the effect of placing the multinational majors, which had been employing a major media and lobbying campaign against the NEP, back on the defensive.

The government did, however, make some concessions to the U.S. government and the foreign-owned sector of the industry. In May 1981, Ottawa offered compensation for the 25 percent Crown interest by way of ex gratia payments. Ottawa also amended the industrial benefits legislation to ensure competitive conditions for foreign suppliers. In July 1981, Finance Minister Allan MacEachen asked the Canadian banks to help slow down the rate of takeovers of foreign firms by Canadians, by making loans less readily available to Canadian firms. In February 1982, Ottawa dropped plans to give Canadian-controlled firms preference in gas exports. In April 1982, Marc Lalonde announced he would not proceed with legislation to give Canadian oil companies power to force out their foreign shareholders. In an additional response to its opponents—either tactical or sincere—Ottawa announced in the November 1981 budget document,

"Economic Development for Canada in the 1980s," that it rejected the idea of using the NEP as a model for the Canadianization of other largely foreign-owned sectors of the Canadian economy.[66]

The Alberta and Provincial Agreements

After months of hard bargaining and political brinksmanship, Ottawa and Edmonton signed a new Memorandum of Agreement on energy pricing and taxation on September 1, 1981.[67] (The dynamics of bargaining are examined in Chapter 8.) Larry Pratt characterized the deal as follows: "In essence, Alberta and the federal government each made concessions to achieve an outcome that permits the province to protect its jurisdiction, Ottawa to extend its Canadianization program and both sides to collect more revenues (at the expense of energy consumers). The petroleum industry appeared to improve its position slightly."[68] The industry and other experts did not necessarily agree with the latter part of Pratt's assessment, however. Energy experts such as Helliwell and McCrae strongly criticized the NEP both on the grounds that it would harm industry cash flows far more than Ottawa projected and that it was, in total, going to be uneconomic in the sense of macroeconomic policy.[69] Scarfe and Wilkinson also strongly criticized the revenue sharing implications arguing that Ottawa's share, when one included *both* taxing *and* prices, was now at virtually 47 percent of revenues rather than at the 20 percent figure Ottawa was claiming.[70] Somewhat later, following the takeovers by Canadian firms and the onset of the recession, other assessments began to conclude that it was the Canadian firms that were in the greatest financial difficulty.[71] We examine these various evaluations in greater detail in Chapter 10.

The key underlying flaw of the September 1, 1981 Agreement, which was to appear within weeks of the signing and become clearer within the following few months, was that the taxation and revenue-sharing provisions of the agreement were based on a pricing scenario which assumed that world prices would continue to rise by 2 percent in real terms throughout the life of the agreement, that is, until December 31, 1986. Both the New Oil Reference Price (NORP) and the price ceiling for old oil (75 percent) were tied to world price. The inaccuracy of the single scenario price assumption of the agreement (the politics of which we have already examined in Chapter 2) would create serious problems for the signatories within a year and a half.

Meanwhile, on September 24 and October 26, 1981 respectively, agreements were reached with the producing provinces of British Columbia and Saskatchewan. On March 2, 1982 the Canada–Nova Scotia Offshore Oil and Gas Agreement was announced. At time of writing, an agreement between Canada and Newfoundland had proved unattainable. Newfoundland has long asserted its ownership over its continental shelf, basically on the strength of the argument that it brought the resources of the continental shelf into Canada when it joined Confederation. The Clark Conservative government was sympathetic to this view and to the other arguments in favour of provincial ownership of the offshore, and agreed in principle in September 1979 to transfer ownership of offshore resources to the provinces. The Liberal government, on the other hand, has argued that Ottawa has and must maintain, in the national interest, jurisdiction over offshore resource development. The Liberals have attempted to negotiate a regime of administrative arrangements in which the provinces would have a major say in how offshore resources are developed, and in which, until they become "have" provinces, the coastal provinces would receive the same kind of revenues as are derived by provinces for onshore resources. While Nova Scotia may have found such an arrangement to its satisfaction, at least in part because it gave it a leg up over Newfoundland in the competition to become the major offshore supply centre for the burgeoning east coast petroleum industry, for Newfoundland the memory of having been so close to its coveted position of constitutional supremacy was still strong and it flatly refused to agree to a Nova Scotia-style deal. Instead, in mid-February 1982 the Newfoundland Conservative government announced a reference case concerning ownership of offshore resources to the Newfoundland Supreme Court, which it subsequently lost, and called a provincial election for April 6, 1982, which it won handily. On March 8, 1984, the Supreme Court of Canada decided unanimously that the federal government had jurisdiction over offshore resources.

Politics, Recession and the Partial Unravelling of the NEP

On February 26, 1982 the government tabled in the House of Commons Bill C-94, the omnibus Energy Security Act. The Tories opposed not only the energy aspects of the bill (for example the number of new Crown corporations), but the disregard for Parliament as represented by the bill's format: they charged that it was really eight bills.[72] This objection is particularly salient, given that the memory of the government's parliamentary conduct with respect to the **Constitution Act** was still fresh in the minds of the opposition Tories. This caused what was to be known as the Bells Affair: the Tories called for a motion of adjournment, caucussed, and refused to report for division until the Liberals broke the bill down into its component parts. The division bells rang from March 2 till March 17 as the three major parties negotiated outside of the House. The affair ended in a compromise, including the break-up of the bill into eight new bills.

In the spring of 1982 a number of factors dovetailed to dampen the short-term outlook for the industry. Continued high interest rates; the deepening of the world-wide recession; the softening of demand for oil in Canada and world-wide, along with the growing realization that the emerging glut of oil on world markets may be more than a short-term temporal condition; the maturation of many of the conservation and substitution programs put in place since 1973 in the western consuming world; the subsequent softening of world price and the growing dissension within OPEC, all combined with the new, higher royalty and taxation provisions of the September 1981 Canada–Alberta Agreement, to squeeze industry cash flow and profits. Provincial approval of the Alsands tarsands project (Shell) and Cold Lake heavy-oil project (Imperial Oil) was withheld by the Alberta government as part of its retaliatory campaign against the federal government and the NEP. By the time the Canada–Alberta Agreement was signed ten months later, the "economics" of these massive $13 and $12 billion projects, respectively, had become clouded. Despite the extensive, high level negotiations between the companies and the two levels of government, including the provision of generous taxation and fiscal incentives by the governments, the industry sponsors decided to cancel the projects.

In response to the industry's situation, the Alberta and federal governments made significant adjustments designed to get increased revenue into industry coffers. On April 13, 1982 the Alberta government announced a $5.4 billion program consisting of royalty reductions and special grants and credits with the objective of increasing revenue flows to the industry in 1982–83.[73] At the end of May, Ottawa unveiled the NEP Update. It included a $2 billion assistance plan designed primarily to aid the Canadian juniors of the oil and gas industry. Some taxes were suspended while others were reduced, and higher prices were offered for certain categories of oil. As a result of the September 1981 Agreement, old oil (discovered before December 31, 1980) was allowed to more than double from $14.75 a barrel in January 1980 to $29.75 in January 1983. New oil was allowed to achieve world price. As a result of these price increases and the above adjustments, industry's cash flow was projected to increase from $6.5 billion in 1982 to $8.6 billion in 1983.

The NEP Update published in the spring of 1982 also stressed the adjustability and flexibility of the NEP. It stated that:

> The National Energy Program is not a single document ... nor is it a static set of policies, ... prices, taxes or direct initiatives. ... The National Energy program is a dynamic and comprehensive set of evolving responses to a changing world—whether through compromise with the provinces, or through necessary mid-course corrections in specific initiatives or the fiscal burden.[74]

In reality this meant that the initial NEP and the Alberta Agreement had produced excessive cash flow effects on the oil and gas industry as the recession took hold.

In 1982, Petro-Canada acquired the refining and distribution assets of BP Canada for $347.6 million. By April 1983 the earlier Petro-Canada purchase of Petrofina had virtually been paid off via revenues collected through the Canadian Ownership Charge. Petro-Canada now had assets in excess of $7 billion and the Canadian public continued to favour it. Petro-Canada retail sales in 1982 were up by as much as 30 percent in a shrinking market. One of the reasons given for the purchase of the 2357 BP outlets was that Petro-Canada needed to have more service stations to meet public demand, and because of public demand the stations are more valuable assets to Petro-Canada than to BP.

The same success cannot be claimed for the private sector Canadian giant Dome Petroleum. After having enjoyed tremendous success in the '70s and having led the Beaufort play and pioneered in Arctic exploration, Dome overextended itself in 1980 with the acquisition of

Hudson Bay Oil and Gas from U.S.-based Conoco. In the late 1970s Dome had become what was sometimes referred to as Ottawa's "chosen instrument" aiding the "need to know" (about Canadian reserves) objective of the federal government.[75] Dome President Jack Gallagher is often credited with convincing the federal government to introduce the "super-depletion allowance" for wells costing over $5 million. Super-depletion applied to only the most expensive offshore drilling, such as that which Dome was doing in the Beaufort. Super-depletion was scheduled for cancellation in the Tory budget of 1979 and expired in April 1980. Depletion on provincial lands was done away with in the NEP. Depletion on Canada Lands was phased out by the Canada–Alberta Agreement.

In order to take advantage of the maximum grants under the NEP for its Beaufort Sea exploration program, Dome created a wholly Canadian-owned subsidiary, Dome Canada. The combination of high interest rates, and, in the summer and fall of 1982, shut-in oil production and decreased gas sales, made it impossible for Dome to meet its loan obligations. To rescue it from its financial difficulties, Dome's Canadian banks and the federal government agreed in the fall of 1982 to an equity infusion package which, if fully implemented, would see the banks and Ottawa attain effective control of the company. At the time of writing, Dome's management and directors were still hoping to avoid having to use the banks' and Ottawa's rescue package, and falling interest rates were working in Dome's favour. However, Dome remains, for the present, an asset-rich, cash-poor company, but with good long term prospects if it can survive the short term.

Just as Dome's interest rates problem resulted partly from international events beyond its control—the Reagan administration's high interest rate, monetarist anti-inflation policy—another international development beyond its control may have had further harmful impact on Dome. Since late 1981 the combination of the recession, restructured energy consumption patterns in the industrial countries, and the post-1973 emergence of much new non-OPEC production (Britain, Norway, Mexico, U.S.S.R.) has resulted in decreased demand, increased supply, a shrinking share of the world oil market controlled by OPEC and subsequently downward pressure on international oil prices. This situation resulted in much internal feuding within OPEC (two of whose members were at war with one another) over price levels and production quotas and led to a two-week summit negotiation among the OPEC countries in London in March 1983. The outcome of this summit was a reduction in the OPEC benchmark price, adjusted within OPEC for quality, to $29 U.S. per barrel.[76] As mentioned above, this has had the effect of putting pressure on the Canada–Alberta Agreement, which forecast the 1983 world price for oil to be $58.50 (Canadian) when it is in fact $29.00 (U.S.). Consequently, Canadian old oil exceeded its ceiling of 75 percent of world price. Ottawa and Edmonton agreed to cancel a price increase due for July 1983.

While Dome retains strong assets in the Canadian prairies (in addition to Dome's original reserves, Hudson's Bay Oil and Gas was a major producer of oil and gas in Alberta), its flagship operation was its Beaufort Sea program. The decreasing world oil price has cast a major shadow of doubt across most of Canada's frontier developments because of the tremendous costs of exploration, production, and transmission in the harsh environment of the Arctic and East coast. Extraordinarily expensive projects such as the Alaska Highway Pipeline, the Polar Gas Pipeline, and the Arctic Pilot Project have been placed in limbo. As a result of the NEP "carrot" (the grants which pay most of the costs of exploration, depending on a firm's Canadian ownership rating) and "stick" approach (COGLA's renegotiation of stricter work programs and a system of land relinquishment in the exploration agreements with existing lease holders), exploration momentum has been maintained on the frontiers for the time being. If the grants are not significantly reduced, this could prove to be a very farsighted move if the world supply glut turns out, for whatever reasons, to be a short-term phenomenon. If, on the other hand, world oil demand and prices stay soft for the next decade, it could prove to be a case of pouring good money after bad. It has not been determined yet what price a barrel of Beaufort Sea oil would have to demand in the market to make major production development economically feasible. In addition, Beaufort Sea exploration had not yet produced the massive discoveries that were hoped for. Canada has no immediate need for frontier gas and may very well not need Beaufort oil in the 1990s either, which raises further questions about export markets. For strategic reasons, the Hibernia oil play on the East coast appears to be the key frontier project, but it suffers from serious environmental risks and the political impasse between Ottawa and St. John's.

As stressed above, these combined events in 1981 and 1982 were putting extraordinary pressure on the Canada–Alberta agreement. On June 30, 1983 a new eighteen-month deal was struck, this time without the acrimony of the 1980–81 negotiations.[77] Under these arrangements, conventional oil prices are frozen at the current price of $29.75 a barrel (about 83 percent of the world price). The $4-per-barrel price increase scheduled for July 1, 1983 was cancelled as would be those scheduled for 1984 if the world price did not rise. Domestic gas prices, initially scheduled to rise by twenty-five cents per thousand cubic feet every six months, would be held to 65 percent of the oil price. Thus gas producers would get the August 1, 1983 increase and part of that of February 1, 1984. Ottawa would absorb the increased costs to consumers through reductions in its gas excise tax. The new agreement also extended the new oil reference price, which was at or near the world price, to include oil discovered after March 31, 1974, and oil produced from wells drilled in gaps in existing oil fields. The effect of these measures was that about 35 percent of Alberta oil would qualify for the world price. Industry cash flow would increase by about $250 million, and both governments would benefit from the stability created.

A further post-NEP event to note was the change announced in August 1983 to help put a cap on the burgeoning costs of the Petroleum Incentive Payments (PIP).[78] The PIP costs would be partially controlled through a mechanism in which wells costing over $50 million would henceforth have to receive individual ministerial approval to be eligible for PIP grants. Companies would also have to show that their drilling costs were competitive. The demand-driven nature of the multi-billion dollar PIP expenditures had made them difficult to control. And these costs, as we show in Chapter 9, were becoming increasingly visible in a period of massive federal deficits. Thus the other side of the "visibility coin" was beginning to rear its head.

In 1984, several other events and changes occurred which, each in its own particular way, reflected either further adjustment to the NEP, or to the realities of oil and gas markets. The Federal Budget of February 15th, 1984, indicated two further changes. The Incremental Oil Revenue Tax (IORT) was suspended for another year to provide additional fiscal stimulus to the industry. In addition, revenues from the Canadian Ownership Account were being treated as general revenues.[79] This was owing to three factors. First, further takeovers were highly unlikely, and funds for the Dome rescue package seemed unlikely to be needed. Second, the money was needed to make a visible contribution to the reduction of the size of the huge federal deficit, or at least to the appearance of reduction. Third, in the event of legislative changes, the funds could now be more readily used for other energy purposes, including PIP payments and Petro-Canada. These probabilities are assessed in Chapter 10.

The improved position of Dome Petroleum, reflected in the increased confidence that the rescue funds would not be needed, did not, however, indicate that all was now well. In February 1984, a news story said that Japan would end a large $400 million financing arrangement with Dome. This proved to be untrue, but Dome had to reassure investors. Dome itself announced a 10 percent write-down of its assets a few days later. The $980 million write-down was the largest in Canadian corporate history, but was taken to improve investor confidence.[80] Further turbulence in energy markets was reflected in the scramble for gas markets, given large amounts of supply. The U.S. Economic Regulatory Administration issued a report that set out new policy guidelines and deregulation orders on the regulation of imported natural gas.[81] Canada had, earlier in 1983, lowered its single border price and offered incentives for extra volume purchases, but the new U.S. policy put further pressure on Canada if it was to maintain its 4 percent share of the U.S. gas market, let alone increase it. The report clearly wanted the market, not interventionist governments, to set prices. Price and competitiveness with other fuels were to be key criteria, but there were also general references to others. These could easily be interpreted to read that the United States would look unfavourably on import proposals when the source of the gas involved investment discrimination. Such a field would be the Venture project, to which the NEP's 25 percent Crown interest would apply. Market pressures, layered over with political muscle, were by no means confined to the United States. The Ontario Energy Board, in response to Ontario industrial pressure, urged the Ontario Cabinet to endorse the principle of direct purchasing of gas by Ontario industries and/or by permitting industrial users such as INCO Ltd. to become involved in the production of their own natural gas.[82] Such action would clearly involve a significant form of deregulation, and could adversely affect not only Alberta producers but pipeline monopolies such as Trans-Canada Pipeline. A 1984 federal task force report on the petrochemical industry added to this pressure by favouring reduced gas prices and gradual deregulation to take advantage of promising opportunities to expand the industry.

Finally, as an election drew nearer and as more sustained criticism of the NEP continued to be made, alternative policies, or at least policy themes, emerged. Thus in May 1984, the Canadian Petroleum Association presented alternatives which, if adopted, would basically have gutted the NEP. The Economic Council published a major report on energy policy which was critical of the NEP's lack of economic coherence. The Council too leaned strongly towards a less interventionist stance. While these views struck similar pro-market themes, they did not show up in undiluted form when the soon to be triumphant Mulroney Conservatives announced a pre-election energy package as part of its policies for western Canada. The new Conservative package included a non-retroactive "Canada share" provision to replace the 25 percent Crown interest; a replacement of PIP grants with transferable tax credits; the replacement of the Petroleum Gas Revenue Tax with a tax on profits; some form of protection for Canadians from sudden price increases; and market-sensitive pricing for exported natural gas, with the caveat that Canadians will always pay less than Americans for Canadian natural gas.[83]

Summary

We have traced the history of energy politics and policy in four broad periods with an increasingly detailed account of the last decade since 1973, when the growing politicization of energy was most noticeable. The sheer chronology of these events is presented so as to provide the basic minimum background for the analysis to follow. In the next two chapters in particular, we revisit these events. Some repetition of this kind is necessary since we now wish to analyse these events, first in a government–industry context, and then in relation to the intergovernmental relationships of power. The numerous post-NEP events in the 1981–84 period also require a chronological description, to be re-examined in Parts III and IV. In relation to the heightened politicization of energy in the 1970s, it is also of no small importance that many of the same political and bureaucratic leaders who were central players in the NEP had their own political experience, and hence political memories, cast in these events.

Notes

1. On the broader energy endowments of Canada, see Economic Council of Canada, *Strategy for Energy Policy* (Ottawa: Supply and Services Canada, 1984) and Department of Energy, Mines, and Resources, *Energy Futures for Canadians* (Ottawa: Supply and Services Canada, 1978).
2. See Donald Creighton, *John A. Macdonald: The Old Chieftain* (Toronto: Macmillan of Canada, 1958), chapter 6; and Vernon Fowke, *The National Policy and the Wheat Economy* (Toronto: University of Toronto Press, 1957).
3. See H.V. Nelles, *The Politics of Development* (Toronto: Macmillan, 1974).
4. G. Bruce Doern, *Government Intervention in the Nuclear Industry* (Montreal: Institute for Research on Public Policy, 1980).
5. See Barbara Hodgins, *Where the Economy and the Constitution Meet in Canada* (Montreal: C.D. Howe Institute, 1981), pp. 14–30.
6. See Arlon R. Tussing, "An OPEC Obituary," *The Public Interest*, No. 70 (Winter 1983), pp. 3–21.
7. See Robert Bothwell, Ian Drummond, and John English, *Canada Since 1945* (Toronto: University of Toronto Press, 1981); and G. Bruce Doern and Richard W. Phidd, *Canadian Public Policy: Ideas, Structure and Process* (Toronto: Methuen, 1983).
8. David Crane, *Controlling Interest: The Canadian Gas and Oil Stakes* (Toronto: McClelland and Stewart, 1982), pp. 39–40. Statistics based on Russell S. Uhler, "Oil and Gas Drilling Activity and Success by Selected Companies in Alberta" (Calgary: Energy Resources Conservation Board, 1980).
9. John N. McDougall, *Fuels and the National Policy* (Toronto: Butterworths, 1982), p. 58.
10. John Richards and Larry Pratt, *Prairie Capitalism: Power and Influence in the New West* (Toronto: McClelland and Stewart, 1979), p. 83.
11. *Ibid.*, p. 66.
12. See William Kilbourn, *Pipeline: Trans-Canada and the Great Debate, A History of Business and Politics* (Toronto: Clarke Irwin, 1970); and

Robert Bothwell and William Kilbourn, *C.D. Howe: A Biography* (Toronto: McClelland and Stewart, 1979).

13. McDougall, *op. cit.*, p. 57.
14. Canada, House of Commons, *Debates*, March 13, 1953, pp. 2928–9.
15. Kilbourn, *op. cit.*, pp. vii–viii.
16. Government of Canada, Royal Commission on Canada's Economic Prospects, *Final Report* (Ottawa: Queen's Printer, 1957).
17. McDougall, *op. cit.*, pp. 9–10.
18. *Ibid.*, p. 84 and pp. 94–95.
19. Government of Canada, Royal Commission on Energy, *First Report* (Ottawa: Queen's Printer, 1958), p. 11.
20. McDougall, *op. cit.*, p. 86.
21. J.G. Debanné, "Oil and Canadian Policy," in E.W. Erickson and L. Waverman (eds.), *The Energy Question: An International Failure of Policy*, volume 2: North America (Toronto: University of Toronto Press, 1974); see also Peter Eglington, "Historical Notes on Canada's Energy Industries" (Mimeo, Ottawa), François Bregha, "Canada's Natural Gas Industry," in James Laxer and Anne Martin (eds.), *The Big Tough Expensive Job: Imperial Oil and the Canadian Economy* (Toronto: Press Porcépic, 1976); and James Laxer, *The Energy Poker Game: The Politics of the Continental Resource Deal* (Toronto: New Press, 1970).
22. Debanné, *op. cit.*
23. Crane, *op. cit.*, pp. 55–56.
24. McDougall, *op. cit.*, p. 90.
25. Government of Canada, Royal Commission on Energy, *Second Report*, Chapter 6, p. 22. For an overall critique of the NOP, see also John R. Baldwin, "Federal Regulation and Public Policy in the Canadian Petroleum Industry: 1958–1975," *Journal of Business Administration*, vol. 13, nos. 1 and 2, 1982, pp. 57–97.
26. Government of Canada, Royal Commission on Energy, *op. cit.*, pp. 18–19.
27. Government of Canada, House of Commons, *Debates*, July 18, 1958, p. 2373.
28. Debanné, *op. cit.*, p. 131.
29. Crane, *op. cit.*, p. 46.
30. McDougall, *op. cit.*, p. 101.
31. See A.R. Lucas, "The National Energy Board" in G. Bruce Doern (ed.), *The Regulatory Process in Canada* (Toronto: Macmillan, 1978); and John B. Robinson, "Pendulum Policy: Natural Gas Forecasts and Canadian Energy Policy 1969–1981," *Canadian Journal of Political Science*, vol. XVI, no. 2 (June 1983), pp. 299–320.
32. Quoted in James Laxer, *The Energy Poker Game* (Toronto: New Press, 1970), p. 1.
33. Honourable Joe Greene, "Speech to Petroleum Society of the Canadian Institute of Mining and Metallurgy," Banff, Alberta, June 1, 1971.

34. See E.J. Dosman, *The National Interest: The Politics of Northern Development 1968-1975* (Toronto: McClelland and Stewart, 1975), chapter 3. For other views see Gurstan Dacks, *A Choice of Futures: Politics in the Canadian North* (Toronto: Methuen, 1981); François Bregha, "Arctic Pilot Project: CARC's Memorandum to Cabinet," *Northern Perspectives* 10:3 (April–May, 1982); and "Arctic Gas Hunt: Folly or Energy Insurance," *Toronto Star*, March 13, 1983, p. B3.

35. See Allan Tupper, "Public Enterprise as Social Welfare: The case of the Cape Breton Development Corporation," *Canadian Public Policy*, 4 (Autumn 1978), pp. 530–546.

36. See Donald J. Lecraw, "Uranium Supply and Demand: Implications for Policy," in G. Bruce Doern and R.W. Morrison (eds.), *Canadian Nuclear Politics* (Montreal: Institute for Research on Public Policy, 1980), chapter 5.

37. See Gordon Sims, "The Evolution of AECL," M.A. Thesis, Carleton University, 1979.

38. See Aidan R. Vining, "Provincial Hydro Utilities," in G. Allan Tupper and G. Bruce Doern (eds.), *Public Corporations and Public Policy in Canada* (Montreal: Institute for Research on Public Policy, 1981), chapter 4; Neil Swainsen, *Conflict Over the Columbia* (Montreal: McGill-Queens Press, 1979); L. Copithorn, "A Search for Common Ground: Canada's Regional and National Energy Policy Conflicts Defined," Economic Council of Canada (Ottawa, May 1982); and Government of Québec, *An Energy Policy for Québec: Insurance for the Future* (Québec City, 1978).

39. Two of the best sources on this period of oil politics are John M. Blair, *The Control of Oil* (New York: Vintage, 1978); and Peter R. Odell, *Oil and World Power*, Sixth Edition (London: Penguin, 1981); see also David H. Davis, *Energy Politics* (New York: St. Martins Press, 1974); and R. Engler, *The Brotherhood of Oil* (Chicago: University of Chicago Press, 1977).

40. For a good review of this period see Richards and Pratt, *op. cit.*, chapter 9, pp. 215–249.

41. *Oilweek*, January 21, 1974, p. 8.

42. *Financial Post*, August 5, 1978, p. 1.

43. For a more detailed analysis of this period see Glen Toner and François Bregha, "The Political Economy of Energy," in Michael S. Whittington and Glen Williams (eds.), *Canadian Politics in the 1980s* (Toronto: Methuen, 1981).

44. For a partial chronology of events during this period see Government of Canada, Department of Energy, Mines and Resources, *An Energy Strategy for Canada* (Ottawa: Supply and Services Canada, 1976), pp. 152–158.

45. H.V. Nelles, "Canadian Energy Policy 1945–1980: A Federalist

Perspective," in R. Kenneth Carty and W. Peter Ward (eds.), *Entering the Eighties: Canada in Crisis* (Toronto: Oxford University Press, 1980), p. 100.

46. Two reviews of this period on the theme of energy and federalism are A.D. Hunt and R.B. Toombs, "Canadian Energy Policy and Federalism— A Background Paper," and D.W. Stevenson, "Energy Issues Facing Canada: Three Perspectives," in Livia M. Thur (ed.), *Energy Policy and Federalism*, (Toronto: The Institute of Public Administration of Canada, 1981), pp. 53–96 and 151–169; for a good overview of energy in the 1970s see John F. Helliwell, "Canadian Energy Policy," *Annual Review of Energy*, 4 (1979), pp. 175–229.

47. See Robin W. Broadway and Harry M. Kitchen, *Canadian Tax Policy* (Toronto: Canadian Tax Foundation, 1980), pp. 147–151.

48. Department of Finance, *Federal-Provincial Resource Taxation Review* (Ottawa: Department of Finance, 1978), p. 30.

49. For the history of Petro-Canada see Larry Pratt, "Petro-Canada," in Allan Tupper and G. Bruce Doern (eds.), *Public Corporations and Public Policy in Canada* (Montreal: Institute for Research on Public Policy, 1981), pp. 95–148.

50. The best analysis of the northern pipeline saga is François Bregha, *Bob Blair's Pipeline: The Business and Politics of Northern Energy Development Projects*, Updated Edition (Toronto: Lorimer, 1979); see also Dacks, *op. cit.*, McDougall, *op. cit.*, and John McDougall, "Regulation Versus Politics: The National Energy Board and the Mackenzie Valley Pipeline," in Andre Axline, et al. (eds.), *Continental Community: Independence and Integration in North America* (Toronto: McClelland and Stewart, 1974).

51. Thomas Berger, *Northern Frontier, Northern Homeland*, Report of the Mackenzie Valley Pipeline Inquiry, Volume 1 (Ottawa: Supply and Services Canada, 1977).

52. National Energy Board, *Reasons for Decisions: Northern Pipelines* (Ottawa: Supply and Services Canada, 1977).

53. See Allan Warrack, *The Alberta Heritage Savings Trust Fund: An Historical Evaluation.* Paper prepared for the Economic Council of Canada, October 1982.

54. See Jeffrey Simpson, *Discipline of Power* (Toronto: Personal Library, 1980), chapters 12 and 13.

55. Honourable John Crosbie, "To the Caucus," memorandum, December 11, 1979. Reproduced by permission of Honourable John Crosbie.

56. From Premier Peter Lougheed's television address to the province in reaction to the Federal Budget and NEP, 30 October 1980, p. 9.

57. Premier William Davis, quoted in the *Globe and Mail*, 1 November 1980, p. 13.

58. An analysis of the impact of the NEP on Canadian-American relations can be found in Stephen Clarkson, *Canada and the Reagan Challenge*

(Toronto: Canadian Institute for Economic Policy, Lorimer, 1982). See also Edward A. Carmichael and James K. Stewart, *Lessons from the National Energy Program* (Toronto: C.D. Howe Institute, 1983).

59. Canadian Petroleum Association, "Public Opinion Poll on the NEP," 1981, question 41, p. 8.

60. Gallup Poll, no. 456-2, December 1981, p. 1.

61. Quoted in Judy Steed, "Canada's NEP: The Beauty or the Beast," *Globe and Mail*, March 19, 1983, p. 10.

62. Prime Minister Pierre Trudeau, quoted in the *Globe and Mail*, November 1, 1980, p. 14.

63. Honourable Marc Lalonde, quoted in the *Globe and Mail*, November 1, 1980, p. 14.

64. Major Projects Task Force on Major Capital Projects in Canada to the Year 2000, *Major Canadian Projects: Major Canadian Opportunities*, June 23, 1981. See also G. Bruce Doern, "The Mega-Project Episode and the Formulation of Canadian Economic Development Policy," *Canadian Public Administration*, vol. 26, no. 2 (Summer 1983), pp. 219-238.

65. Director of Investigation and Research, Combines Investigation Act, *The State of Competition in the Canadian Petroleum Industry*, volumes 1-7 (Ottawa: Supply and Services Canada, 1981).

66. Government of Canada, *Economic Development for Canada in the 1980s*, November 1981, p. 12.

67. *Memorandum of Agreement between the Government of Canada and the Government of Alberta relating to Energy Pricing and Taxation*, September 1, 1981.

68. Larry Pratt, "Energy: The Roots of National Policy," *Studies in Political Economy*, no. 7 (Winter 1982), p. 56.

69. See John F. Helliwell and Robert N. McRae, "The National Energy Conflict," *Canadian Public Policy*, vol. vii, no. 1, 1981, pp. 14-23; and "Resolving the National Energy Conflict: From the National Energy Program to the Energy Agreements," *Canadian Public Policy*, vol. viii, no. 1, 1982, pp. 15-23.

70. Brian L. Scarfe and Bruce Wilkinson, "The New Energy Agreement: An Economic Perspective." Revised edition of paper presented to the Ontario Economic Council Outlook and Issues Conference, October 28, 1981

71. Carmichael and Stewart, *op. cit*. See also Peter Foster, *The Sorcerer's Apprentices: Canada's Super-Bureaucrats and the Energy Mess* (Toronto: Collins, 1982).

72. See Bruce T. Henbest, "Making Energy Legislation," Research Paper, Department of Political Science, Carleton University, Ottawa, 1983.

73. Announcement by Premier Lougheed and Energy Minister Merv Leitch, *The Alberta Oil and Gas Activity Program*, Calgary, 13 April 1982.

74. Government of Canada, Department of Energy, Mines and Resources,

The National Energy Program: Update 1982 (Ottawa: Supply and Services Canada, 1982), pp. 3 and iii.

75. See J. Lyon, *Dome: The Rise and Fall of the House that Jack Built* (Toronto: Macmillan of Canada, 1983).

76. "OPEC's Pack Spurs Mexico to Cut Oil Cost," *Globe and Mail*, March 15, 1983, p. 1.

77. *Globe and Mail*, July 1, 1983, pp. 1–2.

78. *The Financial Post*, August 13, 1983, p. 1.

79. Government of Canada, *Budget Papers* (Ottawa: Department of Finance, February 15, 1984), p. 28.

80. See *Globe and Mail*, March 2, 1984, p. B1 and *Alberta Report*, March 5, 1984, p. 19.

81. U.S. Economic Regulatory Administration, *New Policy Guidelines and Deregulation Orders on the Deregulation of Imported Natural Gas* (Washington, United States Government Printing Office, 1984).

82. *Globe and Mail*, February 29, 1984, p. B1.

83. *Globe and Mail*, July 6, 1984, pp. 1–2.

CHAPTER 4

GOVERNMENT-INDUSTRY ENERGY RELATIONS: THE PRE-NEP YEARS

This chapter assesses the pre-NEP legacy of the government–industry relationship through a more detailed analysis of six key events of the 1947–1979 period introduced in Chapter 3. These events are: the Trans-Canada Pipeline (TCPL); the Borden Commission's decisions on natural gas exports and the Alberta–Montreal oil pipeline, and the Diefenbaker government's subsequent decision to establish a National Oil Policy; the establishment of Petro-Canada; the Syncrude bailout; the northern pipeline decision; and finally, the Clark government's 1979 energy policy. A re-examination of these events, through a focus on the government–industry relationship of power, will help us develop a comprehensive understanding of this relationship as it evolved and as it stood in 1980, when the Liberals formulated and introduced the NEP. This understanding is necessary in order to appreciate the impact of the NEP and to comprehend the changes it caused in the basic relationships of power.

The Trans-Canada Pipeline

The key interests involved in the TCPL conflict were the initially competing pipeline companies which later combined into TCPL, Gulf Oil Corporation, the federal Liberal government—then entering its third consecutive decade in power—the opposition parties, in particular the Tories, and the governments of Alberta and Ontario. It must be remembered that while the Trans-Canada debate reflected a clash of interests similar to that which took place in the other 1950s decisions to build and not to build various pipelines, it was unique in that the federal Liberals exposed in the TCPL case a much stronger commitment to creating a national market for gas than they had for oil, and for ensuring that this project be built entirely within Canadian jurisdiction under Canadian ownership, than was the case with the other pipelines.

The TCPL case reveals a clash of objectives among the key government, industry, and partisan interests in Canadian energy politics in the 1950s. One focal point for the clash of interests was the underlying tension "between east–west nationalism and north–south continental-ism."[1] John McDougall has amplified and clarified this tension between nationalist and continentalist logic as exhibited in the pipe-lines debates. The debates "pitted nationalists who felt that Canadian markets should be served entirely with Canadian fuels and delivered by means of pipelines built exclusively within Canada against 'free marketers,' who felt that Canadian markets should be served by Cana-dian sources only if necessary and then only by means of pipelines built along the cheapest possible routes. The former would maximize inter-provincial trade while the latter would do the reverse."[2]

More specifically, the nationalist position argued that national integration and national unity could be enhanced by overcoming the imposed divisions of geography and federalism and thereby strength-ening Canadian energy security and specifically self-sufficiency in natural gas by linking Canadian markets with Canadian resources; strengthening Canadian sovereignty by constructing the line solely within Canadian jurisdiction; and maintaining Canadian control by ensuring that the pipeline company be majority Canadian-owned. Regional objectives were reflected by arguments about both the need to ensure that Canada's major population and industrial base in central Canada was guaranteed a stable and secure supply of Canada's premium fuel, and at the same time, the need to support the energy base of the Alberta economy.

On the other hand, concerns for efficiency, as expressed by the continentalist position, dictated a view that less expensive markets could be found for the Alberta gas producer's product in the U.S., but that if it was to be mandated by public policy that Canadian markets were to be served, then the costs of constructing the lines and trans-mitting the gas should be lowered for Canadian producers and con-sumers by building an export component into the line. Alberta producers, it was argued, had to be given ample markets for their natural gas production even if this meant exporting, since expanding markets were needed to ensure the producer's cash flow, economic viability and a healthy exploration and development environment. The inclusion of the "joint service" concept in the four major oil and gas transmission systems meant that neither the purely nationalist nor continentalist arguments prevailed. As McDougall has noted, the result of the systems put in place between 1949 and 1961 was a quasi-national or semi-continental pattern.

The upshot was that national integration of Canadian markets and resources was achieved, but at the cost of reduced national sovereignty—the U.S. Federal Power Commission had to grant import licenses for the gas exported by the line at Emerson, Manitoba—and for a time national control, as the line became temporarily majority American-controlled. In the end, however, the political will exercised by the Liberals ensured that the company would be Canadian-owned and controlled. The result, as is often the case in a country which includes both producer and consumer interests, was that the pressures for regional sensitivity more or less equalled each other, and both national and continental integration were strengthened simultaneously.[3]

The government–industry relationship between the main private sector interests, Gulf and Trans-Canada, and the federal government reveal a consensus over the shared objective of ensuring the projects' completion, but also exposes instances of industry pressure and government accommodation which reflect the power of both private sector interests. The Gulf Corporation of Pittsburgh's policy of refusing to sell oil or gas to a company controlled, or potentially controlled, by government sounds positively archaic in the 1980s environment of energy politics, and indeed it provides a very trenchant example of how the government–industry relationship has changed over the last thirty years. As stressed in Chapter 3, this action by Gulf led to the Federal Liberal's temporary acceptance of majority foreign ownership of the pipeline company in 1956–57.

In the early 1950s the "seven sisters" of the international oil industry, including Gulf, had openly conspired to boycott the production of "hot oil" from Iran, which had nationalized the Iranian holdings of British Petroleum. The successful boycott contributed, along with the financial and organizational talents of the Central Intelligence Agency, to the overthrow of the offending Mossadeq regime.[4] Given this sort of heady success in manipulating the political fortunes of third-world governments, the American and British oil companies had little hesitation in pressuring, for both ideological and practical reasons, for various restrictions on the policy options of sovereign western states such as Canada. The refusal of the Canadian government to challenge Gulf's actions gives credence to Gulf's interpretation of its own power. The fact that the parent U.S. company totally domi-nated the decision-making power of its Canadian subsidiary, even at the potential risk of harming Gulf Canada's image, is instructive. Whether this dominant parent–submissive subsidiary relationship has changed by the early 1980s is open to empirical investigation.[5]

The relationship of Trans-Canada and the federal Liberal govern-ment is also revealing. By being committed for political and policy purposes to the construction of the project entirely within Canada, yet by refusing, for ideological reasons and for fear of the consequences for Canadian–U.S. and government–industry relations, to consider the option promoted by the Cooperative Commonwealth Federation (CCF) in Parliament, namely to construct the project by public enterprise, the Liberals weakened their negotiating position vis-à-vis Trans-Canada. While Trans-Canada did not get everything it sought, it continually came back to the government for aid and assistance, gaining in the process government bond and loan guarantees (even when the company became temporarily U.S. owned). TCPL also obtained the license to export up to one quarter of its throughput, a government commitment to take action according to the company's schedule, and finally government agreement to finance and construct, and later sell back to Trans-Canada, the most expensive section of the line through the rugged Canadian Shield of northern Ontario. All of this reflects the possession of considerable bargaining power.

Partisan interests also conflicted in a major way as a result of the Trans-Canada. It is generally acknowledged that the Liberal govern-ment's performance in, and treatment of, Parliament during the Pipe-line Debate contributed directly to its defeat by the Conservatives in 1957. Thus, the bitter partisan conflicts over the respect for Parlia-ment, the role of foreign capital in the Canadian energy industry, the role of energy projects in national economic development, the appro-priateness of public enterprise, the interests of producer and consumer regions, and the control and management of national resources must be acknowledged not only for their importance to Canadian energy politics but also for their importance as currency in the ongoing partisan struggle. Virtually all of these issues were still central, twenty-five years later, to the partisan and parliamentary battles surrounding the NEP.[6]

The Borden Commission: Natural Gas Exports, the Alberta-to-Montreal Pipeline and the National Oil Policy

As noted in Chapter 3, the establishment of the Royal Commission on Energy, headed by Toronto industrialist Henry Borden, was one of the first acts of the newly elected Diefenbaker government and a direct outcome of the Trans-Canada controversy. As John McDougall has argued, the fact that the terms of reference for the Commission were couched in vague generalities suggests that the Diefenbaker government had not determined the substance of a new energy policy or indeed, even the national interest on energy questions. In effect, the Diefenbaker government seemed to abdicate its responsibility for energy questions to the Commission. The Borden Commission's entry into this policy vacuum meant that it could not help but have a significant impact on Canadian energy politics. A number of its proposals revealed the nature of the industry–government relationships.

The oil and gas industry, for a variety of reasons, enjoyed prodigious power in Canadian energy politics during this period. And within the industry the multinationals were much stronger than the Canadian-owned firms. A key factor in the power of the multinationals in this pre-Energy, Mines and Resources, pre-Petro-Canada period, was their control over a pivotal, political resource, namely, information. Because of their control of geological, technical, economic, and financial information and knowledge and their skillful way of presenting it to the Commission and to governments, the industry enjoyed great success in winning both the Commission's and government's support for its positions. In part because of this, the Borden Commission and the federal and Alberta governments adopted throughout the 1960s an approach to energy questions which reflected to a considerable extent the logic, interests, and ideas of the global and continental planning system of the multinational majors.

With respect to gas exports, two related industry arguments were quickly accepted by the Commission. These were: 1) that exports were necessary, even before long-term supplies for Canadian consumers were assured, and 2) that the increased prices that would accompany heightened demand would result in higher revenues to the industry and thus would stimulate further exploration and development.

In the case of the proposed Alberta-to-Montreal oil pipeline, the Commission's preferences were also instructive about the underlying relationships of power. The major competing interests were the Canadian independents led by Home Oil[7] and the integrated majors led by Imperial Oil. As noted in Chapter 3, because of the impact of its Mandatory Oil Import Program in exacerbating the shut-in oil problem of the Alberta producers, and secondly because of its concerns with Venezuelan oil production, the U.S. government must be considered a key interest. In arguing the advantages of an oil line from the Alberta fields to the major Montreal market, Home Oil appealed to diverse concerns for regional sensitivity, security, and national integration. The line would supply Alberta crude oil producers with a guaranteed market, increase national security by eliminating the dependence of Montreal refineries on imported oil, create industrial activity across Canada, aid the national balance of payments by ending the annual $350 million per year outflow of capital to pay for foreign oil, and create a major stimulus for new exploration and production in the west. Imperial Oil challenged this line of argument by appealing to concerns for efficiency and regional self-interest in leading the fight against the line. It argued that the use of western oil in Montreal refineries would be more expensive than imported oil and would necessitate additional costly government regulation of the industry. Imperial and the other majors appealed to regional concerns by arguing that Québec consumers would have to bear the additional expense of using higher-cost western crude. The lack of support for the line among Québec politicians suggests this argument had some impact. Imperial also argued that western producers would be better off to pursue a continentalist strategy of attempting to secure further U.S. markets closer to home.

As outlined in Chapter 3, the majors had other concerns which appealed primarily to the needs of their own global production and marketing networks. The U.S. government, by its imposition of oil import quotas and tariffs in support of its own western independent producers created much of the shut-in problem for the Alberta producers, but for its own geo-political reasons also opposed the use of Alberta oil in the Montreal market. What is interesting about this decision is the lack of support of other significant interests for the project; the lack of support of the Ontario and Québec governments, federal politicians, and Montreal industrialists is particularly noticeable. The Borden Commission clearly bought the economic-efficiency

argument of a continental market as proposed by the majors in rejecting the development of a national crude oil market.

In rejecting a line to serve Montreal markets with Canadian oil
and in explicitly promoting a continental energy policy, the Borden
Commission's views led inexorably to the National Oil Policy (NOP).
By establishing the Ottawa Valley Line, or Borden Line as it came to be
known in 1961, the Diefenbaker government added political legitimacy to the established practice of the multinationals, and in the
process shut the offshore imports of the U.S. independents out of the
rapidly growing Ontario market. The decision not to allow Alberta oil
into Montreal would handicap later national governments, result in
supply worries, and establish the necessity of creating the Oil Import
Compensation Program in 1974 when the once plentiful and cheaper
Middle Eastern and Venezuelan oil suddenly became less secure and a
lot more expensive. At the same time that it rejected the establishment
of a secure and nationally integrated Canadian oil market serving all
three of Canada's major markets, the NOP also strengthened continental integration by making additional surplus Canadian oil and gas
available for export to the United States. It must be acknowledged,
however, that the NOP also strengthened national integration to the
extent that it caused the forced integration of Ontario markets with
Alberta oil fields.

Yet, from the perspective of the main interests involved, the NOP
was surprisingly non-controversial. In the pre-OPEC environment of
cheap and plentiful international oil, and the control of the international oil economy by the Seven Sisters, the arguments of those
private-sector and public-sector interests who supported mixed
concerns for efficiency, equity, and regionalism carried the day. The
bargain offered something to Québec via lower prices, to Alberta via
the safeguarding of its higher-priced crude from competition from
cheaper imports in the Ontario market, and to Ontario via the concentration and expansion of the refining and petro-chemical industry
there. The support of the opposition Liberals for continental energy
planning ensured that the CCF was the lone opposing voice in
Parliament. The support of the relevant provincial governments and
of the U.S. government and the multinationals isolated those Canadian-
owned firms such as Home Oil and the downstream independents in
Ontario who were still unhappy with their market situation.

Syncrude

The politics surrounding the massive 125 000 barrel-per-day oil extraction plant in the tarsands of the Athabaska regions of northern Alberta are complex and intriguing. The project, and its evolution from a $500 million plant at the pre-construction stage in 1972 to a $2 billion project which had to be rescued from collapse by the equity investment of three Canadian governments in February 1975, provides a revealing glimpse into the government–industry relationship by exposing the levels and kinds of leverage that a consortium of foreign-owned companies was able to exert over Canadian governments at the time. There were two key periods of leverage and hence of power: one primarily with the Lougheed Cabinet in August 1973, and the second primarily with Ottawa in January 1975. In the latter period, the consortium threatened to abandon the already-under-construction project unless both governments met a further set of demands by making an additional set of concessions. The original Syncrude consortium (Imperial Oil 30 percent, Atlantic Richfield 30 percent, City Services 30 percent, and Gulf 10 percent) and the governments of Canada, Alberta and Ontario were the key interests involved in shaping the outcome of the issue.

The Lougheed Conservatives, as we saw in Chapter 3, had come to power in Alberta in 1971 on a campaign promise to use the province's increasingly valuable oil and gas reserves to stimulate the diversification of the provincial economy. The world-scale, non-conventional oil producing Syncrude project became a symbol of that diversification, and much of the government's prestige was tied to its success. As Larry Pratt puts it, "Peter Lougheed had deliberately created public expectations of growth and spectacular progress and his personal image and credibility were now bound up with Syncrude's fate."[8] The Lougheed government rejected the advice of a group of senior civil servants[9] that it break with the historical precedent established by the development of the province's conventional oil and gas reserves. The past approach had, the officials charged, resulted in "tremendous and unregulated growth," "short-term benefits" to the province and "long-term costs" arising from exported energy, technology, job opportunities, and environmental damages in addition to the depletion of nonrenewable resources."[10] Specifically, Lougheed was urged to develop the bituminous tarsands in a way which would reverse the "historical trend of ever increasing foreign control of nonrenewable resource development in Canada" by consciously employing Canadian technology and services and by emphasizing orderly growth and development to ensure the protection of the environment and thereby enhance the benefits to Canadians and Albertans.

In part, the Lougheed government's rejection of this strategy can be explained by the fact that the senior civil service was still associated, to a certain extent, in the new government's mind with the previous longstanding Social Credit regime. Yet, it is unlikely the developmental approach promoted by the civil servants would have proved acceptable for a Social Credit government either. Ultimately, the nationalist and interventionist approach of the civil servants was rejected by the Conservatives on ideological grounds. By being committed to tarsands development, but having rejected an approach which would have entailed strict developmental regulation and the explicit utilization of Canadian technology and services, the Government was faced with negotiating the terms of development with the multinational majors:

> In negotiating with the affiliates of these giant corporations governments are often at a decided disadvantage, for the highly centralized companies can pit provinces, countries, regions, even different fuels, against each other in order to win the terms they seek. And where a government is isolated and sees no alternative to the multinational corporation and its priorities, then that government will have little power to dispose of its resources as it thinks best. It is this situation which accounts for the rise of international organizations like OPEC, founded to counter the bargaining power of the world oil cartel. And it is precisely the same situation which has placed Canada's future energy supplies in question and left our governments open to corporate blackmail. Governments who play poker with companies like Syncrude are playing against a stacked deck.[11]

In order to achieve its objective of provincial development and economic diversification, the Alberta government yielded to Syncrude's demands in August 1973. The consortium got the concessions it wanted in terms of taxation and other fiscal conditions, pricing, altered labour laws, provincially financed infrastructure, weakened environmental laws, exemption from pro-rationing, and others. When Lougheed announced on province-wide television on September 18,

1973 that the project was to proceed, he added that the whole thing depended upon Syncrude winning some important tax and pricing concessions from Ottawa. He publicly assured the industry and Albertans that he would lobby hard to make sure the concessions were granted.

Ottawa did in fact respond with major concessions, especially on the fiscal side. For example, Ottawa recommended that any reference to royalties be deleted and the concept of a joint venture be substituted in the Alberta–Syncrude agreement. Among other advantages, this would provide a loophole for tax purposes and in effect exempt Syncrude from Ottawa's then recently announced decision to disallow royalty payments to provinces as deductible for federal income tax purposes as well as qualify for the resource allowance. With respect to pricing, Ottawa agreed to let Syncrude oil move toward international prices, provided such prices were "fair and reasonable" to the economy and citizens of Canada. In addition, Ottawa agreed not to subject Syncrude production to any pro-rationing scheme, thereby guaranteeing that full production could be marketed, in export markets if necessary.

In agreeing to these arrangements Ottawa was reacting to regional pressures and was trying to do its part to ensure that a project to which the Alberta government was committed went ahead. It is worth mentioning that at about this same time in 1973 the Liberals had held a Western Economic Opportunities Conference to try to boost their dismal presence in the west in the midst of a minority parliament. Consequently, the Liberals were anxious to be seen supporting a high-profile western project. Initially, security was not a major consideration, as the Syncrude partners planned to export part of the production. In the words of Jerry McAfee, president of Gulf Canada, the tarsands provided "the best prospects for maintaining Canada's important oil export trade with the United States."[12]

After Atlantic-Richfield announced it was pulling out of the project on December 4, 1974, the remaining consortium partners unveiled, on January 16, 1975, a new set of demands which Edmonton and Ottawa would have to meet by January 31, 1975 to ensure completion of the project. These included guarantee of world price, fresh guarantees for exemption from the non-deductibility provisions of the Turner budget and from any future pro-rationing of oil production, and the public sector infusion of a billion dollars in equity and/or further tax concessions. Ottawa responded to the threat by reiterating its pledge that the project would be exempt from the budget provisions whereby royalties, or payments in lieu of royalties would no longer be deductible for income tax purposes, by providing, as it refused to do in 1973, categorical assurances that Syncrude oil could be sold at world price. Ottawa once again reaffirmed the project's exemption from pro-rationing, and invested $300 million in public funds in the project in return for 15 percent ownership. Alberta invested $200 million for 10 percent and Ontario $100 million for 5 percent ownership.

The Liberal federal government clearly yielded to the industry power play. By complying with the industry's demands, Ottawa could claim to be aiding Albertans by contributing a major regional development project which would also have advantageous industrial spinoffs for other parts of Canada. Most importantly, in the emerging post-OPEC crisis situation of Canada's perceived deteriorating oil supply position, Ottawa could be seen to be enhancing Canadian oil security by strengthening Canada's domestic supply of accessible oil. This last factor could be seen to benefit Canadians from British Columbia to Québec who rely on Canadian crude, and improve the domestic balance of payments by reducing net imports of oil.

Nearly a decade later, it is reasonable to argue that given the continued uncertainty and instability of international oil markets, it is a good thing Syncrude was built. It is debatable, however, whether the governments paid too high a price for its completion. There is no question that the private sector interests, represented by the consortium partners, exacted a high price from the governments of Alberta and Canada. The consortium argued that there were no economic rents to be captured and that the project would yield only normal returns on investment.[13]

In terms of what this case reveals about the possession and exercise of power, however, Pratt's argument about why the politicians negotiated from a position of weakness is, in general, persuasive. He argued that "three essential failings destroyed that possibility [of turning the January 1975 crisis into an opportunity] and fatally weakened the bargaining power of the governments." One major impediment in those pre-Petro-Canada days to effective bargaining by the political leaders was their lack of crucial information. Second,

Canada's balkanized political system weakened the common interests of the governments and, indeed, presented exploitable divisions for the consortium. Third, for ideological reasons the "governments involved were literally incapable of seeing alternatives to capitulation." As Pratt further argued, had they been bargaining from a self-perceived position of strength, the governments could have made "a public statement to the effect that Syncrude would not be shut down: that if the oil companies chose to cut and run, they would lose their investment in the project, be sued for breach of contract and shut out of any future development of the tarsands. If required, the tarsands would be developed by Crown corporations—but they would be developed."[14] Pratt therefore concluded that:

> The point is not a philosophical one; it is purely a question of power politics. By renouncing the option of public ownership and development of the tar sands the political leaders lost their sole opportunity to checkmate what we have called the oil industry's monopoly veto power—its power to threaten to block development of resources such as the Athabasca sands. Without such an option in reserve, without a bargaining card of last resort, the politicians simply lacked credibility when they bravely asserted that they would not be intimidated or pressured into concessions. To put it even more categorically, the governments could not have won the showdown with the oil companies without being prepared to nationalize Syncrude and develop the tar sands on their own.[15]

Indeed, both governments appeared incapable of exercising much strength against the consortium. It is difficult to find any issue of substance on which the consortium failed to achieve its basic objectives.

Petro-Canada

One of the most far-reaching features of Prime Minister Trudeau's December 6, 1973 eleven-point oil policy statement was the decision to create Petro-Canada. This decision was but one of a spate of control-expanding initiatives spawned by a coalescence of political and bureaucratic imperatives induced in response to an externally generated crisis of uncertainty and instability. By rejecting the option of nationalizing a subsidiary of one of the major multinationals, the government avoided the option that would have most shocked the existing relationship. While the creation of a new state enterprise in the petroleum industry has been described even by its first chairman, Maurice Strong, as an alternative to, rather than an instrument of, nationalization,[16] it nevertheless considerably strengthened the federal government's arsenal of instruments that it brought to its side of the relationship with the industry. In combination with the emergence throughout the 1970s of a few large and powerful Canadian-owned and controlled private sector firms, the genesis and growth of Petro-Canada in the years since 1975 has in a significant way restructured the composition of the petroleum industry in Canada. As a result of this development, the various relationships of power between the two major levels of the state and the various sectors of the industry have changed markedly as well.

A state enterprise in the energy field had been considered in the document **An Energy Policy for Canada,**[17] produced by EMR in 1973. The OPEC crisis and the resultant vulnerability of oil consumers in Québec and the Maritimes (a direct result of the Alberta-to-Montreal oil pipeline and NOP decisions taken over a decade earlier) militated in favour of developing an instrument over which Ottawa had direct control and which could enter into state-to-state bilateral arrangements. The latter were becoming increasingly popular with OPEC and other producer nations. Concerns for security and stability of supply were reflected in the other key mandate of the state company. Given the recently acknowledged instability of international oil markets, and the recently recognized limited control the federal government had over the oil and gas industry, the federal government wanted Petro-Canada as an instrument for expediting frontier exploration in pursuit of the objective of "needing to know" what Canada's reserves of oil and gas were. The record profits of the foreign-dominated industry in Canada in 1973, the tarnished image of the industry as a result of its flip-flops on the size of Canada's oil and gas reserves, the public's suspicion about the industry's role in the 1973 crisis and questions about its potential for profiteering from the dramatic price increases, along with Ottawa's growing fear of being totally dependent on the foreign-controlled industry for crucial information, all combined to convince the federal government that they needed a direct window on the machinations and operations of the industry in Canada.

The NDP, who advocated the creation of a state oil company, held the balance of power in the 1972–74 minority Parliament. While there is no question that the NDP pushed hard for a state oil company and made this a condition of their continued parliamentary support of the Liberals, Larry Pratt disputes the NDP's claim of having fathered Petro-Canada by arguing that the Liberal Cabinet and caucus had come to a similar conclusion as to the need for a government-owned company, and indeed the Liberals created Petro-Canada after they had regained majority government status in the July 1974 election.[18] The Conservatives, on the other hand, strongly opposed Petro-Canada's creation, arguing that it was an unnecessary and inefficient intrusion of the state into the economy. The Conservatives mounted a filibuster at the committee stage during the parliamentary passage of the Petro-Canada Act. Their intense dislike of Petro-Canada must not be under-estimated, as four years later they would ignore the strong public support Petro-Canada had developed and make its "privatization" the centrepiece of a short-lived campaign to reduce state involvement in the economy. The Alberta government certainly didn't like the idea of Petro-Canada, which they darkly viewed as yet another attempt by the federal Liberals to extend federal influence and power into areas of provincial jurisdiction.

An additional major impetus for the creation of Petro-Canada was the growing realization among the officials of EMR that a state oil company would allow them to strengthen their control over the petroleum industry as well as enhance their authority over energy matters within the bureaucracy:

> The concept of a national oil company found its strongest advocates *within* the government, notably in an Energy Depart-ment attempting to extend its control over the petroleum industry. Large permanent bureaucracies crave predictability and stability. Confronted in late 1973 with an international supply crisis whose outcome it could not determine, and lacking influence over a multinational business notoriously resistant to political influence, Canada's federal bureaucracy sought to reduce uncertainty and to increase its knowledge of, and control over, the petroleum industry. Petro-Canada was created as an *enterprise témoin*—a bureaucratic device to witness what actually happened and why.[19]

In a world of an ever-increasing number of state oil companies, North America had remained the exclusive domain of private oil, and the oil companies, despite government assurances that Petro-Canada would benefit them, were not initially happy with its arrival on the scene. Indeed some elements of the industry were bitterly opposed to it and virtually all private sector interests criticized the idea of giving Petro-Canada preferential rights. Yet the creation of Petro-Canada did provide the federal government with an important new instrument to bring to its relationships with both the industry and the producing provinces. Not only did the company provide Ottawa with its first significant data-gathering and window-on-the-industry functions, it was an operational instrument which could be used to influence the outcome of developments. It would also later become an important symbol of security and national identity for Canadians.

The Alaska Highway Pipeline

The decade-long northern pipeline issue is important not only for what it reveals about the government–industry relationship but also for what it divulges about the shifting balance of power within the industry. As mentioned above, one important feature of the 1973–1980 period of Canadian energy politics was the emergence of large Canadian-controlled majors. One of the major developments contributing to this new configuration within the industry was the outcome of the northern pipeline issue. The much smaller Canadian-controlled Foothills consortium successfully challenged the foreign-controlled giants of the industry which were allied in the Canadian Arctic Gas Pipeline consortium (CAGPL). "Foothills and Arctic Gas epitomized the confrontation between David and Goliath, East and West, nationalists and continentalists."[20] By offering the government a pipeline option that not only crossed less environmentally, socially, and politically sensitive areas but which also represented a major energy mega-project which would be designed, built, operated, and controlled by Canadians, Foothills achieved a victory which marked a major milestone in the maturation of the Canadian-owned and controlled sector of the industry.

The outcome was pivotal in that it signified the emergence of a Canadian-controlled major. It was, however, additionally important in that Alberta Gas Trunk Line was headed by Robert Blair, a self-proclaimed Canadian nationalist—in an industry renowned for its anti-nationalist and anti-statist sentiment—who was not in the least hesitant, as many small Canadian-owned firms were, to acknowledge and indeed highlight the national ownership and control divisions within the industry and the implications thereof for company procurement policy, independence of company decision making, and for Canada's national balance of payments, research and development effort and the like. François Bregha, in his exhaustive chronicle of the pipeline saga, noted that in response to Imperial Oil's attempt to have the federal government force a merger between Foothills and Arctic Gas, similar to that which transpired in 1972 between the Northwest Project and Gas Arctic, Blair indicated his unwillingness to share power with the foreign majors:

> Having won, Foothills was in a position to dictate its terms. It did so just as Imperial's board was meeting: it was ready to welcome new partners but not the major oil companies. "Exxon tried to exercise too much muscle" in pushing Arctic Gas, Blair explained, referring to Imperial by its corporate parent's name.[21]

The key interests involved in shaping the outcome were the Foothills consortium (Alberta Gas Trunk Line and Westcoast Transmission), CAGPL (Imperial Oil, Gulf, Shell, TCPL and others), the Canadian government, the U.S. government, and a coalition of northern native groups, their southern support groups, and a number of environmental organizations.

As the northern pipeline issue evolved through its various stages, and as extraneous circumstances changed, the concerns reflected in Ottawa's justification for the project also changed. In the early '70s, a northern line was defended as a means of maintaining U.S. markets for Canadian oil and gas and for precluding the necessity of tanker traffic down the B.C. coast carrying U.S. oil to west coast markets in the United States. As shortages of Canadian gas loomed in the mid-'70s, efficiency and security concerns came to the forefront, with the pipeline being touted as the most efficient means of gaining access to new Canadian supplies of natural gas for the Canadian market. As Canadian need for northern gas declined in the late '70s, regional and economic concerns became more explicit as the project was championed as a means of providing a substantial stimulus to the Canadian economy, both along its northern and western route and in industrial Ontario, as well as a worthwhile friendly gesture to the United States.

In addition to the two private-sector consortia which sponsored the competing projects, the key interest was the federal Liberal government. Since the late 1960s the Liberal Cabinet and federal bureaucracy had been active and enthusiastic promoters of a northern mega-project. As Helliwell argues, an increasingly important theme of Canadian energy politics is that "Canadian federal and provincial governments alike are overly inclined to appear in too many conflicting roles at the same time; acting as resource owners, as project entrepreneurs, as taxing authorities, as economic and environmental regulators, and as providers of subsidies. This excessive jumble of roles often makes it difficult to establish either credibility or accountability for the resulting policies."[22] Helliwell's critique, while focussed more generally, is particularly applicable to the northern pipeline issue. Various components of the federal government—the National Energy Board (NEB), Mackenzie Valley Pipeline (MVPL) Inquiry, the Task Force on Northern Oil Development (TFNOD), Alaska Highway Pipeline Inquiry, Environmental Assessment Panels, the Northern Pipeline Agency (NPA), and Cabinet—have all had a role to play in the ultimate outcome. In some respects the roles complemented one another; in other respects, they were blatantly in conflict.

With respect to the government–industry relationship, the most important components of this mix of governmental actors was the political leadership in Cabinet and the bureaucratic leadership in the TFNOD, NEB, and the Northern Pipeline Agency, which never wavered in their support for a northern pipeline mega-project. For ideological and political reasons, the Canadian political and bureaucratic leadership was unable to comprehend a range of options which would have strengthened their bargaining position with the consortium sponsors and with the U.S. government. Consequently, the pipeline saga reflects a sense of drift, a continuous series of concessions both to the pipeline sponsors and to the Americans.

For a number of reasons the government proved incapable of taking a stance that would allow it to maximize Canadian benefits through negotiations with the industry sponsors. In order to maximize its bargaining position, the government would have had to have been prepared to refuse to approve the project unless it met the country's and the government's conditions. A major bias in the government's attitude towards resource development precluded such an option, however. "Throughout the 1970s, the question of whether to exploit the Mackenzie Delta reserves was never asked: the only question was always when and how ... This is a policy by rote of growth for growth's sake. It helps to explain how the government was able to shift its support so effortlessly from pipeline proposal to pipeline proposal. Each in the end meant the same thing: faster development, more jobs, more exports, more wealth."[23] This hard and fast commitment to a northern pipeline by key political and bureaucrat interests contributed to the attenuation of government neutrality and independence and resulted in the creation of a highly consensual government–industry relationship, but one in which the government is the weaker partner in relation to the industry's ultimate control or veto power over the actual construction, decision and production process:

> Surely one of the most remarkable characteristics of the pipeline decision-making process has to be what can only be called the symbiotic relationship which prevailed between government and industry. In 1972, government pressure helped Gas Arctic and the Northwest to merge. In 1979, government policy favoured the realignment of gas export applications behind Pan Alberta. In the former case, the most powerful alliance of oil and gas interests ever forged in the country was created; in the latter, the government backed itself into a corner by contributing to the momentum behind pre-building without receiving any of the assurances that the rest of the Alaska Highway pipeline would follow.
>
> The government–industry partnership in large resource projects, of course, is not just a recent phenomenon in Canada. [Trans-Canada Pipelines, Panarctic Oils, Syncrude] . . . The government's role as a developer, while it has undoubtedly fostered economic growth, has also been of direct economic benefit to large resource companies. Moreover, it has led to a confusion of interests, the government's function as the protector of the public good being tempered by its association with the companies it ostensibly regulates.[24]

The government's performance throughout the 1970s showed that its major objective was to ensure that a northern pipeline was built, and it did virtually everything it could to ensure the project's success short of agreeing to backstop it financially. There are a number of relevant government actions throughout this period which show the symbiotic nature of the government–industry relationship.

From 1968 to 1972, the TFNOD became the "central body for determining northern resource policy." A secretive, senior-level committee composed of the deputy ministers of EMR, Transport, Indian Affairs and Northern Development, and the chairman of the NEB, quickly became "a transmission belt for industry initiatives requiring speedy approval by Cabinet," "a secret forum . . . where senior officials could meet in confidence with business executives." The TFNOD was entirely development-oriented and adopted an active approach to the promotion of a Mackenzie pipeline corridor over its major competitor. As Dosman puts it, the Committee saw as its task the need "to convince the oil industry of the merits of a Mackenzie pipeline system."[25]

The TFNOD and the government supported the consortium approach to northern development even though the more appropriate objective would have been to promote private sector competition to avoid "a common front of corporate interests backed by Washington. Consortia of this kind would exert formidable pressure on senior officials." In 1970 the TFNOD determined that its central problem would be to convince the competing groups to pool their capital and expertise into a single consortium, so that government and industry "might plan together the pattern of northern resource extraction and delivery." In June 1972, after considerable trouble in overcoming tensions between Gas Arctic and Northwest, success was achieved with the merger of the two competing groups into CAGPL.[26]

As outlined below, when the government realized that Berger might interpret his mandate more broadly than the narrow instruction to "determine under what conditions a pipeline would be built," the government tried to intimidate him. As Bregha argues, the government exhibited indifference, if not hostility, "to the principle of public participation." It refused to provide public interest groups with "the means to articulate alternatives to pipeline development; it denied them funding to challenge Foothills' and Arctic Gas' arguments before the NEB; it also denied them access to much of its own information, gathered, one must point out, at the taxpayers' expense."[27]

In the final negotiations in the spring and summer of 1977 the federal government, as it had throughout, continuously accommodated the Canadian decision-making process to meet U.S. deadlines. Because the Americans, in a wise bargaining strategy, threatened right up until the time of signing in September of 1977 to reject the two Canadian alternatives in favour of the all-American El Paso project, the Canadian government became, as a result of its commitment to a northern pipeline, the major lobbyist for the Mackenzie Valley and then the Alaska Highway pipelines in Washington. This was hardly a position from which to negotiate advantageous conditions from either the U.S. government or the pipeline sponsors.

Thus, the most important conflicts here were not between government and industry, but between sectors of the industry, and between all of these pro-development interests and that element of northern society opposed to a pipeline. One of the unintended but most far-reaching consequences of the northern pipeline issue was that it thrust the issue of aboriginal rights and aboriginal land claims and the environmental sensitivity of the north onto the main stage of Canadian politics. The politicization of the northern aboriginal groups and the nurturing of a new generation of aboriginal political leaders may prove to be the major legacy of the northern pipeline.[28] The major vehicle for the participation of aboriginal people and the major forum for exposing southern Canadians to the cultural, social, economic and environmental concerns of the northern aboriginal people was the MVPL Inquiry. Justice Thomas Berger of the British Columbia Supreme Court, a well-known Indian rights lawyer and former leader of the NDP in British Columbia, was named to head the Inquiry in March 1974. The establishment of the Inquiry and the appointment of Berger by the Liberal government were both intended, at least in part, to assuage the NDP, which held the balance of power in the 1972–74 Liberal minority government. Berger's insistence on visiting the communities along the pipeline route to hear the concerns of the people first hand, and his commitment to provide funds to major northern interest groups and aboriginal and environmental organizations so that they could present their cases more effectively, may have gone beyond what the government had anticipated—indeed, it is well known that when Berger adopted a broader view of his mandate, "the government tried to intimidate him by threatening to change his terms of reference, withhold documents, make a decision before his report was ready and limit his budget"[29]—but it reflected the government's need to ensure or at least to appear to ensure that all interests were treated fairly and judiciously in the determination of the outcome.

Indeed, this period of Canadian energy politics is important in that it represented the emergence of a significant aboriginal–environmental coalition both in the north and in southern Canada, which, largely through its access to the media via the Berger Inquiry,[30] was able to help turn public opinion against the MVPL. Despite the expenditure of millions of advertising dollars, the CAGPL consortium was unable to counter this. Bob Blair—his ear always to the newly sensitive political ground—attended a number of northern community hearings and polled southern Canadian opinion, and as a result developed the political acumen to realize that northern political, environmental, and social issues would help turn the political tide against the Yukon Northern Slope–Mackenzie Valley route, if, given the government's long-standing commitment to a northern pipeline, a reasonable alternative was available. The Liberal government had decided in the early 1970s that a northern pipeline was in the national interest. Foothills won because it was able to adapt its proposal to meet the government's needs. CAGPL, perhaps because it was dominated by the major multinationals which had grown used to the Canadian government changing its needs to accommodate the oil companies, was unwilling or incapable of change and therefore lost the battle.

Government–Industry Energy Relations under the Clark Conservatives

Energy was not a major issue in the May 1979 federal election campaign[31] despite the fact that the Islamic revolution was raging in Iran, OPEC's second largest producer. Despite gaining only a minority government and 35.9 percent of the popular vote (less than the Liberals' 40.1 percent), Joe Clark somehow interpreted his victory as a mandate for fundamental change. That the Conservatives were elected at all was in fact more a function of the peculiarities of the electoral system than the result of a massive shift of support to the Conservatives. Clark hired as his economic advisor Jim Gillies, an ex-MP, who was well known as a conservative, neoclassical economist and a member of the party's right wing. Gillies, who had been involved in forming the party's energy policy while in opposition, was far less interested in kowtowing to public opinion than in leading the country, whether it liked it or not, down a conservative path. The key symbol of the fundamental change the Tories hoped to institute was the privatization of the state oil company, Petro-Canada. "To the Tories Petrocan was a symbol. By getting the state out of the state oil company, they would be able to prove that they were, in fact, different from the Liberals, that they were serious about cutting back the role of government, that they meant what they said about promoting individual and private enterprise."[32]

Along with the privatization promise, the Conservative energy policy was initially quite thin in that it amounted to a general objective of achieving self-sufficiency by 1990 and a vague idea of promoting Canadianization. As a result of spending sixteen consecutive years in opposition, the Tories brought copious volumes of political naiveté to the government benches, particularly where their assumptions about the degree of cooperation they could expect from the Conservative premiers on such fundamental issues as oil and gas pricing were concerned.

Like the actions by Khadaffi and the Shah of Iran in 1972–73, the victory of the Ayotollah Khomeini and the Iranian revolution in 1979 had a dramatic impact on both global and Canadian energy politics. Indeed, as Joe Clark and the Conservatives were basking in the euphoria of electoral victory, the spot market price for oil was more than doubling to around $40 U.S. a barrel. This generated a crisis for the Clark government, but one different from that faced by most of the rest of the industrialized world. The Canadian crisis was a result of the fact that Canada is both a producer and a consumer-importer of oil. The geographical and federal cleavages of the Canadian political economy, which are accentuated by the location of oil and gas reserves and markets, were once again stimulated by the dramatic escalation in world price.

The Alberta government and the Canadian oil industry began recalculating what the market price of their oil was and, therefore, how much they were subsidizing Canadian consumers. The dramatic international price increases were a godsend to the industry and Alberta since the existing pricing and revenue-sharing agreement, which was due to expire on July 1, 1980, was up for renegotiation. Hence, the producing provinces and the oil industry geared up the arguments about higher prices being good for Canada because it is a producer. They noticed that the Clark Conservatives identified oil self-sufficiency as their prime energy objective, and noted that Joe Clark had returned from the June 1979 Tokyo Summit having promised to reduce Canada's oil imports by 100 000 barrels a day by 1980. Given that Canada was importing 450 000 barrels a day, and that it was unlikely new Canadian production could make up the shortfall, the producing provinces and the industry assumed this meant the federal Tories were willing to use the price mechanism to reduce consumption. Both Alberta and the industry were well plugged into the Clark government and both were determined to get higher prices. Furthermore, officials at EMR were not opposed to higher prices either, though they pointed out to the new government and the public that substantially raising prices while maintaining the present revenue-sharing regime (10 percent federal government, 45 percent provincial government, and 45 percent industry) would have major consequences for other policy fields.

Not surprisingly, the Conservative government of Ontario and the Conservative MPs within the Ontario and Atlantic caucuses were less enchanted with the prospect of dramatically higher oil prices, whether international or domestic. Much higher international prices would substantially increase Canada's oil import bill and thereby significantly worsen the federal deficit, placing greater pressure on Canadian interest rates and the dollar. Higher domestic prices would raise the cost of the Canadian-produced oil and gas used by their consuming constituents to the benefit of the Alberta Treasury and the oil company profit margins. Ontario alone accounts for over 30 percent of Canada's oil consumption, and over 90 percent of its oil comes from western Canada.[33] The Clark government, struggling to get a grip on governing after sixteen years in opposition, and burdened by a number of ill-considered election promises, hardly needed an energy crisis which would turn their two provincial support bases in Alberta and Ontario against one another. Yet that is precisely what they had.

Concern for security and stability were reflected in the Conservative's overriding objective of moving Canada off the international oil market by 1990 and thereby away from the clutches of OPEC. Clark continually stressed the fact that unlike Japan and Germany, for example, which are forced to go to OPEC, Canada could become self-sufficient in oil and thus in energy, if Canadians were prepared to face up to reality, that is, to pay the price. The Canadian Energy Bank concept introduced by the Conservatives was justified as a means to a secure energy future for Canada. It was intended as a new financial institution, the vehicle to help Canadians invest in Canadian resource development, particularly in frontier regions. It would support projects like pipeline construction, which need high front-end financing; development of hydro, coal, and more experimental sources. It would also help fund home insulation, furnace retrofits, fuel substitution, urban transit, and other conservation measures.

The Conservatives were in the process of approving major new natural gas exports as they prepared their budget and were anxious about being seen to be granting new natural gas exports at the very moment when they were supposed to be most concerned with Canadian security. But new natural gas exports and higher prices could be justified as a means of filling industry coffers with more revenues, which could then be used to undertake further exploration in pursuit of the self-sufficiency objective.

The eighteen-cents-per-gallon increase in the excise tax on gasoline to twenty-five cents per gallon was an explicit attempt by the Conservatives to use the price mechanism to force Canadians to be more efficient in their use of gasoline and thus to reduce oil imports. The pricing policy chosen for natural gas, that is, to have it rise at 85 percent heat content parity with oil for production under contract and at 65 percent for new volumes, was designed to encourage both conservation and the efficient substitution from oil to natural gas.

Most of the principles of the Conservative energy program were supported by the industry. Yet it was the fundamental issues of price and revenue sharing which would ultimately determine the nature of the relationship of the industry and the Clark government. The Conservatives also hoped that their policy on Petro-Canada would enhance their relationship with the industry. The Petro-Canada privatization objective reflected the anti-state intervention bias of the neo-conservative right wing of the party. It ran into difficulty with the public, in part, because it conflicted with two main concerns in Canadian energy politics, security and national identity, both of which Petro-Canada embodied. As a result, the opposition parties were able to exploit the public's concern with the insecurity of the international energy situation in 1979–80 and its suspicion of the major foreign oil companies, both of which were issues which Petro-Canada directly addressed. Furthermore, it caused division within the party, caucus, and Cabinet, as those Conservatives who did not share their more conservative colleagues' convictions about state intervention and public enterprise were not willing to throw their support behind the proposal.

It is in this overall context that the key industry interests and those of the three relevant Conservative governments can be understood. The governments were more directly in conflict over the issue of pricing and revenue sharing, a dispute outlined in detail in Chapter 5. In the context of this chapter's focus, however, one should appreciate the industry's general response to the Conservatives as well as their view of the Petro-Canada issue.

The petroleum industry as a whole had great expectations from the arrival in Ottawa of a strongly pro-business Conservative government, which had apparently taken heed of industry arguments and made oil self-sufficiency its prime energy policy objective. The industry was well plugged into the Conservative party, both through the Alberta caucus and through the influence of the Toronto business community, much of which was Conservative, and much of which shared the oil industry's sentiments about high prices and state intervention. The industry had strong allies in Jim Gillies, Clark's economic advisor, and Harvey André, Clark's close friend, MP for Calgary Centre, and ex-energy critic. Two ex-Imperial Oil employees were senior officials on the staff of energy minister Ray Hnatyshyn.

The industry wanted the Tories to move to world price or at least to a formula which connected Canadian price to a high percentage level of world price. With respect to Petro-Canada, some of the harder-line elements within the industry clearly wanted to see it privatized. Others, though, particularly the majors, saw advantages to having Petro-Canada around. In the 1960s and 1970s, the multinationals had faced nationalizations or other impositions on their freedom in many countries, and as a defensive tactic had developed a strategy of bringing the host country government, either directly or through the state oil company, into an equity position in energy developments, preferably as a minority partner. This strategy could be especially beneficial in a country like Canada where expensive and risky frontier or non-conventional developments were involved. Such an approach has the advantage of giving the government a direct equity stake in the viability of the project, and with a financial stake in a project a government is much less likely to let it collapse or otherwise become delayed. This strategy also brings into the position of producer that element in society which is responsible for taxation and the regulation of environmental, labour and other relevant law. Most importantly, perhaps, it provides access to the state's pool of capital.

The hard-line free-enterprisers in the Conservative party led by Jim Gillies, not expecting that big oil could develop such a pragmatic stance regarding Petro-Canada, were shocked and angered when Imperial Oil and some other major private sector interests let it be known to the task force which Clark had created to devise a way to privatize Petro-Canada, that they did not think having Petro-Canada around was so bad.

The Conservatives never got a chance to introduce their new energy taxes and for industry–Conservative Party relations it is just as well. The industry would not have been very pleased with the new "windfall profits" tax, or, as it was more attractively called, the Energy Self-Sufficiency Tax, which would have given Ottawa 50 percent and the provinces 50 percent of any price increase over two dollars per barrel and thirty cents per thousand cubic feet of gas per year. The new taxes and revenue-sharing scheme presented in the ill-fated budget would have had the effect of increasing the federal share almost entirely by reducing the industry share. The federal–provincial–industry split would have changed from 10–45–45 to 19–44–37.

As a party and as a government, the federal Conservatives never quite came to grips with either of the major planks of their energy policy—Petro-Canada and oil and gas pricing. This was, in part, because the Progressive Conservative Party embodies two major lines of division: the ideological cleavage between right-wing and moderate elements, and the regional division between its Ontario and Alberta power bases. For the Petro-Canada privatization issue, the right-wing–moderate cleavage was key; for pricing, the Ontario–Alberta cleavage had primacy. As Jeffrey Simpson has noted, "Petro-Canada stuck in the party's craw like a bone in a dog's throat":

> Nothing so clearly illustrated the divisions within the Conserva-
> tive Party as the question of what to do with Petro-Canada.... The
> party's initial position that a crown corporation in the energy field
> was unnecessary reflected the views of those within the party who

deeply distrusted state intervention in the economy. They happened to occupy the key shadow Cabinet positions shaping the party's energy policy, but once the party came to power a wider range of views within the party was brought to bear on Petro-Canada. Representatives of another strain of Conservative thinking supportive of state undertakings to expand Canadian ownership of industry made their objections known to their hard-line, free enterprise colleagues.[34]

The pro-privatization element, including Gillies, Clark, Lowell Murray, William Neville, Robert de Cotrêt and Sinclair Stevens, was impervious to public opinion, which was strongly in favour of retaining Petro-Canada. Other prominent Tories, including Ray Hnatyshyn, Bill Jarvis, John Fraser, John Crosbie, David McDonald, and Flora MacDonald, from the Clark inner Cabinet, opposed the privatization proposal. The Conservatives' polling expert, Allan Gregg, provided evidence that the latter group was much more in line with the public mood, which saw Petro-Canada as an important instrument of energy security in an increasingly uncertain environment:

> The reason that this particular issue area is going to present a problem for us is not because the people of Canada are either for or against institutional changes to Petro-Canada as a crown corporation. Rather, the public is increasingly aware that the future is, at best, uncertain.
>
> More particularly, the entire energy issue and energy-related issues tend to bring this belief into focus for the average individual. Our action, therefore, is being presented through the opposition and the media as fueling the uncertainties of the future.
>
> In other words, in the face of an *impending* "energy crisis" and excessive profits by multinational companies, we are seen to be dismantling the only *Canadian* entity standing between the people and the problem. We must, therefore, when explaining these changes to Petro-Canada, present something more than a kneejerk commitment to free enterprise.[35]

Nevertheless, and ironically enough in large part through Clark's personal commitment to see the privatization through, the anti-Petro-Canada element prevailed, to the party's electoral peril. The Conservative government of Ontario had access to the same public opinion polls and they knew of Petro-Canada's popularity in Ontario. Bill Davis left no doubt where he stood on the issue. He opposed the federal Conservative's plans for Petro-Canada. As he told the provincial legislature:

> Our Government believes the present national responsibilities of Petro-Canada should be retained and that the federal government should retain ownership of Petro-Canada as a national publicly owned petroleum institution. . . . I do not feel the federal government and our mixed economy have anything to fear from a financially viable Petro-Canada operating as a Crown corporation to enhance energy security for all Canadians.[36]

Canadianization was clearly the weak part of the Conservative energy policy. In part, because they were not able to pass a budget, the Tories never actually devised a strategy for Canadianizing the national oil industry. To the extent that they articulated a strategy—in the face of trying to privatize Petro-Canada, the growth of which had increased levels of Canadian ownership and control—it amounted to vague generalities about altering the tax system to provide incentive for Canadians to buy shares of foreign-owned firms. Some foreign-owned firms simply were not interested, however, in offering stock to Canadians.

Thus, the government–industry relationship during the Tory interregnum was varied. There were issues which resulted in some conflict in the relationship, as well as much agreement on many broad parameters of an energy program.

Summary

The overall tendency in the government–industry relationship of power over the pre-NEP post-war period was toward greater government intervention in the industry and therefore toward a diminution of the previous industry dominance of the relationship. Throughout the post-war period, partisan conflict and nationalist-versus-continentalist debates characterized the government–industry relationship. While industry dominance of the relationship has diminished somewhat, the importance of the industry to energy developments has not. The federal government decided not to challenge the fundamental power of the industry in the mid-1970s by nationalizing one of its members, but rather chose to start a new Crown corporation. Despite Petro-Canada's rapid growth between 1975 and 1979 and the state ownership of shares by several governments in other firms involved in the oil business, the industry was still primarily privately owned at the end of this period. Owing to the control of the private firms over the vast majority of the productive apparatus, the major sources of technological and geological information, and the major capital pools, the private oil sector retained a great deal of its power. An important development for the industry which had implications for the overall government–industry relationship was the emergence within the industry of public and private Canadian-controlled firms capable of competing, as commercial rivals and project sponsors, with the traditional foreign-controlled majors. While it appeared, briefly in 1979, that the industry would once again move into a more dominant position in the government–industry relationships, there were signs that even the Conservatives would not allow the industry the autonomy it had enjoyed in the glory years prior to 1973. The Liberals obviously did not feel that the government–industry relationship, at least as far as the federal government was concerned, was equal enough. They felt that fundamental changes had to be made to effect changes in the intra-industry relationship as well as in the Ottawa–industry relationship. These would emerge in the NEP.

Notes

1. William Kilbourn, *Pipeline* (Toronto: Clark Irwin, 1970), p. vii.
2. John N. McDougall, *Fuels and the National Policy* (Toronto: Butterworths, 1972), p. 57.
3. For a deeper conceptual analysis of this issue, see Glen Toner, "Oil, Gas and Integration: A Review of Five Major Energy Decisions," in Jon Pammett and Brian Tomlin (eds.), *The Integration?: Political Economy and Public Policy in Canada and North America* (Toronto: Addison-Wesley, 1984).
4. See Anthony Sampson, *The Seven Sisters* (London: Coronet, 1980), chapter 6 and John M. Blair, *The Control of Oil* (New York: Vintage Books, 1978), chapter 4.

5. There is no question, however, that since the NEP, Gulf Canada has expended considerable effort and vast sums of money in a major advocacy advertising campaign to convince a suspicious public that: a) it, in fact, has autonomy and is different from tightly controlled "100 percenters" such as Mobil, Amoco and Chevron, and b) Gulf Canada's operation provides all sorts of benefits to Canada. The primary modes of advertisement for Gulf were full-page ads in prominent daily newspapers like the *Globe and Mail*, two-page ads in major Canadian news magazines such as *Maclean's*, and a widely touted new monthly magazine, "Commentator," aimed at a broad public readership.

6. Bruce Henbest, "Making Energy Legislation: The Role of Political Parties, the Public Service, and Interest Groups in the Parliamentary Stage of the Canadian Policy Making Process" (Masters Thesis, Department of Political Science, Carleton University, Ottawa, 1983).

7. P. Smith, *The Treasure Seekers: The Men Who Built Home Oil* (Toronto: Macmillan, 1978).

8. Larry Pratt, *The Tarsands* (Edmonton: Hurtig, 1976), p. 163.

9. Alberta, Conservation and Utilization Committee, "Fort McMurray Athabasca Tar Sands Development Strategy," Mimeo, August 1972.

10. *Ibid.*

11. Pratt, *op. cit.*, p. 26.

12. Cited in *ibid.*

13. The federal government felt, in retrospect, that it had fared particularly poorly in a fiscal sense in the 1975 Syncrude deal, gaining only a negligible tax take. The memory of this was still fresh on the minds of federal officials as they entered the 1979 and 1980 revenue-sharing negotiations. They were determined this would not be the outcome of the new negotiations.

14. Pratt, *op. cit.*, pp. 166–170.

15. *Ibid.*, p. 170.

16. Maurice Strong, "Canada's Energy Future: The Role of Petro-Canada," Speech to the Canadian Club, Toronto, April 18, 1977, p. 9.

17. Government of Canada, Energy, Mines and Resources, "State Participation in the Canadian Energy Industry," in *An Energy Policy for Canada— Phase 1*, Volume 1 Analysis (Ottawa: Information Canada, 1973), pp. 179–195.

18. Larry Pratt, "Petro-Canada," in Allan Tupper and G. Bruce Doern (eds.), *Public Corporations and Public Policy in Canada* (Montreal: Institute for Research on Public Policy, 1981), pp. 108–109.

19. *Ibid.*, p. 109.

20. François Bregha, *Bob Blair's Pipeline*, Updated Edition (Toronto: Lorimer, 1979), p. 16.

21. *Ibid.*, p. 139.

22. John F. Helliwell, "Canadian Energy Policy," *Annual Review of Energy*, 1979:4, p. 176.
23. Bregha, *op. cit.*, pp. 195–196.
24. *Ibid.*, p. 195.
25. Edgar Dosman, *The National Interest* (Toronto: McClelland and Stewart, 1975), pp. 24–26.
26. *Ibid.*, pp. 66–69 and 99–115.
27. Bregha, *op. cit.*, p. 194.
28. See Gurston Dacks, *A Choice of Futures: Politics in the Canadian North* (Toronto: Methuen, 1981).
29. Bregha, *op. cit.*, p. 193.
30. Thomas Berger, *Northern Frontier: Northern Homeland*, The Report of the Mackenzie Valley Pipeline Inquiry, Two Volumes (Ottawa: Supply and Services Canada, 1977).
31. See Harold Clarke, Jane Jenson, Larry Leduc and Jon Pammett, "Voting Behaviour and the Outcome of the 1979 Federal Election: The Impact of Leaders and Issues," *Canadian Journal of Political Science*, xv:3 (September 1982), pp. 517–552.
32. Geoffrey Stevens, "The Petrocan Two-Step," *Globe and Mail*, January 2, 1980, p. 6.
33. Statistics Canada, "Energy Supply and Demand in Canada," 57–003, August 1983.
34. Jeffrey Simpson, *Discipline of Power* (Toronto: Personal Library, 1980), p. 159.
35. Cited in *ibid.*, p. 165.
36. Ontario Legislature, *Debates*, October 16, 1979, p. 3519.

CHAPTER 5

INTERGOVERNMENTAL ENERGY RELATIONS: THE PRE-NEP YEARS

This chapter examines the pre-NEP legacy of intergovernmental energy relationships as they evolved throughout the post-war period to 1979. Intergovernmental energy relations in Canada can only be understood in the context of the evolving constitutional and interregional relationships which have developed since World War II. Thus, we revisit key issues sketched initially in Chapter 3. However, before examining the issues of oil and gas pricing, revenue sharing and resource management, it is essential to review first the constitutional powers of each level of government with respect to energy policy, as they stood in the pre-NEP period prior to the promulgation of the **Constitution Act 1982**, and second, the historical relationship of western and central Canada and thus the roots of western alienation. Within this more detailed analysis of constitutional and historical patterns, one can then see the emergence of the two key relationships we focus on here, namely, the federal–producing province relationship, and the Alberta–Ontario interprovincial relationship.

Division of Powers with Respect to Non-Renewable Natural Resources

The constitutional division of powers is at once the essence of federation and an area of constant friction between legislative authorities. This is particularly the case for the administration of natural resources, as the Constitution provides for both strong federal and provincial powers, while at the same time containing controversial areas of both overlapping and uncertain jurisdiction. Thus, in order to discuss the politics of the control of natural resources, one must examine the rights of the provinces as owners of the resources within their boundaries, and consider the ways in which the federal government might, in the exercise of its constitutional jurisdiction, restrict the exercise of those ownership rights.

Under section 109 of the **British North America Act 1867**, all lands, mines, minerals and royalties belong to the province "in which the same are situate." This is a very important provision in relation to energy resource development, granting as it does authority to the provinces to manage their own energy resources. Provincial ownership is reinforced by the property and civil rights clause [92(13)], the power to levy direct taxes [92(2)], and the authority over the management and sale of public lands belonging to the province [92(5)]. These powers together confer on the provinces far-reaching authority over the management of all lands in the province, even those that are not public lands. It has been conceded for many years that the provinces have primary responsibility for the regulation and management of natural resources and primary access to natural resource revenues. The federal government exercises these "provincial powers" of land ownership in the Yukon, the Northwest Territories, and in offshore areas.

There are a number of significant bases for federal involvement in the natural resources sector as well. The "trade and commerce" power [91(2)] gives Parliament jurisdiction over all aspects of interprovincial and international trade. This includes interprovincial pipelines and oil and gas exports, and consequently is an important authority with respect to marketing. The "declaratory power" as spelled out in section 91(10)(c) gives Parliament control over provincial works it "declares" to be "for the general advantage of Canada" or "of two or more of the provinces." This declaratory power was used by the federal government to attempt to gain control over all aspects of atomic energy. The courts later conferred federal jurisdiction on other grounds. The "emergency power" of section 91 gives Parliament extensive authority to legislate and maintain "peace, order and good government." Section 91(3) provides virtually complete freedom to employ any mode or system of taxation, the only limitation being the prohibition of section 125 against taxation of "Lands and Property" belonging to a province. This power is important with respect to the provision of incentive systems for resource development. "The spending power" is Parliament's power to make payments for purposes other than those for which it can legislate. This was used to provide direct grants to home owners for home insulation, notwithstanding the fact that jurisdictionally, provincial governments are responsible in this field. Finally, even though this power has not been used since 1943, the federal Parliament may reserve or disallow provincial legislation.

In addition, in the wake of the 1973 energy crisis, the producing provinces and the federal government passed new legislation pertaining to the management and pricing of oil and gas. Ottawa's **Petroleum Administration Act** gives it the power to fix the domestic price of oil and gas in the absence of an agreement with a producing province. The Alberta government's **Petroleum Marketing Act** gives it the power to set oil prices within the province, and the **Natural Gas Administration Act** gives it the same power with respect to gas.[1]

Offshore resources were placed on the agenda of the constitutional discussions at the request of the provinces in October 1978. However, complete agreement on the issue has proved impossible to reach. Newfoundland has consistently asserted its ownership of the continental shelf and has proposed the constitutional entrenchment of the principle that resources of a province's continental shelf be treated in the same manner as resources located on land. While all coastal provinces have a stake in having offshore resources treated equally in constitutional terms with onshore resources, Newfoundland has clearly been the driving force behind this movement. Newfoundland's case rests on three principles—one unique to Newfoundland, the other two common to all coastal provinces. First, Newfoundland claims that the ownership of these resources resided with the Dominion of Newfoundland before Confederation and was not alienated from Newfoundland in that process. Second, it argues that in the interests of fairness those provinces which have some of their resources covered with water should be granted equal constitutional treatment with those whose resources are located on land. Newfoundland also argues that Ontario has always owned and controlled the underwater resources of the Great Lakes, and that since both the Great Lakes and the water covering the mineral resources of the continental shelf are international waters, the mere fact that water is fresh or salt should not detract from equality of treatment. Finally, Newfoundland feels that because it is the adjacent provinces which will experience all the adverse impact which attends offshore resource development, it is crucial that they have the legislative authority to manage such development. They claim this authority can only come from the rights of ownership.

The federal Conservative government of Joe Clark was sympathetic to these arguments and agreed in principle in September 1979 to transfer ownership of offshore resources to the provinces. However, the Clark government was defeated in February 1980 by the Liberal administration of Pierre Trudeau, which argued that Ottawa had and must maintain jurisdiction over offshore development. The Liberal government proposed a regime of administrative arrangements in which the provinces would have a major say in how offshore resources are developed, and in which, until they became "have" provinces, the coastal provinces would receive the same kind of revenues as are derived by provinces for onshore resources. Beyond that point they would share an increased proportion of offshore resources with all Canadians.[2]

Thus, while it appears that the provinces have sufficient constitutional authority to decide when, how, and under what conditions natural resources will be developed, there are also ample grounds to justify a federal presence in this policy area. A natural consequence of this situation of substantial jurisdictional overlap is, of course, federal–provincial conflict.

A Brief History of Western–Central Canadian Relations

The debate over the management of energy resources illuminates the underlying tension that exists in the Canadian political economy between the industrialized manufacturing core of central Canada and the natural resource staple-producing western periphery. The hostility exhibited by western Canadians and their provincial governments towards a number of Ottawa's energy policies in the 1970s was not unique. Rather it was a continuation of a decades-long tradition of regional dissent resulting from the region's frustration with its economic role. The pattern of economic development which cast Canada in the role of an economic satellite and marginal supplier of resource staple products to other more advanced countries, chiefly Great Britain and the United States, is roughly analogous to the historical relationship of western Canada to central Canada. Just as the United States and Great Britain had for Canada as a whole, central Canada acted as a source of capital, manufactured goods and immigrant labour as well as a market for some of the staple products of the west. The federal government under John A. Macdonald played a major role in this developmental process by establishing policies designed to facilitate the production and export of staple products from the west. This concept was anchored in the National Policy of 1879, and in related policies that ensured the completion of the Pacific Railway, encouraged western settlement, and created a new frontier of investment opportunities through tariff protection for the commercial, manufacturing, and financial interests of central Canada.

In addition, control over the land of western Canada was instrumental to Ottawa's plan for transcontinental expansion and western agricultural settlement. Consequently, when the province of Manitoba was created in 1870, it was given an inferior constitutional status. Specifically, Crown lands in the new province were retained by the central government "for the purposes of the Dominion." When the provinces of Saskatchewan and Alberta were carved out of the old Northwest Territories in 1905, Ottawa once again retained control over natural resources. It took nearly three more decades of protest and provincial rights agitation before control over natural resources was transferred to them in 1930.

By then, western Canadians already resented their colonial status within Canada. The transfer of control over natural resources did little to alleviate this resentment, for 1930 also marked the advent of the decade-long drought which, together with the economic depression, had devastating consequences for the Prairies. After World War II, as the western economy expanded and diversified, new grievances, largely focussed on oil, gas, potash and mineral wealth, joined the column of historical grievances. In addition to the natural resource disputes, the tariff, and the activities of the banks, transportation policy—particularly railroad freight rates—federal monetary policy, and the regional distribution of manufacturing remain the cornerstones of western economic discontent.

It should be noted that there is no general agreement about the relative degree to which the west's disadvantages are the fault of federal policy or simply the logic of market economics for a vast, sparsely populated market geographically peripheral to the national and continental centres of economic power. Nevertheless, there is general agreement that, on resource taxation and energy pricing in the post-1973 period, the west was placed in a uniquely discriminatory position by national policies. The prime examples of this discrimination were the federal government's two-price policy for oil and its export tax on oil. The former kept the price of domestically consumed oil below its international commodity value. The federal government used the revenues derived from the latter to help subsidize eastern consumers who were dependent on imported crude. In an oft-cited quotation, former Saskatchewan Premier Allan Blakeney articulates a widely held western view about federal policies:

> We in the West find it passing strange that the national interest emerges only when talking about Western resources or Eastern benefits. If oil, why not iron and steel products? If natural gas, why not copper? If uranium why not nickel? And to add insult to injury, we in the West are now being told that the national interest demands a rail transportation policy in which the user pays full cost. What user will pay the most under that kind of system? Land-locked Saskatchewan. Air transport is subsidized. The Seaway runs monumental deficits. Our ports are all subsidized. Truck transport is subsidized by many provincial highway systems in Canada. But in rail transport—the one upon which we depend—we are told the user must pay.[3]

In essence, however, it does not even matter that much whether the west's economic grievances are carved in solid economic stone, but rather that they exist, are part of the political culture and, as such, influence political behaviour. Regardless of whether regional discontent is subject to partisan manipulation by provincial political leaders, there is no question that in the past it has influenced political behaviour in the west with respect to both the provincial and federal arenas. Moreover, it continues to do so.

For most of its history the west was a high-risk society—farmers were reliant on outside capital and volatile commodity markets, and vulnerable to distant decisions affecting communications and transportation. Western farmers often felt themselves to be at the mercy of the railways, the banks, the manufacturing trusts, and the grain trade. In the face of these political and economic insecurities, the farmers organized themselves through the cooperative movement, the wheat pools and their farm organizations to better their position. The farmers' organizations became effective lobbies, and up until the end of World War I, the farmers tried to rectify their problems within the traditional party system.

However, as the disillusionment of westerners with the two traditional parties grew, it took a new partisan twist. When the traditional parties were no longer perceived as adequate forums for the articulation of western views, agrarian protest moved to form alternative parties. The emergence of the Progressive party at the federal level in 1921 and the victories of the United Farmers of Alberta in 1919 and the United Farmers of Manitoba in 1922 were the first manifestations. The western protest against central Canadian institutions and political parties was aggravated by the Depression and the failure of the Progressives, whose platforms and leadership were partially co-opted by the Liberals under Mackenzie King.[4]

As a result of these factors, and in keeping with the populist tradition of prairie politics, two new protest parties were born during the Depression. Social Credit was a right-wing populist movement established by the lay preacher "Bible Bill" Aberhart. It focussed its critique of the causes of the economic depression on the actions of eastern financial institutions and came to power in Alberta in 1935.[5] The left-wing populist Co-operative Commonwealth Federation (CCF) was founded in 1932 and attempted to unite farmers and workers with a more wide ranging and general critique of capitalist society. The CCF became the government of Saskatchewan in 1944.[6] Both the Social Credit, in 1953, and the New Democratic Party (successor of the CCF), in 1972, went on to win elections in British Columbia. The NDP has also been elected in Manitoba, forming a government there for the first time in 1969.

Since the Depression, with the exception of two brief interregna in the late 1950s and 1970s, the Liberal party has, as a result of its domination of the large central Canadian electorate, dominated the federal electoral scene. In the words of one of the leading authorities on prairie politics, westerners have developed a perception of the Liberal federal government as an "imperial government," which, when necessary, will sacrifice western interests in the name of national unity, but in reality, in the interests of central Canada.[7]

Not surprisingly then, the Liberal electoral success in central Canada has been matched by their lack of success in the west. Moreover, the affiliation with the federal Liberals has proven to be a major thorn in the side of western provincial Liberal parties; in 1980, there was but a single Liberal Member of the Legislative Assembly in the four western provinces (Manitoba). In the mid 1970s, in the wake of major energy conflicts, provincial Conservative and NDP governments in Alberta and Saskatchewan respectively were returned to office with increased majorities after fighting elections based on strengthening provincial powers over resource management. In the 1980 federal election, the Liberals returned only two MPs from the west. Since westerners see themselves in a position of permanent political disadvantage in federal politics, they have turned to their provincial governments for protection.[8]

The coincidence of international circumstance (the energy crisis) and jurisdictional responsibility (control over resources) provided western Canada (and potentially the Atlantic provinces) with the opportunity to redress the perceived historical economic and political inequalities within the Canadian federation. The governments of the western provinces wished to seize the opportunity to diversify their economies beyond the historical boom-bust syndrome of dependence on the traditional staples and to localize decision-making power over the region's economy and society. The key to the provinces' economic development strategy was thought to be the control over the management and revenues of the natural resource sector, particularly the depleting reserves of non-renewable conventional oil and natural gas. The western provinces' intention to use the considerable leverage provided by increased natural resource revenues to encourage a fundamental diversification of the regional economy has, as a concomitant, the alteration of its traditional role within the national economy and, hence, of the structure of the national economy itself.

Since the Leduc discovery, the Canadian society and economy have developed a way of life dependent upon both cheap and abundant energy. That energy, however, is not evenly distributed. Ontario and Québec (which together used about 55 percent of the oil and gas consumed in Canada in 1981) produced almost none of either fuel. Conversely, the three western provinces supplied virtually all of Canada's domestic oil and all of its natural gas.[9] Depleting Canadian supplies and rapidly rising international prices after 1973 saw the ill-prepared federal government attempting to reconcile the competing interests of the major energy-producing and energy-consuming provinces, while at the same time maintaining its own unique set of interests. The energy debate also saw the government of Ontario become increasingly critical of the western producing provinces and vice versa. It is within this historical context of the west's development within the Canadian political economy that the energy controversies which strained federal–provincial and western–central Canadian relations in the '70s must be viewed.

Intergovernmental Energy Relations: 1949 to 1972

Richards and Pratt have traced both the government–industry and intergovernmental energy relationships, as they relate to the two prairie producing provinces, back to their earliest stages in the period surrounding the transfer of jurisdiction over natural resources to the two provinces by constitutional amendment in 1930. In the following quotation, they capture the importance of natural gas for the sensitive intergovernmental relationship in the early period. It is important to note that in the post-1973 period, as international supplies of oil became more expensive and less secure and as oil achieved a new status as a political and economic weapon, worth a great deal both financially and psychologically to those who controlled it, oil would come to assume a status similar to that of natural gas for intergovernmental relations:

> Natural gas has been viewed as a crucial fuel for industrialization by "nation-builders" such as C.D. Howe as well as "province-builders" such as Peter Lougheed and the reconciliation of national and provincial interests has tested the flexibility of Canada's federal political system on a number of occasions over the past three decades.
>
> From Alberta's perspective, the most important economic and political influences on the growth of provincial powers over the gas industry were, first, pressures to prevent the wastage of gas through flaring or unsound methods of development; second, the threat of federal encroachment over provincial resource jurisdiction; and third, political pressures from Alberta consumers, industrial interests, opposition parties, and the media to give priority to provincial gas requirements.[10]

As mentioned in Chapter 3, oil and natural gas had in the 1930s and 1940s a different status in the eyes of the federal and provincial policy-makers. Whereas oil was treated pretty much as a regular mineral commodity, natural gas was treated as a birthright; as a provincial and/or national patrimony to be carefully managed and used to aid the industrialization and diversification of the provincial and/or national economy. This had not always been the case however, as vast volumes of natural gas were flared off in the Turner Valley field from 1914 through the 1920s. The growing opposition to and sense of loss from this wasteful practice led to the introduction of various conservation measures by the Alberta government subsequent to its acquiring responsibility for natural resources in 1930.

Concerns about exports from the province, the proper rates of production and the cost of natural gas to Albertans as consumers stimulated a good deal of political controversy in the province and showed the special place natural gas held in the hearts and minds of Albertans. These political disputes and, ultimately, the policies chosen by the Alberta government, reflected concerns about security and regional development. In the face of public concern about these interrelated issues, the Alberta government established in November 1948 the Dinning Natural Gas Commission to inquire into the proven and estimated reserves of natural gas in the province, and to investigate the present and estimated future consumption in the province. The issue of exports and their impact on depletion and local costs was extremely important at this point, because pipeline companies were agitating to export Alberta gas to central Canada and to the U.S.

In its March 1949 report, the Dinning Commission supported the principle, consistently voiced by Alberta interests which had appeared at the Commission's hearings, that the people of the province should have first call on provincial natural gas supplies and that Canadian consumers should take priority over foreign users if and when a surplus developed. With respect to determining a surplus, many Albertan interests insisted that Alberta's requirements be assured for up to fifty years before exports were approved. The Alberta government eventually settled for a thirty-year period. The Alberta government's formula for determining if a surplus was available for export was pivotal, as in September 1949 the Board of Transport Commissioners ruled that a company required the Alberta government's permission to export gas from the province *before* the Board could hear its application for permission to build a pipeline.

The federal Liberal government also realized the role that natural gas could play in the industrial development and space heating needs of other Canadian provinces, and their policy objectives tended to reflect concern for national integration and equity among all Canadians. In April 1949 the federal government moved to strengthen its control over the interprovincial and international trade in oil and gas by introducing the **Pipe Lines Act**. In sponsoring the bill the Minister of Transport justified its introduction by arguing that "the importance of the oil and gas industries to the economic welfare of Canada cannot be overemphasized."[11]

In reaction to the Dinning Commission Report and the federal Pipe Lines Act initiative, the Manning Social Credit government in a turbulent special session of the provincial legislature in July, 1949, pushed through several new pieces of legislation, including the **Gas Resources Conservation Act**. This new legislation greatly strengthened Alberta's wellhead control over gas. It also empowered the Oil and Gas Conservation Board to control the removal of gas from the province by issuing export permits. The Manning government considered this a necessary move because it had failed to convince the federal Liberal government to insert protective clauses in federal pipeline legislation requiring provincial permission before gas could be exported.

Impending approval of the Trans-Canada project in early 1954 necessitated a further controversial intervention by Alberta into the natural gas industry. As Richards and Pratt have stressed, "the precondition of new gas sales was the creation of a corporate instrument to defend the province from predatory encroachment into its resource base by outside monopolies backed by an acquisitive federal Liberal government."[12] This instrument, as we saw in Chapter 3, was the creation of Alberta Gas Trunk Line (later to become Nova, an Alberta Corporation). The Manning government was concerned that via its jurisdiction over federal incorporated pipelines, Ottawa could extend its control over resources into the province. Alberta Gas Trunk Line would provide a single integrated gathering system and act as a common carrier inside Alberta, distributing pooled gas to export companies such as Trans-Canada at the provincial border:

> This would keep the export companies—and Ottawa—out, and prevent encroachments on the province's jurisdiction. If the ostensible threat was constitutional, it was Alberta's underlying fears of the empire-building instincts of Mr. Howe and his

corporate allies that alerted Social Credit to the threat and provoked its defensive response. The parallels with the Lougheed administration's reaction in 1973 to the federal export tax on oil are striking.[13]

No issues of great significance affected the intergovernmental relationship in the 1960s. The Alberta-to-Montreal pipeline and National Oil Policy decisions were resolved in a manner that was acceptable to the governments of Alberta and Ontario and the federal government. Alberta production increased steadily throughout the 1960s even though Alberta and Ottawa both would have preferred to have exported greater volumes of oil to the United States. In fact, the single most frustrating issue for both levels was the restricted access to U.S. markets for Alberta production. Yet, by the latter part of this period in the early 1970s, the portents of change for the intergovernmental relationships were imminent. Shifting power relations in certain OPEC countries and the election of the Lougheed government in Alberta on an activist platform of utilizing energy developments to diversify the provincial economy prepared the way for the shocks that visited the intergovernmental relationships in the 1970s.

Intergovernmental Energy Relations: 1973-1979

The dramatic price increases internationally, and the consequent raising of the stakes domestically, had the effect of unveiling with shocking clarity the intergovernmental conflict of interests in Canadian energy politics. The combination of spectacular oil price increases, the spectre of unstable supplies, the magical creation of huge economic rents, and the emergence of oil as a strategic commodity resulted in the dawning realization among the eleven senior Canadian governments that with respect to pricing, revenue-sharing and control of resources, many of them had different and even opposing interests. However, owing to the peculiar nature of the Canadian Constitution and the Canadian political economy, only a few of the governments could actively intervene to influence the situation. The producing provinces and the federal government had constitutional authority in respect of these various contentions, and the 1973-74 period saw a remarkable bout of constitutional sparring between these two levels of jurisdiction. The opposition between the interests of producing and consuming regions, which had erupted into a full-blown conflagration internationally, produced more constrained conflict in Canada. Donald Smiley summarizes the issue:

> The dramatic increases in oil prices imposed by the Organization of Petroleum Exporting Countries (OPEC) in 1973 has conferred upon national governments the imperative of attempting to ensure energy supplies within their respective jurisdictions. Just as the crisis has resulted in fundamental shifts in geopolitical power between oil importing and oil exporting nations and opened up new cleavages and conflicts among nations, so in Canada new advantages have been realized by provinces with endowments of fossil-fuels and new vulnerabilities experienced by provinces and regions deficient in such resources. In general terms, the energy crisis has directly or indirectly joined a group of crucial issues in public policy, federal–provincial relations, and the most fundamental aspects of national life—foreign ownership; the rights of native peoples; the protection of the natural environment; the respective roles of public and private enterprise in economic development; interprovincial fiscal equalization and other attempts to reduce interprovincial disparities; and persistent patterns of production and consumption developed on the basis of cheap and seemingly inexhaustible sources of energy.[14]

The following section will analyse this period of intergovernmental energy relations by focussing on the contentious themes of: a) oil and gas pricing; b) revenue-sharing; and c) resource management.

Intergovernmental Relations: Oil and Gas Pricing

The division of the Canadian oil market in 1961 by the National Oil Policy (NOP) instituted a two-price system for the Canadian oil market. The market east of the Ottawa Valley received cheaper imported oil, while the more expensive Alberta crude was reserved for Ontario and the west. It is important to remember that the price of oil in Toronto was based on the posted price of Alberta oil which was set at the equivalent to the Chicago gate price for Texas oil, which was protected by U.S. import controls. This is a major indication of the strength of the industry in determining price, and indicates the degree to which price was in many ways politically contrived rather than only a product of market forces. Between 1961 and 1970, compliance with the NOP was voluntary. By 1970, however, the differential between the cost of foreign oil in Montreal and the cost of domestic oil in Ontario was great enough, around a dollar a barrel, that independent marketers were willing to risk selling imported oil from Québec in Ontario. At the request of the majors, the NEB prohibited this practice by forcing the licensing of all imports into Canada and by refusing to allow the further movement of petroleum products across the NOP line.[15]

The rapid escalation of international oil prices in 1973 upset the traditional relationship of domestic and foreign oil prices, vitiated the NOP and forced the federal government to address fundamentally the issue of oil and gas pricing in Canada. The issue of oil and gas pricing is so basic to a large, cold country like Canada that it involves all of the dominant concerns of Canadian political life, security, national integration, redistribution, efficiency, regional sensitivity and equity. Virtually all of the major interests in Canadian energy politics are affected by major pricing changes. Interests such as the federal government and the governments of the major producing and consuming provinces, the petroleum industry, Canadian consumers and the major industrial sectors which have oil or gas as a key input—such as the manufacturing, transportation, agriculture, mining, and petrochemical industries—are all directly affected. To the extent that the value of their product is influenced by relative changes in the cost of their major competitive energy sources, the non-petroleum energy sector is also directly affected. Dramatic escalations in price also affect the clientele and mandates of many provincial and federal government departments, though the two most directly involved, for the relevant governments, would be the departments of energy and finance. Two other important institutions, the first ministers' conferences and the equalization system, were also directly affected by the 1973 price increases.

The federal government faced a dilemma as a result of the price escalation. Alberta oil had held a privileged position in the Canadian economy, while Québec and the Maritime provinces had enjoyed access to cheaper offshore oil. The increase in the cost of imported oil reversed this relationship. Given the magnitude of the increase in the international price, a decision to maintain the two-price system would have had severe repercussions for the economies of the already most depressed regions of Canada. The continuance of the two-price system would have clashed fundamentally with the redistributive objective of various federal programs designed to reduce regional disparities. In other words, the poor would have gotten poorer and the rich richer. In addition, for a federal government fighting a war against separatism in Québec, the prospect of subjecting Québec consumers to an oil price substantially above that of Ontario was not attractive.

It would hardly be fair to subject the citizens of Québec to high and unstable international oil prices when the reason they did not have access to secure, stably priced Canadian sources was the federal government's decision a decade earlier to reject the Edmonton-to-Montreal pipeline. Thus, in order to protect the security of Québec consumers, a pipeline would now have to be built to Montreal. In order to provide itself and the country with a breathing space to consider the alternatives and to let the international scene unfold further and become a little clearer, the federal Liberals instituted in September 1973 a six-month oil price freeze.

This price freeze marked a major conjuncture in Canadian energy politics. It was the first direct application of the federal government's authority over interprovincial trade and commerce with respect to energy pricing—much to the vexation of the producing provinces. Second, the price freeze transferred for the first time in Canada the price-setting function from the industry, and in particular Imperial Oil, to the federal government. This power to set the price of oil used in Canada outside of the producing province was one that Ottawa would jealously guard. Moreover, the way in which the price freeze and export tax decisions were made and imposed was a precursor of the type of unilateralism that was to characterize energy policy decision making over the next few years and in the process contribute to a high level of distrust among governments. The Liberals made the decision to impose the price freeze and the export tax in a hurry over the Labour Day weekend in 1973. These were not normal times, and the government did not feel it could wait for the next budget, which was not expected until 1974, to deal with the issue. In any event, they had just been through the stormy period of the post-Carter Tax Commission reform conflicts and hence were not keen to fiddle around with the tax system. Earlier in the century an export tax had been applied to exports of Ontario hydro power to the United States, so the Liberals felt they were on safe constitutional ground in deciding on an export tax on oil. In the meantime they had asked Alberta to design a better royalty system, and Alberta felt rebuffed when a major new federal tax was imposed before they had finalized and responded with their review.

This action set in train the rapid-fire, ploy-counterploy which characterized relations in the following two years.

Even prior to the events of the fall of 1973, there were important precursors to the new aggressiveness of the Alberta Lougheed Conservatives. When in opposition, Peter Lougheed and his energy critic, Don Getty, were persistently critical of the Social Credit government for their passivity vis-à-vis Ottawa. Alberta owned the resource, they charged, but was not involved in crucial decisions made in Ottawa. They were especially suspicious of the National Energy Board, and did not regard it as a neutral, quasi-judicial body. Before the OPEC events hit, Alberta was under strong pressure from Ottawa to sell more of its then exceedingly cheap gas to Ontario via the Trans-Canada Pipeline. Lougheed said no, unless two conditions were met: first, assurances of genuine consultation; and second, a better price for gas sold to the rest of Canada. As pointed out in Chapter 3, hearings in Alberta had shown that natural gas was undervalued relative to its substitutes. At about this time, Lougheed held a meeting with the president of Trans-Canada Pipeline (TCPL), and asked the president of TCPL how the pipeline monopoly was going to facilitate price increases. Lougheed was told abruptly that Alberta did not set prices—TCPL did. The meeting ended abruptly when Lougheed left the room. By the summer of 1973 Alberta and Ottawa were on the verge of agreeing to an upward movement in gas prices, and seemed to have developed a modus vivendi regarding consultation. But then came the sudden events of the Labour Day weekend of 1973, as well as the OPEC crisis in October, and the spate of new policies that emerged from Edmonton and Ottawa in December 1973.

On December 6, 1973 in the parliamentary energy speech which outlined the federal Liberal government's response to the OPEC crisis, Pierre Trudeau announced that the federal government would abandon the two-tier system in favour of a commitment to a single price of oil for all Canadians, adjusted only for transportation charges. A unified price was to be achieved by extending the Interprovincial pipeline to Montreal and thereby making Canadian crude available to Canada's second largest and import-vulnerable market, and by establishing an Oil Import Compensation Program (OICP), financed by revenue from the oil export tax, to reimburse refiners who purchased offshore oil. The subsidy would amount to the theoretical difference between the price of Alberta oil transported to Montreal and the cost of foreign oil landed there.

Even if the federal government committed itself for reasons of equity, regional sensitivity, and redistribution to a unified price in Canada, the level of that price still had to be determined. "Was it to be equal to the price of foreign oil landed in Montreal or to the Edmonton price, which was still linked to the lower U.S. price? The controversy over this question was to dominate the Canadian energy scene for most of the 1970s and during the early part of the 1980s."[16] Initially the federal government resisted moving to world price for Canadian-produced oil, arguing that the international price was inappropriate for Canada because it was totally unrelated to the cost of producing oil in Canada. Ottawa insisted that the Canadian price reflect the "fraternal responsibilities" that existed between Canadian regions, and that while prices must rise they must be fair to all Canadians.

Alberta argued that because oil and natural gas are depleting, non-renewable resources they should be sold "only at prices that reflect fair value." As the producer of 85 percent of Canada's oil and gas, Alberta obviously had a strong material interest in oil prices moving as rapidly as possible to the world level. To strengthen its control over pricing the Alberta government established, as part of the aforementioned spate of legislation passed in December 1973, a provincial Petroleum Marketing Commission, a Crown corporation. As Richards and Pratt put it, "the purpose of all the legislation was to strengthen the province's ownership and control of its resources, including the pricing of these resources in interprovincial and international commerce."[17]

Ontario, on the other hand, as the major consuming province, had little interest in higher prices, though it nevertheless recognized that prices would have to increase. It therefore pressed for restrained price rises, arguing that the majority of price increases would go to the federal and producing province's treasurers and would result in little additional discovery of oil and gas, and that price increases would contribute to the already severe inflationary pressures and to even higher levels of unemployment. By convincing Ottawa and the producing provinces to maintain oil prices below world levels, Ontario and the other oil-importing provinces would ensure that individual and industrial consumers captured a certain share of the economic rents that were being generated by the escalation in world price.

At the Federal–Provincial Conference on Energy on January 22–23, 1974 it was agreed that there should be a unified single price for oil throughout Canada. On March 27, 1974 the Prime Minister and premiers agreed that until July 1, 1975 the price of Canadian crude oil would be set at $6.50 per barrel. Upon returning to power with a majority government after the July 8, 1974 election, the Liberals moved to strengthen their constitutional position with respect to the regulation of the price at which oil and natural gas are sold in Canada. The **Petroleum Administration Act** (PAA) provided the federal government with the authority to set the price of Canadian oil and gas in the event that a negotiated price could not be arrived at through agreement with the producing provinces.

In defending the bill, the Liberals presented the federal government as the final arbiter of provincial interests, as the only government able to strike a compromise between producer and consumer interests. The parliamentary debate on the bill juxtaposed "firms, governments, and MPs from the producing provinces [who] tended to argue the merits of a higher price in ensuring long-term security of supply, [and] their counterparts from the consuming provinces— especially the central Canadian ones—[who] argued the merits of a lower price in holding down the cost of living and maintaining the competitiveness of Canadian manufacturing industries."[18] It also raised the question of the constitutionality of the bill, which some Conservative members argued was a violation of the principle of the provincial control of natural resources. Yet, as John McDougall concludes from his study of this period, "the Conservative members and the conflicting (or at best, extremely vague) positions they took with respect to the desirable price level of oil in Canada create the impression that the party was either unable to resolve the conflict between consumer–province and producer–province interests within its own ranks, or (probably more likely) was attempting to promote, or at least defend, producer interests without appearing to be obviously abandoning the interests of consumers, especially those in Ontario."[19] The NDP made even fewer nods in the direction of producer interests than the Liberals, and this reflected their belief that with proper public-sector management, long-term self-sufficiency could be realized at much lower prices than the Liberals or Conservatives would concede. Ultimately, the PAA was passed with the support of the two opposition parties. Given our focus on the behaviour of key interests, McDougall's overall conclusion about the PAA debate is important:

> ... almost without exception, increases of any magnitude in the Canadian oil price—whether they were to go all the way to world price or were to be held well short of that level—tended to be supported solely on the basis of their contribution to Canada's future security of supply: higher prices were reluctantly or enthusiastically endorsed, but in either case were endorsed only to the extent that they would contribute to the national interest in the long-term availability of supplies. There were few voices expressing the idea that higher prices were justified simply by virtue of making their owners, the citizens of Alberta and Saskatchewan, rich.[20]

A First Ministers' Conference was convened on April 9–10, 1975 to discuss what to do with oil prices once the existing agreement expired on July 1. The federal government had by this point come around to accepting that higher prices were necessary. "This position seems to have resulted from the pressures of the producing provinces, the decreasing activity in oil exploration by private companies, the increasingly pessimistic estimates of domestic reserves of oil, and a recognition of the need for energy conservation."[21] The Ontario government opposed new price increases, arguing that 90 percent of the increased revenues resulting from the increase in domestic price from $2.70 per barrel to $6.50 per barrel over the previous eighteen months had gone to the coffers of the federal and producing governments and had done little to enhance the supply of oil and gas. Consequently, the conference was adjourned with no agreement. This marked the demise of the federal–provincial First Ministers' conference as a forum for oil price setting. The federal government later raised the price of a barrel of oil to $8.00 when the previous agreement expired. In reaction, the Ontario government imposed a ninety-day freeze on the increase from $6.50 to $8.00 a barrel on oil sold within Ontario, arguing that Ontario consumers should not have to pay the higher prices on oil in transit or in storage which had been purchased at the old price. In May 1977, Ottawa and the producing provinces concluded an agreement that would allow Canadian prices to move to world price by $1.00 increases twice a year. By late 1978 Canadian prices had reached 80 percent of world levels. By mid-1979 the world price skyrocketed in the wake of the Iranian revolution, and Canadian prices once again fell well short of the international mark.

Without question, then, oil and gas pricing was a major source of conflict in the intergovernmental relationships between 1973 and 1979. It would soon once again be a major source of contention between governments. Related to the issue of oil and gas pricing is the issue of revenue sharing. Once price levels have been determined—in other words, once the size of the pie has been determined—the question of who gets what still has to be settled. Consequently, the two issues are usually, and often painfully, decided in tandem.

Intergovernmental Relations: Revenue Sharing

Revenue sharing among governments and between governments and the industry cuts to the heart of the federal and capitalist systems upon which the Canadian political economy is built. Like pricing, all of the dominant concerns are reflected in the various positions taken by the key interests.

The acrimony of the Ottawa–Edmonton, Ottawa–Regina relationship was highlighted by the rapid-fire action/reaction of the 1973–74 period over revenue sharing. The initial salvo was fired by the new Lougheed government in 1972 when it informed the industry, as outlined in Chapter 3, that it planned to introduce new measures to circumvent the restrictive Social Credit royalty limits and thereby to increase the province's share of oil and gas generated revenues. U.S. oil production peaked in 1970, and in April 1973 U.S. oil import quotas were removed. Between 1970 and 1973 Canadian oil exports to the United States increased by 83 percent. Fearing that this rapid growth in exports might deprive Canadian refiners of their crude oil supplies, the federal government imposed export controls in March 1973. To the extent that export controls restrained Alberta production, it reduced Alberta's revenue from royalties. In the face of the strong U.S. demand, Canadian crude prices had increased substantially, and reached $3.80 per barrel at the wellhead by August 1973. It was at this point that the federal government increased the intensity of the intergovernmental tensions by freezing oil prices and levying an export tax on oil exported to the United States.

The rapid escalation in world price which followed the outbreak of the Arab–Israeli war and the ensuing oil embargos created the potential of realizing massive new economic rents if the Canadian price followed the world price. Economic rent is the excess income generated over and above that necessary to provide a "normal" return to the capital and labour employed. In other words, they are not costs of production but a residual item which remains after all production costs, including a normal rate of profit, have been paid. It was the contest for the relative shares of the new rents that would be created by the new price increases which fueled the three-cornered conflict between the federal government, the producing provinces, and the industry.

Alberta realized that the rapidly emerging seller's market would provide it with the revenues to put into operation its ambitious development strategy, which was, in brief, to "encourage local industrial processing of its energy and agricultural resources and, through its ownership of most of Canada's oil and natural gas, to negotiate a transfer of secondary industry, high-income jobs, and decision-making from central Canada to the West."[22] By capturing the bulk of the new economic rents, Alberta would have the leverage to utilize subsidies and incentives, as well as to create the most attractive tax system for both corporations and individuals in Canada, in pursuit of its larger development strategy. As Richards and Pratt have argued, "federal intervention was a threat, but it was also a golden opportunity for the Conservatives: Ottawa's actions could be used as justification for abandoning Social Credit's dated inflexible royalty arrangements with the petroleum industry." Thus in early October of 1973, after Ottawa's imposition of the export tax and the price freeze, but before the major escalations in world oil prices, "the Lougheed cabinet startled the oil industry by suddenly abandoning its new royalty plans, the subject of months of lengthy negotiations and public hearings, and announcing that royalties would henceforth rise with international oil prices." This strategy revealed that despite Alberta's reliance on the oil and gas industry as the major economic force to restructure the place of the provincial economy within the Canadian economy, the province had developed a more fluid and ambivalent relationship with the industry and was willing to use it as a bargaining chip in Alberta's conflicts with Ottawa: "the province's primary objective was evidently to force Ottawa to withdraw its export levy by squeezing the industry; damage done to the oil industry could be repaired by Alberta later on."[23]

Saskatchewan also felt the export tax was an appropriation by Ottawa of revenues that should have gone to the provinces, which owned the resources. The Saskatchewan NDP government was also determined that the industry was not going to achieve windfall profits from the price increases, and accordingly imposed in October 1973 a royalty surcharge which would have the effect of capturing for the Saskatchewan government virtually 100 percent of any further increase in Canadian oil prices. British Columbia, for its part, increased its royalty rates on oil and established the British Columbia Petroleum Commission (BCPC) which, through the assumption of the bulk of the contracts of Westcoast Transmission and other B.C. gas carriers, could appropriate most of any future increase in natural gas prices. In that regard, royalties on the small volumes of gas not under contract to BCPC were raised 25 percent up to twenty cents/mcf and 50 percent on prices in excess of twenty cents/mcf. In early 1974 Alberta raised its royalty rates on natural gas to 50 percent of the price between thirty-six cents and seventy-two cents/mcf, and 65 percent of the price in excess of seventy-two cents/mcf. Royalty rates were also restructured so that the provincial government would collect sixty-five percent of the price in excess of $4.41 per barrel.[24]

The federal government rejected the provinces' charge that the export tax was either an infringement on provincial authority or part of the federal share of revenues, since it was used entirely to subsidize Canadian consumers who were forced to use imported oil and thus was necessary to maintain the agreed-upon principle of one price for all Canadians. As part of the very generous taxation regime put in place in the earlier post-war period to stimulate the growth of the Canadian oil and gas industry, the oil companies had been able to deduct royalties, taxes, and other like payments made to provinces from their federal corporate income tax. The federal Department of Finance saw Saskatchewan and Alberta's new higher royalties as thinly disguised income taxes. Given the impact of rising energy prices on the macroeconomy in general, and the equalization formula (though, as we saw earlier, energy revenues were not totally included) in particular, the federal government was in no mood to relinquish its authority or tax base. Shaffer has captured the essence of the federal motivation:

The federal government, for its part wanted the economic rents not only for its own revenue needs but also to retain its control over the country. If the bulk of the rents flowed into the coffers of the provincial treasuries, the economic power of the provinces would grow relative to that of the federal government. It would then become increasingly difficult, it not impossible, to formulate any effective national economic policy. With their increased economic base, the provinces would be in a position to wield far more political power than in the past. This dispersion of power from the centre to the periphery would pose the danger of the balkanization of Canada. In more specific terms, Alberta, as the chief recipient of economic rents, would become the most powerful province in Confederation and would be in a position to undermine federal jurisdiction over the nation's affairs. The federal government was not inclined to abdicate its role, especially to a province containing only one-tenth of the population. Thus, it was essential for the federal government that it obtain a certain minimum share of the economic rents before it consented to large increases in prices.[25]

To counter the province's royalty increases which were eroding the federal tax base, and which would as a consequence reduce Ottawa's share of energy revenues, the federal government introduced in the May 1974 budget a provision to amend the **Income Tax Act** in order to disallow the deduction of provincial resource royalties in the calculation of taxable federal corporate income. The minority Liberal government was defeated on this budget, but subsequent to their return to power on July 8, 1974, it reintroduced the measure as part of the November 1974 budget. "In presenting the November budget the Minister of Finance, John Turner, noted that the federal government had drawn back from many of the provisions in the May budget. He invited provincial authorities to reconsider their fiscal regimes in responding to the needs of the industry and the nation."[26]

The federal action enraged the province and angered the industry, which felt it was being injured in the crossfire.[27] Richards and Pratt have argued that "the major petroleum companies confronted all three western producing provinces with a well co-ordinated capital strike—withdrawing drilling rigs, cancelling new projects and investments, and laying off employees. This campaign was particularly effective in Alberta, as it threatened many of the province's oil-dependent businesses with sudden recession."[28] While it is debatable how "co-ordinated" the industry actions were, the provinces were nonetheless forced to respond to the industry pressure and the federal power play. In December 1974, Alberta implemented a Petroleum Exploration Plan which was estimated to cost $2.5 billion. It reduced royalties and introduced new drilling incentives, among other measures. Saskatchewan also introduced measures to rebate a portion of the increased tax liabilities arising from the non-deductability of royalties. Throughout the summer and fall of 1975 the producing provinces introduced additional royalty deductions and other incentive schemes.

Ontario was not directly involved with Ottawa, the producing provinces, and the industry in the competition for the increased energy revenues. Nevertheless, higher prices and increased taxes directly affected Ontario consumers. For example, on July 1, 1975, Ottawa introduced an excise tax of ten cents a gallon on sales of motor gasoline for non-commercial use to help finance the Oil Import Compensation Fund, when the export tax revenues would no longer cover import subsidy costs. Canadians east of Ontario benefited from the subsidy, while the producing provinces enjoyed the benefits from higher prices and royalties. As mentioned above, in an economic climate of increasing unemployment (from 6.0 percent in December 1974 to 7.2 percent in March 1975) and increasing inflation (the annual rate of increase in consumer prices was in excess of 11 percent) Ontario rejected a new round of price increases at the April 1975 First Ministers' Conference. Moreover, throughout the 1973-75 period and beyond, Ontario continually reminded Ottawa of its national responsibilities with respect to economic management and the need to develop offsetting policies to counter the effects of increased prices.

The magnitude of the revenue involved, and the importance of its capture for the economic and fiscal policies of governments, raised the stakes and clarified the conflicts and coincidences of interest between governments. Of no small importance in this context was the visible burgeoning of the Alberta Heritage Fund. The fund was in part established at Ottawa's suggestion as a way of avoiding excessive fiscal equalization problems. At the same time, the larger it grew, and the more visible the projections about its future multi-billion dollar growth into the 1990s became, the greater was Ottawa's interest in having the major say in the recycling of petro-dollars. It is interesting to compare Alberta to Saskatchewan in this regard. Saskatchewan too was accumulating oil and gas revenues, but it did not parade its wealth in one place, such as in a heritage fund only. Saskatchewan had its own similar fund (albeit of much smaller size), but as an NDP government it was more inclined to diversify its wealth investment through several instruments, including its several Crown corporations. Saskatchewan's energy revenues were therefore a less visible target.

In the final analysis, however, the struggles over pricing and revenue sharing were as acrimonious and as hard fought as they were precisely because each of the relevant governments had the constitutional authority and/or political power to defend their interests, as they interpreted them, against the encroachments of other governments. Yet, this question of constitutional authority, and the jurisdiction over resource management which emanates from it, was itself a major issue of contention in this fractious period of intergovernmental energy relations.

Intergovernmental Relations: Resource Management

> ... the energy situation has impelled governments to evolve more comprehensive and coherent policies towards energy, and such policies have led directly to severe intergovernmental conflict. When energy was cheap and in seemingly inexhaustible supply the public authorities did not much concern themselves with alternative energy sources, the impact of energy policies on the economy or energy conservation. These circumstances have changed.[29]

Ultimately the federal–provincial conflicts over pricing and revenue sharing reflect the larger struggle over the constitutionally defined need and politically defined desire of the producing provinces and Ottawa to strengthen their control over the management of energy resources. As shown above, the control over energy resources and the revenues generated by them is central to the historical relationship of the producing provinces and Ottawa and the historical relationship of central and western Canada. The emerging seller's market of the early 1970s kindled hopes in the hearts of westerners that they could use their resource strengths to diversify the prairie economy away from the historic vulnerability of the boom–bust syndrome endemic in a dependence on primary resources. The 1973 Western Economic Opportunities Conference was pervaded by the themes of resource control, economic diversification, and industrial development. The various assertions of provincial authority over the control of natural resources undertaken by Alberta and Saskatchewan must be understood in this context.

The changes to the provincial royalty regimes, the establishment of the Alberta Petroleum Marketing Commission, the BCPC, Sask-Oil, the Alberta Energy Corporation, the Alberta Heritage Savings Trust Fund, for example, were all attempts by the producing provinces to put in place new instruments which would strengthen their control over resource management and thus their capacity to pursue their respective provincial development strategies.

By the same token, the events of the mid-'70s required the federal government, which has its own set of obligations and constitutional authorities with respect to energy policy management, to strengthen its position. The extension of the Interprovincial Pipeline to Montreal to displace 250 000 barrels per day of imported oil, the March 1973 export controls, the autumn price freeze and export tax, the PAA, the establishment of Petro-Canada, increased funding of Panarctic Oils, the support of Syncrude and the northern pipeline as well as the royalty deductability legislation, are all examples of initiatives undertaken to pursue energy policy goals and to enhance federal authority over resource management.

It is not surprising, given this flurry of activity in the mid-'70s, that in pursuing their own objectives the federal government and governments of the producing provinces would come into conflict over the management of resources. Nowhere was the conflict more striking, however, than when the federal government joined as co-plaintiff in the oil industry challenge to the **Saskatchewan Oil and Gas Conservation, Stabilization and Development Act.**

The Act was introduced in December 1973 as part of Saskatchewan's attempt to extend and strengthen its constitutional control over its oil and natural resources. The Act was a complex piece of legislation, but its central function was to nationalize (with compensation) virtually all freehold oil and gas rights, and to impose a "royalty surcharge" on all Crown production. The intent of the surcharge was to impose a 100 percent tax on all incremental rents arising from future price increases:

> To prevent evasion of the surcharge by transfer pricing among divisions of an integrated oil company, Bill 42 empowered the Minister of Mineral Resources to specify for purposes of calculat-

ing the surcharge due, the market price whenever he deemed oil
was being sold at a price below it.... The Calgary-based oil industry
decided that one of its members should challenge the constitutionality of Bill 42 and in February 1974 Canadian Industrial Gas and
Oil Ltd. (CIGOL), an independent company producing oil in Saskatchewan, initiated such an action.... After May 1974, the constitutional challenge to Bill 42 assumed an enhanced significance.
Whereas it began as a manifestation of the oil industry's traditional
mistrust of the NDP, it became the arena for a major constitutional
battle between the federal and provincial governments over resource jurisdiction.[30]

At the level of the Court of Queen's Bench and the Saskatchewan
Court of Appeal, the constitutionality of Bill 42 was upheld. However,
in an important November 1977 decision, the Supreme Court of
Canada ruled that the sections of the Act establishing the royalty
surcharge were *ultra vires*. The details of the case are analysed in detail
elsewhere; for our purposes it will be necessary only to highlight the
key features of the decision and to consider some of its larger political
implications.

The thrust of the Supreme Court judgement was that the royalty
surcharge was a tax and not a royalty. A majority judgement placed
great stress on the powers granted to the Minister by Bill 42 to specify,
for purposes of calculating the surcharge, the market price of oil. Because of this power, it was argued, the producing company would
become a conduit passing on the surcharge to the purchaser of the
crude oil. Thus the surcharge constituted an indirect tax and was *ultra
vires*. Second, because provincial legislative authority does not extend
to fixing the price of goods sold in export markets, which they found
the price setting powers of Bill 42 to do, the Supreme Court majority
judgement ruled that the bill infringed on federal jurisdiction over
trade and commerce. Such an unqualified conclusion strengthened the
constitutionality of the federal PAA which, as we saw earlier, authorizes
Ottawa to negotiate agreements with producing provinces for oil
prices, and in the event of failure to agree, to establish unilaterally the
maximum price for oil entering into interprovincial trade.

As Richards and Pratt stated in 1979 in the wake of the CIGOL case
"the uncertainty surrounding the current constitutional division of
powers over resources has increasingly prompted Saskatchewan and
Alberta (plus certain other provinces) to exercise their proprietary

rights." They further speculated that given this uncertainty, an increasingly attractive option for producing provinces would be to establish Crown corporations which could retain ownership to the point of sale to a final customer, thereby enabling the province "to garner economic rent via the Crown corporation's profits, potentially obviating the constitutional proscription on indirect taxation by a province."[31] Alberta had established such a vehicle in December 1973 with the creation of the Petroleum Marketing Commission. There was some speculation at the time that given the setbacks to the Saskatchewan resource management strategies in the CIGOL and Central Canada Potash cases, that the industry or federal government might also challenge the Alberta resource management legislation. No legal challenge to Alberta's legislation was launched, however, and no further legal action was taken until Alberta, as part of its retaliation to the NEP, drilled three wells near the U.S. border and challenged the federal government's authority to tax exports from them (as provincial property) in a Supreme Court reference case. Alberta's position was upheld.

Thus we can see the constitutional ambiguity where resource management is concerned. What is less ambiguous is the political acrimony engendered by various governments moving into one another's perceived constitutional territory. The constitutional battles over resource management were both the cause and effect of the overall intergovernmental conflicts stimulated by the OPEC-induced 1973 price escalations. These disputes caused the provincial governments to redouble their efforts via the constitutional patriation negotiations which were underway in the late 1970s, to restrict federal involvement where provincial resources are concerned.[32] The government of Alberta took a strong provincial rights position in this debate, motivated by a largely defensive response to what it felt was a federal campaign to reduce and abridge the powers of the provinces over natural resources. In their 1978 constitutional discussion paper, "Harmony in Diversity: A New Federalism For Canada,"[33] the Lougheed Conservatives called for the termination of the federal powers of disallowance and reservation and for severe limitation on the federal declaratory and emergency power. They also wanted to entrench provincial powers over resources by strengthening provincial ownership and control over natural resources; reaffirming provincial authority to tax and collect royalties from the management and sale of their natural resources; establishing provincial jurisdiction over offshore mineral resources; giving provinces access to direct and indirect taxes; and establishing a provincial role in certain areas of international relations. Alberta further proposed that the provinces have the right to appoint 40 percent of the members of federal regulatory agencies such as the National Energy Board, and that a new representative constitutional court be created to settle constitutional disputes. Such a package of amendments would have essentially emasculated federal power in this area and, not surprisingly, only a small part of it actually materialized in the new **Constitution Act of 1982**.

In conclusion, then, it seems abundantly clear that the political and constitutional energy wars of the 1970s did have a significant impact on the relationship of governments to one another as well as the relationship between governments and industry. Donald Smiley has suggested three major impacts of the 1970s energy wars on the federal system, Canadian institutions of government, and intergovernmental energy relations:

> First ... on the organizational side prior to 1973 responsibility for energy matters was divided in the federal and provincial governments among several departments and agencies which carried on their activities with little relation to each other. These thrusts have been reflected as clearly as anywhere in Ontario where there has been established a Ministry of Energy with responsibilities for various energy policies and an Ontario Energy Corporation to develop energy sources. In general terms this new degree of coherence has given rise to intergovernmental conflict as the various jurisdictions define their interests in respect to energy in a more clear-cut, expert and comprehensive way. ... Secondly, the energy crisis has rapidly extended public involvement in energy matters and has launched the country on experiments in joint public–private ownership. ... It is possible to foresee complications in such arrangements, not only between their public and private components but also in circumstances as that of Syncrude where one or more governments holds equity shares under the jurisdiction of another; this was presumably the kind of consideration which has led Ottawa to block the participation of the government of Quebec in the Pan-Arctic consortium. ... and perhaps most crucially, the energy crisis has led, in respect to these matters, to a resurgence of power and purpose by the central government. ... these new im-

peratives projected the national government into many new activities in which it had hitherto done little or nothing—energy conservation, the development of new energy sources, the building of new pipelines for oil and natural gas, the control of the domestic price of petroleum, emergency legislation allowing Ottawa to control the domestic supply of oil and so on. In all these circumstances, and others, new patterns of relations with the provinces have evolved.[34]

1979: Intergovernmental Energy Relations under the Conservatives

The conundrum the Clark Conservatives had to master, with respect to oil and gas pricing and revenue sharing, was to increase prices enough to induce conservation and to increase exploration without being seen to be caving in to the industry and capitulating to the Alberta government, while at the same time getting a larger share of energy revenues for the federal government to help reduce the federal deficit and to pay for the various conservation, substitution, and redistribution programs they had devised as part of their larger energy strategy. As the outcome of the February 1980 election showed, they failed to pull it off: in fact, they were essentially defeated by Ontario voters. The Conservatives' attempt to walk a tightrope between the demands of their Alberta and Ontario brethren, while pursuing their own independent set of interests, is a revealing glimpse into both the government–industry and intergovernmental relationships as they stood in 1979.

Energy pricing negotiations between Ottawa and the producing provinces are always complex and fraught with frustration. No one, however, feels the frustration more than the "outsiders," in this case the industry and the governments of the consuming provinces. The industry, because it does not sit at the bargaining table, is limited to attempting to influence public opinion and lobbying decision makers in both levels of government beforehand. Though it normally finds a more responsive ear in the capitals of the producing provinces, it is also sometimes shocked by the outcome of negotiations. The same holds for the governments of the consuming provinces. Because they have not sat at the negotiating table since the demise of the premiers' conference as a forum for determining energy prices in 1975, they are largely restricted to trying to exercise some leverage by influencing public opinion in their provinces. In his analysis of the Clark Government, Jeffrey Simpson has captured the essence of the relationship of energy to partisanship and intergovernmental relations:

> Nothing had adequately prepared either Joe Clark or his party for the task at hand. In Opposition, the Conservatives drafted an unrealistic energy policy based on a number of misconceptions and a refusal to confront the key question in any sensible energy policy: the price of oil and natural gas. Once in power, the Opposition party found its illusions shattered by the civil service, which produced a series of policy recommendations for which the Conservatives were unprepared. Similarly, the Conservatives had convinced themselves, more by constant repetition than by cogent analysis, that energy and other federal–provincial problems could be solved if the new Government in Ottawa spread sufficient good-will around the country. ... It had taken months of excruciating bargaining with Lougheed even to approach an agreement, and the story of these months is, in part, Joe Clark's slow disillusionment with the Alberta premier and the shaking of the young Prime Minister's conviction that the Conservative premiers of Canada really wished him to succeed. He was naive on entering the negotiations; nothing in Opposition had prepared him for the intractability of provincial governments. He believed that by showing good-will and making early concessions he would consummate a speedy energy agreement that would fulfill his election promise to end the warring between Ottawa and the provinces. ... he discovered that the premiers cared at least as much about their own provinces as about the national interest, and cared much more about their own political necks than about helping Joe Clark. ... Clark learned a lesson that a more experienced Prime Minister would have understood. In federal–provincial relations, premiers are colour-blind when the vital interests of their provinces are at stake; in fact, it is often easier for them politically to have a federal government of a different political stripe to blame at provincial election time.[35]

The Conservative governments of Canada, Alberta, and Ontario were clearly all major interests where oil and gas pricing and revenue sharing was concerned. Even though the industry had insiders such as James Gillies and Harvey André representing their positions at the centre of power within the Clark government, the government proved willing to take on the industry to the extent that they would heavily tax away the windfall profits created by a new pricing regime. Gillies for ideological reasons, and André for regional as well as ideological reasons, accepted the Alberta position and that of industry, and even went so far as to try to argue that huge price increases could somehow be disassociated from their larger economic and fiscal consequences. In so doing they showed themselves to be inflexible, and lacking in political acumen. As a consequence, they became increasingly marginal players. Even Lougheed argued that Ottawa should tax the oil companies heavily unless the companies re-invested their profits in new energy-related projects.

While the Clark government was willing to go to higher prices, they were still cognizant of the need to make the connection for the public between higher prices and energy self-sufficiency, that is, to show that something was to be gained in exchange for higher prices. With respect to revenue shares, Clark claimed that while he had no problems with a rapidly growing Alberta Heritage Fund—it was speculated that if the Alberta proposal in the negotiations was accepted the Fund would have grown to $30 billion by 1985 and by 1990 could have amounted to $100 billion—there was still the question of the federal responsibilities for national economic management, in which the recycling of petro-dollars within Canada was a key issue. The Clark government initially offered Alberta a major price hike, $6 per barrel a year, in exchange for Alberta's agreement to recycle oil revenues through two new federal institutions, the National Energy Bank and a Stabilization Fund. Alberta refused to make an equity contribution to either, so the federal government decreased its price offer in the December 1979 budget to the $4.00–4.50 range, with the energy self-sufficiency tax.

In addition to this direct interest in revenue sharing, the federal Conservative government had an indirect interest in the flow of revenues created by petroleum price increases. For example, because the federal government derived most of its revenue from the non-energy sectors of the economy, it had to be cognizant of the impact of higher oil and gas prices on the revenues of these other sectors. Faster price increases would also restrict the utility of the excise tax. In other words, the federal government had to take the larger view of the impact of higher prices on the national economy, and more specifically, of the impact of the vast shifts of revenues to the Alberta Treasury and to the multinationals-dominated oil industry on the federal government's credibility and authority over national economic management.

The fact that Joe Clark headed a Conservative government made little impression on the Lougheed Conservatives. The Alberta government started from the principled position that Alberta owned the non-renewable oil and natural gas resources, that these resources were being depleted, and in the process were undervalued and underpriced in Canada relative to their international commodity value. One legacy of the bitter 1973–74 energy wars was the Alberta position that it was subsidizing Canadian consumers by the difference between the world price and the Canadian price. The dramatic increases OPEC was able to enforce in the aftermath of the Iranian revolution significantly increased the size of this subsidy, though no one in Canada had done anything; a poignant reminder of how developments halfway around the globe can have a major impact on domestic Canadian politics.

The Alberta–Ontario and Alberta–Ottawa struggle over pricing and revenue sharing since 1973–74 reflected the fundamental interregional and federal–provincial tension that exists in Canada over the past and future development of the Canadian economy. To further its objective of restructuring the Canadian economy, Alberta was determined to extract large price increases out of Ottawa; this time, they wanted to entrench a formula that would tie Canadian price to the U.S.–Chicago price. Despite these structural and historical factors, the partisan and personal determinants cannot be ignored. After fighting for years with the centralist Trudeau Liberals, the Alberta Conservatives saw the Clark image of Canada as a community of communities and his rhetoric about improved federal–provincial relations as an opportunity. This sense of a strategic opportunity was reinforced by their view that key Alberta oil sands and heavy oil developments were essential to the federal Conservatives' self-sufficiency objective and that therefore they could take a hard line. Simply put, they thought they could stare-down the inexperienced, pro-business Clark government, and thus were not willing to negotiate very much. The importance of the personalities involved should not be underestimated:

> The fact that Joe Clark was a Conservative scarcely moved Peter Lougheed. Clark had once worked for Lougheed, and the Alberta premier considered Clark to be his intellectual inferior. He simply did not have much respect for the Prime Minister of Canada, whom he felt was poorly briefed and not quite up to the job.[36]

In essence, the Alberta government wanted higher prices and at least the same share of revenues (45 percent) as before; if Ottawa wanted additional revenues they could take them out of the industry. While this is another case of Alberta's distinguishing between its own interests and those of the industry, Alberta did warn Ottawa about imposing too high a windfall profits tax, one which would turn the industry off. Alberta also opposed the nature of the energy self-sufficiency tax, which it charged was a royalty at the wellhead. Alberta wanted to retain control over decision making with respect to granting concessions on the prices for new volumes of natural gas. That is, if concessions were being made regarding natural gas prices in order to encourage new contracts, Alberta wanted it to be clear that *it* was making the concessions and not being forced to do so by the federal government. This is, of course, a classic case of politicians and governments wanting visibly to capture the political credit for popular programs.

Alberta rejected the concept of an Energy Bank and Stabilization Fund if they were conceived to be primarily instruments to recycle petro-dollars. The Lougheed government let it be known that if there was any recycling of Alberta's share of resource revenues that they would do it. Alberta was willing to lend $2 billion over five years to the Energy Bank but only at near-commercial, not concessionary rates; this was a far cry from the grants and cheap loans the federal Conservatives had been looking for. Finally, in mid-November 1979, Lougheed accused the Clark government of giving in to Ontario. As Lougheed put it, "In examining your position, I find considerable symmetry between your position and the one advanced by the Government of Ontario."[37] Lougheed was also angered over Ontario's policy paper counselling the federal government to be prepared to use its declaratory power if necessary in order to fulfill its national responsibilities.

The William Davis-led Conservative government in Ontario had a set of interests quite distinct, to say the least, from those of the industry and those of the producing provinces and Ottawa. It was well known, even pointed out in the federal Cabinet's own energy background paper, that inflation would rise roughly 0.6 percent and unemployment 0.2 percent for every $1.00 increase in the price of a barrel of oil. Ontario was solely a consumer province. It and its industrial base would suffer the most in terms of the inflationary and unemployment consequences of higher prices. Furthermore, higher prices would represent the outflow of billions of consumer dollars to the producing provinces and the industry over the life of a multi-year agreement. Ontario knew price increases over the $2.00 per barrel a year increase of the previous agreement were inevitable, but when they heard that the federal Conservatives were offering $6.00 per barrel a year increase for three years, they were outraged. The provincial Conservatives led a minority government; their polls, like the provincial Liberal and NDP polls, showed that major price increases were unpopular in Ontario. Because Ontario did not sit at the bargaining table, its best hope for some success in influencing the outcome lay in galvanizing public opinion in Ontario against a rapid escalation in price. Consequently, Davis made a series of speeches denouncing huge price increases. He charged that the federal–Alberta deal, as he understood it, was "an excessive and imprudent response to the claims of the producing provinces and the petroleum industry." Davis felt frustrated and alarmed by what appeared to be a "seemingly unrelenting commitment to chase an artificial, erratic and *soaring* world price—a price set by interests and circumstances foreign to Canada and to *our* economic realities."[38]

Recognizing that higher prices were inevitable, that they would increase inflation and unemployment and hurt economic growth in Ontario, the Davis Conservatives wanted the federal government to take a bigger slice of oil and gas revenues and to recycle them through the economy in order to offset the impact of higher prices. Ontario also insisted that the producing provinces relinquish some of their revenues to help mitigate the economic consequences of higher prices in the consuming provinces. If the producing provinces balked, then Ontario urged Ottawa to consider using its draconian constitutional power to alter unilaterally the revenue flows.[39] This suggestion, along with Ontario's resistence to immediate and large price increases, incensed the Lougheed Conservatives.[40]

In the end, the federal Conservatives found themselves caught between the hard-line position taken by their provincial cousins, both of whom accused the Federal Tories of siding with the others. Just as Davis gambled and lost in 1975 when his intransigence at the April First Ministers' Conference led to the demise of the Conference as a forum for price negotiations and thus removed Ontario and the other consuming provinces from the negotiating table, the Lougheed intransigence with the Clark government also proved to be a strategy that backfired: it ultimately contributed to the demise of the Clark government and the return to power of a Liberal government willing to take a much tougher stance with Alberta.

The sole intergovernmental energy issue on which the Clark government achieved strong provincial support from the relevant provincial governments was the issue of offshore resource ownership. This is not surprising given that the Clark government was willing to transfer ownership of offshore resources to the coastal provinces, as it agreed to in principle in September 1979.

Quite clearly, then, the fact that Conservatives occupied the government benches in Edmonton, Queen's Park, and Ottawa did not preclude energy issues from causing considerable stress and conflict in intergovernmental energy relations. This, of course, reflects the fact that vital energy issues such as pricing, revenue sharing, and resource management play into a complex structural and historical relationship in the Canadian political economy that has the key governmental interests representing distinctive concerns and claims. It is one of the features of Canadian political development that provincial governments, when and where they have the capacity to do so, strive actively to shape the development of their provincial economies and societies. When an issue is as pivotal as oil and gas pricing and revenue sharing and can have a major impact on economic growth provincially as well as regionally and nationally, it is not surprising that provincial governments will fight hard to achieve their objectives—using all the resources available to them. Federal governments of whatever political stripe, because of their structural responsibilities in this area, will also want to satisfy their obligations. Given the power that each of these interests can bring to this issue, it is not surprising that intergovernmental conflict is a natural feature of Canadian energy politics.

Summary

Two sets of interim observations can be offered at this stage of the analytical journey. One concerns the substantive energy issues to which the NEP was responding and at the same time attempting to influence. The second concerns the two relationships of power.

In respect of the immediate nature of the cumulative pre-NEP legacy, one can see from Chapters 4 and 5 what a troubled state both the government–industry and intergovernmental relationships were in during the 1979–80 period. A number of developments in the 1979–80 period contributed to the troubled state of these relationships. Among these were: the Iranian revolution, the supply cut of 2.5 million barrels per day it caused, and the subsequent 150 percent increase in world price; the outbreak of the Iran–Iraq war and the renewed fears of shortages it engendered; the federal Conservative budget and Petro-Canada privatization debacle; Alberta's intransigence in the 1979 and 1980 price and revenue-sharing negotiations; the emergence of massive new economic rents; fear of petroleum industry acquisitions of other sectors of the Canadian economy and the expatriation of capital by foreign-owned oil companies; the concern of the federal and Ontario governments with the prospect of huge interregional trans-fers of wealth from consuming provinces to Alberta and the resulting continued spectacular growth of the Alberta Heritage Trust Fund; anger in western Canada over Ontario's abandonment of the federal Conservatives in the 1980 election; and the intergovernment quarrel-ing over the patriation of the constitution in general and the sections on natural resources in particular.

While developments in the 1979–80 period both reflected and aggravated the strained government–industry and intergovernmental relationships, these relationships were troubled for deeper structural reasons. In the 1947 to 1972 period of Canadian energy politics, both relationships were basically characterized by consensual relations. Both government and industry fundamentally and consciously agreed on what basically should be done. Despite the fears expressed in the Gordon Royal Commission about foreign domination of the industry, little heed was taken by governments, and the government–industry relationships (federal and provincial) were predominantly industry-oriented, in that industry was knowingly given wide latitude by both the federal and provincial governments in the development of Canada's oil and gas reserves. Furthermore, the federal and provincial governments shared the objective of encouraging oil and gas produc-tion and of stimulating the growth of the domestic petroleum industry. Hence, there was a basic consensus of values between the federal and provincial governments over the management of Canada's growing oil and gas reserves. This period of Canadian energy politics was one of minimum government interference in the interplay of market forces. The price and supply shocks induced by the 1973 OPEC crisis ended all that.

The quadrupling of world oil price dramatically raised the stakes of energy politics in Canada, and in the post-1973 period it became increasingly clear to the producing provinces, the consuming provinces, the federal government, and the industry that they each had distinct and, to some degree, different interests with respect to oil and gas pricing, and revenue sharing. This realization resulted in, arguably, the most acrimonious intergovernmental and government–industry conflict in post-war Canadian history, as each of the key interests mobilized to protect its position and to stalemate "the opposition." The overall result of the 1973–74 confrontations was increased governmental assertiveness and intervention and strengthened state authority in the energy policy field. As a direct consequence the industry's predominance in the government–industry relationships was also changed. The effect, then, was that the government–industry and federal government–producing province relationships became much more equal, with the federal government relative to the producing provinces and both levels of government relative to the industry strengthening their capabilities and positions. The Alberta–Ontario relationship shifted decidedly in favour of Alberta, and Ontario came to rely more and more on the federal government to guard its interests. This is particularly true after the breakdown in 1975–1976 of the first ministers' conferences as a meaningful forum for establishing oil and gas prices. The industry, of course, as a result of its control over the productive apparatus and major capital pools, remained a powerful interest. With respect to the intraindustry configuration of power, one of the key developments of the 1973–1980 period was the emergence of large Canadian-controlled companies capable of competing in a meaningful way with the foreign-controlled majors.

By 1978, following three and a half years of relative calm on the international oil scene and decreasing real world oil prices, things had quieted down in Canada as well, and many of the wounds created by the 1973–74 conflicts had begun to heal. Because the conflicts were the result of fundamental differences of interest within these two relationships of power, many of the old sores were reopened and new wounds were suffered as a result of the next dramatic raising of the stakes in 1979. It was out of this period and the events since 1973 that the NEP emerged.

Notes

1. This was the state of constitutional affairs pertaining to resource owner-ship and management throughout the 1970s. After years of frustrated efforts and hard federal–provincial bargaining, the Constitution Act was proclaimed in April, 1982. Canada's new Constitution consists of the Constitution Act of 1982 and the B.N.A. Act of 1867 and all the amend-ments thereto. While the Constitution Act of 1982 does affect jurisdiction over oil and gas directly through the resource amendment and perhaps indirectly through the Charter of Rights, the real substance of legislative jurisdiction is still to be found in the 1867 Act, the important features of which are described above. The resource amendment is found in Section 50 of the Constitution Act 1982, which adds Section 92A to the 1867 Act. It will suffice here to note only three subsections of 92A. 92A(2) enables a province to make laws in relation to the export from the province to another part of Canada of the primary production of a resource, with the qualification that such laws may not discriminate in prices or in supplies exported to another part of Canada. Subsection (3) states that nothing in Subsection (2) derogates from the authority of the federal government to enact laws in relation to the same matters. Most important in terms of provincial jurisdiction is section 92A(4), which expands the taxation power in respect of non-renewable natural resources. Whereas prior to the amendment the province was limited to direct taxation within the province to raise revenue for provincial purposes, it is now empowered to make laws in relation to the raising of money by any mode or system of taxation in respect of non-renewable natural resources, including indirect taxation of resources. Depending on how the courts interpret it, certain aspects of the Charter of Rights could also have ramifications for energy activities. All one can really do at the present, is acknowledge that the "stakes involved in jurisdiction over natural resources, both in terms of revenue and political power, are so astronomical that any changes or concessions will be made carefully and grudgingly," and that "the new

constitution has increased the legislative base of the provinces with regard to non-renewable natural resources, but has done nothing to shift the overall balance of power between the two levels of government." John B. Ballem, "Oil and Gas Under the New Constitution," Inaugural lecture delivered at the official opening of the Canadian Institute of Resources Law, Calgary, Alberta, December 2, 1981. See also John B. Ballem, "The Energy Crunch and Constitutional Reform," *The Canadian Bar Review*, Volume 57 (1979), pp. 740–756.

2. The Liberals reasserted the federal government's jurisdiction over these resources in the NEP, designating them as part of the Canada Lands. Nova Scotia and the federal government have agreed to put the ownership issue aside, however, and in March 1982, the two governments signed an agreement outlining the administration and management of Nova Scotia offshore resources. Newfoundland has refused to do so, and instead referred the question of jurisdiction to the Court of Appeal of the Supreme Court of Newfoundland in February 1982. Three months later, in May 1982, Ottawa sent a reference to the Supreme Court of Canada on this same issue. Newfoundland lost its case in the provincial Supreme Court, and on March 8, 1984, the Supreme Court of Canada, in a unanimous judgement, ruled that the federal government had jurisdiction over offshore resources.

3. Allan Blakeney, "Resources, the Constitution and Canadian Federalism," 1977 speech reprinted in J. Peter Meekison (ed.), *Canadian Federalism: Myth or Reality*, Third Edition (Toronto: Methuen, 1977), p. 181.

4. W.L. Morton, *The Progressive Party in Canada* (Toronto: University of Toronto Press, 1950).

5. See J.R. Mallory, *Social Credit and the Federal Power in Canada* (Toronto: University of Toronto Press, 1954); C.B. Macpherson, *Democracy in Alberta: Social Credit and the Party System*, Second Edition (Toronto: University of Toronto Press, 1962); and J.A. Irving, *The Social Credit Movement in Alberta* (Toronto: University of Toronto Press, 1959).

6. Seymour M. Lipset, *Agrarian Socialism*, Updated Edition (New York: Doubleday and Company, 1968).

7. David E. Smith, "Western Politics and National Unity," in David Jay Bercusson (ed.), *Canada and the Burden of Unity* (Toronto: Macmillan, 1977), p. 150.

8. Joseph Wearing, *The L-Shaped Party: The Liberal Party of Canada, 1958–1980* (Toronto: McGraw-Hill Ryerson, 1981).

9. Government of Canada, Energy, Mines and Resources, *The Energy Statistics Handbook*, 1981.

10. John Richards and Larry Pratt, *Prairie Capitalism* (Toronto: McClelland and Stewart, 1979), pp. 61–62.

11. Government of Canada, House of Commons, *Debates*, April 8, 1949, p. 2509.

12. Richards and Pratt, *op. cit.*, p. 66.

13. *Ibid.*, pp. 66–67.

14. Donald Smiley, *Canada in Question: Federalism in the Eighties*, Third Edition (Toronto: McGraw-Hill Ryerson, 1980), pp. 193–194.

15. See Government of Canada, Director of Investigation and Research, Combines Investigation Act, *The State of Competition in the Canadian Petroleum Industry* (Ottawa: Supply and Services Canada, 1981), vols. 1 and 2.

16. Ed Shaffer, *Canada's Oil and the American Empire* (Edmonton: Hurtig, 1983), p. 215.

17. Richards and Pratt, *op. cit.*, p. 226.

18. John N. McDougall, *Fuels and the National Policy* (Toronto: Butterworths, 1982), p. 137.

19. *Ibid.*, p. 138.

20. *Ibid.*, p. 139.

21. Smiley, *op. cit.*, p. 200.

22. Richards and Pratt, *op. cit.*, p. 216.

23. *Ibid.*, p. 225.

24. Government of Canada, Energy Mines and Resources, *An Energy Strategy for Canada: Politics for Self-Reliance* (Ottawa: Supply and Services Canada, 1976), pp. 156–157.

25. Shaffer, *op. cit.*, p. 226.

26. *An Energy Strategy for Canada, op. cit.*, p. 34.

27. Many of the industry officials interviewed traced the beginning of the "crossfire" to this period.

28. Richards and Pratt, *op. cit.*, p. 227.

29. Smiley, *op. cit.*, p. 200.

30. Richards and Pratt, *op. cit.*, pp. 288–289.

31. *Ibid.*, pp. 293–294.

32. See Ballem, *op. cit.*

33. Government of Alberta, *Harmony in Diversity: A New Federalism for Canada*, Position Paper on Constitutional Change, 1978.

34. Smiley, *op. cit.*, pp. 201–202.

35. Jeffrey Simpson, *Discipline of Power* (Toronto: Personal Library, 1980), pp. 178–179, 204.

36. *Ibid.*, p. 194.

37. Cited in *ibid.*, p. 201.

38. William Davis, Opening Remarks to the Special First Ministers' Conference on Energy, Ottawa, November 12, 1979, p. 543.

39. See William Davis, "Oil Pricing and Security: A Policy Framework for Canada," August 14, 1979, p. 18.

40. The day following the release of the Ontario "Framework," Premier Lougheed responded with a four-page, fourteen-point rebuttal. See Statement by Premier Peter Lougheed of Alberta in response to Ontario position paper entitled "Oil Pricing and Security," August 15, 1979.

PART III

ENERGY POLITICS
AFTER THE NEP: 1981-1984

CHAPTER 6

GOVERNMENT–INDUSTRY ENERGY RELATIONS AND THE NEP

We now turn to an examination of the impact of the NEP on the government–industry relationships of power. In our analysis of the broad historical periods in previous chapters, it was acceptable to treat the industry as a single interest vis-à-vis the key state interests. For the most part the only distinction that was made between the various elements which comprise the industry was to focus on the division of the industry on the basis of ownership, that is, between foreign- and Canadian-owned and controlled firms. In this chapter, we differentiate among the interests in the industry on the basis of national ownership and size. The specific objective here is to identify, describe, and assess the reactions of key industry interests to the NEP.

As shown in Chapter 4, one of the key developments for energy politics as a whole in the 1970s and for the intra-industry configuration of power in particular, was the emergence of three large Canadian oil and gas companies. The three firms, Dome, Petro-Canada and Nova are diversified into a variety of activities in the petroleum business, and each has expanded in recent years by both acquisitions and expansion of their industry activity. They make a difference in Canadian energy politics because, as the Alaska Highway Pipeline case shows, they are capable of mounting an intra-industry challenge to the former dominant financial and technological power of the multinationals. Another important impact is that they provide the federal government in particular with an alternative set of major industry interests and a very real option to the power of the multinationals.[1] Indeed, one of the main objectives of the NEP's Canadianization initiatives was to facilitate the emergence of other Canadian majors.

While there are several criteria one could adopt to divide the industry (see Table 6.1), the most important—and perhaps widely accepted in terms of differentiating the common interests of various firms—are the criteria of ownership and size: that is, foreign majors, foreign juniors, Canadian majors and Canadian juniors. While the majors are clearly identifiable by the size of their operations, the juniors are a less discrete category in that the term tends to be used to mean non-majors, and as such includes both intermediate and small companies. In this chapter we focus attention on some of these intermediate firms which we label the "second-line" Canadian firms. There is also the traditional division of the global industry into the "seven sisters" (Exxon, Gulf, Shell, BP, Texaco, Mobil, Standard Oil California), the "independents," including other large private U.S. (Occidental, Continental, Hess, Getty) and non-U.S. state-owned firms (CFP, ENI), and in recent years the state-owned companies of major OPEC and non-OPEC producers (Pemex, BNOC, Statoil). For space and analytical reasons, we will have to limit the number of industry interests we can focus on here. The most important individual firms in Canadian energy politics fall into the categories of foreign majors, Canadian majors, second-line Canadian firms, and Canadian juniors. Thus we will not deal with the category of foreign juniors here.

Multinationals. These are, of course, the Canadian subsidiaries of the seven sisters, some of which, like Imperial and Gulf, have some significant Canadian minority shareholdings (20 to 25 percent). They include Texaco which has less than 10 percent, and the "100 percenters" such as Mobil and Chevron which, as their nickname suggests, are 100 percent owned by the foreign parent. Given that U.S. ownership of Canadian industry is an overwhelming feature of Canadian energy politics, we will focus here on the three major U.S. firms: Imperial, Gulf, and Texaco. In later chapters we deal also with Mobil, Shell, and Chevron.

Canadian Majors. The three acknowledged majors in the Canadian-owned sector are Dome, Petro-Canada, and Nova. Though on a strictly "reserves" rating Pan Canadian, the subsidiary of Canadian Pacific, is larger than Nova, the latter's importance in a number of key energy projects and the stature of its president, Bob Blair, compels its ranking as a Canadian major.

The Second-Line Canadian Firms. As Table 6.1 indicates, the second-line firms embrace a category of about ten quite diverse, medium-sized

TABLE 6.1
THE TOP 20 OIL AND GAS COMPANIES IN 1983

Overall Proven Reserves[1]	Oil and Gas Liquids Production[2]	Natural Gas Production[2]
Imperial Oil Ltd.	Esso Resources	Shell Canada
Petro-Canada	Texaco Canada	Dome Petroleum
Dome Petroleum Ltd.	Gulf Canada	Petro-Canada
Shell Canada Ltd.	Dome Petroleum	Amoco Canada Petroleum
Gulf Canada Ltd.	Chevron Canada	PanCanadian Petroleum
PanCanadian Petroleum Ltd.	Petro-Canada	Gulf Canada Resources
Texaco Canada Inc.	Mobil Oil Canada	Esso Resources Canada
The Seagram Company Ltd.	Amoco Canada Petroleum	Mobil Oil Canada
Canada Development Corp.	Shell Canada	Alberta Energy
Husky Oil Ltd.	Suncor	Chevron Canada
Hiram Walker Resources Ltd.	PanCanadian Petroleum	Canterra Energy
Alberta Energy Co. Ltd.	Husky Oil	Canadian Superior Oil
Norcen Energy Resources Ltd.	Canterra Energy	Norcen Energy Resources
Nova, An Alberta Corp.	Norcen Energy Resources	Texaco Canada Resources
Noranda Mines Ltd.	Canadian Superior Oil	Canadian Hunter
TransCanada Pipelines Ltd.	Home Oil	Home Oil
B.P. Resources Canada Ltd.	TCPL Resources	BP Canada
Sulpetro Ltd.	Union Oil of Canada	Ocelot Industries
Bow Valley Industries Ltd.	BP Canada	Sulpetro
Dome Canada Ltd.	Saskoil	Canadian Occidental

Sources: 1. *Financial Times*, July 9, 1984.
2. *Oilweek*, June 18, 1984.

firms, six of which we examine in an illustrative way in this chapter. These include such firms as Pan Canadian, Norcen, Home Oil, Canterra, Husky, and Bow Valley. A full list could easily be broadened to include the Alberta Energy Co., Sulpetro, Trans-Canada Pipelines, and Noranda Mines, depending upon the criteria used.

Canadian Juniors. This group includes disparate interests, from firms as large as Ocelot to very small, one- to five-person exploration outfits. No attempts will be made here to trace the reactions of specific firms to the NEP, but rather, the reaction of this group as a whole is assessed.

It is clear that the foreign domination of the industry was a problem which, in the eyes of the Liberal government, "required fundamental change . . . in the structure of the oil and gas industry."[3] The introductory section of the NEP entitled "The Problems" outlined in detail what the government understood to be the peculiar problem of foreign domination of the oil and gas industry. The NEP stressed that "the Government of Canada believes that the oil and gas sector is a unique case, and that special measures not required in other sectors are needed to ensure more Canadian control."[4] It is worth citing at length from the "Problems" section of the NEP, as it essentially provides the official rationale for the ambitious initiatives introduced in the NEP to alter the government–industry and intra-industry configurations of power:

> A major objective of national policy over the years has been to foster a strong petroleum industry, through pricing and tax incentives more generous than those available outside the resource sector. . . . The most important reason for developing these national policies was a determination to promote the domestic oil industry and encourage economic growth in Western Canada, even though it meant imposing higher direct costs on other parts of the country, and left the Government of Canada with little income from the petroleum industry. These policies have succeeded. The petroleum industry enjoys unprecedented prosperity and growth. No other industrial sector in Canada can match its vitality and outlook. The financial facts are striking. Net oil and gas production revenues in Canada have risen from $1.2 billion in 1970 to $11.1 billion in 1979. . . . the effect of the [OPEC] price increases is a massive transfer of wealth, now and in the future, from consumers

to producers. Most of these producers are foreign-owned; the wealth transfer is therefore away from Canadians.

Yet, the oil and gas industry, far from drawing in foreign capital, has—since the 1974 oil crisis—been a capital exporter. The industry, in addition to maintaining its normal dividend and interest payments, supported net capital outflows abroad of $2.1 billion in 1975-79. . . . If dividends and interest payments are added to this total, the total outflow over the period 1975–79 becomes approximately $3.7 billion. Dividends rose from $200 million a year in 1973 to $600 million in 1979. In addition, the foreign parents have received fees for technological, operating, and managerial services.

Moreover, the prospect is for these capital exports to grow. The continued increase in oil and gas prices that will occur means a further large foreign wealth transfer from Canadians to foreign shareholders. By ignoring the problem of foreign ownership in the past, Canadians have lost a significant share of the benefits of having a strong resource base. If we fail to act now, Canadians will lose once again.

Indeed, the loss may become permanent. Each year brings a further windfall gain to the foreign-owned firms. The value of these firms and, therefore, the cost to Canadians of securing control over them, has increased three- to four-fold—equivalent to tens of billions of dollars. A further delay will put the value of companies in the industry so high as to make the cost prohibitive, leaving Canada with no choice then but to accept a permanent foreign domination by these firms.

Reinforcing the impact of buoyant cash flow, the system of tax incentives inadvertently fostered concentration in the industry and, with it, foreign control. While the incentives have served the purpose of encouraging investment, they have not been available on the same basis, or to the same extent to all investors. For example, the Income Tax Act for many years allowed only firms whose "principle business" was resources to claim favourable write-off rates for petroleum exploration expenditures. Except in special situations, the Act permitted only investors with resource income to claim depletion allowances for such expenditures. The net result was to favour those who were already in the industry. Since these were predominantly foreign companies, the result unintentionally worked against Canadian ownership objectives.

Of the top twenty-five petroleum companies in Canada, seventeen are more than 50 percent foreign-owned and foreign-controlled, and these seventeen account for 72 percent of Canadian oil and gas sales. This is a degree of foreign participation that would not be accepted—indeed, simply is not tolerated—by most other oil-producing nations.

... foreign-controlled firms control the future through their control of the land in which exploration takes place. The frontier land permits are largely held by foreign-controlled companies.... Similarly, the existing oil sands plants are dominated by foreign-controlled firms.... The rapid growth that is inevitable for the energy sector in Canada over the next decade or two would strengthen further the position of these foreign oil companies, giving them even greater power in the Canadian economy than they have today.... Yet over that period, Canadian consumers and taxpayers would contribute the cash and provide the tax support for much of the investment made by these companies.[5]

The NEP then specified three goals which would rectify the problem of foreign domination:

- at least 50 percent Canadian ownership of oil and gas production by 1990;
- Canadian control of a significant number of the larger oil and gas firms;
- an early increase in the share of the oil and gas sector owned by the Government of Canada.[6]

The Multinationals: General and Individual Responses

As that element of the industry singled out for criticism in the NEP and whose dominance of the industry the Canadianization measures of the NEP were intended to challenge, the foreign-owned majors could be understood to have reacted angrily to the program. The federal government expected as much. Both as individual firms and as a group through the Canadian Petroleum Association (CPA), the foreign majors condemned virtually all aspects of the NEP. They charged that the restrained oil and gas price increases in combination with the increased taxes would make it impossible to achieve self-sufficiency by 1990 because the industry would not have the requisite capital to undertake the required exploration. While generally agreeing that security ought to be the chief objective of Canadian energy policy, the multinationals denounced the pricing and revenue-sharing aspects of both the NEP and the subsequent September 1981 Canada–Alberta Agreement, which, while it raised prices, also raised taxes.

While they did not criticize the concept of Canadianization, or the other objectives for that matter, the foreign majors as a whole condemned the instruments employed by the government to achieve

Canadianization. These firms vigorously denounced the 25 percent Crown interest as confiscatory and strongly criticized the Petroleum Incentive Program which would discriminate against them by providing larger incentive grants to Canadian firms. These companies pressured their home governments in the United States, Great Britain, and the Netherlands to apply pressure on the Canadian government to change the Canadianization, procurement, and other aspects of the NEP which favoured Canadian firms. The majors also utilized their position within the multilateral energy forum, the International Energy Agency, to criticize Canadian policy. Within Canada, they lobbied the Alberta government and the federal Conservatives to force the Liberals to make fundamental changes to the NEP. The key action which the majors employed both to signal their dissatisfaction with the NEP, especially its fiscal aspects, and to pressure the Liberals to alter the NEP was to slash, amid great fanfare, their planned exploration budgets for 1981.

While a number of the multinationals had indicated to the commission which Joe Clark had established to determine a way to privatize Petro-Canada that they were not opposed to having Petro-Canada around, virtually all of these companies opposed and attacked the Petro-Canada expansion called for in the NEP. Some firms, such as Imperial Oil, expressed doubt that the Canadian firms favoured by the NEP could succeed in the frontiers and the non-conventional plays. Yet, the foreign majors knew that despite the expenditure of millions of advertising dollars throughout the 1970s, they had a poor public image.[7] This was enhanced by the world price increases in 1979 and reflected in the NEP's polemical attack on them. In the immediate aftermath of the NEP the multinationals, through the CPA, commissioned a major public opinion survey to investigate public opinion on the industry, energy issues and the NEP. The study concluded that the multinationals had, at best, a mediocre public image and that the NEP and particularly Canadianization were popular. To counter this state of affairs, the CPA developed a $3 million advocacy advertising campaign to help improve the overall image of the industry. A number of the individual multinational firms also organized multi-million dollar advocacy advertising campaigns. The issue of the foreign majors' image escalated in importance after the highly publicized **State of Competition in the Canadian Petroleum Industry** report, in March

1981, charged them with ripping off Canadians by $12 billion (in 1981 dollars) between 1958 and 1973.[8]

When it became clear that the September 1981 Canada–Alberta Agreement would not provide the sorts of improvements in their fiscal arrangements that they had hoped for, the foreign majors responded by maintaining their exploration budget cutbacks. Arguing that they could not go ahead with the mega-projects given the inadequate returns that they could expect (specifically, less than a 20 percent discounted rate of return), Imperial Oil abandoned the Cold Lake heavy oil project in the fall of 1981, and Shell cancelled the Alsands project in April 1982. When it became apparent that the NEP would for the most part remain intact, a number of the foreign majors decided to hedge their bets and decrease their costs by farming out sections of the Canada Lands leases to Canadian-controlled firms eligible for PIP grants.

To develop a better understanding of the tenor of the multinationals' response, it is useful to investigate the reactions of some specific companies. It will not, however, be possible, nor necessary, to assess the reactions of all the foreign majors. Imperial Oil, Texaco, and Gulf are all integrated internationals, subsidiaries of members of the fabled "seven sisters" of the international industry, but all three also have strong roots and lengthy records in Canada. It is adequate to assess the nature of their reactions to the NEP to obtain an illustrative sense of the different corporate interests at stake. Other foreign majors such as Mobil, Chevron, and Shell are examined in more specific contexts in later chapters.

Imperial Oil
Imperial Oil is the largest oil company in Canada and has for decades been recognized as the industry leader. It is about 70 percent owned by the world's largest oil company, Exxon of the United States. In many respects Imperial was more restrained in its public reactions to the NEP than were other members of the industry. Throughout the 1970s, Imperial had become increasingly involved in non-conventional oil plays including Syncrude, of which it was the major partner. Indeed, Imperial is often criticized for having made a strategic error in writing off conventional exploration in the Western Sedimentary Basin too quickly and as a result missing out on some of the major late 1970s

conventional discoveries, such as Elmsworth, into which it later bought at considerable expense. Given its major stake in two of the key non-conventional plays, namely the Beaufort Sea and the Cold Lake heavy oil project, Imperial had stressed throughout the 1979–1980 period the importance of raising prices for oil and for pursuing oil self-sufficiency as the prime objective of Canadian energy policy. Both Cold Lake and the Beaufort were high-cost alternatives to conventional production, involved long lead times, and made sense economically only if Canadians were willing to pay high prices in order to be less dependent on imported oil. Thus, J.G. Livingstone, President of Imperial, stressed that, "the plain fact is there just isn't any cheap oil around anymore. Unless Canadians are willing to pay a realistic price for energy, we will not only fail to develop our indigenous resources, but our dependence upon foreign suppliers will grow more desperate each year."[9]

In one of his major reactions to the NEP, Livingstone focussed on the widely diverging views of the country's energy future represented by the NEP's projected supply–demand projections and those of the industry. He said that Imperial estimated that net oil imports, then running around 350 thousand barrels per day, could rise to 600 thousand barrels per day by the mid-1980s. His explanation for the disparity of views centred on differing expectations of industry performance under the NEP. "The federal government clearly believes that its program offers the industry sufficient inducement to enable it to develop new supplies in sufficient quantities and at sufficient speed to meet NEP projections. Equally obviously, a large portion of the industry does not share this opinion and therefore takes a different— and to its way of thinking, a more realistic—view of the situation."[10] Livingstone also used this dual focus on the non-conventional projects and the idea of self-sufficiency to criticize the Canadianization objectives of the NEP: "Unfortunately some—though certainly not all—of the companies who allegedly stand to benefit from the budget have not yet developed the expertise and resources necessary to tackle the really mammoth projects—in the oil sands, and in the Arctic and the Atlantic offshore—on which future self-sufficiency will depend to a major extent."[11]

Livingstone criticized the pricing, taxation, and incentive features of the NEP which, in his opinion, constrained an all-out effort to bring on additional supplies. While he applauded the "positive" directions of the NEP to encourage "conservation and the substitution of oil by other more available fuels," Livingstone argued that "at the same time we have to face the fact that we cannot conserve and substitute our way to self-sufficiency. Along with an all-out effort to conserve and substitute we must have a corresponding all-out effort to develop new supplies— with all speed from all possible sources."[12] Livingstone's "gravest reservation" about the NEP—and a theme he stressed on several occasions before September 1981—was that "by reducing industry cash flows and severely curtailing incentives to reinvestment, the program is bound to have a marked effect on the industry's ability to find and develop new petroleum supplies."[13] He particularly emphasized the PGRT which, he argued, had "hidden" impacts. "One hidden effect of the tax is that by reducing a company's producing revenues, it also reduces its ability to take advantage of tax credits related to resource revenue that could be ploughed into reinvestment."[14]

Imperial's emphasis on the fiscal regime is not surprising. Approval for Cold Lake and the Alsands tarsands project had been withheld by Alberta as part of its retaliation against the NEP. Imperial tried to influence the outcome of the post-NEP federal–Alberta negotiations by continuously arguing that unless the new oil pricing and taxation agreement provided a 20 percent discounted cash-flow return for Cold Lake, it would have to be abandoned. Imperial was aware that the NEP anticipated that the tarsands and heavy oil projects would make a contribution to Canadian oil supply by 1990, and therefore felt they were in a strong position to demand such a high return.

Imperial also reacted to the changed environment of energy politics represented by the NEP by upgrading its Ottawa office by assigning a company vice-president to act as the company representative. In March 1981, Imperial Oil took out full-page ads in thirty-seven daily newspapers across Canada to refute the allegations of the **State of Competition in the Canadian Petroleum Industry**.

On September 17, 1981 Livingstone responded that overall he was disappointed with the terms of the Canada–Alberta Agreement. He said that while the agreement had some positive elements—an agreement had been reached, the agreement brought some stability to the regulatory environment, the export tax on natural gas was effectively removed, and the pricing schedule for new oil was bound to encourage exploration—there were a number of very disappointing aspects to the agreement. Livingstone identified these as the high tax rate imposed on old oil through the PGRT increase and the incremental oil revenue tax, and the failure to improve industry cash flow on anything like the scale required. Livingstone's major concern was for the future of oil-sands development in light of the agreement. With respect to Cold Lake he stressed that

> under the pricing and tax regimes provided, including the restric-
> tions on tax credits, we can foresee about a 15 percent discounted
> cash flow return for the Cold Lake project. In our discussions with
> both the federal and Alberta governments we have consistently
> said that we would need to receive a 20 percent DCF before we could
> proceed with this high risk investment. Without some adjustment
> therefore, the terms of the new agreement do not appear to
> provide an adequate return to allow Cold Lake to be reactivated at
> this time. . . . I will hasten to add, however, that Imperial remains
> extremely anxious for Cold Lake to be reactivated and that all our
> efforts continue to be directed towards this end.[15]

In fact, in late 1983 Imperial Oil announced that it planned to reactivate the Cold Lake project, though on a much smaller scale. While Imperial cancelled the Cold Lake mega-project in late 1981, they largely maintained their exploration program in the Beaufort Sea. They farmed parts of their land holdings out to Canadian controlled firms eligible for high PIP grants, and built a new $150 million drilling system. As Chapter 11 shows in greater detail, in sponsoring this latter project Imperial adopted an approach which garnered it much good will in Ottawa. Imperial prepared its system design through Canadian design contractors. Then, at each subsequent contract stage, Imperial came to Ottawa and showed its requirements, went out of its way to obtain Canadian sources, and broke up its contracts into component parts rather than require one total package contract. It bought its own Canadian steel for the project, and shipbuilders bid knowing they had to use this steel. Canadian content in the construction phase is said to be over 70 percent, even though the caisson was actually built in Japan. Imperial was praised in Ottawa as being helpful and open. In addition to high Canadian content, more fundamental Canadian long-term benefits (technology transfer, improvement of capabilities in design, production, and management) are high was well. Imperial is also rated high by federal officials in maximizing northern participation (in employment, service, and contracts), as it did in the expansion of its Norman Wells, N.W.T. oil field, as well as its Beaufort Sea operation.

Texaco Canada

Texaco Canada is 91 percent owned by the U.S. parent. It had a reputation, in the immediate pre-NEP years, as being a highly conservative company, tightly controlled by its parent, which reinvested only a small percentage of its cash flow in Canada and did little frontier exploration while funneling most of its revenues to the parent company. Of all the fully integrated foreign majors, Texaco is identified as the one most like the "100 percenters" or "red phone" operations such as Mobil, Amoco, and Chevron, which are 100 percent owned by and tightly controlled from head office in the United States.

Not surprisingly, given the company's extremely high level of foreign ownership and its limited autonomy over decision making, Texaco Canada's opposition to the Canadianization measures of the NEP were central to its response. Although Texaco never criticized the principle of Canadianization, they were very critical of the government's chosen methods. In particular, Texaco focussed its attack on the government acquisitions and the PIP grants. Texaco consistently indicted the NEP as being excessive. In the wake of the Petro-Canada acquisition of Petrofina, Texaco charged that "the NEP is clearly excessive. . . . there is no need for more government control of the oil industry. . . . governments already hold all the levers of power that determine the supply, distribution, and pricing of oil and gas in this country."[16] Texaco consistently labeled the Canadianization measures as arbitrary and discriminatory. In his remarks to the April 1981 annual meeting of Texaco shareholders, R.W. Sparks, Chairman of the Board and Chief Executive Officer spoke of the misguided priorities of the government which led it to impose a system of discriminatory incentive grants for exploration. He was perhaps even more concerned however, that "government takeover of an established efficient affiliate of an international company does not give Canada more oil. It only turns more private industry over to the state, and sends out of this country billions of Canadian dollars that are needed for investment here."[17]

By September 1981, the emphasis in Texaco statements began to shift away from worries of government takeovers and shift towards worries about the system of "discriminatory incentive grants." This shift may have been a result of the fact that the enabling legislation for the PIP grants was awkwardly making its way through the House of Commons, first in the form of C-94, the omnibus Energy Security Act, and later as Bill C-104. Texaco's presentation to the House of Commons Standing Committee on Energy Legislation argued that "with the requirement for 50 percent Canadian participation in productive Canada Lands already assured by the Canada Oil and Gas Act, there is no need for further discriminatory measures based on the degree of Canadian ownership, as proposed in Bill C-104."[18] Texaco further argued, at some length, that the discriminatory measure of Bill C-104 would be counterproductive to the primary NEP objective of oil self-sufficiency. In its public criticism of Canadianization, Texaco, despite being 91 percent U.S. owned, stressed the Canadian origins of the Company which "goes back 108 years—to the era of the Fathers of Confederation. We intend to remain here for a long time to come, and with your continued support we will continue to grow, to prosper and to serve Canadians across the length and breadth of this great land."[19]

Texaco tended to deal with the Crown interest provisions of Bill C-48 separately from the Canadianization measures. On March 12, 1981, in the company's opening statement to the Standing Committee on National Resources and Public Works which, at that time, was hearing testimony on Bill C-48, Texaco argued that the forfeiture of the 25 percent interest disregarded the circumstances under which the interest had been acquired and disregarded the holders' efforts to evaluate that interest by risky, expensive means. The company statement said that

> it has been stated that the forfeiture of 25 percent to the Crown is justified because the Canadian taxpayer by way of tax deductions granted to the industry, actually footed the bill for a substantial part of the $5 billion spent on Canada Lands. The tax deductions were provided by the government as an incentive, and indeed these incentives formed an integral part of the decision making process of industry to make the high-risk investment necessary to explore Canada Lands. We are most concerned over the frightening realization that the Federal Government now proposes to penalize those who responded positively to its policy. Texaco, in good faith,

made significant investments in response to the economic ground rules in effect and it should not have to retroactively give up 25 percent of its interest in Canada Lands. . . . If Government policy dictates that a 25 percent interest must be retained by the Crown, such policy should apply only to future Crown dispositions and the interest should be on a participating basis.[20]

This line of reasoning would be repeated in future executive speeches and presentations. The company had made investments in good faith and now the government was ready to change the rules of the game and *confiscate* existing rights retroactively and without compensation: "The [back-in] measure is unfair to any company which invested large sums of money . . . took the risks . . . did the work, then found the ground rules changed. If this back-in provision were to apply only for new exploration on federal lands, that would be one thing; but making it retroactive is simply unfair."[21]

With respect to the fiscal implications of the NEP, there was a shift in emphasis in the company's statements after September 1981. In April 1981, Texaco Canada's president, Roland Routhier, had listed the four most objectionable measures of the NEP: the PGRT; the back-in privilege; the withdrawal of depletion allowances; and the Canadian-ization measures. But by March 1982 the Canada–Alberta fiscal regime was identified as the major problem while the back-in provision had been relegated to a list of "other regressive measures." Texaco had calculated that the 8 percent PGRT would actually reduce cash flow at the wellhead by approximately 25 per cent because government royalties were not deductible in determining the levy and the levy was not deductible for income tax purposes. Like other companies, Texaco Canada had hoped that their cash flow position would be improved as a result of the September 1981 Agreement.

Because they felt this did not happen, Texaco's argument against the PGRT was broadened to embrace the entire fiscal regime created by the Energy Agreement. Focussing on the cash-flow problems facing the industry, Texaco Canada's Annual Report for 1981 stated:

> The larger companies such as Texaco Canada . . . must be allowed to generate and retain enough cash flow to be able to invest in an all-out drive that is necessary to find and develop sufficient new domestic oil reserves . . . The inadequate return for "old oil" results primarily from the combination of heavy provincial royalties and

taxes and the federally imposed Petroleum and Gas Revenue Tax, which is currently set at 16 percent. These royalties and taxes are not deductible for the determination of taxable income and are only partially offset by "resource allowances" which were introduced in lieu of deductibility. Consequently, substantial portions of the revenues of Texaco Canada and other oil companies are subject to the onerous burden of double taxation.[22]

Texaco Canada's position over the entire 1981–1984 period was, however, quite healthy financially. This was in part because, between 1978 and 1982, Texaco Canada spent only about 8.7% of cash flow on exploration compared to over 23% by the other multinationals.[23] Moreover, by 1984 Texaco Canada was becoming a gas-rich but oil-vulnerable company. Only in 1983 did Texaco begin to increase its level of exploration activity. This included a joint venture with Sun Life Assurance Co. of Canada and Atco Ltd. to form ATS Exploration Ltd. to increase activity on the frontiers.

In conclusion, then, a review of Texaco Canada's position on the NEP reveals a shift in emphasis and content over time. Between October 1980 and the signing of the Canada–Alberta Energy Agreement in September 1981, relatively less criticism was directed at the fiscal regime than at the Canadianization measures and, in particular, the back-in provisions of Bill C-48. After September 1981, the company's criticism was directed at the effects of the PGRT on the company cash flows (especially when the PGRT was taken together with provincial royalties and the pricing arrangements for old oil) and at the discriminatory features of the proposed Petroleum Incentives Program. It was the most reluctant of the three foreign majors examined here to engage in frontier exploration in the post-NEP period.

Gulf Canada

Two consistent themes of Gulf's statements on the NEP were that the government had placed its objectives in the wrong order of priority and that the government had failed to provide the necessary measures to achieve the desired first objective of self-sufficiency. In February 1981, Gulf stated that they interpreted Ottawa's broad energy policy objectives, in order of priority, to be:

1. Fifty percent Canadian ownership and control by 1990;
2. Equitable and effective energy revenue sharing arrangements;
3. Economic growth through energy development;
4. Oil self-sufficiency for Canada by 1990.

Gulf claimed to have "no disagreement with these objectives in their broadest sense," though they argued that "our analysis of the impact of the NEP . . . shows that the program places these objectives in the wrong order of priority."[24] In Gulf's view, the proper order of importance was the reverse of the above list.

In his December 1980 speech, John Stoik, President of Gulf Canada, acknowledged that the NEP contained some positive aspects, such as the idea of encouraging the use of Canada's natural gas or coal in order to reduce imports of costly and insecure oil; measures designed to reduce energy consumption; measures to increase oil supply, such as the incentive price for tertiary oil; and the $38 per barrel price offered for production from the oil sands. Subsequent to December of 1980, however, there would be few words of praise for any aspects of the NEP.

Stoik's criticisms of the NEP in December 1980 were wide ranging:

- To the extent to which energy tax revenues would be recycled into the energy sector, they would be applied mainly to conservation measures and would therefore do little to promote new sources of supply.

- The increase in the federal revenue share would be taken almost entirely from the industry revenue share.

- The only significant incentives provided for exploration were in the frontiers, on Canada Lands. But the new grants would be heavily biased against the multinational affiliates who had done the most to establish Canada's frontier potential.

- Frontier exploration would continue to qualify for the 33⅓ percent depletion allowance and companies would be eligible to apply for incentive grants of up to 25 percent of exploration costs. However, in the case of companies not classed as "Canadian," the incentive payments would be nullified by the requirement to carry the cost of the new 25 percent back-in. Furthermore, the proposed incentive payments would be taxable.

• There would, under the NEP fiscal regime, be a reduction of cash flows for even Canadian companies.

• The withdrawal of earned depletion on all development work could jeopardize the viability of some frontier projects, since development programs were predicted to be in the order of ten times as costly as the exploration phase.

• The problem with Petro-Canada or other government agencies buying out multinational affiliates would be that a lot of money would go out of the country, while not one barrel of oil or cubic foot of natural gas would be added to Canada's reserves.[25]

In his first speech on the NEP, Stoik announced Gulf's investment cutbacks. He said that Gulf estimated its reduced cash flow as a result of the NEP to be about 30 percent. He said that "after a month of intensive study, we have come to the conclusion that we will have no alternative but to reduce our spending plans for this period [five years] by 15 percent or $900 million."[26] Stoik also made it clear that if the NEP were revised or if new negotiated settlements satisfactory to Gulf could be arrived at with the provinces, "we are prepared to reinstate spending to the limit of the additional cash that will be available to us."[27] Indeed, during the period from December 1980 to September 1981, Gulf appeared to assume that the fiscal regime would be altered in the federal–Alberta negotiations in favour of the industry. The company therefore concentrated its efforts on lobbying for an acceptable fiscal regime rather than criticising specific pricing or taxation features of the NEP. Thus Gulf, like most other companies, was disappointed with the results of the September 1, 1981 Canada–Alberta Agreement:

We said [in December of 1980] that we were prepared to reinstate spending to the limit of additional cash made available to us through revisions to NEP or through agreements to be negotiated between Ottawa and the producing provinces. But last September, when the producing provinces and Ottawa signed the oil and gas pricing and taxation agreements, it was the signal to the industry that *the door was closed.* The federal–provincial agreements further reduced cash flow in the early years of those agreements; but I still hope for relaxation of some of the National Energy Program's most onerous provisions.[28]

While Gulf's reaction to the NEP's pricing and taxation proposals was relatively subdued between October 1980 and September 1981, its criticism of the government's approach to Canadianization of the industry was loud. In December 1980 Stoik observed that: "As a Canadian, I can understand the government's desire to see increased Canadian content in the industry. But when we examine the very rapid growth of the Canadian sector over the past few years, we seriously question whether the discriminatory and confiscatory measures contained in the new policies are justified."[29] He argued that by the end of 1979 Canadian control of industry assets had already reached 34 percent and, if this trend had continued for just two more years, then the government's original objective of 50 percent of the industry assets by 1990 would have been achieved in 1981. However, added Stoik: "In view of this trend, it is not surprising that the government, in August, suddenly abandoned its previous objective of having 50 percent of the *assets* in Canadian hands by 1990, and changed it to 50 percent of the *production revenues*—72 percent of which it claims are still going to multinational affiliates."[30] Stoik felt that since a company has no control over who buys its shares, a preferable approach to Canadianization would have been for the government to create incentives for Canadians to buy and hold industry shares: "Governments already have complete control over the industry, so the focus should be on increasing Canadian equity ownership, which would keep more of the dividends in Canada."[31]

Stoik's stress on government incentives to encourage Canadians to buy and hold oil and gas industry shares must be understood in light of Gulf's secondary share offering which had been made in the spring of 1980. At that time the parent company of Gulf Canada, Gulf Corporation, had acquired Amalgamated Bonanza Ltd. This acquisition had been paid for with Gulf Canada shares. Also at that time, a five-for-one stock split of Gulf Canada shares, together with a Gulf Canada secondary offering, had increased the float of stock available to the general public by almost 40 percent. These events allowed Gulf Corporation's holdings in Gulf Canada to be reduced by approximately 8 percent to 60.2 percent. Commenting on this opportunity for Canadians to buy into Gulf Canada in the spring of 1980, Stoik stated in his December 1980 speech that: "As you know, Gulf Oil Corporation reduced its interest in our company by about 8 percent during the past year. We were hoping this would result in a significant increase in our Canadian ownership, but foreign investor enthusiasm for our future prospects was such that our Canadian ownership increased by only one percent, to about 21 percent."[32] In future public statements, especially during the spring of 1981, Gulf would use the 1980 secondary offering as an example of: ". . . reasonable, logical movement toward increased Canadianization,"[33] that would have succeeded if only the government had provided sufficient tax incentives to Canadians.

Gulf's criticism of the NEP pricing and taxation regime was subdued until after the Canada–Alberta Agreement. The Canadianization measures and the back-in provision of bill C-48 were, however, consistently attacked by Gulf's public statements. "[The government's] line of reasoning does not answer the basic unfairness of retroactively changing the rules and taking assets found in good faith under previous agreements. In our case, a 25 percent back-in on successful frontier discoveries would far exceed the value of any incentives we have received, and whatever compensation we will eventually get under the revised regulations."[34]

While many of the foreign majors downplayed the Bertrand Report and chose not to highlight it in their 1981 annual shareholder's meeting, noting that an inquiry was underway which would in the end exonerate the industry, Gulf's J.C. Phillips, Chairman of the Board, devoted his entire speech to refuting "many of the irresponsible allegations which it contains. . . ." Phillips made three main points in his speech. First he argued that the high prices charged consumers by the majors as compared to those charged by the independents merely reflected the additional services being provided by the majors to the consumer: "People were not just looking for gasoline—which was the only product most of the small independents provided. They also wanted convenience, accessibility, and a range of services. Prices that provided this complete range of services just had to be higher than prices that delivered only gasoline." Second, Phillips allowed that overbuilding of service stations had occurred in the 1950s in response to the demand of a rapidly expanding car-driving public, but also noted that consolidation and conversion of retail outlets followed: ". . . a classic example of market forces dictating correction." Finally, Phillips rejected the charge that consumers were overcharged as a result of paying unnecessarily high prices for foreign crude between 1958 and 1973. The underlying assumption behind the latter allegation, said Phillips, was that all companies should have been buying crude oil on the spot market which, in the period under review, was frequently below the official price. Phillips stated that such an assumption overlooks the fact that no responsible firm would build a multi-million dollar refinery without assurance of continuous feedstock supply at reasonably predictable cost—predictability that was not available when purchasing crude on the spot market.[35]

Despite its extensive criticism of the NEP, Gulf maintained its commitment to its major Beaufort Sea exploration program. In a series of negotiations between mid-1980 and the end of 1983, with the federal government over the approval of its radical new drilling system and its exploration agreements, Gulf developed a reputation throughout the COGLA–OIRB network as a difficult project sponsor which gave inadequate regard to maximizing Canadian content and industrial benefits. Gulf was criticized for not giving Canadian firms adequate time to bid for contracts, for not providing complete information on performance requirements, and for "designing out" Canadian equipment. Only after the application of power at the top through a series of meetings between the Minister of Industry, Trade and Commerce and the President of Gulf was Gulf brought around to giving Canadian companies full and fair opportunity. During this same period, Gulf ran a series of full-page newspaper advertisements stressing the Canadian roots of its executives and the benefits to Canadian businesses all across Canada of Gulf's procurement policy, right down to listing the local cafés frequented by Gulf employees in prairie oil towns. It is now estimated that after all the government arm twisting, Canadian content in the massive, nearly $700 million drilling system is about 50 percent.

Gulf later tried to depreciate the $700 million drilling equipment over three years. This escalated the cost per well and was widely regarded as an attempt by Gulf to exploit the PIP grant system. The upshot of this escalated cost would be higher PIP grants from the federal treasury. Gulf Canada's Canadian partner, Canterra Energy Ltd., a subsidiary of the half federally owned Canadian Development

Corporation, objected to the use of the equipment and its cost and eventually withdrew from some segments of the project for this and other reasons.

Early in 1984 the fate of Gulf Canada in the post-NEP era took on a new potential twist when Gulf Corporation, its U.S. parent, was bought by the Standard Oil Company of California (SOCAL).[36] This greatly increased the probability that Gulf Canada's assets would be sold, both to help SOCAL pay for the takeover and to assuage U.S. anti-trust regulators.

For the foreign majors, as a whole, there is no doubt that the first two post-NEP years, in combination with their own tactical responses as well as other important factors such as the recession and the permanent effects of conservation and off-oil incentives, produced reduced earnings.[37] Imperial Oil reported a doubling of taxes from $1.1 billion in 1980 to over $2 billion in 1982 with earnings decreasing about 52% over the same period. Texaco reported a 13% decrease from 1981 to 1982 and Gulf Canada and Shell Canada were down by 32.7% and 43.6% respectively in the same period. Most of the majors, however, attributed the strong decline primarily to what were increasingly regarded as permanent reductions in the level of downstream sales. This led to the closing of seven refineries, and paralleled twenty-seven such closings in the United States and twenty-eight in Europe. It also meant significant staff cuts, including 1200 at Gulf Canada and 800 at Imperial.

These overall effects must be put in some context. The majors also benefited from the PIP grants, especially since many of the PIP funds flowed indirectly to the multinationals via farm-ins with Canadian firms. Second, it must be remembered that the multinationals still have the best capacity to plan "for the long haul." They operate on ten- and fifteen-year time frames and so were well suited to wait patiently for a new government or new policies more suitable to their interests. We examine the multinationals' overall position as a result of the NEP in greater detail in Chapters 9, 10, and 11.

The Canadian Majors: General and Individual Responses

Even though Petro-Canada and the two private sector majors Dome and Nova were among the most sanguine voices in the industry on the Canadianization issue, they quite naturally shared with the rest of the industry opposition to the pricing and taxation features of the NEP. For example, Dome's chairman, Jack Gallagher, and president, Bill Richards, told their shareholders in April 1981 that

> there are a number of negative factors in the National Energy Program including the wellhead revenue tax and excise tax on natural gas and natural gas liquids. These new taxes will affect the cash flows of all oil companies operating in Canada. It is hoped that current provincial and federal government negotiations will result in a modification of these new taxes or a reduction of royalty or an increase in price, or a combination of these so that the producer's share will be increased sufficiently to encourage a major exploration effort.[38]

Indeed, in a less prosaic moment, Bill Richards labeled the NEP as "confiscation without compensation." Dome was, in particular, not pleased with most of the changes destined for the Canada Lands. Dome was one of the leading frontier explorers and had, via super-depletion allowances and other arrangements, managed to couch its operation in a very favourable fiscal policy blanket. The changes to the royalty system, the Crown interest and the shifts in the incentive system, all directly affected Dome. Nova's operations were confined to the western basin in 1980 and it too argued the inadequacy of the price rises and the onerous combined federal–provincial tax take. It was marginally happier with the outcome of the 1981 Canada–Alberta Agreement. Petro-Canada, as an oil company, would also have preferred higher prices and lower taxes, but found itself, by the very nature of its lineage and favoured status, defending, or at least "explaining," the pricing, taxation, and other aspects of the NEP.

The NEP, by providing higher incentive grants for Canadian firms, by encouraging the acquisition of foreign-owned firms, and by requiring a minimum of 50 percent Canadian ownership on projects on the Canada Lands, had included specific measures to move the industry toward the objective of 50 percent Canadian ownership by 1990. While the chief executives of these three firms, Bob Blair, Jack Gallagher, and William Hopper had all called for greater Canadianization of the industry in the past, they and their companies had mixed feelings about the instruments chosen to achieve the objective. Dome and Petro-Canada's reactions were the most celebrated. Dome created Dome-Canada, retained 48 percent ownership and offered the other 52 percent to Canadians via a share offering. It also purchased a large foreign-owned firm, Hudson's Bay Oil and Gas, from Conoco. Petro-Canada purchased Belgian-owned Petrofina for $1.45 billion and the refining and marketing assets of BP Canada for $347.6 million. Nova had in 1979 made a significant purchase of the foreign-owned firm Husky Oil, which in turn made a smaller acquisition in the post-NEP era of Uno-Tex Petroleum for $371 million. Nova did, however, become far more active in the Canada Lands as a result of the NEP incentives.

Nova

In Nova's **1980 Annual Report** the company stated that under the National Energy Program:

- The price of oil to consumers in Canada and the netbacks being offered to producers in various producing arenas are both too low to allow the domestic balancing of supply and demand by the early 1990's.

- Primary production of many heavy oil wells under the existing royalty structure in Saskatchewan, combined with the new federal taxes and pricing, cannot recover basic costs, and other wells are not generating sufficient cash flow to support routine maintenance requirements.

- The combined impact of current tax, royalty and pricing provisions for tertiary and enhanced heavy oil production does not encourage such production to meet previous expectations.[39]

In February 1981, Robert Blair stated that the Nova group of companies had not yet changed its investment plans as a result of the National Energy Program. Apparently, Nova did not revise its investment plans because the company anticipated significant changes in the NEP's fiscal regime: "Back in October 1980 when the National Energy Program was outlined, the NOVA group of companies reviewed the documents carefully and with our customary optimism. Our thoughts were also tempered because we knew that the National Energy Program was developed in anticipation of stiff provincial opposition so that there were likely components that would 'give way' so to speak during Federal/Provincial negotiations."[40] However, by February 1981, Blair observed that: "It is growing apparent however that the flexibility we thought would exist, which would include some fundamental aspects of the National Energy Program, has not been shown."[41]

During the first half of 1981, Blair argued that a large increase in the price of domestic oil was essential for three reasons: (1) to assure producers of adequate netbacks (2) to encourage substitution to gas and (3) to provide more room for negotiation between federal and provincial governments. This last reason was stressed repeatedly by Blair in his public statements. For example, in his message to shareholders in March 1981, Blair stated:

> . . . I suggested in January that if there were an increase instantly, or with a few months' forewarning, of $10 per barrel in the Canadian oil price, coupled with an instant start of gas-for-oil substitution, the overall effect on the Canadian economy would be a plus.
>
> . . . I do not suggest the $10 increase to make oil companies richer, but to give the situation more room for negotiation. If ever and wherever petroleum producing companies start making much more than they need to develop next year's supply, or more than society trusts them to hold in their possession as a matter of public concern, then set the tax rates accordingly and let them work with the balance. What a private sector petroleum company needs is enough net price, after royalty and tax, to justify its new investments on the expectation of making a return reasonable to the associated risk.[42]

The new pricing schedule of September 1981 was regarded by Blair as providing an "excellent incentive right now to find and produce new light oil" in Alberta; especially when the NORP price was combined with the NEP update changes and the Alberta government royalty initiatives.[43] It should be noted that by September of 1981 Nova was in a good position to take advantage of the NORP. In August of that same year Husky Oil had purchased Uno-Tex for $371 million. Whereas Husky had previously been confined in Canada primarily to heavy oil extraction, it now possessed, as we see later in the chapter, a vehicle for expanding its activities in conventional oil production.

In June 1979 Nova, then AGTL, acquired a controlling interest in the foreign-controlled Husky Oil, in the process snatching Husky from Petro-Canada's grasp. This acquisition represented not only a major enlargement of the company's range of activities, but also represented a major change in main revenue sources for the company. In 1975 gas transmission had accounted for 90 percent of AGTL's net operating income. By 1979 gas transmission contributed only 46 percent, while petroleum contributed 40 percent. Petrochemicals and manufacturing accounted for the residual. In keeping with the newly diversified base of the company, AGTL changed its name to Nova, an Alberta Corporation in August of 1980. With respect to the name change, Nova's 1980 Annual Report noted that

> it is important to note that while NOVA is proud of its ability to change and diversify, its Board wanted to be sure the Alberta base of the Company continued to be emphasized. It is as true as ever that by far the majority of NOVA's assets are located in Alberta as are its permanent headquarters and most of its employees and offices.[44]

On the subject of Canadianization, Bob Blair stated that while "I have been counted among those who maintain that it will be better when there is more resident ownership, full management, professional and expert authority and technical investigation at all levels in the petroleum industry in Canada . . . I would not be prepared at all to be counted on the side of any who argue that petroleum companies who are not majority owned or substantially owned by Canadians, should get out of Canada or become scorned as operators."[45]

One of the Canadianization elements of the NEP is the COR/PIP regime. In November of 1980, Blair observed that the PIP grants would only help Husky if the company was able to shift from more development to exploration commitments and from provincial to federal lands. Blair had no criticism to make of the shift from tax-based incentives to the PIP direct-grant system. As we have previously seen, Husky was able to make the shift from production to exploration through its acquisition of Uno-Tex. By 1982 Husky was also investigating possibilities for frontier participation. Blair noted in a January 27, 1982 speech to a Financial Analysts seminar in Calgary that

> we . . . have good reason to expect that throughout 1982 and 1983 Husky will emerge as one of the half dozen leading investor vehicles for exploration off the east coast of Canada and with some participation in the Canadian Arctic. . . . A shortage of semi-submersible vessels is anticipated, and we believe has provided Husky/Bow Valley the opportunity to put ourselves forward to the federal and provincial governments having jurisdiction and desiring exploration action and to the major companies who have

the main land spreads, as business-like participants who will bring the indicated contribution of Canadian Ownership Rating and a special element of Canadian content to the provision of equipment and services.[46]

Although Nova was able to take advantage of PIP, it felt that in some respects the program went too far. In September of 1982, Blair criticized the complexity and intensity of Canadian Ownership Rating under the NEP:

> The general point of some greater incentive to domestically controlled companies is supportable. But this rigorous inquisition on the exact degree of Canadian ownership is inefficient and even more important is insulting by its exact comparisons to some excellent corporations in Canada who do everything else right, but just do not happen to maintain a high level of Canadian ownership. For some, their rating stays low because one foreign parent maintains a control block, for others just because more non-resident than resident individuals have chosen them for investment through the stock markets. Anyhow, the rating process did not need to be turned into such an elaborate degree-of-citizenship comparison.[47]

While Nova did not extensively comment on the 25 percent Crown interest on Canada Lands, it did consistently voice concern over the "public ownership" thrust of the NEP, feeling it had been unduly stressed in the original NEP document. In September of 1982, Blair would wax reflective to Ottawa to

> back away from some of the factors in the National Energy Plan which have caused the greatest upset, starting with the "retroactive" back-in provision. I understand that the provision was not expected to be seen as badly discriminatory, but it certainly is so perceived. In principle, it was not anti-foreign, but practically it affected foreign companies mainly. Whatever the merits of professionals' arguments about 25 percent back-in matching 25 percent incentive payments, I think that the foreign perception of unfairness should be acknowledged by this time, and some other tax technique substituted. Any sign of a government acting retroactively as to a right of ownership can be serious in shaking confidence of an industry.[48]

Nevertheless, Nova moved aggressively into the east-coast offshore play, building drilling rigs in partnership with Husky and Bow

Valley and operating them primarily in the Nova Scotia area. Although Nova was on balance a supporter of the NEP, it was by no means all smooth sailing between 1981 and 1984. This will be more evident when we review the Husky and Bow Valley links below, but it was also present, as Chapter 4 noted briefly, in the overall financial status of the company. In February 1984, for example, Nova revealed that it would write its assets down by about $120 million. The writedown was due to the development costs incurred on the long-delayed northern section of the Alaska Highway Gas Pipeline. Some interpreted the writedown as an admission that the pipeline would never be built.[49]

Dome

Reflecting its major potential role as a key frontier producer, Dome took particular exception to the NEP's adjustment of the Progressive Incremental Royalty on Canada Lands. On Canada Lands the government royalty consists of a basic royalty of 10 percent of the value of production, plus 40 percent of "net profit" implemented according to a Progressive Incremental Royalty (PIR) scheme, plus the Petroleum and Gas Revenue Tax, plus an income tax on the remainder. PIR is designed to levy a royalty only to the extent of net annual profit in excess of a 25 percent floor rate of return. The PIR had been in place prior to the announcement of the NEP. Between 1975 and 1977, industry and the federal government had discussed a number of possible amendments to the PIR for discoveries made on Canada Lands. Following these discussions, Bill C-20 was drafted, which provided for a three-year PIR exemption for discoveries made on Canada Lands before December 31, 1982. However, Bill C-20 was never passed and Bill C-48 reduced the previously proposed three-year holiday to any discovery made prior to December 31, 1980. Therefore, Bill Richards told the House of Commons Committee on National Resources and Public Works that

> our programs designed to take advantage of these opportunities are already scheduled for three years hence. Consequently, we have already taken commitments in the expectation that the PIR holiday would be provided for in Bill C-20, and consequently we feel again that this is the reduction of a right which we felt we had already received. We feel that the substantial unexpected changes in the

fiscal regime tend to be damaging to the financeability of these
[energy] projects, tend to be detrimental to Canada's reputation as
a stable country with sound policies.[50]

In April 1981, Dome Petroleum requested the government to amend
the PIR exemption in Bill C-48 to take into account the "understanding
with government as stated in Bill C-20."

Dome Petroleum is the largest natural gas liquids producer and
marketer in Canada. This foremost position is well illustrated by
Dome's 20 percent participation in the Arctic Pilot Project, the Cochin
Pipeline, and by Dome's proposed $4 billion LNG export facility on
British Columbia's northwest coast. As previously mentioned, Dome
had hoped the natural gas tax would be modified in the federal–provincial negotiations during 1981. However, despite the fact
that the agreement of September 1981 reduced the export tax on
natural gas to zero, Dome still argued that further tax relief and pricing
measures were needed if the "critical cash flow shortage facing gas
producers was to be alleviated."[51]

Along with the September 1981 gas taxation and pricing
measures, Dome also listed the statement on gas marketing, contained
in the accord, as being unsatisfactory. The Alberta–Ottawa accord
stated that: "If the National Energy Board determines that there is an
exportable surplus, it is the intention of the Government of Canada to
authorize additional exports."[52] Dome's Senior Vice-President John
Beddome responded: "Although this offers a clear promise of
improved sales via increased exports the real issue lies in answering
the question of whether in fact there is an exportable surplus. Our
industry has long felt that this very surplus exists and we must get on
with the task of moving this gas."[53] Dome's continuing campaign for
greater gas exports was carried on throughout 1982. For example, in
December 1982, Dome's president, Bill Richards, argued that the
"development of export markets provides the economic justification
for the exploration necessary to provide Canada with a secure supply of
natural gas." Richards added the caveat: "We don't, of course, intend to
pursue export sales without developing the domestic market as fully as
is practical."[54] Thus Richards took a position compatible with that of
the NEP Update of May 1982.

Dome Petroleum did not find the fiscal regime of the NEP or
subsequent energy accords completely satisfactory. While Dome did

state that the NORP of the Alberta–Ottawa accord would provide significant new incentives for the exploration of provincial lands,[55] it also felt that the taxation burden on industry, particularly on that industry segment committed to the frontiers, was onerous. In October 1982, Jack Gallagher stated: "We suggest that some of the more prolific fields in the frontier areas can stand the original base royalty of 10 percent plus PIR and the income tax, but to my knowledge, there are no oil fields that have been found in the frontier areas to date that are economic to develop with the additional PGRT tax and the 25 percent retroactive back-in by the federal government."[56]

Dome clearly had the highest profile response to the Canadianization objective with its creation of Dome Canada and its acquisition of Hudson Bay Oil and Gas (HBOG).[57] While the PIP ownership levels for maximum grants were later reduced to a lower level, as stated in the NEP they required that firms be 75 percent owned and controlled by Canadians to be eligible for the maximum PIP grants. Despite its Canadian roots and management, Dome Petroleum was about 65 percent foreign owned. During November and December 1980 and January 1981, Dome's management discussed the effect of the new incentive regime on Dome's Beaufort operations with federal government representatives. In the last week of January 1981, Jack Gallagher and Marc Lalonde held a joint news-conference in Calgary at which Dome announced the creation of a new Dome subsidiary, Dome Canada. A public offering of Dome Canada shares was made, constrained to Canadian individuals and institutions. This offering represented a 52 percent interest in the new company. Dome Petroleum would take up the remaining 48 percent through a cash purchase of stock and the transfer of some of its Trans-Canada Pipeline shares (Trans-Canada was a subsidiary of Dome Petroleum) to the new Dome Canada.

An agreement was entered into between Dome Canada and Dome Petroleum which allowed Dome Canada to earn a 50 percent interest in Dome Petroleum's provincial lands in return for Dome Canada's paying all exploration costs. On Dome Petroleum's Canada Lands, Dome Canada would be eligible to earn between a 10 percent and 50 percent interest in return for paying all exploration costs. Because Dome Canada would be over 75 percent owned by Canadians, the company would be eligible for the maximum PIP grants. In addition, the transfer of Trans-Canada shares to Dome Canada increased the

Canadian ownership rating of Trans-Canada to the extent that it was eligible for maximum PIP grants.

As part of the Dome Canada–Dome Petroleum agreement, and as a further public commitment to Ottawa's Canadianization goals, Dome Petroleum announced its intention to raise its own Canadian Ownership Rate per the following schedule:

35 percent by December 1982
40 percent by December 1983
45 percent by December 1984
50 percent by December 1985
60 percent by December 1990[58]

This commitment was related to yet another component of the same agreement which allowed Dome Petroleum an option to purchase up to 55 percent of Dome Canada's shares (up from Dome Petroleum's original interest of 48 percent) within six years. If Dome Petroleum wished to exercise this option and still have Dome Canada retain full government PIP grants, then Dome Petroleum would have to increase its Canadian Ownership Rating.

In Dome Petroleum's **1980 Annual Report** the company stated that the creation of Dome Canada, together with its own commitment to increasing levels of Canadian ownership, should be regarded as a "positive response to the Federal Government's policy to encourage increased Canadian ownership of the oil and gas industry."[59] A fuller explanation for the establishment of Dome Canada, and one perhaps less directly related to Dome's good will towards the federal government, was provided by Dome's president, Bill Richards, in April 1981. Richards told the House of Commons' Committee on National Resources and Public Works (conducting hearings on Bill C-48) that

> immediately following the introduction of the National Energy Program, we in Dome found ourselves, so to speak, off-side; that is to say that we had a Canadian ownership rating of substantially under 75 percent and we had no reasonable expectation of being able to increase our Canadian ownership rating, in any reasonable period of time, to that rate. We found ourselves, therefore, in an extremely difficult position. We had plans for the commitment of approximately $400 million in capital expenditures by the end of 1981, in order to keep our planned schedule to be on stream by the end of 1986.

With no availability of the substantial incentives that were offered by the National Energy Program, our program was in deep difficulties. To respond to the initiative taken by the Government of Canada, we formed a company, Dome Canada Limited. . . .[60]

The HBOG acquisition involved the purchase of 53 percent of the shares from the American oil company Conoco for $1.8 billion in June 1981, and the follow-up acquisition of the remainder a few months later. The later part was necessary to allow Dome access to HBOG's cash flow. Altogether the deal cost Dome $4 billion, and together with high interest rates and softening gas markets contributed to Dome's debt management problems.

Dome appeared also to have mixed feelings regarding the incentive grants scheme as opposed to the previous tax-based incentives or other incentive options open to the government in 1980. Dome's 1980 Annual Report did state: "The Company has endeavored to take advantage of the positive features in the National Energy Program, specifically the exploration incentives in both Federal and Provincial areas . . ."[61] However, in January 1981, Jack Gallagher told the Toronto Board of Trade that interest-free federal loans, repayable out of production, "would have a better chance of political survival" than the PIP grants.[62] The concern voiced by Gallagher in January of 1981—on the political vulnerability of PIP—became of greater importance as the company's debt position worsened during 1981 and 1982.

Dome had banked heavily on the PIP grants and was owed $130 million for its 1981 exploration activity, with even higher sums payable for 1982. Suffering under a heavy debt load and inadequate cash flow, Dome was naturally anxious about the long delays in the passage of PIP legislation in the Commons. In his spring 1982 appearance before the House energy legislation committee, Bill Richards strongly urged the members to expedite passage of Bill C-104, the PIP grant legislation.

Dome opposed the 25 percent back-in provisions contained in Bill C-48. The company argued that as a result of industry representations to government during 1976 and 1977, an agreement had been arrived at that Petro-Canada would have no production take on any lands where a significant discovery had been made or where Canadian ownership was over 35 percent. If, however, Canadian ownership were under 35 percent, then the interest accruing to Petro-Canada would vary according to the degree of Canadian ownership. This agreement, said Dome, was embodied under certain amendments to the Canada Oil and Gas Land Regulations in July of 1977. On the basis of these regulations (or "understandings," as Dome characterized them), Dome involved itself in expenditures in excess of $600 million. "It is our view," said Bill Richards in April 1981, "that the present provision for a Petro-Canada take is contrary to the arrangements we understood we had at that time, and we feel that it is unnecessary in view of the large share of the profits which the government already owns."[63]

In late 1982, Dome was forced by its increasingly critical debt situation to sign an arrangement with the federal government and its Canadian bankers which would see Ottawa and the banks gain substantial control over Dome's management decisions in exchange for the infusion of $1 billion. Fortunately for Dome, it had not, by the end of 1983, been forced to activate this arrangement. Dome managed to stay afloat by selling assets and cutting corporate costs. It also benefited from lower interest rates (a decrease in the interest rates of 1 percent saved Dome around $50 million a year). In late 1983, Jack Gallagher and Bill Richards were replaced by a new management team headed by Howard McDonald.[64] These and other aspects of "the Dome dilemma" are examined in Chapters 10 and 12.

Petro-Canada

Petro-Canada vice-president Joel Bell agreed with his private sector counterparts that prices must increase. Even though "increased oil prices are not popular and can be expected to have an adverse impact on the rate of inflation, it is evident that higher oil prices are needed both to reduce the growth in demand and to encourage the development of new sources of supply."[65] This is a line Petro-Canada would often take throughout the post-NEP period, particularly after softening world prices dampened the escalation of domestic price increases in 1982–83.

We have seen that, particularly between September 1981 and mid-1982, much of the industry argued that the cutbacks and layoffs in the oil industry were the fault of the NEP, in particular the PGRT and the IORT. Petro-Canada officials, however, were attributing the ills of the industry less to the NEP than to changing market conditions by no means unique to Canada: "There is a great deal of gallows humour going around Calgary these days. . . . Much of the blame for this pessimism has been focussed on the National Energy Program and indeed, while some of this blame is justified, most of the reasons for the serious problems facing the oil and gas business today have world roots that have nothing to do with the NEP."[66] While acknowledging that the fiscal regime of the NEP was designed for buoyant times, Joel Bell said: "We do work in an industry which is looked to for government revenues—partly because the prevailing values are not established by a free market and partly because our industry has been the one real strength of producing country economies in recent years, and hence a logical place to turn for the needs of public treasuries."[67] The fiscal regime cannot solve the problems of extreme debt leveraging or the absence of gas markets for shut-in reserves. Changing the fiscal regime, said Bell, would not fully compensate for dashed presumptions of constantly rising real-world prices and never-ending demand growth.

In part because the federal government did such a poor job of defending the NEP after it introduced it, in part because of the favoured status provided Petro-Canada under the NEP, and in part because Petro-Canada officials such as Joel Bell had been involved in the preparation of the NEP, Petro-Canada found itself in the position of having to carry much of the defence of the Canadianization aspects of the NEP.

One of the more notable "defence tactics" Petro-Canada employed in the immediate aftermath of the NEP against its critics was the downplaying of its size within the energy sector and the importance of its role within the context of the NEP. For example, in March 1981 Bell would state: "Acquisitions by Petro-Canada, or other agencies of Government also sounds ominous to many observers. Petro-Canada only need achieve a certain size and revenues base to perform the basic role designed for it—to be able technically and operationally to make a challenging project go; to provide additional risk capital to fund large and risky projects; to participate in the international market to protect Canadian interests; to help Government understand the industry; to add to the level of activity in priority areas; and to increase the Canadian content in those activities. In fact, it would be dangerous for Petro-Canada to be conceived of as a giant-sized firm representing a large part of the industry."[68] And in the following month Bell would again downplay the role of Petro-Canada, this time with respect to the

NEP: "Once again, the objectives of government policy of which Petro-Canada is part, do not only turn to Petro-Canada for their implementation. The more responsible and entrepreneurial Canadian companies, including some not previously in the oil business, have and will spearhead part of the change sought in the complexion of the Canadian oil and gas industry. In fact, the extent of this response will affect the extent to which recourse is had to Petro-Canada or other Government vehicles for the realization of the goals."[69]

Petro-Canada did not deny that a national oil company enjoyed certain advantages over private sector firms, but it argued that these advantages were "minimal," even with respect to the back-in privilege, ". . . the government is now proposing to take a 25 percent carried interest through the exploratory stages on federal lands, offer a 25 percent grant to all spenders regardless of nationality, and could transfer that carried interest to any agent, including Petro-Canada. . . . The government has, however, required of us that we meet the highest work level commitments on our land holdings and expects us to use our land position aggressively to draw new participants, especially Canadian participants into the activity where they are inclined to join with us."[70]

The retroactive nature of the Crown interest provision in Bill C-48 was readily admitted by Petro-Canada, but the corporation argued that there was nothing especially new about retroactivity in public policy:

> This element [back-in] was criticized as being retroactive and it is, in the same sense that any change in tax or other form of government take is retroactive when imposed where previous investment has occurred. The effect of this provision is to have the government participate in 25 percent of the future value of production. This is clearly more flexible than a direct tax or royalty on production. The government must spend its 25 percent of all costs on exploring and developing the fields. . . . In the Canadian context, the selection of this technique is motivated by the Government's desire to have a greater understanding and capacity to influence activities on Canadian Lands. It is also important to understand that this provision increases Canadian ownership and reduces the difficulty of achieving 50 percent Canadian ownership requirement, since despite being a fiscal provision, it also counts toward the ownership requirement.[71]

Petro-Canada also attempted to deflect criticism of its activities under the NEP by emphasizing that its existence was merely a pragmatic response by government to new problems in the energy sector of the economy: "The proliferation of [national oil companies], even in jurisdictions of widely divergent political philosophies, suggests that a government oil company should be seen more as a matter of policy expedience for the government to serve its goals conveniently rather than a reflection of political philosophy. Too much of the debate on national oil companies has turned on philosophies and on the extremes of either public ownership or private enterprise rather than on the utility of a government company to complement or replace other public policies aimed at achieving energy goals. This has deflected the discussion from the more appropriate consideration of the productive co-existence of public and private goals and bodies."[72]

But of course, Petro-Canada, as a major government instrument in energy policy, did enjoy special advantages in the NEP. The Liberals were responding to both strong public support for Petro-Canada and to strong support within the caucus and party when they mounted a stout defence of Petro-Canada in the face of the Clark government's privatization plans and during the election. Indeed, Trudeau's January 25, 1980 Halifax election speech identified Petro-Canada as a key instrument for pursuing both security and Canadianization goals.[73] He promised to strengthen and expand Petro-Canada. Consequently, as we see in detail in Chapters 9 and 11, Petro-Canada enjoyed major equity infusions from the government and access to the Canadian Ownership Charge revenues to finance its acquisitions. This, of course, was a major focus of criticism of NEP critics. What Petro-Canada did *not* do is of as much interest as what it did. The NEP stated that "for these reasons, the government of Canada (through Petro-Canada and other instruments) intends to acquire several of the large [foreign] oil and gas firms."[74] With the exception of Shell, the ten largest foreign-controlled firms were American. Despite polls which showed strong public support for Petro-Canada acquiring one of the largest foreign-owned firms,[75] Petro-Canada did not acquire any of them, but rather purchased Belgian-owned Petrofina, the eighteenth largest oil company in Canada (in February 1981), and then later the refining and marketing assets of British-owned British Petroleum (Fall, 1982), the twentieth ranked company. The U.S. companies that were acquired were bought by privately owned Canadian companies. Via these purchases, Petro-Canada moved from being the seventh largest to the fourth largest oil company in Canada.[76]

In a speech given exactly a year after the introduction of the NEP, Petro-Canada Chairman William Hopper revealed some of the anger which Petro-Canada felt toward other Canadian-owned elements of the industry which had been very vocal in their criticism of Petro-Canada:

> Finally, I would like to return to my comments made earlier by industry about the state of gloom and doom that the industry is creating. Petro-Canada has been a member of the Independent Petroleum Association of Canada since we were invited to join in 1976. We have not been an active member nor have our views on policy issues been sought. Over the last year many statements have been made by IPAC that we have disagreed with strongly. In fact, they have attacked us—one of their own members. Their strong attack on the National Energy Program and the Energy Pricing Agreement is in my view wrong and harmful to the interests of its member companies, shareholders in those companies, and Canadians in general. As a consequence, Petro-Canada will resign its membership in IPAC as of today.[77]

Earlier in his speech, perhaps as a result of the purpose of his speech, Hopper had directly spoken to the charge that the NEP and Petro-Canada were another example of "creeping socialism" and a further erosion of free enterprise:

> Government intervention in the economy, particularly to favour Canadian companies and especially Petro-Canada, is characterized by critics as inherently, and by definition, bad. Government intervention wasn't inherently bad for this industry when the federal government stepped in to protect the young Canadian oil industry in 1960 with the protection of the Ottawa Valley line. Many Canadians paid higher oil and gas prices for a decade to assist and protect this industry. That wasn't what was said when government was asked to assist the building of the TransCanada Pipeline. That certainly wasn't what was said by three members of the Syncrude Consortium when the fourth dropped out. Then government intervention was not only welcomed, it was demanded. The simple fact is that the oil business can't have it all their own way. . . . Simply put, oil is now a strategic commodity. Since 1973 it has become the object of governmental concern all over the world.

> Anyone who thinks that government intervention in the economy
> is going to decrease probably also believes in Unicorns. As to
> creeping socialism; if the NEP is the final word, this industry, and
> all others, can sleep comfortably at night.[78]

Petro-Canada officials were better able to withstand the barrage of criticism directed at them by foreign and Canadian critics, because they knew Petro-Canada had strong support among the mass of Canadians. It had weathered its major crisis to date, one that threatened its very existence, and emerged, according to the polls, as a very popular national symbol. In the post-NEP period Canadians continued to favour Petro-Canada, whose retail sales were up by as much as 30 percent in a shrinking market. It was also clear that a larger number of private sector executives and employers were willing to work for the state company. After all, it was one of the companies still growing in the industry in 1982–83. Petro-Canada sought to maintain its appeal by conducting an extensive television and newspaper advertising campaign which appealed to Canadians' nationalist sentiments by distinguishing itself and the consequences of its efforts from those of the multinationals, with slogans such as "Petro-Canada: It's Ours" and "Buy Petro-Canada and pump your money back into Canada."

The Second-Line Canadian Firms

Located between the Canadian majors and the Canadian juniors are about six to ten firms which we designate as the second-line Canadian firms. They are of particular interest because they were, in a very real sense, the prime intended beneficiary of the NEP. As Table 6.1 indicates, there is no uniform way to rank these companies since one has to differentiate their oil versus gas activities, their level of involvement in upstream and downstream activities, their involvement in other resource sectors, and their links to parent firms or larger holding companies. Nonetheless, as a group they deserve special attention, and we examine them in numerous contexts throughout the book. In this chapter, we describe and analyse some of these firms in an illustrative way, pointing out their divergent circumstances and the basic strategies they followed in the wake of the NEP, both economic and political. In this sense we are focussing on their role as a more or less distinct interest, in line with the broad themes of Part III of the book. In Part IV we examine them again in relation to more specific aspects of the NEP. At the end of Chapter 10, after a detailed treatment of the tax and pricing regime and of energy expenditures, especially the PIP grants, we review the fiscal and overall viability of these firms to be major players in the development and production stage of development on the Canada Lands, especially in pursuit of the NEP's goal of 50% Canadian-owned participation. In Chapter 11 we examine them in relation to the COGLA regulatory regime in general and to the process of obtaining farm-ins from the multinational majors who still held most of the land being explored in the Canada Lands.

While in a broad sense we wish to distinguish these firms as a separate group, it is absolutely critical to recognize that assessments of them can never be wholly separate from their economic and political links to the foreign-owned and Canadian majors. The NEP sought to make some of these firms more aware of their potential as a distinct political interest and to get them to act accordingly. Whether the policy has succeeded depends greatly on the time frame used to assess results; on a mixed range of evidence; and on the political values of those doing the evaluating. This too will be more evident in Part IV.

Given the illustrative nature of our analysis and the sheer impossibility in the space available of dealing with each company in any detail, we will profile the strategies of this group of companies in two ways. First, we summarize each firm separately in a brief, perfunctory way. Second, we comment on the overall political views of the group as reflected in their response to the NEP. Six companies are examined briefly—Pan Canadian Petroleum Limited, Norcen, Home Oil Company Limited, Canterra Energy Ltd., Husky Oil Ltd., and Bow Valley Industries Ltd.

Pan Canadian Petroleum Limited

Pan Canadian is 87.1 percent owned by Canadian Pacific Enterprises Ltd. In 1983 it ranked seventh overall in the Financial Times list of the top 100 oil and gas companies in Canada. It was fifth in natural gas production. Pan Canadian traces its roots to the late nineteenth century and the railroad era, when Canadian Pacific Railroad received a land grant of 25 million acres, most of it in Alberta.[79] Much of this land was later sold for settlement, but about 9.6 million acres were retained. The petroleum rights became especially valuable because it is freehold land: no Crown royalty is collected, and as a result Pan Canadian's profitability, as measured by return on capital, has historically been much higher than the industry average.

Pan Canadian had some early involvement in the Canada Lands as an original shareholder in Panarctic, but in general it had focussed on its Alberta holdings. The NEP presented as range of dilemmas and opportunities. The company was generally sceptical and critical of the NEP for several reasons. First, it was a company whose senior management believed that equity and internal cash flow were the only sound way to expand. The NEP was viewed as a device to promote Canadianization through borrowing. It was a kind of "Robin Hood" policy to help smaller Canadian firms by diverting cash flow from the larger integrated firms. Pan Canadian stood in a sense right at the edge of the fine line between the majors and the second-line firms. While it opposed the interventionism of the NEP, its initial economic view was that, on balance, the plan would have a neutral effect on the company. One specific test of this view was that the expected gains from the receipt of PIP grants would be about equal to the losses suffered by the new NEP taxes, especially the PGRT. By 1983 the PGRT losses slightly exceeded the PIP gains.

Since Pan Canadian's parent firm, Canadian Pacific Enterprises Ltd., was itself a large multinational firm, it also communicated its opposition to the NEP by stressing the discouraging signals it gave to foreign investors. Nonetheless, Pan Canadian did decide to avail itself of the opportunities presented by the new PIP incentives in particular. While it was much more cautious in its commitment than some of the other second-line firms, it did become much more active on Crown lands both in Alberta and on the Canada Lands. Its main new activity was in the eastern offshore in farm-ins with Mobil on lands 60 to 120 miles northeast and northwest of Mobil's Hibernia discovery. In general then, Pan Canadian took a relatively cautious position. It is perceived in the industry as a company with an excellent overall position, considerable financial stability and one of the few second-line firms to be well positioned to become a main player in the development phase on the Canada Lands if it chooses to do so.

Norcen

Norcen Energy Resources Limited was formed in 1975. It is ranked thirteenth in the *Financial Times* list. It operates extensive conventional oil and gas operations in Canada and the United States, and frontier and heavy oil operations in Canada.[80] Through subsidiaries, Norcen also owns and operates natural gas distribution systems in Ontario and Manitoba. Under an acquisition arrangement with Conrad Black's Argus empire, Norcen also has iron ore and other mineral resource interests. As a result, Norcen obtained a more diversified cash flow, but it also increased its debt by a considerable amount. By 1984 Norcen was generally viewed as being in the middle of the pack of the second-line firms in terms of its overall financial and technical capability to gain from the benefits conferred by the NEP. Norcen viewed the new grants regime as being inherently objectionable in a political sense but felt compelled to take advantage of them. By 1984 its PGRT losses had slightly exceeded its PIP gains. On the other hand, compared to Pan Canadian for example, it had a much higher percentage of NORP or world price oil. On balance its cash flow and net income positions by 1984 had not reached their buoyant 1980 levels, but had returned to their 1977–78 levels.

Norcen already had a corporate policy to be involved in the frontier and escalated its involvement to a considerable extent. In frontier lands, its exploration capital expenditures went from $3.1 million in 1980 to $45.5 million in 1981 to $103 million in 1983. It entered into a major farm-in agreement with Gulf Canada Resources in the Beaufort Sea, with Mobil and Gulf off the shore of Newfoundland, and with Shell Explorer off Nova Scotia. Norcen has thus stretched itself to a point where it is quite dependent on the PIP grants. This is counterbalanced to some degree by the fact that it has the Black empire behind it; as well, its gas distribution is not only a regulated utility, and hence assured of a fairly steady rate of return, but also has been encouraged by the NEP regime. Norcen would favour a return to a tax-based regime, but would need to have the regime grandfathered or phased in gradually.

Home Oil Company Limited/Hiram Walker Resources Limited

Formed in 1925, Home Oil was at one point in the mid 1940s Canada's largest independent oil company. Its post-NEP responses, however, can only be understood in relation to two corporate takeovers in 1979 and 1981. In 1979 Home Oil became a wholly owned subsidiary of Consumers' Gas Company Ltd., one of Canada's largest natural gas distribution utilities. In 1980 Consumers' Gas merged with Hiram Walker resulting in the establishment of Hiram Walker Resources Limited.[81] The latter owns 100 percent of Home Oil as well as other energy companies. In 1983 Hiram Walker Resources Limited was the eleventh largest company in the *Financial Times* list of oil and gas companies.

Because of the inevitable consolidation problems following such a major reorganization, Home Oil was a delayed participant in the NEP sweepstakes. This delay was also a product of the fact that its chief executive officer in 1981 was Al McIntosh, who had served in the same capacity at Pacific Petroleum when the latter had been taken over by Petro-Canada. This had left him with a strong distaste for interventionism of the kind represented by the NEP. Accordingly, Home Oil was initially unwilling to avail itself of the PIP incentives. This corporate strategy changed markedly in 1982 when Dick Haskayne became the chief executive. The company increased its frontier exploration activities in a major way. Its capital expenditures on exploration increased from about $6.9 million in 1980, to $23.9 million in 1982, to $497.6 million in 1983. Home entered into extensive farm-in arrangements with Esso Resources in the Beaufort Sea area. It also took advantage of Dome's vulnerability by farming into about 20 million gross acres of Dome's lands in western Canada, as well as 12.8 million gross acres of Dome's land in the Beaufort, as well as other Dome land off Nova Scotia and in the Arctic. As we point out in Chapter 12, when we examine the farm-in process more closely, these farm-in choices involved a tradeoff between some very good Dome land and some marginal land which Home would rather not have acquired.

Earlier, Home Oil had gotten into difficulty with its acquisition in 1981 of Davis Oil, a U.S. company. Financed by increased borrowings, this purchase exerted a heavy interest burden and drained the company's cash flow. As was the case with Dome, but obviously on a much smaller scale, this acquisition was partly a function of the seductive but illusionary beckoning of the greener pastures then believed to be available in Ronald Reagan's new America, as well as the initial visceral opposition to the NEP.

The post-NEP regime produced a mixed fallout of effects on the Home Oil/Hiram Walker Resources enterprise. It is a net beneficiary of PIPs and gains from the NEP's gas expansion initiatives. Its cash flow suffered from the Davis takeover, but the overall merger with Hiram Walker gives it a broader financial base than it had previously enjoyed. While it has extended itself into the Canada Lands, it has also strengthened its western Canadian holdings.

Canterra Energy Ltd./Canada Development Corporation

Canterra is a wholly owned subsidiary of the Canada Development Corporation (CDC) which is in turn about 48 percent owned by the Government of Canada.[82] Formed in 1981, Canterra owns the assets of the former Aquitaine Company of Canada Ltd., CDC Oil and Gas Limited, and the Canadian oil, gas and sulphur assets formerly owned by Texasgulf Inc. On the *Financial Times* list the CDC is the ninth largest company in Canada and the fourth largest Canadian-owned company. About 72 percent of its net proven reserves are gas. The Aquitaine takeover, financed through borrowings, produced a severe cash-flow effect. This was in turn exacerbated by the fact that its parent firm, the CDC, also suffered from the recession and from doubts about the federal government's intentions towards the future role of the CDC. At one point in 1980, the federal government tried to put Petro-Canada initiator Maurice Strong in charge of the CDC in order to convert it into a more aggressive instrument of the Liberals' then burgeoning industrial policy. When the bid to insert Strong failed, the Liberals shifted their attention to the establishment of the Canada Development Investment Corporation (CDIC) and declared their intention to divest their CDC shares as market conditions permitted.[83]

While Canterra's overall financial circumstances were not entirely propitious, it did have one decided asset, namely, the considerable oil and gas expertise it acquired from Aquitaine. As a result it both farmed out some of its lands to other companies and farmed in extensively. On the Canada Lands, Canterra negotiated new exploration agreements that almost tripled its holdings or interests, including interests near the Hibernia field in the Avalon Basin, and on the Scotian Shelf. It has a strong PIP versus PGRT balance in its favour, and company executives now confidently present themselves as having the third or fourth largest exploration program on the Canada Lands. If the PIP grants were to disappear it would have to curtail its exploration program significantly. On the other hand, the more that the PIP program is grandfathered as a transitional measure towards a future tax-based incentive system, the more Canterra believes it will benefit relative to other medium-sized Canadian companies. Despite its acknowledged geological expertise, the company in the mid 1980s was in general viewed by its competitors as being in the lower half of the second-line firms, in terms of its overall financial viability over the long term, and especially in relation to the later development phase.

Husky Oil Limited

Husky describes itself as the largest Canadian-owned, publicly traded, fully integrated oil and gas enterprise.[84] In the *Financial Times* list it ranks as the twelfth largest company. Husky's post-NEP role is intricately tied to two other Canadian firms, Nova and Bow Valley Industries. Husky is about 68 percent owned by Nova; Husky's chairman of the board is Bob Blair, who also heads Nova and whose decisive nationalist role we have already examined above. The post-NEP connection to Bow Valley is found in the two companies' extensive joint operations off the east coast through Bow Valley Resource Services Ltd. Indeed, in the Calgary oil patch the combined name of Husky-Bow Valley is often used to designate the total operation. While Husky, Nova, and Bow Valley remain distinct companies, it is of interest to note that if their reserves were combined they would rank as the eighth largest company overall.

Among the second-line firms, Husky is characterized by other company spokespersons as the company that most openly and enthusiastically sought to take advantage of the NEP incentives. This is hardly surprising in view of what we have already seen about Bob Blair's role vis-à-vis Nova. Blair stated his position to Husky shareholders in May 1982:

> In the east coast offshore exploration area the policy environment has become attractive to Canadian-owned companies. . . . The concept which we have developed jointly with Bow Valley Industries is to position our companies in the creation of a new Canadian-owned exploration operator capability, as completely equipped as Petro-Canada, but private sector owned, and thereby contribute equipment and exploration expertise and action. Our joint venture is also featuring Canadian-serviced equipment to a new level for offshore operations, to fully meet the national and regional government policy objectives. . . . A shortage of both equipment

operators having Canadian content continues to be projected for that area. We know we can do a useful job from the point of view of all of those parties and expect that by taking every effort and our share of the risks, can get the rights to some very worthwhile positions in the Canada Lands.[85]

In the spirit of this commitment, Husky embarked on an aggressive frontier exploration program. This included not only the Bow Valley drilling equipment ventures, described below, but also two major farm-ins on the Scotian Shelf. Husky also shared in the direct issuance of four exploration agreements by the Canada–Nova Scotia Offshore Oil and Gas Board. Farm-ins were also negotiated with Gulf in the Beaufort Sea area.

Though Husky therefore benefited greatly from PIP grants, its enthusiasm also exacted a price in other dimensions. In August 1981, before the Canada–Alberta Agreement, Husky acquired the properties of Uno-Tex Petroleum Corporation for $371 million through borrowing. Husky did improve its Alberta reserves and future development prospects through this transaction but in the short term weakened its cash flow markedly. Some diversification of Husky's reserves was necessary, however, since Husky was otherwise dependent on its heavy oil activities in Saskatchewan and Alberta. Its heavy oil assets were nonetheless also central to its post-NEP strategy as well. In 1982 it proposed to the federal, Alberta, and Saskatchewan governments a $3.2 billion heavy oil project. In June 1984 negotiations on the project were successfully concluded. As we show in Chapter 9, large projects of this kind became entwined in the fiscal gamesmanship and uncertainty that followed in the wake of the NEP, the recession, and falling oil prices. On balance then, Husky was a fairly enthusiastic respondent to the NEP, but found itself financially strained. Its activities were linked to the role of Bow Valley Industries, the last of the second-line companies to be surveyed in this chapter.

Bow Valley Industries Ltd.
Bow Valley was incorporated in Alberta in 1950. Originally involved primarily in the manufacturing, supply and drilling aspects of the energy business, it had by 1980 become the twenty-first largest company with significant oil and gas operations conducted in nine countries, including significant North Sea operations.[86] Its Canadian

reserves were mainly in gas, whereas its international operations were primarily in oil. Bow Valley, however, significantly expanded its frontier exploration activities in response to the NEP incentives and as a way to diversify its heretofore almost exclusive Alberta-based production activity. Major farm-ins were negotiated on the Scotian Shelf. As we have already indicated, however, its most extensive commitment was in its drilling and manufacturing operations in concert with Husky.

Bow Valley's 78 percent owned subsidiary, Bow Valley Resource Services Ltd., became the chief instrument for capitalizing on what, it was hoped, would be a growing service and supply market on the Canada Lands. By 1983 Bow Valley Resource Services had three semi-submersible drilling rigs off the east coast. One was under contract to Petro-Canada until 1985, and the other two were contracted to Bow Valley and Husky Oil Operations Ltd. In addition, the company had an equal interest with Husky in six supply boats then being built to service the rigs.[87] These were large undertakings which may in the long run prove profitable, but in the interim they strained the companies involved, especially because the recession and the declining level of world exploration in this period made it a buyer's market in the drilling supply business. Given the large world supply of rigs, it quickly became more economic for companies to "buy" rather than "make" their own supply capability.

The above profiles show the diversity of corporate circumstances that conditioned the response of the second-line firms. We have by no means been exhaustive in our treatment of this group. For example, a full inventory of such firms would also have to include companies such as the Alberta Energy Corporation (half owned by the Alberta government), Noranda Mines Ltd., Trans-Canada Pipelines Ltd., and Sulpetro Ltd., to name a few of the others. Our discussion has been primarily an illustrative one, but absolutely essential, if one is to appreciate the political interests at stake as well as the later dynamics of NEP implementation examined in Part III.

Though none of the firms liked the general thrust of the NEP as an act of intervention and most complained of the rigidity of the price system and the excessive bureaucracy of COGLA and related aspects of the regulatory regime, the companies did move, albeit with varying rates of speed and commitment, to take advantage of the incentives that favoured them. As a group, the firms generally suffered in terms of reduced cash flow, along with the industry as a whole, but none of them appears to have seriously overextended itself as a corporate entity or in relation to its parent company. Some, of course, are more extended than others. The key question, however, remains the degree to which the second-line firms in concert with the Canadian majors are well positioned to become major players in the development phase of activities on the Canada Lands and in the future activity on the Western Sedimentary Basin as well. We return to this larger question in different ways in Chapters 9, 10, and 11.

The Canadian Juniors: Reactions to the NEP

The category "Canadian Juniors" includes literally hundreds of exploration and production companies. Most of these firms are members of the Independent Petroleum Association of Canada (IPAC), though so are the Canadian majors and the second-line Canadian companies identified above, with the exception of Petro-Canada, which withdrew in 1981. Thus IPAC's reactions and positions were not identical to those of the juniors. Because there are so many juniors, and because individual companies' responses varied in tone and substance, it will not be possible to deal with specific companies. There were, however, enough similarities in the general response to make it possible to distill an overall reaction to the NEP by the juniors.

It can safely be said that the reaction of the Canadian-owned juniors surprised the federal government and perhaps did more than anything else initially to tarnish the credibility of the NEP. Critics of the NEP could point to the reaction of this element of the industry as proof that the NEP authors did not really know what they were doing. After all, it was this element of the industry—the aggressive, ambitious, dynamic, small Canadians—along with the Canadian majors, and the second-line firms, which the Canadianization features of the NEP were supposed to favour. Like the rest of the industry they could have been expected to oppose the pricing and taxation provisions of the NEP. It is virtually part of the credo of the oil patch to oppose all increases in taxation and to press constantly for higher oil and gas prices. To the extent that oilmen felt the federal government really did deserve a larger share of energy revenues, they felt they should take it from the provincial share. However, the vociferous opposition of the juniors as a group to the Canadianization provisions of the NEP, which had both an ideological and material basis, was more of a surprise. To an extent this can be attributed to the political and psychological composition of the people who run the juniors. Many of these oilmen are not particularly interested in or knowledgeable about politics and of those who are, most tend to see politics as a low form of activity, an inherently less important activity than wealth creation. Consequently, many of these people were unaware of the extent of the politicization of oil and gas over the previous decade; of the degree to which both energy politics and energy policy had expanded to involve much more than solely energy issues. Many were therefore shocked by the breadth, political motivation, and polemical nature of the NEP.

Ideologically, this element of the industry tends to be on the most conservative end of the Canadian political spectrum. Psychologically, the people who run the juniors tend to embody the stridently independent, free-enterprise concept of small business. Many of them have had career experience in the large bureaucracies of the major oil companies and were uncomfortable in technocratic functions and with the committee decision-making structures of the large firms. They preferred the direct decision-making authority which is possible in a small company. While some of these firms have grown to quite a large size in recent years, they are still the most vulnerable interests in the overall context of Canadian energy politics. They are vulnerable to the majors, to government policies, and to the market place. For example, past generations of Canadian juniors were taken over by the majors during the periods of great expansion by acquisition in the 1950s, 1960s, and 1970s.[88] Moreover, the juniors have neither the capital to outbid the majors for exploration land, nor the technology or capital to challenge the majors in the frontiers. Consequently, they have in the past been largely restricted to the Western Sedimentary Basin and even there they end up with the land the majors chose not to bid for, or they do farm-in exploration on leases already tied up by the majors. They are also vulnerable to decisions of government policy makers. For example, tax expenditures built into the Canadian tax system in the late 1970s provided them with access to the tax-saving investment dollars of high-income Canadians via drilling funds, which many of the juniors came to rely on for a significant part of their working capital.

The threat to remove these in the MacEachen 1981 budget for a series of unrelated reasons exposed the juniors to losing one of their key revenue sources. National Energy Board, Cabinet, and U.S. regulatory agency decisions regarding oil and natural gas exports, and the price of these products in export and domestic markets, directly affect their ability to sell their main products. They are also vulnerable to the vagaries of the market with respect to the demand for their products, the level of interest rates, and the like.

The juniors shared with the rest of the industry the opposition to the limited price increases allowed by the NEP. This is an obvious focus of opposition as it decreases the potential value of the assets of the oil and gas companies. In addition, one of the security features of the NEP affected the juniors in a significant way. Specifically, one of the key measures of the NEP regarding enhanced energy security was to induce Canadian consumers, both residential and commercial, to switch from scarce oil to abundant natural gas for space heating needs. In addition to providing financial grant incentives to convince consumers to switch, the NEP utilized the price mechanism by promising that the natural gas price would be held at approximately 65 percent of the blended oil price in Canada. Given that most of the juniors are primarily gas producers, this cap on the price of natural gas was perceived to have restricted their revenues.

With respect to taxation, the two new taxes introduced in the NEP (the PGRT and the NGGLT) and the removal of the incentive program from the tax system had direct consequences for the cash flow of the juniors. Because upstream revenues are usually their only source of revenue, the fact that the PGRT was imposed at the wellhead and allowed for no write-offs affected the juniors even more than the integrated majors which had revenues generated from other links of the integrated chain. Most of the juniors were active in 1980 in the western provinces and, therefore, the NEP's intention to phase out the earned depletion allowance for exploration on provincial lands and to eliminate the depletion allowance for expenditures on conventional oil and gas development would have a direct impact on those firms that were in a tax-paying position. Of course, the tax-based depletion allowances were replaced in the NEP by the direct incentive grant program, which allowed the federal government to target the incentives according to Canadian ownership levels and location of exploration and development. However, there were two practical problems associated with this program for the juniors, in addition to a major ideological dislike among many of them for the influence the PIP grants gave the government over the decision making of the individual companies.

First, throughout the 1970s the juniors had often gone to the foreign equity markets to raise capital and in the process had taken on foreign equity to the extent that, in some cases, the Canadian juniors did not have the requisite 75 percent ownership level to qualify for the highest PIP incentive payments. Secondly, given that the PIP objective was to channel exploration dollars to Canadian firms, many of the juniors were upset that the levels of the PIP grants were dramatically higher for the Canada Lands, where few of them had the expertise or the capital to become involved, than the provincial lands, where most of them saw the bulk of their future exploration taking place. While the obvious reason the PIP grants were higher on the Canada Lands was that the costs and risks were much higher, many of the juniors felt the NEP had prematurely de-emphasized the potential of the Western Sedimentary Basin to contribute to Canada's future oil supplies. None of the juniors was active in the frontiers, and few felt they had the necessary expertise to operate there or, even with the high PIP payments, the financial capacity to carry a debt load for frontier exploration, given the long payback periods. On the other hand, some of the larger Canadian juniors, who were interested in potentially rich frontier plays, recognized that interventionist measures, such as the high PIP payments and the requirements for 50 percent Canadian ownership for a production licence on Canada Lands, were necessary incentives, given that the majority of the best land was already leased by the foreign majors.

With respect to the NEP's stated objective of increasing Canadian ownership levels by encouraging the acquisition of foreign firms, a number of the larger Canadian juniors engaged in or contemplated engaging in takeovers.[89] This did not prevent many juniors, largely for ideological reasons, opposing Petro-Canada's expansion through acquisitions.

Coincidental developments south of the border had the effect of making the NEP appear even more onerous. The election a week after the introduction of the NEP of the aggressively pro-business Reagan administration in the United States on a conservative platform of reducing government regulation of the economy in general, and completely deregulating oil pricing and phasing out the regulation of gas prices in particular, was music to the political ears of the oil juniors, particularly when juxtaposed with the sour notes of the NEP. The prospect of deregulated prices, markets for full production, and an overall lower state/federal tax burden in the United States, compared with constrained price increases for oil and particularly for gas, assumptions of limited market expansion for gas, increases in federal taxes and the prospect of further federal–provincial wrangling over revenue shares in Canada, combined with the juniors' hostility to the federal Liberals' centralism and interventionism and ideological attraction to the Reagan neo-conservative message, coalesced to convince a number of the juniors to cut back on their exploration activity in Canada and shift a greater share of their activity to the United States.[90] Thus it can be seen that there was both a material and ideological basis to the reaction of the juniors.

The introduction of a New Oil Reference Price, essentially world price, for "conventional new oil" (that is, oil from pools discovered after December 31, 1980) in the September 1, 1981 Canada–Alberta Agreement was an improvement to the pricing picture for the juniors, though the Agreement as a whole was much less efficacious than many of them had expected, and had the effect of shaking the faith of some of these companies in the Government of Alberta. One of the additional consequences of the Agreement and the largely negative reaction to it by the CPA, IPAC, a number of the majors and some of the juniors was to restrict to an even greater extent the investor interest in oils. As mentioned above, the stock market and particularly the drilling funds are far more important to the juniors than to the larger firms who can finance more of their exploration from retained earnings and other internal revenues. Most of the juniors belong to IPAC, and as mentioned IPAC took a very critical position on the Canada–Alberta Agreement. As a result of this position and the high profile political campaign that IPAC and some of its member companies chose to engage in in attempting to reverse the NEP, the organization became increasingly alienated from the federal government. As a consequence, a number of IPAC members decided that to get their message across in Edmonton and particularly in Ottawa, they would have to negotiate separately from IPAC.

A loose organization of 157 juniors including some IPAC and other firms came together to lobby federal energy officials for changes in the tax and pricing structures, and they felt they were able to have an impact. By late spring of 1982, it had become obvious that the single-price scenario upon which the revenue sharing assumptions of the Memorandum of Agreement were based had been quickly dated by changes in the world energy prices. Consequently, the industry had not benefited from the Canada–Alberta Agreement to the extent the governments had projected. After the passage of eight months and much hard industry lobbying and political agitation, both levels of government concluded that further alterations were needed with respect to prices, royalties and taxation. On April 13, 1982 the Alberta government announced a $5.4 billion program consisting of royalty reductions and special grants and credits. On May 31, 1982 the federal government announced the NEP Update, which included a number of pricing and taxation changes which were generally thought to be a response to the lobbying efforts of the 157 juniors. Both IPAC and the CPA acknowledged the improvements in the NEP Update but were not satisfied that it had gone far enough; consequently, they maintained their critical stance.

For the juniors the most important features of the NEP Update were the exemption of the first $250,000 of production revenues from the PGRT, which constituted $900 million of the $2 billion in benefits involved in the package, and the introduction of the category "new/old" oil, or oil discovered between 1973 and 1981, which would be allowed to move to a price level of 75 percent of world price. Since the juniors found the vast majority of their oil in the period since 1973, they would therefore benefit the most from such increases. The Incremental Oil Revenue Tax (IORT) introduced in the September 1981 Agreement was reduced to zero for a year.[91] While these changes are not everything the juniors would have liked, they were seen as positive "proof of exactly how specific that cause and effect relationship" between the 157 juniors and Ottawa had become.[92]

The juniors continued to lobby both levels of government throughout 1982 and 1983, and the 1983 Amendment did extend world price to oil produced between 1974 and 1980 and to oil from infill wells, thereby covering most of the production of the junior firms. While some of the juniors farmed-in to the leases of the foreign-owned majors in the Canada Lands, most strove to find NORP oil in western Canada. The most severe problem faced by the juniors as a group was that of shut-in natural gas. Throughout 1983, the juniors and other gas producers lobbied both governments to take measures to increase gas exports to the United States, such as decreasing the export price, but the major problem remained the existence of surplus U.S. production and soft U.S. markets.

While we have covered a large portion of the oil patch in this chapter, we have by no means covered it all. For example, the petrochemical industry interests have not been treated. By early 1984 they were pressing government to reduce gas prices and deregulate, in part because this segment of the industry saw excellent opportunities to compete and expand on a world scale.[93]

Conclusions on the Industry Response and Government–Industry Relations

This analysis of the overall reactions of various firms and elements within the industry to the NEP shows that there were variations on certain themes of the industry response to the NEP depending on the companies' size, ownership, and major sphere of operation. The industry as a whole agreed that the price increases allowed in the NEP were inadequate, and when combined with the increased taxes would make the achievement of self-sufficiency impossible because the overall effect, even with incentives, would be inadequate netbacks to the industry. The foreign majors were especially critical of the Crown interest provision and were highly critical of the shift in the incentive system and the Petro-Canada expansion. Their response involved lobbying their home governments to pressure Ottawa for changes, slashing their exploration budgets, and cancelling the non-conventional mega-projects. They also attempted to improve their public image and to refute the Bertrand Report by employing major advertising campaigns. Once it became clear the NEP would remain largely intact, they attempted to take advantage of the PIP system by farming-out parts of their Canada Lands leases to Canadian-controlled firms, by working with COGLA to address Canadian benefits standards, and by trying to take advantage, where possible, of loopholes in the PIP program. As a group they developed through the CPA an alternative energy program which could meet the concerns of all CPA members. This is discussed in greater detail in Chapter 9.

The three Canadian majors used their access to the federal government to lobby for changes in pricing, taxation, COR regulations and natural gas exports and pricing. While they were critical of aspects of the Canadianization program, they also moved to take material advantage of it by (in Nova's case) using their high PIP payments to transfer more of their exploration to the East Coast, and in Dome and Petro-Canada's case by making significant acquisitions, as well as maintaining their leading roles on the Canada Lands.

The second-line Canadian firms were critical of the overall thrust of the NEP, but nonetheless felt compelled to profit from it, especially via the PIP grants. Among the six companies reviewed above in an illustrative way, the responses varied from the cautiousness of Pan Canadian to the enthusiasm of Husky and Bow Valley, and ranged across the permutations and combinations of the various asset positions, debt-load factors, and overall health of the firms themselves, and of their parent holding companies.

As a rule the junior firms reacted with anger to the centralist and interventionist thrust of the NEP. Most of the companies cut back their exploration programs and a number shifted a percentage of their exploration activity to the United States. They, of course, continued to lobby the federal and provincial governments for changes to the pricing, taxation, and royalty regimes, and met with some success. While as a whole they were quite critical of the chosen means to increase Canadianization, a number of the juniors sought to achieve advantages for their shareholders by acquiring foreign firms or farming-in to the Canada Lands.

The federal government responded to the industry in a number of ways, both verbal and concrete, in the three-year period following the introduction of the NEP. Chapter 3 briefly chronicles and Appendix A lists the full range of federal actions. We do not examine them here since they are the focus of Part IV of the book.

Quite clearly, the NEP and subsequent developments reveal several attempts by Ottawa and the various industry interests to exercise the power they possess in Canadian energy politics. With the NEP, the federal government exercised its powers of exhortation, taxation, expenditure and regulation in an attempt to effect fundamental change in both the Ottawa–industry and the intra-industry relationships of power. In turn, the various industry interests employed public denunciations of the NEP or other appeals to public opinion, and exercised their control over capital spending, exploration budgets and corporate borrowing, as well as their connections with other governments to signal their various positions to Ottawa and to attempt to force the federal government to alter aspects of the NEP. There were clearly features of the NEP that the industry as a whole disagreed with. Yet, the various corporate interests within the industry were treated differently enough by the NEP, that, particularly for the Canadian-controlled firms, it was necessary to calculate whether it was possible to take advantage of aspects of the NEP, even if, as a whole, the company or its chief officials were ideologically or personally opposed to the NEP.

In response to the reaction of the various industry interests to the NEP, the federal government used both verbal and concrete measures to lash out at certain elements of the industry—especially in defending its Canadianization program and Crown Interest proposal—and to appease others. While some of its reactions can be considered direct reactions to the application of power by the industry, others were in part reactions to pressure being applied to it by other governments. In fact, the government–industry and inter-governmental relationships have to be understood as part of a complex, interrelated, three-sided arrangement. In order to consider the two relationships in an integrated way, we must consider the impact that the NEP had on the inter-governmental relationship.

Notes

1. An analysis of the relative influence of various oil companies and industry groups in Ottawa published October 27, 1980, the day before the introduction of the NEP, argued that Dome, Nova and Petro-Canada "probably have more clout than the rest of the industry put together." Their influence was considered an exception in that the industry as a whole lacked credibility. The foreign companies, "a group that public opinion polls say is as popular with most Canadians as a skunk at a garden party," were divided into two groups. "Companies with considerable Canadian content and a commitment to the country such as Imperial, Shell and Gulf . . . can get access to Mr. Lalonde when they want to." "Another group of multinationals is not trusted at all. Texaco, Amoco, Mobil and Chevron are regarded in Ottawa as quintessentially bad corporate citizens, ugly Americans intent on taking Canadians for all they can get with no regard to Canadian interests." James Rusk, "Powers in the Oil Lobby Cull Clout from the Flag," *Globe and Mail*, October 27, 1980, p. 9.

2. This profile of the industry is not meant to be exhaustive. For example, one element of the industry not dealt with here but of considerable importance to energy politics in Alberta is the Alberta-based oil industry supply, service and manufacturing sector. This sector is also of importance federally because of Ottawa's often-stated objective of encouraging the development of Canadian manufacturing, supply, and service companies capable of capturing greater industrial spinoffs from oil and gas exploration and production. The Energy Services Association (ESA), the Canadian Association of Oilwell Drilling Contractors (CAODC), and the Canadian Oilfield Manufacturers Association (COMA), are three of the organizations representing this element of the industry. The reactions and concerns of the juniors as a group to the NEP, outlined below, reflect many of the concerns of this element of the industry as well. For further analysis, see Chapter 9.

3. Government of Canada, Department of Energy, Mines and Resources, *The National Energy Program* (Ottawa: Supply and Services Canada, 1980), p. 49.

4. *Ibid.*, p. 48.

5. *Ibid.*, pp. 16–22.

6. *Ibid.*, p. 49.

7. The majors' public image was further damaged in 1979 when Exxon Corporation of New York unilaterally diverted offshore crude oil supplies destined for Imperial Oil refineries in eastern Canada. The federal government attacked Exxon's move which, Ottawa argued, raised further questions about Imperial's autonomy (and by implication the autonomy of the other Canadian affiliates of the foreign majors). While the diversion did not actually cause a crude shortfall, the resulting publicity increased already high public suspicion about the operation of the foreign-controlled majors in Canada.

8. Government of Canada, Director of Investigation and Research, Combines Investigation Act, *The State of Competition in the Canadian Petroleum Industry*, seven volumes (Ottawa: Supply and Services Canada, 1981).

9. J.G. Livingstone, "Remarks to Annual Meeting of Shareholders," Toronto, April 25, 1980, p. 9.

10. _____, "Remarks to the Energy Symposium organized by the Liberal Party of Canada (Québec)," Montreal, May 7, 1981. p. 3.

11. _____, "The New Budget and Energy Self-Sufficiency," Remarks to the Canadian Club of Vancouver, December 2, 1980, p. 6.

12. _____, "Remarks to the Canadian Institute of Chartered Accountants," Halifax, September 17, 1981, p. 3.

13. _____, "The New Budget and Energy Self-Sufficiency," *op. cit.*, p. 6.

14. _____, "Remarks to the Montreal Chamber of Commerce," May 12, 1981, p. 2.

15. _____, "Remarks to the Canadian Institute of Chartered Accountants," *op. cit.*, p. 8.

16. R.W. Sparks, "To the Shareholders," in *Texaco Canada Inc.: Annual Report 1980*, March 17, 1981, p. 2.

17. _____, "Remarks to the Annual Meeting of Shareholders, 1981," April 24, 1981, p. 10.

18. W.A. Gatenby, "Statement Concerning Bill C-104 to the House of Commons Standing Committee on Energy Legislation," May 4, 1982.

19. Sparks, "Remarks to the Annual Meeting of Shareholders, 1981," *op. cit.*

20. _____, "Opening statement on Bill C-48 to the Standing Committee on Natural Resources and Public Works," March 12, 1981, p. 4.

21. R.N. Routhier, "Remarks to the Equipment Lessor's Association of Canada on behalf of the Canadian Petroleum Association," Québec City, September 21, 1981, p. 21.

22. R.W. Sparks and R.N. Routhier, "To the Shareholders," in *Texaco Canada Inc.: Annual Report 1981*, March 16, 1982, p. 2.

23. See *Financial Times*, March 5, 1984, p. 1. See also *Oil Week*, July 4, 1983, pp. 14–16.

24. Gulf, "Opening Statement," Presentation to the National Energy Board, February 1981, p. 2.

25. J.L. Stoik, "Notes for a presentation to the Canadian Association of Petroleum Investment Analysts," Toronto, December 2, 1980, pp. 4–7.

26. *Ibid.*, p. 15.

27. *Ibid.*

28. R.H. Carlyle, "Remarks to the Canadian Association of Petroleum Investment Analysts," March 3, 1982, p. 3.

29. Stoik, "Notes for a presentation to the Canadian Association of Petroleum Investment Analysts," *op. cit.*, p. 7.

30. *Ibid.*, p. 8.

31. *Ibid.*, p. 9.

32. *Ibid.*, p. 8.
33. J.L. Stoik, "Remarks to the Annual Meeting of Shareholders, Gulf Canada," April 23, 1981, p. 15.
34. _____, "Presentation to the New York Society of Security Analysts," New York, June 16, 1981, p. 3.
35. J.C. Phillips, "Remarks to the Annual Meeting of Shareholders, Gulf Canada," April 23, 1981, pp. 4–6.
36. See *Globe and Mail*, March 6, 1984, pp. B1 and B5.
37. See *Oilweek*, July 4, 1983, pp. 14–16, and *Oilweek*, January 9, 1984, pp. 22–27.
38. Jack Gallagher and Bill Richards, "Report to the Shareholders," *Dome Petroleum: Annual Report 1980*, April 1981, p. 4.
39. H.J.S. Pearson and S. Robert Blair, "Report to Shareholders," *Nova, An Alberta Corporation: Annual Report 1980*, March 13, 1981, p. 2.
40. Robert Blair, "Notes for a Speech to the Financial Post Conference," Toronto, February 25, 1981, p. 8.
41. *Ibid.*
42. _____, "President's Message," in *Nova, An Alberta Corporation: Annual Report 1980*, March 13, 1981, p. 5.
43. _____, "Notes of a Speech to the Annual Meeting of the Canadian Life and Health Insurance Association," Edmonton, June 1, 1982, p. 6.
44. Pearson and Blair, *op. cit.*, p. 2.
45. Robert Blair, "Notes from a Speech to the Conference on the Canadianization of the Petroleum Industry," Ottawa, January 23, 1982, pp. 2–3.
46. _____, "Notes for a Speech to the Financial Analysts Federation Seminar," Calgary, January 27, 1982, p. 6. It should be remembered that Blair was co-chairman of the Major Projects Task Force which recommended in June 1981 that a larger Canadian procurement, management, engineering and construction capability be developed and actively employed in Canadian natural resource projects. That Husky became an active frontier participant between 1981 and March 1983 is reflected in its status as the seventh largest PIP grant recipient at $40 million. It followed Dome Canada ($486 million), Petro-Canada ($431 million), Canterra ($130 million), Norcen ($92 million), Gulf Canada ($56 million) and Mobil ($46 million). See *Globe and Mail*, December 27, 1983, p. B1.
47. Robert Blair, "Statement for Panel Discussions on Economic Nationalism in Canada," Ottawa, September 8, 1982, p. 9.
48. *Ibid.*, p. 12.
49. See *Alberta Report*, February 1984, p. 14.
50. Bill Richards, "Comments to the House of Commons Standing Committee on Natural Resources and Public Works," April 1, 1981.
51. John Beddome, "Speech to the Canadian Petroleum Tax Society on the September 1, 1981 Pricing Accord," September, 1981.

52. *Memorandum of Agreement between the Government of Canada and the Government of Alberta Relating to Energy Pricing and Taxation,* September 1, 1981, p. 8.

53. Beddome, *op. cit.*

54. Bill Richards, "Canada's Petroleum Industry and Quebec: The Necessity of Increased Natural Gas Export Sales," December 6, 1982.

55. Beddome called NORP a "powerful incentive mechanism for the production of new sources of oil." The NORP system, in his estimation, represented dramatically higher prices and provided for increases in the before-tax netback on new oil of over three times those provided under the original blended price proposal of the NEP. Natural gas, on the other hand, received the least favourable pricing treatment. Beddome, *op. cit.*

56. Jack Gallagher, "A Speech on Oil and Gas Development and Exploration in the North," October 28, 1982.

57. For a detailed analysis of the HBOG and Dome Canada period, see Jim Lyon, *Dome* (Toronto: Macmillan, 1983).

58. See Dome and EMR press releases, January 29, 1981.

59. *Dome Petroleum: 1980 Annual Report,* p. 21.

60. Richards, "Comments to House of Commons . . . ," *op. cit.*

61. *Dome Petroleum: 1980 Annual Report, op. cit.,* p. 4.

62. *Globe and Mail,* January 27, 1981, p. B2.

63. Richards, "Comments of House of Commons . . . ," *op. cit.*

64. See Robert Bott, "Up to His Kilt: Why the Scot Who's Taken Over at Dome Yearns for Home," *Energy,* October 1983, pp. 72–73.

65. Joel Bell, "The Outlook for Canada's Oil and Gas Sector in the Next Two Decades," A speech to the Canadian Association of Business Economists, Toronto, April 14, 1980, pp. 7–8.

66. _____, "Notes for a Speech to the 1982 A.A.P.G. Annual Convention," Calgary, June 29, 1982, p. 1.

67. *Ibid.,* p. 13.

68. Joel Bell, "Notes for an Address to the Canadian–American Committee," Chicago, March 28, 1981, p. 14.

69. _____, "National Oil Companies—'Quo Vadis'," Paper prepared for the International Bar Association Energy Law Seminar, Banff, Alberta, April 27, 1981, p. 34.

70. *Ibid.,* p. 46.

71. Joel Bell, "Canadian Energy Policy: Anti-Americanism or New Partnerships," Notes for an Address to the 45th Chicago World Trade Conference, Chicago, March 15, 1982, pp. 7–8.

72. _____, "National Oil Companies—'Quo Vadis'," *op. cit.,* pp. 3–4.

73. Rt. Hon. Pierre Trudeau, "Energy Policy Speech," Halifax, January 25, 1980.

74. Government of Canada, National Energy Program, *op. cit.,* p. 51.

75. A December 1981 Gallup Poll indicated that 55 per cent of respondents

favoured the expansion of Petro-Canada into Canada's largest oil company by buying one of the four major foreign-owned oil companies— Imperial, Shell, Gulf or Texaco. Twenty-eight per cent of respondents opposed and 17 per cent didn't know. See Gallup Poll number 456, p. 4.

76. See Government of Canada, Department of Energy, Mines and Resources, *The National Energy Program: Update 1982* (Ottawa: Supply and Services Canada, 1982), pp. 48–49.

77. W.H. Hopper, Notes for a Speech to the Financial Post Conference on "Year One: What's Ahead after 12 Months of NEP," Calgary, October 27, 1981, pp. 8–9.

78. *Ibid.*, pp. 4–5.

79. See Pan Canadian Petroleum Ltd., *Annual Report 1982.*

80. See Norcen, *Annual Report 1982*, and Norcen, *Annual Information Form 1983.*

81. See Hiram Walker Resources Ltd., *Annual Report 1983*, and Home Oil, *Annual Review 1983.*

82. See Canterra Energy Ltd., *Annual Report 1982*, and Canada Development Corporation, *1982 Annual Report.*

83. See Steven Brooks, "The State as Entrepreneur: From CDC to CDIC," *Canadian Public Administration*, Winter 1983, vol. 26, no. 4, pp. 525–543.

84. See Husky Oil Ltd., *Annual Report 1982.*

85. Robert Blair, Speech to the Annual General Meeting of Shareholders of Husky Oil Ltd., May 6, 1982, Calgary, Alberta, pp. 4–5.

86. See Bow Valley Industries, Ltd., *Annual Report 1982.*

87. See Bow Valley Resource Services Ltd., *1982 Annual Report.*

88. See "Acquisitions by Imperial, Shell, Gulf and Texaco," Appendix E, *The State of Competition in the Canadian Petroleum Industry* (Ottawa: Supply and Services Canada, 1981), pp. 217–240; and "Will Independents Survive Take-Overs?," *Oilweek*, October 8, 1962.

89. Some of those engaging in takeovers were: Sulpetro; United Canso Oil and Gas Ltd; Fairweather Gas Ltd; Drummond Petroleum Ltd; Turbo Resources Ltd; Aberford Resources Ltd; and Francana Oil and Gas Ltd. A number of the acquiring companies later experienced financial difficulties as high interest rates and softening international prices increased their costs and decreased the value of the assets they had purchased.

90. Many of the juniors that bought into the U.S. during this period later had to take embarrassing writedowns on their U.S. assets when they proved to be less valuable than expected: "the value of all U.S. oil and gas reserves fell when world oil prices fell; some reserves were smaller than the purchasers had been led to believe; some deals were over-priced; some accounts receivable were worthless when partners and customers went bankrupt; and the rules of the game could change abruptly in the maze of regulations by states, federal authorities and even Indian tribes." Juniors were not the only Canadian companies to experience this, however.

Dome had to write down its U.S. properties by $214 million in 1982, and Hiram Walker Resources (Home Oil) experienced a writedown of $177 million on the assets it purchased from Davis Oil of Denver. The Canadian affiliates of the American multinationals did not engage in this shift of activity to the U.S. as they are not mandated by corporate policy to operate outside of Canada. See Gillian Steward, "Southern Discomfort: How Canadian Oilmen Lost Their Shirts in the U.S.," *Energy*, October 1983, pp. 73–74.

91. See NEP *Update, op. cit.*

92. In terms of the relationships among the juniors, the key actors in the group of 157 took credit for the advantageous features of the Update. "Lobbying as 157 companies we got hundreds of millions poured in the juniors. . . . we give Ottawa the biggest bang for the buck in getting the exploration and development industry back to work," said Peter Aubrey, a director of Zephyr Resources Ltd. Moreover, this group was increasingly disenchanted with IPAC's political posturing and the resulting negative image this was portraying of the industry's prospects for potential investors. "If we had not done our presentations independent of IPAC we wouldn't have got what was in NEP-II" said Uldis Upitis, president of Pancontinental Oil Ltd. "It's absolutely paramount that we form our own organization and spread the word to the country. This is a profitable industry. We've got to tell the conventional sources of capital—the doctors, dentists, lawyers—that this is the time."

93. See *Report of the Petrochemical Industry Task Force*, Report to the Minister of Regional and Industrial Expansion (Ottawa: Supply and Services Canada, February 1984).

CHAPTER 7

INTERGOVERNMENTAL ENERGY RELATIONS
AND THE NEP

The constitutional division of power and the geographical division of the Canadian political economy have assured the intergovernmental relationship a primary position in Canadian energy politics. In this chapter we continue to focus on the two key provincial governments of Alberta and Ontario and the federal government as we investigate in detail the dynamic and turbulent post-NEP period of intergovernmental energy relations. Reference will also be made briefly to the responses of other provincial governments as well, since these affect the total constellation of events and interests. One of the overall conclusions of Chapter 5 was that while there were a number of specific developments in the 1979–80 period which aggravated relations along both dimensions of the intergovernmental relationship, there were also larger structural reasons for the troubled state of the relationship in the immediate pre-NEP period. Indeed, many of the wounds resulting from the 1973–74 intergovernmental energy battles had begun to heal by 1978–79, yet the fundamental, structural differences of interest which underpinned the conflicts were intact, and revealed once again by the 1979 price shocks internationally and the defeat of the Clark government domestically.

Chapter 5 analysed the three key governments as major interests. By assessing their positions on pricing, revenue sharing, and resource management throughout the post-1973 period, we were able to (a) discern where their various positions and interests converged and diverged, and (b) appraise the reasons for the ways in which energy decisions caused developments in the federal–provincial and interregional relationships.

In this chapter we first identify more precisely the federal government's motives with respect to those aspects of the NEP which directly affected the provinces. We then examine Alberta's response to the NEP and Ontario's response to the NEP and Alberta. Our objective here is to clarify the specific characteristics of the intergovernmental relationship in order to contribute to the development of a better understanding of the larger world of Canadian energy politics.

In the "Problems" section of the NEP entitled "Energy Benefits and Burdens," the Liberals provided the rationale for the pricing and revenue sharing features of the NEP which would most directly effect the producing (and consuming) provinces and therefore effect not only the federal–provincial but also the interregional dimensions of the intergovernmental relationship. It is worth citing at length, as it outlines the federal critique of the existing situation, and rationale for the major changes introduced in the NEP:

> The impact [of oil price increases] on Canada's economy is not borne equally by all parts of Canada; the petroleum-producing areas benefit from OPEC actions, while the rest of Canada is penalized. . . . A large proportion—approaching one-half—of the revenue from these higher domestic prices accrues to the governments of the petroleum-producing provinces; most of it to Alberta. The resulting inter-regional transfers of wealth are now so large, and growing so rapidly, that they have become a national issue.
>
> The national and provincial governments in Canada have specific rights, powers, and obligations under the provisions of the British North America Act. However, there is no legislatively-defined arrangement under this Act for the sharing of revenues arising from the exploitation of natural resources, including petroleum. The revenue share accruing to each level of government is a function of a mixture of fiscal instruments that has evolved over time. The result is a distribution of benefits that is extraordinarily unfavourable to the national government. . . .
>
> . . . The Government of Canada has a legitimate claim to a share of the energy industry's revenues to support its energy initiatives, and its broad economic management responsibilities— to cushion individual Canadians from the adverse economic effects, to facilitate industrial adjustment, and to see that fair play is done. As already noted, OPEC price rises provide a windfall to Canadian energy producers; they also hit hard at the economy, driving inflation rates up, and growth and employment down. . . . This is a crucial difference between Canada and most other energy-rich countries, among them federal states like Australia, or unitary states such as Norway and the United Kingdom. In these countries, the national government obtains most of the revenues accruing from the increase in price of domestic petroleum; it captures the

"upside" appreciation; it gets the financial wherewithal to offset the negative economic consequences of world oil price shocks. In Canada, one provincial government—not all, and not the national government—enjoys most of the windfall under current policies. These policies are no longer compatible with the national interest. . . .

To rely entirely on new taxes upon the industry would be unfair. It would also be ill-advised, for it would put in jeopardy our energy supply objectives. Finally, it would miss the basic point: *what is the appropriate distribution of oil and gas revenues among governments?*

What share of revenues reflects the needs and responsibilities of the two levels of government? At present, provincial governments receive more than three-quarters of the oil and gas production revenues accruing to governments. Alberta, with 10 percent of Canada's population, receives over 80 percent of the petroleum revenues gained by provinces.

Under existing arrangements, the Government of Alberta is enjoying rapid increases in its oil and gas revenues. Its revenues have grown faster than its expenditures, even though those expenditures have risen faster than those in any other province. Alberta has been able, moreover, to reduce substantially its tax rates for non-resource corporations, and its citizens enjoy the lowest tax burden, and the highest disposable incomes in Canada. With rising oil and gas prices, the revenues accruing to the province are sufficient to allow the Government of Alberta to have growing budgetary surpluses for the foreseeable future. . . . Canadians must decide, however, whether the current arrangements, which concentrate the financial benefits of higher oil prices in one provincial government and give little benefit to the national government, are appropriate. The Government of Canada believes the present system is inappropriate and unfair.[1]

Restrained price increases and a new series of federal taxes were the methods chosen by the Liberals to redistribute a larger share of economic rents to the national government and to energy consumers; that is, to equalize the energy benefits and burdens.

The upshot of the NEP pricing package for the producing provinces was, of course, to restrain in a major way, when compared to world prices, the price they would receive for their oil and gas resources. Even though the NEP scheduled conventional oil to reach

$66.75, Oil Sands Reference Price to reach $79.65, and Tertiary Recovery Oil to reach $62.85 by 1990, the assumption in 1980 was that world prices would increase to much higher levels, as world price was already around $39 Canadian. In addition to the absolute limits, the pace of increases was in dispute. Conventional oil was scheduled to rise $1 every six months until the end of 1983; from then until the end of 1985 it would increase by $2.25 every six months, and thereafter by $3.50 every six months "until it reaches its appropriate quality-determined level relative to the oil sands 'reference price.'"[2] This was considered to be far too slow by the producing provinces.

The producing provinces consistently used two arguments: (a) that their oil and gas were rapidly depleting, non-renewable resources, and (b) that in fairness, oil and gas should be treated like any other province's natural resources, to buttress their case for prices closer to the international price. The Liberals addressed both of these arguments in the NEP. In a special "box" section of the NEP, the Liberals rejected the Alberta government's claim that their resources were rapidly depleting, allowing at most that reserves of conventional crude oil had declined:

Alberta's Oil and Gas Resources—Rapidly Depleting?

In total, Alberta's remaining established reserves of oil and gas were larger in 1979 than in 1970, despite the production of huge quantities of oil and gas during the decade. What has changed is the mix; reserves of conventional crude oil and equivalent have declined, while natural gas reserves and oil sands resources committed to operating plants have increased.

The oil sands reserves in the table are those dedicated to the existing Suncor and Syncrude plants only. Total oil sands reserves are far greater. The Alberta Energy Resources Conservation Board (AERCB) estimates established surface-mineable oil sands reserves to be about 25 billion barrels from the Athabasca deposit alone. Total non-conventional petroleum reserves in Alberta are far higher again.

For natural gas, the table below reflects an increase in remaining recoverable reserves from 48 trillion cubic feet in 1970 to about 61 trillion cubic feet in 1979.

Alberta Oil and Gas Reserves*

	1970	1979
Total remaining established reserves	18.5	18.7
(billions of barrels of oil equivalent)		
Relative shares		
Conventional crude oil and equivalent	53%	36%
Natural gas	45%	56%
Oil sands	2%	8%

*Based on estimates by the Alberta Energy Resources Conservation Board.[3]

The argument that oil and gas resources should be treated like any other is also rejected. On a number of occasions the NEP argues that "energy has always been a special case":

> No Canadian can escape the impact of changes in its availability or price. Its influence on other activity—other products, other services—is pervasive. Reliance upon it is enormous. None of us can eliminate this reliance. Governments in Canada and elsewhere have long recognized and responded to this uniqueness. In Canada, for example, trade in the major forms of energy has been closely regulated by federal agencies for many years. Special procedures governing energy exports have been in place for some time, reflecting a national consensus that Canadian needs are to be served first, and that only surplus energy may be exported. At the international level, creation of institutions such as the International Energy Agency reflects a view that energy's role in today's world is extraordinarily important.[4]

Given their objective of strengthening the fiscal capacity of the national government, and the rationale that this was necessary to prevent the further balkanization of the Canadian economy and the excessive accumulation of financial surpluses in Alberta, the Liberals had to increase taxes on the industry. The two major new tax sources were the Petroleum and Gas Revenue Tax (PGRT) and the Natural Gas and Gas Liquids Tax (NGGLT). While the PGRT had more direct impacts on the industry, the NGGLT amounted to the next federal salvo in the continuing federal–provincial dispute over export taxes:

> For all these reasons the proposals presented to the producing provinces incorporated a federal tax on natural gas exports. The

Government of Canada was prepared to introduce a system in which the economic rent resulting from higher international prices for gas exports would have been shared between the producers, the federal government and the provinces. The Government of Canada also indicated that it was prepared to introduce a tax on electricity exports in order to ensure that energy exports were treated on an equitable basis.

The governments of Alberta and British Columbia have strongly opposed a natural gas export tax. They have argued that such a tax is an intrusion on the resource ownership rights. They also argue that taxes on gas exports are discriminatory.

The Government of Canada rejects these arguments. There is no doubt of the federal government's constitutional right to impose export taxes on any commodity. To deny this is to attempt to extend provincial powers well beyond their present constitutional limits. The federal government imposed an export tax on electricity for 38 years, from 1925 to 1963. Similarly, the federal government established a tax on oil exports in 1973. It continues to impose this tax.

A tax on natural gas exports is not discriminatory. These exports have earned enormous economic rents as their price has soared due to OPEC's price increases. Taxation based on the ability to pay is in accord with long-established principles.

Recognizing, however, the strong opposition of Alberta and British Columbia to the gas export tax, the federal government offered to discuss arrangements whereby there would be a sharing of provincial revenues when a province's revenues grew very much larger than those of other provinces. This offer to pursue an alternative which would have yielded the federal government little revenue, but would have worked towards reducing disparities between provinces, was also rejected. The Alberta government took the view that this proposal was neither feasible nor appropriate as an alternative in the context of the current oil and gas pricing negotiations. . . . It is a time when all governments must temper principle with flexibility.

The Government of Canada is, therefore, not proceeding with a natural gas export tax.[5]

The best that can be said about there not being an export tax imposed, was that the government pulled a quick sleight-of-hand. They imposed a new natural gas and gas liquids tax to which all natural gas sales would be subject, including those to the export market. The producing provinces were, of course, enraged.

On the larger issue of resource management, the NEP was clearly intended to give the national government greater control over one of the real commanding heights of the Canadian economy. The energy sector had become the brightest star of the Canadian economy. However, some observers charged that the same forces which had caused a boom in oil industry activity and fattened petroleum company profit margins had hurt other sectors of the economy. "For example, a recent Department of Finance study concluded that rates of return in Canada's manufacturing industries have been cut in half by 1978, as a consequence of the increases in the real price of oil that had occurred in the 1970s."[6] The dramatic OPEC price increases of 1979–80 and their ominous implications for inflation, economic growth, and unemployment both galvanized the Liberals to use the pricing and taxation measures to soften the impact on Canada, and provided them with an opportunity to assert federal direction on energy policy and the economy.

Alberta's Response

I frankly do not think it is possible for us,—as we move into the 1980s—to develop a Canadianism that responds to the diversity of our nation without some major, major readjustments in the way we have operated as a nation in the past. . . . The attitude of Western Canada towards Confederation today is dissatisfaction and frustration. . . . Alberta is being pressured to continue to sell its oil for less than 50 percent of its value. Alberta has foregone— as a contribution to Canada, from a depleting resource—over $17 billion. That is $8,500 for every man, woman and child in our province. . . . Any unilateral action by the federal government— particularly one by a federal government that's been rejected by western Canada—will be resisted by our citizens in the strongest and most determined ways. It would be a tragic miscalculation by Ottawa if they misjudge the resolve of Albertans in this matter. (Peter Lougheed, April 16, 1980)[7]

As the above quotation testifies, the Lougheed government began preparing its populace for the inevitable early in the spring of 1980. When the attack came on October 28, the Alberta government switched their three-pronged retaliation into operation and mobilized provincial public opinion. Given its political position as virtually that of a one-party state, at least in legislative power, this was not difficult to do. The retaliation itself consisted of the production cutback of 180 000 barrels of oil per day in three equal stages over nine months; the withholding of provincial approval for the Alsands and Cold Lake projects; and, the mounting of a constitutional challenge to the legality of Ottawa's proposed tax on natural gas. The Lougheed government explained its actions and rallied public opinion by developing a high-powered speech and pamphlet campaign designed to exploit traditional Alberta suspicion and resentment of Ontario and the central Canadian-determined Liberal federal government. This was particularly easy to do in the wake of Ontario's abandonment of the federal Tories in the 1980 election, which resulted in the defeat of a government well represented by westerners and its replacement by a government virtually devoid of western representation. The Alberta government fundamentally rejected both the policy thrust and the political motivation of the NEP, and in its response highlighted both the federal–provincial and interregional dimensions of Canadian energy politics.[8]

In his prime-time provincial television response to the NEP on October 30, 1980, Premier Lougheed stated that he could "only surmise that Mr. Trudeau wants to see control of Alberta's resources essentially in the hands of Ottawa."[9] He later went on to charge that if the oil had been owned by Ontario, Canadians would be paying world price. Lougheed denounced the federal initiatives in graphic terms and used fiery rhetoric to stir provincial passions:

> As far as I am concerned, the NEP consists of proposals not programmes and they are not national, they are Ottawa.... We will sit down and again try to negotiate. Ottawa made no attempt to do so last summer despite some very major concessions and compromises made by Alberta in an attempt to settle our differences on this very vital question for Canada. We are not optimistic about these negotiations but we are never the less still prepared to seek alternative solutions. However, no matter how stormy the weather, we will not capitulate. We will not give away the heritage of this province (*standing ovation*)....[10]

Merv Leitch, the provincial Minister of Energy, charged that the federal government had been bargaining in bad faith:

> I have no hesitation in saying to members of this Assembly that I'm convinced the present Ottawa government decided shortly after the last election that they were not going to reach an energy

agreement with the province of Alberta. I am convinced that shortly after the election, they concluded that now was the time, and oil and natural gas were the issues upon which to insure that the provinces with small populations would be dominated by the provinces with large populations.[11]

One of the political tactics employed by the Lougheed government in an attempt to diminish the legitimacy of the federal government, was to refuse to call it the federal or national or even central government, but rather to insist upon identifying it as the "Ottawa government." Another constant theme of the Alberta position was to link the NEP and the constitutional proposals and portray them as part of a larger scheme to take control of provincial resources:

> Mr. Speaker, one cannot divorce the energy issue from the constitutional proposals. I view those proposals, in essence, as saying that if a provincial government, if Alberta endeavours to stand on its ownership rights, its ownership over natural resources, to resist the decisions of the Ottawa government, they will then have in place a means whereby the constitution can be amended again by the majority population, by those provinces having a majority of Canada's population. What I've said is a harsh judgement of the Ottawa government, but I'm convinced that the history of our energy negotiations, the budget of October 28, the energy program of October 28, and the constitutional proposals, leave us with no other conclusions.[12]

Indeed the moral "high road" of Alberta's positions, and the theme the government drilled home at every turn, was the argument that the NEP was part of a larger plan to change fundamentally the nature of Canadian federalism. On November 19, 1980 Lougheed argued:

> It is my belief that the Prime Minister's plan to unilaterally change Canada's constitution over the opposition of the majority of the provinces, is closely linked to resource development and western Canadian development. . . . If the country proceeds as intended by the Prime Minister, we will have a very different kind of Canada. It will be a much different federal state—if a federal state at all. In my judgement, it will primarily be a unitary state with provinces other than Ontario and Quebec—being in a second class position. . . . [The NEP's] objectives are an attempt to take over the resource ownership rights of this province. The taxing and pricing powers of the federal government are clearly discriminatory and obviously

primarily directed at the two million citizens of Alberta and to a lesser degree, B.C. and the other western provinces. I believe very strongly as you know (and I believe many Albertans also believe), that it is unfair and basically changes the rules of Confederation. It changes the rules in a very significant way from the history of this country in terms of resource ownership rights of the provinces.[13]

This theme of Ottawa wanting to establish a unitary state in which the residents of all the provinces except Ontario and Québec would be "second class citizens" was one Lougheed would consistently return to: "They really want a unitary state where any decision of substance is made in Ottawa. They recognize they have to cater to Ontario and Quebec to stay in office but this select group cannot accept any other province becoming moderately independent and not subservient to them for federal discretionary grants. . . . upstart provinces will never do."[14]

In addition to portraying the NEP as a tool of federal and central dominance, Lougheed identified it as an instrument of nationalization and laid blame on the EMR officials.

In 1979, with the Clark administration, we had difficult negotiations because the senior officials involved in the Department of Energy, Mines and Resources wanted—as they do today—to nationalize the industry. I seriously believe that there is a select group in Ottawa that want to nationalize the industry so that they can fully control it from Ottawa. They have no seats to lose, no Chrysler or Massey Ferguson manufacturing in Alberta. . . . We look at the automobile industry—talk about foreign ownership! Look at the petroleum industry—they are already very heavily regulated and sovereignty is protected by resource ownership rights of the provinces. It is control from Ottawa—not Canadianization—that is the motive. It is an obvious smokescreen to say that it is Canadianization.[15]

The nationalist and centralist motivations of the NEP were seen as being virtually synonymous for Alberta. Both the pricing and Canadianization components of the NEP were portrayed as central Canadian inspired, and imposed by "their" federal government. With respect to the relationship of pricing to regionalism, Lougheed stated in October, 1979 during the peak of the Ontario–Alberta battle:

. . . the very serious oil pricing dispute. You are aware of the intensity of it—it is primarily between Ontario—the largest consuming province—and Alberta who produces 85 percent of Canada's oil. It is over prices. I bear you no apologies in terms of presenting Alberta's determination in this issue. . . . Ontario also argues that oil (and natural gas by implication) are somehow different in jurisdiction from other resources—so they want to change the rules of Confederation when circumstances suit them. They try to argue that oil revenues do not belong to the owner of the resource—but this position doesn't apply to other resources— to Ontario Hydro or Quebec Hydro—but only Alberta's oil . . . This position is repugnant and disturbing to Albertans—to generations who have paid to protect industry in central Canada and they now want us to pay twice—it is not acceptable.[16]

Alberta would continue to stress throughout this period that Canadian pricing policy had resulted in Alberta's subsidizing Canadian consumers, the majority of whom are in central Canada, by $17 billion since 1973. This was far greater than the $4 billion subsidy that Ontario had paid to Alberta and the industry between 1961–1973 by paying higher than world price. In January 1981, Merv Leitch would again make the connection between oil prices and the prices of central Canadian manufactured goods:

Frankly, I have the greatest difficulty understanding why anyone is arguing about paying world price for oil produced from the oil sands. We have lived for over a hundred years in this country totally accepting the philosophy that it was good for Canada, good for our national economy, good for the development of technology, to pay *more* than the world price for manufactured goods such as cars, radios, fridges, textiles, and a host of others. And even when we were paying more than world price, many of those activities were not very profitable and therefore didn't return any large tax revenues to any level of government. Two examples we can all quickly call to mind are Chrysler and Massey-Ferguson.[17]

Even though the proposal to impose an export tax of 4 mills per kilowatt-hour on electricity exports was discussed in previous federal energy positions, Leitch noted that "it is worthwhile observing that the proposal is not found in the current federal budget or in the energy program. I think it is worthwhile observing that the two provinces which currently export electricity to the U.S. are the provinces that have sent far and away the vast majority of the Members of Parliament that form the Liberal majority."[18] Despite the fact that public opinion polls showed that Canadianization was popular throughout Canada, and despite the support given to Canadianization by the government of the neighbouring province of Saskatchewan, the Alberta government depicted Canadianization in regionalist terms:

> It is fashionable in parts of this country to attack multinational corporations—who [sic] we invited into this country. It ignores the history, the contribution, and the potential for research and development. It is serious in terms of jobs for Canadian oil and gas companies. It seems that they care not a whit in some parts of Ottawa about jobs in this part of Canada. We look at the treatment of a company like Chrysler—the different ways in which they are treated is a disturbing sign of discrimination in the extreme to me. I am trying to control my emotions! I favour Canadianization but not Ottawa's way. Incentives to Canadians—yes, but not penalties to those who are already here.[19]

Alberta charged that the PGRT, which was a tax on production revenues and did not allow for any write-offs, was a wellhead tax, a veritable royalty. Royalties were considered a sacrosanct provincial right and its application in combination with the introduction of the NGGLT incensed Alberta. As a program of energy policies, the NEP was identified by Lougheed as "economically stupid." Alberta consistently claimed that the consequence of the NEP would not be energy self-sufficiency and security of supply by 1990; rather, the NEP would send the economy into a tailspin. The points explicitly outlined by Lougheed were:

- Reduced cash flow and fewer jobs for Canadians.
- A shift in exploration and production to the United States.
- "Expropriation" of more of the funds from Alberta oil and gas production to the federal treasury and a Canadian consumer subsidy.
- Damage to the Canadian owned segment of the industry.
- Opportunity for Petro-Canada to prey upon companies most unable to withstand the storm.
- Canada becomes increasingly dependent on insecure supplies.
- Natural gas is put on the back burner.[20]

It is clear then that Alberta's response to the NEP was strident and condemning. The content of the verbal response portrayed the NEP as a centralist attempt to make the smaller provinces second-class citizens; a plot by a small cabal of federal civil servants to nationalize the industry so that they could control it from Ottawa; a plan designed to reward the Liberal party supporters and electorate in central Canada, as opposed to their opposition in the west; a program which, together with the constitutional changes, was intended to turn Canada into a unitary state; and finally, as stupid economic policy. The production cutbacks, the withholding of mega-project approval and the court challenge, made it clear that Alberta was also willing to act in concrete ways to challenge the federal policy. Throughout November and December 1980, both the federal Liberals and the Alberta Conservatives flexed their muscles, each having recently been returned to power with fresh, majority governments. Through the early months of 1981, an agreement seemed anything but imminent. Both governments showed their resolve, and Lougheed steeled the will of his supporters by graphically warning Albertans "to be prepared to suffer and bleed."

However, as the impasse dragged on into 1981, both business and the other governments became increasingly impatient with the instability it was causing in the Canadian investment environment and pressured both Edmonton and Ottawa to reach an agreement. The President of the Canadian Chamber of Commerce said, "I, like many of you, am rapidly running out of patience with the political pugilists who persist in putting the nation's affairs on hold while they pursue their personal vendettas."[21] The oil industry itself began to criticize the stance of the Lougheed as well as the Trudeau government. J.M. Macleod, president of the Canadian Petroleum Association, suggested that Alberta may be too greedy in its demands for higher oil revenues. "Both governments must bend," he said, "to provide greater revenues to the companies."[22] Last, but certainly not least, in the summer of 1981, all the premiers urged the two disputing governments to settle their dispute. The dynamics of the 1981 negotiations are examined in more detail in Chapter 8.

Despite the return to power in Ottawa of a Trudeau Liberal government, the Alberta government still felt throughout the summer and fall of 1980 that it was bargaining from a position of strength. The two Alberta mega-projects were ready to go, and Alberta knew that the federal government was counting on production from them to contribute about 20 percent of Canadian oil supply by 1990. Canadian oil consumption had not yet started to drop, and therefore, Alberta felt, the threat of production cutbacks would have real force. Yet Alberta recognized that in imposing the cutbacks they would have to stress that the cutbacks would not be allowed to endanger the oil supply of other Canadians, thereby giving the federal government an excuse to utilize its overriding emergency powers. As a result of this, however, the cutbacks lost much of their clout.

By the summer of 1981 the Alberta government, by its own admission, was in a less advantageous position. There was plenty of oil available on world markets, so the importation of additional crude oil to replace cutback Alberta production was more a nuisance than a serious problem for Ottawa. Moreover, Ottawa was even able to gain publicity points by imposing a levy on Canadian consumers to pay for the additional imports and calling it the "Lougheed Levy." Indeed, the production cutbacks most hurt the Alberta producers whose oil sales were reduced. In fact, the entire Alberta provincial economy was beginning to feel the effects of the energy dispute, and Edmonton was being roundly criticized from all quarters for being intransigent and too demanding. Especially crucial were the pressures being applied on the Alberta government by the Alberta-based juniors and the Alberta-based supply and service industries. The latter were suffering the brunt of the exploration cutbacks and the shift of exploration activity to the United States. Ottawa had exercised its power with the NEP. Alberta was forced into a reactive position and found it could really have little effect in forcing changes to what was generally acknowledged to be a popular policy with Canadians, especially its Canadianization features.

Over the summer of 1981, as we see in detail in Chapter 8, senior Alberta and federal officials got down to the task of determining a mutually acceptable pricing scenario, which was the first step to arriving at an agreement. In late August 1981 Energy Ministers Merv Leitch and Marc Lalonde and their respective teams engaged in a marathon bargaining session in Montreal in which a final agreement was hammered out. On September 2, 1981, one day after the last Alberta production cutback came into effect, Canadians witnessed the two arch foes, Peter Lougheed and Pierre Trudeau, toasting each other on the successful negotiation of an energy agreement. At long last, Lougheed referred to the federal government instead of the Ottawa government.

For his part, Lougheed called the agreement the most significant event in the ten-year period during which his administration had been in office. "The long term consequences and benefits to Alberta are great," he said. "The Minister of Energy and Natural Resources and I believe most Albertans are pleased with the result."[23] The agreement gave Alberta what it wanted the most—a re-affirmation of its ownership of the resources. Secondly, there was no export tax on natural gas, although the federal government insisted on putting in writing that such a tax could be levied, but for the present it would be at a rate of zero percent. Thirdly, it provided a pricing schedule and revenue sharing regime the Alberta government was prepared to live with (see Appendix III for details). In order to maintain control over, or more specifically to keep federal officials away from, exploration in the province, Alberta agreed to fund and administer the Petroleum Incentives Program in Alberta. Alberta also agreed to make Market Development Incentive Payments (MDIP) to the federal government to facilitate the expansion of gas markets east of Alberta.

Even with a new agreement in place, the energy policy environment was to be anything but stable. At home, much of the industry was upset with the Lougheed government for allegedly taking care of its own interests at the expense of the industry in the September Agreement.[24] By 1982, international factors intervened once again, this time with a softening of the world oil market. Suddenly, the key assumption on which the NEP and the Canada–Alberta agreement had been based was no longer valid. Without continually rising international oil prices (but with rising interest rates), many of the non-conventional projects envisaged for Canadian energy development were not considered economically feasible. Moreover, the industry had been squeezed harder than Alberta had anticipated. By early 1982, the two major non-conventional mega-projects were doomed by the softening prices. The Alsands and Cold Lake projects, whose approval had been put on hold by Alberta during the earlier wrangles, were abandoned because their sponsors could not be convinced of a satisfactory rate of return and a sufficiently high world oil price. This happened despite federal and Alberta promises and commitments of assistance and guarantees.

Throughout late 1981 and early 1982, the Alberta government came under increasing pressure from the Alberta-based industry to assist it through a difficult period. On April 13, 1982 Alberta responded with "the Alberta Oil and Gas Activity Program." Through a series of royalty reductions and grants, Alberta hoped to increase the revenue flows to the industry by $5.4 billion between 1981 and 1986.

Alberta continued to lay most of the blame for the sagging fortunes of the industry on Ottawa.

While Alberta agreed in the spring of 1983 to amend the 1981 Agreement, it continued its verbal attack on the federal government. In August 1983, Peter Lougheed said:

> After the stupidity of the National Energy Program and the rape of western Canada I just don't believe that there's any conceivable way with a region such as the west suffering the economic difficulties of that stupid policy to see a re-election of that government.
>
> Because there's a growing awareness, I believe, in central Canada of how ill-advised that policy was.[25]

Ontario's Response

The Ontario government and Ontario-based industries were directly attacked in the Alberta response. Interprovincial sparring between Ontario and Alberta had become, of course, a prominent feature of Canadian energy politics. As shown in Chapter 5, the Davis Conservative government was a vocal and assertive defender of Ontario's interests during the period when it appeared the Clark Conservatives were willing to accede to rapid price escalations. Ontario's position reflected the interests of Ontario industry, Ontario motorists, Ontario householders, Ontario taxpayers, and of course, the interests of the Ontario government itself as a dominant force in Canadian federalism.

One of the key tactics of the Ontario government's strategy was to identify the interests of the Ontario economy with the national interest. Davis' dual concern for the Ontario and national economies covered the spectrum from the impact of rapid price escalation on economic growth, inflation, and unemployment, to the need for adequate recycling of oil and gas resource revenues throughout the Canadian economy. It is clearly debatable whether Davis' attack on the Clark government's efforts at negotiating with Alberta was intended only to make Clark aware of Ontario's concerns and to build a public attitude on energy issues in Ontario which Clark could not ignore, or whether Davis actually intended to "hammer another nail in Clark's political coffin," as Simpson has argued, with every expression of his "systematic campaign to discredit Clark's energy policy."[26] What is clear, however, is that Davis ultimately denounced the proposed energy deal between Alberta and the Clark government as "an excessive and imprudent response to the claims of the producing provinces and the petroleum industry."[27]

It is useful to juxtapose Davis' public stance in the wake of the NEP with his posture in the Clark era. Obviously Davis felt Ontario's back was to the wall in the Clark period, and he came out fighting. The following summary of his speech to the special First Minister's Conference on Energy on November 12, 1979, provides a sense of the breadth and bite of Davis' campaign:

> . . . Massive price increases would be unjust, unnecessary, and damaging to the Canadian economy, if not to the fabric of Confederation. . . . the people of Ontario are quite prepared to pay what is necessary to achieve self sufficiency. Certainly, in terms of the real costs of oil development, we are not getting it on the cheap today. . . . last year the petroleum industry enjoyed 360 percent more revenue than was the case in 1970. . . . it is misleading to suggest that Ontario is afraid of change or that we wish to protect an "obsolete" industrial base with the illusion of cheap energy. Indeed, throughout the 60s we accepted oil prices that were above world levels. . . . I am alarmed at the widespread temptation to turn national economic development policy into a zero-sum game, seemingly at the expense of Ontario.
>
> Any notion that energy development must inevitably lead to a poorer Ontario is not only bad economics, it is also grossly unfair. It would be ironic and unacceptable if the goal of crude oil self-sufficiency—which is supposed to help secure our nation— becomes a weapon for settling what some perceive as old scores between our regions. . . . surely those who want to build Canada dare not make their case by appealing to regional prejudice and inward myths.
>
> When massive and unprecedented interregional shifts of tax dollars threaten to distort the economy and enfeeble the capacity of our national economy to meet its national responsibilities, then provincial royalties are of legitimate national concern. . . . I cannot accept the argument that [Alberta] must enjoy a world rate of return, or go for broke on oil revenues, because it is a "depleting" resource. . . . conventional crude oil reserves are . . . only *one* source of revenue: in total, Alberta's revenue base is not running out, but is increasing steadily and will do so for decades. . . .
>
> . . . The stark prospect before all of us is that our differences over the pricing of crude oil really have less to do with energy policy than they have to do with conflicting aspirations and convictions about the management and future of our country. . . . We

in Ontario are firm in our conviction that energy policy must be defined within a national, not merely provincial context.

There is a view being advanced that Canada is a community of communities or a nation of provinces, and that our country is made stronger not by building the whole but by strengthening the separate parts. In some measure, that may, in fact be true, so long as province-building does not replace nation-building as the most ambitious goal of Canadians. Thus, the Government of Canada must stand not merely as an arbitrator of community differences, but the guardian of the nation as a whole.[28]

With the introduction of the NEP, in which the protection of consumer interest and the recycling of petro-dollars were prominent aspects, Davis adopted a rather different tack. He remained relatively restrained in his response to Lougheed's charges and taunts, and later adopted a generally conciliatory attitude toward the west. It is obviously much easier, in Canadian energy politics, to be magnanimous in victory. Nevertheless, Davis was critical of the production cutback by Alberta. He responded to Lougheed's October 30 speech in the following manner:

It is my view that the nature of last night's statement by the Premier of Alberta, while restrained and careful in some respects, is nevertheless a matter of deep regret. While no direct threat is posed to security of supply for Ontarians or Canadians, it will add a liability of $1 billion to the oil compensation fund in 1981 and $1.8 billion in 1982, based on present world prices. This will add to the national deficit and the debt load carried by all Canadians. . . .

The impact of last night's statement is economic. It imparts an extra financial burden upon an already tight national economy. This burden is not imposed on Canadians by any foreign power or by any international collapse but by a Canadian provincial government. This has been done despite one conservative estimate which places Alberta's cumulative revenue from oil and gas from 1980 to 1990 in the $100 billion range.

It is sad and of deep concern that one provincial government, presiding over what is the most rapidly expanding economy in the country, should respond to a continued and prolonged disagreement by imposing deep economic penalties on the working men and women, the pensioners, the business men and the people of Canada. I note and respect that Alberta will not allow its actions to pose a threat to security of supply.[29]

Davis also felt obligated to respond to Lougheed's charge that if Canada's oil was owned by Ontario, Canadians would be paying world price, and that western Canadians have always paid extra to protect central Canadian industry. Davis did not actually respond directly to either charge, but instead argued that Ontario has more than paid its way via equalization, while getting in a soft dig about Alberta's "jealousy" of Ontario:

> Last night the Premier of Alberta asked whether Canadians would be paying world prices if the oil and gas were here in Ontario. Let me say this to him, neither in anger nor sadness, but in a spirit of frankness and understanding: We have many wonderful resources in this province, both human and natural. Oil and gas in large quantities are not among them. Our wealth, our manufacturing, our industrial heartland is a source of envy and perhaps frustration to some. It is at the core of a feeling of alienation and regionalism for others.
>
> I answer Mr. Lougheed's question by saying that the record on our sharing of our wealth is clear. Ontario corporate profits, Ontario farmer's incomes, Ontario wages have all been taxed by the national government and redistributed nationwide to advance development elsewhere to help build schools, roads, and hospitals in other provinces.[30]

Additional evidence of the Ontario government's overall satisfaction with the thrust of the NEP is contributed by provincial Treasurer Frank Miller's October 30, 1980 response to the NEP and the Mac-Eachen budget in the Ontario Legislature. While Miller denounced the budget as "an inadequate response to the resolution of Canada's economic problems," he claimed that it "does present a constructive approach to a national energy strategy."[31] On the issue of pricing, Miller reiterated a key element of Ontario's position, specifically that energy price increases "must be accomplished by a reinvestment strategy designed to support consumer adjustment, provide industrial restructuring incentives, promote conservation and substitution and increase domestic energy supplies."[32] While Miller conceded the necessity of increased domestic oil prices, he insisted that the revenue produced from them serves the national economic priorities, and that the increases be balanced by some offsetting programs to protect consumers from the inflationary impact that increases generate.

Both of these are essentially questions of redistribution. On the latter point, Miller charged that the Liberal budget contained no such offsets, "no measures to assist the Canadian public to adjust to the inflationary effects of higher energy prices."[33] Ironically, given the Davis government's opposition to most of the energy measures of John Crosbie's December 1979 budget, Miller pointed to it approvingly for having proposals "to cushion the impact of energy prices on low income groups least able to absorb the changes."[34] On the former issue of regional distribution and adjustment Miller was also critical:

> Four billion dollars will be pumped into the western economy through the western economic development fund. This is in addition to the $38 billion that will flow to the producing provinces as a result of the federal energy package over the next few years. . . . The federal government also plans to consider initiatives relating to industrial diversification and to re-examine trade and industrial policies to serve western development better. . . . I commend these objectives but there should also be concerted efforts to address the same needs across the entire country.[35]

Miller implicitly took some credit for federal positions, stating that "I am pleased to note the federal government has accepted Ontario's position with respect to a blended price structure for oil pricing and has moved to develop a revenue-sharing arrangement that provides increased funds for national priorities."[36] Both of these proposals were outlined in the Ontario Government's August 1979 document, **Oil Pricing and Security: A Policy Framework for Canada**.[37]

Miller's utterances about Canadianization revealed some division within the Ontario Conservative government. In this same legislative speech Miller stated, "I believe strongly that more of the nation's petroleum industry should be Canadianized, but I make a very clear distinction between Canadianization and nationalization."[38] He went on to argue that Canadianization as the NEP proposed it was simply a euphemism for nationalization. He accused the Liberals of "using our money from a tax base to purchase for the government of Canada shares in those companies. That is quite different from encouraging the purchase of shares by individuals and investors in the country, the route I, and I am sure my party, firmly believes." It would appear that Miller was speaking more for himself than for the Ontario government. In fact, his comments on Canadianization would come back to haunt him in the legislature a year later when the Davis government purchased 25 percent of the shares of U.S.-owned Suncor. Central to Davis' explanation for the expenditure of $650 million was the NEP goal of Canadianization:

> This purchase will assist the Canadianization of the petroleum industry and fulfils a policy commitment announced by the Minister of Energy a year ago for greater Ontario participation in the Canadian petroleum industry. . . . Over the past several months the Ontario Energy Corporation has considered a number of potential opportunities to determine which investment would most effectively contribute to Canadianization of the industry and other policy objectives including a stronger voice for Ontario and its people in the energy business.[39]

Thus, it is clear that one of the Ontario government's motivations behind the Suncor purchase was to show direct and concrete support for the NEP's Canadianization objective. Davis went on to say in his Suncor speech that it was his desire to bring other Canadian investors into Suncor so that at least 51 percent of Suncor's shares would be owned by Canadians as soon as possible. As a new minority owner of a foreign-controlled-and-owned firm, Ontario wanted Suncor to continue to Canadianize so as to be eligible for higher federal exploration incentives. "The initiatives I have announced today signal a new phase in the activities of the Ontario Energy Corporation and represent a commitment by this government to contribute to crude oil self-sufficiency for Canada and to provide Ontario with a stronger voice in the determination of energy policy in this country."[40] In that regard, that very evening Energy Minister Robert Welch announced that Ontario would participate, via the Ontario Energy Corporation, in a joint venture with other firms to explore for oil in Hudson Bay. It is clear then that Miller, who initially couched his opposition to Canadianization in conservative ideological language, and later said he did not see a compelling enough practical reason to spend $650 million of public money for intervention in the private sector, especially in a period in which the government was supposed to be practicing restraint, was outgunned by those in Cabinet who felt the need to signal their support for the embattled federal energy policy (perhaps as a quid pro quo for the federal energy policy's having recognized Ontario's interests) and who saw direct intervention in an industry in which Ontario interests had not traditionally been paramount, as necessary to achieve the larger provincial security and economic goals.

Ontario was obviously pleased by the general thrust of the NEP, and did not respond in any major way to the alterations to the NEP which took place in 1981, 1982, and 1983. But then the blended-price concept was never seriously challenged, and softening world prices alleviated the Ontario government's worst fears regarding price increases. It is also important to note, of course, that the Ontario Conservative government was the federal Liberal government's closest ally in the constitutional patriation debate which raged along-side the NEP controversy in 1981–82.

Other Provincial Responses

While the Alberta and Ontario responses are obviously central, it is also essential to appreciate in a general way the responses of some of the other provinces.

The provinces of Manitoba, New Brunswick, and Prince Edward Island were either unable to present, or did not wish to provide, an articulate response to the National Energy Program. Given their minimal energy demands and marginal contributions to energy supplies in Canada, these three provinces had little interest in entering the national energy policy debate. From the perspective of these provinces, entering such a debate appeared to carry considerable political risk with the prospect of minimal political return.

The government of Québec was caught in a philosophical and pragmatic quandary by the NEP. The economic interests of Québec should surely have dictated that the Parti Québécois government join with the other major consuming province, Ontario, and actively champion lower oil and gas prices as contained in the NEP. Philosophically, however, the Québec government had such a hard-line provincial rights policy, it was inconceivable that it could actively support the federal government's aggressively interventionist energy policy, especially since the major producing provinces took their stand against the federal government on jurisdictional grounds. The Lévesque government, moreover, had just lost the 1980 Referendum on Sovereignty Association, and was a chief protagonist of the Trudeau constitutional proposals.

It is one of the great ironies of this period that the Parti Québécois government was able to extricate itself from its energy policy dilemma by relying on federal Liberal representatives from Québec to "do the right thing." The question of who governed Québec energy policy in the post-NEP period was answered by the Québec government by their very refusal to enter into the national energy debate. The Lévesque government, however, was not totally silent. We will see in Chapter 10 how it ensured that Hydro-Québec was not harmed by excessive conversion from oil to natural gas.

The other western provinces, Saskatchewan and British Columbia, joined Alberta in its call for world price. Saskatchewan's Minister of Energy and Mines called the continued subsidization of imported oil "ridiculous" when the revenue could be used for developing energy resources within Canada. Like Alberta, he claimed that "the federal government chose to sacrifice the interests of western producers and governments for the interests of consumers in the East."[41] Premier Blakeney also emphasized the relationship between regional discrimination and energy pricing. As he told one audience:

> The major benefit of low oil prices goes to Ontario, a province very much richer than oil producing Saskatchewan. We see this as reversing Robin Hood—or to give to the rich. There is a pervasive feeling in Western Canada that those policies are against our region and in favour of Ontario. It is no accident that the current federal government policies on constitutional reform and the National Energy Program are supported by every political party represented in the Ontario Legislature and opposed by every political party represented in legislatures of Alberta and Saskatchewan. Party lines are irrelevant. Regional views totally dominate. That is no accident but it is a national tragedy.[42]

While Saskatchewan opposed the pricing provisions of the NEP, the province did not implement any of the retaliatory measures such as Alberta had implemented.

Because of British Columbia's marginal oil production, the province took a back seat to Saskatchewan and Alberta in the oil-pricing conflict. British Columbia was more concerned with natural gas prices and the proposed natural gas taxes. The province did, however, fully support Alberta's position that oil prices should rise significantly. In the provincial government's policy statement, **An Energy Secure British Columbia**, released before the NEP in February 1980, the Bennett government stated: "The price of energy commodities must continue to be adjusted to reflect long-term replacement costs and the value of the resource. While there may be compelling reasons to hold the prices below market levels in the short term, this approach discourages production, encourages consumption, and relies on imports to fill any supply gap."[43] The British Columbia government continued to promote this line of reasoning in its public statements after October 1980.

Nova Scotia and Newfoundland focussed on their claim to ownership rights of the offshore resources. Thus, the proposed **Canada Oil and Gas Act**, which claimed those lands and all accompanying revenue benefits for all Canadians, angered the two eastern provinces. Both provinces insisted that offshore resource development was the catalyst to the general economic development of the region. Therefore, it was felt that a fair share of resource revenues accruing from that development was necessary and required in order to address the development needs of the region. In their minds, for the Government of Canada to claim ownership of those lands precluded the possibility of the provincial governments' enjoying the normal provincial benefits associated with resource development, and hence was unacceptable.

The Nova Scotia government condemned the proposed act. Premier Buchanan warned: "Should Parliament pass and proclaim this legislation, the province . . . will consider it ultra vires and will not recognize it as valid legislation."[44] Prime Minister Trudeau then called Buchanan's bluff, challenging the Premier to take Ottawa to court to determine ownership of offshore resources. In his response to the federal government's challenge, Buchanan questioned the practicability of a Supreme Court reference and assessed the dispute as political rather than legal. Further communications between the two governments revealed no shift in the federal position. On July 27, 1981, in his reply to Buchanan's inquiry regarding possible negotiation on the offshore, Trudeau stated:

> The present divergence of views regarding ownership has introduced an element of uncertainty which would eventually impinge adversely on an orderly development of the offshore hydrocarbon potential. The issue cannot remain unresolved much longer. It is therefore the intention of the Federal Government to see the matter resolved through the legal process while Federal–Provincial discussions concentrate on the more germane aspects of administrative mechanisms and revenue-sharing.[45]

He suggested that negotiations be undertaken in the fall, and then set February 1983 as the deadline for a political settlement, after which the conflict would be resolved through litigation.

Discussions between federal and provincial officials commenced in late October 1981. On October 6, the Buchanan government received a strong endorsement from the provincial electorate. Buchanan had called the election to secure a mandate for the province's stand on offshore ownership.[46] The Conservatives captured 47 percent of the popular vote and thirty-seven of the province's fifty-two seats. In the view of the government, these results would give their demands additional clout in the upcoming negotiations.

Nevertheless, when negotiations concluded nearly six months later, with the signing of the Canada–Nova Scotia Agreement on Offshore Oil and Gas Resource Management and Revenue Sharing, it was clear that the province had failed to achieve several objectives. On March 2, 1982, the two governments announced that the question of ownership would be set aside. On the issues of administration and management, the Agreement provided for the establishment of a five-member, federally controlled Offshore Oil and Gas Board, to oversee the management of offshore resources, but whose decisions could be overturned by the federal Minister of Energy, Mines and Resources. The minority provincial representation on the Board would be given the power to delay some major decisions for periods of up to one year. The Agreement provided for the establishment of an Executive Committee to co-operate with the Board in setting objectives regarding economic and social benefits from offshore activity.[47]

The province's concessions on offshore management may have been compensated by its share of revenues. Nova Scotia would receive all "provincial-type" revenues and additional revenues derived from a basic 10 percent royalty on gross production revenues; a progressive incremental royalty of up to 40 percent on net revenue; provincial corporate tax and retail sales tax applied in the offshore region; bonus payments; rentals and license fees above administration costs; and the federal petroleum and gas revenue tax (PGRT) at an effective 12 percent rate. The province would receive these revenues until its financial capacity exceeded the national average, and thereafter, the revenues would be increasingly shared with the federal government.

The Agreement also established a $200 million development

fund, financed initially by the federal government, for infrastructure costs associated with offshore development. Nova Scotia would have to repay the amount once it had begun to receive production revenues. However, federal approval would be required before expenditures were made from the fund. Among its other salient features, the Agreement granted the Nova Scotia government the right to acquire, at a price based on federal government's costs, a 50 percent portion of the Crown share of offshore gas fields and a 25 percent portion of the Crown share of offshore oil fields. Finally, and of no less importance, the Agreement provided that if another province should conclude a better deal, then the same terms would be available to Nova Scotia.

The Newfoundland government, as expected, denounced the federal initiatives as "devices to confiscate resource income that rightfully belongs to the province."[48] It reserved particular criticism for the Petroleum Incentives Program which "deliberately encourages exploration on lands to which the federal government claims ownership and discourages exploration on provincial lands (and, on a note of optimism, that) . . . when the province . . . succeeds in confirming its ownership over the offshore, most likely these lands would then not be subject to the Petroleum Incentives Program."[49] The province retaliated by transferring almost 10 million acres of petroleum rights on the continental shelf to its Crown corporation (NLPC).

For its part, the federal government, in May 1981, indicated its willingness to negotiate a settlement on shared management of the offshore resources and set aside, at least for the moment, the question of jurisdiction. Prime Minister Trudeau reiterated the federal position on revenue sharing:

> A coastal province should receive the same kinds of revenues as are derived by the provinces from onshore revenues until it becomes a have province. After that point, it would have to share an increasing portion of these revenues with the rest of Canada.[50]

The Newfoundland government accepted the Prime Minister's suggestion to negotiate, but only after the federal government agreed to delay the proclamation of its Oil and Gas Act. In return, the federal government fixed February 28, 1982, as the deadline for a negotiated settlement. By mid-1984 negotiations had still not succeeded, although the federal government's hand was greatly strengthened by the

Supreme Court's decision in March 1984 that confirmed federal jurisdiction.

Much of the federal response to Alberta and Ontario, as well as to other provinces, has already been introduced in Chapter 3, and will be examined in depth in Part IV. For the purposes of this chapter, it is sufficient to note that the immediate federal reaction to the Alberta retaliation was to lament the delay in the commencement of the two mega-projects and to impose a special levy on consumers to cover the cost of the additional imported oil. To lay the blame for the additional charge on the Alberta government, the Liberals informally called this the Lougheed Levy. In most of his speeches in the post-NEP, pre-Memorandum of Agreement period, Marc Lalonde avoided directly attacking the producing provinces. Criticism of the provinces was usually done implicitly when discussing the fiscal responsibilities of the federal government, equalization, the problems created by large increases in economic rents, and Ottawa's role in distributing the benefits and burdens of oil and gas price increases. After Ottawa and the producing provinces signed agreements in the fall of 1981, and Nova Scotia signed in March 1982, Lalonde would cite these as examples of co-operation in Canadian federalism. When Jean Chrétien became energy minister he promoted a conciliatory, co-operative, consultative tone with the provinces, though he was still unable to conclude an agreement with Newfoundland.

In a more concrete sense, the concessions made in the September 1981 Agreement reflected both the power of Alberta and the pressure placed on Ottawa by the other provinces and the business community. The concessions in the NEP Update were a direct response to Alberta's earlier package of concessions. The industry was very receptive to Alberta's package and challenged Ottawa to match Alberta's effort. The federal government continued to adjust in terms of its share of energy revenues with the 1983 Amendment to the 1981 Agreement. Alberta charged that Ottawa was not allowed by the 1981 Agreement to roll back the price of old oil which had exceeded 75 percent of world price. The Liberals argued that they had this power, but in the Amendment agreed to freeze wellhead prices rather than roll them back. The federal government also agreed to increase the amount of oil that could receive world price. While Alberta had continued to press for higher prices, this can probably more accurately be portrayed as a concession to the industry, particularly the juniors. The federal government absorbed through reductions in the NGGLT the major losses in revenue in order to maintain the price of natural gas at 65 percent of that of oil.

Summary

The most striking feature of post-NEP intergovernmental relationships is the virtually opposite reactions of Alberta and Ontario to the NEP. This of course reflected the different ways in which they were treated by the NEP, and their opposite positions on the key issues. While Ontario had reacted vigorously to the direction of energy policy under the Clark Conservatives, they quietly endorsed the NEP, even investing in a foreign oil company to signal their support. Alberta, which on the other hand, had been close to achieving many of its objectives with the Clark government, reacted angrily to the NEP. It adopted a tough rhetorical response and exercised its powers over production authorization, authority over the mega-project developments, and constitutional rights to fight the federal initiative. While it reached various accommodations with Ottawa over the intervening period, and was able to have some success in gaining higher prices for greater quantities of oil, it continued vigorously to oppose and criticize the overall thrust of the NEP into 1984. As was the case during the 1973–74 period the governments clashed over all three dimensions of pricing, revenue-sharing and resource management.

Because of a lack of intra-Alberta partisan opposition, the Lougheed government had carte-blanche in devising Alberta's response to the NEP. Throughout the 1970s the Lougheed Conservatives had been increasing their stranglehold on legislative power and during the NEP battle the legislative opposition was miniscule. Moreover, strong popular opposition within Alberta to the NEP, combined with strong provincial public support for provincial control over oil and gas, provided the Conservative government with a fertile attitudinal basis of support. If anything, the outburst of western separatist activity that followed the return to power of the Trudeau Liberals and the NEP caused the provincial Tories to take an even more strident stand. There was also a good deal of consensus in Ontario between the three major provincial parties over how Ontario should respond on energy issues. While the Ontario Conservatives returned to majority government status after being a minority government during the Clark interregnum, the fact that the Conservatives in Ontario had a provincial partisan opposition to cope with meant the intraprovincial dynamics were different than in Alberta. In fact, the Ontario Conservatives took as tough a stance as they did during the Clark-Lougheed negotiations because of the pressure being applied on them by the provincial opposition Liberals and NDP.

For its part, Ottawa did make a series of concessions on pricing and taxation which can be interpreted as accommodations to the power of the producing provinces and the various industry interests. It was able to do so, however, without alienating Ontario because global developments had softened the upward pressure on oil prices.

The focus of the last two chapters on the key governmental and industry interests in the post-NEP era has shown both the range of variations and common positions which emerged within the relationship between key interests. For example, the strains that visited the Alberta–industry relationship, particularly concerning the junior firms, in the wake of the September 1981 Alberta–Canada Agreement, reveal the interrelated nature of the government–industry and intergovernmental relationships. Indeed, as one traces these key relationships of power over the post-war period and observes them at close range in the post-NEP period, it again becomes increasingly clear that energy politics must be understood as the outcome of interactions between a number of key interests organized around a series of relationships of power.

Notes

1. Government of Canada, *The National Energy Program* (Ottawa: Supply and Services Canada, 1980), pp. 10–16.
2. *Ibid.*, pp. 25–26.
3. *Ibid.*, p. 15.
4. *Ibid.*, p. 11.
5. *Ibid.*, pp. 33–34.
6. *Ibid.*, pp. 10–11.
7. Hon. Peter Lougheed, "Speech to the Canadian Daily Newspaper Publishers' Association," Toronto, April 16, 1980, pp. 1–2.
8. The Alberta government followed the Lougheed speech of October 30 with the production of an extensive ten-page brochure which it distributed in December 1980 to Alberta households. The brochure contained thirty-three points which explained the Alberta government's position on energy issues and the constitution. It attacked the federal energy program, explained Alberta's reaction and posed and answered a series of other questions, including the following:

   • Are we being unpatriotic when we insist on protecting provincial ownership rights?

   • What about the charges that Alberta is being too selfish?

   • What features of the Alberta proposal would specifically help other provinces?

   • Do the energy issues relate to the constitutional issues?

   The brochure closed with an exhortation to Albertans to "send a copy of this brochure describing Alberta's position to friends and relatives in other parts of Canada. . . . they must realize that we do care for our country. . . . we are willing to make a very large contribution to Canada. We have already done so." See Government of Alberta, *Energy Issues and the People of Alberta*, December 1980.
9. Hon. Peter Lougheed, "Transcript of Address to the Province of Alberta in Reaction to the Federal Budget," October 30, 1980, p. 3.
10. _____, "Address to Annual P.C. Convention," Calgary, March 21, 1981, pp. 12, 14.
11. Alberta Legislature, *Debates*, November 3, 1980, p. 1338.
12. *Ibid.*
13. Hon. Peter Lougheed, "Speech to the Edmonton Chamber of Commerce," Edmonton, November 19, 1980, pp. 1–2.
14. _____, "Speech to Calgary Chamber of Commerce," Calgary, February 13, 1981, p. 7.
15. _____, "Speech to the Edmonton Chamber of Commerce," *op. cit.*, pp. 3, 6.

16. _____, "Speech to Vancouver Board of Trade," Vancouver, October 29, 1979, p. 8.

17. Mervin Leitch, "Speech to Vancouver Board of Trade," Vancouver, January 14, 1981, pp. 15–16.

18. Alberta Legislature, *Debates*, November 3, 1980, p. 1339.

19. Hon. Peter Lougheed, "Speech to the Calgary Chamber of Commerce," *op. cit.*, p. 7.

20. _____, "Speech to the Edmonton Chamber of Commerce," *op. cit.*, p. 5.

21. *The Globe and Mail*, February 28, 1981, p. 13.

22. *Ibid.*

23. Alberta Legislature, *Debates*, October 14, 1981, p. 1092.

24. IPAC, on behalf of the industry, offered to make industry officials available to work for the Alberta team during the negotiations leading to the September 1981 Agreement. Alberta politely declined the offer. While Alberta felt it had the necessary technical sophistication within its own energy department to cope with Ottawa, the industry was later suspicious of Alberta's motives when Alberta appeared to fare better in the outcome than the industry felt it did.

25. *The Ottawa Citizen*, August 6, 1983, p. 6.

26. Jeffrey Simpson, *Discipline of Power*, (Toronto: Personal Library, 1980), chapter 7.

27. Hon. William Davis, "Opening Remarks" to the Special First Ministers Conference on Energy, Ottawa, November 12, 1979, p. 5.

28. *Ibid.*, pp. 10–23.

29. Ontario Legislature, *Debates*, October 31, 1980, p. 3949.

30. *Ibid.*

31. Ontario Legislature, *Debates*, October 30, 1980, p. 3861.

32. *Ibid.*, p. 3864.

33. *Ibid.*, p. 3862.

34. *Ibid.*, p. 3861.

35. *Ibid.*, p. 3863.

36. *Ibid.*, p. 3864.

37. Hon. William Davis, Oil Pricing and Security: A Policy Framework for Canada, August 14, 1979. It was in this document that Davis told Joe Clark that "if necessary, the federal government must use its influence and constitutional authority to direct oil and natural gas revenue flows in accordance with agreed national objectives," p. 18. This argument, indeed the entire document, incensed the Lougheed government which the next day released a four-page, fourteen-point rebuttal. See "Statement by Premier Lougheed of Alberta in response to Ontario position paper entitled 'Oil Pricing and Security,'" August 15, 1979.

38. Ontario Legislature, *Debates*, October 30, 1980, pp. 3863–3864.

39. Ontario Legislature, *Debates*, October 31, 1981, p. 2442.

40. *Ibid.*

41. *Leader Post*, October 29, 1980, p. 1.
42. Hon. Alan Blakeney, "Notes for March 21, 1981 Speech," pp. 10–11.
43. Government of British Columbia, Department of Energy, *An Energy Secure British Columbia*, February 1980, p. 4.
44. See Barbara Yaffe, "Will Ignore Federal Energy Bill, N.S. Says," *Globe and Mail*, May 14, 1981, p. 1.
45. Government of Canada, Office of the Prime Minister, *Press Release*, July 28, 1980.
46. Lyndon Watkins, "Buchanan Seeks Resources Mandate, Calls October 6 Election," *Globe and Mail*, August 29, 1981, p. 13. See also Michael Harris, "PCs Win Crushing Victory in N.S.," *Globe and Mail*, October 7, 1981, p. 1.
47. Government of Canada, Department of Energy, Mines and Resources, *Canada—Nova Scotia Agreement on Offshore Oil and Gas Resource Management and Revenue Sharing*, March 2, 1982. In June 1984 it became known that there was a further secret element to the agreement. A separate letter contained a provision that would ensure that Nova Scotia would not lose a dollar of equalization payments for every dollar it earns offshore. See *Financial Post*, June 2, 1984, p. 1.
48. Government of Newfoundland and Labrador, Newfoundland Petroleum Directorate, *Effects of the Federal Energy Policy on Offshore Newfoundland and Labrador*, PD81-1, February 1981, p. 1.
49. *Ibid.*, p. 9.
50. Government of Canada, Prime Minister's Office, Letter to Stephen A. Neary (Newfoundland Liberal M.H.A.), July 6, 1981.

PART IV

POLICY AND IMPLEMENTATION IN THE POST-NEP PERIOD

CHAPTER 8

ENERGY POLICY AND IMPLEMENTATION:
IDEAS, STRUCTURES AND PROCESSES IN ACTION

With the dominant intergovernmental and government–industry relationships of power and the interests they contain fully examined, we can now in Part IV proceed to give greater attention to the NEP as a public policy, including its implementation between 1981 and 1984.[1] Before beginning the more detailed analysis of the NEP, however, it is important to have in mind some basic concepts so that the view of public policy presented in this section, that of an interplay between ideas, structure and process, can not only be understood but can also be related to the broader political interests analysed in previous chapters, and to the realities of implementing a policy as complex as the NEP.

Public Policy Concepts: Ideas, Structure and Process

Chart 8.1 conveys some of the detailed terrain to be covered in this section. In one sense it contains a checklist of the key components of the energy policy system. **Ideas** refer to the broad normative content of energy policy. These have been examined earlier and have been related to the specific objectives of the NEP and to its rhetorical language in Chapter 1. Throughout the following chapters we continue this examination particularly in relation to what we have called the NEP evaluation game. As we have stressed, the NEP objectives were almost universally applauded. But the differences arise in the relationship among the objectives, and the evaluations that emerged reflected the political interests at stake as they pursued ideas that were not always compatible. **Structures** refer to organizations and the persons who head them. Structures embody ideas and they have a stake in the policy process and its outcomes. Public policy is the product of the need to structure and organize political power and influence. At the time of their establishment new structures often "are" the policy, but thereafter they take on lives of their own, not just in some perverse sense of "bureaucracy" run amok, but in the sense of having a mandate enshrined in law and approved through a democratic process. They are therefore bounded in some general way by the larger political institutions and interests that we focussed on in Parts II and III. **Processes** refer to the changing dynamics which arise when decision makers are required to deal with uncertainty, with risk, and with divergent perceptions of how to deal with a changing environment. Processes also refer to the subsidiary patterns of behaviour that arise in several different ways and which interconnect with the larger overall intergovernmental and government industry politics and processes that were the focal point of Parts II and III. One process, for example, is the government's overall priority-setting process and the agenda as it sees it. We saw this clearly in Chapter 2 on the origins of the NEP. The formulation of energy policy at any given time cannot be understood unless it is explicitly linked to the larger view of priorities and to how larger priorities change. But there are other processes as well. These include those that accompany the main instruments of government such as pricing and taxing, spending and regulating.[2] The price-tax process, the spending process and the regulatory process take on lives of their own. These latter processes are the main basis on which the chapters in this section are organized. There are also the processes that accompany large projects, that is, highly visible, capital-intensive events that create a unique, highly focussed kind of politics and risk sharing. The dynamics of projects are examined in Chapters 9 and 11. There are also the processes in which the arts of forecasting, analysis, and evaluation interact with ideas and interests. Finally, there are the processes imposed by imminent deadlines and the leverage gained or lost by the fluctuations in public opinion and of sustained pressure applied in timely ways.

Public Policy Concepts: Implementation as Public and Private Behaviour

But before proceeding to outline these processes, we must deal with another concept central to the public policy focus of this section of the book, namely, policy implementation.[3] "Implementation" is perhaps one of the most misleading words in the English language and in one's classic view of "the policy process." The mere sound of the word lulls one into a dull but serene sense of a world of routine predictability. It is, is it not, what bureaucrats do? When one thinks of the classic description of the "stages" in the policy process, namely, initiation; formulation; the search for, and analysis of, alternatives; decision; and

CHART 8.1

A PROFILE OF KEY COMPONENTS OF THE ENERGY POLICY SYSTEM

Ideas	Structures	Processes
Efficiency	Cabinet	Overall priority setting
Individual liberty	EMR	Prices and price setting
Stability	Finance Department	Taxes and tax expenditures
Equity	COGLA	Expenditures
Redistribution	NEB	Regulation
Nationalism and national	Petro-Canada	Major projects
integration	Provincial energy agencies	e.g., Alsands, TQM Pipeline
Regionalism and regional	and boards	Forecasting, analysis
sensitivity	Environmental assessment	and evaluation
	panels	Deadlines and other
(Expressed both directly	Office of Industrial and	temporal pressures
and through the official	Regional Benefits	Uncertainty and risk
and unofficial goals,	Crown corporations	taking
objectives, and language	Petroleum Monitoring Agency	
of the NEP and the reaction	OPEC	
of interests to it.)	International Energy Agency	

"implementation," the last takes its appointed place at the hind end of the policy beast.

There is no doubt that many features of policy implementation are indeed routine, the production of reliable, predictable behaviour according to the dictates of law and policy arrived at in a general democratic way. But one need only think about government for a few concerted minutes to realize that the nature of this seemingly benign activity in fact takes on many forms and involves different combinations of public *and* private behaviour. Far from being just what bureaucrats or public servants do, implementation also involves behaviour by private sector implementors. Some public services involve a passive relationship—e.g., the mailman delivers the mail to your door. Some involve a co-determination of services—e.g., the citizen calls the cops and the police respond. While these everyday examples may seem far removed from the world of energy policy and the NEP, they are not.

The problem with the word "implementation" is that it does not sufficiently capture that part of the real world of policy implementation that goes beyond routine predictability. In short, it does not sufficiently embrace the frequently wide areas of discretion and hence power involved, a world that includes both public and private discretion by sometimes willing and sometimes unwilling "implementors."

The NEP is an example par excellence of a pervasive public policy reality, namely that the implementation of public policy increasingly involves both public and private behaviour. It is not just a function of what public officials do but also of how private decision makers— corporations, consumers, citizens—respond to and/or attempt to escape the consequences of the policy itself or particular parts of the policy. Public policy in its full sense therefore involves not just one kind of power but two kinds. The first involves power as revealed by the victory of one minister over another or one interest over another in the pursuit of some general ideas or specific goals. But the second kind of power is more difficult to achieve. This is the kind that seeks to insure that human behaviour actually changes over time in a sustained way and in the desired direction. This is ultimately what implementation is all about; in this sense, it profoundly embraces politics and power in a continuous and persistent way.

The chapters in this section, and the arenas of implementation that each separately covers, are intended to capture and analyse these broad dimensions of policy implementation. While in the case of the NEP, we can of course cover only its first few years of implementation, it is precisely in this sense that one must put these early post-NEP years in the context of the pre-NEP legacy and events. The NEP is clearly a major event, but it does not represent a de novo start. There is considerable analytical danger in thinking of policy development in terms of stages. Policy is embedded in history. Decision makers have memories. Old ideas persist through time. New structures more often than not do not replace old structures, but rather are added to the status quo.

This view of implementation is all the more necessary in the case of the NEP because of its three essential attributes. First, as stressed in Chapter 2, the NEP was itself in part a major bargaining ploy intended to break a political logjam and induce and force a response. Second, as stressed in Chapter 1, the NEP embraced a range of official and unofficial objectives that partially were in conflict and thus gave key interests considerable room for both rhetorical and de facto manoeuvre. And third, as this and later chapters show, the NEP contained several program elements that were virtually "one line" items and that therefore were not well defined nor well thought out. Examples of these are the proposals for a natural gas bank, for Petro-Canada International, a new subsidiary of Petro-Canada, and for the Trans-Québec and Maritime Pipeline (TQM). Thus, far from being ready to implement, these policy elements were yet to be developed.

For all these reasons, policy implementation must be viewed as a far more dynamic and elusive process, indeed a series of processes. In Part IV we have chosen to examine the different processes by grouping them into the main instruments of public policy inherent in the NEP. Thus we devote separate chapters to the dynamics of pricing and taxing, spending, and regulation respectively. But while doing so, one must remember that public and private decision makers were interested in, and were responding to, the entire package of NEP initiatives in all of these "arenas" of implementation simultaneously. Thus one has both to unravel the component instruments and processes and then put them back together again, recognizing all the while that the policy environment was not conveniently standing still.

The titles of the chapters in this section convey a sense of the implementation dynamics inherent in each area of the NEP. The notion of having to "run a gauntlet" through the maze of post-NEP taxes and prices is not an excessive metaphor for the nature of the relationships between the public and private implementors of the NEP. Private interests were being induced and required to change their behaviour so as to implement the policy. How were they to respond to the fiscal regime, not only in general, but in specific corporate contexts? The notion of a "paradox of control" in the world of energy expenditures conveys a vivid reality of the NEP implementation dynamics in that control took on various and quite elusive dimensions. First, it implied a capacity to control revenues so that projected energy expenditures could be carried out. Second, it involved controlling spending when the basic initiative resided in the hands of private decision makers as to just how much, and to what ends, they would avail themselves of new grants. The concept of developmental regulation involved a form of highly discretionary bargaining and negotiating over discreet projects and over the pace of "development," and hence stood in contrast to the more traditional kinds of policing and public utility regulation practised by bodies like the NEB.

The three arenas covered in Chapters 9, 10, and 11 do not of course exhaust the ways any government might try to implement its policy. Woven into our analysis are the other ways in which suasion, exhortation, and propaganda were used by both sets of implementors, public and private. The use of Crown corporations is also central to the analysis in this chapter and in later chapters as well.

To pave the way for these various portraits of the implementation of the NEP, one first needs to have a more detailed understanding of the structures and processes of energy policy. We first describe the general federal energy decision process. We then examine basic features of the key structures, namely, the Cabinet, EMR, and Petro-Canada. In later chapters we examine bodies such as the NEB, COGLA, and the Office of Industrial and Regional Benefits. While our focus here is on federal structures, we also refer periodically to other structures in provincial governments and in other countries, especially the United States. The next section of the chapter restores some life and flesh to these static structural portraits by examining two very different immediate post-NEP implementation dynamics, namely the federal–Alberta negotiations that led to the 1981 Canada–Alberta energy agreement and which altered key features of the NEP, and the work of the Alberta Technical Advisory Committee (ATAC), the committee established late in 1980 by Economic Development Minister Bud Olson to reestablish contact with parts of the industry immediately after the announcement of the NEP, and to which we referred briefly in Chapter 3.

Basic Federal Energy Policy Structures and Decision Processes

The NEP created its own dynamics within the federal decision making system, and energy prices, taxes, and expenditures were in turn buffeted and affected by external events, pressures and perceptions both in the energy policy field and in other related areas such as fiscal and economic policy. We have already examined many of these dynamics in Chapter 2, where we focussed on the key ministers and officials involved, and where we distinguished the views of old-line EMR officials from the newer "policy types" who entered EMR in the late 1970s.

The somewhat static description of the energy decision process and its main structural components presented in this section must be viewed in this light. The description is organized in three parts. First, we note briefly the pre-NEP decision process. The second part describes the post-NEP decision process. Finally, we describe the main decision structures, and stress again the importance of personalities and individual dynamics.

In the immediate pre-NEP period of 1978 and 1979 energy decisions, especially those involving expenditures, were nominally a part of the purview of the economic development committee of Cabinet (the Board of Economic Development Ministers under the Liberals, and the Cabinet Committee on Economic Development under the Conservatives). In principle then, energy decisions and expenditures were to be traded off and assessed in relation to the whole array of economic development departments and programs. In practice, however, energy decisions during this period were, like the NEP and post-NEP periods, the product of "special" processes outside this Cabinet committee. This was because energy issues were central to the economic and political fate of the government. Thus under the Clark government in 1979, major elements of energy policy were handled by the Prime Minister and examined primarily through the inner Cabinet.

As we have already stressed in Chapter 2, the NEP itself was forged through a process virtually separate from the "normal" Cabinet decision process. The main contours of the NEP were developed while the Liberals were in opposition, through a small group of political party advisors during the 1980 election campaign. Many of the main features were revealed in Prime Minister Trudeau's election speech in Halifax on January 25, 1980 and included the concept of a blended national "made in Canada" price, an expansion of Petro-Canada, and a commitment to support Canadian oil and gas producers and to increase Canadian ownership of the industry significantly.

Once in office, the Liberals forged their new plan in greater detail with a handful of ministers and their deputy ministers, including the Prime Minister, the Minister of Finance, and the Minister of Energy, Mines, and Resources. At the deputy minister level, the trio of equivalent deputies became known as ENFIN for "energy–finance." Two major factors dictated this concentration of power. The first was the need to have a small core group to negotiate with the Alberta government over the critical twin issues of prices and revenue shares. The second was the decision in the summer of 1980 that the NEP would have to be part of a budget, since it involved major issues of taxation and fiscal policy. A further related reason for a cohesive and concentrated decision process, and one closely entwined with the first two, was the growing determination on the part of the incoming key Liberal ministers and on the part of the senior EMR and Finance department officials that there was a need for decisive action to break the logjam in negotiations with Alberta. As we have seen in Chapters 2, 3, and 5, these negotiations had stalled even under the somewhat sunnier partisan climate expected to arise from the Clark government's dealings with a fellow Conservative government. The post-NEP decision process flows inexorably from these immediate pre-NEP dynamics. Figure 8.1 attempts to portray the several routes that energy decisions have taken. Each of the main structures involved is described briefly below.

FIGURE 8.1

THE GENERAL POST-NEP ENERGY DECISION AND RESOURCE
ALLOCATION PROCESS

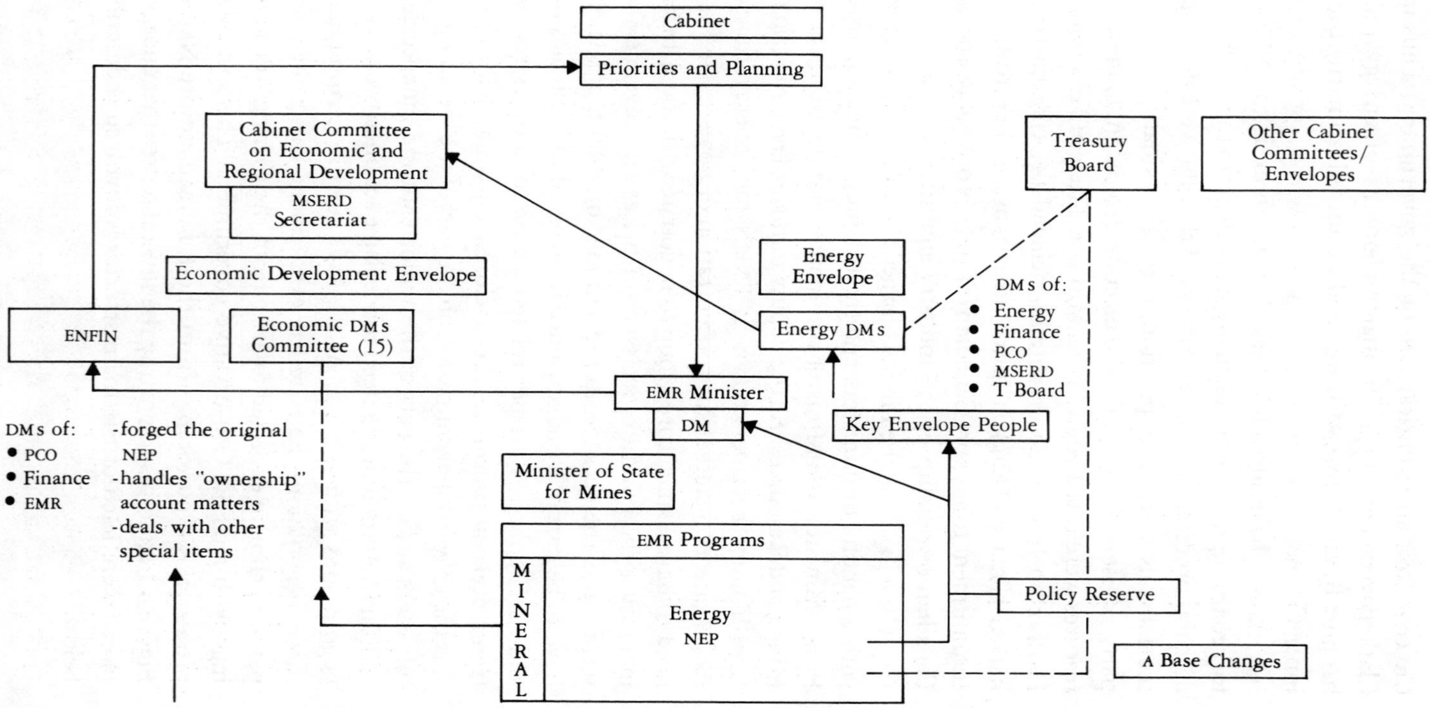

Cabinet Committee on Priorities and Planning (P&P)

Chaired by the Prime Minister, P&P makes the major determinations of the government's priorities, its fiscal position and the size of the policy reserves (money for new initiatives) for each expenditure envelope including the energy envelope (see Chapter 10). Since P&P included the key ENFIN ministers, its role overlapped with that of ENFIN.

ENFIN

ENFIN was the dominant decision making body. It cannot be stressed too much that it functioned outside the normal Cabinet decision process. Technically, ENFIN is the trio of deputies, but in reality it should also be viewed to contain the three key ministers, Trudeau, Lalonde and MacEachen, since if the three acted informally in concert, ENFIN could be said to have decided, in a de facto way. ENFIN was the fulcrum in forging the NEP itself, assisted as we saw in Chapter 2 by another small handful of EMR and Finance officials. As well it handled issues arising from later takeover decisions using funds from the Canadian Ownership Account. The Petrofina and BP acquisitions by Petro-Canada were handled through ENFIN. Such decisions by their nature must be kept tightly controlled since negotiations are delicate and financial, and stock market rules and proprieties must be adhered to. ENFIN also dealt with any other major energy issue it chose to deal with, such as the 1982 NEP Update package and the failed negotiations on the Alsands project.

The Cabinet Committee on Economic and Regional Development (CCERD)

CCERD contains ministers of the major economic departments and is responsible for policy and resource allocation decisions. It has jurisdiction over the economic and regional development and the energy envelope.[4] With respect to the energy envelope, however, as we see below and in more detail in Chapter 10, its stewardship is less direct. CCERD is chaired by the Minister of State for Economic and Regional Development (MSERD) whose staff advise him and other CCERD ministers. In the case of post-NEP decisions, the CCERD practice was to group together a number of energy items or proposals and then hold periodic "energy" meetings of CCERD. Because of the high priority and political sanctity accorded the NEP, particularly in 1981 and early 1982, other CCERD ministers did not feel particularly disposed to challenge such proposals as they might other proposals at a normal CCERD meeting.

The Treasury Board

The Treasury Board under Ottawa's Cabinet committee and expenditure and decision system retains its primary role of approving detailed expenditure and person-year plans and of monitoring the continuing allocations from the "A base" of expenditures, that is, *existing* expenditures. Since it has more detailed knowledge of actual programs than any other central agency, its advice is also part of the detailed financial assessment of new initiatives (that is, so-called policy reserve initiatives). The Treasury Board role vis-à-vis energy envelope initiatives was somewhat abnormal, however. This arose primarily out of a decision in December 1980 that several major post-NEP decisions would *not* be subject either to extensive CCERD review or to review and prior scrutiny by Treasury Board. Several items were sent to the board, but the political momentum behind the NEP was such that not much Treasury Board opposition would be brooked. The board of course also retained its role over regular EMR pre-NEP "A base" programs. It must be stressed that the NEP resulted initially in a huge element of new programs (often referred to as the "B" Budget) being added to a much smaller A base. This is the reverse of the typical situation for most departments in most years. A further point must be stressed about the Treasury Board's overall posture on the NEP. That is, that from the outset the board was concerned that the NEP contained numerous "one-line" program entries whose integrity as viable programs had not been fully assessed. This concern increased because of the fact that EMR was historically primarily a scientific and technical department, not a program-oriented department—but would have to gear up *very rapidly* to become one.

Other Cabinet Committees

Other Cabinet committees, such as those on Social Development (CCSD) and External Affairs and Defence are involved in energy and energy-related matters in two respects. First, some issues overlap, such as in expenditure allocations for Petro-Canada International (which involves Official Development Assistance funding levels and hence affects the external and defence envelopes). Energy issues in the north have also involved disputes over which envelope (e.g., social development versus energy) should fund all or part of a northern hydrocarbons and oil and gas development program. Second, other committees are invariably involved in an indirect but equally real way, through the normal expenditure pressure and demands that occur within any highly political Cabinet. Thus other ministers, departments, and Cabinet committees increasingly envied, especially beginning in 1982, the generous funding that seemed to flow into and out of the energy envelope. As the economy declined precipitously in 1982 and 1983, the pressure from other ministers and from outside interests to put scarce dollars to non-energy uses increased greatly.

The Energy Deputies

The Energy Deputies are a committee composed of the Clerk of the Privy Council, the Secretary to the Treasury Board, the Secretary of the Ministry of State for Economic and Regional Development, and the deputy ministers of Finance and Energy, Mines and Resources. The committee was established to help manage the energy envelope by establishing a "mirror" deputies' committee similar to the larger economic and regional deputies' committee that supported the work of CCERD on general economic development envelope issues.

Most major post-NEP energy decisions (including non-NEP items such as nuclear issues), except for those that went through the ENFIN route shown on Figure 8.1, were sent first to the Energy Deputies. Proposals were usually assessed at a lower level by senior analysts from EMR and the central agencies involved, before going to the Energy Deputies' meeting per se. From December 1980 to the end of 1983 the Energy Deputies met about fifteen times, with the frequency decreasing as the main NEP components were put into place.

The Minister and Department of Energy, Mines and Resources

Within EMR the post-NEP decision process and related envelope activities were in the hands of a small handful of persons. The focal point was obviously the Minister, Marc Lalonde, and the deputy, Mickey Cohen. They had direct and instant access through P&P, ENFIN, the Energy Deputies, CCERD, MSERD and any other structure or modus operandi deemed necessary. Within EMR they were advised primarily by the senior ADM, Ed Clark, and the ADM Energy Sector, George Tough, and their small core of advisors. Other ADMs in EMR were involved in relation to their specific program responsibilities only.

Other Departments and Agencies

Just as other Cabinet Committees have a role in energy policy directly and indirectly, so also do some individual departments and agencies. Some of these, such as Indian Affairs and Northern Development and the Department of the Environment, were referred to indirectly above and are analysed further in Chapter 11. There are others as well, including Petro-Canada (whose obviously central role is explored later); the Ministry of Transport and the CTC (vis-à-vis transportation technologies and routes, and energy use in the transport sector as well as public safety); the Department of Regional and Industrial Expansion (DRIE), especially its Office of Industrial and Regional Benefits; and the National Energy Board (exports, pipelines). These are a list of the major departments only. Several dozen agencies could claim some "energy" role.

This, then, is the basic inventory of federal energy policy structures. It is a necessary list to keep in mind. The dynamics of energy decisions, however, though influenced by the ideas inherent in energy and related policy issues and by the structures, are also a product of the interaction, skills, and power of individual ministers and senior officials. Of special overall importance is the simple fact that during the four-year period examined, EMR was headed by two ministers and two deputies who functioned at very different times in the "life cycle" of the NEP and in the fiscal and political fortunes of the government. These personality factors are reintroduced below in the context of a more specific look at the Cabinet, EMR, and Petro-Canada.

The Cabinet, EMR and Petro-Canada

In the context of our analysis in Chapter 2 of the genesis of the NEP, we have already made a number of observations about the three core structures involved in energy decisions. These were made in the general context of the relations between ministers and senior public servants. We stressed the relative balance of power and influence between ministers and bureaucrats. This was based on several factors, including the personal power of Prime Minister Trudeau, Energy

Minister Marc Lalonde, and Finance Minister Allan MacEachen; the impetus of the 1980 "energy election" and the federal–Alberta deadlock, and the particular nature of, and the alternatives foreclosed by, specific provisions of the NEP. The bureaucracy's influence was clearly present in particular elements of the NEP, and the overall package was given greater coherence because of the tactical influence of Mickey Cohen and the ideas, powers of advocacy, and integrative skills of officials such as Ed Clark. Finally, we also stressed the concern expressed then by other segments of the Ottawa machinery that the NEP would bureaucratize the energy policy process because it contained such a complex price and program structure.

All of the above was set in the immediate *pre-NEP* context as the NEP decisions were being made. Several other observations need to be made about the core structures in the context of the evolving *post-NEP* period and in the light of the general description of the energy decision processes presented above.

First the Cabinet as a whole, which had not in real terms had much to say in the initial NEP decision (since the latter was a pre-emptive strike by three ministers and their bureaucratic allies) gradually began trying to reassert some larger notion of collective Cabinet government (albeit after the horse was out of the barn). Senator Bud Olson, the Minister of Economic Development, established the aforementioned ATAC group (see also below), out of frustration at not being involved and out of concern that the government had lost all communication with the industry. Treasury Board President Donald Johnson, a conservative in fiscal orientation, attempted to have the Treasury Board scrutinize NEP program elements. Other ministers simply wanted to know more about the NEP in order to explain it better to their own constituents.

Any real protests about the NEP, however, were generally lost in the heady euphoria of 1981. The NEP was popular and Marc Lalonde, by dint of personal skill and the Prime Minister's backing, held sway without much difficulty, cocooned with his own multi-billion dollar envelope of funds. It was not until the fall of 1981, after the Canada–Alberta agreement, after the disastrous MacEachen budget of November 1981, and after it became evident that the economy was sliding into deep recession, that the pace of ministerial criticism picked up. As Chapter 10 shows, Finance Minister Allan MacEachen soon had to demand the return of funds from the energy sector to help shoulder the growing deficit. Other ministers saw dwindling dollars for their programs and accordingly related their financial demise, in part at least, to the NEP.

It must be stressed, however, that none of these protests were a direct attack on the NEP. Rather, they were indirect "second thoughts" inserted as the economy declined and as the government's extremely aggressive and ambitious priorities unravelled. Only in 1982, with the recession in full swing, was it deemed necessary to begin adjusting the NEP. Marc Lalonde presided over the development of the NEP Update package announced in May 1982, the chief feature of which was an amended fiscal package that funnelled about $2 billion in additional incentives to improve the cash flow of the industry, especially the smaller Canadian firms. Lalonde subsequently left EMR to become Finance Minister, taking his deputy, Mickey Cohen, with him. From then on the government's priorities shifted to the wounded economy.

Lalonde's successor, Jean Chrétien, was clearly a different kind of minister presiding at a very different time in the fate of both the NEP and the government. Less interested than Lalonde in the conceptual basis of policy and anxious to mend fences with the industry, Chrétien made it clear that his priority was to make the energy climate more stable and to speed up Ottawa's response time to the numerous individual concerns being raised by companies. His deputy minister, Paul Tellier, shared this view of the need for consultation and stability.

Thus it is important to stress that as the NEP was implemented, both personalities and the political and economic context of the NEP changed markedly. This was also evident in the more specific circumstances of the evolving role of EMR and Petro-Canada. There can be no doubt that initially a mutually supportive bond existed between EMR and Petro-Canada.[5] This dated back to the early 1970s when its then new deputy minister, Jack Austin, advocated the need for such a state corporate presence in the even then increasingly turbulent energy world. Only after the 1973 OPEC crisis did the Trudeau Liberals agree, spurred on by new energy realities plus the minority government pressure of the NDP. The initial intention was that Petro-Canada would play only a role as a catalyst in the risky frontier exploration game and that it would improve Ottawa's intelligence in, and knowledge about the oil and gas industry. As pointed out in Chapter 3,

Ottawa and EMR were embarrassed at their lack of knowledge of, and their degree of dependence on, the oil and gas industry. Thus at this early stage EMR and Petro-Canada shared a common need in that both were intended, in a general way, to improve Ottawa's policy capability in the energy policy field.

This mutual bond was strengthened during the brief Clark government, when senior EMR officials defended the role of the state oil company in the face of Tory promises to privatize all or parts of it. As defenders of Petro-Canada the Liberals in 1980–81 brought the EMR/Petro-Canada symbiosis to its zenith, but thereafter the relationship began to change, the product of the same circumstances noted above in the more general setting of the post-NEP period.

The key to the relationship between the two structures in this period is found in the approval process for Petro-Canada's five-year corporate plan and its annual capital budget. In formal terms, approval must be given by both the energy and finance ministers in December of each year after receipt of the two sets of documentation earlier in the fall. The plans are analysed by senior central agency advisors but usually in the context of a last minute rush of meetings. Meanwhile the real evaluation process is occurring at a far more senior level among a small handful of ministers and officials. The key to this process was the personal lobbying network of Bill Hopper and Joel Bell, Petro-Canada's president and vice-president, respectively. Bell in particular shepherded the plans largely through his personal access to Lalonde and Trudeau. The relationship was obviously a mutual one, since the two key ministers were prepared to give Petro-Canada virtually carte-blanche support.

The degree of this support was evident in 1981 when Petro-Canada's capital budget reference levels were set that December to include new government equity investments of $450 million in 1983 and $600 million in 1984 growing at 10 percent per year thereafter. These figures did not include the moneys Petro-Canada would receive either through the Canadian Ownership Charge which would pay for some acquisitions or from PIP grants. By the fall of 1982, however, in an "X budget" cutting exercise, Petro-Canada's equity infusions had been pared to less than $370 million, $480 million, and $510 million in 1983–84, 1984–85, and 1985–86, respectively. Moreover, several of Petro-Canada's major projects were cancelled or deferred in 1982.

The changing status of the EMR/Petro-Canada relationship was also reflected in the BP acquisition in the fall of 1982. Petro-Canada, with approval from Trudeau and Chrétien, decided to buy the down-stream assets of BP at a cost of $347 million for shares and about $670 million in total including other inventory, legal and interest costs. In this case the government said that new funds would not be required because Petro-Canada would be able to finance it. Petro-Canada was able to finance the acquisition because its financing capability was increased by the fact that its commitments to the Alsands and Cold Lake projects were no longer needed. These had been approved by the Cabinet in Petro-Canada's earlier capital budgets. Technically no new money was involved in the BP acquisition, but this was based only on the assumption that Petro-Canada did not later come back to Ottawa for more equity or other financial benefits to "make room," so to speak, for the partially reallocated Alsands and Cold Lake funds.

The BP takeover typified a larger set of problems about the capacity of the Cabinet and of EMR to control Petro-Canada. Although Petro-Canada presents much more information to Cabinet than virtually any other Crown corporation, the advance time available to scrutinize the Petro-Canada capital plan and its five-year corporate plan is still extremely limited. There is little doubt, however, that ministers and central agency officials are no longer prepared to give Petro-Canada the virtual carte blanche it had been accorded in 1981. Tougher questions were being asked about its role in the downstream sector, the pro-gas export pressure it was exerting on the government, its possible further expansion into coal, and its delays in proposing Canadian benefits policies for its own contracting needs, a problem examined in Chapter 11. Although there can be little doubt that Petro-Canada's easy entrée into the corridors of power through the rapport between key officials such as William Hopper and Joel Bell and minis-ters such as Marc Lalonde was a major factor in its capacity to obtain massive funds and infusions of equity, this chemistry too was changing, the cumulative product of changes in personality and position as well as the factors noted above. Both Lalonde and Bell, for example, departed for other positions in 1983.

We return to these key energy structures in the chapters which follow. They clearly influenced the NEP, but equally they were affected in different ways by the NEP itself and its many intended and unintended effects. While the somewhat static portrayal of key structures and a listing of the basic processes of policy formulation and implementation are essential preparation for the analysis in Chapters 9, 10 and 11, they must be brought to life by examining other realities and dynamics that followed immediately in the wake of the NEP. Two of these are briefly examined, namely the federal–Alberta negotiations that led to the 1981 Canada–Alberta Agreement, and the work of the Alberta Technical Advisory Committee (ATAC). The former illustrates the implementation processes that occurred at the centre of power in an essentially intergovernmental domain. The latter illustrates the implementation processes that occurred for those who were not at the centre of power and which involved essentially government–industry relations.

The 1981 Federal–Alberta Negotiations: Implementation at the Centre of Power

By far the most important post-NEP implementation dynamics were centred in the federal–Alberta negotiations that led to the September 1, 1981, Canada–Alberta Agreement on pricing and revenue sharing. This was simultaneously a "hardball" exercise in implementation and a further exercise in policy development. The Liberals wanted Alberta to react to their initiatives. The nature of the dynamics involved must be related to our earlier analysis in Chapter 2 of the pre-1980 negotiations or, more accurately, discussions. The key players were the same but the balance of power now tipped decisively in favour of the federal government.

The Liberals now had a major and decisive policy document in full public view and with apparent widespread public support. They were now the initiators and Alberta would have to react. This could not help but affect the nature of the bargaining. This is not to suggest that Alberta was not well prepared. Knowing that something highly unfavourable to their interests was going to be contained in the NEP, the Alberta government had prepared their contingency plans months before so that it was prepared to announce, without hesitation, the tough measures that Premier Lougheed launched a few days after the NEP.

These included the phased-in production cutbacks and the withholding of approval for the mega-projects. The cutbacks were real but their de facto leverage was curtailed by the Alberta promise that Canadians in other parts of Canada would not be denied supply in any emergency. The Alberta government also found it difficult to counter in any effective way, at least in the short run, the Canadianization theme of the NEP. On this point they were also put on the defensive. Moreover, the production cutbacks, in real terms, had adverse effects mainly on Alberta producers and on the even larger oil field service sectors of the Alberta economy. These interests were at the core of the Lougheed Conservatives' political support, and as the negotiations dragged on over the summer of 1981, they applied extensive pressure on the Alberta Tories to settle. Alberta negotiators also faced another reality. If they did not settle on a deal, Ottawa would act on its full NEP programs. This would have been far worse for Alberta, and there was no doubt now that the federal Liberals would act.

Whereas in 1979 and even 1980 Alberta was well positioned to bargain, by 1981 the balance of real power had changed. Nonetheless, negotiations had to be conducted. Almost immediately after the NEP, first in November 1980 and then in early January 1981, the two key deputy ministers, Mickey Cohen and Barry Mellon, met to discuss the approach to be followed. The sequence of the issues that had to be resolved was quickly established—first, prices, then revenue shares, and finally items such as PIP, Canadianization, and specific projects.

The first substantive meeting with ministers Lalonde and Leitch present was held in Winnipeg in April 1981. Its chief purpose was to establish and confirm a common data base. Both sides tabled their data. It is at this point that one should relate our earlier comments in Chapter 3 about the relationships between the art of forecasting and analysis with the realities of pressure politics and political deadlines. While both Alberta and federal data were based on buoyant expectations about real increases in world oil prices, the federal projections were much higher than Alberta's. Federal negotiators produced high forecast numbers in part because of their tactical strategy. They believed that the bigger the pie that could be shown to exist the easier it would be to strike a deal with Alberta. To obtain final agreement on the data to be used, the two sides averaged Ottawa's high numbers with Alberta's lower figures.

Since, in relation to actual proposals, Lalonde had done most of the talking at the April meeting, it was the Alberta decision makers who were under pressure to respond with counterproposals. After an extensive and often heated three-day debate by the Alberta Cabinet energy committee at Jasper in late April and early May 1981, Alberta eventually brought its pricing proposals to a June meeting at Banff involving the two sides. The federal response to these proposals in a July meeting in Toronto essentially nailed down the pricing issues. The nature of the compromise was essentially to move from Ottawa's single blended-price concept to the more complex price system (which we examine in detail in Chapter 9) based on old and new oil, and schedule the phase-in of price increases to a pace that was slower than Alberta wanted but somewhat faster than the NEP schedule.

Even though price issues seemed to be largely settled by July, there was still much doubt that an agreement would be reached. Ottawa was putting on pressure by arguing that an agreement had to be settled by September 1 so that the federal government could present a budget in the fall. Meanwhile there was strong pressure on both sides to reach agreement, but much of this favoured Ottawa in terms of the final leverage available. Alberta had at the outset said that Ottawa should have more revenue than in the past, but how much more was the key. The precise tradeoffs here became very complex and are entwined with the time pressures. Alberta fought hard for the principle that no export tax be levied on natural gas. Ottawa said it had the right to tax but agreed to set the tax at zero percent. Alberta also, in support of its firm belief in provincial resource control, did not want Ottawa bureaucrats administering PIP grants in Alberta. For this principle they paid several hundred million dollars, a dubious victory in the total scheme of things.

Despite some further quarrels over each side's apparent "monkeying" with the data base heretofore thought to be established, the negotiators met again in Montreal in early August and finalized items in a marathon bargaining session over the final ten days of August. As to the optimistic pricing and economic assumptions behind the agreements, both sides had some inkling by early August that these forecasts were perhaps unrealistic. But this evidence was not overwhelming. Private sector forecasts were still buoyant. In any event, both sides knew that to reopen the numbers game now would unravel the agreement. The pressure to settle was too great.

While the substantive effects of the agreement are the subject of later chapters, some aspects of the policy process and implementation dynamics are worth noting, especially in the light of the energy policy structures described earlier in the chapter. First, in both governments involved in the negotiating process, the finance or treasury ministers were essentially not primary participants. Their officials had an analytical and advisory role but, despite the fiscal importance of the deal that was being struck, they were not a major part of the action. Merv Leitch was a former Alberta Treasurer, and Mickey Cohen and Ed Clark had been senior finance officials, but in the crunch of negotiations the fiscal perspective did not prevail. A second point to note is that the forecasting and analytical component, while always an important element of such dynamics, is impossible to understand except in relation to the kinds and levels of political pressure involved and the ideas inherent both in the pressure itself and in the analytical assumptions. Finally, there is the simple issue of deadlines and memories of past dead-ends. An agreement did have to be reached by the early fall. The then current level of conflict and anger could not be tolerated.

The ATAC Committee and MSED: Implementation Discussions at the Periphery of Power

The Alberta Technical Advisory Committee (ATAC) was described briefly in Chapter 3, where we noted its role as a device initiated by Senator Bud Olson, the Minister of State for Economic Development, to help restore communication with the energy industry in the explosive early months after the NEP was announced. As we have already seen, Olson, despite his Alberta base, was not involved in the NEP or the negotiations described above. Nor were MSED and the Cabinet Committee on Economic Development, despite the latter's custody of the energy envelope and of economic development policy, involved. They were, in short, on the periphery of power. They devised their own way of being involved, not in the intergovernmental arena, but in the government–industry arena.

Composed of selected Canadian oil and gas company executives, ATAC was not allowed to challenge the fundamental principles and components of the NEP. Its mandate was to suggest ways to improve the detailed implementation issues. It did, however, reveal something of the perceived early impacts and uncertainties of the NEP, and shows why the supposed radical character of the NEP lay not in its official objectives per se but in the complexity of the new fiscal regime and its impact on accepted ways of doing things in the oil patch. The company reactions and perceptions discussed below must of course be placed in the larger context of industry interests examined in Part III, but they are illustrative of the overall implementation dilemmas as seen by a major segment of the industry, indeed that part of the industry that was the main targeted beneficiary of the NEP.

The overall concerns raised in the earliest meetings in November 1980 were about the impact of the new taxes. ATAC members asserted that they would have a large negative impact on corporate balance sheets, especially for the non-integrated and therefore mainly Canadian firms. Not surprisingly, there were concerns about key concepts in the NEP such as the precise meaning of Canadian owner-ship and control, how distinctions would be made between exploration and development, and what would constitute approved costs. There were also concerns about the "paper burden" effects of all the new requirements, especially for small Canadian firms.

The bottom-line concerns were very evident and were often expressed in specific, individual company contexts (as opposed to the ATAC group as a whole). Concern centred, for example, on how the PIP grants would be treated in accounting terms. Under current accounting practices endorsed by the accounting profession in the interests of accurate disclosure, such grants would not be reflected as a source of income on income statements. This could then have an adverse effect on a firm's capacity to raise funds in the financial markets, since their financial statements would not look as robust. Therefore some firms wanted an arrangement whereby they could waive the right to a grant by a corresponding reduction in the PGRT tax. Other firms objected that this would destroy the credibility of the industry, which had been making loud noises about the negative impact of the NEP.

Other interesting divisions and views occurred in the realm of policy information and forecasting. Discussions arose over the pros and cons of giving "more numbers" to Ottawa. If Ottawa had better information, would it make better policy? Some ATAC members believed that more information would only lead to more and more comprehensive cost-based pricing systems and to the mistake of creat-ing a myriad of reference prices. But a majority of ATAC members seemed to conclude, at least at this initial stage in the post-NEP politics of implementation, that if Ottawa was determined to move towards a kind of "utility rate of return" regime then Ottawa would not be deterred by a lack of industry cooperation. In this regard it is likely that ATAC members had little trouble recalling other information-seeking interventions of the not-too-distant past, namely Petro-Canada's role as a window on the industry, and the establishment in 1978 of the Petroleum Monitoring Agency. These ATAC members also pointed out that smaller Canadian firms with few reserves of cheap old oil favoured a higher price for higher-cost new oil, and thus wanted a more complex pricing regime. Therefore, it was thought best under the circumstances to supply Ottawa with the best information in a form Ottawa found useful.

There were also concerns raised about Ottawa's data and modelling techniques. The concern was a dual one, not only because such models, as we saw in Chapter 2, informed the construction of the NEP itself but also because similar approaches were likely to underpin future policy. Therefore, the reasoning went, "next time" the industry should help shape the results as they used to do in the glory days of the 1950s and the 1960s. EMR officials explained to ATAC members that two levels of modelling had been involved, a macro-model dealing with pricing and revenue shares and related items, and a micro-model dealing with the financial performance of different types of companies regarding cash flow and investment behaviour. ATAC members zeroed in on the micro-model. It is worth noting at this point that in the larger federal–Alberta negotiations going on, it was the macro-model that was the focus of dispute.

It was explained by EMR analysts that the micro-model projects company income, capital expenditures, and cash flows over the decade for both the pre- and post-NEP fiscal regimes. The model, it was said by EMR spokespersons, had held up moderately well in comparisons with some companies' own estimates. EMR officials acknowledged, however, that there were a number of behavioural relationships that were difficult to model. These included changes in current taxes; reinvestment and redeployment of capital expenditures; the relationship between current exploration and development and future company production; and the lack of consideration given to pools of tax write-offs that individual companies may have accumulated. EMR modeled fifty-eight companies and concluded that in the 1981–83 period there would be about a 15 percent difference in cash flow between pre- and post-NEP, and that capital expenditures could be lessened by about 18 percent. EMR also concluded that between 1984 and 1990, cash flow would be about even between the pre- and post-NEP regimes, and there there might be an 8 to 9 percent drop in capital expenditures.

Needless to say, the model and the projections based on it aroused considerable opposition and criticism within ATAC. Company representatives zeroed in on several problems and effects. For example, by not including claimable tax pools, companies' initial cash flow was artificially reduced in the modelling of data, and the impact of the NEP was accordingly underestimated. Another example concerned grants. In the model, grants were treated by EMR as an automatic part of corporate cash flow. Grants, however, were not included in cash flow in industry accounting practices, and therefore ATAC members estimated a reduction of cash flow of 30 to 40 percent. This refers in part to the accounting problem noted above, since these net figures, in the industry view, are the real cash-flow numbers that concern shareholders and investors when they look at the underlying investment value of the firm. ATAC members also argued that EMR's estimates of exploration and development activity by Canadian firms on the Canada Lands were extremely optimistic. As we see in Chapter 9, there was also sharp dispute about the relevant pre- and post-NEP years to compare.

These various bottom-line, cash-flow, data and modelling–forecasting issues are themselves implementation issues of no small import. One should not be surprised to find out that different, though basically medium-sized Canadian companies, even within the group of companies on ATAC, saw their interests differently. The modelling cannot possibly capture the *individual* company effects, even under the most stable of circumstances. Nor can better consultation before the fact give better intelligence, since energy associations and other groupings must also aggregate their positions to some kind of acceptable lowest common denominator. It is in this very real sense (a sense repeated in numerous other policy fields as well) that the "idea" of equity as set out in Chapter 1—the notion of having to treat people or companies in equal situations equally and those in unequal situations unequally—is rampant in the very design and implementation of the NEP.

One must also keep in mind that the illustrative glimpse supplied by the ATAC example, is, in the case of the entire NEP, but a small sampling of the implementation dynamics. They were issues perceived to be occurring at a very early post-NEP stage, and as seen by a few of the medium-sized Canadian firms. This was *before* the Canada–Alberta Agreement, the onset of the recession, and the decline of world oil prices. The larger protests and investment postponements by key interests referred to in Part III were going on concurrently with the ATAC exercise. Nonetheless the flavour of the detailed concerns expressed in the ATAC process is indicative of the issues, uncertainties, and conflict of ideas about prices and taxes, expenditure incentives, and regulatory rules and understandings unleashed by the NEP.

Key Implementation Issues in the Pricing, Taxing, Expenditure and Regulatory Arenas

In any period of implementation following a major policy initiative, there is bound to be much uncertainty. Persons and interests do not like to be subject to too much uncertainty because, in the face of it, one senses one's own powerlessness and vulnerability. Uncertainty was endemic in the NEP, and a preliminary view of its component parts gives us, along with the main official and unofficial objectives of the NEP discussed in Chapter 1, a clue as to why. The NEP was an act of political risk taking. Its scope, complex price, tax and program structure, and its analytical assumptions produced marked uncertainty. This was aided and abetted by powerful opposition to it, and by its occurrence just prior to a largely unforeseen, but massive, recession.

In the realm of prices and taxes, the NEP was underpinned by assumptions and forecasts made in 1980 about the expected steady real increase in world oil prices throughout the 1980s. As we have already seen, these forecasts did not materialize. Revenue intakes by both Ottawa and the producer provinces were in turn based on assumptions about prices. A complex new array of taxes was imposed, the initial effect of which was to create extraordinary uncertainty among firms, each one of which had to calculate overall net effects, not only from the taxes, but also from the loss of other tax incentives, *plus* the possible addition of PIP grants, *plus* the net mix of old and new oil. Gas companies had prices pegged at 65 percent of oil prices, but faced widely varying domestic and export market situations depending on the state of gas surpluses in the United States and competition from electricity and heavy oils in the regional markets in Canada. On large projects there were further complications, because such projects are always in some respects treated as special cases involving special mixtures of prices and taxes. This was all the more the case when the Trudeau Liberals gave great fanfare in the summer and fall of 1981 to their so-called mega-project strategy.

On the expenditure side, the NEP contained a new array of grants and incentives whose overriding characteristic, as we see in Chapter 10, was that they were demand-driven. That is, the volume of expenditure was determined primarily by the level of activity initiated by private decision makers, be they private corporations deciding how much exploration activity to undertake in the Canada Lands, or individual homeowners deciding the extent to which they would take up COSP and CHIP grants.

Finally, on the regulatory front, the NEP would involve an elaborate new regulatory regime on the Canada Lands centred in COGLA and designed to increase the pace of activity, enhance Canadian participation and public sector involvement in each play, and ensure improved Canadian content in the procurement of contracting services and supplies as well as capital equipment.

In the midst of all of the price, tax, spending, and regulatory turmoil stood Petro-Canada, involved in and affected by the new maze of policy instruments. What mattered was not just these policy devices in isolation, but their combined effects in a short period of time and in the midst of recession.

Summary

As an introduction to Part IV and an entrée into the more policy-oriented issues inherent in the NEP, this chapter has provided some further necessary background for the detailed analysis to follow in Chapters 9, 10, and 11. We have reviewed the overall federal structures and processes of energy decision making in the post-NEP period, and linked them back to our earlier account of the role of ideas. We have stressed particular changes and attributes of key structures such as the Cabinet as a whole, EMR and Petro-Canada, and have reminded ourselves of their connection to key personalities examined in Chapter 2. We have also stressed the importance of both public and private behaviour in policy implementation. This has been done both in relation to the main separate arenas of implementation—prices and taxes, expenditures, regulation and public enterprise—and their interconnections, and in the context of varying concerns about the politics and effects of modelling and forecasting and about numerous versions of the corporate bottom line. We have also presented preliminary and illustrative glimpses of two implementation dynamics: the federal–Alberta negotiations in 1981, which were at the centre of power; and the ATAC committee, which fell on the periphery.

Policy implementation is in one sense a "stage" in the policy process. But in the case of the NEP it was hardly the stage at which serene predictability and monotonous routine took hold. Rather it was, for many good reasons, a stage where more policy was made, where ideas in conflict were rejuggled and reinterpreted, where deadlines and pressures loomed large, and where interests tried to adjust to a world that refused to sit still while the NEP policy experiment was undergoing a giant version of a "once only" field test. There were implementors galore, but not all of them were willing participants.

Notes

1. On the interplay approach, see G. Bruce Doern and Richard W. Phidd, *Canadian Public Policy: Ideas, Structure, Process* (Toronto: Methuen, 1983).
2. See *ibid.*, Chapters 4, 11, and 12.
3. For related views on implementation, see J.L. Pressman and Aaron Wildavsky, *Implementation* (Berkeley: University of California, 1973); Robert T. Nakamura and F. Smallwood, *The Politics of Policy Implementation* (New York: St. Martin's Press, 1980); and Charles E. Gilbert, ed., *Implementing Governmental Change*, special issue of *The Annals*, American Academy of Political and Social Science, March 1983.
4. See G. Bruce Doern, ed., *How Ottawa Spends* 1981, 1982, 1983 (Toronto: Lorimer) for an analysis of the evolution of this Committee and of MSERD.
5. For assessments of EMR and Petro-Canada, see J.E. Hodgetts, *The Canadian Public Service: A Physiology of Government* (Toronto: University of Toronto Press, 1972), Chapters 3 and 4; Richard W. Phidd, Administrative Change and Policy Development: A Case Study of Energy, Mines and Resources Canada, unpublished paper, University of Guelph; Peter Foster, *The Sorcerer's Apprentices* (Toronto: Collins, 1982), Chapters 6, 7, and 8; G. Bruce Doern, "Energy, Mines and Resources, the Energy Ministry and the National Energy Program," in G. Bruce Doern, ed., *How Ottawa Spends Your Tax Dollars* 1981 (Toronto: Lorimer 1981); and Larry Pratt, "Petro-Canada Tool for Energy Security or Instrument of Economic Development?," in G. Bruce Doern, ed., *How Ottawa Spends* 1982 (Toronto: Lorimer, 1982), pp. 87–114.

CHAPTER 9

PRICES AND TAXES: RUNNING THE NEP GAUNTLET

Above all else, the National Energy Program and the subsequent Canada–Alberta Agreement established a veritable gauntlet of new taxes and prices through which the main energy players now had to run and slither. As Table 9.1 shows, the relatively simple pre-NEP fiscal regime was transformed into a dog's breakfast of complex new prices and taxes. The overall fiscal regime epitomized the degree to which energy policy had become imbued with the many ideas and interests inherent in Canadian political life. Heaped on its stooped shoulders was the task of promoting simultaneously efficiency, stability, equity, nationalism, and regionalism collected under the trio of NEP objectives—security, fairness, and opportunity, all defined and ranked variously by key energy interests.

In this chapter we look at the post-NEP fiscal regime in greater detail than has been possible in previous chapters. The first section describes briefly the nature of the tax and pricing changes. The second section looks at the price and tax dynamics and assesses their general effects on consumers and taxpayers; revenue shares between Ottawa and the producing provinces; industry cash flows for both the foreign-owned and Canadian sectors; and the overall economy. The third section explores selected dynamics and more specific effects in such areas as the fate of Dome Petroleum, the takeover spree, and the bargaining over mega-project fiscal deals. Finally, we offer some concluding observations about the politics of implementation as revealed in the tax and pricing arena. Throughout the chapter we draw attention to the politics of evaluating the NEP: in short, the NEP evaluation game, since this is itself indicative of the dynamics of the implementation process and of the selective but sustained pressure that key interests brought to bear both for, but primarily against, the NEP.

Before proceeding to a description of the NEP fiscal regime, however, it is essential to recapitulate briefly the key points about prices and taxes that we have already examined earlier. This list can be considered a kind of analytical inventory that must be related to the dynamics discussed below:

TABLE 9.1

A PROFILE OF THE PRE- AND POST-NEP TAXING AND PRICING REGIME

Pre-NEP		Post-NEP*	
Taxes	Prices	Taxes	Prices
Federal Income Tax (Deductions incl.): • capital cost allowances • exploration and development expenses • special resource allowance • depletion allowance Tax at about 36% of taxable income	Single crude oil price subject to transportation differences: moving towards but less than world price	Same as pre-NEP but with *additions* as follows: The Petroleum and Natural Gas Revenue Tax (PGRT)	Blended price concept New Oil Reference Price (NORP) i.e. world price for new oil as defined
	Oil Import Compensation Program (financed by regular tax revenue)	The Natural Gas and Gas Liquids Tax (NGGLT)	75% of world price ceiling for old oil
	Synthetic crude oil producers allowed to sell at world price	Incremental Oil Revenue Tax (IORT)	Schedule of gradual price increases
Provincial Income Tax (11-15%)	In 1975 domestic gas price at about 85% of equivalent oil. Policy was to close the gap over the next three to five years	The Petroleum Compensation Charge The Canadian Ownership Charge	Gas prices linked to but not rigidly tracked to 65% of oil price
Provincial Royalties • 30–40% for old oil • 40–50% for new oil		Elimination of Depletion Allowance	
Special Syncrude levy to subsidize purchasers of synthetic crude		Stricter definition of Canadian Exploration Expense 10% royalty + 40% incremental royalty on Canada Lands	

*Including Canada–Alberta Agreement

- It was the dual world price shocks, in 1973 and 1979, that ultimately changed the energy pricing and then taxing game. It must be remembered, however, that from 1975 to 1979 Canadian prices had been moving to the then world price, by stages agreed to through a process of federal–provincial negotiations.

- Canada, perhaps more than any other Western state, embodied within its own political–economic boundaries the producer–consumer, importer–exporter energy conflicts that were reflected in the larger world scene.

- The link between federal revenues and the deficit, including burdensome expenditure items such as the then $4 billion Oil Import Compensation Program, produced a genuine fiscal issue. When linked to the massive transfer of wealth to the Alberta Heritage Fund and the failure to get agreement on a mechanism to reallocate petrodollars for national purposes, it raised the stakes to a genuine national crisis involving deep partisan and regional differences.

- In the context of the basic policy options available in 1979 as analyzed in Chapter 2, the choice between a simpler world-price oriented regime and complex cost-based regime was not an easy one. It was ultimately *politics* (that is, the process of balancing and allocating ideas and interests) as judged by *elected* politicians, rather than bureaucratic conspiracies, that pushed the process toward the latter regime.

- The 1980 "18 cent" election fought in consumer Toronto's swing ridings added to the complexity of the price-tax regime by inducing the Liberals to create new price "charges" in order to be able to say that energy "taxes" were lower than the Tory 18 cent tax on transportation fuels, a key feature of the Crosbie budget.

- It was a combination of events, issues and forces, some energy related, some not, that led to an aversion, in the federal energy and finance bureaucracies, against using the tax system as the prime instrument for providing incentives to the oil and gas industry. The tax system was too complex. Items like the super-depletion allowance were viewed as outrageously generous. Tax treaties did not allow policy to discriminate in favour of Canadian firms; grants would. Tax complexity, however, was not a concern when it came to revenue raising—hence the five new taxes and charges imposed as part of the NEP and the Canada–Alberta Agreement.

• High price assumptions and forecasts drove the NEP. But it also drove the energy industry lobby for much of the 1970s and well into the fall of 1981, when the Canada–Alberta Agreement was signed.

• The 1982–1983 recession and its high interest rates greatly complicated the task of assessing the NEP. As Chapter 1 pointed out, the NEP evaluation game was already mired in shifting political sands. The recession and interest rate factor converted it into quicksand.

• The weakening of OPEC caused by, and reflected in, declining world oil prices and the addition of new supply due to both new non-OPEC discoveries and the impact of several years of Western conservation policies, was not expected. The subsequent amendment to the Alberta Agreement in 1983 reflected the need of all energy players to hedge their bets.

This inventory of items on the tax and pricing front demonstrates, in somewhat staccato fashion, what a moveable political and economic feast the post-NEP fiscal regime ultimately became.

A Profile of the Pre- and Post-NEP Tax and Pricing Regime

Reading a description of energy taxes and prices is somewhat like reading the yellow pages of the telephone directory. Not even your fingers can really help you do the walking. Accordingly, our description of the NEP fiscal regime will contain only the most basic information necessary to understand the main dynamics examined in this chapter. Table 9.1 helps guide the way.

The Pre-NEP Fiscal Regime

The pre-NEP tax system consisted of two main charges, federal and provincial income taxes and provincial royalties.[1] Also in existence was the so-called Syncrude Levy, a special charge of $1.75 a barrel that Ottawa collected to subsidize purchasers of synthetic crude oil where such purchases were required to be made at world price levels. Federal income tax is 46 percent, less 10 percent tax room for the provinces' income tax, in effect 36 percent of taxable income. Provincial income tax rates in 1980 were 15 percent in British Columbia, 11 percent in Alberta and 14 percent in Saskatchewan. "Taxable income" was a figure calculated after allowing for major deductions. These included capital cost allowances; exploration and development expenses; a special resource allowance; and depletion allowances. The provincial royalties varied among provinces and between oil and gas. In the 1960s and early 1970s the provinces collected a royalty generally averaging between 12.5 to 16.7 percent of the value of production. The royalty structure became much more complex after 1973 as the producing provinces sought to capture the majority of economic rent while, in their opinion, still leaving a fair return to the industry. The new royalty regimes averaged around 40 to 50 percent for old oil and gas production and 30 to 40 percent for new oil and gas production.[2]

As shown in Chapter 3, the deductions from gross revenues enabled the large oil and gas firms to pay much lower effective tax rates.[3] Moreover, it was the multinational firms that could best take advantage of such incentives. But these incentives and low effective tax rates were also a matter of deliberate public policy to encourage the development of the industry. Hence there arose a classic and often repeated clash of basic ideas, that spilled over the boundaries of energy policy, as it inevitably must. At the broader level of the tax system as a whole, for example, the argument was increasingly mounted in the 1970s that ad hoc marginal new tax incentives, each *separately* desirable in promoting a more efficient "industrial climate" were, *in the aggregate*, producing a system that was increasingly inequitable and inefficient. Equity was of course definable along several dimensions, depending on the interests arguing the case. The tax system could be viewed to be unfair in its treatment of various industries, in its treatment of Canadian as opposed to multinational firms, and in relation to revenue shares captured by the various governments, to name only three dimensions.

Thus, in general, it must be continually stressed that the tax system as a whole (and the energy component within it) was constantly buffeted by its conflicting ideas and purposes, that is: efficiency (will it increase overall GNP and produce initiative and risk taking?); equity (will taxpayers at similar income levels be treated equally and, simultaneously, will dissimilar companies and projects or different kinds of new and old oil be treated differently—that is, "fairly"?); stability (will the new system produce a "climate for investment"?); and redistribution (will the system redistribute income from rich to poor?). The pre-NEP tax system was simple in relation to the *number of taxes* but not in relation to the *number of ideas and interests* with which it had to deal.

A final overall question obviously is whether the tax system will generate enough *total* revenues to meet the needs of governments? In this regard, it is important to remember the relative proportions of revenue accounted for by resource taxes in the two levels of government. We pointed out in Chapter 3 that in the mid-1970s the entire sector provided only about 1.2 percent of all provincial revenues and 0.5 percent of federal revenues. By the late 1970s resource revenues were over 50 percent of Alberta's budget revenues, even *excluding* the revenues directed to the Heritage Fund. By 1983–84, however, even after Ottawa's "revenue grab," energy revenues were only 6.0 percent of total federal budgetary revenues.[4] While these relative percentages are important, the key in the 1980–81 period was that, at the margin, the buoyant energy sector was viewed, by Ottawa especially, as the best place to look for significant additional revenues.

The pre-NEP pricing regime is somewhat simpler to describe than the tax regime. The federal position since the OPEC crisis of 1973 was that there should be a single price for crude oil in Canada, subject to transportation cost differences. This principle was agreed to by the provinces at federal–provincial conferences in 1974 and 1975. A second feature was that there should be a *gradual* movement towards world prices to allow time for industrial and consumer, economic and social adjustment to occur, but this was not a full world-price commitment because it was argued by Ottawa, and Ontario in particular, but also by some of the "have not" provinces, that the world price was not wholly a market price. Rather, it was a politically contrived cartel price.

One essential corollary to the single price policy was the Oil Import Compensation Program referred to in previous chapters. Under it, refiners processing imported oil were subsidized. A second special pricing feature involved the Syncrude Levy, noted above. Domestic synthetic crude oil producers were allowed to sell their production to refiners at world import price levels.

Meanwhile natural gas prices in 1975 were about 85 percent of the commodity-equivalent value of delivered crude oil. Federal policy was that the remaining 15 percent gap would be eliminated over a three-to-five-year period. In actual fact the gap remained. Table 9.2 shows the overall administered price regime for oil and gas that evolved between 1973 and 1979. In the mid-1970s there was strong pressure from the governments of British Columbia and Alberta, the main gas producers, to increase gas prices. Since new export sales were not then open (owing to the 1972–73 concern about shortages) Alberta increased its field price to $1.15/mcf compared to 22 cents in early 1974. Ottawa sought to moderate such a price increase. It would have meant a Toronto city-gate price of $1.60 to $1.65, and thus through Ottawa–Alberta haggling, a price of $1.25 was accepted. Export prices were put under upward pressure by the B.C. government's decision to establish a new Crown corporation—the B.C. Petroleum Corporation (BCPC). B.C. gas was exported but on long-term contracts at prices around 30¢/mcf. BCPC became the main vehicle for collecting a return on the Crown-owned gas. Export prices were pushed up as a result of B.C.'s manoeuvres. Ottawa had to respond to set gas export prices closer to those for crude oil.

The Post-NEP Fiscal Regime

As Table 9.1 shows, the NEP introduced a major quantum jump in the number of taxes and in the complexity of prices.[5] These are listed on the right side of the table. As we have already seen in previous chapters, the PGRT and the NGGLT were the two taxes most characterized by NEP opponents as a "revenue grab" by Ottawa. This is of course exactly what they were; it is hard to think of a tax that is not. The PGRT was initially set at 8 percent on oil and gas production revenue. In the Canada–Alberta Agreement it was raised to 16 percent with a 25 percent resource allowance for an effective rate of 12 percent. The key feature was that it was "off the top," that is, levied before profits are determined. Alberta initially opposed this kind of tax on principle, since it was a tax on production and hence a direct threat to the principle of provincial resource ownership and control. The NGGLT was a tax on all natural gas sales under the Excise Tax Act. Initially intended to apply to all sales, domestic and foreign, export sales were later excluded after the Canada–Alberta Agreement of September, 1981. The NGGLT has been varied so as to insure that natural gas prices would be at about 65 percent of crude oil prices, the latter being a key feature of pricing policy and of the "off oil" conservation elements of the NEP.

The Canada–Alberta Agreement also yielded the Incremental Oil Revenue Tax (IORT). It would tax the incremental revenue earned by producers of "old oil" in Alberta. Taxed at a rate of 50 percent, less

TABLE 9.2
POLICY-DETERMINED PRICES FOR CANADIAN CRUDE OIL
AND NATURAL GAS 1973–1980

Date when new prices were established	Crude oil wellhead price ($/bbl)	Natural Gas Prices (Can. $/mcf)	
		Toronto city-gate wholesale price	Export price
Sept. 1974	3.80		
April 1, 1974	6.50	0.62	
Nov. 1, 1974		0.82	
Jan. 1, 1975			1.00
July 1, 1975	8.00		
Aug. 1, 1975			1.40
Nov. 1, 1975		1.25	1.60
July 1, 1976	9.05	1.405	
Sept. 10, 1976			1.80
Jan. 1, 1977	9.75	1.505	1.94
July 1, 1977	10.75		
Aug. 1, 1977		1.68	
Sept. 20, 1977			2.16[a]
Jan. 1, 1978	11.75		
Feb. 1, 1978		1.85	
July 1, 1978	12.75		
Aug. 1, 1978		2.00	
May 1, 1979			2.30[a]
July 1, 1979[b]	13.75		
Aug. 1, 1979		2.15	
Jan. 1, 1980	14.75		
Feb. 1, 1980		2.30	

[a]Beginning with the September 1977 export price increase, export prices of natural gas are listed in U.S. rather than Canadian dollars.
[b]In December, 1978, previously agreed price increases of $1/bbl for oil and of 15¢/mcf for gas originally scheduled to be implemented Jan. 1 and Feb. 1, 1979, respectively, were deferred until the mid-1979 dates shown in the table. The revised agreement also includes provision for a further oil and gas price increase in 1980 as shown. Note that the 15¢/mcf figures are approximate.
Source: John Helliwell, "Energy Policy." See Footnote 1, p. 189. Reproduced, with permission, from the Annual Review of *Energy*, Vol.4. © 1979 by Annual Review Inc.

Crown royalties, the incremental revenue would not be subject to income taxation by either Ottawa or Alberta. This tax was later suspended for one year in June 1982 and further one-year extensions of the suspension were given in the April 1983 and February 1984 federal budgets.

The Petroleum Compensation Charge was the new charge designed to enable payment of the oil import compensation program previously paid out of general revenues. The new charge was levied on domestic refiners and was to be an integral part of the "made in Canada" price regime described below. The depletion allowances were also radically altered by the NEP. They would in fact be gradually phased out. There were also changes to the definition of the "Canadian exploration expense" which narrowed eligibility. This change was later postponed for two years.

The Canadian Ownership Charge, to which we have repeatedly referred, and which we examine in greater detail in Chapter 10, was the "nationalist" flagship of the NEP. Levied on gasoline and petroleum products and gas consumers, it was to finance the acquisition of one or more foreign-owned oil companies, and thus help meet the 50 percent Canadian ownership goal.

Last but certainly not least was the overall royalty regime on the Canada Lands. The 25 percent Crown interest, already examined in Chapter 2, was a central provision. This interest would have to be paid for by Ottawa. In addition, each holder of a production licence would have to pay the PGRT a 10 percent basic royalty and a progressive incremental royalty of 40 percent of net profit, as defined in the legislation.

The portrait that emerges from the post-NEP tax package is obviously one of byzantine complexity. Figures 9.1 and 9.2 capture the flow of taxes and charges that accrue for gasoline and natural gas respectively. They do not, however, capture another aspect of energy taxation, namely the treatment of large energy *projects* such as the Alsands and Cold Lake projects. As we return to these items later in the chapter, it is sufficient to note here that special deals had to apply. For example, post-NEP concessions resulted in a federal policy to allow a reduction in the rate of the PGRT as applied to these projects until the particular projects received a payout.

We have in part already dealt with some aspects of the NEP pric-

FIGURE 9.1
ESTIMATED INCIDENCE OF TAX
AND SHARING OF GASOLINE REVENUES
(SPRING 1982—¢/LITRE)

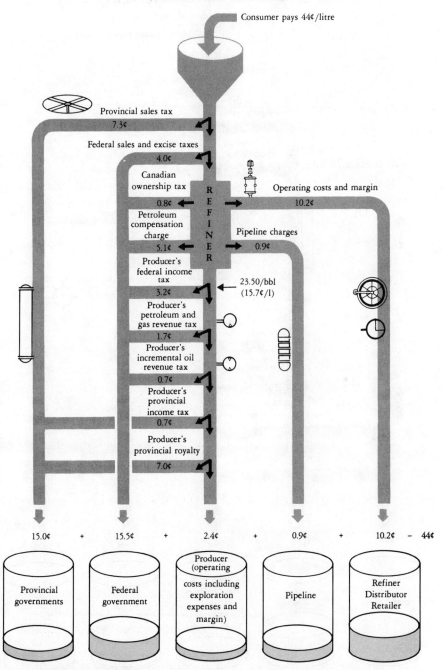

FIGURE 9.2
ESTIMATED INCIDENCE OF TAX
AND SHARING OF NATURAL GAS REVENUES
(SPRING 1982—$/MCF NATURAL GAS)

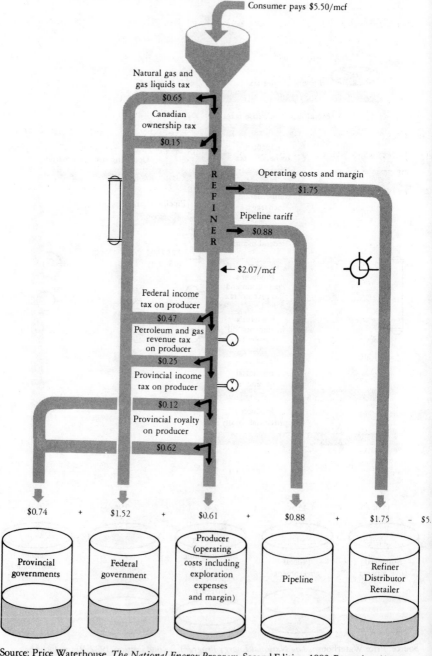

Source: Price Waterhouse, *The National Energy Program*, Second Edition, 1982. Reproduced by permission of Price Waterhouse.

ing regime in the above inventory of taxes. The "charges" noted above were part of the pricing regime. However the centrepiece of the NEP regime was the overall "made in Canada" blended-price concept as amended by the Canada–Alberta Agreement. Under the NEP there would have been one weighted average price to consumers, and Canadian prices would not have reached world price levels for the reasons repeatedly emphasized in previous chapters. After the Canada–Alberta Agreement, however, separate producer price schedules were established for old and new oil. The latter could reach 100 percent of the international price under the provisions of the New Oil Reference Price (NORP). Old oil prices could not exceed 75 percent of the world price. Gas prices would not be set so as to be "lock-step" at 65 percent of crude oil prices, as originally set out in the NEP, but would be varied through changes to the NGGLT to price it significantly below oil prices but around the 65 percent range.

The post-NEP price regime also contained a phase-in schedule of regular price increases, a schedule that had to be altered radically when the expected pattern of world oil prices failed to materialize in 1982 and 1983.

To see the pricing regime in yet another way, it is helpful to end our descriptive inventory by referring to Figure 9.3. It shows roughly the sequence of Canadian oil price determination. Oil imports at Montreal are the starting point. The lagged average cost of imports at Montreal is the base point for oil price determination, measured in Canadian dollars. The price of new oil (NORP) is set at the world price level after adjusting the average import price for quality differences between imported and domestic crude. NORP is paid to frontier, synthetic, and some categories of enhanced recovery and conventional oil discovered after 1980. By 1984, about one-third of Canadian oil was NORP oil. Domestic wellhead prices are calculated by subtracting the appropriate transportation costs. The average refinery acquisition cost is established at Toronto and is a weighted average of old and new domestic oil prices and the price of imports, with the weights deter- mined by the volumes used. The Petroleum Compensation Charge is then determined as the difference between the average refinery acqui- sition price and the world price.

These, then, are the basic features of the post-NEP fiscal regime in the realm of taxes and prices. The total regime, of course, also includes

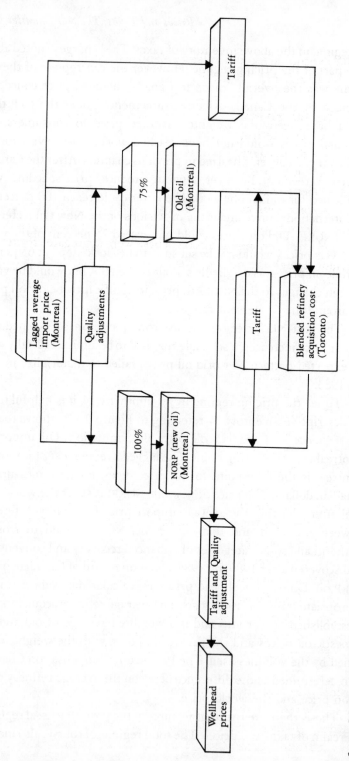

FIGURE 9.3
CANADIAN OIL PRICE DETERMINATION

Source: L.J. Murphy, "Adapting Canadian Energy Policy to Changing World Energy Trends,"
Canadian Business Review (Spring, 1983), p. 36. Reproduced by permission.

the NEP expenditure and regulatory elements, which are examined in Chapters 10 and 11.

Price and Tax Dynamics: General Effects and the Politics of Evaluating Them

There were three aggregate levels or kinds of effects that most concerned those who began to engage in evaluations of the NEP and the Canada–Alberta Agreement tax-price juggernaut. These were the effects on consumers and taxpayers, revenue shares between Ottawa and the producing provinces, foreign-owned versus Canadian-owned firms, and overall economic effects. These were aggregate effects; and important though the debate over these effects may be, they do not sufficiently portray the implementation politics involved since the myriad permutations and combinations of fiscal effects on individual companies and governments—in short, on different interests—are not captured by the aggregate numbers.

Effects on Consumers and Taxpayers

Undoubtedly the most clear-cut general effects are those on the consumer-taxpayer. Energy prices as a whole doubled in two years, but gradually the rate of increase leveled off when world prices declined and a new amended Canada–Alberta agreement was signed in July 1983. The only real contentious debate was whether the Liberal energy tax increases were kept below the rate that they would have been had the Tories' Crosbie budget provisions been implemented. The Liberals insist that their key 1980 election promise has been kept, but if it has it has only been possible through the invention of new "charges" described above. Thus taxpayers as consumers have paid a higher total amount than would have been the case under the Tory plan. Moreover, low-income Canadians received no protection through an energy tax credit, as had been contained in the Tory package. The Liberals' 1980 increase in the Guaranteed Income Supplement helped older Canadians, but certainly not all low-income Canadians.

Effects on Federal–Provincial Revenue Shares

The second most clear-cut aggregate effect is that Ottawa did secure, as intended, a larger share of the revenues vis-à-vis the producer provinces from 7 percent before the NEP to 16 percent in 1984. What is also not in dispute is that the total amount of money to be shared shrank drastically from the amounts originally calculated at the time of the 1981 Ottawa–Alberta agreement. Table 9.3 shows the aggregate drop in the total estimated percentage shares from the time of the original agreement, as forecast at the 1982 NEP Update, and then as achieved in 1984. By early 1984 federal budgetary data showed that the $36 billion in revenue that Ottawa said (in the NEP Update) it would obtain between 1981 and 1986 (already down from $61 billion forecast less than a year earlier), was now reduced to forecasts of just over $20 billion for the period 1982–83 to 1987–88. The rapidly shrinking pie was due to the interrelated effects of declining oil consumption; restrained price increases, and the sharp drop in gas exports which resulted from reduced international prices; and the deeply depressed economy.

TABLE 9.3
REVENUE SHARE PERCENTAGE ESTIMATES

	September Agreement* September 1981	NEP Update* May 1982	Senate Committee**
Federal	29%	22%	16%
Provincial	35%	32%	28%
Industry	36%	46%	56%
Total	100%	100%	100%

Source: NEP: Update 1982, p. 77, and EMR presentation to Senate Committee on Natural Resources, Proceedings on the National Energy Program. Issue No. 1, April 4, 1984, pp.
13–14.
*Estimates for 1981 to 1986.
**Actual 1984 percentages.

As was the case before the NEP, there was much dispute after the NEP as to just how big Ottawa's increased revenue share "in fact" was, and should be. A 1983 EMR paper concluded that the "average share of the Government of Canada over the 1981–1986 period is expected to be about 22 percent, or roughly double that of the 1975–1980 period."[7] Other interpretations occurred not only at different times but were based on different combinations of the total fiscal package. For example, a 1982 paper by University of Alberta economists Brian Scarfe and Bruce Wilkinson concluded that Ottawa's real share in the wake of the projections available after the Canada–Alberta Agreement in the fall of 1981 was closer to 47 percent. They reasoned as follows:

> ... the part going to reduce the price of imports is essentially a tax the federal government is levying on domestic producers to pay foreign oil producers. This part should be included in the federal government's revenue share, since it is essentially only a federal government decision to provide a subsidy to consumers of petroleum products. Over the 5½ years of the agreement, the subsidy on imported oil is expected to total approximately $15 billion, remaining close to $3 billion annually for 1981–1986.
>
> Once the federal revenues are adjusted by adding back the estimated PIPs on Canada Lands and the PCC on imported oil, its share rises to 32.2 percent from the original 25.5 percent, while the Alberta and industry shares drop to 27.5 percent and 40.3 percent respectively.
>
> These are not the only adjustments that might be made. The Ottawa policy of keeping oil and gas prices below world market levels is equivalent to taxing producers of oil and gas and using the tax to subsidize consumers. Therefore, it makes sense to count the value of this "tax" as part of the federal revenue share as well. Even assuming that the "world" market price for natural gas is somewhere between 80 percent of the world oil price and the price of gas exports to the United States, the value of this federal "tax" over the life of the agreement is enormous—about $40 billion from natural gas alone and $28 billion for oil.
>
> With this adjustment, the federal slice of revenues from oil and gas production rises dramatically, to 47.4 percent, while the Alberta and industry shares diminish to 21.3 and 31.2 percent respectively. The federal negotiators have indeed done well.[8]

Scarfe and Wilkinson went on to conclude further:

> Thus, the revenue implications of the new agreement may be likened to a situation in which the Alberta government has agreed to transfer a substantial portion of its non-renewable resource revenues to a National Energy Bank. One portion of the revenues transferred may well be used to finance the federal government's own energy conservation and conversion programs. Another part may be used for redistributive purposes, for example to finance a refundable energy tax credit or more probably to fund the existing federal–provincial revenue equalization program. Indeed, we would recommend the implementation of a refundable energy tax credit to low income Canadians.

In any case, a rent-sharing scheme has implicitly been put in place, in which Alberta has already made major concessions in sharing potential petroleum and natural gas revenues with the rest of Canada. No one should now expect Alberta to agree to contribute substantially to a further inter-provincial rent-sharing scheme as some have suggested should result from the upcoming negotiations on federal–provincial fiscal arrangements. Other provincial jurisdictions with substantial hydro-electricity generating capacity capture large-scale economic rents for the public sector, and/or choose to distribute them to consumers within the province instead. These must also be accounted for in any revised federal–provincial equalization scheme. Finally, Alberta must be permitted to continue saving, not only for the days when its non-renewable resource revenues are substantially lower in real per capita terms than they are today, but also to provide essential capital funds to help finance the large-scale investment program that Canada must inevitably undertake over the next decade. The anticipated growth in the Alberta Heritage Savings Trust Fund should not be thought to create a problem of fiscal drag; rather it should be recognized as a useful addition to the necessary Canadian savings pool.[9]

These two mid-course interpretations reflect the difference in ideas and interests inherent in the politics of assessing the NEP. EMR's paper, as we show below, did not include criteria that the Scarfe–Wilkinson paper chooses to include. The Alberta academics, for their part, accept without the slightest question the Alberta government's line of argument that world prices in 1981 are "market" prices and hence, by a stroke of the analytical pen, derive the other additions to the federal revenue column. They also lump consumers with the federal government's gains. They imply, when one includes these assumptions, that Alberta's negotiators were overwhelmed by Ottawa's, since Ottawa then secured a triumphant four-fold victory from 10 percent to 47 percent rather than 11 percent to 22 percent. Such conclusions may well flow from the questionable assumptions of the analysis, but as they virtually ignore the other criteria that a federal government must consider, their case is not persuasively argued. Moreover, they deal only with selected parts of the NEP.

Later, of course other assessments emerged in the light of the realities of 1982 and 1983. The loss of expected federal revenues exacerbated the ballooning federal deficit and showed the problem of hitching energy policy too closely to fiscal policy. Within the space of less than eighteen months, Ottawa's estimated deficit went from about $10 billion to 19.6 to 23.6 and then to over 30 billion dollars. Most of this was due to the operation of automatic stabilizers such as unemployment insurance and social programs during the recession. However, some of the deficit, about $2.5 billion according to a C.D. Howe Institute study, can be attributed to lower oil prices and lower energy related taxes. Revenues from the PGRT, IORT and NGGLT were well below expectations, as were corporate income tax collections from the oil and gas firms.[10]

An even more broadly based analysis by Helliwell, MacGregor and Plourde, which looked at several declining price and economic outlook scenarios, concluded:

> In the main, our results indicate that by far the largest part of the direct revenue losses have accrued to governments. The combined effect of the energy agreements and the subsequent policy adjustments, including the 1983 amendments, has been to put the producing industry in almost exactly the same position that it would have had under the higher prices forecast in the original 1981 energy agreements.
>
> The loss of energy revenues in the government sector as a whole is partially offset by the macroeconomic effects of the lower oil prices, because the increases in domestic activity cut the price of government purchases, reduce the required size of transfer payments, and raise the real revenues from non-energy taxes. The government of Alberta loses revenues because of the lower oil prices but nevertheless remains in a substantially stronger fiscal position than either the federal government or the governments of the other provinces.[11]

In this instance, however, the federal government could and did argue that such a conclusion merely showed the flexibility of the regime, not its rigidity. That is, the system was intended to work in precisely such a way so that when prices went up, government would gain the most, and when they went down, it would lose the most. Of the two governments, it would be the federal government that would gain the most on the upswings and lose the most on the downswings.

Industry–"Bottom Line" Effects and the Overall Economy

When it comes to the aggregate effects of the NEP and post-NEP developments on the industry, the picture becomes much less clear cut. We have already seen some of these effects and the various *perceptions* of effects by key interests in previous chapters, but it is useful to return to the same range of views as portrayed above in the assessment of the intergovernmental revenue share. The previously mentioned EMR paper attempted in 1983 to address the issue of the government–industry shares and to defend Ottawa from the charge that the industry was in a worse net position than before the NEP and that therefore, Ottawa's consistent claim, that the principal issue in the NEP was the disposition of revenues between the two levels of government, was accurate.

The EMR study attempted to assess the net fiscal effect, by which it meant the combined tax and grants regime. It also was based on what EMR regarded as a fairer time frame for comparison. It rejected what it regarded as the industry's penchant to compare only 1980 with 1981, arguing that both of these years were not only too short a time period, but were highly abnormal as well. 1980 was abnormal because the energy industry was abnormally buoyant in the wake of the 1979 OPEC price increases; 1981 was abnormal because of the shakedown from the NEP and the Ottawa–Alberta stalemate that existed for much of the year. It therefore presented a comparison between the 1975–1980 period as a whole with the projected 1981–1986 period as a whole. It also sought to deal explicitly with the effects of higher interest rates as distinct from the effects of energy policy. The paper reached three conclusions:

- over the period 1981–86, the NEP fiscal regime, in combination with provincial royalties, taxes and incentives, will impose a fiscal burden on the industry which is projected to be *no higher*, on average, than that borne by the industry in the 1975–80 period.
- since 1979, the industry's interest cost burden has increased significantly and, in part, it is the failure to disentangle the different effects of fiscal and interest burdens which is at the root of misdirected criticism of the NEP regime.
- while the conclusions above are valid for the industry as a whole, it is also the case that some segments of the industry fare better than others under the NEP fiscal regime. Nevertheless, even those companies which benefit least from the incentives provided in the NEP do well in terms of after-tax cashflow relative to the levels of cashflow in the 1975–80 period.[12]

Tables 9.4 and 9.5 capture the two global snapshots. The former is based on actual data, while the latter is based on *projections*. There can be no doubt that it is more reasonable to compare five-year periods, but the EMR projections are obviously just that—projections. The study asserted, for example, that the projected increase in the revenue base was far in excess of projected increases in production costs and there-

TABLE 9.4
HISTORICAL OIL AND GAS REVENUE SHARING, 1975–1980

	Net operating income	Federal		Provincial		Industry	
	($B)	($B)	(%)	($B)	(%)	($B)	(%)
1975	5.3	0.6	(11.3)	1.9	(35.8)	2.8	(52.9)
1976	6.3	0.6	(9.5)	2.6	(41.3)	3.1	(49.2)
1977	8.1	0.9	(11.1)	3.8	(46.9)	3.4	(42.0)
1978	9.2	0.9	(9.8)	4.2	(45.7)	4.1	(44.5)
1979	11.1	1.0	(9.0)	5.6	(50.5)	4.5	(40.5)
1980	13.4	1.1	(8.2)	6.0	(44.7)	6.3	(47.0)
Total	53.4	5.1	(9.6)	24.1	(45.1)	24.2	(45.3)

Source: Energy, Mines and Resources, "Do Governments Take Too Much?" (Ottawa: Energy, Mines and Resources, 1982), p. 5. Reproduced by permission.

TABLE 9.5
FUTURE REVENUE SHARES, 1981–86

	Total revenues to be shared	Federal		Provinces		Industry	
	($B)	($B)	(%)	($B)	(%)	($B)	(%)
Projection							
1981	17.0	4.0	23	6.0	36	7.0	42
1982	22.2	6.2	28	6.7	30	9.3	42
1983	26.5	6.3	24	8.2	31	12.0	45
1984	29.1	6.3	22	9.6	33	13.2	45
1985	32.0	6.4	20	10.4	33	15.1	47
1986	35.1	6.3	18	11.6	33	17.2	49
Total	161.9	35.5	22	52.5	32	73.8	46

Source: Energy, Mines and Resources, "Do Governments Take Too Much?" (Ottawa: Energy, Mines and Resources, 1982), p. 6. Reproduced by permission.

fore reflected primarily a windfall gain. But no industry cost projections, nor the basis of calculating them, were presented: a curious omission to say the least.

The study also attempted to show the historical after-tax cash flow for the main subdivisions of the industry. Tables 9.6 and 9.7, respectively, show this without, and then with, the interest rate burden included. The EMR study concluded:

> In short, after-tax cashflows per barrel for all company groups of the industry have increased significantly from the levels of the late 1970's although, in relative terms, Canadian firms have fared better. It also needs to be recognized that 1981 represents a relatively high water mark in terms of industry net fiscal burden because of the significant price increases and royalty reductions that were introduced in 1982.
>
> It is only when one examines the impact on these cashflows of rising debt charges (Table 9.7) that the financial picture of the industry begins to deteriorate seriously. A comparison of Tables 9.6 and 9.7 indicates that Canadian firms, many of which have been involved in debt financed acquisitions (e.g., Dome, Canterra, Sulpetro), have been particularly hard hit by increases in interest charges. Foreign juniors have also been adversely affected but to a more limited extent. Foreign majors appear not to have been significantly affected at all. Thus, whereas Table 9.6 suggests the fiscal impact of the NEP has been greater on foreign majors than on the rest of the industry, the impact of higher interest costs has been correspondingly more severe on the Canadian segment of the industry.[13]

TABLE 9.6
HISTORICAL AFTER-TAX CASH FLOW*
($/OIL EQUIVALENT BARREL)

	1977	1978	1979	1980	1981
Foreign Majors	4.06	4.61	5.42	7.65	6.49
Canadian Majors	3.71	5.45	6.89	8.40	9.94
Foreign Juniors	3.54	4.78	5.73	8.04	7.90
Canadian Juniors	3.44	4.39	4.85	7.48	8.99
Total	3.96	4.79	5.74	7.84	7.46

*After Tax Cashflow: production revenue less operating costs, royalties and all taxes, plus incentives. *Interest charges have not been deducted.*
Source: Energy, Mines and Resources, "Do Governments Take Too Much?" (Ottawa: Energy, Mines and Resources, 1982), p. 15. Reproduced by permission.

TABLE 9.7
HISTORICAL NET CASH FLOW*
($/OIL EQUIVALENT BARREL)

	1977	1978	1979	1980	1981
Foreign Majors	3.95	4.44	5.27	7.47	6.29
Canadian Majors	3.21	4.83	6.02	6.45	6.38
Foreign Juniors	3.54	4.78	5.42	7.56	7.01
Canadian Juniors	3.13	3.78	4.09	5.58	2.90
Total	3.76	4.52	5.42	7.18	6.23

*Net Cashflow: production revenue less operating costs, royalties, all taxes *and* interest expenses, plus incentives. Interest costs on a total corporate basis have been allocated to different segments (i.e., upstream, downstream) of the industry by the companies themselves in their reports to the PMA.
Source: Energy, Mines and Resources, "Do Governments Take Too Much?" (Ottawa: Energy, Mines and Resources, 1982), p. 16. Reproduced by permission.

Interestingly, the EMR study attempted to go somewhat beyond these two main subdivisions and presented stylized scenario portraits of different kinds of firms with different kinds of characteristics (ownership, vintage of oil, size of firm, debt burden, and reinvestment ratio). This was summed up in Table 9.8, virtually without explanation. In general the study concluded:

> Clearly, the new system will affect firms in different ways, both in terms of comparison with the former system and in terms of differences between companies. For example, a low-reinvesting company fares worse under the new system than before; a high reinvestor does better. A Canadian company, all other things being equal, does better than a foreign-controlled firm. Some companies will pay PGRT and receive no PIP; others will pay no PGRT and receive PIP. These structural effects complicate comparisons between the two systems, but it is possible to assess both the aggregate situation and some typical cases.[14]

The quotation itself is not an unreasonable one and accords with the reality that a myriad of different corporate interests and situations exist. The point to stress, however, is that these various stylized scenarios are not explained or supported with concrete data.

The oil and gas industry and interests within it were obviously not just sublimely responding to studies such as the EMR one examined above. Many were privately derisive about the study, but the industry "evaluation" took many other forms, including some of the actions that were traced in Chapters 3 and 6: speeches, lobbying, advertising campaigns, decisions not to invest, to invest elsewhere and to take advantage of various NEP-based incentives. It is essential in this and other fields of public policy not to equate the evaluation of policies with cerebral analysis only, that is, the kind that shows up in tidy reports. Most evaluation in a political setting also involves verbal and substan-

TABLE 9.8

COMPARATIVE COMPANY SHARES OF NET OPERATING REVENUES*
UNDER PRE- AND POST-NEP REGIMES (1982–86)

	Pre-NEP	Post-NEP
	(%)	(%)
1. Large foreign Old oil Low debt Low reinvestor	43	38
2. Large foreign Old oil Low debt High reinvestor	51	46
3. Small Foreign New oil High debt High reinvestor	74	74
4. Large Canadian Old oil Low debt High reinvestor	51	63
5. Large Canadian Old oil High debt High reinvestor	52	67
6. Small Canadian New oil High debt High reinvestor	74	102

*Taking into account the payment of all taxes and royalties and the receipt of all incentives.
Source: Energy, Mines and Resources, Canada. "Do Governments Take Too Much?" (Ottawa: Energy, Mines and Resources, 1982), p. 20. Reproduced by permission.

tive pressure from those who have some degree of power but which is exercised in relation to quite different or particular interests. It is in this sense that the views of individual firms expressed in the ATAC committee, examined in Chapter 8, and the views of key interests of the above-noted EMR report coincide. These views are based on a realistic appreciation that aggregate and even middle-level "modelling" and analysis simply cannot capture all or even most of the individual permutations and combinations that interests face, let alone the divergent ideas and, therefore, criteria involved. This also applies to governmental interests. For example, the NEP Update published by EMR was also an evaluation that painted a view of positive progress. But it also contained a large package of fiscal concessions thus revealing both external pressure and the government's own view that it had indeed hit the industry too hard, especially the smaller Canadian firms struggling in the midst of a deep recession.

By 1984 several other kinds of overall evaluative activity by the critics of the NEP were in evidence. The Canadian Petroleum Association (CPA) presented a brief to the Senate Committee on Energy and Natural Resources in April 1984 which was part of CPA's concerted effort to lobby the government to change the NEP. The CPA was careful to point out that its subcommittees, created to study policy alternatives, consisted of balanced representation from multinational and Canadian firms, a gesture to the new politics of Canadianization. It presented economic forecasts that showed significant economic benefits over the 1984–1992 period if the NEP were "modified." The list of "modifications," however, when added together meant in fact the virtual elimination of the NEP, or at least its fiscal regime. It is worth noting that the CPA study showed industry with only 46 percent of the revenues, thus continuing the "numbers game" with EMR which, as Table 9.3 indicated, showed the industry share at 56 percent.[15]

In 1983 and 1984 the Business Council on National Issues (BCNI) organized "energy summits" that brought together federal and Alberta energy ministers, the banks as well as oil company representatives, many of whom were BCNI members. A common set of themes emerged in these meetings which reinforced the network of critical opinion that was being formed. These included the need to "reward success and not activity" in reference to the PIP grants; to re-establish stability and predictability; and to restore market forces.

A Progressive Conservative caucus energy policy team also began a systematic canvass of opinion that showed similar themes. Even the 1984 Liberal leadership race contained criticism of the NEP by John Turner and Donald Johnston. In the fall of 1984, the Economic Council of Canada also sharply criticized the lack of explicit concern in the NEP for economic efficiency.[16] It presented a detailed assessment which also favoured significant deregulation. It was, however, more sympathetic to features of the NEP such as Petro-Canada and the 25 percent Crown interest.

Individual energy academics such as Brian Scarfe, whose work with Barry Wilkinson was referred to earlier, also began to broaden their analysis. Scarfe's 1984 paper still pronounced the NEP an economic failure, but did concede that the Canadianization program had had some success.[17]

It is also instructive to ask how evaluations of the combined effects of the NEP and the 1981 Canada–Alberta agreement were officially viewed by key Alberta government agencies. The 1983 annual report of the Alberta Department of Energy and Natural Resources stressed that the oil and gas industry declined further from the depressed level of 1982, attributing this to be the result of "a lingering worldwide recession, uncertain markets, and the continuing effects of the National Energy Program" in that order.[18] Well completions dropped 12 percent from the 1981 figures, and exploratory drilling dropped 24 percent with sharp adverse effects in employment, especially in the small companies engaged in drilling or in supplying these firms. The 1983 budget address, however, took a different tone. It reversed the order of variables, putting the "Ottawa Energy Program" first, but in the very next paragraph the Alberta Treasurer, Lou Hyndman, stressed that "Albertans now realize that our economy was flying artificially high in recent years."[19] He stressed that "oil and gas drilling activity in 1982 returned to the levels experienced in 1977 and 1978," and pronounced the industry in Alberta to be "well placed to pursue a normal path of development."[20]

Another mode of evaluation of the NEP worthy of mention was that presented by the primarily Alberta-based drilling and support service sector of the industry, especially from the Canadian Association of Oilwell Drilling Contractors (CAODC). We have already referred in Chapter 1 to the exodus of drill rigs to the United States after the NEP but the views of interests such as the CAODC, composed primarily of the small business segment of the industry, must be looked at over the entire period. In 1980 there were about 425 rigs operating at the height of the 1979–80 boom period. The rapid expansion had been fostered by easy bank credit and the euphoria over prices. Even CAODC officials and members knew, however, that this level of capacity could not be sustained. By early 1984 there were about 200 rigs working out of about 500. Figure 9.4 shows the levels of rig activity from 1977 to early 1984.

In the wake of the initial anger at the NEP the highly entrepreneurial drillers issued monthly "casualty reports" with considerable fanfare. About 150 rigs went south to the United States but about fifty came back the wiser since the United States too had a huge oversupply of rigs despite the preferred ideological climate of the Reagan government and the energy deregulation practices of that administration. However, relative to the 1979–80 period, this highly employment-intensive sector was truly hurting. There is no doubt the decline contributed much to the rapid increases in Alberta's rate of unemployment. The NEP and the recession also brought with it changes in the structure of industry interest group organization. In the wake of the NEP, that part of the service sector less directly involved in actual drilling broke away from the CAODC to form their own group, the Petroleum Services Association of Canada (PSAC). This was partly because the latter, also employment intensive, indeed even more so than the CAODC, believed that its interests were insufficiently recognized in the new political context of the NEP.

Gradually the CAODC and PSAC adopted somewhat different evaluative and political stances. For example, late in 1982 both prepared studies of well costs.[21] These clearly showed how much more economic in every way the investment in Alberta and in the Western Sedimentary Basin was over similar magnitudes of investment in Hibernia. For example, one Hibernia well might cost $35 million. In Alberta this would drill six deep wells or twenty-five medium wells. Moreover, in contrast to the east coast, where there is little Canadian content, Alberta would involve a high level of Canadian content. The CAODC, however, did have to exercise much more care in casting too many aspersions on the east coast, since some of its own new members were operating there. For similar reasons it had to mute its general dislike of the PIP grants. Its approach by late 1983 was, like other

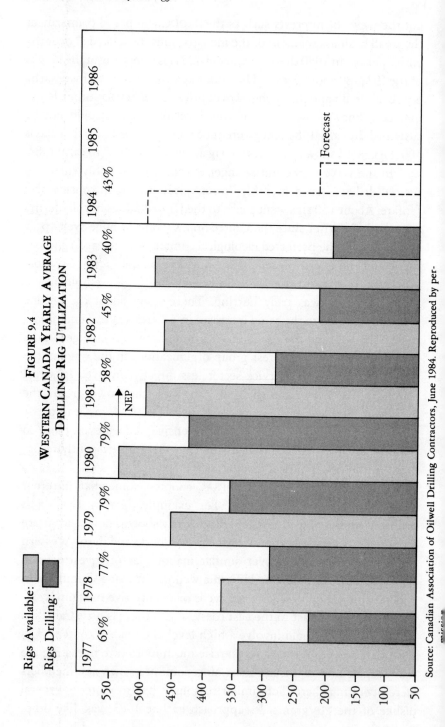

FIGURE 9.4
WESTERN CANADA YEARLY AVERAGE
DRILLING RIG UTILIZATION

Source: Canadian Association of Oilwell Drilling Contractors, June 1984. Reproduced by permission.

energy interests, to chip away at the fiscal regime. It was lobbying the Alberta government to give simple incentives such as the one-year royalty holiday that the Saskatchewan government had given and which had greatly spurred activity in that province, using primarily Alberta-based drillers, in 1983.

To show a final version of evaluative ingenuity linked to different interests, we can cite the case of the Dome empire. In an hour-long cable television program aired on Calgary's TV10 station on February 27, 1984, the president of Canadian Marine Drilling (a Dome subsidiary) showed viewers an "oil barrel" graph. It was in response to a question about whether PIPs were a waste of money. The barrel represented a billion barrel oil find in the Canada Lands (presumably, the Beaufort). He explained that over its life such a field would yield $40 billion in revenue. Of this, 29 percent would go to development, 56 percent to government, and 15 percent to the industry. At the bottom, the barrel graph showed a thin sliver of yellow that represented about 1 billion in PIP grants for exploration. The message was clear. PIPs would yield handsome returns over the long haul. Efficiency in the long run would prevail. This was not at all unlike the view and/or the hope of EMR advocates when the NEP was being designed. If there was even one "big play" found, PIP would pay for itself many times over.

Two points need to be stressed about the more independent studies that were published in the 1982–1984 period. First, most of them looked only at *parts* of the NEP rather than the whole package, and secondly, most of them did not examine the politics of the NEP, or where they did, did it badly. The absence of a sophisticated political dimension in the evaluations was surprising given what was generally known about the origins of the NEP. For example, the previously cited Scarfe–Wilkinson paper focussed primarily on the intergovernmental revenue shares. It was also critical of the takeover elements and of the capital outflow that resulted from it and of the utility of certain specific taxes compared to the corporate income tax as an incentive to explore. We have already noted the shaky conceptual grounds on which they based their notion that Ottawa's negotiators had whipped their Alberta counterparts.[22] The C.D. Howe study focussed more on the "takeover binge" effects (as we see in greater detail below) and on the effects on the actual achievement of the security of supply goals.[23] It ignored other elements of the NEP and confined its political analysis to a simple view that power was too concentrated in Ottawa and that there should be better consultation. Finally, the Helliwell, MacGregor and Plourde study couched in the later 1983 period of lower prices concluded that "the producing industry is in almost exactly the same position that it would have been under the higher prices forecast in the original 1981 energy agreements."[24] It was happily devoid of any haphazard look at politics, and stuck to basic economic modelling.

The point to stress again is that interests and authors initially were generally assessing *particular* features of the NEP in flexible ways. The basis of the criticism shifted as *one* component of the NEP was used to support and/or criticize other parts of the NEP. Later the NEP, the recession, and overall Liberal policy came to be viewed as one amorphous mass in the recessionary politics of 1982 and 1983. As oil and gas and other private sector interests mounted a sustained attack along general common lines, the evaluations broadened to become a more general political critique. Evaluations varied with the interests having a stake in the evaluation in much the same way as we saw in Chapter 2, in our account of the pre-NEP forecasting exercises. There were, of course, some independent analyses, such as the Helliwell studies. In general though, the role of evaluation must be linked to the broader domain of the political ideas and interests at stake.

None of the studies, moreover, compared the *overall* 1975–1980 period to projections of the 1981–1986 period, or to actual results in the 1981–1984 period, in all the main dimensions of the NEP. This especially slippery, but necessary, aspect of the politics of the NEP evaluation game was reflected again when the Petroleum Monitoring Agency reported in July 1983 on the 1982 energy year. The PMA had since 1981 increasingly been viewed as one of the only federal agencies that the oil and gas industry felt it could trust for the presentation of fairly unbiassed data. The press greeted its 1983 report by citing evidence presented in the PMA document that the profits of Canadian controlled firms had dropped from $1.2 billion in 1981 to a small loss in 1982 compared with a much smaller 19 percent *year over year* profit decrease for foreign-controlled firms.[25] Virtually ignored was the PMA's account of the *five-year* summary of industry finances. The PMA concluded:

• Revenues have more than doubled—growing at an annual

compound rate of nearly 20% for both the upstream and down-stream industry segments.

- Net income has followed a much more erratic course, peaking in 1980 and tailing off in the last two years. The level of up-stream and downstream profits, however, in 1982 was slightly higher than four years earlier.
- Internal cash flow has declined from the peak levels of 1980 but still increased nearly 50 percent between 1978 and 1982.
- Both capital expenditures and dividends have doubled over the five years.
- Outstanding long-term debt, now $14 billion, is nearly triple the level in 1978. Most of this increase occurred in 1981 when additional debt was raised to finance acquisition activity.[26]

As these uses of data continued to show, evaluations turned on the eye of the beholder and, as we see again in the next section, on the time frame one used in one's assessment.

While in this initial portrait of aggregate effects we have often spoken of the oil and gas industry as if it were one industry, it is necessary to remind ourselves that the issues for primarily gas firms were different than for the general oil business. Conversion to gas from oil was being encouraged by the NEP, as was the expansion of the gas distribution network in Québec. But gas firms also tended to be both smaller and more heavily Canadian owned. Thus these firms faced a different configuration of problems that were increased significantly by the loss of U.S. markets. We have not dealt with these issues here since they require a closer look at energy expenditures as well, a task we leave for Chapter 10. Suffice it to say that the gas industry faced severe problems.[27] Diminishing sales to the United States forced Canada in April 1983 to cut its uniform border export price from $4.94 (U.S.) to $4.40 per thousand cubic feet. Later Canada offered an incentive price of $3.40 for additional contracted volumes. Still further pressure was exerted by U.S. authorities when it was announced in Washington in February 1984 that U.S. policy would favour competitive market pricing.

More Specific Price and Tax Dynamics: Dome, Takeovers and Mega-Project Financing

While the various views of the general effects of the NEP provide a view of one element of the implementation of the policy, it is also essential to see other more particular implementation dynamics. In this section we look at three: the impact on Dome Petroleum, the takeover spree more generally, and the financing of mega-projects.

The Dome Dilemma

We have already referred in Chapters 3 and 6 to basic features of the post-NEP events related to Dome Petroleum. Here we are more interested in the "causal chain," that is, the mix of public and private behaviour that produces particular implementation results and decisions, intended and unintended. In the case of Dome the chain of interests and responses includes those of the federal government, Dome and its board of directors, and the four major Canadian banks.

There can be no doubt that the NEP helped create an explicit climate of encouragement for the takeover by the Canadian firms of foreign-owned oil and gas companies. It did so in at least two ways. First through general exhortation and verbal urging, it let it be known that takeovers would be looked upon favourably. While Petro-Canada would be a chief vehicle for takeovers, it is clear in the NEP that private takeovers were also wanted. Second, in more concrete terms, the overall fiscal regime (including the PIP grants) favoured Canadian-owned and -controlled firms and hence inherently made the shares of foreign-owned firms somewhat less valuable relative to Canadian firms in a similar scale and range of operations. The assets of U.S.-owned firms were not, however, devalued in absolute terms, since higher prices under the NEP increased their value. Nor were they subject to "fire-sale" or devalued prices, as some U.S. interests charged in the 1981–82 period.

In the Dome situation, Ottawa's interests were first expressed as an **energy policy maker**. It wanted more rapid Canadianization but it could not control the timing or the magnitude of the response. Later, in 1982, Ottawa's interests as **economic policy manager** became dominant. The Dome rescue package, in league with the banks, was perceived in the depth of the 1982 recession to be a vital act of economic policy to prevent massive bankruptcies, particularly in western Canada by Dome's numerous suppliers.

But if the NEP provided the "climate," the rest of the decision chain moved clearly out of the realm of public behaviour and into the realm of private behaviour. It was the senior management and board of

Dome and the banks that made the decisions, particularly the decision to take over Hudson Bay Oil and Gas (HBOG), from the U.S. giant, Conoco. Even before the HBOG takeover decision in the spring of 1981, Dome Petroleum had a heavy debt position of over $2.5 billion versus $5 billion in assets. The decision to acquire HBOG through further debt was not taken *before* interest rates soared in 1981. They were already at 19 percent, and Dome had no difficulty obtaining bank loans for the first phase of the takeover. The banks, particularly the Royal Bank, the Commerce and the Bank of Montreal, though normally conservative in image and practice, figuratively grovelled over the opportunity to cash in on the euphoria that seemed then in 1981 to surround Dome. Later in 1982, when Dome attempted to complete the takeover in order to get at the considerable cash flow of HBOG, the banks became much more concerned. By this time, however, a consortium of foreign banks headed by Citi-Bank of New York were also involved. As both interest rates and Dome's debt rose perilously, the struggle became increasingly one of protecting the security of loans on the part of the many banks now involved, and in the case of Dome, on avoiding bankruptcy and the collapse of the Beaufort northern dream nurtured for three decades by Dome's two entrepreneurial leaders, Jack Gallagher and Bill Richards.[28]

With the advantage of hindsight, it is now recognized that private decision makers also bit off more than they could chew. This behaviour cannot all be attributed to the NEP or to Ottawa. Both the Lyon and Foster books on the Dome situation, while stressing the importance of the NEP climate, clearly apportion a higher part of the causal chain (or blame) on Dome's own board and on the banks.[29] In the case of the former, Dome had itself become so complex an organization and its leaders so smitten by the self-styled (and partly true) myths of the Dome empire, that its internal checks and balances had failed to function. In the case of the banks, not only was there the issue of plain bad judgement, but in addition there was the impact of the larger cumulative inflation psychosis of the 1970s that increasingly seemed to propel decisions into a pursuit of inflation profits rather than those based on real economic growth.

The banks, it should be pointed out, were also in a somewhat ambivalent position. On the one hand, most of the key bank executives were ideologically opposed to the interventionist nature of the NEP and said so publicly, but on the other hand the NEP provided extensive opportunities to profit not just in financing takeovers, as was the case in the example discussed here, but also in the larger context, in that numerous firms were increasingly dependent on their banks to obtain advice and interim transition financing to find their way out of the pre-NEP regime and into the post-NEP regime.[30] As we have stressed earlier, ideological views and material interest did not coincide, a reality in which the bankers were clearly not alone.

Ottawa did not remain aloof from these events in the world of private sector public policy implementation. When Dome announced early in 1981 that they had established a subsidiary, Dome Canada, as a Canadian-owned-and-controlled vehicle to obtain the maximum PIP grants and fiscal advantage, Ottawa used the occasion for maximum public relations effect to show how some of the "wiser" (in Ottawa's view) elements of the industry were cooperating and benefiting from the NEP. Later, in November 1981, Ottawa had to re-enter the fray to repair an unforeseen effect of the ill-starred MacEachen budget. The budget had sought to close some so-called tax loopholes, including one previously available to investors in share exchange deals. This was vital to Dome's HBOG deal. After an intensive Dome lobby, this provision was announced as not being applicable to the Dome and a few other transactions, since they were underway at the time of the budget.

Interest rates, which later reached 22 percent, clearly applied the coup de grâce to Dome and led to the need for the Dome rescue package announced in September 1982. In 1983, as interest rates declined and as Dome sold off some of its assets and pruned expenditures to the bone, there emerged some reasonable prospect that the rescue package might not have to be implemented, and that Dome could meet its financial obligations. This brief account obviously does not do justice to the larger aspects of Dome as an energy interest. Part of the larger picture was examined in Chapters 3 and 6, and other aspects of Dome's Canadian benefits activity are examined in Chapter 11. We have dealt only with the overall fiscal effects on this one particular but important company, and with the causal decision chain involved in one dimension of the implementation phase of the NEP.

The Takeover Spree and Canadian Ownership

The Dome case leads logically to the need to discuss a related aspect of NEP implementation, namely the more general takeover spree of 1981 and 1982. In addition to the $1.45 billion takeover by Petro-Canada of Petrofina examined in Chapter 8 and the HBOG takeover by Dome examined above, over a dozen other Canadian companies acquired foreign-owned oil and gas companies in the wake of the NEP. Between February and July 1981, $6.6 billion was spent. As was the case with Dome, these takeovers were financed through the banks with debt financing involving a large outflow of capital to the United States. For example in 1981, nine companies acquired foreign companies valued at $7.2 billion, but borrowed $9.2 billion. Borrowed at relatively high interest rates, the interest expenses for the acquiring companies increased by over $700 million.[31] As early as July 1981, this had produced such strong downward pressure on the Canadian dollar that the Minister of Finance, Allan MacEachen, had to use moral suasion to persuade the Canadian banks to reduce their lending activities that involved takeovers of foreign-owned firms.

The U.S. reaction to the takeovers was also extremely strong at this time. Congressional opposition increased as U.S. firms protested at being the targets of takeovers at alleged fire-sale prices and contrasted the ease of Canadian takeovers with the roadblocks erected by FIRA in U.S. takeovers of Canadian firms. The overall historical injustice of this view did not really matter much, since it was the immediate *short-run* perceptions and realities, fuelled in a U.S. political setting flush with the free-enterprise ethos of the recently elected Reagan administration, that really mattered. Moreover, it must be stressed that some of the acquisition attempts by Canadian firms were not responses to the NEP itself, that is, to increase Canadian ownership of the industry in Canada, but a response to the buoyant outlook for oil companies in the United States in the post-1979 period.

Some of the immediate effects of the takeover spree are now not in dispute. Canadian ownership increased from 28 percent to 38 percent in the 1980 to 1983 period. Ownership was measured as a percentage of upstream revenues (i.e., basically revenues from production but not refining and marketing).[32] Carmichael and Stewart's analysis for the

C.D. Howe Institute shows that, *in the short term*, the costs of the improved level of ownership were great and exceeded likely benefits.[33] Whether these benefits are greater when one takes a *longer-term* view, and whether all the costs can be attributed to the NEP, is another matter with which we have already grappled, at least in part. In respect of its effects on the Canadian dollar and interest rates, Carmichael and Stewart conclude that the takeovers "were largely responsible both for the downward pressure on the Canadian dollar and the upward pressure on interest rates in the first half of 1981."[34] According to this view the chain of causality starts with the NEP because it is argued that these effects *preceded* the later, more general effects of U.S. monetarist policy. The effects of American and related Canadian monetary policy were the important engine of high interest rates later in 1981 and 1982.

Tables 9.9 and 9.10 show that the short-term effects on the acquiring companies were also distinctly unfavourable when compared with both other firms in the oil and gas industry and with other industries. The now familiar themes in the chain of causality and in the politics of evaluating the NEP (or in this case parts of the NEP) re-emerge in the above assessment. Once again, as was the case in the Dome takeover, one is required to note that it was ultimately private decision makers who made the great majority of the decisions and it was the banks that agreed to finance them. The NEP clearly set a climate but it taxes the imagination to attribute the instincts of these private decision makers to the NEP only.

TABLE 9.9
FINANCIAL RESULTS FOR ACQUIRING COMPANIES (CAN. $ MILLION)

	1980	1981	Change
Net income	337	288	–49
Cash flow	762	656	–106
Interest expense	375	1 083	708
Assets	7 720	18 284	10 564
Long-term debt	3 889	13 112	9 223
Shareholders' equity	2 504	3 507	1 003

Source: E.A. Carmichael and J.K. Stewart, *Lessons From the National Energy Program* (Toronto: C.D. Howe Institute, 1983), p. 29. Reproduced by permission.

TABLE 9.10
SELECTED FINANCIAL STATISTICS FOR ACQUIRING
COMPANIES AND ALL INDUSTRIES

	Return on equity[a]	Return on Capital employed[b]	Working capital ratio[c]	Debt--equity ratio[d]
Acquiring companies				
1980	18.4	7.5	1.28	1.463
1981	6.1	1.3	1.00	3.573
Other petroleum companies				
1980	19.3	14.4	1.84	0.345
1981	12.2	9.1	1.96	0.339
All industries				
1980	19.3	12.9	1.56	0.497
1981	14.6	9.0	1.51	0.628

[a]Net income before extraordinary items as percentage of shareholders' equity.
[b]Net income before extraordinary items as percentage of shareholders' equity plus long-term debt.
[c]Ratio of short-term assets to short-term liabilities.
[d]Ratio of long-term debt to shareholders' equity.
Source: E.A. Carmichael and J.K. Stewart, *Lessons from the National Energy Program* (Toronto: C.D. Howe Institute, 1983), p. 30. Reproduced by permission.

The assessment of the takeover spree again points out the central issue of the time frame used to assess the NEP and its implementation. It is instructive to note that the Carmichael and Stewart assessment pointedly does not refer to the potential *future* profitability that might arise out of the virtual tripling of the acquiring firms' asset base. In one sense this omission is understandable. The great thing about short-term effects is that they show up in the short term. Data comparing 1980 and 1981 can be assembled quickly. Acquiring firms are in difficulty—ergo the NEP is a failure, since the supposed beneficiaries are not benefiting. The problem with the longer-run effects is that there is no data. Moreover, when one has such data, say in five years, it will be relatively easy to say that the then observed adverse effects are not due to the NEP since, of course, many intervening events and forces will have occurred. Or, conversely, all the good effects can be attributed to the NEP for similar reasons. This is also where economic and political criteria and ideas conflict, since they assign different values and time frames to the implementation/evaluation game in the same way that there were differences in attributing causes to the genesis of the NEP, as set out in Chapter 2. There can be little doubt, for example, that the takeover spree was inefficient in the short term. It did not produce a barrel of new oil. Will the domestic ownership of a higher percentage of assets of the pivotally important and still dynamic (compared to other industrial sectors) energy sector result in greater efficiency in the long run, as well as the achievement of other private and public objectives? This remains an open question.

This is partly a different question, not only because of the time frame dilemmas cited above, but also because of the problems of calculating the benefits when the latter are expressed in qualitative political terms such as sovereignty or security, let alone when they are based on ideas such as a desire to restructure the balance of power vis-à-vis Ottawa and the industry, as was the case in the NEP. Those who see the NEP primarily in terms of economic efficiency have a right and indeed a responsibility to assess it in relation to this important criterion. But equally it must be acknowledged that other ideas and time frames are a central part of the NEP evaluation/implementation agenda, and are central to a more complete understanding of the slippery causal chain of the post-NEP world of energy politics. A brief look at the financing of mega-projects will give us a further glimpse of the particular effects of the fiscal regime and hence of the implementation dynamics of the NEP.

Financing Mega-Projects

In 1981 the term "mega-projects" came to denote the large capital and mainly energy projects proposed or planned for the 1980s and 1990s. Arbitrarily defined to be projects costing over $100 million, mega-projects included items such as the Alsands and Cold Lake projects. About eight months after the NEP, Ottawa released the report of the business-labour "Major Projects Task Force on Major Capital Projects in Canada to the Year 2000" (the Blair–Carr task force). It projected projects in excess of $440 billion, and suggested ways of maximizing Canadian benefits from them. This latter issue is examined more fully in Chapter 11. In the context of this chapter, our focus is on the fiscal implementation issues raised by some of these projects in the immediate post-NEP period, and on the economic and public policy climate engendered by the mega-project episode in 1981 and 1982.

The mega-project episode raises in more particular ways the issue stressed in Chapters 2, 3 and 5, namely, the contending views of whether energy policy was being seen as the prime "engine" of economic development (i.e., in line with a staples theory of development), or whether it was viewed essentially as a factor of production or as an industrial sector, much like any other industry. In Chapter 2 we argued that the NEP was not couched in a larger overall "economic" view or concept. Economic concerns were a part of the policy context, but the 1980 Liberal agenda was not dominated by concerns for the economy. Indeed, in specific terms, energy preceded economic policy issues in the Liberal policy queue of 1980. As we already know, however, the political and policy agenda do not conveniently stand still while previous policy is routinely implemented. So it was that the mega-project episode interceded.[35] The "episode" included not only the Blair–Carr task force in July 1981, but also the November 1981 Statement on Economic Development for Canada in the 1980s, presented with the ill-fated MacEachen budget to which we have already referred. This statement gave particular emphasis to the mega-projects issue and to a kind of "resources first" view of economic development. Although its route through the Cabinet decision process was a tortuous one, the MacEachen statement was partly influenced by an economic forecast for the 1980s which suggested that Canada could in part ride the crest of an expected increase in real terms of the value of its overall resource endowment, owing to favourable increases in the terms of international trade.[36] This referred to all resources including energy, minerals, forest and food products. While there was a plausible basis to these forecasts, they entered the policy cycle precisely at the time in the late summer and early fall of 1981 when Ottawa's (and many other) policy makers were seriously misreading the state of the economy. A severe downturn in the economy was already underway, but was not detected in time to assist in the development of the MacEachen budget of November 1981. Similarly, the downturn and the imminent decline in world oil prices were not detected, as we saw in Chapter 2, in time to influence the Canada–Alberta Agreement of September 1981.

While this larger collage of events was unfolding and permanently muddying the economic–energy policy connections, the fate of particular mega-projects was being determined. Alberta Premier Peter Lougheed's retaliatory package of actions against Ottawa immediately following the NEP had included an explicit refusal to give Alberta approval to the Alsands and Cold Lake projects. At this stage, politics was therefore the key obstacle to the start-up of these projects. But later, after the September Canada–Alberta Agreement, and the beginning of the economic downturn, economic issues took precedence.

It is necessary to appreciate all of the above to understand the context and evolution of the mega-project financing dilemmas to be reviewed below. But in addition, one needs to be reminded of the larger politics—indeed, geo-politics—contained within the larger projects at stake. Thus it is essential to remind ourselves of the point stressed in Chapter 2, namely that each of the major reserves of new energy supply—Alberta tarsands and heavy oil, the Beaufort Sea, Hibernia, and high Arctic and east coast gas—were under different political jurisdictions, faced different and uncertain technological and economic cost factors, and were owned by different interests and consortia with different degrees of political allegiance with the national and provincial governments. While all of these sources of supply were more or less a part of Ottawa's security of supply scenario, there were no firm rules as to which of these was at the head of the geological, economic and political queue, other than that Ottawa in a general sense preferred a Canada Lands-located supply option. The NEP had counted on the Alsands and Cold Lake projects as part of its projections for oil self-sufficiency by 1990, but when they were held hostage to the events of 1981, the firmness of the view was quickly dissolved.[37]

In the nexus of Alberta–Ottawa and Ottawa–industry relations, moreover, there was also the memory of the earlier mega-project negotiations. We have already referred to the Syncrude and Alaska Highway Pipeline arrangements in Chapters 3 and 4. The point to be stressed here is that these deals were not so distant as to be forgotten by the main protagonists. They had themselves involved tough bargaining and much political brinkmanship on the part of all the interests involved.

In this context, and keeping in mind our related goal of trying to understand the dynamics of implementation and the public and private behaviour that it involves, it is worthwhile to pause briefly and note some of the general characteristics of "projects" and how they alter the policy process, in comparison with what one might call the normal policy process.

Large projects are by definition capital intensive. As events in 1981 and 1982 have shown, they are therefore especially sensitive to financing and capital market conditions, including interest rates, inflation rates and medium- and long-term price movements. They induce all parties involved in a project to try to deflect risk as much as possible on to others. Because many projects involve joint ventures or consortia, they present different problems for different companies and governments, depending on their particular fiscal position and attitudes towards risk. The gradual breakdown of the Alsands consortium in 1982 showed this clearly, in that various consortium members fell out separately.

The projects impose on the political system a need to consider a longer-term planning period. In the regular federal policy process, three years is a long time. The realities of obtaining initial approvals and financing and the period of sheer physical construction make some kind of longer-term planning and project management essential. When these temporal and physical attributes are added to the technological novelty and risks of many of the projects, uncertainty is increased and the drive to share or to displace risks on others is overwhelming. Projects such as the Alsands, Cold Lake, Hibernia, Beaufort Sea, Heavy Oil Upgraders, and the Arctic Pilot Project all involve technological experimentation in the recovery and production process or in transportation and distribution processes.

The first two characteristics combine to produce a third. Large projects involve high political visibility. In the initial decision and construction phase, they have a distinct beginning and end. They allow political actors and their private sector partners to experience a visible success, including successful experiments in labour relations, environmental and procurement practices. Or they suffer a conspicuous failure. Sometimes the same politician can experience both over the same project. A potential white elephant in the short term can become an act of courage and foresight in the long term. The reverse can also happen.

The political visibility of a project is not one-dimensional. A substantial portion of large resource development projects are hinterland-based and thus physically remote from national and provincial capitals and other large urban centres. There is high political visibility for the project in urban Canada at the time of decision and perhaps construction, but many of the social effects of the project are in the hinterland and in small surrounding communities. Thus, the socially or environmentally deleterious effects can be, as it were, "out of sight, out of mind."

A large physical project has an even higher probability of triggering concerns and ideas in several policy fields concurrently than does a normal policy initiative. Because each project is partly unique and occurs at a different time, it "tests" these policy fields in different ways *each* time. Although efforts will be made to "be fair" to each project and to treat them equally, there will also be a need to "be reasonable," in short, to strike a new composite policy deal every time. The kinds of policy fields that can be and have been involved concurrently in large projects include energy and resources, economic and fiscal, social and environmental, labour relations and employment practices, regional policy, foreign policy and trade and technology. Each of these is under the custody of different ministers and officials in numerous departments, agencies, and boards of several levels of government, federal, provincial, local, and foreign.

If several policy fields are involved, it follows that several policy instruments are likely to be involved to ensure that the right, or at the least, the acceptable mix of public and private behaviour occurs in relation to each project and, over time, in relation to all or most projects. Thus, packages of spending grants and subsidies, verbal understandings, procurement activity, taxes or tax breaks, regulations (including administered prices) and direct public investment through Crown or mixed enterprises, could be involved. These packages are not easily assembled, partly because there are always political disputes about how much of the carrot and the stick are necessary to achieve the many purposes of the project. Moreover, the custodian departments and boards must constantly decide, when a project arises, how much of an exception, if any, the project should be to their normal policies and policy responsibilities. Such judgements must be made in the context of legal as well as political and financial constraints. These judgements become all the more difficult as more and more mega-projects queue up at the governmental trough. Which ones deserve the most support, and on what grounds? Which ones should come onstream first, and why?

Large projects are therefore politically visible and volatile events, each one of which is somewhat unique. This was all the more the case in late 1981 and early 1982. The pricing and taxing issues in particular converge on these projects, but they do so in the context of the larger policy climate set out above. A brief review of the Alsands project will illustrate the dynamics in a more specific case.

The Alsands Project was cancelled in the spring of 1982.[38] As originally projected, it would have had a capital cost in excess of $13 billion with start-up to begin in 1988 and a production capacity of 140 thousand barrels per day. For some sense of the rate of cost escalation (even taking into account the different sizes of the earlier oil sands plants), consider that the 1967 Suncor plant cost $350 million and the 1978 Syncrude plant cost $2.5 billion. One forecast of the economic stimulus that the Alsands project might have generated suggested 16 000 jobs during construction, 6 500 at the operating phase, with a similar number of indirect jobs. Half of the construction phase activity would have provided economic benefits outside Alberta. The planning of the project began in 1977, but there was an eleven-year lead time, since production would not begin until 1988. Full capacity would not be achieved until 1995.

At the point of cancellation the rate of return on equity for the Alsands project was estimated to be 20 percent.[39] This calculation took into account both the reduced oil price forecasts then emerging and included the elimination of the PGRT for such projects until the project achieved a pay-out. If such returns were possible, it seems difficult to see why the Alsands did not proceed. The fact is, however, that the Alsands was a nine-member consortium, and each firm was in a different set of circumstances. A senior Nova executive placed most of the blame on the lack of consistency of "the policy environment and government attitude towards equity investment in energy projects."[40] Given the concurrent impact of both the recession and the post-NEP shakedown in late 1981 and early 1982, it is not surprising that policy inconsistency was a factor. With interest rates rising, however, it is also clear that the private interests were doing their very best to deflect as many of these risks as possible on to the governments involved. This is why the Alsands and other large projects produce contradictory objectives from all the interests. The industry wants policy and political consistency—in short, stability and predictability. But at the same time, because each project is indeed different and special, private interests also want special deals and concessions—in short, "inconsistencies," in order to share risks and to "be fair" to the unique circumstances involved. Governments might like to be consistent across all such projects but each time one occurs, the times have changed and the situation is different.

For example, the final offer made by the Alberta and federal governments in April 1982 to the then remaining members of the consortium (Shell Canada 25 percent, Gulf Canada 8 percent, and Petro-Canada 17 percent) and to those who had conditionally withdrawn, involved a proposed participation of 50 percent by the private sector, 25 percent by Alberta and 25 percent by Ottawa (including the Petro-Canada involvement). The deal would have involved, in addition, loan guarantees from the two governments for almost 70 percent of the private sector's equity investment in the period prior to production. The loans were to be repayable by ensuring that about 60 percent of private net revenues were assigned to debt payments. Minimum royalties and no taxes would be levied until the loans were repaid. Thereafter taxes would be payable, including income taxes, a 16 percent federal PGRT, and provincial royalties set at the greater of 5 percent of gross revenues or 30 percent of net revenues.

The private and public returns on such a scheme are subject not only to the normal problems of assumed discount rates, but obviously on the future pattern of oil prices and interest rates. If rising real oil prices did not materialize, there would have been heavy public subsidization, but the private sector could have lost as well. Only if there were rising real oil prices would the project have produced roughly equal returns to the public and private sectors. In the final analysis, the project did not proceed in 1982 because both parties would not accept the risks, economic or political.

The cancellation of the Alsands and other projects appeared to be more calamitous than it might otherwise have been precisely because of the fanfare that the Liberals themselves gave to the mega-project industrial strategy, and because the Lougheed government, even though it had made them a central bargaining chip in the 1981 stalemate, had remained overwhelmingly confident in 1980 and 1981 that the project would proceed. The cancellation of some large projects, however, and the subsequent effort by their sponsors to go the route of smaller scale, modular projects, may well be a blessing in disguise, not only given the uncertainty of future price trends, but also the need to solve the numerous technological problems that are bound to arise.[41]

By late 1984 several such scaled-down projects appeared on the verge of commercial reincarnation, aided undoubtedly by lower interest rates, and a sense that the grumpy histrionics of the immediate post-NEP era simply could not continue. Thus scaled-down versions of a Cold Lake project, a Wolfe Lake project, and a Saskatchewan heavy oil upgrader project were announced as being underway, after the appropriate special fiscal concessions/incentives were given by the governments concerned.

Summary
In our first portrait of the post-NEP implementation world, we have focussed on the overall taxing and pricing regime. This regime is far more complex than in the pre-NEP era in the sense of the number of taxes and prices. The distinction between pre- and post-NEP is perhaps less obvious when one considers the diverse ideas that had to be accommodated by the fiscal regime. This diversity was present in the latter part of the 1970s as well. But the overall complexity was itself illustrative of the larger problem that various public and private interests had in reacting to the NEP itself. Moreover, even though we have had to focus on the taxing and pricing regime, the chapter shows how easy and even necessary it is to slip beyond the tax-price elements to the other features of the NEP, especially the PIP grants. Nonetheless, we have looked at the tax-price effects, and the contending interpretations and perceptions of them, in two major ways—aggregate effects and selected particular effects.

We have looked at aggregate effects on consumers and taxpayers, on revenue shares between governments, on the effects on the oil and gas industry in general, and on the economy. When one sifts one's way through the many interpretations of data it is possible to conclude that Canadian taxpayers and consumers are clearly paying double the pre-NEP prices for oil and gas and that Ottawa has increased its share of energy revenues vis-à-vis Alberta and other producer provinces from about 7 percent in 1980 to 16 percent in 1984. However, the total energy revenue pie has shrunk rapidly from the amounts forecast even as late as May 1982. Judgements of industry effects are very much dependent upon the time frame chosen for analysis and the weight one places on the effects of the recession and of high interest rates as opposed to the NEP. It must be remembered that in the late 1970s it was the most prosperous industrial sector, and that, even in the midst of the NEP and the recession, it fared much better than many other sectors, such as forestry, mining, and several manufacturing areas. According to this comparison, the industry was no worse off in 1984 than it was in the latter half of the 1970s, despite having been significantly buffeted by the NEP. The industry's overall view in 1984 was that its share of revenue was too low given the risks involved in frontier and non-conventional exploration and development.

When judged, however, in its immediate context in the 1980–84 period, the NEP clearly produced a loss in potential GNP and economic growth, in part from the actual outflow of capital, and in part because of its indirect effects on the climate of investment. These latter effects, however, are also interwoven with the recession, extremely high interest rates, and the practice of fiscal and monetary policy.

But industry and economic assessments are also dependent upon the second portrait we have taken, namely that of more particular effects. This second view has included a look at the effects on one major firm, Dome Petroleum, the effects on other firms that engaged in takeovers, and on the effects on *projects* in which there were several corporate and governmental interests at stake. This second look is essential, though by no means exhaustive, since it is effects on, and the response of, particular firms in the foreign-owned versus Canadian-owned sectors, the oil versus gas sectors, and in different regional geopolitical settings that produce the variety of implementation dynamics and views of success or failure. Thus the illustrative items covered in this chapter must be added to the earlier portraits of the responses of particular companies presented in Chapter 6.

The evolving nature of the NEP evaluation game has been stressed as well. Various evaluations both in the form of studies and political pressure emerged between 1981 and 1984. Initially these were highly selective, but gradually they were broadened into a fairly sustained line of criticism that focussed on the lack of emphasis in the NEP on economics and efficiency. This was part of a cumulative effort, especially by private interests to change the NEP, indeed, to remove its basic fiscal underpinnings by simplifying the price system, deregulating and recognizing the reality of world markets. But evaluative pressure and actual behaviour were not always moving in a similar direction. Behaviour was more fluid between 1981 and 1984 because of the intensity of the post-NEP rhetoric, the conflict of ideas and evaluative criteria that lay beneath it, and the perceived need by industry interests to overcome (at least partially) their ideological opposition to the NEP, and to the government that sponsored it, precisely at the same time that they had to discover how best to profit from it in the interests of their own shareholders.

The chapter has also dealt more explicitly with the relationships between energy policy and fiscal policy, and its link to federal deficits. Accordingly it shows the increasing rigidity of the fiscal-energy maze, even though, for the federal government, energy revenues are only about 6 percent of total budgetary revenues. A more complete view of these connections, however, must await the analysis in Chapter 10 of energy expenditures, which present the other side of the energy–fiscal coin.

Notes

1. See John F. Helliwell, "Canadian Energy Policy," *Annual Review of Energy*, vol. 4, 1979, pp. 175–229; Department of Finance, *Federal–Provincial Resource Taxation Review*, Discussion Paper (Ottawa: November 1978); Department of Energy, Mines and Resources, *An Energy Strategy for Canada* (Ottawa: EMR, 1976); Price Waterhouse, *The National Energy Program*, 2nd ed. (Toronto: Price Waterhouse, November 1981); and Anthony Scott, ed., *Natural Resource Revenues: A Test of Federalism* (Vancouver: University of British Columbia Press, 1976).

2. These are approximate averages. For exact details see the first two references in Note 1.

3. See Department of Finance, *op. cit.*, pp. 29–31. On the larger tax policy and tax incentive debate see Allan Maslove, "The Other Side of Public Spending: Tax Expenditures in Canada," in G. Bruce Doern and Allan Maslove, eds., *The Public Evaluation of Government Spending* (Montreal: Institute for Research on Public Policy, 1979), chapter 9; and Robin W. Boadway and H.M. Kitchen, *Canadian Tax Policy* (Toronto: Canadian Tax Foundation, 1980), pp. 131–152.

4. See Government of Canada, *The Fiscal Plan* (Ottawa: Department of Finance, February 1984). Calculated from Table 2.1, p. 10.

5. See Government of Canada, *The National Energy Program* (Ottawa: Supply and Services Canada, 1980); Government of Canada, *The National Energy Program Update 1982* (Ottawa: Supply and Services Canada, 1982). On world price changes, see The Economist Intelligence Unit, OPEC *and the World Oil Outlook* (London: The Economist, 1983); L.J. Murphy, "Adapting Canadian Energy Policy to Changing World Energy Trends," *Canadian Business Review* (Spring 1983), pp. 32–39; and Edward P. Neufeld, "International Financial Stability in the New Oil Price Scenarios," *Canaer 28, 1981*, pp. 18–21.

6. Government of Canada, *The Fiscal Plan, op. cit.*, p. 10.

7. Energy, Mines and Resources Canada, "Do Governments Take Too Much? An Examination of Pre- and Post-NEP Fiscal Regimes" (Ottawa: EMR, 1983), p. 7.

8. Brian L. Scarfe and Bruce W. Wilkinson, "The New Energy Agreement: An Economic Perspective." Revised edition of paper presented to the Ontario Economic Council Outlook and Issues Conference, October 28, 1981, pp. 18–21.

9. *Ibid.*, pp. 22–23.

10. Edward A. Carmichael and James K. Stewart, *Lessons from the National Energy Program* (Toronto: C.D. Howe Institute, 1983), pp. 41–42.

11. John F. Helliwell, M.E. MacGregor and A. Plourde, "The National Energy Program Meets Falling World Oil Prices," *Canadian Public Policy/Analyse de Politiques*, vol. IX, No. 3 (September 1983), p. 294.

12. Energy, Mines and Resources Canada, *op. cit.*, pp. 1–2.

13. *Ibid.*, pp. 15–16.

14. *Ibid.*, p. 1.

15. See Senate of Canada, Proceedings of the Standing Senate Committee on Energy and Natural Resources, Issue no. 2, April 10, 1984 and Issue no. 4, April 17, 1984 (Ottawa: Supply and Services Canada, 1984). It was explained that the wide difference in shares was due not only to the fact that EMR was using an *actual* number for 1983 versus CPA's *projected* nine-year average, but also because CPA projected a higher corporate tax take, lower PIP grants, and slightly higher provincial royalties.

16. Economic Council of Canada, *Strategy for Energy Policy* (Ottawa: Supply and Services Canada, 1984).

17. Brian Scarfe, "The National Energy Program after Three Years: An Economic Perspective" (Edmonton: University of Alberta, 1984).

18. Alberta Department of Energy and Natural Resources, *Annual Report March 31, 1983* (Edmonton, 1983), p. 59. Interestingly, the widely read news journal, *Alberta Report*, carried a story on this report titled, "The Lingering NEP Disaster," thus attributing the economic downturn to the NEP. See *Alberta Report*, December 12, 1983, p. 18.

19. See Alberta, *1983 Budget Address* (Edmonton, March 24, 1983), p. 7.

20. *Ibid.*, p. 10.

21. See Petroleum Service Association of Canada, *Well Cost Survey* (Calgary: Petroleum Association of Canada, December 1982). For the evolving view of this sector see Canadian Association of Oil Drilling Contractors, *Annual Report*, 1981, 1982 and 1983; Canadian Association of Oil Drilling Constractors, Submission to Alberta Government Department of Energy and Natural Resources, September 1983; and Petroleum Services Association of Canada, *Annual Report*, 1982 and 1983.

22. Scarfe and Wilkinson, *op. cit.*, pp. 9–12, and pp. 23–27.

23. Carmichael and Stewart, *op. cit.*, pp. 32–36.

24. Helliwell et al., *op. cit.*, p. 294.

25. See, for example, *The Globe and Mail*, July 27, 1983, p. 1.

26. Petroleum Monitoring Agency, *Canadian Petroleum Industry: Monitoring Survey, 1982* (Ottawa: Supply and Services Canada, 1983), p. 9-2.

27. For a good review of gas industry problems see Economic Council of Canada, *Strategy For Energy Policy, op. cit.*, Chapter 5.

28. On the Dome dilemma, see Jim Lyons, *Dome: The Rise and Fall of the House That Jack Built* (Toronto: Macmillan of Canada, 1983); Peter Foster, *Other People's Money* (Toronto: Collins, 1983); Dome Petroleum, Submissions to the Special Committee of the Senate on the Northern Pipeline (Calgary: Dome Petroleum, 1982); Dome Petroleum, Brief submitted to the House of Commons Standing Committee on Natural Resources and Public Works (Calgary, April 1981); and Evidence (by W.E. Richards), House of Commons Committee on Energy Legislation, May 4, 1982, pp. 11:5–11:23.

29. See Lyons, *op. cit.*, chapter 15.

30. See *Financial Post*, September 24, 1983, pp. 1–2 for a brief review of some of the impact on the banks.

31. See Carmichael and Stewart, *op. cit.*, p. 28; and Petroleum Marketing Agency, *op. cit.*, pp. 2.1–2.3.

32. See Senate of Canada, Proceedings of the Senate Standing Committee on Energy and Natural Resources, Issue no. 1, April 4, 1984 (Ottawa: Supply and Services Canada, 1984), p. 13. See also Footnote 12 of Chapter 1 for a review of the various measures of ownership.

33. Carmichael and Stewart, *op. cit.*, pp. 22–31.

34. *Ibid.*, p. 26.

35. See G. Bruce Doern, "The Mega-Project Episode and the Formulation of Canadian Economic Development Policy," *Canadian Public Policy*, Vol. 26, No. 2 (Summer 1983), pp. 219–238.

36. For details, see Doern, *op. cit.*, pp. 229–232.

37. Government of Canada, *The National Energy Program* (Ottawa: Supply and Services, 1980), p. 94.

38. See G.W. Douglas and J.A. MacMillan, *Alsands Energy Ltd. Economic Impact Study* (Calgary: Canadian Energy Research Institute, June 1981); John E. Feick, "Prospects for the Development of Mineable Oil Sands," *Canadian Public Policy*, vol. IX, no. 3 (September 1983), pp. 297–303; and Peter Eglington and Maris Uffelman, "An Economic Analysis of Oilsands Policy in Canada—The Case of Alsands and Wolfe Lake," Discussion Paper no. 259 (Ottawa: Economic Council of Canada, 1984).

39. Feick, *op. cit.*, p. 301.

40. *Ibid.*, p. 300.

41. See "Now . . . Mini-Mega Projects," *Financial Times*, July 11, 1983, pp. 11 and 19.

CHAPTER 10

ENERGY EXPENDITURES AND THE NEP:
THE PARADOX OF CONTROL

The total expenditures initially projected in the NEP were impressive. Table 10.1 shows the projections for the period between 1980 and 1983, and conveys the array of new programs. About $8.2 billion in new energy programs would be added to the $3.4 billion of existing programs. As set out in 1980, however, these figures were misleading in that they excluded the $3.3 billion cost of the then ballooning Oil Import Compensation Program and the then projected $4 billion Western Development Fund referred to earlier in Chapters 2 and 3. Thus in effect about $19 billion was potentially available in the energy or energy-related pot.

Beyond these impressive global figures, however, there is little that is straightforward about energy spending in the wake of the NEP. The analysis in Chapter 9 shows clearly one reason why, namely the volatility of both the economy and energy prices which were in turn the prime determinants of the actual, as opposed to the projected, amount of energy and tax revenues flowing into the federal coffers. To understand the continuing fate of energy expenditures, however, one also needs to penetrate the mysteries of Ottawa's system for allocating money, as well as understand the nature of energy expenditures, particularly their demand-driven characteristics. These are discussed briefly in the first section of the Chapter, prior to our examination of key expenditure dynamics in the implementation of the NEP. Given the broad scope of these expenditures, we must of necessity be selective. Not all programs are looked at since our overall focus is on the implementation dynamics including the interaction between public and private behaviour, and the interplay between ideas, structure, and process.

The chapter shows that energy expenditures produce a paradox of control. On the one hand, key parts of the expenditure package, in particular the Petroleum Incentive Program (PIP), were intended to

TABLE 10.1

ENERGY EXPENDITURES FOR 1980–1983 AS PROPOSED IN THE NEP
($ MILLIONS)

Industry incentives 2 550	**Special Atlantic Canada Program** 460
Exploration	Utility off-oil fund
Development	Lower Churchill Development
Non-conventional oil	Corporation
Heavy crude oil upgrading	Coal utilization package
	Coal R&D
Gasbank 440	P.E.I. conservation and renewable
Oil substitution 1 620	energy agreement extension
Conversion grants	Industrial Conservation upgraders 310
Conversion of federal buildings	Research and Development 260
Distribution systems incentives	Petro–Canada International 200
Transmission system support	Future Initiatives 1,200
Propane vehicle initiative	
Propane demonstration	
(government fleets)	

Conservation and renewables 1 150

Expanded CHIP
Industrial audits
Seminars and workshops
Mileage standards
Retrofit federal buildings
Arctic community demonstration
Arctic housing demonstration
Solar demonstration
(Residential hot water)
FIRE extension
Municipal energy management program
New housing guidelines
Remote communities initiative
Agricultural sector initiatives
Super-efficient housing demonstration
Small projects fund
Super-retrofit (Newfoundland,
P.E.I., Yukon, N.W.T.)

Source: *National Energy Program*, p. 90.

make the oil industry more visibly dependent on Ottawa as well as allow Ottawa to target incentives on Canadian-owned firms and encourage and or force activity away from Alberta and onto the Canada Lands which Ottawa controlled. Thus control in this political sense was a central objective. On the other hand, the very nature of key expenditure elements was that they were not controllable precisely because they were demand-driven and hence dependent upon private behaviour.

The Energy Envelope and the Expenditure System

Most energy expenditures are contained within the energy "envelope." The energy envelope is one of the ten parcels of spending into which the federal government's expenditures are divided. Located within the larger envelope system known as the Policy and Expenditure Management System (PEMS) and thus linked to the Cabinet decision process already examined in Chapter 8, the envelope's origins and characteristics have their own unique features as well as features which they share with other envelope sectors.

A separate energy envelope was established for several reasons. The first was that because the NEP would be visibly taking energy revenue from several classes of taxpayers, particularly in Western Canada, there was concern that it be seen that these revenues would be used for energy policy purposes. There was also a concern that the energy expenditures were of such magnitude and involved such a high proportion of unpredictable demand-driven programs that they would require special treatment. Had they been placed in the economic development envelope, where energy expenditures had been prior to 1980, they would have distorted it. Ultimately, however, a separate envelope was deemed essential to ensure decisive and speedy decision making. Put simply, the NEP was the government's overriding priority, and the political power of key ministers was mobilized behind it. From the outset, therefore, it was inevitable that the energy envelope would partially contradict the intentions of those who designed the envelope system as a whole, the latter being a system, in theory, to produce careful considered analysis and trade-offs.

PEMS was introduced by the Clark Conservative Government in 1979 and was maintained by the Trudeau Liberals on their return to power in 1980.[1] The system assigned the blocks or "envelopes" of expenditure to different cabinet committees. The main principles of the system are:

- the integration of policy and expenditure decision-making to ensure that policy decisions are taken in the context of expenditure limits with full consideration of the cost implications and that, in turn, expenditure decisions are taken with an understanding of and responsibility for the policies and priorities of Ministers.

- the decentralization of decision-making authority to Policy Committees of Cabinet in recognition of the increasing range and complexity of government responsibilities, the interrelationships of policies and programs, and the requirement for the Cabinet Committee on Priorities and Planning to focus on the central strategic issues and overall priorities of the government.

- the publication of a longer-term fiscal plan encompassing government revenues and expenditures over a five-year period thereby setting out the overall resource constraints within which policy and program choices are made.

- the establishment of expenditure limits (i.e., "resource envelopes") for policy sectors consistent with the fiscal plan and the government's priorities, with appropriate Policy Committees of Cabinet assigned the responsibility to manage their envelopes.

- the development of policy sector strategies by Policy Committees as a means of providing an overview of their sector to integrate the individual actions and responsibilities of Ministers in a common government approach for that sector.[2]

When one places the NEP and the "uniqueness" of the energy envelope and of energy politics between 1980 and 1984 alongside the PEMS and its requirements for "normal" decision making, it is clear that there are some problems of compatibility.[3] As we have stressed throughout our analysis, there are several competing official and unofficial criteria for assessing the substance and processes of energy expenditures. The NEP itself imposes three overt criteria—security, Canadianization, and fairness. The dynamics of the introduction of the NEP add two implicit criteria: revenue protection, and speed and decisiveness in the decision process in order to put the main features of the NEP in place. The broader governmental priorities between 1980 and 1984 add a further criterion, namely a view that energy decisions reflect concern for overall economic development and efficiency as well as regional sensitivity. Indeed, as we saw in Chapter 8, the energy envelope is nominally the responsibility of the Cabinet Committee on Economic and Regional Development (CCERD). Now, in addition the PEMS system itself imposes further overall criteria, namely that ministers on CCERD make their choices knowing the resource implications of new energy initiatives, and based on careful and considered prior analysis and with some sense of longer-term implications.

Not surprisingly these several criteria do not meld easily. Indeed they are bound to conflict, at least in some respects. For example, speed and decisiveness do not always augur well for the judicious consideration of resource implications, especially over the medium term. Concerns for security and efficiency may conflict, at least in the short run, and perhaps over the long run as well. This chapter deals with these conflicts in greater detail. They are stressed at the outset, not out of the mistaken expectation that they can be somehow permanently solved, but rather out of the view that they present basic problems in judging the overall management of energy expenditures depending upon which criteria are used or emphasized. This problem of course applies to all features of the NEP.

In addition to the overriding tensions between the NEP and PEMS criteria and dynamics, a key characteristic of energy expenditures is the demand-driven nature of many of the main expenditure items. These include the PIPS and the 25 percent Crown Interest provisions as well as the Canadian Home Insulation Program (CHIP) and the Canadian Oil Substitution Program (COSP). CHIP was established in 1977 and provided grants to home owners who installed increased insulation as an energy conservation measure. COSP was an NEP initiative that gave grants to consumers to encourage them to switch from oil to alternative sources of energy. Each is dependent upon levels of private action and/or consumer take-up rates. A second and closely related characteristic is the sensitivity of the envelope to energy tax and pricing changes. Not only did these affect the general inflow of revenue (to the Consolidated Revenue Fund and other separate accounts, and then to the envelope itself) but there was also the combined effect of revenue-tax-pricing issues on programs (e.g. on COSP and CHIP take-up rates), on the issue of how generous PIP and other incentives had to be, and on issues such as Alberta's Market Development Incentive Program (MDIP) revenues, gas pipeline expansion and the Québec Laterals Fund. Finally, there is the issue of funding Petro-Canada in particular and energy Crown corporations in general (including other new smaller companies such as Petro-Canada International and Canertech). These issues involve concerns about the adequacy of the vetting and review of capital budgets and corporate plans and of equity advances to such enterprises.

Another characteristic of the energy envelope and expenditure universe which should be understood is the existence of several special funds and accounts. In principle, the PEMS is not supposed to tolerate such special funds (envelopes within envelopes, so to speak) since it violates the symmetry of control and the open trade-offs among expenditure items that are supposed to characterize the budgetary decision process. More than a fair share of these exist in the energy envelope and outside it. They therefore add to the slipperiness or the "amoeba-like" quality of energy expenditures. These funds are examined later. They include the Canadian Ownership Account, the Market Development Incentives Program (MDIP) and the Laterals Fund.

Energy Expenditure Dynamics: Issues and Problems

In the post-NEP evolution of the energy expenditure decision process several overall issues quickly emerged. These include the status and adequacy of the policy reserve and the revenue-expenditure imbalance that quickly materialized, the control of demand-driven programs, and the issue of special funds and accounts. Each is examined below.

The Revenue–Expenditure Shortfall

An overriding issue in the post-NEP period has been the rapidly changing state of the energy "policy reserve" (the PEMS name given to the amount of money in the envelope for "new" initiatives) in the face of declining federal revenues, EMR's desire to protect the reserve from other governmental uses of it, and several budget cutting (X-budget) exercises. It is necessary to appreciate a brief history of the overall state of the envelope and its changing policy reserve.

The energy envelope was officially established by a Priorities and

Planning Committee decision taken at Lake Louise on July 15, 1980. The envelope included EMR's pre-NEP energy programs; the capital and operating budgets of energy Crown corporations including a yearly reference level of $100 million for Petro-Canada's equity contribution; allocations for NEP initiatives, and finally a substantial annual policy reserve that exceeded $400 million in 1982–83 and in the two subsequent years. The large policy reserve was essential if EMR was to have the flexibility to respond to changing circumstances. An operating reserve was created later to cover potential cost over-runs and minor adjustments to existing or "A-Base" programs in the envelope. This was financed out of the energy policy reserve, leaving overall funds allocated to the envelope unaffected.

Almost immediately, Ministers of the Cabinet Committee on Economic and Regional Development (CCERD) approved several non-NEP or quasi-NEP energy programs, including: assistance to Donkin and Prince Mines; compensation payments for Coleson Cove; financial assistance for the Lepreau I nuclear station; an advance of $40 million for the Cold Lake project; $100 million to enter into a joint venture with the prairie cooperatives; and significant increases in the reference levels for Petro-Canada's equity contributions. These initiatives were financed out of the energy policy reserve, and coupled with the need to have an operating reserve, effectively put the energy envelope into a significant deficit situation.

Given the deficit situation in the policy reserve, EMR adjusted some NEP initiatives through expenditure reductions, program deferrals, and the use of funds committed by Alberta to Market Development Incentive Payments. These MDIP payments are examined below. Significant savings in PIP expenditures were achieved through the energy agreement with Alberta since Alberta would take over PIP in Alberta itself.

These envelope adjustments temporarily brought the envelope within its limits. Indeed, they re-established a positive policy reserve. However, at the Priority and Planning meeting at Keltic Lodge in September 1981, the Minister of Finance recommended reducing the Energy Envelope not only by the PIP "savings" but also by $200 million in each year from 1982–83 to 1984–85. As a result, problems in the policy reserve re-emerged. It was hoped that this situation might be ameliorated somewhat by the Minister of Finance's subsequent offer to restore to the energy envelope $230 million, if required, to cover cost overruns in the energy demand-driven programs or for new energy initiatives of overriding national interest, but this offer was overtaken by other fiscal realtities.

As part of the NEP Update in 1982, EMR undertook once again to eliminate the estimated envelope deficits both in order to free funds to finance the new programs in the Update, and to create a positive policy reserve. A series of program cuts and deferrals were approved by the Minister and presented to the Department of Finance. The EMR X-budget exercise represented envelope savings of over $1.2 billion over the period 1982–83 to 1984–85, and therefore again established a positive reserve.

The Minister of Finance later sought the Minister of EMR's approval in using $280 million of the policy reserve to finance the Update's fiscal measures. He also suggested a further cut of $320 million in the 1982–83 energy envelope. If this were to be agreed to, it would not only have invalidated the effect of EMR's X-budget exercise in creating a policy reserve for the 1981–82 fiscal year, but it would have generated a new deficit of more than $300 million in 1982–83 when new programs would have to be financed. The Minister of Energy, Mines and Resources offered $140 million of the anticipated 1982–83 policy reserve towards a general reduction in the federal deficit.

This was followed by yet another X-budget exercise in the fall of 1982. Following the Meach Lake annual priorities exercise, a further $800 million-cut was ordered, covering the period ending with the 1984–85 fiscal year. These reductions were to help fund a new job creation package announced in the Finance Minister's economic statement. Marc Lalonde, now the Minister of Finance, knew well the budgetary games and the padding left in the energy envelope.

It is clear that several strategies were adopted by the main budgetary players. Both the central agencies and EMR knew that many of the initial NEP initiatives were soft, "one-line" items and that other programs could not get started as quickly as planned. There was therefore a strong incentive for the energy minister and key EMR officials to portray the energy envelope as being in perpetual deficit in order to ward off those anxious to use scarce federal dollars in other policy areas. At the same time central agency officials saw the energy envelope, even when in deficit, as a ripe target for short-term X-budget cuts, because they knew there was soft money buried not only in the reserves but in the envelope in general.

While it can be readily and even validly argued that much of this budgetary gamesmanship was induced by the overall fiscal volatility the government faced and by the demand-driven nature of key NEP initiatives, it remains nonetheless true that the envelope could scarcely be well managed, in any ordinary sense of these words, under the circumstances. This was particularly the case because current X-budget savings were being drawn down from future years, and were therefore only postponing some of the reckoning. This was true without even considering some of the problems of capping the demand-driven programs discussed below.

The fate of the energy policy reserve typifies the underlying conflict between the special nature of the NEP and the energy envelope and the normal PEMS process. Judged against the NEP, the volatile reserves are understandable. Judged against the PEMS criteria, the energy envelope management falls well below the standard required.

Demand-Driven Programs
Several key demand-driven programs obviously posed a major dilemma. The three most obvious ones are the PIP, CHIP and COSP programs, but there are demand-driven features in the 25 percent Crown interest provision as well. This chapter does not describe or evaluate all these programs per se but rather examines the uncertainties they create in estimating and containing costs and in managing NEP energy expenditures as a whole. It must also be remembered that some similar problems were present under the pre-NEP regime as well, that is, when incentives were conferred through the tax system. This involved difficult problems of estimating *tax revenues* rather than expenditures. The problem of control, however, is neither as large or as visible as it is under the NEP grants regime. We first offer a brief assessment of the control problems of each program, and then of the general issues of NEP implementation they create.

PIP Grants and the PIP-COGLA Connection
The PIP grants were intended to meet not only the Canadianization and self-sufficiency goals but also the "need to know" goal.[4] The grants

effectively reduced the after-tax cost of an exploration dollar for a Canadian company exploring on the Canada Lands to 9 cents, versus about 31 cents on provincial lands. Foreign-owned companies received much less generous PIP grants, but even their after-tax cost is 34 cents per dollar on the Canada Lands, versus about 48 cents on provincial lands. PIP grants are administered by the Petroleum Incentives Administration (PIA), but the level of expenditures is especially tied to the regulatory regime centred in the Canadian Oil and Gas Lands Administration (COGLA). Though we examine COGLA in detail in Chapter 11, it is essential to stress at the outset two features of COGLA directly related to the interpretation of the "need to know" mandate of COGLA and hence to the PIP grants. The first feature was the decision to limit the size of holdings in wildcat areas to about two million acres for each exploration agreement approved by COGLA. The second feature was the decision to enter into agreements in all major areas of the Canada Lands, namely, the Scotian Shelf, the Grand Banks, the Labrador Shelf, the Beaufort Sea and the Arctic Islands. Designed to ensure that exploration was not concentrated in one area, the "need to know" mandate was interpreted in this dual way to require a broad-scale search. In other words, the "need to know" mandate could have been focussed exclusively on a more intensive exploration of blocks closer to the more promising areas, such as the Grand Banks or the Beaufort Sea, rather than spread more thinly across to include areas such as the high Arctic and the Labrador coast. As pointed out in Chapter 11, some geological targeting was done in that the size of blocks was smaller near Hibernia and in the Beaufort Sea, but in general the system opted for a broad-scale search, rather than a focussed one. A further central dilemma was that COGLA was not responsible for the PIP grants but influenced the pace of drilling in a major way. The PIA administered the grants program but could not control costs.

Total PIP grants were $1930 million in the 1981–83 period and were projected in 1982 to be $1150 million in 1983–84, $1474 million in 1984–85 and $1850 million in 1985–86. But these estimates for later years must be considered to be extremely tentative. The pace of drilling is a function not only of the exploration agreements but of the volume of farm-ins. The PIP regime encouraged the multinationals to farm out some of their lands to Canadian firms. Drilling levels as a whole were also uncertain because of falling world oil prices, the recession, and because of uncertainty about the degree of future recovery in 1985 and 1986. These uncertainties, combined with major revenue shortfalls, could easily produce some "billion dollar" surprises. If exploration activity increases, PIP expenditures will increase significantly. If the economy improves, so also will federal revenues. But the key point to stress is that there is no guarantee that incremental revenues which flow from economic recovery will be allocated to *energy*, since demands to reduce the deficit, and/or allocate it to other economic recovery programs, will be extremely strong.

The PIP conundrum is a very real one. There was almost immediately a strong suspicion in the oil and gas industry that the PIP would be cut back one way or another. There was, accordingly, a strong desire on the part of the government not to appear to be holding back on PIP. Yet sufficient money might not be available. The Liberals had to control PIP, but not do so directly. The only major way to cap PIP expenditures in the short run was via administrative means through the PIA.

The COGLA approvals process is a contentious one, not only in the general ways examined in Chapter 11, but also in terms of its net effects on the magnitude of the PIP expenditures. The general concern was that COGLA's enthusiastic "pro-exploration" and broad scale "need to know" mandate was inducing more activity and therefore more PIP grants than would otherwise be the case. Between 1981 and 1983 there were, however, some sobering economic and financing realities which partially counterbalanced this pro-exploration tendency. These countervailing pressures perhaps made it less likely that companies were engaged only in "grant-driven" exploration activity.

On the other hand, other features of the COGLA process made the costs of PIPs difficult to control. COGLA's exploration agreements set *minimum* levels of exploration activity, not maximum levels. If more is carried out, more PIP money is required. Exploration agreements with the multi-nationals may produce later farm-in arrangements with Canadian firms, thus producing PIP expenditures unforeseen at the time of the original approval of the exploration agreement. Agreements, moreover, are for several years, thus making it potentially more difficult to estimate any *one year* period's money needs. PIP costs, well over initial estimates, were evident by early 1983. As we noted in Chapter 3, EMR announced in August 1983 a scheme to help control costs. This would be done by requiring individual ministerial approval through the PIA for each well over $50 million and by a requirement that companies would have to show that their drilling costs were "competitive." In the longer run, however, the real and visible problems of expenditure control can only be made more manageable by eliminating the PIP regime through a gradual phase-out or by targetting the PIP grants to those areas which have the best geological and commercial prospects. The phrase "made more manageable" is used advisedly, because a purely tax-based system would also involve problems of control, owing to foregone tax revenues.

It should not be surprising that the PIP grants would induce private sector firms into new strategies about how to take advantage of their availability. "Grantsmanship," the use of grants at least somewhat on an "activity for the sake of activity" basis, was easily parlayed into the system. The incentive to use grants in this fashion was aided and abetted by the severe recession, and hence the desire by some firms to put idle exploration equipment to work to earn PIP dollars, dollars worth as much as 90 cents per exploration dollar. Some firms were also motivated to use PIP dollars and increase the pace of their "normal" exploration activity precisely out of an expectation that the grants were so rich that Ottawa could not and would not continue them for very long. A further issue that triggered concern about PIP gamesmanship and hence about costs was the attempt by Gulf Canada to depreciate its almost $700 million Beaufort Sea high-technology drilling equipment over three years. This escalated the cost per well and hence the PIP grants paid out of the federal treasury. Gulf Canada's partner in the project, Canterra Energy Ltd., a subsidiary of the half-federally owned Canadian Development Corporation, objected to the use of the equipment and its cost, and eventually decided to withdraw from the project. Other stories of PIP abuses were also going the rounds off the east coast as well. Here, Mobil, aware of the political pressure to get offshore exploration visibly underway, and faced with a slowdown of its own drilling activity in other parts of the world, took advantage of "PIP-able" activity. The point to stress here is not that this kind of activity was illegal or a malfeasance. Rather, it was corporations taking advantage of the system in their own interests. Thus the responses, abuses, and effects were many and varied.

Meanwhile, the executives of some of these companies, particularly the multinationals, were continuously voicing their political opposition to the grants on the grounds that they rewarded "activity" and not "success," and on general grounds of efficiency. The latter included a view that too much was being spent on the offshore and the Canada Lands, given the new economics of declining oil prices.

It was some of these practices, coupled with the larger federal fiscal straightjacket, that prompted Ottawa to impose the previously noted new procedures announced in August 1983. As a result, by the end of 1983 EMR officials were claiming that the PIP expenditures were basically under control, that is, within about $50 million of original estimates of $1.15 billion for 1983–84. The total five-year prediction of $8.2 billion in PIP expenditures made in 1981 is expected by EMR officials to be on target. It is clear, however, that it would not have been, had the new control measures not been adopted. Indeed, there are other factors, as noted above, which could still result in a serious lack of control.

But lack of control was in the nature of the PIP game just as it had been under the demand-driven nature of the multi-billion dollar Oil Import Compensation Program prior to the NEP. Control in the sense of inducing Canadian firms into exploration in the Canada Lands was meanwhile having some of its intended effects. (The full range of intended and unintended effects is explored in more detail below and in Chapter 11.) As Table 10.2 shows, Canadian firms were the main recipients of the $2.4 billion spent on PIP grants between 1981 and 1983. These included not only Petro-Canada and Dome Petroleum, but the firms we have referred to as the second-line Canadian firms, whose investment responses we surveyed in Chapter 6. By 1983 it was clear that several such firms had changed their investment and corporate strategies. These included Home Oil, Canterra Energy, Norcen Energy Resources, Pan Canadian, and Husky Oil. We have more to say about the overall fate of these "second-line" Canadian firms at the end of this chapter and again in Chapter 11, since it is the total fiscal and regulatory regime that must be taken into account.

The 25 Percent Crown Interest

It is important to link the 25 percent Crown interest provision to the PIP dilemma, since it presents the need for further large expenditures and/or financing requirements when projects reach the *development* and production stage. It is presumed that the 25 percent Crown

TABLE 10.2
TOP 20 RECIPIENTS OF FEDERAL PIP PAYMENTS
FOR THE PERIOD JANUARY 1, 1981 TO DECEMBER 31, 1983

	$ Million
Dome Canada Limited	615
Petro-Canada Exploration Inc.	576
Canterra Energy Ltd.	199
Norcen Energy Resources Limited	111
Gulf Canada Resources Inc.*	57
Mobil Oil Canada. Ltd.*	45
Exploration SOQUIP Inc.	43
Husky Oil Operations Ltd.	39
Teck Frontier Corporation	38
Panarctic Oils Ltd.	37
Home Oil Company Limited	37
PanCanadian Petroleum Ltd.	32
Bow Valley Industries Ltd.	30
Roxy Petroleum Ltd.	27
Forward Resources Ltd.	25
Ranchmen's Resources (1976) Ltd.	22
Mackenzie Delta Energy Limited	21
Nova Scotia Resources (Ventures) Limited	19
Esso Resources Canada Limited*	19
Canalands Energy Corporation	17

*Foreign owned

[1]For those applicants offsetting incentives against their Petroleum and Gas Revenue Tax liability, applications will not be received until the second quarter of 1984; adjustments and supplementals may be received beyond June 30, 1984. Hence, these figures are not final for the period designated.

Source: Adapted from EMR, Petroleum Incentives Administration Report, January 1981 to December 31, 1983, p. 17.

interest will not be auctioned off to a private company. (If it were, it would obviously generate revenues for the government.) Therefore, further expenditures or financial commitments, certainly in the multi-billion dollar range, can be expected in the late 1980s, when the federal government will have to pay for its 25 percent interest in production and development costs. There will of course also be additional revenues when projects come onstream. Petro-Canada or other Crown agencies may be the vehicle for the exercise of the Crown interest.

The 25 percent Crown interest is perhaps less urgent than the PIP issue but it presents similar dilemmas in terms of where to focus scarce energy dollars as well as other federal dollars. At present it is fair to say that these future dollar commitments are not well in hand in terms of basic estimates, policies, and financing and/or revenue needs. Uncertainties also remain because the U.S. government continues to object strongly to this provision, and the Mulroney Conservative government may well abolish it as a conciliatory gesture to the Americans.

The role of partisan politics and governmental interests is a major issue in the disposition of the 25 percent Crown interest debate. The prospect of the Conservative government actually abolishing the provision is problematical in that a Conservative provincial government, Nova Scotia, is likely to press to have legislatively enshrined with the federal government their half of the revenues that would flow from the 25 percent interest. For Nova Scotia this would provide legislative protection for the Canada–Nova Scotia Agreement, which is now only an agreement between the two Cabinets. The dilemma for the Conservative party is obvious, since it would create major policy differences on an issue that is regionally very visible and essential, all the more so because provincial governments would have a concrete revenue interest.

CHIP, COSP and "Off-Oil" Incentives

The demand-driven nature of the CHIP and COSP programs presents problems of a lower dollar magnitude and of less uncertainty than the PIP and 25 percent Crown interest aspects of energy expenditures. In 1982–83 CHIP and COSP expenditures were $224 and $153 million, respectively, or $377 million in total. A combination of events—the recession and hence lower consumer take-up rates, an evaluation of CHIP, controversy over urea-formaldehyde insulation, and insulation company irregularities regarding CHIP, and the restraint of X-budgets—helped control these programs somewhat. Economic recovery may produce an upsurge in take-up rates and hence in expenditures. Conservation and off-oil consumer consciousness, on the other hand, may dissipate in the wake of falling oil prices and the publicity given to them. Uncertainties therefore obviously remain, but the problems seem to be containable.

The CHIP and COSP programs and the future need for them are, of course, bound up in the larger debate, not only about the total costs of energy programs vis-à-vis other demands on the government, but also of the demand management aspects of energy policy and of the role of prices versus grants as the main vehicle to secure off-oil and conservation policies. As the energy debate heated up in the 1970s, one question centred on whether the price mechanism, if allowed to work, would itself produce the right signals to businesses and home owners to conserve and be fuel efficient. We have already seen how prices were politically determined and hence unavailable to perform fully these policy chores. There still remained, and remains today, the relative choice of "how much" of a special incentive is necessary to induce the right behaviour. Are the CHIP and COSP grants just inducing persons to do what they would have done anyway?

EMR calculated that COSP and CHIP contributed to about 4 percent of the reductions achieved in the total demand for oil, with COSP being the more efficient program.[5] By 1984, EMR argued that the overall demand management aspects of the NEP, such as COSP and gas pricing incentives, plus the recession, had resulted in a 22 percent reduction since 1980 in the demand for oil, and had therefore in itself appreciably contributed to the security of supply and self sufficiency goals.[6] The major closure of refineries by the multinationals referred to in Chapter 6 certainly indicates that the NEP policies, as well as the cumulative effect of other conservation programs initiated in the 1970s, had produced permanent effects. As usual, the figures used, the energy sources covered, and the periods compared vary, but other sources do confirm that conservation effects have been real. The Economic Council's 1984 energy study showed overall conservation gains of 17 percent between 1973 and 1982, measured in terms of primary energy consumption per unit of real domestic product.[7] Regionally, the improvement varied from 8 percent in Ontario to 24 percent in Atlantic Canada. In a general sense, therefore, partial success for the NEP can be claimed. The argument is nonetheless still raised, that a fuller reliance on the price mechanism would have allowed the same or better results without the need for large grant programs. It would also have involved different costs and benefits to different income classes.

Different interests intrude in this substitution and conservation game in different ways. For example, in Québec a political and economic battle arose over the preferred "off-oil" energy source to which consumers and businesses should switch. Officially, Ottawa's policy between fuels was characterized as neutral in parts of the NEP.

This was wise at the level of the individual consumer, since to intervene in any decision given the "good housekeeping" seal of approval by Ottawa was fraught with dangers, as the CHIP and urea-formaldehyde health controversy had made abundantly clear. But at another level, the NEP was hardly neutral. Gas was to be given incentive pricing. In Québec, the TQM pipeline would be extended with major federal subsidies. Meanwhile, the Parti Québécois government of Québec, whose relations with Ottawa were in a state of perpetual conflict, wished to give some preference to electricity as the alternative fuel. Its political interests were in part in league with that of Hydro-Québec which it owned and which had, in the wake of the James Bay development and the recession, large amounts of excess capacity. To complicate matters still further, in the midst of the oil glut of 1981–82, residual fuel oils were extremely competitive for heavy industrial users (the major energy users in terms of total volume).

All of this must be related to the politics of the TQM pipeline to which we have previously referred. The pipeline was not favoured by many EMR officials, but was inserted into the NEP primarily at the insistence of ministers to show visibly and concretely that the NEP was a national program. The construction of the pipeline ran into huge cost overruns. Moreover, as we discuss in Chapter 11, in relation to the Sable Island Venture project, the availability of Nova Scotia gas led to provincial government demands that the TQM be made a reversible pipeline so that Alberta gas could flow east and Nova Scotia gas could flow west into Québec, even though in the first instance it was destined overwhelmingly for U.S. markets. These issues quickly became entwined in the rather curious interconnected aspects of the Québec-based Natural Gas Laterals Program and the Gas Marketing Assistance Program discussed briefly below.

Natural Gas Laterals Program and the Gas Marketing Assistance Program

The Natural Gas Laterals Program involves expenditures of $40.0, $184.6, $223.8 and $41.0 millions in 1982–83 to 1985–86 respectively to build distribution lines from the extended TQM pipeline in Québec. It has been capped at a $500 million total. At first glance, therefore, one may be hard pressed to label it a demand-driven program. The laterals program deserves concern, however, because it still contains the seeds of future expenditure pressure caused partially by demand pressures that could exceed the $500 million ceiling. It must also be linked to the Gas Marketing Assistance Program (GMAP). GMAP provides monthly contributions to the gas distributors developing the new gas market areas in Québec and the Maritimes. The total projected cost of GMAP through fiscal year 1986–87 is almost $100 million. This is funded presently by Alberta MDIP revenue, which is itself subject to considerable instability (see below).

The laterals program warranted concern because it appears to have been established partly or even primarily to *protect federal tax revenue* rather than for "off-oil" energy policy reasons. The laterals were initially part of the TQM costs. As cost overruns occurred, revenue from the natural gas and gas liquids tax declined. These revenue declines would have mushroomed had there been a failure to expand gas sales via the laterals to Québec markets. The fund was established to protect the revenue source as much as anything else. The reality of the revenue protection goals was borne out by the fact that the use of Alberta MDIP funds was ruled out as a source of funding for the laterals program (but not the GMAP.) Commitments were made to finance the building of laterals and the marketing of gas in the Québec market in the face of growing uncertainties about whether gas has sustainable economic advantages over electricity and residual fuel oil, especially in the large industrial market. If gas expansion does not materialize, the federal government will be left with the potential political need to sustain further support, especially given the fact that laterals and GMAP activity is spread through numerous constituencies held by Liberal MPs.

The "revenue protection" goals of the laterals program may have made sense in an overall fiscal and revenue management sense (especially in a time of rapidly rising deficits) but it is not clear that it makes much energy policy sense. In any event, it clearly adds yet another layer of potential future surprises for energy decision makers. Admittedly, the dollars are not as big as the previously mentioned demand-driven programs, but they do add to the total.

While each of the above demand-driven items is of different expenditure magnitude and undoubtedly presents problems unique to each individual program item, in general, they lead to an energy expenditure situation that is potentially out of control, particularly in respect of PIP. They involve future expenditure commitments of several billions without a reasonable prospect of adequate revenue to pay for them, not only within the five-year framework of energy envelope planning, but also in subsequent years. They also show the different contexts in which control can be viewed, not only on a program-by-program basis but on the mixture of programs, their connections with each other, and on the economic and political engines which drove the expenditures as the NEP unfolded in the middle of a deep recession.

Special Funds and Accounts
Any system of policy and expenditure management has to have room for some special funds and discretionary spending. There are, however, limits to this practice, especially when such funds in total, or even separately, begin to exceed the size of the official policy reserve for each envelope. The energy envelope and the broader energy expenditure domain contain several such pools of spending (as do other envelopes as well). Several of these are examined briefly below. Each special fund has its own usually desirable rationale, but in total they create problems for expenditure and policy implementation. Space does not allow a full description of these funds. Once again our focus is on the expenditure and implementation dynamics they present. The special funds examined are the Market Development Incentive Payments (MDIP) and the Canadian Ownership Account.

Market Development Incentive Payments (MDIP)
Under the terms of the Canada–Alberta Agreement, the government of Canada obtained a new source of funds in the form of Market Development Incentive Payments (MDIP) from the government of Alberta. These payments have the express purpose of expanding markets for Alberta-produced gas and hence cannot be treated as general revenues accruing to the government of Canada. Indeed, the government of Canada has a legal obligation to make an annual accounting to the government of Alberta on the manner in which these funds are used. Key features of the arrangements, including the eligibility criteria underlying MDIP, specified that funds could be used for:

(a) gas transmission utilities to assist in the extension of gas transmission systems into new domestic market areas east of Alberta for Alberta-produced gas, and

(b) gas distribution utilities to obtain new domestic markets east of Alberta for Alberta-produced gas.[8]

This new source of revenue permitted substantial reductions from the original allocations in the Energy Envelope for NEP programs aimed at natural gas infrastructure and market expansion. Specifically, the $80 million per annum for the Distribution System Expansion Program (DSEP) was reduced to $20 million per year, thus effectively reducing the potential draw of the program on federal monies by $300 million for the planning period ending 1987. As well, MDIP revenues are to finance a new range of initiatives approved as part of the NEP Update: the Industrial Conversion Assistance Program, the GMAP referred to earlier (formerly known as Developmental Pricing), and assistance to vehicle conversion to compressed natural gas. However, some federal funds are required for these programs to be applicable nationally. MDIP funds can be used only where Alberta gas is sold (currently Saskatchewan, Manitoba, Ontario and Québec).

The conditional nature of the MDIP funding, and the timing of its payment (program expenditures are incurred before all MDIP receipts for a particular year are known) has necessitated special accounting procedures which were agreed upon in the spring of 1982. Problems arose because program planners had to make commitments on the basis of anticipated MDIP revenues, which in turn depended on accurate forecasting of future natural gas sales. In November 1982, forecasts of revenues showed a reasonable balance between total MDIP receipts and anticipated program expenditures. Indeed, at that time forecasts of $418 million over the five-year period showed no need to draw funds from the envelope. Later, however, the recessionary climate produced low natural gas sales and resulted in far lower revenues than anticipated, especially in 1983–84. This in turn affected the capacity to fund programs such as GMAP, as noted above.

MDIP is thus couched in some of the same uncertainties of the larger energy revenue-expenditure dilemmas already examined. A major attempt was made to manage it carefully. For example, the decision not to use MDIP funds for the Natural Gas Laterals Programs (referred to above) was undoubtedly a wise one, not only in relation to accountability to Alberta, but because of the size of the laterals program relative to anticipated MDIP funds.

The Canadian Ownership Account

The Canadian Ownership Account is not part of the energy envelope but is important in the broader realm of energy finances. Established initially under the authority conferred by EMR Vote 5C of the Appropriation Act No. 4, 1980–81 and later made part of the **Energy Administration Act** (Section 65.26 to 65.27) the account receives proceeds from the Canadian Ownership Charge. At the discretion of the Governor in Council on the recommendation of the Minister of EMR and the Minister of Finance, these funds may be used for "investment in shares, debentures, bonds, or other evidences of indebtedness and or for property acquisitions from any person in order to increase Canadian public ownership of the oil and gas industry in Canada and to repay loans or expenses incurred for that purpose" (Section 65.26 3.b).

The account's funds were used to finance Petro-Canada's acquisition of Petrofina and are earmarked for use to pay the federal government's $500 million loan package to Dome Petroleum should the latter be necessary. Decisions on the use of the fund and on the imposition and level of the ownership charge are not channelled through the envelope machinery. They are made directly by the two ministers and the Prime Minister. However, an order made under subsection 65.26(3) must be tabled in the House of Commons where it may, under certain conditions, be subject to a three-hour debate followed by a vote on the resolution.

By 1984, the combined pressures of significantly higher-than-expected energy expenditures and much lower-than-expected revenues, accompanied by intense government-wide competition over the reduced total revenue pie, had resulted in the government broadening the uses of the account. This means that it could be used for PIPs or specific kinds of project financing without necessarily meeting the test originally applied to the account, namely, that it was *increasing* Canadian ownership. While it can be argued that the ownership account has served a useful purpose in the context of the NEP's explicit goals, it is a debatable point, in the context of energy expenditures, and indeed in the context of the broader issues in economic development, whether the account should be used in this more open-ended way.

Expenditure Implementation and the Paradox of Control

Our review above of selected expenditure items, in combination with our account in Chapters 8 and 9 of energy decision structures and pricing and tax dynamics, respectively, reveals several additional aspects of the implementation of the NEP. The first point to stress, lest it be lost sight of in the dynamics of the 1981 to 1984 period, is that key elements of the NEP were indeed implemented. That is, action was taken, legislation was passed, and large sums of money were in fact spent. The COGLA–PIP regime was put in place. The off-oil incentives of the COSP were quickly put into operation very efficiently, especially compared to the earlier CHIP program. The Petro-Canada expansion and takeover initiatives were carried out, albeit with reduced amounts of money than originally envisioned.

But the paradoxes of control remain a dominant reality in the complex world of NEP expenditure implementation. One must keep in mind the various, partially contradictory notions of control that produce these paradoxes. First, there is the notion of control as "power politics" inherent in the whole shift from the pre-NEP tax incentive regime to the post-NEP grants incentive approach. There can be little doubt that as a short-term exercise, the industry and Alberta took notice and are aware that the relationships of power are now altered. Second, there is the notion of control as "enhanced federal visibility." This also probably worked in the short run, but was quickly followed by the "downside" realities of Ottawa's visibility penchant. That is, the volatility of the PIPs and other expenditures at a time of skyrocketing deficits provided a fairly constant reminder, and an especially visible one, that Ottawa's overall economic management was not under control. It did not matter that the pre-NEP tax regime was equally demand-driven and difficult to control as well. In the latter case, the lost revenue that resulted could be more easily hidden in the byzantine crevices of the tax system. Under the NEP the dollars were now all "up front."

Finally, there is the notion of control inherent in the managerial context of "well analyzed and properly planned programs." Here there was, not surprisingly, a mixed bag of successes, partial successes, failures, and boondoggles. How could there be anything else, when one considers the blast of spray-gun expenditures inherent in the NEP and in the concentrated time in which it was both conceived and implemented. Thus, as we noted earlier, COSP seemed to be a well-conceived program and contributed in a significant way to the off-oil substitution goals, and hence to self-sufficiency goals of the NEP. On the other hand, the proposal for a gas bank was not well conceived and was mercifully aborted before the NEP Update in 1982. The TQM pipeline ran into a swirl of cost problems and Ottawa's Laterals Fund, as we noted above, was established as much to protect the federal tax revenue base as to promote off-oil gas expansion. And then there were the expenditure "minuets" (if one is charitable about these things) or "horror stories" (if one is wearing one's citizen Auditor General hat). One of these, at least in respect of the *way* the decision was made, was the \$100 million expenditure on the prairie co-operatives venture, the project referred to in Chapter 2. Though energy related, it was as much a part of the Western Canada strategy then being hatched in the PMO. In the heady early days of the post-NEP period when \$100 million here or there did not seem to matter much to the Liberals, the commitment was made. The figure was literally "announced" out of the blue by an exuberant Marc Lalonde, on a western speaking tour. It was the first time energy envelope officials had heard of the number. This was a triumphant example of ministerial victory over bureaucratic good sense, an example of which we could use fewer.

. Residing somewhere in the middle of this continuum of well-run versus questionable expenditure programs were the PIP grants. The PIP grants were clearly difficult to control, but judgements of their overall utility are caught up in the conflicts among the program objectives of PIP, including the controversy that inevitably arises as to how much one should spend to meet a broad-scale "need to know" objective. This in turn, is entwined with the regulatory role of COGLA and the 1990 date for achieving the Canadianization targets, both in general and on the Canada Lands.

So it was that the NEP implementation process produced some expected as well as peculiar expenditure scenarios and vignettes. Large problems remain. Can the PIP grants be transformed so as to be better targeted on viable exploration activity? If so, who will pick the winners? If not, then does one revert to the pre-NEP tax regime and, if so, will Canadian firms, so recently enticed into the Canada Lands by the PIP–COGLA carrot and stick, be financially able to stay the course Ottawa planned for them? This last issue deserves a separate concluding comment.

The Fiscal Regime and the Future of the Canadian Majors and Second-Line Firms

While we have focussed in this chapter on energy expenditures, it is appropriate to draw together several aspects of the overall fiscal regime, that is, the combined effects of the pricing and taxing elements examined in Chapter 9, and of energy expenditures as examined above. While the overall regime can obviously be looked at in a number of ways, we believe there is one litmus test that is of major overall importance. This concerns the medium- to long-term capacity of the second-line Canadian firms to become major players in the *development* stage on the Canada Lands and elsewhere in the industry. We have stressed that the overall regime was intended to favour Canadian firms vis-à-vis the multinationals. In Chapter 6 we examined in a general way the responses of the Canadian majors, especially Petro-Canada and Dome. Chapter 9 demonstrated that Dome's headstrong participation in the takeover game, along with other factors, has left it wounded but still potentially viable. Chapter 8 has shown that Petro-Canada has clearly benefitted from massive equity infusion, PIP grants and Ownership Account funds, but faces a serious period of both consolidation and probably reduced equity and political support. But what of the next group of second-line privately owned firms which we looked at first in Chapter 6, and some of whose bottom-line concerns we examined in Chapters 8 and 9.

Can second-line firms such as Pan Canadian, Norcen, Home Oil, Canterra, Husky Oil, and Bow Valley Industries, plus perhaps three or four others, become active players in the expensive development stage? In the short run, as we observed in Chapter 6, each has suffered to some extent from reduced cash flow, due both to the effects of the energy taxes and the recession. Each made varying degrees of commitment to new exploration activity, and hence exhibited different degrees of dependence on PIP grants. Each had different combinations of old and new oil, and oil versus gas operations. Each had varying degrees of involvement in other parts of the world. Judgements about the group as a whole are therefore difficult to make, especially in the medium- and long-term extending into the early 1990s. Their overall viability is dependent upon a host of factors including their cash flow, extent of indebtedness, the future level of world prices, geological and technical abilities, and the financial strength of parent holding companies that range from the Conrad Black Argus empire and Canadian Pacific to Hiram Walker Resources and the Canada Development Corporation. They depend also on the future state of royalties and taxes.

The future viability of these firms can be seen in different contexts. They are in general well-run companies. Even those that are particularly dependent on PIP grants have been wise enough to protect themselves from the demise of PIPs. By participating in extensive farm-ins they have gained considerable experience which will stand them in good stead. If the farm-ins yield land holdings near one or two of the main development prospects on the Canada Lands, they will have valuable property and reserve assets that they can either sell to others or attempt to develop. None of them has abandoned the Western Sedimentary Basin, and thus all could be well placed to shift priorities to western Canada depending on corporate strategies. In short the companies, as corporate entities, have every prospect of being viable and prosperous operations.

In relation to the long-range thrust of the NEP, however, the judgement must of necessity be much more cautious. The NEP's ultimate reason for tilting the exploration incentives in favour of the Canadian firms was that only in this way would they be in a position to be major players at the development stage on the Canada Lands, where 50 percent Canadian-owned participation was the policy requirement. Otherwise, the past pattern of foreign ownership would simply repeat itself. The key question is, will this happen anyway, despite the NEP, and the gobs of PIP money? Several scenarios exist as to the probable outcomes. First, it is possible that the 50 percent goal will be altered in order to work towards it more gradually. This is the view of many who see no combination of Canadian firms able to participate to the tune of 50 percent in total. Second, others see the 50 percent goal as viable only if the 25 percent Crown interest is retained. Then the remaining 25 percent could be found among a combination of the second-line firms, as well as a rejuvenated Dome and/or Nova. The assumption here is that Petro-Canada would be the main agent for exercising the 25 percent Crown interest. Under this scenario the federal government would have to pay for its interest, and so there are, as we have seen in this chapter, large financial implications. Third, still others are convinced that even the largest of the multinationals will be unwilling to want to go it alone, given all the risks, and thus will gladly seek out Canadian partners, including governments, to share them. This view often uses the giant Syncrude and Alsands projects as the model of what will happen. That is, the main developer starts out preferring only one other major partner, but, as reality creeps in, is content to bring in several smaller partners to share the risks, even though this complicates the initial negotiations needed to get the project into full developmental gear. A fourth scenario sees the possible infusion of new Canadian capital from outside the oil and gas industry per se.

The gloomiest scenario is that the effect of the NEP fiscal regime, including the PIP grants, will be to strengthen the multinationals, the very opposite of the intended purpose. Some have already reached this conclusion. In general, we find this view unpersuasive. Though it is true that some Canadian firms, especially those that engaged in take-overs, were financially weakened in the short, and perhaps medium term, the question of whether Canadian firms as a group will be viable at the development stage can only be answered in the context of the long term. It also requires a more detailed look at the NEP regulatory system, especially COGLA, and the nature of the developmental task to be faced on the Canada Lands.

Notes

1. See Sanford F. Borins, "Ottawa's Envelopes: Workability, Rationality at Last?" in G. Bruce Doern, ed., *How Ottawa Spends Your Tax Dollars 1982* (Toronto: Lorimer, 1982), chapter 3, and Rick VanLoon, "Ottawa's Expenditure Process: Four Systems in Search of Coordination" in G. Bruce Doern, ed., *How Ottawa Spends 1983* (Toronto: Lorimer, 1983), chapter 4.
2. Treasury Board, "Policy and Expenditure Management System: Envelope Procedures and Rules" (dated July 1, 1981), pp. 1–2.
3. We do not wish to imply that other areas of Ottawa's envelope system are inherently better managed. The social, economic, and defence areas face dilemmas of their own. But energy expenditures faced an extremely unique set of circumstances as to scale and political power. For other elements of the PEMS see the references in Note 1 above as well as G. Bruce Doern and Richard W. Phidd, *Canadian Public Policy: Ideas, Structure, Process* (Toronto: Methuen 1983), chapters 11 and 12.
4. For general information, see *Petroleum Incentives Administration Report, January 1981 to December 31st, 1983* (Ottawa: Energy, Mines and Resources, 1984). See also Senate of Canada, *Proceedings of the Standing Senate Committee on Energy and Natural Resources*, Issue nos. 7 and 8, May 15 and 16, 1984 (Ottawa: Supply and Services Canada, 1984).
5. W.D. Jarvis, Comments on John B. Robinson's Paper "Insurmountable Opportunities: A Review of Canada's Energy Demand and Supply Sources," paper presented to Conference on Energy in the 80s: The Next Steps, University of Waterloo, May 14, 1984, p. 2. (Jarvis is Director of Market Analysis and Statistics, Energy Strategy Branch, in Energy, Mines and Resources.)
6. See Senate of Canada, *Proceedings of the Standing Senate Committee on Energy and Natural Resources*, Issue no. 1, April 4, 1984 (Ottawa: Supply and Services Canada, 1984), p. 12.
7. Economic Council of Canada, *Strategy for Energy Policy* (Ottawa: Supply and Services Canada, 1984), Table 7.9.
8. Memorandum of Agreement between the Government of Canada and the Government of Alberta Relating to Energy and Taxation, September 1, 1981.

CHAPTER 11

ENERGY REGULATION: FROM PUBLIC UTILITY POLICING TO DEVELOPMENTAL BARGAINING

In the post-NEP era two major new regulatory structures were put in place, the Canada Oil and Gas Lands Administration (COGLA) and the Office of Industrial and Regional Benefits (OIRB). The former was a direct outcome of energy legislation and therefore a regulatory agency in the fullest sense. The latter was a product of the larger concerns about economic development and thus reached beyond energy matters. Moreover, the OIRB did not possess its own direct regulatory powers and thus was a negotiating body per se. These are the agencies that we focus on in this chapter. Some attention is also devoted to the Petroleum Incentives Administration (PIA) since it is one of the links between COGLA and the PIP program already examined in Chapter 10. The PIA is the cheque-writing agency for PIP grants but also has some regulatory responsibilities in the realm of cost control, especially after changes made in 1983, as well as in the area of determining the ownership and control ratings of companies. It should not be surprising, however, to discover that the difficult politics of getting the post-NEP rules right cannot be wholly explained by examining only these agencies. The "new boys" on the energy regulatory block joined a number of older "regulars" such as the National Energy Board, key provincial bodies such as the Alberta Energy Resources Conservation Board and other agencies listed in Chart 11.1.

To understand the new regulatory regime, one must therefore appreciate the nature of the regulatory transformation from old to new, keeping in mind that the new are additions to, and enlargements of, the old. We do not cover all features of the post-NEP regulatory systems. We give only limited attention to environmental issues and to the land claims of aboriginal peoples. These are important aspects of developmental regulation as the experience with the Berger Inquiry has shown. We focus here on the exploration activities per se and on the overall developmental challenge. The first part of the chapter

CHART 11.1
CANADA'S ENERGY REGULATORS AND QUASI-REGULATORS

Federal	Alberta and other provinces (examples)
• National Energy Board	• Alberta Energy Resources Conservation Board
• Canadian Oil and Gas Lands Administration	• Alberta Petroleum Marketing Commission
• Petroleum Incentives Administration	• Alberta Department of Energy and Resources
• Petroleum Monitoring Agency	• Ontario Energy Board
• Foreign Investment Review Agency	• Canada–Nova Scotia Offshore Oil and Gas Board*
• Environmental Assessment Panels and Department of Environment	• Various provincial energy boards, and environmental and energy departments
• Department of Indian Affairs and Northern Development	
• Restrictive Trade Practices Commission	
• Northern Pipeline Agency	
• Atomic Energy Control Board	
• International Energy Agency**	

*Joint federal–provincial body
**An international body to co-ordinate emergency supply-sharing arrangements among twenty-one western consuming nations.

surveys briefly the nature of the pre-NEP regulatory apparatus. This is followed by our examination of COGLA and the OIRB in the second and third parts of the chapter.

One can view regulation in several ways, each of which highlights different attributes and dilemmas. For example, one can visualize it in relation to governmental efforts to affect conduct at the various "stages" in the production cycle of the industry. Thus regulation occurs at the point of initial exploration, at later development and production stages and in the transportation and marketing stage. Environmental regulation and the regulation of competition also enter the "energy" regulation cycle when viewed in this way. A second way to view regulation is to visualize the "types of behaviour" that regulation is attempting to affect, such as "policing" versus "developmental" behaviour. Regulation can be directed towards "preventing" things from happening, in short a policing function, or a public utility style of regulation designed to prevent abuses of monopoly power such as in the case of pipelines. Developmental regulation, on the other hand, involves an attempt to induce/require certain positive kinds of preferred behaviour as well. Such distinctions are often not entirely clear but the transformation of regulation over time suggests the need to make these distinctions. The reference in the title of this chapter to developmental bargaining tries to capture some of the dynamics involved when "the rules" are developmental and therefore multi-valued in nature, when the new regulators try to act simultaneously as brokers on the one hand and advocates on the other, and when the regulators act on behalf of the federal government which is also the owner of the resource.

Both of the above ways of viewing regulation are inextricably linked to the contending ideas of political life. The first is linked inevitably to the "degree' of intervention considered acceptable at any given time by different interests. The second addresses specific ideas, since it involves preferences for regulation intended to "restore" efficiency in natural monopoly situations such as those involved with pipeline regulation (often characterized as public utility regulation); promote stability in the gradual development of markets (the NOP); redistribute resources (by regulating prices), and so on through the now familiar list of ideas.

It must be stressed that the energy industry was heavily regulated at the federal and especially the provincial level before the NEP and already embraced many of the concerns noted above. The NEP brought a major increase in federal regulation, particularly of the developmental bargaining kind. Some of this was not a surprise to the industry, however, since it had urged in the latter half of the 1970s the need for a new regime particularly to overcome the multiple agency system they were already experiencing in the Canada Lands. Thus the following points already examined in previous chapters should be kept in mind in understanding the post-NEP regulatory dynamics:

- The initial point of regulation is the system of exploration permits and production leases. Forged in Alberta's early oil and gas era, the system was intended to ensure appropriate technical and engineering standards but also to ensure public control of the pace and nature of development. Thus Alberta's system included procedures to proration production. At the exploration end it was based on an auction or bonus bid system in which firms bid for the right to explore and develop land. A regulatory system was put in place at the federal level under the 1961 COGL regime noted in Chapter 2. The COGL was not very stringent partly because there was only limited activity on federal lands. Moreover, it involved separate kinds of permits for exploration and then for development.

- When interprovincial trade in oil and gas emerged, Ottawa moved via the National Energy Board into classic public utility-style regulation to prevent monopoly abuses and to ensure the orderly expansion of the industry as examined in Chapter 3.

- The National Oil Policy provided a mode of regulating markets. As shown in Chapters 3 and 4 it was a form of regulation without legislation. Most of the key private interests and even some key governmental interests regarded it as an exemplary form of voluntary consensus-based regulation and contrasted it later with the non-consultative basis of the NEP.

- The NOP also partially regulated prices. Between 1973 and 1975 the tradition of managed prices moved to the arena of federal–provincial First Ministers' conferences which reached agreement about phased in price increases. Between 1975 and 1979, prices were set through bilateral federal–Alberta negotiations.

• New hybrid quasi-regulators emerged in the mid- and late 1970s with mixtures of statutory, persuasive, and information-gathering powers. These ranged from the Berger Inquiry, to the Petroleum Monitoring Agency, and from the Northern Pipeline Agency to the inquiry of the Restrictive Trade Practices Commission into the oil and gas industry under the provisions of the Competition Act. It also included new environmental assessment procedures at the federal and provincial level.

• Throughout this period Canadian developments were partly dependent on the processes and decisions of U.S. regulatory bodies.

In point form, these were key elements in the flow of regulatory change that preceded the NEP. Before proceeding further, however, we need to look somewhat more closely at the basic criticisms the pre-NEP regulatory regime centred in the National Energy Board.

The Old Regulatory Regime: The NEB and Energy Dynamics

The origins of the NEB were examined in Chapters 3 and 4 in the context of the Borden Royal Commission; in the wake of the heated controversy over the Trans-Canada Pipeline in 1956; and the election of the Diefenbaker Conservative government in 1957. Intended to preside over an orderly expansion of pipelines and markets, the NEB's task was made possible by the larger quasi-voluntary, quasi-regulatory framework of the National Oil Policy and by low and stable world oil prices. Given the political heat of the mid- and late 1950s, the NEB was also intended to depoliticize energy matters. In many ways the NEB succeeded remarkably in this latter task.[1] For much of the 1960s it went about its prime appointed task of being, in part, a public utility style regulator and, in part, a technical referee in the construction and operation of pipelines. Under its regulatory powers it granted certificates "of public convenience and necessity" for pipeline construction and approved utility rates, tariffs and tolls. It also issued licences for the export and import of electrical power, natural gas and oil.

Its decisions on export licences and construction certificates are subject to Cabinet approval. When combined with the NEB's statutory role as an advisor to the Minister of Energy, Mines and Resources and its role in carrying out studies of energy issues on its own volition or at the minister's request, it is evident that the NEB was never a fully independent regulator. It was a quasi-regulator, quasi-manager of the industry operating with constant contact and interaction with the energy department. Indeed prior to 1966, when EMR was established, it was the main source of energy expertise in the government. Even after EMR was created and until the early 1970s, the NEB retained its role as the most influential agency. During the early 1970s the Alberta government viewed it with considerable suspicion, because key ministers believed that its quasi-judicial role only masked its role as Ottawa's key voice in energy matters.

It is probably fair to say that the NEB's classic public utility regulatory role was carried out, certainly in the 1960s, without much sustained controversy. Populated primarily by technical engineering people, the board performed with technical style and competence. However, it was in its export licencing and advisory role, both inextricably tied to its determination of the adequacy of Canada's future oil and gas reserves, that produced the most heated controversy. Since most of Canada's oil and gas was in Alberta, this meant that the NEB's link to the Alberta Energy Resources Conservation Board (AERCB) was also important since it was from the AERCB that it obtained its best information on reserves.[2] The latter oversaw Alberta's exploration and pro-rationing system and hence was one step closer to the industry. It was the industry itself, however, that had the most first-hand knowledge about reserves and which had a profound stake in not being too willing to share information about them, especially with the NEB regulators.

The NEB had powers to compel information, but it was nonetheless in a state of extreme second- and third-hand dependence on others. It must be remembered that as recently as 1973, when Canada's oil production was near 2 million barrels per day, well over 50 percent of it was being exported to the United States. This was several years after the optimistic speeches by energy minister Joe Green, referred to in Chapter 2, which envisaged a veritable energy millenium. There could be little doubt, in retrospect, that the development of estimates and forecasts of reserves was increasingly part geology, and involved some economics, but it was overlaid with a heavy dose of politics from all the key interests.

The causal forces worked in both directions. Optimistic forecasts of reserves allowed demonstrable room for exports. Exports, on the other hand, were good for the economy and for the industry, at least in the short term, and so forecasts would have to be generous. This does not mean that there were no technical/geological limits to the forecasting game. It does mean that there were wide areas of latitude, and these were exacerbated by the NEB's dependence on the industry. The lack of plausible forecasts was also exacerbated by the NEB's practice of assessing demand "one fuel at a time," so to speak: oil and gas demand were examined separately.[3] It was not until the late 1970s that integrated demand estimates were developed, and hearings conducted with different economic assumptions applied to gauge different supply and demand scenarios.

By the mid-1970s the NEB's central position in the federal energy regulatory and advisory apparatus was being challenged in several ways. EMR was beginning to compete successfully for the attention of energy ministers. OPEC jarred all of the assumptions on which pre-1973 energy policy had been constructed. Petro-Canada was on the verge of creation as a window on the industry. The decision on a northern pipeline involved special mechanisms such as the Berger and Lysyk inquiries. The Northern Pipeline Agency was established in 1978 to give statutory clout to the regulation of Canadian industrial benefits on this particular project.[4] It was therefore a precursor to the OIRB and to COGLA, at least conceptually.

Thus the old regulatory regime centred on the NEB was joined by a new regime that was crystalized under the NEP. It was not that the NEB can be said to have failed. Rather, it is more accurate to say that, as an integrated managerial arm of the federal apparatus, it partially succeeded and partially failed, and was eventually overtaken by larger energy events of a political and economic kind in the post-1973 era. The NEB did help foster a growing but stabilized industry and it did offer, for a time, what one author accurately labelled "symbolic reassurance"[5] to Canadians that its energy needs were competently in the hands of experts.

The New Regulatory Regime I: COGLA
The last word in COGLA, "administration," is a profound misnomer. A more accurate title might be the Canadian Oil and Gas Lands "Negotiating Chamber and Developmental Agency." This would more

accurately capture the nature of COGLA as well as convey the kind of regulation it encompasses in the post-NEP regulatory regime. Our examination of COGLA proceeds in three stages. Its overall mandate and approach is first described as it and the government officially present it. We then juxtapose against this view the broader realities it faces in "regulating" oil and gas development on the vast northern and off-shore Canada Lands. Finally, we look at some of the early regulatory dynamics in COGLA's first few years of operation, keeping in mind its intricate connections to the PIP grant regime already examined in Chapter 10.

Mandate and Process
The Canada Oil and Gas Lands Administration was established to manage oil and gas activity over the vast Canada Lands[6] and to contribute, especially in association with the PIP program, to the Canadianization, self-sufficiency and "need to know" objectives. The lands are made up of 6.4 million square kilometres (under the juris-diction of the Minister of Indian and Northern Affairs in the Yukon, the Northwest Territories and other areas north of 60 degrees latitude), and about 3.8 million square kilometres (under the juris-diction of the Minister of Energy, Mines and Resources off the east and west coasts).

COGLA is the main operational contact for the industry working in the Canada Lands for most phases of exploration, development and production activity. It reports to the Minister of Energy, Mines and Resources with respect to the government's energy policy and to the Minister of Indian and Northern Affairs with respect to the govern-ment's northern policy, according to the jurisdiction of each in the Canada Lands. The oil and gas management functions of the two departments were pooled in COGLA and thus it is an integral part of both departments. Table 11.1 summarizes its organizational components. The first four branches existed before the NEP while the last two were new.

COGLA works in co-operation with other departments and agencies of the federal government. For example, COGLA has close ties with the Department of the Environment and the Department of Fisheries and Oceans on environmental concerns and with the Office

TABLE 11.1

THE FUNCTIONS OF COGLA'S BRANCHES

COGLA is organized into six branches and has regional offices in Newfoundland and Nova Scotia. The **Land Management Branch** takes the lead in negotiations with companies seeking exploration rights in the Canada Lands. The **Resource Evaluation Branch** advises on the resource potential of lands under negotiation and on geology for the **Engineering Branch,** which oversees the way in which companies carry out their work programs.

The Administration, through its Resource Evaluation and Engineering Branches, issues the work program approvals and specific well approvals which operators had to obtain before they could begin work. As well as insisting on prior approval of operators' plans, COGLA inspectors regularly visit work sites to ensure activities are carried on safely.

COGLA engineers also approve floating and fixed structures used by the industry, assess oil and gas reservoirs, and monitor management and development. Petroleum processing and production systems and pipeline systems within production fields are also licensed and inspected.

The **Environmental Protection Branch** scrutinizes operators' plans and regulates their activities to ensure that the highest standards of environmental protection are maintained. Included in this process is the determination of measures to be taken in the event of an accident. This

planning complements recommendations for environmental studies designed to assess the impact of resource development.

The **Canada Benefits Branch** examines company plans to ensure Canadian businesses get a full and fair chance to compete for the economic opportunities oil and gas exploration and development offer and that jobs are provided for Canadian workers. Working with other agencies of government, the Branch advises companies on the preparation of acceptable Canada Benefits packages. The Minister ultimately must approve all proposals.

The **Policy Analysis and Coordination Branch** is responsible for the analysis, development, interpretation and implementation of policy for the management of oil and gas activity in the Canada Lands. The Branch liaises with other policy groups within Energy, Mines and Resources and Indian and Northern Affairs, coordinates policy-related work of the COGLA Branches and provides secretarial support to the Policy Review Committee and to the Canada–Nova Scotia Offshore Oil and Gas Board. The Branch is also responsible for coordination between COGLA and other federal departments and provincial government bodies.

of Industrial and Regional Benefits and the Canada Employment and Immigration Commission to promote maximum economic benefits for all Canadians from resource development.

COGLA also works with provincial governments to ensure that their needs and responsibilities are addressed. It is the Government of Canada's intention that COGLA's mandate be integrated with that of other levels of government. In March 1982, the federal and Nova Scotia governments signed an agreement creating the Canada–Nova Scotia Offshore Oil and Gas Board. Through the Board, which is chaired by the COGLA Administrator, representatives of the federal and Nova Scotia governments jointly manage resource development off the Nova Scotia coast. Under the agreement, the Nova Scotia representatives can if necessary delay decisions for up to one year in order to ensure full consideration of provincial concerns.[7] The agreement also establishes a regime for the sharing of resource revenues between the two levels of government which will provide a significant new source of revenues for the Nova Scotia government when offshore production begins.

Activities of the oil and gas industry in the Canada Lands are managed by COGLA through a multi-phased approval system. Exploration agreements between companies and the federal government essentially establish the area where companies will explore for petroleum resources. They usually have a term of less than five years. During the term, companies agree to *minimum* exploration work to be performed, including seismic and drilling programs and related environmental work. COGLA also monitors drilling results and gives technical approvals to actual drilling programs.

To ensure prudent Canada Lands resource management, new exploration agreements provide for the return to the Crown during the term of agreement of a portion of the lands included in the agreements, usually about 50 percent. Companies keep all discoveries they have made, as well as additional prospects which they are prepared to drill, and also have first choice of the additional land blocks which they believe to be most promising. But COGLA, through an alternating process of selection with the company, also has an opportunity to choose land blocks for the Crown. This process is in keeping with the government's policy that land should be held by the oil and gas companies only to the extent that they can actively explore it. It is intended to ensure that lands are constantly being returned to the Crown to be held or reissued, enabling establishment of an appropriate pace of exploration.

The Canada Oil and Gas Act requires submission of a "Canada benefits plan" satisfactory to the Minister before commencement of any work program under an exploration agreement or a development plan. This is to ensure that Canadians are given full and fair access on a competitive basis to the industrial and employment benefits arising from exploration programs. This incudes a program of related social and economic activities designed to ameliorate local and regional impacts. Affirmative action plans to aid disadvantaged groups such as native people may also be required. Other relevant aspects include the extent to which Canadian partners will be active participants in exploration and acquire the technical knowledge that they need to enable them in time to become Canada Lands operators in their own right.

The Developmental Task: Reactive versus Active Regulation

The NEP sought to shift the geo-political focus of oil and gas to the Canada Lands. It was therefore both an energy policy and a policy for the North. Even while COGLA was being put in place the two key departments, EMR and Indian Affairs and Northern Development, were urging the need for a still more active role. While exploration and the "need to know" objective were pursued through the COGLA-PIP regime, the equally critical need was that of anticipating, planning, and otherwise being ready for the developmental stage of energy production. This would have energy dimensions as well as environmental, social, and native land claim issues, not to mention major decisions about transportation and Canada's exercise of sovereignty.[8]

A profile of the developmental setting and issues can be quite easily stated. (Controlling and managing the pace and the nature of development is a far more difficult task.) In the early 1980s, production north of the 60 degree parallel was extremely limited, encompassing about 3000 barrels of oil per day (at Imperial Oil's Norman Wells operation) and less than 60 million cubic feet of natural gas per day. Only at Norman Wells was expansion in the short term feasible, to about 25 000 barrels per day. A 1984 EMR report concluded that "established" reserves of oil are 754 million cubic metres, and of gas

2111 billion cubic meters, all located in western Canada. The frontier areas add an estimated 419 million cubic meters of oil and 902 million cubic meters of gas. Other "potential" reserves also exist.

Future developmental activity would be dependent not only on new exploration activity but on a host of factors, including: whether the fields are large enough to sustain the costs of the extremely expensive field and transportation development; the relative costs of developing reserves in the north versus those in the conventional areas through enhanced recovery, and in the offshore; whether the reserves are oil or gas (oil being the more pressing need); the environmental and social effects, many of which could not be assessed until accurate project–specific proposals had been obtained from the developers; and transportation costs and technology, the latter involving, whether in the marine or overland mode, challenges where past practice would be an utterly insufficient guide. And if this was not enough, towering above all these factors was the medium- and longer-term price of oil and gas.

The example of transportation costs is as good an example as any of the giant regulatory dilemmas on COGLA's as well as EMR and DIAND's agenda. In July, 1982 a Treasury Board study was completed on Beaufort Sea oil transportation alternatives.[10] It attempted to analyze the relative merits of pipeline versus ice-breaking tankers. It was the first such study to be carried out in any systematic way by any federal department of the implications of alternative transportation modes. Even this study, however, is filled with so many caveats and cautionary notes on virtually every page, that its value as a guide is very doubtful. Its authors do not disguise their own serious doubts. Seven transportation scenarios are examined based on variables such as volume profiles, pipeline versus tanker, eastern and western destinations, and at least three pipeline route options. It is conducted without knowing the actual proven reserves in particular supply sites. Future financing costs, discount rates and inflation costs had to be assumed. Exact project costs are impossible to acquire because no one has proposed a specific development project. What then do conscientious policy makers and regulators do?

The dilemma is a real one. One must anticipate and actively plan for development. But one cannot plan if one does not know the most important facts and costs. One does not want to be "reactive" because projects have long lead times. But when specific projects have not yet been proposed, how can one be anything else but passive and reactive? Besides, there is more than one conscientious regulator involved. Environmental regulation is in general non-statutory and resides in the Department of the Environment.[11] EMR has energy concerns; DIAND has northern concerns. Many of these partial policy conflicts and trade-offs are reproduced *within* COGLA. Thus the overall regulatory conundrum is inescapable. The rate and pace of development must be managed and controlled, but everyone knows that the main power of initiative resides with private decision makers whose interests dictate that it is better to delay telling regulators too much until they are themselves ready to move ahead. One element can propose; the other can delay. No one source of power controls the development in any ultimate sense.

One must also relate the overall developmental challenge to past experience with major energy projects and development. Writing in 1979, energy economist John Helliwell cited some probable benefits from the so-called "regulatory lags" that resulted from the elaborate Berger inquiry and other procedural requirements that accompanied the mid-1970s Mackenzie Valley pipeline decisions.[12] He related this point to a central theme in his analysis of energy policy in Canada, namely that there was no adequate basis for the "swings in government and energy industry forecasts of future supplies and demands" that had been prevalent in the 1970s. He also linked it to his view that energy policies in Canada (federal and provincial) had been excessively concerned with increasing energy supplies without "ensuring that demands (for appropriate uses) were likely to be large enough to justify the new high-cost projects."[13]

In Helliwell's view the existence of regulatory lags softened the two excessive tendencies noted above. He concluded that the "often decried lags in getting regulatory approval for large new energy projects have performed a valuable function in reducing the extent to which supply is likely to overshoot demand in the 1980s." Helliwell cautions that these "favourable effects . . . arise only in circumstances where the lag permits a false justification to be exposed as such. . . ."[14] He does not, however, indicate how one can tell *a priori* what will be a false case, hence the perceived need for regulatory procedures of the kind that the post-NEP period has brought.

General COGLA Dynamics: Start-up Problems

In its first few years of existence, however, COGLA's regulatory dynamics were driven more by the immediate "exploration" phase of the energy play. To parallel our account of the tax and expenditure dynamics in previous chapters, we discuss the COGLA dynamics in three ways: first we look at what are best described as "start-up" dynamics; then we look at general effects; finally, we examine some selected particular effects. In each case one must bear in mind that the term "effects" refers to only a few years of activity to date. One must also keep in mind that, even with several years' data, regulatory effects are usually more difficult to assess, since they do not show up either as speedily or necessarily even in the form of governmental dollar budgets. Regulations normally have their largest dollar effects on *private* budgets, though in the NEP regime PIP dollars do reveal some of these effects in *public* budgets as well.

As to start-up issues, two in particular need to be highlighted. First, the COGLA legislation stipulated that all existing interests in the Canada Lands had to be renegotiated. This involved over 200 agreements, about 25 percent of which were completed in the first year and the rest in 1983–84. This alone was a formidable task that pulled COGLA staff in three directions at once. They were tugged by the need to show that there was indeed exploration momentum and impetus behind the new post-NEP regime to contribute to future supply. They were simultaneously propelled by the notion that the new regime was not supposed to be like the old; hence they would have to proceed carefully in order to be able to bargain hard with the industry over Canadian benefits and to show that the new regime was serious in its broader regulatory mandate. At the same time the "need to know" objectives, operationalized in part by the decision that at least one well had to be drilled in each area covered by exploration agreements, drove COGLA into its practice of not differentiating the geologically most promising and economic areas.

Inevitably in the process there was some hard learning to be done. Problems were compounded by the need to bring in some new and inexperienced personnel. Most of COGLA's personnel came from existing departments. The personnel were not therefore raw regulatory rookies, but many were inexperienced in two respects; in the specifics and interactions required by the new multi-agency COGLA-centred process, and in knowledge of the oil and gas industry's operational problems. COGLA was one step closer than the NEB to having direct knowledge, since its geologists received detailed drilling results. But it shared, to some extent with the industry, the "knowledge" gap about *northern* and offshore exploration. Knowledge for everyone was less certain than in the conventional southern exploration game, a fact which exacerbated the growing pains and the uncertain regulatory climate. Even though we define these personnel problems here as a start-up problem, there is a sense in which, even in mature regulatory agencies, it remains a problem without a solution. In other words, regulators can never either acquire the same level of knowledge, nor, where common knowledge exists, should they necessarily view it in the same way as the industry. Their interests differ, in part at least.

An understanding of the way COGLA functions is dependent on some appreciation of its links to the key departments involved and of its internal processes. COGLA's first head or administrator is M.E. Taschereau, who came to COGLA from the Asbestos Corporation. A mining engineer, he had previously worked for twenty-five years for Noranda. He was not an EMR "policy type"; indeed, the policy analysis issues or the grand NEP game plan were tasks he much preferred to leave to others. Taschereau gave emphasis to the energy (and therefore EMR) side of the COGLA mandate as opposed to its northern or environmental aspects. DOE was the weak sister in the early COGLA years, partly because the thrust of the NEP was not environmental but energy-supply and security oriented, and partly because DOE could not exercise any enforcement powers. On issues north of 60 degrees latitude, Taschereau was legally bound to report to the Minister of Indian Affairs and Northern Development. In fact, however, the internal working relationship was functional in nature. EMR has primary responsibility over energy items on both sides of the 60 degree line, whereas DIAND offers policy guidance on northern policy only. As to Canadian benefits, Taschereau made it known that, though COGLA had a role to play, it would rely primarily on the competitive bidding process. Hence COGLA was somewhat less aggressive on these matters than the OIRB. COGLA had the legal muscle but the OIRB, as we see below, did most of the "jawboning" or persuading.

Given the immense early start-up task faced by COGLA, this interpretation of the mandate was hardly surprising. The key task was an energy one, namely to put in place a better regime on the Canada Lands that would actually ensure that exploration and delineation occurred and developments proceeded. This emphasis was ensured also by the fact that COGLA's Policy Review Committee was chaired by Ed Clark for the first year or so of its existence. Clark had been the chief proponent of the need for a tough new regime on the Canada Lands.

The old COGLA regime had been extremely lax and ad hoc. About 900 million acres of land had been virtually given away without imposing firm minimum drilling and exploration obligations on the companies holding the rights. The new COGLA process sought to divide the Canada Lands into reasonable parcels in which companies were expected to carry out agreed minimum amounts of exploration within specified periods, or return the land parcels to the Crown. Blocks of lands in the so-called "wildcat" areas are about 2 million acres, and at least one hole per block must be drilled. The blocks are smaller in areas judged by COGLA as being geologically more promising. For example, in the Beaufort Sea area the blocks are smaller and larger numbers of holes are drilled, though not necessarily in each exploration agreement. In south Hibernia, off the east coast, the blocks are smaller still.

A key feature of the system is that COGLA receives confidential information from the companies on every hole that is drilled, but it cannot share this detailed information with EMR or DIAND. Aggregate data are prepared to assist in overall policy formulation, but the well-by-well data are not. Thus the principle of commercial privilege has to be balanced with the public policy concept of the need to know. Both principles are supportable in a mixed economy. A related issue, however, is whether a public presence is needed on each separate development—in short, not just a "window on the industry" (the early rationale for Petro-Canada), but a "window" on each project. Obviously this does not necessarily involve a presence on each exploration well, but at some point the task of managing the pace of development of actual proven reserves is critically dependent upon knowledge of the field in question. This point is obviously linked to the issue of the 25 percent Crown interest and to the role of Petro-Canada in various joint ventures at both the exploration and developmental stages.

An important feature of the early exploration agreements is that they were primarily for old tracts of land renewed from the old 1961 COGL regime. With the exception of a few new tracts off Nova Scotia, no new lands had been involved. Many of the larger agreements were ¬igned, moreover, before the decline in world oil prices. Thus by 1984 the key questions were: how much more exploration did the government want on these new lands, and where did the best prospects lie geologically? economically? politically?

General COGLA Dynamics: The Farm-in Process
Under the Canada Lands regime all the players had to experience various "learning curves." The negotiation of exploration agreements was not the only process involved. Also central to the process was the series of farm-ins that the multinational majors who still held the prime land or offshore sites entered into with the smaller Canadian firms. The trade-offs were obvious. The foreign majors could get exploration done by the Canadian firms, who were eligible for high PIP grants, often using the majors' own equipment, but without giving up de facto control as the operators. Thus PIP dollars flowed to the Canadian firms, and then benefited the foreign majors. Farm-ins were negotiated directly between the operators that had the exploration agreement permit and the farm-in firm or consortium of firms. Typically these were based on a "2 for 1" concept: the farm-in paid 100 percent of the costs of drilling and acquired a 50 percent interest in the particular well or group of agreed wells. The Canadian firms gained an interest in the offshore and, for some of them, they also gained critically needed operational experience in the Canada Lands environment. Once a farm-in had been arranged, or in some cases concurrent with the inter-company bargaining, COGLA and the PIA became involved. COGLA's interest was in part to see that the farm-in did not violate the existing exploration agreements held by the operator, especially the levels of ownership. This could happen through an actual transfer of interest or a potential transfer. COGLA also wanted to see that wide farm-ins occurred so as to ensure that good land was farmed out and to give Canadian firms greater operational experience.

PIA's interest was to keep a cap on PIP costs by examining how the drilling would be done (e.g., renting versus buying equipment), and so on.

The key issues in this process were the quality of the land or parcels offered by the majors in the operation, and the degree of leverage that COGLA itself could exercise, or wanted to exercise, in getting the best quality land sites, geologically speaking, for the Canadian farm-in firms. Needless to say the experience on both these issues varied greatly, not only in practice at different times as COGLA and the companies learned the ropes, but also in the perception of the companies, which were in turn coloured by their overall views of the NEP. Three examples will illustrate some of the dynamics.

Mobil Canada is the key operator in the Hibernia fields. It is also the operator of the Hebron and Ben Nevis fields. Mobil steadfastly refused offers, principally from Petro-Canada, for farm-ins that would delineate Hebron and Ben Nevis. Petro-Canada pressured COGLA to force the pace, but COGLA refused. Petro-Canada took the view that COGLA's job was precisely to force the pace. COGLA's refusal could be attributed to any number of reasons, ranging from a desire to be fair to companies, especially given the then strong U.S. criticism of the NEP; greater trust in Mobil's expertise; and a desire to use the COGLA lever to keep Petro-Canada "in its place" given that its entrée into other aspects of the NEP had given it more than its share of NEP largesse. In the final analysis, senior COGLA officials saw their role as brokers rather than "musclers" of the industry. There is, of course, often a very fine line between brokering and "muscling."

A second example concerns Husky Oil Ltd. and its farm-ins. As a firm with much less experience and expertise in the offshore than some other firms, Husky did get saddled with what is known in the oil patch as "moose pasture" land, but then acquired farm-ins off the Grand Banks that were geologically good. They also combined with Bow Valley to acquire rigs and boats. In the latter process Husky officials are complimentary about COGLA in that its industrial benefits process led to the provision by DRIE of federal industrial grants as well.

Finally, one can cite the example of Home Oil. It had farm-ins with Esso Resources in both the Beaufort and Mackenzie Delta. They were quite confident that the land they obtained was geologically promising relative to what they had in the Western Sedimentary

Basin. Later, in farm-ins with financially troubled Dome, they obtained deals that were only partially favourable. In the East Sable play, for example, they obtained good land, but as part of the deal they also had to farm-in to some of Dome's Arctic holdings. This was in part also because they were arranging simultaneous farm-ins in Alberta on Dome's vast western Canadian lands. Thus the quality of land varied widely, depending on the circumstances.

The dynamics varied with the permutations and combinations of circumstances, interests, geological judgements, and commitments to take risks. There was clearly a flow-through of PIP cash indirectly to the majors, but the ultimate verdict on whether this PIP investment was worth it depends on the many factors already noted. It will also be dependent on what happens at the development stage in the late 1980s and early 1990s, a point to which we return later in the chapter.

One final point about the farm-in process and the overall land tenure system deserves emphasis. This is that despite numerous farm-ins between 1982 and 1984, there has not yet been a radical change in the pattern in which companies hold the main lands as operators. The multinational majors hold the land in much the same proportions as they did in the mid-1960s under the former COGL regime. This was because, as we have noted above, the first main task of COGLA was to renegotiate the old agreements where the work obligations were not at all onerous. There have, however, been increased opportunities for Canadian companies to earn an interest. In 1980 they held an interest in 38 percent of the Canada Lands versus 62 percent in 1983.[15]

As the current batch of agreements expires in 1986 and beyond, however, there will be a major "relinquishment" round. In all probability this will mean that in marginal areas such as the Arctic and Labrador, a majority of the land may be relinquished. In the southern offshore, about 50 percent could be relinquished. It is at this point that a far larger stock of land, some favourable, some unfavourable, will become available. As Chapter 10 has already shown, Canadian firms then may or may not be geologically and financially ready not only for further exploration, but also for the even more costly development phase. It is not, of course, clear that COGLA would automatically put out all of the relinquished land for further exploration, since this would depend on a range of geological and economic factors that could only be determined at the time.

One can thus view the overall pattern of exploration activity and the new COGLA regime in several ways. For example, Figure 11.1 portrays the pattern of exploration activity for the period from 1972 to 1983. The post-NEP period, as viewed in 1984, obviously shows significant drilling activity slowly developing by 1983. It does show, however, a major jump in seismic activity. Such seismic activity is usually followed one or two years later by actual drilling. Table 11.2 presents data on the exploration agreements reached in the period from May 1982 to February 1984. Supplied by COGLA, these data can be looked at in various ways. There were 135 agreements involving the eventual drilling of a total of 71 wells. The total program value is just over $8 billion or about $113 million per well. If one simply tallied the percentage Canadian content column from Table 11.2, it would show about a 70 percent average. Much more meaningful, however, are the data on the ten largest programs as listed in the program value column. These involve about $6.7 billion of the $8 billion, approximately half under agreements with Canadian-owned firms and half under the multinationals. In this group, the proportion of Canadian content was expected to be about 54 percent for the foreign-controlled operators and 56 percent for the Canadian holders of exploration agreements.

The direct COGLA effects are not easy to discern in the short term. As we have seen, however, the COGLA process of negotiating exploration agreements involves a direct link to the PIP expenditures and raises important issues about the exercise of discretionary power by a handful of senior officials and the two ministers who head EMR and DIAND. Numerous individual decisions on the approval of wells involve over 100 million dollars. To put this in some perspective, this is a sum which *exceeds* the total discretionary *new* money available to some entire Cabinet committees.

As pointed out in Chapter 10, there have been persistent charges that the COGLA–PIP regime is promoting exploration of a frivolous or wasteful kind. Both of these points are linked, but satisfactory evidence about the "appropriateness" of COGLA's behaviour is difficult to come by. There are many anecdotal cases about PIP grantsmanship and about wells being approved because of their local employment benefits rather than their geological probability, but such "evidence" is not easily grouped into numeric columns, one for "prescient exploration

FIGURE 11.1

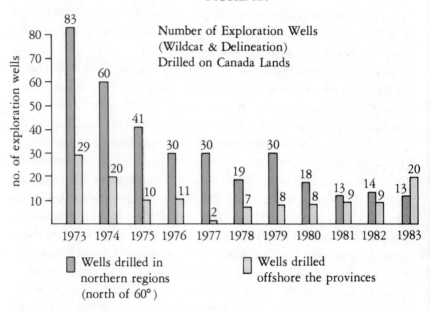

Number of Exploration Wells
(Wildcat & Delineation)
Drilled on Canada Lands

■ Wells drilled in
northern regions
(north of 60°)

□ Wells drilled
offshore the provinces

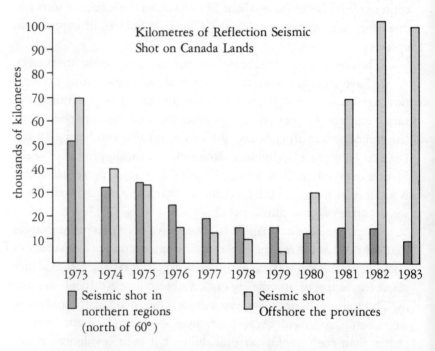

Kilometres of Reflection Seismic
Shot on Canada Lands

■ Seismic shot in
northern regions
(north of 60°)

□ Seismic shot
Offshore the provinces

Source: Canadian Oil and Gas Administration, *Annual Report*, 1983, p. 13. Reproduced by permission.

activity" and the other for "wasteful exploration activity." After all, even oil company executives constantly assert how risky the exploration business is, and how nine dry holes out of ten drilled is not uncommon, especially in the frontier. The pursuit of the "need to know" goal further complicates such judgements. At the same time, it would be extremely surprising, given the nature, complexity, and scope of the COGLA mandate, if considerable wasteful activity did not occur. The difference is that, to the tune of about $100 million per mistake, this "waste" is directly paid for by visible tax dollars. Even under the pre-NEP regime, of course, it can be argued that some equivalent waste of public money occurred through the tax incentives that companies received, assuming of course that such incentives are viewed as "lost" federal revenue. This is precisely where basic ideological views of what constitutes governmental intervention arise. The earlier tax incentives are not viewed as either intervention or as "government" money by oil and gas interests. It is *their own* or their shareholders' money that they are investing and risking and the tax rules are merely the appropriate ones needed to define a legitimate cost of doing business.

The politics of assessing COGLA are thus subject to the same kaleidoscope of ideas and perceptions as the other NEP components have been. The general dynamics of COGLA are, moreoever, linked to the even larger issues of the price and taxing regime, but also to the expenditure process and to the specific problems of controlling the PIP expenditures. In this regard it is essential to recall the items of expenditure uncertainty examined in Chapter 10. The overall magnitude of PIP expenditures is difficult to estimate, not only because the power of initiative rests with the industry, but also because exploration agreements only specify a *minimum* amount of exploration activity. If in fact more exploration is pursued, PIP expenditures increase in ways that cannot be predicted on the basis of the agreements themselves. Similarly, agreements with multinational firms, which otherwise would have lower PIP grants, may later involve much higher PIP grants if the multinationals bring Canadian firms into their exploration activity through farm-in arrangements. These may or may not be known for the later years of the agreement.

TABLE 11.2
EXPLORATION AGREEMENTS CONCLUDED*

Operating company	Date	Number of agreements	Area million hectares	Location	Term	Well commitment	Program value (M $ CND)	% Canadian Content	Peak employment/ % Canadian	Notable aspects
Esso	May 1982	6	2.4	Mackenzie Delta– Beaufort Sea	5 years	5 offshore 4 onshore	600	72	525/100	
Shell	June 1982	6	3.8	Scotian Slope	2–6 years	6	188	45	/99	
Canterra	July 1982	1	0.8	Davis Strait	5 years	2	200	44	187/48	
Petro-Canada Husky–Bow Valley	July 1982	4	1.7	Scotian Shelf	3 years	8	500	58	/85	Training program of $1.4 million; $2 million, or 3 of expenditures, allocated to supplier development.
Shell	Sept. 1982	7	1.9	Scotian Shelf	3 years	9	553	45	458/99	
Panarctic	Nov. 1982	20	14.0	Arctic	5 years	25	713	79	500/100	
Mobil	Nov. 1982	3	1.3	Scotia Shelf	18 mos. to 4 years	6	307	50	474/94	Significant transfer of knowhow undertakings.
Gulf	Jan. 1983	1	0.6	Beaufort	5 years	5	1110	64	/100	
BP	Feb. 1983	6	5.3	Newfoundland Shelf	2–5 years 4 years	6	258	51	/90	$1.25 M training and education commitment.

Source: Canada Oil and Gas Lands Administration, March 1984. Reproduced by permission.

TABLE 11.2 (Cont'd)
EXPLORATION AGREEMENTS CONCLUDED*

Operating company	Date	Number of agreements	Area million hectares	Location	Term	Well commitment	Program value (M $ CND)	% Canadian Content	Peak employment/ % Canadian	Notable aspects
Dome	March 1983	5	3.5	Beaufort	5 years	8	960	82	629/97	
Gulf	March 1983	1	.4	Beaufort	5 years	1	214	44	/100	
Labrador Group	April 1983	10	9.0	Labrador Sea	5 years	10	500	-	530/84	
Chevron	April 1983	2	1.3	Gulf of St. Lawrence	3 years	2	28	-	189/90	
Dome	April 1983	1	.24	Scotian Shelf	2.5 years	2	113	42	189/100	
Mobil	July 1983	9	2.61	Grand Banks	22 months -4 years	13	636	41	781/83	
Canterra	July 1983	1	.3	Labrador Shelf	5 years	1	32	-	180/62	
Petro-Canada	July 1983	6	2.5	Grand Banks	3–4 years	8	505	64	496/100	
Petro-Canada	Aug. 1983	9	6.5	Mackenzie Valley	4 years	11	120	88	328/100	
Dome	Aug. 1983	1	.68	Mackenzie Valley	4 years	2	7.5	90	102/90	
Esso	Aug. 1983	1	.64	Mackenzie Valley	4 years	2	7.5	90	102/90	

Source: Canada Oil and Gas Lands Administration, March 1984. Reproduced by permission.

TABLE 11.2 (Cont'd)
EXPLORATION AGREEMENTS CONCLUDED*

Operating company	Date	Number of agreements	Area million hectares	Location	Term	Well commitment	Program value (M $ CND)	% Canadian Content	Peak employment/ % Canadian	Notable aspects
Amoco	Aug. 1983	5	.99	Mackenzie Valley	4 years	5	30	75	145/80	
Coho	Aug. 1983	1	.80	Mackenzie Valley	1–5 years	2	5.3	75	120/50	
Texaco	Aug. 1983	2	.20	Mackenzie	4 years	2	5	40	100/40	
Dome	Dec. 1983	1	.589	Northumberland	2½ years	1	14.25	-	180/60	
Placid	Dec. 1983	1	.685	Beaufort	5 years	1	180	80	180/-	
Suncor	Dec. 1983	1	.109	N.W.T.	5 years	1	22.6	85	140/100.	
Petro-Canada	Dec. 1983	1	.805	N.W.T.	5 years	1	11	89	82/100	
Dome	Dec. 1983	1	.545	N.W.T.	4 years	3	9.2	84	107/100	
Amerada	Dec. 1983	1	.210	N.W.T.	4 years	1	6.6	100	100/100	
Pan Mackenzie	Dec. 1983	1	.024	Yukon	4 years	1	16.0	85	60/100	
General American	Dec. 1983	1	.003	Yukon	3 years	-	-	-	-	
Pan Canadian	Dec. 1983	1	.013	Yukon	-	-	-	-	-	Significant discoveries.

Source: Canada Oil and Gas Lands Administration, March 1984. Reproduced by permission.

TABLE 11.2 (Cont'd)
EXPLORATION AGREEMENTS CONCLUDED*

Operating company	Date	Number of agreements	Area million hectares	Location	Term	Well commitment	Program value (M $ CND)	% Canadian Content	Peak employment/ % Canadian	Notable aspects
Suncor	Dec. 1983	1	.006	N.W.T.	-	-	-	-	-	
Fairholme	Dec. 1983	1	.039	George's Bank	5 years	-	-	-	-	Moratorium.
Shell	Feb. 1984	1	.025	N.W.T.	4 years	1	9.8	100	69/90	
Shell	Feb. 1984	1	.649	Davis Strait	6 years	1	35.7	53	244/90	
Shell	Feb. 1984	2	.393	Mackenzie	5 years	2	15.3	85	110/65	
Sulpetro	Feb. 1984	1	.191	N.W.T.	4 years	1	2.6	80	106/-	
Gulf	Feb. 1984	2	.589	Mackenzie	5 years	2	23.2	81	110/-	
Chevron	Feb. 1984	1	.025	Delta	4 years	1	9.8	100	104/71	
Chevron	Feb. 1984	3	.107	Delta	5 years	3	34	-	234/-	
Westmin	Feb. 1984	2	.527	Yukon	4 years	2	15.4	33.5	135/-	
Dome	Feb. 1984	1	.469	Beaufort	5 years	1	-	-	-	
Western Delcalta	Feb. 1984	2	.947	N.W.T.	4 years	2	6.2	76	-	

Source: Canada Oil and Gas Lands Administration, March 1984. Reproduced by permission.

Specific COGLA Dynamics: The Venture Project and Mobil Oil

The world of regulatory implementation cannot be even remotely understood by looking only at real or purported general effects. Selected particular effects must also be briefly explored, since many individual large decisions or projects cannot help but involve idiosyncratic combinations of political, economic and technical-physical circumstances not easily accommodated by "the rules." In this section we look at the dynamics of the Venture gas project off the coast of Nova Scotia.[16]

The Venture project was sponsored by Mobil Oil, the multinational which, as noted in Chapters 3 and 7, allowed, arguably, the least amount of decision making independence for its Canadian subsidiary. Mobil's exploration lease expired in the summer of 1982 and would have to be renegotiated through the COGLA process. At the time Mobil's total lease acreage, including Venture, other Scotian Shelf leases, George's Bank, and the Bay of Fundy, exceeded 12 million acres. As one energy official put it, this was "too much for any one company to say grace over." Mobil briefed COGLA and other federal officials in July 1982, indicating that Mobil wished to proceed as quickly as possible. They felt the Venture project was commercially viable, provided that marketing arrangements, gas price and royalty arrangements fell into place appropriately.

At this time federal pressure was being exerted on Mobil to speed up its dilineation drilling, but Ottawa's pro-development urges were not uniformly applied. This was because Petro-Canada, a partner in the project, was itself not in a position to move any faster. Moreover, delays had occurred before since Ottawa and Nova Scotia had only in March 1982 concluded their oil and gas offshore agreement examined in Chapters 3 and 5. COGLA's negotiations nonetheless centred on conditions related to the continued pace of drilling activity in the Venture project area. At the same time it must be remembered that Mobil's corporate strategy was not confined to the Venture project only. It was the major player in the Hibernia oil project as well. Thus its political and economic calculus was informed by the larger Ottawa–Newfoundland deadlock and by its own view of what pace of total development best met its corporate interest and that of its shareholders. In some respects, it was in Mobil's interest to proceed quickly, since this might increase their leverage over the trio of governments they were dealing with. COGLA and the federal government for example, mired in deep recession and with no mega-projects in sight, had short-term political incentives to speed up the pace of development to show that the NEP was working. Thus a more favourable fiscal regime might be negotiated by Mobil under these circumstances.

The alternative policy strategy also arises, namely: should the regulator slow down the process to ensure that environmental and Canadian benefits provisions can actually be secured through tough bargaining? Even these choices, however, are not the sum total of the regulatory agenda. The viability of the Venture project depends upon the marketing of gas beyond the small Maritime market into the eastern United States. In 1982 Ottawa was forecasting scenarios for Venture which by 1990 could see the Maritime provinces' consumption of gas at anywhere from 40 to 200 mcf per day of the total 360 mcf, and U.S. exports at anywhere from 320 to 140 mcf per day. It must be remembered that concurrent with these events, as we saw in Chapter 10, Ottawa was strenuously promoting the expansion of Alberta gas into Québec.

Mobil in 1982 favoured a "maritime only" gas pipeline with an export lateral to the United States. Such a pipeline would provide access to the more lucrative U.S. export market and would involve a much lower gas transmission cost than the alternative TQM proposal for a longer and more costly connection with Québec City. However, a reversible TQM (not envisioned in the original NEP) was promoted by the Nova Scotia government on the grounds that it could provide greater future flexibility. In the reversible TQM option (quickly rejected by Ottawa), Venture gas would back out Alberta gas in eastern Canadian markets all the way to Montreal and would be tied to the approval of incremental Alberta gas exports to the United States. These kinds of regulatory decisions resided in the hands of the old regulators on the energy block, including the NEB.

Nor do the now familiar export and pipeline dilemmas of such decisions exhaust the dynamics. There was also the fiscal regime. Mobil officials indicated in 1982 that although the project was not viable under the royalty system of the Canada–Nova Scotia offshore agreement, there was ample scope to "induce viability" through modifications to the royalty system. But since under the agreement most of the royalty revenues accrue to Nova Scotia, these concessions would have to be made by Nova Scotia. As Chapter 7 has shown, Nova Scotia had displayed its strong desire for economic development through the engine of oil and gas, precisely by signing a fast agreement with Ottawa rather than holding out as Newfoundland had. Probably Mobil has properly judged Nova Scotia to be the most vulnerable "bargainer" from which to secure fiscal concessions. There are of course other avenues of fiscal support that would be potentially necessary to make the Venture project viable. These include grants for pipeline construction, equity participation (for Petro-Canada's involvement) and perhaps changes to the gas pricing regime. The latter could conceivably include a two-price system for gas, thus transferring the subsidy element to consumers much as in the case of administered oil prices.

The fact that the Venture decision goes well beyond the COGLA mandate is abundantly evident. COGLA did sign new agreements on the Scotian Shelf with Mobil, but the regulatory politics continued to be played out as the anticipated development stage of Venture approached. By the fall of 1983, following more delineation drilling, Mobil was reporting that its results were disappointing in that the total size of the Venture play may not be as large as first thought, and hence its economic viability was even more in doubt. More drilling would be necessary. The question arises as to whether this is just another form of regulatory and fiscal brinksmanship, or whether it reflects genuine geological/economic uncertainty. The tendency to identify regulatory villains and heroes usually rises to the surface in these circumstances. Mobil is known as a tough company, unsympathetic to the nationalist instincts of host countries. But in this case, Petro-Canada and Nova Scotia Resources (a provincial Crown corporation) are Mobil's partners along with Texaco Resources Inc. and East Coast Energy Ltd. Given Petro-Canada's interest in particular as a "window on a project," the question arises as to how much geological information remains proprietary to the main developer, and how much is shared. One must also consider the extent to which it is in Petro-Canada's corporate interest to share or withhold information and to bargain with the governments involved, since Venture is not the only project on its plate, either.

This perilously brief account of the Venture project does not do full justice to the actual complexity of the dynamics of the situation as it stood early in 1984, let alone to its earlier evolution as a project. We have not dealt with its "Canada benefits" industrial policy dynamics, nor with environmental issues. We have used the account only to give a practical flavour to some of the particular effects and dynamics that arise out of the COGLA regime, but which quickly slither into the tax and expenditure dynamics traced in previous chapters. It is but one project mirrored at but one point in time.

Specific COGLA Dynamics: Petro-Canada and Canadian Benefits

A further glimpse into the particular effects of COGLA regulatory dynamics can be obtained by looking at a firm that is, nominally at least, the polar opposite of Mobil or any other multinational oil company, namely Petro-Canada. We have already examined Petro-Canada in several different respects, but both the COGLA and closely related OIRB regulatory aspects are instructive in the domain of industrial benefits. The key question here is whether Petro-Canada can or should play a leading role as a Canadian-owned corporate citizen in fostering spin-off benefits to Canadian industry, and thus itself become an instrument of economic development rather than just of some defined view of energy policy.[17] In short, should COGLA and the OIRB properly expect Petro-Canada to behave in a more exemplary fashion than strictly private firms would? Several elements are interwoven in this regulator–regulatee relationship.

The first is that both COGLA and Petro-Canada report to the Minister of Energy, Mines and Resources. But EMR's minister is not the minister of economic development. When push comes to shove, just how much should Petro-Canada use its funds to foster such development? As late as 1984, eight years after the company's establishment and two years into the COGLA and OIRB mandate, there was strong criticism that Petro-Canada had not yet developed a clear industrial development policy. Petro-Canada argued that there was no governmental policy on the question as to this aspect of its public policy mandate. Petro-Canada was already criticized as being inefficient by some of its private sector competitors. Its frontier exploration role was already a large public policy obligation. Should it be expected to pay a premium for Canadian-produced supplies and if so, how often? On all projects? On some projects? Should it be given special funds over and above its normal allotment to play these additional economic development roles? If so, should EMR have to pay for these, or should they come out of some industrial development fund or department?

Contradictions also arise out of the dual COGLA expectations. If Canadian benefits are stressed, this could potentially drive up costs. But when PIP grants are given, the COGLA concern, in alliance with the Petroleum Incentives Administration, is also to keep costs down so as to keep a lid on PIP spending. Thus the pressures are concurrent, but not wholly compatible. Nor have we included in this account the other dimensions of the Canada benefits regime which we discuss in the next section of the chapter.

None of these issues were fully worked out, nor are they likely to be cast in the form of firm rules. Though Petro-Canada is clearly not the same as Mobil or other private firms, it is not at all exempt from having to wend its way through the negotiating maze of the post-NEP regulatory process. Its interests are not wholly the same as those of EMR or any other single structure in the new regulatory regime.

The New Regulatory Regime II:
Office of Industrial and Regional Benefits (OIRB)

As Chapters 2 and 3 showed, there has been a longstanding concern, since the 1950s resource boom, that Canadians had not benefited adequately from the generation of new skills, technologies, and products made possible by large development projects, especially those sponsored by the multinationals.[18] The Gordon Commission had raised concerns in the late 1950s. In 1966 the federal government issued "Guiding Principles of Good Corporate Behaviour" for foreign-controlled Canadian subsidiaries, requiring them to search out and develop economic sources of supply in Canada. They were to set up Canadian research and design capabilities to enable their companies to compete in markets abroad as well as in Canada. So little of that occurred in a decade that fourteen "New Principles of International Business Conduct" were issued by the same Liberals in 1975. These principles, too, sought to increase research and development in Canada, to increase Canadian sourcing of goods and services, and to develop advanced-technology, Canadian products for export.

In 1975 an Advisory Committee on Industrial Benefits (ACIB) was established, representing thirteen federal departments and agencies and the provinces. It was to advise ministers on how well the owners/sponsors of projects on Canada Lands were meeting industrial benefits objectives; later it advised on all major projects having significant federal involvement—i.e., almost all major projects—anywhere in Canada. It had no powers, had a secretariat of three part-time officers, and achieved little.

The NEB hearings of 1977 and the 1978 Northern Pipeline Act broke some new ground in *requiring* from Foothills Ltd., the builders of the Canadian leg of the Alaska Highway Gas Pipeline, a procurement plan ensuring "a fair and competitive opportunity" for the supply of Canadian goods and services. The government's claim is that Canadian content, as a result, has been over 87 percent.

Events thereafter followed more quickly. The Throne Speech of April 1980 talked of using Canada's resources "as a building block of a vigorous industrial policy." The National Energy Program announced that there would be "requirements for the use of Canadian goods and services in exploration, development and production programs on the Canada Lands, and in major non-conventional oil projects" (i.e., heavy oil and tarsands). The Canada Oil and Gas Act required companies applying for exploration and development projects to present a satisfactory plan of employment of Canadians and of providing Canadian manufacturers, consultants, contractors, and service companies with a full and fair opportunity to participate. The Trudeau government's economic development statement of November 1981 talked of harnessing the resources of the economy as a national enterprise through the national government, using major instruments for managing and exploiting the development opportunities and ensuring that the benefits are shared fairly.

The Blair–Carr task force of seventy-six business and labour leaders in June 1981 stressed that in order for Canadian firms to develop world-scale design, production, and management capabilities out of projects, the traditional reluctance of the Canadian subsidiaries of foreign-based multinational enterprises to employ Canadian-owned firms on their Canadian projects must be addressed. In a climate of economic malaise, yet of apparent promise that new economic pinnacles were within reach through a favourable energy future, the government was apparently ready to override oil industry and U.S. political opposition. And the priority task of the new Regional and Industrial Expansion department (DRIE) was to concentrate the federal government's efforts to derive industrial benefits from major projects, though an Office of Industrial and Regional Benefits (OIRB).

OIRB Mandate and Process

The Cabinet decided in June 1981, and announced in August, that owners/sponsors of major projects would have to work closely on manpower and procurement policies with a new Committee on Megaproject Industrial and Regional Benefits (C-MIRB) before letting any contracts. They were not only to consult in advance, but to help identify and provide necessary and timely information to prospective Canadian bidders. They were to report periodically to C-MIRB on progress made. C-MIRB is the strengthened successor to the puny ACIB mentioned earlier, with the same key departments and agencies represented, but supported by the now thirty-member staff of the OIRB.

The C-MIRB representatives report to their respective ministers and bureaucracies their assessment of a proposed or existing project from their perspectives (regional benefit, industrial benefit, employment potential, research and development opportunity, foreign market possibility, large-project design and management potential). As one observer put it, they contribute a less definable but no less important "climate of opinion," a consensus that Company A is trying hard and can be accommodated this time, or that Company B is "stalling and needs to be squeezed." Remarkably little is put on paper. Telephone calls and meetings produce a "network view," a drift of opinion wafted upwards that conditions ministers when they meet to decide upon prepared options laid before them or, as will be seen, whether a company's firm decision on procurement in, say, Japan, cannot indeed be reversed.

For Canada Lands projects the sanction is clear. COGLA approves through the Ministers of Energy and of Indian Affairs and Northern Development applications for exploration and for development. COGLA says yes, no or (usually) "yes, with conditions." One major criterion is regional and industrial benefits, based on plans submitted. Following COGLA-initiated meetings, the OIRB calls in the company, inquires carefully into its Canadian regional and economic spinoff intentions, requires a detailed plan specifying targets and how they are to be reached, and then advises COGLA. It also advises COGLA and C-MIRB periodically as to how the company, having had its project approved, is carrying out the plan. COGLA's Canada Benefits Branch has a representative on C-MIRB, but also keeps in regular touch with OIRB by telephone and memorandum.

The OIRB also works with FIRA when foreign enterprises seek to acquire control of a Canadian business or to establish a new business in Canada. The OIRB advises FIRA with respect to such companies that are, or could be, suppliers to major gas and oil projects. The National Energy Board, as quasi-judicial agency, cannot be used directly as a lever, but the OIRB does work with the NEB's technical and commercial staffs providing them information for their investigation into applications. The Canada Employment and Immigration Commission has the role of enhancing employment benefits from major projects. It works with the OIRB and COGLA to try to see that Canadians are appointed to key positions in project design and management. In a pinch, this means using the hard lever of rejecting a foreigner's visa application.

Explicit sanctions do not exist for projects in the provinces, but here again the OIRB is the focus, through its own networking and through C-MIRB, for federal concerns with a major project in a province. It provides information and assessments to provinces pondering approval or rejection of an application. It is the OIRB that investigates and advises on the benefits aspect when Saskatchewan or Alberta and the federal government consider a heavy oil or tarsands project; or a Trans-Québec-Maritimes pipeline is being proposed; or a major coal development has to be approved by British Columbia, but the federal treasury builds the necessary railway and ports.

The OIRB deals directly with companies through its Operations and Project Review unit. A second component of OIRB, Planning and Analysis, gathers and distributes information. It tells project sponsor/owners about Canadian suppliers. It tells suppliers about project opportunities, current and downstream. OIRB organizes and chairs C-MIRB meetings and provides it with information and analysis.

OIRB states that it "operates mainly through the powers of persuasion and its abilities to demonstrate that sourcing in Canada makes good business sense." However, where COGLA is involved, "compliance with the industrial benefits provision of the Canada Oil and Gas Act is a major factor that is weighed in the granting of licenses" for exploration or development.

The applying company is asked to present an industrial benefits plan, outlining in detail corporate procurement policies and its procedures to implement those policies. It wants to see evidence that the company will identify in good time its requirements for goods and services. The company must open bidding to the widest possible number of Canadian firms. It should have programs to seek out and inform potential Canadian suppliers. "An appropriate plan will also maximize opportunities for research and development in Canada and for local and regional sourcing, and give special consideration to sensitive contracts or "designated items."

The OIRB zeroes in on "designated items" which it identifies from the company's description of its project. These are products and services that the OIRB believes "could prove crucial to supplier development." This covers all research and development contracts, all contracts for project management, engineering, procurement, and construction services. It also covers items that the OIRB feels meet the following criteria:

• Canadian capability exists but is being denied supply access;
• there is strong potential for regional diversification;
• there is nascent Canadian capability but no track record;
• market prospects justify encouragement of Canadian supply.

Where COGLA is involved, the OIRB reports and discusses the company's plan so that COGLA may determine its negotiating position. The OIRB takes part in such negotiations, led by COGLA. The OIRB and the Minister of Industry, Trade and Commerce and Regional Economic Expansion (ITC and DREE, now DRIE) provide their advice through COGLA to the Ministers of Energy and of Northern Affairs. When the company gets the project, its bidders' lists and its bid evaluations are reviewed by the OIRB and industry sector branches and regional offices of DRIE. Finally, the OIRB participates in annual reviews with COGLA "of the company's performance in all its aspects."

The OIRB also works with the DRIE industry sector branches and with other federal granting or loaning agencies to help Canadian companies equip themselves technologically or with expertise to design and build products for major ventures. It helps set up joint ventures and sub-contracting arrangements, as well.

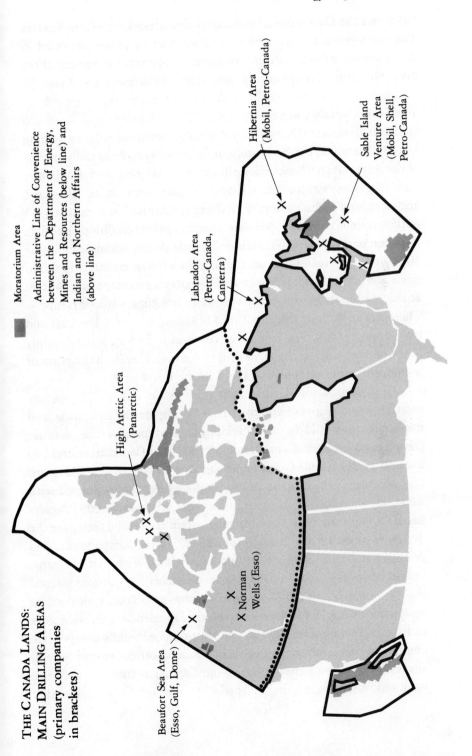

THE CANADA LANDS:
MAIN DRILLING AREAS
(primary companies
in brackets)

■ Moratorium Area

Administrative Line of Convenience
between the Department of Energy,
Mines and Resources (below line) and
Indian and Northern Affairs
(above line)

Hibernia Area
(Mobil, Petro-Canada)

Sable Island
Venture Area
(Mobil, Shell,
Petro-Canada)

Labrador Area
(Petro-Canada,
Canterra)

High Arctic Area
(Panarctic)

Beaufort Sea Area
(Esso, Gulf, Dome)

X Norman
Wells (Esso)

OIRB and the Dynamics of Industrial Benefits: Three Case Studies

The main projects with which the OIRB is involved are indicated in Appendix B. To illustrate the dynamics, however, we present three case studies involving Gulf Canada, Dome Petroleum, and Esso.

The Gulf Canada Case Study

Gulf Canada came to Ottawa in mid-1980 to seek approval for a drilling system that would cost $526 million, later to rise to $674 million. Part of the system is an 81-metre long barge of 27 500 tonnes whose circular hull and downward conical shape are supposed to sit passively, anchored, and break up sea ice pushing against it. It was to cost $171 million and to operate without resupply while drilling one well. Another part was a $164 million "mobile deep caisson" containing 30 000 tons of steel, to sit on the bottom with its centre core full of stone and gravel to hold it there. A 284-foot octagon at the top, 364 feet at the bottom, it is to operate two wells at a time without resupply. There are to be four ships costing $143 million, two icebreakers and two supply vessels. The rest of the cost was to be for an arctic supply base and for bringing the giant drill system vehicles from the point of manufacture and establishing them in the Beaufort Sea.

Gulf Canada told Ottawa that the caisson was too big for any existing world shipyard and the barge too big for any in Canada, and the contracts would be let outside. But a preponderance of other contracts to be let in Canada would bring total Canadian content to over 50 percent. Gulf Canada was vague as to how that would occur.

Meetings between the ACIB (C-MIRB's forerunner) started with some suspicion on Ottawa's part, since Gulf Canada had used a Calgary-based Canadian firm for a preliminary system design and then gave the design work to a San Francisco subsidiary of a U.S. company that had designed and built offshore drilling rigs before. With that company, industrial spin-offs for Canada had been notably few. Ottawa warned that it would be unhappy if the company, as before, continued to design, for example, for the Electro Motor Division of General Motors in its rigs. Bombardier-MLW of Canada produced a fully competitive engine for this application but, as one federal official put it, "It was always designed-out; they designed-out Canadians consistently." The issue was raised at a meeting in April 1981, and Gulf Canada ignored it:

the San Francisco company got the job (and later went on to "design-out" Bombardier).

With the design issue lost, further meetings and further pressure by Ottawa moved the consortium leader to words and promises, but not deeds. Both major contracts, for the caisson and for the barge, went to Japan. The reason given was time—the Japanese could meet the tight deadlines. A problem for the Canadian shipyards certainly was time—they were given a short period of time in which to bid. The winning Japanese said they would incorporate Canadian products in the two giant vehicles, but gave no details. Ottawa told Gulf Canada to press the Japanese. Gulf said it had no power to require the Japanese to use Canadian goods and services. ACIB took strong exception to that, saying the company could include whatever they wish to include in a contract.

A modest victory was won, in Ottawa's view, when super-winches on three-inch cables worth over $10 million, rather complex equipment that all northern exploration work is likely to require, went first to a U.S. firm after Gulf Canada put out bids and gave ten days in which to respond. The bid was old hat for the U.S. firm; a Toronto firm hastily cobbled together a rough bid but it was high. Ottawa intervened, protested, and got a rebidding. With more time to work its bid through, the Toronto firm was competitive and won. It was helped financially by IT&C with grants to upgrade its plant to do the job. It now is claimed to be fully competitive in a new field with a good future. This is one key instance of OIRB people (in a predecessor unit for part of the time) interceding on behalf of a Canadian company to ensure it a fair chance at getting a contract—then interceding with grant-givers in the same department or elsewhere in government to help the firm equip itself to carry out that contract (and, more importantly, future contracts).

At the April meeting, Gulf Canada had no specific sourcing policy. It said it simply had to get the best world experience and get the results into the Arctic within a tight time frame, in the summer of 1983. Warnings of unhappiness by federal ministers were received politely by the company's five middle officials. (Two public relations men, two project engineers, and a manager of engineering faced twenty-four federal and four provincial officers.) The civil servants concluded that there was a clear lack on the part of Gulf Canada of a genuine commitment to maximizing Canadian content and industrial benefits. They pressed for a meeting of IT&C Minister Herb Gray with the company's president. This kind of pressure must have had some other related effects, because Gulf Canada began in 1982 to run full-page newspaper ads showing how its contracting produced benefits across Canada.

Ottawa reluctantly approved the Japanese contracts, but stated it was interested in the four support vessels, in massive deck modules for the caisson and generators, winches and other equipment for the barges. It demanded a review of bidders' lists and bid documents before bids were requested and then a review of the selected placement (the bid winner) prior to commitment with the proposed supplier.

Gulf Canada had a general statement of sourcing policy which the ACIB believed fell short of a policy that would ensure Canadian companies a full and fair opportunity to participate in the project. Gulf came back with a list of major equipment still to be tendered for—but it had little idea of possible Canadian suppliers for the equipment. Ottawa sent it a list of eight possible Canadian suppliers. The company selected bid winners and almost all the $28 million in contracts purported to qualify as Canadian content because they were ordered from abroad through Canadian subsidiary companies.

As mentioned above, Gulf ruled out Bombardier for engines. The drilling system was designed for engines bought from General Motors (Canada) but made by General Motors diesels in the United States. Gulf Canada first argued it was a matter of timing. OIRB was by then in existence, but it lost that battle as well, giving a reluctant go-ahead to buy GM Diesels. Then the OIRB said it was interested in Canadian sourcing of the main generators and main switchgear. Gulf Canada, in the federal view, failed to give Bombardier a crack at the three main generators.

In the early fall of 1981, Herb Gray met Gulf Canada's president and received assurances of co-operation in Canadian sourcing. At about the same time, Gulf officials informed the OIRB that price bids for equipment were being sent to Canadian and other suppliers with a closing date of October 13, just two weeks later. The officials added that if the OIRB wanted to suggest other possible bidders, they notify Gulf accordingly within forty-eight hours. Later Gulf informed the OIRB that Bombardier engines were ruled out beause they could not stand the cold. A check found these engines were used on Baffin Island, at

James Bay, in the North Sea, on icebreakers and drilling rigs. Gulf then advised that they were concerned about Bombardier's ability to meet delivery, price and service requirements. Bombardier, in the view of OIRB officials, was able to meet all these and had done so on other contracts. Gulf then argued that the priority of rapid development of northern petroleum resources was greater than objectives for industrial benefits.

In October 1981 the OIRB advised DIAND in respect of Gulf Canada's application for approval of its drilling program that C-MIRB was not satisfied because Canadian companies were not given adequate time to bid, were not given full information on performance requirements, and were "designed-out."

The two icebreakers and one supply vessel went to Canadian yards; one supply vessel went to Japan. Herb Gray advised Gulf's president that these procurements had proceeded acceptably, but that he was unhappy about other procurement for the same reasons noted above. Now it transpired that the giant caisson that had been awarded to Japan for reasons of timing, would be delayed by a year. The Japanese yard had been granted a year's extension by Gulf; Ottawa yelled foul play. Gray wanted the company to state how it proposed to stop its habit of precluding Canadian companies from a competitive opportunity to bid by timing, sole sourcing, or design restrictions.

As the pressure from the DIAND and IT&C Ministers was applied, tenders were called for fourteen large steel modules weighing from 65 to 545 tons each. They were to be built to provide accommodation for 100 workers and for mud-pumps, power, and utilities. The modules would be built, tested, packaged, and delivered to the caisson-maker in Japan. After interested companies were assessed, six were asked to bid—one Japanese, one U.S., two Canadian, and one a Canadian subsidiary of a U.S. parent. The companies were given three weeks to bid on a $30 million contract. Canadian companies pulled out except for one rough and hasty bid, which came in high.

At about the same time, in January 1982, the Canada Benefits Branch in COGLA sought the OIRB's advice as to action necessary to hold the company accountable. The OIRB responded as it had to DIAND. Gray met senior Gulf Canada executives in February 1982 to express concern. To that date, contracts worth $521 million had been let. Canadian content totalled $176.24 million, or less than 34 percent.

Two Canadian companies out of three had declined to bid because of insufficient time.

One of the drop-outs was a Canadian-controlled multinational which had requested more time to bid but had been refused. Meanwhile, OIRB went on to urge the possible Canadian bidders that they bid seriously if an extension could be arranged. Late in February, Gulf Canada advised that it was reopening its bids, but was concerned that this change may be construed as a departure from accepted professional standards.

The pressure had worked. In April, the Canadian-owned multinational learned it had won the $33 million contract. Six of the modules were of complex design, new to Canadian manufacturers, and thus the contract would add to the industry's capabilities to supply the oil industry's offshore equipment needs. A new Canadian entry had been created into what is expected to be a large market for fabrication of modules. Typical of other such instances and of the way this new developmental regulatory system works, there was a hard core of proven company experience and capability, coupled with government pressure in its favour (applied, here, to a company deemed by network consensus to be unsympathetic). The Canadian firm had persuaded Gulf Canada of its practical capability to do the job. But its bid came in about $8 million high. Gulf was about to reject the bid. Federal ministers told Gulf it should take the bid anyway, because its overall Canadian content record on the project was low. As for Gulf's taking an $8 million blow, OIRB officers stressed that Gulf was getting from the federal treasury many times $8 million in PIP grants, for its exploration activities.

In October 1982 Gulf sought approval from COGLA to drill eleven wells from 1983–1990 in the Beaufort Sea at an estimated expenditure of $1.7 billion in 1982 dollars. Of its capital costs of $674 million to be completed in 1984, about 51 percent are said to be Canadian content, a significant improvement from what Ottawa viewed as a bad start.

For its part, the OIRB now thinks that Gulf Canada, one of the more difficult mega-project sponsor/owners it has had to deal with, now has satisfactory procurement policies and procedures. Gulf Canada has come around, after much pushing and hauling, to the following practices:

- A large expansion of its Canadian sourcing lists; better identification of Canadian firms capable of supply; identification of
Canadian firms not now fully capable but that could be further
developed to handle more advanced technology;
- fully briefing large and small Canadian companies on supply
requirements; packaging bids so as to allow more Canadian
companies to bid for component parts rather than the whole
thing; provide winning foreign contractors with information
on the availability of components in Canada;
- require all winning contractors, consultants and service
companies to buy and hire Canadian.

The Esso Case Study

Esso (or Imperial Oil), as we have seen in earlier chapters, was viewed
in an unsympathetic way by EMR officials in the mid- and late 1970s.
But gradually it came to be viewed much more sympathetically by the
OIRB network. Esso came in early to see Ottawa officials about its own
Arctic drilling system plans for the Beaufort Sea. It had been drilling
from artificial islands in shallow waters and wanted to move into
waters somewhat deeper but not deep enough for drillships. There
were no nearby deposits of gravel. So it had decided on steel islands of
eight sections cabled together, containing power generators and
equipment for pumping, ballasting and de-ballasting. Tugs, barges,
dredges and drilling equipment brought the total cost of the project to
about $150 million.

Esso prepared its system design through Canadian design contractors. Then, at each subsequent contract stage, Esso came to Ottawa
and showed its requirements, went out of its way to source Canadian,
and broke its contracts into component parts rather than require one
total package contract. It bought its own steel for the project (from
Algoma), and shipbuilders bid (and later built) with the Canadian steel.

Three Canadian bidders for the eight sections of the steel island,
or caisson, were high, even though the bid was broken down so that
a yard could take part of the job. The time frame for bidding was tight,
and none would assume a time-penalty for lateness. Japanese competitors had the capability and would assume the risk. Esso kept the OIRB
and C-MIRB informed of all this and had relatively easy sailing, when it

eventually chose a Japanese bidder. The caisson was built in Japan, of Canadian steel shipped there. Canadian-made winches were shipped to Japan for installation on the steel island. Esso worked with Ottawa on securing significant Canadian involvement (with a Dutch company) on the towing of the island to Canada and on the continuing dredging work.

A crane barge and a dredge were bought abroad, while a drilling rig and several vessels were made in Canada, thereby enhancing Canadian capability in major project design and manufacturing. As well, five of the ten largest trailer-suction-hopper dredges in the world are in the Beaufort Sea now; they all are Dutch, and have a monopoly on a dredging activity that requires considerable new technology and that will have continuing value offshore Canada and elsewhere. Through the OIRB and DRIE, the Canadian government suggested to the Dutch company owners that they would have a better chance at future contracts if they joined up with Canadians. When the Dutch complied, Esso awarded the dredging contract. Canadian content in the construction phase of this project is said to be something over 70 percent. In the coming operations phase it is estimated at 85–95 percent.

The C-MIRB network congratulated Esso for being helpful and open. It stressed that while Canadian content is indeed high, the more fundamental Canadian long-term benefits (technology transfer; improvement of capabilities in design, production and management) are high as well.

In May 1982 a news release from Industry Minister Herb Gray announced a $600 million program of new exploration agreements with Esso to cover 2.3 million hectares in the North, on land and sea. Esso obtained its approvals with relative ease.

For the work on fulfilling those exploration agreements, which are a small part of their total Canadian drilling program, Esso tells bidders on all sub-contracts that Canadian content will be an important factor in evaluating their bids. Esso is rated high by government officials on maximizing Northern participation (in employment, service and other contracts).

The Dome Case Study

Dome Petroleum, along with a consortium of Canadian companies (and one foreign-owned firm), won Canadian government approval of a $4 billion project to liquefy natural gas taken from Alberta and British Columbia, pipeline it to tidewater, and ship it by special LNG tanker to Pacific-rim markets or to Japan. By mid-June 1982, Dome was leaning heavily toward foreign liquefaction technology (through a Pennsylvania concern) and toward giving the whole contract to a foreign contractor. The OIRB learned of this indirectly, since Dome had conducted little consultation with Ottawa.

The liquefaction process required cooling in aluminium tubing (which Canada makes); further, Canadian design, production and management in just such a process had been formed previously on the Arctic Pilot Project. Joint ventures of Canadian firms with experienced firms from France and Germany had been set up. DRIE had persuaded Canadian consulting firms to join with such foreign companies in order to gain technological expertise and the capability of managing world-class projects. Despite all this preparation, Dome seemed to be going to a foreign (U.S.) firm that had only a token Canadian partner. Dome stated that it wanted a U.S. contractor for demonstrated base-load LNG project construction, management and expertise. Ottawa responded that such Canadian capability had been proven in previous major projects, including one in which Dome itself had been involved; U.S. experience could be tapped through a U.S. firm as a minority partner in a joint venture.

The OIRB contacted FIRA and Herb Gray, the minister to whom both reported. Dome was bringing a Japanese firm to Ottawa to talk about approval of the formation of a Canadian company to buy and deliver the gas. FIRA obligingly passed on the message that they had better get busy discussing industrial benefits with the OIRB. Dome came to the OIRB and was asked for an explicit policy on industrial benefits. It did not have one. Assurances of good intent were offered, but nothing positive transpired.

Concerning the building of LNG carriers, the liquefaction process, and industrial benefits, the Minister advised Dome of the government's desired approach. Dome rejected the advice, stressed that it believed in the government's approach, but that it was in a hurry "on this one."

The OIRB deplored what it regarded as Dome's pro-foreign bias and its rejection of the policy that Canadian projects should bring on competent, aggressive and new Canadian supply capability. This was ironic in the view of OIRB officials, since Dome's strong place in the Beaufort was a direct product of the government's willingness to use the Canadian resource base and the federal tax and grant structure to develop new Canadian capability in oil and gas exploration and production.

Dome told the OIRB that foreign contract winners will include Canadian content in their contracts, but gave no details. The OIRB argued that they did not believe the Japanese would just altruistically do that. Dome's efforts generated the right words, but demonstrated no effective action to produce the proper result. This particular project remains still to be decided. Changed times, the availability of more and cheaper energy, financing difficulties, both for the project and for Dome, have cast doubt on whether the project will go ahead. That doubt is also expressed along the network, where Dome is regarded with a certain lack of sympathy, a sharp contrast to its image in the 1970s.

New Habits versus Bureaucratic Excesses

The three cases must be put in some perspective since the lessons to be derived from them are not just those the OIRB might wish to offer. Consider, for example, the issues raised earlier in this chapter about Petro-Canada. It too was slow in developing a Canadian benefits program, and its arguments were often not all that different than those marshalled by Gulf Canada. There are some limits as to just how large a premium can or should be paid for Canadian content. Yet the Gulf case does show that though old corporate habits lingered, the new regulatory regime could induce new habits. Hence each succeeding time the armtwisting and cajoling would be less evident, and probably less necessary. Esso's response to the new regime, despite its overall opposition to the NEP, was indicative of the fact that new habits could be learned. The Dome case indicated that a virtually Canadian-controlled company did not necessarily behave in expected ways. As in all these cases, however, one must keep in mind that the particular circumstances of the project or the case at hand are different. Timing and other factors are not unimportant at given points in the particular company's evolution or in relation to the risks, technology or profit margins and investment returns on each project.

The degree of progress on overall Canadian benefits has not been measured in any fully accurate or visible way. As we showed earlier in relation to Table 11.2, COGLA data shows "lists" of percentages of Canadian content that average 70 percent. We have already noted, however, that when related to dollar volume, the proportion is closer to 50 percent for both Canadian and foreign-controlled firms. Moreover, these data were largely for exploration activity. Informal judgements of some EMR officials range from 30 to 50 percent when the full range of the oil and gas industry is taken into account. There may even be a reluctance by Ottawa to reveal data for two reasons. If the figures are too low, it will provide ammunition for critics of the NEP. If too much progress is shown, it may indicate that federal policies are too discriminatory, and thus lead to further charges, especially from the United States, that policies violate the General Agreement on Tariffs and Trade (GATT) and other trade obligations.

Another less evident, but in the long run, equally critical dimension of the Canadian benefits issue is the simple question of the information or data base on Canadian suppliers. It is not at all clear that either Ottawa or individual firms, including many large ones, really have knowledge of the capabilities of Canadian suppliers. This is true of suppliers that are now capable of competing for business. It is even more true, of course, for suppliers in related fields who might adapt their business or engage in joint ventures to become suppliers. It is obvious that in some aspects of this activity of "creating suppliers"— another name for industrial and regional policy—the oil and gas firms have a legitimate point of contention. Most firms have experienced the joys and frustrations of "single sourcing," that is, of being dependent on one supplier, when questions arise as to how technologically reliable the supplier is, or how much premium to pay for experimenting with a new supplier. How fast and how much—in short, questions of degree—become critical both for those who wish to enhance Canadian industrial benefits and want to see demonstrable progress, not just promises of progress, and for private firms and Crown corporations who are in the business of profit and/or of getting projects done on time and as viable, healthy enterprises.

Finally, one must relate the pros and cons of the new kind of regulatory bargaining revealed by the OIRB and the COGLA processes to the charge that this politicizes the decision process and brings "bureaucrats" into the board rooms of the oil and gas business. There can be no doubt that oil and gas firms resent being given a regulatory "massage," so to speak. One enters the new regulatory chambers being required to "do a deal," but often not knowing exactly what kind of a deal has been done. Politics, in the sense of the insertion of ideas other than efficiency, certainly are a part of the new regime. Private firms do not like being "fine-tuned" in this way, but the art of fine-tuning is a two-way street. It is at this point that one must remember that the same firms are not at all reluctant to fine-tune the government as they seek to lever the public purse into special fiscal deals on a project-by-project basis.

Nonetheless the federal regime can be usefully compared as to its *degree* of bureaucratization to the Alberta regime for industrial bene-fits. The Alberta industry does have a high percentage of Canadian sourcing. This has been built up over the years by a less interventionist (in this instance) à priori system of regulations. It must be remembered that the overall system of Alberta regulation is extensive indeed. Based on several decades of relative trust, the industry knows that there are high expectations by the Alberta government that Canadian sourcing will occur. At the exploration stage, however, it is done without regulatory requirements per se. Large development projects, including the oil sands, however, do require permits which presuppose the presentation of procurement plans. These are then monitored closely by ex-post reports. COGLA is a much more detailed system but could, in time, evolve into a system such as Alberta is. But the comparison is not a wholly fair one: the Canada Lands *are* different, especially in the context of the offshore, and in the range of interests and ideas that have to be accommodated by a national regime, which are politically and economically different from those of a provincial regime. Nor can all of the bureaucratization inherent in the COGLA–OIRB processes be attributed to bureaucrats. Sectors of the industry wanted procedures put in place that, they hoped, would be better than the old divided pre-NEP regime, then split in even more obvious ways between EMR, DIAND, and DOE. It is in this sense that COGLA sees itself in a "one-stop" broker role. Some industry spokespersons also cite instances where the sheer bureaucracy involved has in fact saved some companies, especially smaller ones, from expensive mistakes simply because the COGLA hoops had to be jumped through.

The Post-NEP Regulatory Regime:
Possible Future Directions

The role of COGLA–OIRB, and of the NEB to a lesser extent, could change in the medium-term future, in significant though gradual ways. As one moves away from the early problems of start-up and exploration to the development stage, the dynamics shift. For example, if PIPs are phased out gradually some of the bureaucracy of the PIA and the detailed ownership determination apparatus could be jettisoned. But the Canadian benefits and environmental issues are likely to loom even larger. Big projects mean big stakes in both the industrial and environmental sense.

When a major relinquishment of land occurs in the late 1980s, the stage will be set for more potential exploration activity by Canadian firms (depending on the fiscal and price regimes in place). It is also the point at which hard realities will set in as to whether the 50 percent Canadian-owned participation in the actual development of projects can be realized. While most industry spokespersons, as we have seen in Chapter 9, seem to doubt the feasibility of Canadian participation at this 50 percent level, there is still a strong likelihood that the larger relinquishment of land will make the regulatory game different. This is because the focus is likely to fall much more on the Hibernia and Sable Island areas. Some suggest that then, for this relinquished land, one could resort to a less interventionist system by moving towards a land sale or cash bonus system of bidding, as opposed to the current system which is primarily a work bonus system. COGLA has issued guidelines that would invite bids on several kinds of criteria, including cash bonuses. A cash bonus system would be more like the Alberta and U.S. systems. Not surprisingly, however, this type of choice is not politically neutral. A cash-based bonus system might also favour the big integrated firms, and therefore the multinationals. Once again it would depend on the connections and contradictions between the regulatory regime and the fiscal regime, and of how different interests gauge the risks involved, including the presence or absence of the 25 percent Crown interest.

All of these possible dynamics nonetheless suggest that some form of COGLA–OIRB regime, albeit mellowed by more experience and perhaps trust between industry and government, is necessary over the long term.

Summary

In this chapter we have examined the last of our trio of implementation arenas, the regulatory arena. As we have successively traversed the three arenas of "implementation," it has become increasingly difficult and unrealistic to try to hold any one of them constant while examining the other. This was perhaps especially the case in the regulatory field, not only because of the COGLA–PIP connection, but also because of the transformation in the nature of the regulatory task being attempted by the two agencies which most epitomize the post-NEP regime, COGLA and OIRB. Although we have focussed on the newer agencies, one should not forget that the NEB also plays a central role and will do so even more as the development stage is reached. We have also given short shrift to the role of U.S. regulatory bodies, especially vis-à-vis gas exports and pricing. These too must be kept fully in mind.

We have stressed the transformation from the old somewhat more reactive public utility style of regulation epitomized by the NEB to the more active "development-oriented" mandate inherent in the COGLA and OIRB processes, the latter being more accurately labelled as multi-purpose, multi-idea negotiating chambers. While the transformation to this new kind of regulation is clearly important, we have cautioned the reader against attributing all of this only to the interventionist outburst of the NEP. The movement from old to new was more gradual, since both the agencies examined derive their mandate from previous regulatory and quasi-regulatory experiments in the 1970s and earlier. There had been, in short, a considerable amount of learning from previous experiences at both the exploration and the development stages of the energy regulatory cycle.

The analysis has shown in various ways the profound dilemmas involved in controlling or managing the nature and pace of development in the activist regulatory regime. The limits of regulation are evident in the developmental dynamics. They are bound to arise both between governmental regulators and private proponents of projects and activities, and between and among different regulatory agencies and different proponent interests. How does one control the pace and the nature of the development? The answer is that no single source of power can, and thus the composite portrait is a distinctly untidy one. We have also raised questions about whether the regulatory system can be made simpler or indeed be "deregulated," but this question in turn raises corollary questions about how we got to where we are in the first place.

At the extreme ends of the reform continuum one might have a system where proponents are left to develop and invest as they see fit. At the other end one might envisage only direct state ownership. Neither of these are very likely, given not only Canada's overall history, but even taking into account Canada's interventionist energy events after 1973. The next prospect which arises is to roll back parts of the current complex regulatory mandate. If so, which concerns should it be? Industrial benefits? Environmental concerns? Northern and regional policy? In each of these areas a "guidelines" approach has already been tried over many years, and in some instances, over many decades; but such approaches occur to the dissatisfaction of significant bodies of political opinion, and to particular interests dissatisfied with the old rules.

The central problem in developmental regulation is that the "rules" are really not rules in the sense of reliable, predictable codes of conduct. Rather, what exists is a cumulative collection of ideas and instruments housed partly in the new array of regulatory "negotiating chambers" and partly in bodies like the NEB that deal with transportation issues and export permits. There is undoubtedly some waste of resources in the process. But significant political interests do not regard the regulatory regime as being invariably inefficient, precisely because they assert or bring to bear other ideas such as the need for stability, national integration, or regional development. Moreover, they assert arguments which essentially address the long-term growth and efficiency of the Canadian economy, and thus introduce the familiar temporal dimensions of regulation and of public policy.

This chapter has shown that the politics of assessing the regulatory apparatus of the NEP is even more replete with analytical quicksand than were the previous arenas. This arises partly for the same reasons outlined in Chapters 9 and 10 but also because regulation produces even less short-term "data" than that found in the other realms of implementation. Thus one is left with a form of soft evidence, or a "trial by anecdote." This makes it hard to assemble tables of data, but does not make the evidence cited unreal. Regulatory dynamics are untidy because proponents line up at the regulatory negotiating window asking simultaneously to be treated like everyone else, but also to be treated as a special case. The regulatory bodies, moreover, are part of a government which also owns the resource, and whose regulations apply to Crown and mixed enterprises, whose very purpose is to give the government greater leverage and knowledge on how to manage and control development in the face of an otherwise overwhelmingly privately owned industry.

So it is that regulatory implementation, like the other arenas of implementation, involves heavy doses of public and private behaviour. In Canada's vulnerable and uncertain northern and offshore Canada Lands, however, the dynamics of implementation are couched in even larger amounts of uncertainty, technological novelty, and environmental fragility. Yet it is here that the NEP's geo-political objectives, along with those of security of supply, are rooted.

Notes

1. See A. Lucas, *The National Energy Board* (Ottawa: Law Reform Commission, 1977); Ian McDougall, "The Canadian National Energy Board: Economic Jurisprudence in the National Interest or Symbolic Reassurance?" *Alberta Law Review*, vol. 11, no. 2 (1973), pp. 327–382; John N. McDougall, *Fuels and the National Policy* (Toronto: Butterworths, 1982); and John R. Baldwin, "Federal Regulation and Public Policy in the Canadian Petroleum Industry: 1958–1975," *Journal of Business Administration*, vol. 13, nos. 1 and 2, 1982, pp. 57–96. Our discussion of the transformation of regulation from a "policing" to a "development" mode draws on Richard Schultz, "Regulatory Agencies and the Dilemmas of Delegation," in O.P. Dwividi, ed., *The Administrative State in Canada* (Toronto: University of Toronto Press, 1982), pp. 89–106.

2. For an account of the evolution of the Alberta regulatory system, see John Richards and Larry Pratt, *Prairie Capitalism: Power and Influence in the New West* (Toronto: McClelland and Stewart, 1979), chapters 3 and 4.

3. See David Brooks, *Zero Energy Growth for Canada* (Toronto: McClelland and Stewart, 1981), chapters 5 and 6. For an assessment of the politics of energy forecasting, see John B. Robinson, "Pendulum Policy: Natural Gas Forecasts and Canadian Energy Policy 1969–1981," *Canadian Journal of Political Science*, vol. XVI, no. 2 (June 1983), pp. 299–320.

4. See Senate of Canada, *Marching to the Beat of the Same Drum: Transportation of Petroleum and Natural Gas North of 60°*, Report of the Special Committee on the Northern Pipeline (Ottawa: Supply and Services, March 1983).

5. Ian McDougall, *op. cit.*, p. 327.

6. The description of the COGLA mandate and process is taken from official government publications. See Department of Energy, Mines and Resources, "Presentation by COGLA to Special Committee of the Senate on the Northern Pipeline" (Ottawa: EMR, September 14, 1982) and Canada Oil and Gas Lands Administration, *Annual Report* 1982 and 1983 (Ottawa: EMR, 1983, 1984). See also Senate of Canada, Proceedings of the Standing Senate Committee on Energy and Natural Resources, no. 7, May 15, 1984 (Ottawa: Supply and Services Canada, 1984).

7. See Roger Voyer, *Offshore Oil: Opportunities for Industrial Development and Job Creation* (Ottawa: Canadian Institute for Economic Policy, 1983).

8. The nature and politics of the developmental task in the north is examined in several books. See E. Dosman, *The National Interest: The Politics of Northern Development 1968–1975* (Toronto: McClelland and Stewart, 1975); Gurstan Dacks, *A Choice of Futures: Politics in the Canadian North* (Toronto: Methuen, 1981); and François Bregha, *Bob Blair's Pipeline: The Business and Politics of Northern Energy Development Projects* (Toronto: Lorimer, 1979).

9. See Geological Survey of Canada, *Oil and Natural Gas Resources of Canada 1983* (Ottawa: Energy, Mines and Resources Canada, 1984), p. 1. See also *Globe and Mail*, October 12, 1983, p. B1.

10. Treasury Board of Canada, *Beaufort Sea Oil Transportation Alternatives*, a report to the Departments of Energy, Mines and Resources and Indian and Northern Affairs (Ottawa: July 16, 1982).

11. See Reg Lang, "Environmental Impact Assessment: Reform or Rhetoric?" in William Leiss, ed., *Ecology Versus Politics in Canada* (Toronto: University of Toronto Press, 1979), pp. 233–251, and William Rees, Reflections on the Environmental Assessment and Review Process: A Discussion Paper (unpublished), School of Community and Regional Planning, University of British Columbia, November, 1979.

12. John Helliwell, "Canadian Energy Policy," *Annual Review of Energy*, vol. 4 (1979), pp. 175–229.

13. *Ibid.*, pp. 221–222.

14. *Ibid.*, p. 223.
15. Senate of Canada, Proceedings of the Senate Standing Committee on Energy and Natural Resources, no. 1, April 4, 1984 (Ottawa: Supply and Services Canada, 1984), p. 13.
16. For general background, see Voyer, *op. cit.*, pp. 42–46, and Peter Eglington and Maris Ufflemann, *An Economic Analysis of the Venture Development Project and Hibernia,* Discussion Paper no. 261 (Ottawa: Economic Council of Canada, 1984).
17. See Larry Pratt, "Petro Canada: Tool of Energy Security or Instrument of Economic Development" in G. Bruce Doern, ed., *How Ottawa Spends Your Tax Dollars 1982* (Toronto: Lorimer, 1982), chapter 4.
18. See Glen Williams, *Not For Export* (Toronto: McClelland and Stewart, 1983).

CHAPTER 12

ENERGY POLITICS: A NEW BALANCE OF POWER?

We have presented as comprehensive a look as possible at the NEP and energy politics in the oil and gas sector. The genesis of the NEP was first examined in the context of the short-term dynamics of the 1979–1980 period. In the second part of the book we located contemporary energy politics and public policy in the larger context of the post-World War II period, showing how energy policy increasingly but persistently became imbued with many of the core ideas and interests inherent in governing Canada. It focussed on the two major relationships of power—intergovernmental and government–industry—in the pre-NEP period, and enabled us to examine in greater detail how different interests interacted. We continued this dual focus in the third part, which covered the post-NEP years from 1981 to 1984. In the fourth part of the book our attention shifted more completely to the NEP itself as a public policy, including a detailed look at the dynamics of implementation where the latter is understood to involve both public and private behaviour. The unfolding of the NEP and of other events was examined in each of the main taxing and pricing, expenditure, and regulatory domains.

Central to our portrayal of energy politics has been the concept of "interests." Interests have the capacity to exercise power. That capacity is rooted in the existence of three core institutions: capitalism, federalism, and cabinet–parliamentary government. We have examined interests in at least two levels of detail. Within the energy industry we have distinguished between the foreign-owned majors, the Canadian-owned majors, the second-line Canadian firms, and the Canadian juniors. At a more detailed level, we have analysed such major firms as Imperial Oil, Dome, Petro-Canada, Texaco, Nova, and Gulf Canada as distinct interests. Similarly within the governmental sector, we have focussed on the divergent positions and actions of the federal government, and the government of Ontario and Alberta.

Other provinces have been examined in much less detail to illustrate other facets of energy politics.

A focus on interests is also essential in the more specific context of the NEP because, as we have argued throughout the book, the fundamental political purpose of the NEP was to alter the structure of power between Ottawa and the industry as a whole, between Ottawa and foreign-owned energy interests in particular, and between Ottawa and Alberta.

Our focus has been on these two major relationships of power and the assessment of their interrelated development over time. Each of the major interests analysed is relevant in that each has exhibited at various points throughout the post-war period that it has power, and that under certain conditions it will attempt to exercise it. The relevance and importance of both public and private sector decisions in the determination of what does and does not happen in the Canadian energy arena shows that power emanates both from private interests and state interests.

The Possession and Exercise of Power in Canadian Energy Politics: The New Balance
1947-1973

Canadian energy politics in this period were essentially characterized by consensual relations. Both industry and government fundamentally and consciously agreed on the need to ensure the growth and expansion of the industry. One of the few expressions of concern during this period was the Gordon Royal Commission's warning about the implications of foreign domination of the petroleum industry. None of the governments paid much attention to the Commission's concerns, in part because government–industry relationships (both federal and provincial) were predominantly industry-oriented, in the sense that the industry was knowingly given wide latitude by both the federal and provincial governments in the development of Canada's oil and gas reserves. Moreover, because the federal and provincial governments shared the objective of encouraging oil and gas production and of stimulating the growth of the domestic petroleum industry during a period of stable world prices, there was a basic consensus of values between federal and provincial governments over the management of Canada's growing oil and gas reserves. Thus, this earliest period of Canadian energy politics was one of limited government interference in the industry and of generally congenial intergovernmental relations. Even so, there were a number of instances where the various interests exercised or attempted to exercise power, and in so doing, differentiated their positions from one another.

The Trans-Canada Pipeline issue underlined two historical debates in Canadian energy politics: the use of public enterprise, as opposed to other governing instruments, to ensure the achievement of government objectives; and the choice between nationalist as opposed to continentalist solutions to Canadian energy problems (particularly as embodied in partisan political debate). The federal Liberal government exposed the considerable power possessed by a majority government by essentially forcing their legislative plan through the frenzied House of Commons. However, the opposition parties showed that they are not entirely without power, as they were able to focus on the Liberals' treatment of Parliament as well as the Liberals' chosen pipeline strategy to convince the Canadian electorate to throw the Liberals out of office in the subsequent election. Both Gulf and Trans-Canada Pipelines Ltd. were able to exercise some considerable power in shaping Liberal policy and in gaining material concessions from the Liberals. Their power was enhanced by the Liberals' commitment to an all-Canadian line but refusal on ideological grounds to build the project entirely by public enterprise.

The Borden Commission's rejection of Home Oil's Alberta-to-Montreal oil pipeline proposal—which reflected the concerns of security and national integration—and the subsequent introduction of the National Oil Policy by the Diefenbaker Conservatives—which particularly reflected Imperial Oil's arguments about economic efficiency and regional self-interest—as well as a range of other Commission and government decisions on pricing and exports, revealed the prodigious power of the industry in Canadian energy politics throughout this period, and the domination of the industry by the multinationals. The NOP, however, also produced benefits sought by Alberta and by eastern provincial governments. One major political resource enjoyed solely by the industry in this period was its control over the vital geological, technical, economic, and financial information necessary to make policy. At least in part for this reason, throughout the 1950s and 1960s the provincial governments, the

Borden Commission, and various federal governments adopted an approach to energy questions which reflected the logic, interests and ideas of the global and continental planning systems of the multinational majors. It is also important to stress, however, that there was a basic consensus between the relevant provincial governments, the U.S. government, and the federal government over the National Oil Policy.

Nevertheless, there were, in the 1950s, several examples of governments identifying their interests as being distinct from those of the other levels of government. The best examples are Ottawa's 1949 move to strengthen its control over the international and inter-provincial trade in oil and gas by introducing the **Pipe Lines Act**. The Alberta government reacted to this as well as to the provincial Dinning Commission's recommendation to satisfy and protect Alberta needs first by passing several new pieces of legislation, including the **Gas Resources Conservation Act**. Alberta moved in 1954 in the face of the impending approval of the Trans-Canada project to create Alberta Gas Trunk Line. The participants in these various government legislative initiatives passed them with an eye on one another, and a sense of mutual suspicion over each other's intentions. While in the process they expanded somewhat the potential role of each government in the oil and gas industry, their initiatives can now be viewed as largely pre-emptive acts in which the various governments armed themselves with legislative instruments that would be useful in future struggles.

1973-1980

The price and supply shocks induced by the 1973 OPEC crisis extinguished the relatively calm and consensual relations which governed the major relationships of power throughout the 1960s. The quadrupling of the world oil price dramatically raised the stakes of energy politics in Canada, and crystalized for the producing provinces, the consuming provinces, the federal government, and the industry the recognition that they each had distinct and, to some degree, conflicting interests with respect to oil and gas pricing and revenue sharing.

The rapidly increasing international price, and the even less rapidly increasing national price, meant there were considerable economic rents up for grabs. The magnitude of the revenue, and the importance of its capture for the participating interests, raised the stakes and clarified the conflicts and coincidences of interest between them. The struggles over pricing and revenue sharing were as acrimonious and hard fought as they were precisely because each of the relevant interests had either the constitutional authority, political power, or economic power to defend their concerns, as they interpreted them.

Despite the expansion of state authority, the increased involvement by both levels of government, and the resultant quantum increase in the number of regulatory instruments with which it had to contend, the industry—as the Syncrude case showed—remained a powerful interest because of its control over the productive apparatus, the major sources of technological and geological information, and the major pools of investment capital for future exploration and production. The establishment of Petro-Canada and a number of provincial state oil companies can in large part be understood as a direct government reaction to this dominance, an attempt to reduce these aspects of industry power. The establishment of Petro-Canada and the outcome of the northern pipeline issue also contributed to a shift in the intra-industry configuration of power. Indeed, one of the major developments of the 1973–1980 period was the emergence of a few large Canadian-controlled companies capable of competing in a meaningful way with the foreign-controlled majors.

The overall result of the confrontations of this period was increased government authority, assertiveness, and intervention in the energy policy field. Concomitantly, the industry's power in both of the key government–industry relationships declined. The net effect, then, was that the government–industry and federal government–producing province relationships became much more balanced than had been the case, with the federal government (relative to the producing provinces) and both levels of government (relative to the industry) strengthening their capabilities and positions. The Alberta–Ontario relationship shifted decidedly in favour of Alberta, and Ontario came to rely more and more on the federal government to guard its interests. This was especially so after the breakdown in 1975–76 of the First Ministers' Conference as a meaningful forum for establishing oil and gas prices.

The period from mid-1974 to 1978 was one of relative calm on the international energy scene, characterized by decreasing real world oil prices. Things had quieted down in Canada as well. The Canadian oil price moved in stages toward the world price, and many of the wounds created by the 1973–74 conflicts began to heal. The Joe Clark-led Conservatives had the misfortune to form their first national government in sixteen years just as the world price for oil was skyrocketing in the wake of the Iranian revolution. The 1973–74 conflicts in Canadian energy politics resulted from the fundamental conflicts of interest within the two major relationships of power. These conflicting interests were still present in 1979. Indeed, they had intensified, because of the increased understanding of the interregional consequences of rapid and large price increases, and by the fact that the same party formed the government in Edmonton, Ottawa, and Toronto. The regional and ideological strains within the minority federal Conservative government made it difficult to develop policy in a period of extreme uncertainty.

The bargaining strategy employed by the Alberta Conservative government revealed the considerable power that a major producing province can wield in Canadian energy politics. While Alberta almost came to an agreement with the Clark Conservatives, their hardline stance during negotiations galvanized the Davis Conservative government of Ontario to mobilize a campaign to discredit the Alberta and ultimately the Clark government's positions on price, revenue-sharing and Petro-Canada. The Davis government's campaign shows that a major consuming province is itself not without power in Canadian energy politics, particularly when it contains one third of all Canadian voters in a period of minority government. If anything, the federal Conservatives overestimated their power to govern or, more specifically, to pass a budget in a minority Parliament. The internecine quarreling between the three Conservative governments, at this point, worked to the distinct disadvantage of two of them. Bill Davis, Joe Clark and Peter Lougheed had each gambled on energy issues at various points in the 1970s and each, at one point, lost in a major way. Just as Davis gambled and lost in 1975 when his intransigence at the April First Ministers' Conference led to the demise of the Conference as a forum for price negotiations, and thus removed Ontario and the other consuming provinces from the negotiating table, so also did the Lougheed government's intransigence with the Clark government prove to be a strategy that backfired, as it ultimately contributed to the demise of the Clark government and the return to power of a Liberal government willing to take a much tougher stance with Alberta. The Clark government, in part at least because of the pressure placed on it by the industry and the Alberta government, proved incapable of making the sorts of concessions which would have allowed it to strike a deal with the ideologically aligned Québec Social Credit MPs, which would have assured the successful passage of the budget.

1980-1984

The NEP was clearly a shock to each of the major relationships of power in Canadian energy politics. This is precisely what it was intended to be. In the immediate sense, the NEP, and its unilateral imposition, was a bargaining ploy designed to force a solution to the pricing and revenue-sharing dilemmas created by the huge increases in the international price. The NEP was directly preceded by two sets of tense and unsuccessful federal–provincial negotiations, a vicious inter-provincial battle, and an angry and hard-fought partisan contest. Given the pervasive assumption that oil prices would continue to rise towards $100 barrels of oil by the end of the decade, energy costs and supplies, it was assumed, would be a major factor governing Canadian political and economic development throughout the 1980s. In the larger context of the Liberals' overall program, once they returned to power after the Clark interregnum, the NEP can be viewed as part of an interrelated effort by the recentralizing Liberals to reaffirm the central government's economic management powers and political visibility. The November 1981 **Economic Development for Canada in the 1980s** document revealed the extent to which the Liberals hoped to use energy developments to fill federal coffers, to revitalize the Canadian economy, and to enhance the economic management role of the federal government. In the historical context of the previous eight years, the NEP—in particular the revenue-sharing, resource management and Canadianization elements—can be seen as an attempt to address some longer-term economic and political problems, and to restructure the main relationships of power. The aggressive "act first, talk later" strategy of the NEP and the polemical tone of the document with its specific differentiation of regional, governmental and industry interests, can best be understood in this context.

The NEP named names, identifying those who were part of the

problem and those who would be favoured in bringing about the solution. As such, it threw up a major challenge to the power of the foreign majors and the producing provinces. As we saw in Chapters 6 and 7, the various affected interests responded both rhetorically and concretely to the NEP. Yet, those who have the capacity only to talk, and not to act, obviously have less clout. Each of the major interests identified and analyzed in this study has the capacity to act, and in order to appreciate the relative balances within the relationships of power, one must assess both the talk and the action of the various interests.

The Alberta Premier and key ministers unleashed a strong series of verbal denunciations of the NEP, linking it to the Trudeau constitutional reform package and the tactics that accompanied it, and charging that together they constituted a plan by the "Ottawa" government and the central Canadian provinces to capture control of the western provinces' resources, and to ensure that all provinces except Ontario and Québec remained second-class citizens. Both because the Ontario government had attacked the Alberta position during the Clark period and because Ontario voters, essentially, turned the Clark government out of office, Alberta focussed its attack on Ontario.

Compared to its strident condemnation of Alberta during the Clark regime, along with its portrayal of the Ontario economy as synonymous with the national economy, Ontario's silence in the wake of the NEP was deafening. Bill Davis indicated he regretted Alberta's attacks on Ontario and was saddened by Alberta's response, in particular the production cutback. Frank Miller argued that the NEP was a constructive approach to a national energy strategy, and the Ontario government continued to express support for Petro-Canada.

As indicated by our analysis of Imperial Oil, Texaco, and Gulf, the multinationals individually and as a group (through the CPA) condemned virtually all aspects of the NEP. The combination of restrained prices and increased taxes, they charged, would vitiate the achievement of self-sufficiency by not providing the industry with the investment capital via netbacks to do the necessary exploration and development. This charge largely remained intact after the September 1981 Canada–Alberta Agreement, since while the agreement raised prices, it also raised taxes. While not criticizing the concept of

Canadianization, the multinationals as a whole condemned the means chosen to achieve it. They all criticized the PIPs, which discriminated against them, and denounced the Crown interest as confiscatory. Virtually all of these firms attacked the Petro-Canada expansion and some, such as Imperial Oil, expressed doubt that the Canadian firms favoured by the NEP had the necessary financial capacity to play a major role on the Canada Lands. The multinationals also challenged the accuracy and legitimacy of the **State of Competition in the Canadian Petroleum Industry Report** and its charges.

The Canadian majors expressed support for Canadianization, though the firms had mixed opinions on whether the PIP approach was better than the tax incentives system. This was particularly the case for Dome as it had been a major recipient of tax incentives. Like the rest of the industry the Canadian majors, including Petro-Canada, doubted the price increases were large enough to stimulate the necessary activity, particularly when combined with the new taxes. The second-line Canadian firms responded in diverse ways. They offered their share of verbal criticism, but also altered their investment strategies to take advantage of the PIP grants. The Canadian juniors are a disparate group, and reacted verbally in various ways. What is clear, though, is that their organization, IPAC, along with some individual firms, unleashed strident condemnations of the overall interventionist thrust of the NEP, the expansion of Petro-Canada, the increased taxes and restrained price increases, and an incentive system which favoured activity in the frontiers far away from their base in the western sedimentary basin.

In addition to their verbal response, the various interests had the capacity for action as well. While their verbal reactions were meant to influence public opinion and to let the other interests know where they stood, these interests are important in Canadian energy politics because they also have the capacity to "put their money where their mouth is." By reviewing the concrete behaviour of the various interests, we have a better understanding of the possession and exercise of power.

The most immediate concrete reaction to the NEP was Premier Peter Lougheed's October 30, 1980, prime-time television address to the people of Alberta. During this address the Premier outlined Alberta's three-pronged retaliation—the production cutbacks, the constitutional challenge to the tax on natural gas exports, and the withholding of approval for the Alsands and Cold Lake mega-projects.

Reflecting their overall satisfaction with the NEP, Ontario government ministers kept a low profile during this tense period, intentionally saying little that could rile the western provincial leaders. At the same time Ontario joined in an alliance with the federal government on the constitutional patriation issue. In October 1981, the Ontario government materially signalled its support for the Liberals' Canadianization objectives by spending $650 million to purchase 25 percent of Suncor.

The reaction of the multinationals was to signal their anger by cutting exploration budgets for 1981 and 1982. When it became apparent that most of the NEP would remain intact for several years, a number of the foreign majors with land-holdings on the Canada Lands decided to take advantage of the NEP and reduce their risks by farming out sections of their land-holdings to Canadian-controlled firms eligible for high levels of PIP grants. The multinationals, through the CPA, commissioned a public opinion survey, and based on its findings, which indicated a poor public image of the oil and gas industry, organized a $3 million advocacy advertising campaign to improve the industry's overall image.

Among the Canadian majors, Dome and Petro-Canada made the most concrete moves in support of Canadianization by making major acquisitions of foreign firms and, in Dome's case, by establishing a new Canadian-owned subsidary. Nova made a minor purchase and extended its operations onto the Canada Lands. Dome and Petro-Canada were already very active on the frontiers. The Canadian banks were falling all over themselves to lend money to Canadian firms to buy foreign-owned oil companies, and in terms of numbers, the majority of the acquisitions were undertaken by the larger juniors. Nevertheless, in the period immediately following the NEP, many of the juniors indicated their anger by shifting some of their exploration to the U.S. western basin. Other juniors spent money to farm-in to the land holdings of the foreign majors in the Canada Lands. In other words, many of the Canadian juniors vigorously attacked the NEP verbally, but also moved to take material advantage for their share-holders of the various inducements embodied in the NEP. Others within the junior camp tried to distance themselves from their more strident peers, and lobbied Ottawa separately from IPAC in an attempt to get some alteration to the NEP taxes and pricing system that would help the junior firms.

While the various industry interests and provincial governments employed these various power tactics in an attempt to change all or parts of the NEP, the federal government itself reacted both verbally and concretely to the charges and actions of the other interests. In March 1981, Ottawa released the **State of Competition in the Canadian Petroleum Industry**. This report conveniently materialized at about the height of the industry media campaign against the NEP. In charging the multinationals with "ripping off" Canadian consumers to the tune of $12 billion between 1958 and 1973, and by commencing a Restrictive Trade Practices Commission investigation, the government was able to force the industry back on the defensive. The government, however, also remained on the defensive, paradoxically, as a result of the run-away success of its own Canadianization policy. By mid-1981 acquisitions worth more than $6 billion had been made by Canadian firms in the wake of the NEP. Concerned about the impact of such a rapid transfer of assets out of the country, Finance Minister MacEachen called on representatives of the major banks to help slow down the rate of takeover by Canadian firms by making loans less readily available. In June 1981 the **Report of the Major Projects Task Force** was released. It argued that energy developments would be among the leading activities of the Canadian economy in the future, and concurred with the NEP that formal steps would have to be taken to ensure maximum Canadian benefits from developments in a sector traditionally dominated by foreign firms.

Responding to growing political and economic pressure from other provinces and other industrial sectors, the Alberta and federal government finally came to an agreement in September 1981.The Memorandum of Agreement represented a compromise which reflected the power of both of these governments. Alberta was able to extract higher prices and therefore more revenue for itself and, it claimed, the industry. As shown above, the industry, which had mistakenly assumed that the Alberta government could force the federal government into the compromises the industry was demanding, was shocked to learn that the outcome of the negotiations reflected Alberta's self-interest. The federal government acceded to the higher prices, and in exchange got the Alberta government to pay for the PIP program in Alberta. Developments on the international stage ended the upward movement of oil prices, on which the Canada–Alberta fiscal arrangements were based. This provided additional evidence to buttress the industry agrument that the combined government take was too great. Both governments responded by providing financial and fiscal incentives to "sweeten the pot" for the Alsands mega-project. Both levels of government responded to industry pressure and the overall recessionary atmosphere by announcing significant financial concessions to the industry. In April 1980, Alberta announced a $5.4 billion program of royalty reductions and special grants and credits. In May 1982 the federal NEP-Update, which included $2 billion worth of federal tax concessions, was released.

When in March 1983 the OPEC countries finally agreed to reduce the benchmark price to $29 U.S. per barrel, it became obvious to everyone that the pricing scenario of the September 1981 Agreement was not to transpire. Canadian price had already exceeded 75 percent of world price, and a price increase scheduled for July 1983 had to be cancelled. As a result, Edmonton and Ottawa were forced to renegotiate the September pricing and revenue-sharing arrangement. By this point both governments had a strong stake in making the system work, and accommodations were arrived at with a minimum of conflict. Ottawa suffered the greatest relative loss in revenue share.

Thus we can see that the dynamic and volatile period which followed the introduction of the NEP was characterized by numerous attempts to exercise power, including charges and countercharges and several concrete acts among the range of interests involved. Dominating energy politics in Canada is an overarching three-sided triad of powerful interests represented by the federal government, the producing province governments (predominantly Alberta), and the industry. Each of these interests, as has been shown, has power or the ability to act independently to realize its will and to achieve its objectives. Yet it is a power that is constrained by the countervailing possession of power by the other contending interests in each of the relationships.

The NEP was, therefore, in some respects, a massive catch-up act. In the 1950s and 1960s the industry was by far the dominant interest because it was the "doer." It had the technology, the skills, the knowledge, and the capital to do something the governments wanted. This gave the industry a great deal of bargaining power with which to secure favourable arrangements. It also gave both levels of government incentive to provide the industry with the "environment" it wanted and needed to get on with developing Canadian potential in oil and gas.

The industry is often portrayed by its critics as the all-powerful leviathan of Canadian energy politics, manipulating governments into doing its bidding, and by the industry itself as a paper tiger, tied down with regulations at every turn, misunderstood by the public, and unappreciated and tightly controlled by government. The historical analysis shows that it is neither of these. Despite what some in the industry argue, the NEP did not strip the industry of power, because it did not fundamentally dispossess the industry of the basis of its power, that is, its control over the productive apparatus and the major pools of investment capital. Moreover, it must be understood that none of the relevant governments viewed the increased state intervention, represented by the NEP and the earlier state regulations, as representing a fundamental challenge to the capitalist organization of the oil and gas sector.

The NEP did, of course, attempt to encourage shifts between the elements of the private sector in pursuit of Canadian ownership objectives. The NEP did not, however (despite some rumblings in the actual NEP document that the state-owned sector would increase significantly), represent a fundamental shift to state capitalism. By far the vast majority of the assets in the Canadian oil industry are privately owned. Despite popular support to do so, Petro-Canada did not attempt to acquire one of the big six foreign-owned firms (Imperial, Gulf, Texaco, Shell, Amoco, Mobil) which led the Canadian Industry in 1979–80. Five of these are American-owned, and the hostile challenge to the NEP by the Reagan Administration can, in part, account for Petro-Canada's reluctance. Interestingly, the two firms from which state-owned Petro-Canada acquired assets were European-owned. Nevertheless, there can be no doubt that as a result of the NEP, the industry now takes much greater notice of the federal government. This is in part because it now knows that Ottawa acted decisively once, and therefore may do so again; because the incentive grant system has made the industry openly more dependent upon federal agencies; and because a new regulatory regime and a greatly expanded Petro-Canada are in place. It is, therefore, clear that in this overall sense, the industry has a much better understanding of the power which a federal government can wield in Canadian energy politics. The days of the industry lobbying primarily the Alberta government and then relying on it to defend the industry's interest in negotiations with the federal government are past. The NEP and subsequent events have taught all elements of the industry that both the federal and provincial governments have both power and their own interests.

Despite the fact that the overall level of federal government intervention increased substantially between 1973 and 1980, the Liberals felt that throughout the 1970s energy developments, in combination with developments in other social and economic policy fields, had resulted in an overall shift of responsibility and activity to the provincial level, with a corresponding weakening of federal authority and power. Indeed many scholars agreed with the Liberal analysis, at least to the extent that "province building" was identified as one of the most important phenomena in Canadian politics in the 1970s. While there are several different contributing factors, as well as contending explanations, of the exact nature of this new surge in province building, the resources boom of the late 1960s and early 1970s, and in particular the increases in oil and gas prices which followed the OPEC crisis, are usually identified as being among the most important catalysts and forces to drive province building. It was the oil-flush Alberta government which produced in 1978 the **Harmony in Diversity: A New Federalism for Canada** document, perhaps the most lucid statement for a decentralized confederation yet developed.

The Liberals only seemed to grasp the extent of the centrifugal movement under way in Canada federalism when they were provided with a new vantage point from which to view proceedings by the May 1979 election of the Clark Conservative government. The NEP, therefore, was intended to be a signal of a revitalized central government as well as a bargaining stance in the continuing price and revenue-sharing negotiations. That is why the NEP, even though it had an economic basis, must be understood as first and foremost a political act which was intended to enhance federal power vis-à-vis provincial and industry power.

We conclude, at least for the short-term 1980 to 1984 period, that the introduction of the NEP, in conjunction with other federal initiatives, did in fact alter the balance of power within both the government–industry and intergovernmental relationships of power. While the industry as a whole and the producing province governments have remained powerful interests, the new-found federal assertiveness in the early 1980s did result in a discernible shift in federal power relative to provincial and industry power.

Can the Power Balance Be Sustained?

The important question in the realm of political power in energy politics is: "to what extent is the greater evenness in power relations likely to continue?" Or stated more specifically, "to what extent is the recent post-NEP federal position in the two power relationships sustainable?" To address such a question is to engage in a speculative exercise. By now one would think that pundits would have been cured from engaging in such exercises, replete as they are with pitfalls and minefields. This is probably particularly true for Canadian energy politics which, as we have seen in the past, are conditioned by and subject to major global factors, such as whether the last half of the 1980s remains a period of relative calm in the international political economy of energy, or whether the world is once again plunged into a period of international energy crisis. Yet our analysis of the post-war period of Canadian energy politics does provide some basis for thinking about the future. Just as the forecasters were humbled by their wildly inaccurate 1979–1981 projections regarding oil and gas price, supply and demand, we too recognize that the volatile and often scabrous world of energy politics can easily humble those who attempt to envisage the future.

There is no question that the NEP was a traumatic experience for the industry as a whole. In both a political and economic sense, the different elements of the industry were treated differently. Reduced demand for oil and gas, dampened prices and, for many companies, high debt levels exacerbated by high interest rates, remain a problem. Natural gas producers, in particular the small Canadian firms whose primary production is natural gas, were suffering in the mid-1980s from the lack of markets for their shut-in gas. It was the multi-nationals who were chastised in the NEP; yet in 1984 it was the multi-nationals who were still in the best economic shape (though some of the Canadian majors and second-line Canadian firms were also in good shape, considering the overall condition of the industry), and they were once again rounding into shape politically. The large oil com-panies, both individually and as a group through the CPA, have extensive analytical and lobbying resources. While the oil companies as a whole and the multinationals in particular are far more aware of Ottawa's potential to act decisively on energy issues, and more cognizant of Alberta's willingness to act independently towards its own ends even at the risk of offending the industry, the industry has not, throughout the entire post-NEP period, ceased applying relentless pressure to alter the NEP. Although it took them a long time (and agreement between the Canadian and foreign-owned firms was arrived at only with considerable difficulty), the big companies developed through the CPA an energy policy strategy which in the spring of 1984 the CPA presented as an alternative to the NEP. The alternative energy program, not surprisingly, comprised a major critique of the NEP and was intended in large part to influence the energy strategy adopted by the Mulroney Conservative government elected in September, 1984. If adopted in its entirety, the program would essentially "gut" the NEP.

The oil industry position, in the largest sense, has, since the NEP, been supported by a series of other interests. Many of the major oil companies are important members of the Business Council on National Issues (BCNI) which in 1984 brought together the key government and industry leaders in a series of private energy meetings. The BCNI is well funded, and the most powerful business lobby in Canada. It can act as a forum for the discussion of conflicts between the major oil and gas producers and the major oil- and gas-consuming industrial sectors. The Canadian banks, despite their rush to lend money to Canadian companies to purchase foreign-owned firms, along with the Canadian business media, have been relentless critics of the NEP. On the issues of pricing, exploration incentives, and Canadianization, for example, the multinationals in particular have found intellectual allies among some of the major Canadian think tanks. The Economic Council of Canada, the C.D. Howe Institute, the neo-conservative Fraser Institute, as well as several university-based economists, have published studies critical of the NEP which have provided useful ammunition for NEP critics, both in and outside of the industry. The combination of their free enterprise ethos and an avowed emphasis on economic efficiency as the dominant evaluative criterion provides a strong political-economic critique of federal policy, in particular its interventionist, centralist, and nationalist dimensions. Private sector supporters of the NEP are few, and it was increasingly clear that the federal government proponents and their intellectual allies in the universities and press were less and less able to match the prowess of the anti-NEP critics.

Clearly, in 1984 the oil and gas industry as a whole was attempting to reduce federal power in Canadian energy politics by gearing up the lobby for the adoption of a less interventionist approach, reflected, for example, in such specific policies as world price, a slow shift of the incentive system from grants back to tax breaks and reduced federal taxes. In this they are supported by much of the rest of the Canadian corporate sector, the business media, and their intellectual allies. Such alterations as the above would indeed reduce the day-to-day involvement of the federal government in energy policy in the latter part of the 1980s, and could result in reduced federal power. This would be the case particularly if the federal government which made such alterations did so precisely to signal less government intervention as a feature of a new approach to energy issues.

The Conservative government of Alberta was clearly challenged by the federal Liberals in the NEP. Yet, electorally, the Alberta government has a massive majority, and will survive to fight again and negotiate further energy arrangements with Ottawa. Moreover, the Alberta energy technocracy is intact and now even more experienced in dealing with Ottawa than in 1979–1981. Nevertheless, the lesson of the NEP for Alberta is that under certain circumstances the federal government can act decisively. As the 1979–1980 period showed, the Ontario government is also prepared to mobilize itself and public opinion on energy policy issues if the policies appear destined seriously to harm the provincial economy. Moreover, the Alberta economy in the mid-1980s is significantly less buoyant than it was in 1979, and there is a more sober sentiment in Alberta about the prospects of using oil and gas developments to diversify or restructure the provincial economy away from its dependence on resources. Yet Alberta can be counted on to continue opposing the NEP and federal policy on pricing, revenue sharing, and resource management. If there are no major price shocks in the next few years, Ontario is more likely to soften its position on pricing and revenue sharing, though if there is a major price increase, Ontario could reasonably be expected to mount the same arguments it marshalled in 1979.

Given the entrenched status of its two major antagonists in the key power relationships, there is no question that the federal Liberal pro-NEP forces are vulnerable. Even before its crushing defeat in the 1984 election there was, within the Liberal Party, a wing which would willingly make major amendments to the NEP, particularly its most interventionist features. Initial evidence for this was present during the 1984 election campaign, when the Turner Liberals announced the partial de-regulation of gas export prices and pledged a rapid movement to world price for oil. At the bureaucratic level, few of the original NEP team remain in the Department of Energy, Mines and Resources. EMR's high-growth days are over, and there is less of a feeling of pride of authorship there than was once the case. Even before the victory of the Mulroney Conservatives in the September 1984 election, opinion in EMR had shifted away from defending NEP programs, even to the extent of raising questions about its key principles.

The Conservatives revealed their energy policy just prior to the start of the 1984 election campaign. The first point to stress about it is that Mulroney actually gives the NEP some credit, noting that "some elements of the NEP have been helpful to the economy in parts of Canada."[1] This had not been said by Tory critics before and reflects, at a minimum, the real politique that Mulroney had to respect in order to protect his support in Atlantic Canada. The Tories, however, do super-impose above the stated "security, Canadianization, and fairness" objectives of the NEP which they retain, an overriding economic objective, namely that of "developing energy resources as an engine of growth." Some of the economic edge to the Tory package won support from the oil and gas industry and from Western Canada.

But closer scrutiny of the Tory package reveals that key concepts in the NEP could have a staying power that one would not at first glance recognize, especially in the light of the virtual hallelujah chorus that has accompanied both Tory and industry rhetoric against the NEP over the past four years. Closer scrutiny suggests that far from "gutting" the NEP, the Tories are repackaging the NEP. The PIP grants are to be replaced gradually by "transferable" tax credits rather than a return to the pre-NEP fiscal regime. This recognizes that Canadian firms must "somehow" be favoured.

The PGRT is to be replaced by taxes on profits. Since the PGRT was the tax most associated with the view that Ottawa was engaged in a "revenue grab," it would appear that Tory Ottawa will grab the revenue in different ways, since there is no disavowal in the Conservative package that the higher share of oil and gas revenues achieved by the Liberals is inappropriate, given the national responsibilities of the federal government. Given the size of the federal deficit, the plain fact also is that the federal government needs the money. The 25 percent Crown interest is to be replaced by a Tory "Canada share" but one that is not retroactive. This is a gesture to the United States, but it is a far cry from earlier promises that the entire concept was unacceptable, indeed, an example of Trudeau "socialism." There is an acceptance in the Tory plan that past tax breaks and grants are indeed a form of public investment that warrants some kind of ownership claim.

On the pricing front, despite the obvious references to a return to market forces, there is a Conservative commitment to their own form of interventionism. Thus, if there are "sudden" price increases (e.g., as in 1979–80), the Tories "will protect the energy consumer,"[2] and although Canadian gas will be sold at "market-sensitive" prices (the new euphemism for administered prices), Canadians will "pay less than their American neighbours" for exported gas.

As for Petro-Canada, whose expansion was a central part of the NEP, the Conservatives now plan to keep it but promise to commit funds only if it is explicitly linked to Petro-Canada's self-sufficiency role as opposed to its downstream activities. The NEP's "off-oil" incentive programs will be combined into one program in the Tory plan and the NEP's important changes in the regulatory regime on the Canada Lands will be left intact.

The underlying reason that the NEP will be altered but not emasculated is that key features of the NEP, despite the economic criticisms of it, are politically attractive and appeal to a range of values important to Canadians as a whole. The NEP was intended to alter the balance of power in the oil and gas industry and the Tory package recognizes, albeit begrudgingly, that it has partly done this.

It is also important to remember that a third of Canada's federal voters still live in energy-consuming Ontario and the federal Liberals and Conservatives both know that public opinion on the issue of foreign ownership and on the acceptability of public enterprise—especially in a crisis situation—is an important political resource. The industry is also aware of this, and is spending large sums of money on advocacy advertising to influence public opinion. In addition, the Davis Conservative government remains strong in Ontario, now has extensive experience in the energy conflicts, and is clearly capable of maintaining a stout defence of Ontario's interests, as would either of the two Ontario opposition parties if they were to form the government.

The overall balance of forces in Canadian energy politics over the last half of the 1980s will, as has consistently been the case since 1973, be in large part influenced by global events. If the conditions as of mid-1984, that is stable world oil prices, plentiful supply, and non-serious interruption of Persian Gulf exports, prevail over the 1980s, then energy policy in Canada is likely to continue to be characterized by the recent return to a "consultative mode." If, on the other hand, a serious conflagration, in the Persian Gulf in particular, erupts and serious and lengthy Middle East oil supply interruptions materialize with world prices escalating sharply, it seems entirely possible that, notwithstanding the "lessons" of 1973–1984, energy politics in Canada could largely be a replay of past conflicts, reflecting the fact that the fundamental concerns of the key interests in Canadian energy politics have not significantly changed.

Related Dimensions of Political Power

While our focus has been on the government–industry and intergovernmental relationships, we have also examined other related dimensions of political power. Accordingly we offer several concluding observations about interpersonal relations among leaders, partisan politics, international and Canadian–American relations, and ministerial–bureaucratic relations.

The role of individual political leaders and the presence or absence of the right interpersonal chemistry among leaders is central to understanding energy politics. Our focus on interests in the first three parts of the book or on ideas, structure and process in Part IV, is not intended to downplay analytically the requisites of individual power. Nor is any of the above intended to gloss over the fact that politics (energy or any other kind), produce their fair share of pure personal aggrandizement, wasteful decisions, and interpersonal conflict. The NEP and the preceding decade, however, alert us to the need to walk a very thin line when one links personalities to ideas, institutions, and interests. Personalities give politics a human face, whether one is speaking of the power of Marc Lalonde; the seeming lack of respect that Peter Lougheed had for his former party and election advisor and then Prime Minister, Joe Clark; the entrepreneurial zeal of Jack Gallagher or Bob Blair; or the mutual mixture of both begrudging respect and dogged mistrust that characterized the relations between Pierre Trudeau and Peter Lougheed. But the basic positions of these individual leaders and others like them also usually emerge concurrently from the larger interests they represent and from their custody of, and belief in, key ideas and concepts. This applies equally to both public and private sector leaders. For example, there can be no doubt whatsoever that the heads of multinational energy firms and their senior executives, most of whom are Canadians, believed strongly that their decisions also served the general interests of Canada. Accordingly, they often resented the NEP in a deeply personal way.

Just as personalities should not be artificially separated from ideas, institutions and interests, so also must one be prudent about the role of partisan politics. At one level, the NEP can clearly be seen to have been forged by a Liberal Party surrounded by a sea of non-Liberal (and primarily Tory) provincial governments. The NEP was partly the result of the Trudeau Liberals' desire to reassert their view of "who speaks for Canada" in response to a decade of provincial aggressiveness, to ensure the survival of the Liberal Party and to repair the historical legacy of the Trudeau regime after the Prime Minister's initial retirement in 1979. Also at a general level, the response to the NEP by the federal Tories was partly based on an ideological opposition to the degree of intervention contained in the NEP. This was a manifestation of genuine belief on the part of many western Conservatives in particular who also saw it, quite validly, as a measure directed primarily against Alberta, thus reinforcing the already strong sense of regional alienation against central Canada. When added to the 1979 defeat of the Clark government, effectively by Toronto voters, it only added insult to injury.

Within this broad partisan configuration, however, there were other partisan variations that did not fit an expected partisan mold, but which are explainable in terms of the interests at stake. The Ontario Tories, reflecting the industrial and consumer base of populous Ontario, aligned themselves with the Liberals, not on all the details of the NEP, but certainly on the key questions of prices and the recycling of petro-dollars as well as on the need to defend and expand Petro-Canada. The early arrangement of an agreement with the Nova Scotia Tories reflected a calculation on the part of the Buchanan government, in the context of a depressed regional economy, that Nova Scotia could, by moving quickly, garner a larger share of the off-shore oil business spin-offs, than its main regional competitor, Newfoundland. The Newfoundland tories, reinforced by both strong belief and the antipathy between Premier Brian Peckford and the federal Liberals, chose to bargain for higher stakes, including control of the off-shore on constitutional grounds.

When it comes to concluding assessments of the role of international politics and Canada–U.S. relations in the energy politics configuration, a diverse array of connections emerges. In the broadest context it was clearly the 1973 and then 1979 oil price shocks that forced a variety of domestic responses and perceptions of responses. In 1979 in particular, it was the 150 percent increase in world prices that "upped the ante," or escalated the stakes, not only for Alberta, but for a federal government anxious to secure more revenue to reduce its ballooning, partly energy-induced, deficit. The Iranian revolution also produced a deep concern, initially short term but nonetheless very real, about security of supply. The oil price shocks also produced almost inevitably a key point of interpretation and belief about price increases that goes to the heart of the domestic dispute. This was more central to the Canadian debate precisely because Canada, more than any other Western country, encapsulated within its own boundaries the larger world dilemma. Thus producer interests could and did argue that world prices were market prices. Consumer interests could characterize the same phenomena as being evidence of political or administered prices. From this central set of contending interpretations and beliefs, one was easily led into deep divisions about how quickly one should "adjust" to these "realities" and about how efficient, fair, equitable, regionally sensitive, and nationally appropriate the results would be.

In the more specific realm of Canada–U.S. relations, two overall features deserve concluding emphasis. Over the entire decade covered, it is evident that the continental dimensions and interdependencies of Canadian energy policy are still a central reality that no government can ignore. Not only are they central to general Canadian–American relations but they are critical to key elements of successful energy policy. Thus U.S. regional gas markets are essential to the Canadian industry. Pipeline decisions by American regulatory and investment decision makers are critical to Canada. The very definitions of energy security and strategic security are entwined in the continental versus national debate. Prior to 1973, Canadian policy could be said to have been quite content with a continental notion of security, since markets were benignly regulated, in part at least, by bodies like the Texas Railway Commission. Obviously the world has changed since then, but the conflict between continental versus purely national notions of security has by no means disappeared.

In the more specific context of the NEP, however, we have argued that the NEP was not itself forged in an anti-American context. The NEP, however, obviously did contain provisions that could not help but jar Canadian–American relations, all the more so because they landed in the heady early days of a decidedly pro-free enterprise Reagan administration, and because they were linked to other industrial policy strings in the Liberals' aggressive policy bow of 1980–81 that included the then proposed strengthening of FIRA, industrial benefits legislation, and an energy mega-project-driven economy. The desire to secure greater industrial benefits from the expected next generation of energy development on the Canada Lands was an understandable one, given any reasonable interpretation of past history. Moreover, the Americans had faced provisions in other countries not at all dissimilar to some of the basic features of the NEP. A decade of third-world and even European nationalism had not apparently phased them. But the United States clearly does not view Canadian nationalism in the same light. Canadians are viewed to be much like Americans themselves, and therefore provisions like the 25 percent Crown interest strike them as being curiously out of step with the "North American way" of doing things. The retroactivity of the Crown interest deserved criticism, but it was apparent that, even apart from this provision, the position taken was that the NEP was "changing the rules" in the middle of the game, and hence was unfair. Strong pressure from within the United States by American energy interests, urged on by their Canadian subsidiaries, clearly reflected this view. The problem is that the energy–economic "game" *never* ends, and thus the logical extension of this sporting metaphor suggests that it is never appropriate to change the rules.

Last, but certainly not least in these related aspects of energy politics, comes the issue of the relationships of power and influence between elected ministers and senior bureaucrats. We have characterized the specific genesis of the NEP as being forged in a balance of power between ministers and bureaucrats rather than, as has been portrayed by other critics of the NEP, a triumph of bureaucrats over ministers. There are several reasons for this view. The first is that the NEP would not have happened if key ministers such as Prime Minister Trudeau and Marc Lalonde had not devoutly wanted it to happen, and had not been prepared to take the risks in what could not help but be an unpredictable and massive policy exercise. They were prepared to take risks and they did. The second reason is based on a need to distinguish the actual role of bureaucrats from the rheotrical role ascribed to them by those who partly wish to rationalize their own lack of political success. Thus in Chapter 2 we have stressed the interconnected bureaucratic roles of both policy advisor to ministers and policy implementor. We have examined these relations by linking them to specific individual features of the NEP, showing that the relationships of influence and power between ministers and bureaucrats vary greatly.

Even these relationships, however, must be placed in the context of the larger struggle *among politicians* and the strategies they followed. Thus the intransigence of the Lougheed government in its negotiations with the Clark government, the concurrent constitutional struggle with its accompanying conflicting visions of Canada, the Trudeau Liberals' attempt to skirt the provinces and foster more direct links between Canadians and national institutions, and the pressure and views of the Ontario Tories, must all be linked before making judgements about bureaucratic versus elected political power.

There can be no doubt that senior officials exerted major influence over some parts of the NEP. There is also no doubt that the knowledge of key federal officials about the oil and gas industry was not a detailed operational knowledge. In this respect, and taking into account the small group of ministers and officials that forged the NEP (and the short time period involved) there is no doubt that the total feasibility of the interconnected parts of the NEP was not adequately thought out. Some critics of the bureaucracy's role properly related this to the fact that the officials involved were "policy types," overly mesmerized and fascinated by the complexity and interrelationships among policy fields. Why, NEP critics often said, didn't they stick to energy matters and talk to the experts who really knew the industry—the industry itself, as it used to be in the old days before 1973? In one sense, this is an understandable view but it is also, in its own way, an extremely narrow and even naive view, not only in the context of energy policy and what it had become *politically* since 1973, but also in relation to what had happened to the nature of government as a whole. Energy policy no longer was energy policy alone. It was no longer just another industrial sector. There were profound interconnections with fiscal, regional, social, and economic policies and interests. Senior bureaucrats and ministers could not help but have to take these into full account. Moreover, bureaucrats were constitutionally not just advisors to one department, but to a government as well.

Discussions of bureaucratic power are always reflective of the selective double standard Canadians often apply to "bureaucrats." These are in turn reflective of the contradictory or at least ambivalent role that bureaucracy plays in a democracy. Bureaucracies are invariably both a necessary (but not sufficient) condition for democracy, and at the same time are a major threat to it. As long as "bureaucrats" are involved in policies that conform to the views of a given interest, that interest attributes virtue to bureaucrats. If policies are unfavourable, then bureaucrats are "power hungry" and "out of control." The fact is, however, that in both of the above instances, bureaucrats exercise influence. In the short-term rhetoric of politics, however, it is usually far more convenient to lay public blame on bureaucrats than to have to admit that a particular interest has simply not had its views endorsed.

Notes
1. Hon. Brian Mulroney, Statement on Energy Policy, Prince Albert, Saskatchewan, July 5, 1984, p. 2.
2. *Ibid.*

CHAPTER 13

THE NEP AND ENERGY POLICY: AN EVALUATION

Throughout the book we have examined the numerous issues involved in assessing the NEP and its effects, intended and unintended. Is it a radical policy change? How does it fare when judged against its official and less official goals? To what extent does it embody the dominant ideas inherent in Canadian politics and therefore the partial contradictions that exist among them? Is it the goals that are in dispute, or only the means? What is the time frame to be used in assessing the NEP in respect of each objective? How does one distinguish the effects of the NEP from those of the recession and other intervening events, such as the Canada–Alberta Agreement and the fall of world oil prices? These are all germane to the task of presenting a report card on the NEP. They are also the issues which take our analysis out of the realm of pure politics and into public policy.

It is hard to dispute that the NEP was a major policy change. It is not, however, a radical policy. Two overriding arguments counsel this view: there was considerable agreement about the official objectives of the NEP, though much dispute about the means; and although the takeover program was perceived to be its most radical element, it must be remembered that even this goal was directed towards achieving only a 50 percent Canadian ownership and control target. In no other Western industrialized country would this be considered a radical goal. Only because of past policy was Canada faced with this "catch-up" situation. In many other respects, the NEP, precisely because it embodied so many of the core ideas of Canadian political life, could not be considered to be radical in intent. What was a major departure from the status quo was the scope of the new arsenal of means. The great reality of politics is that means are also ends. *How* things are done is as valued as *what* is done.

This is why, in our analysis, we have placed alongside the official goals of the NEP its equally important unofficial goals, especially the Trudeau Liberals' desire to restructure the basic relationships of power

478

as they saw them between Ottawa and the industry and between Ottawa and the provinces. Here one inevitably confronts different notions of power and the time frame used to assess the exercise of this power. As we have concluded in the previous chapter, at a broad political level the NEP can be considered to have been successful in that the oil and gas industry now clearly knows that the rules of the game are different and that it can no longer, as it once tended to do, take the federal role for granted. It can also no longer assume that its interests are the same as those of the Alberta government. Similarly, the various producer provinces now know conclusively that Ottawa has the capacity for decisive action. Ottawa's aggressiveness, however, as we have stressed throughout this book, was a product of far more than just energy policy or the NEP; it was linked to other initiatives designed to reassert federal powers over economic management.

But there is a second kind of power that is much more difficult to "restructure." This is the power actually to change *behaviour* in a *persistent*, sustained way over longer periods of time. This is what "implementing" a policy is ultimately about, and where politics and policy become wholly one and the same thing. Has Ottawa restructured power in this sense through the NEP? The answer must be threefold: partly yes, partly no, and, in some respects, we cannot tell.

The partial success is found in the revenue share aspects of the NEP. The NEP was successful to the extent that it did secure a higher share of revenues for the federal government, from about 7 percent to 16 percent, but short of the avowed goal of about 24 percent, because projected price increases failed to materialize. Partial success, in Ottawa's terms, was also in evidence in the expansion of Petro-Canada and in the takeover program in that the level of ownership increased by 10 percentage points, from 28 percent to 38 percent, and may well reach over 40 percent if Gulf Canada is acquired by Canadian interests in the wake of the SOCAL takeover of the parent Gulf Oil in the United States. In addition, a tougher regulatory regime was put in place in the Canada Lands, resulting in Canadian firms' in 1984 having an opportunity to earn an interest in 62 percent of the Canada Lands, compared to 38 percent in 1980 and even lower percentages before that. A pricing system was put in place that reflected the undoubtedly real *political* consensus that, on balance, supported prices that increased less rapidly than Alberta and the industry wanted.

A closer look at the three official objectives, however, also shows that there is ample medium-term evidence to show that there are policy failures as well. A number of Canadian firms, in the short and medium term, have been harmed. In the 1981–1984 period, the combined effects of the NEP and the recession have left some firms financially vulnerable, at least in relation to their capacity to be the vehicle for realizing a 50 percent Canadian participation rate in the development phase on the Canada Lands. The key question here is whether that relatively smaller group of firms *in addition* to Petro-Canada, Dome and Nova—in short the "second line" firms—will be able to survive the medium term, and be poised and able to participate fully and vigorously in the next political–geological era of the oil and gas industry. The evidence here is more judgemental in that not only are facts hard to come by, but also both Ottawa and these individual firms have a common interest in not wanting to reveal what evidence there is, lest it reflect badly not only on their political and business prospects, but also lead to self-fulfilling behaviour. Thus, there are large aspects of the Canadianization objective that remain in doubt, and are equally bedeviled by having to gauge long-term effects when, as usual, the "long-term" continues its maddening habit of always residing in the uncertain future.

Our analysis has shown that the prospects of the Canadian-owned firms are dependent upon a number of factors. Among the Canadian majors, Petro-Canada has been a prime beneficiary of the NEP and is well positioned to take a lead role in the development stage of the Canada Lands. But it is also a company much in need of consolidation. Its easy money days are over, and it would be useful to see its role disciplined by much tougher Cabinet scrutiny.

It is not clear that proposals to have Petro-Canada partially privatized through limited share offerings to the public make sense in energy policy terms, however satisfying it may sound as a measure to ensure greater (albeit probably illusory) Crown corporation accountability. Petro-Canada should retain its higher risk exploration and "need to know" role, a role likely to be sacrificed if private investors interested in immediate profitability are part of its equity component and board of directors.

Dome's shaky present is due much more to its own excesses, aided and abetted by the banks, than it is to the NEP. With luck, it has a good possibility of being a major player. Nova has a strong corporate base, but its overall prospects are best seen in the context of the second-line firms. As a group, firms such as Pan Canadian, Norcen, Home Oil, Canterra, Husky and Bow Valley have been given opportunities by the NEP to extend their operations and experience to the offshore and the Canada Lands. This would not have been as readily possible under the pre-NEP fiscal and regulatory regime. They have gained from the farm-in process of the COGLA regulatory regime. It is clear that without this experience and opportunity, there would be little prospect of achieving 50 percent Canadian participation in the development of the Canada Lands. Even with the NEP and the PIP regime, however, one must still ask whether the 50 percent target is feasible. The conclusions reached in Chapter 10 are cautious, since numerous factors are involved. Development will occur on a project-by-project basis, probably with a fiscal regime that includes royalty postponement, world price, phased in tax takes and perhaps loan guarantees. Among the combined group of the Canadian majors and the second-line firms, it is likely that different combinations of them will be in a position to take part and hence reach the 50 percent target. These prospects increase, of course, if the 25 percent Crown interest is retained and not given away as a concession to the Americans. The prospects of achieving the 50 percent participation rate are also plausible if one relates the financial capacity of some of the firms to their parent companies and to other pools of Canadian capital that may well enter the play through mergers. If all the variables do not fall into place on every project, it would be wise policy not to be rigid about the 50 percent goal. Gradual movement towards it in clear, publicly agreed steps would be a sensible policy position.

As to the multinationals, it is difficult to see them as being victimized by the NEP. In the short and medium term they have been taxed more heavily, especially via the PGRT, but they have gained in the short and medium term by PIP grants in that the latter, via farm-ins, have generated a flow-through of funds to Canadian firms and then partially back to the multinationals. This exploration activity has helped better delineate the land structures held by the multinationals. While in the long run this may lead to 50 percent Canadian ownership, the foreign-owned majors have repeatedly said they agreed with this objective. The multinationals did suffer, along with the entire industry, from the fiscal effects of the NEP, but these were at least equalled and probably exceeded by the effects of the recession, and by the longer-term impacts of the conservation and off-oil programs implemented by Western governments in the 1970s, and contained as a central part of the demand-side aspects of the NEP's security and supply strategy. These effects became pronounced in the early 1980s and thus are partially attributable to the NEP. It is of no small importance to note, however, that it was mainly the multinationals who were in a sound financial position, as early as 1983, to revive their scaled-down mega-projects in the oil sands and heavy oil areas of Alberta and Saskatchewan. Only later, in 1984, was a Canadian firm, Husky Oil, able to announce its $3.2 billion heavy oil upgrader plant.

The "Canada benefits" or procurement aspects of Canadianization are more difficult to gauge than increases in ownership. The COGLA–OIRB processes examined in Chapter 11 suggest to us that new procurement habits are being learned, but that any instincts to label the multinationals as villains and Canadian firms heroes in this respect should be strongly resisted. Percentages of Canadian involvement will probably increase through the muscle supplied by COGLA and the OIRB, but overall economic development objectives in the form of sustainable backward and forward linkages in the industrial and service chain will remain mired in an analytical jumble where clear-cut answers do not emerge.

As to the goal of security of supply and self-sufficiency by 1990, the evidence is mixed. At a minimum level, the NEP has achieved the government's "need to know" objectives regarding basic geological prospects. The demand-side "off-oil" elements of the NEP, aided by the recession and previous conservation efforts, have produced significant results in the form of a 22 percent reduction in oil demand between 1980 and 1983. While EMR's claim that in 1983 self-sufficiency in oil was achieved, because Canada exported more than it imported, is true, it is not sufficient ground on which to make a more sustained claim. Nonetheless, demand has been reduced in a major way, and this contributes to greater security of supply. Simply put, a barrel of oil saved is a barrel of oil discovered and produced. New supply sources of the long hoped for elephant scale on the Canada Lands have not to date materialized. Even if one is discovered in the last half of the 1980s, its commercial viability would not be established until well into the 1990s.

Moreover, aggregate self-sufficiency is not the same as security of supply, since there are still regional security concerns within Canada that cannot wholly be dealt with until transportation and other issues are also resolved. In other words, the four Maritime provinces and eastern Québec are still dependent on imported oil.

The geological reality of the "supply" is, in a sense, the least mysterious. Hibernia and Sable Island are both major supply pools whose discovery slightly predates the NEP. The Alberta tarsands supplies are geologically even more significant. The Beaufort Sea supplies are somewhat more debatable as to their proven size, but also seem to be large. It is the *political economy* of supply that is fundamentally at stake. This was true before the NEP, and it is even more the case after. Which source of supply comes onstream first? No one truly knows, because it is not a wholly controllable phenomenon. No interests, political or economic, hold all the levers, let alone have a monopoly on the ability to foretell the future.

When it comes to the objective of fairness, one enters the most metaphysical but equally real of all the realms where politics and economics meet in energy policy (as in any other policy field in Canada). Fairness and efficiency, in particular, either collide or involve trade-offs. In the NEP, fairness seemed most to be associated with the idea of regionalism and equity. But the judgements here must of necessity vary enormously. There was considerable electoral support for the concept of the blended price, and the slower path toward world price. The Alberta government, however, obviously did not regard the NEP as fair. Foreign-owned firms regarded it as unfair and discriminatory, which of course it was, and was intended to be. Ontario, Québec and Maritime consumers, to the extent that one can gauge them, regarded the blended price as fair. While the Nova Scotia government took advantage of the NEP, Newfoundland strongly opposed it.

All of the above raises the question of the degree to which the NEP was good at promoting efficiency in the global sense of maximizing potential Gross National Product. This was the overriding alternative criterion or idea either explicitly or implicitly used by most of the NEP's critics in the oil and gas industry, in other industrial sectors, in the financial press, and by most economists. For these critics, the NEP was simply inefficient, and its goals could have been achieved in better ways. A rapid movement to world prices was eschewed, and some economic adjustments were therefore postponed. Billions of dollars in capital left the country in the takeover binge, and an inflow of foreign capital in other fields as well was undoubtedly discouraged by the Liberals' overall attitude to foreign investment. The Alberta oil and gas industry and the Alberta economy was driven to considerable under-utilization of capital and a severe loss of jobs. The incentive grants were wasteful, whereas a tax-based regime would have been more efficient. This was the consistent line of argument and, in purely economic terms, some of it is persuasive.

By its commitment to the objectives of Canadianization, security of supply, and fairness, however, the NEP explicitly sought to pay a price in terms of short-term efficiency in order to achieve a restructuring of political power. The Liberals also sought to gain benefits in terms of longer long-term efficiency. These longer-term notions of efficiency embodied a hoped for, more competitive and vibrant Canadian segment of the industry operating in the future development phase of the Canada Lands as well as elsewhere in western Canada. It also embodied the industrial procurement gains to be realized over the longer term and the employment gains that were thought to accrue if Ontario's industries could adjust *gradually* to a slower pace of energy price increases.

Each of the individual policy goals of the NEP, however, could not help but fall well short of the mark, precisely because they partially collided with each other and involved trade-offs. The goals are surrogates for the dominant ideas that govern Canadian political life. These ideas persist. They are not easily or, for long, "muscled off" the political agenda. Someone or some interest always wants them back on.

The discussion above of the official and unofficial goals of the NEP is not only intended to show concretely the links to ideas and interests, but also to show that energy policy as revealed by the NEP is tied to economic policy, regional policy, and social policy. We have stressed that the NEP was not explicitly guided by or preceded by an overall view of economic policy or "economic development" policy. But it was hardly divorced from it either. Energy was partly treated as an industrial sector, albeit a "special" one in the post-OPEC era. It was also partly treated as a staple engine of growth, not only in Ottawa's promotion of mega-projects and Canadian benefits and its efforts to influence the pace of development of large projects, but also in the context of Alberta's Lougheed-era strategy which saw energy as the decisive engine of the historic desire to escape its overall *resource* dependency. It is paradoxical but quite understandable in this regard to note that a large chunk of Ottawa's NEP-generated revenue, namely that part that went into the 1980–1983 $2 billion Western Development Fund, was spent on resolving the historic Crow dispute on grain freight rates. This in turn was largely based on the need to modernize and expand the west's railway infrastructure so as to facilitate in the next decade an expansion of the west's *resource* markets, particularly for the export sector. Despite these economic development themes inherent in the NEP, there were major areas that were not thoroughly considered. The highly important petro-chemical industry was almost ignored in the NEP, as was the role of nuclear power. Economic policy concerns entered the energy policy equation through its link to the issue of deficits, revenue shares and the taxing of resource rents, as well as in relation to the rate at which price increases should be, or could be, absorbed by Canadian industry. Thus there were links to economic development defined in various ways. But the links were episodic and haphazard, in part because the ideas and interests were in dispute, and because no single policy could possibly produce co-ordinated behaviour of this complex kind.

Energy Policy, the Policy Process, and Policy Implementation

What does ten years of energy politics and the NEP itself tell us about public policy formulation and implementation? In this book we have examined public policy as an interplay among ideas, structure, and process. Moreover, in the case of the NEP, we have examined as much of a full "policy cycle" as time and space would allow. That is, we have tried to trace both the genesis of the NEP and its implementation over time until mid-1984. All of this has been done in the context of the larger political setting, especially the government–industry and inter-governmental dimensions. Since key leaders and personalities are the custodians and advocates of ideas and head the institutions and structures, it follows that individuals and their preferences and conceptions of risk and uncertainty are at the centre of energy policy dynamics. Such leaders are sometimes "on top" and confidently in charge, but far more frequently they are "in the middle," in the sense that they must interact with, anticipate and deal with others who have power and varying amounts of political will and determination.

Drawing lessons from the NEP about "the policy process" is difficult, because one must deal with the degree to which the NEP is a unique event. Moreover, one must recognize that over the whole policy cycle covered in this book, there is no single policy process. We have seen this in particular in Part IV where the processes *in* each of the main arenas, the tax-price, expenditure, and regulatory arenas, and *among* them, involve a host of interlocking ideas, structures and dynamics. If one cannot draw lessons as such, then it is certainly possible to draw out some key issues about policy formulation and implementation.

The first concerns the concentration of power within the Cabinet. Barely three key ministers were involved. While among the hundreds of decisions that governments make annually, this is not the normal way, there is a broader sense in which, periodically other decisions of the magnitude of the NEP *do* involve the kinds of concentration of power evident in the NEP. That is, where an issue is central to the mandate and fate of the government and Prime Minister, those few ministers and officials with the most influence, will exercise it. In any given regime or term in office these major occasions are likely to be, almost by definition, few in number. Thus the NEP should perhaps be compared to the handful of other key policies of the past two decades that were central to the regime of the day. Such a list might include the constitutional initiatives of 1981, wage and price controls in 1975, the October crisis of 1970, medicare in 1965–66, and so on. Needless to say, one could see the same phenomenon at the provincial level. The essential decisions of the Lougheed government, for example, were also taken by an equally small entourage of power holders.

It is doubtful that one can reform the Cabinet so as to ensure that these concentrations of power do not occur again. It is in the nature of power that it concentrates or congeals. Democracy faces a constant dilemma about both the need to *mobilize* power to allow for clear decisions and to *constrain* power. Even here, however, one must be careful about what one is talking about. The NEP itself was a major package of decisions assembled as a policy *at a particular point in time*. Power was therefore concentrated around that event. But the NEP was also the product of a larger flow of events in the previous decade.

These realities, in turn, raise issues about the degree and efficacy of prior consultation with the industry and other affected interests. "If only the industry had been properly consulted," was a frequent rallying call after the NEP. The oil and gas industry felt that Ottawa and the key provinces were at the bargaining table, but the industry was not. It was felt by industry spokesmen that, when energy policy was next made, a new process had to be designed in much the same way as unfavourable budgets lead to calls for budget reform, while favourable ones do not.

Consultation is always a central issue of democratic policy formulation. Ideally, consultation *precedes* the decision and reflects some kind of consensus among the interests as to the ideas and priorities at stake. The full decade of energy policy shows the existence of much consultation, albeit grumpy consultation embellished with the normal expressions of dissatisfaction from those who did not get all that they wanted. The NEP itself was *preceded* in 1979 by extensive bargaining by the Clark Conservatives with the Alberta government. The NEP was viewed by the Trudeau Liberals as a way of forcing a reaction from Alberta. In short, it was bare-knuckle consultation, using an "act first—talk later" tactic. Therefore, there are always difficult, and quintessentially political judgements to be made about whom to consult and why and for how long. It is certainly easy to see how, from the federal Liberal perspective, in the summer of 1980, consulting with the industry about expanding the role of Petro-Canada, or about shifting the industry incentives off the tax system and onto direct grants would have been interesting, but its outcome predictably counterproductive from the Liberals' point of view. At the same time, given the later difficulties with the NEP regime and its diverse intended and unintended effects, one can easily see how better consultation might have produced better policy and better results.

Periodically every government faces a situation where it must act first, in a decisive manner, and "talk later." This is then followed by adjustment, strategic retreat, and various responses to changed circumstances. Politically this makes the political leader who launches it look tough and decisive in the first instance, and then "flexible," or "vacillating," as the case may be, in the later stages. The alternative is to consult and compromise early and often. This may make the minister look like a good pragmatic politician or a "wishy-washy" compromiser with no political backbone. One can get from A toB in either way and it is always a moot point as to which produces the best results and from whose point of view.

The problem with the first approach in the context of events in the 1980–81 period is that the overall Liberal strategy was in fact an attempt to take unilateral action on several policy fronts simultaneously. Thus the NEP was initiated in concert with constitutional initiatives, a Western Canada strategy, and an economic development strategy. For the Liberals this was too much, too fast, with too little genuine political legitimacy to back up the efforts. Generating controlled conflict is not always bad for the political system. Democracies often learn from successfully resolved conflicts. But those who seek to generate a lot of conflict as a deliberate strategy had better know how to manage it.

In the specific energy context, however, one cannot avoid returning to the central issue posed throughout this book, namely that there are divergent energy interests and that idyllic consensus is not always possible, because fundamental interests differ. There is nothing in politics and public policy that should lead one to expect that sweet harmony will or should prevail. Over the entire period of energy politics covered there is evidence of both full-scale or reasonable consensus (e.g. the National Oil Policy, and the pricing agreements between 1974 and 1978) and heated controversy and anger (Petro-Canada, the 1956 Pipeline debate, and the NEP). Those who look to the future construction of elegant consultative "technologies" will look in vain if they expect to find either uniform approaches or predictable results.

At the same time, however, the de facto nature of the NEP is that an exceedingly complex policy and set of diverse policy instruments were put in place. As we have stressed, the NEP is an example par excellence where the implementation of policy turns on an elaborate mixture of public and private behaviour. The detailed analysis of the implementation dynamics in Part IV has shown the problems, as the numerous willing and unwilling "implementors" sought to respond to, and/or partially counteract, the effects of the NEP and the recession. In part, the level of uncertainty and complexity is overstated in our analysis in that the immediate post-NEP period, 1981 to 1984 was bound to display the maximum turmoil. An examination over a ten-year period would probably show more stable patterns of behaviour.

We have seen, however in each of the chapters on the main policy instruments, and in our cumulative account of the connections among such instruments, how essential it is to view implementation in this way. The adjectives and metaphors we used for each instrument are not at all misplaced: they tell us much about the limits of grand designs and machine-gun policy-making bursts. The tax and price dynamics did produce a gauntlet through which the interests had to run and slither. The expenditure programs did create paradoxes of control. Control, in the sense of visibility and the inducement of activity out of Alberta and into the Canada Lands, was present, but at the same time the key programs were demand-driven and hence in key respects uncontrollable. The regulatory regime did produce a vague halfway house of developmental bargaining that was added to the old public utility style regulation inherent in the National Energy Board. Cumulatively, the NEP produced a heady mixture of both genuine change and bewildering confusion.

Consultation and implementation responses by unwilling implementors are concepts that must be related to the role of formal analysis and evaluation in the policy process. The role of analysis, both of the "hard" modelling kind and of the "soft" judgemental kind, cannot in the least be understood without relating it to political pressure and the timing and pressure of events. Formal ex post facto evaluations similarly must be judged by looking at the interests that conduct them and the selective and partial criteria that are used. Analysis and evaluation, in short, are acts and processes of both cerebral thought and political pressure and interaction. Obtaining a common data base was essential to the 1981 Canada–Alberta agreement, but the data was so complex and the pressure of interests to manipulate them was so strong that it drove the main actors into a set of propositions about the future that could not be sustained. In one sense there was too much "hard" analysis and not enough "hard" judgement. In other respects, of course, Canada's earlier energy history showed that there was also at times a dearth of analysis and knowledge, for example about future reserves, industry finances, and procurement decisions.

Analysis and evaluation are also related to the relationship between myths and realities. Myths are not necessarily entirely untrue. They may contain kernels of truth, but they are not "the facts" either.

They become interwoven with ideas and entrenched ways of viewing combinations of facts and values. We have seen this in various ways. The Trudeau Liberals' overall aggressiveness in 1980 was in response to a cumulative perception of the provinces as "province builders," to use the academic term often used, or power-hungry regional barons, to put it in the vernacular of power politics. But this was only partly real. The reality of federal–provincial relations in the 1970s was in fact much more complex than that. The same can be said for the perception of western provincial governments that saw all issues through the lens of historic western alienation.

At another level, that of world prices and supply, myth and reality also collided. Concern about immediate security of supply was real in a short-term sense, but was undoubtedly capitalized upon too eagerly, since the underlying conditions of supply and demand were not critical. These in turn drove the psychology of forecasting energy prices. As a result, a function that is already more art than science became even more informed by imagination than judgement. It is not clear that there is any obvious solution to these perverse connections between myth, perception, and reality, save that of encouraging open informed debate in which those who see the world only in terms of "heroes" and "villains" are forced to demonstrate their conclusions and hypotheses more carefully, and are examined more closely.

As if there are not enough paradoxes in the NEP saga, it is none-theless necessary to draw concluding attention to yet another: the issue of "flexibility" versus "rigidity" in energy policy. The general argument about the NEP is that it has resulted in a rigid bureaucratized policy at precisely the same time that Canada needs flexible policy to respond to changes in world oil and gas markets. While we share concern about this excessive rigidity, it is well to remember that "flexibility" and "rigidity," like so many other real and rhetorically expressed ideas and concepts in political life, are words whose meaning depends greatly on who is using them. As we have shown, prior to the NEP, special price arrangements were negotiated to make tarsands projects feasible. These were individual instances of "flexibility" as were the deals to phase in gradual price increases in the general price structure. But collectively, each flexible deal adds up to more rigidity in total. The NEP obviously creates a quantum jump in the total supply of rigidity, but each component of it was also *individually* to respond to the needs for flexibility, that is, a flexible mix of ideas, of regional circumstances, of projects, of interests, and of corporate and international contexts.

A strong case can be made for simplifying energy policy, but how much simplification is desirable? The world price scenario is the favourite example of simplicity. But what if the world price doubled again overnight as it did in 1979? Does anyone who knows the reality of Canadian politics doubt for one minute that a new cry for "flexibility" would arise, this time arguing that Canada should not be "rigid" slaves of a politically fickle world market, and that "special" pricing arrangements should again be designed? Does anyone doubt that if interest rates again reached the high teens that there would be a clamour to renegotiate the financing and fiscal regimes surrounding the large energy projects, regardless of their stage of construction? It is of course highly doubtful that the entire NEP scenario would be repeated. People do learn from experience, even when they do not agree on all the lessons that have been learned. But there are still ways in which history might repeat itself, precisely because of the divergent underlying interests and the ideas they espouse.

None of the above is intended to belittle the seriousness of energy matters or the practice of playing the "flexibility" versus "rigidity" game. Our focus on these manifestations of politics and policy is simply to try and put the current and future energy policy choices in some kind of realistic perspective, but a perspective which still shows the nature of the choices available and the interests that may benefit from them. The NEP has had four years of implementation, but of a hardly routine nature. Parts of the NEP and certainly some of its effects will endure, but hard choices and much compromise remain in a political-economic industry that is no longer just another industrial sector.

We conclude that while some unraveling of the current complex array of policy instruments is both likely and desirable, there are limits as to how much one can or should roll them back, in a more fundamental sense. A radical roll-back package (e.g., getting rid of Petro-Canada, PIPs, COGLA, and the 25 percent Crown interest) would create as much uncertainty as have the past four years, particularly since key Canadian firms have altered their investment practices and would be caught mid-stream. It would also be unwise, given the continuing political need to pursue several desirable national goals concurrently within the realm of energy policy. Beyond these considerations, however, there remains the larger political reality left in the wake of any major policy change, namely that to unravel it too much would be to unravel a host of cumulative explicit and implicit ideas and understandings that have become the political legacy of that policy and of the energy policies of the past decade. The NEP in this sense can no more escape the political and historical legacy it carries than could the building of the CPR, the National Policy, the post-World War II welfare state, bilingualism, the Crow rate, the Diefenbaker and then Trudeau charters of rights, medicare, or any of the provincial government equivalents that make up the mosaic of Canadian political life.

493

CHRONOLOGY OF
MAJOR ENERGY POLICIES AND EVENTS
1945–1984

1944 (Jan)   Eldorado Nuclear Ltd. became a Crown Corporation.

1945   Saskatchewan's Department of Natural Resources issued a statement outlining a plan to gain eventual complete social ownership and management of key industries in the development of its natural resources.

1946   Atomic Energy Control Board established under the Atomic Energy Control Act.

1947   Leduc discovery.

1949 (Mar)   Dinning Commission of Alberta brought down finding that there was insufficient oil and gas to warrant export from the province. Majority of submissions to Commission wanted Canadians, particularly Albertans, to benefit from their petroleum supplies before considering any export of it.

1949 (Apr)   Pipelines Act first introduced in Parliament; gave power of decision over interprovincial and international pipeline transmission of oil and gas to federal government.

1949 (July)   Alberta enacted Gas Resources Act and set up Petroleum and Natural Gas Conservation Board to regulate removal of gas from province.

1949   Saskatchewan's CCF government issued memorandum on principles that were to guide them in their province's resource development: development of resource wealth; raise standards of living; promote economic stability through diversification; prevent physical waste; protect consumer from price gouging; oil majors to be important part of growth.

1949 (Oct)   C.D. Howe decided in favour of shipping Canadian oil to U.S. terminus for subsequent shipping to other Canadian ports in spite of arguments citing need for an all Canadian pipeline to help development of northern communities.

1949   Social Credit government of Alberta enacted into sections of the *Mines and Minerals Act* a ceiling on the maximum royalty rate payable by producers on petroleum and natural gas leases.

1949   Manning government of Alberta introduced legislation to permit prorationing of market demand.

1950 (Oct)   Alberta Natural Gas Bill passed incorporating Alberta Natural Gas Company. (This bill essentially condoned the transmission of Alberta gas through the U.S. to west coast ports.)

1952 (Apr)   Atomic Energy of Canada Ltd. (AECL) incorporated as a Crown corporation.

1953 (Mar)   C.D. Howe energy policy statement advocated transport of oil via least cost routes and marketing of surplus Canadian oil.

1953 (June)   Oil Policy Committee of Saskatchewan government issued memorandum calling for creation of Crown corporation to explore and produce oil and gas.

1954   Saskatchewan's Premier, T.C. Douglas, abandoned nationalization option by pulling back from deal to farm out Crown reserve land to Consumer's Coop. Oil companies had threatened to move out of Saskatchewan if deal not retracted.

1954   Formation of Alberta Gas Trunk Line Co. (AGTL) by Alberta Government.

1956   Trans-Canada Pipeline debates.

1957   Final report of Gordon Commission on Canada's Economic Prospects tabled. Commented on importance of Canada's resources to the Canadian economy and recommended development of comprehensive energy policy; establishment of national energy authority; and regulation of energy exports.

1957 (Oct)   Borden Royal Commission on Energy established. First report (1958) recommended formation of National Energy Board.

1959 (July)   *National Energy Board Act* enacted charging NEB with responsibility of monitoring and reporting on all federal aspects of energy. Given regulatory functions of controlling transportation, exporting/importing of power; and setting utility rates and tariffs.

1959   AECL's Whiteshell Nuclear Research Establishment announced.

1960   Great Canadian Oil Sands project approved by Alberta government. Opened in 1967.

1960   Diefenbaker government declared that Canada Lands oil and gas production licences would be granted only to Canadian-owned corporations. First time Canadian ownership officially mentioned in any Canadian land policy. Declaration required foreign-owned company only to register on Canadian stock exchange, no sale of shares to Canadians necessary.

1961   Canada Oil and Gas Lands Regulations (COGL) promulgated.

1961 (Feb)   National Oil Policy announced. Western Canadian oil limited to markets west of Ottawa Valley.

1963 (Oct)   National Power Policy announced, advocating development of Canadian power through exporting arrangements with United States.

1964	Federal and Ontario governments reached agreement on cost sharing of the construction of Pickering nuclear power station.
1965	Federal and Québec governments reached agreement on cost sharing of Gentilly-1 nuclear reactor construction.
1966 (Oct)	Department of Energy, Mines and Resources created.
1966	Federal government purchased controlling interest (45 percent equity share) in Panarctic Oils Ltd. ($9 million).
1966	Carter Royal Commission on Taxation report released, stating that the multinationals' grievances concerning Canadian tax policy had little justification economically or socially, and that they should be taxed just as other industries are.
1967 (July)	Energy Development Group established within EMR.
1967 (Dec)	Pearson government announced it was entering into partnership with twenty oil and mining companies to carry out joint exploration and drilling programs in the Arctic Islands.
1967–68	West Coast Transmission application to export natural gas to United States resulted in NEB's modifying its three test criteria for export licencing in favour of increasing continentalist energy ties to United States. Alberta and Southern NEB application of 1970 similarly notable for the above reason.
1968 (Dec)	Task Force on Northern Oil Development formed.
1969	Oil discovered at Purdhoe Bay, Alaska.
1969 (June)	*Federal Oil and Gas Production and Conservation Act* enacted.
1970	Province of Québec created public enterprise Société Québécoise d'Initiatives Pétrollières (SOQUIP).
1970 (Jan)	Federal government increased its funding of Panarctic to maintain its 45 percent controlling interest as Panarctic expands exploration program.
1970 (Mar)	Trudeau announced amendments to Atomic Energy Control Act to prevent American takeover bids of Canadian mining companies, thus stopping Hudson's Bay Oil and Gas Co.'s bid to take over Denison Mines.
1970	White Paper, "Proposals for Tax Reform" released by federal Finance Minister, stated that special rules were needed to encourage and control the mineral industry. With respect to oil and gas industry it advocated immediate write-off privileges for exploration and development costs.
1970 (June)	*Nuclear Liability Act* and *Arctic Waters Pollution Prevention Act* enacted.
1971 (June)	Uranium Canada Limited incorporated as a Crown Corporation.
1971	Canada Development Corporation set up with one of its mandates being to encourage Canadian participation in oil and gas industry.
1971 (June)	Referring to Canadian Petroleum Association estimates, the

Federal Minister for Energy, Mines and Resources, J.J. Greene, proclaimed that at 1970 production rates Canada has 923 years of reserve oil and 392 years of reserve gas available.

1971 (Feb) Emergency debate on takeover bid by American-owned Ashland Oil for Home Oil resulted in federal government blocking the transaction.

1971 (Aug) Lougheed's Progressive Conservatives gained power in Alberta.

1972 Lougheed government announced "Natural Resource Revenue Plan," which sought to boost royalty payments.

1972 (Aug) Energy Resources Conservation Board of Alberta, in their "Report on Field Pricing of Gas in Alberta," stated that existing gas prices were well below their commodity value.

1972 (Dec) NEB report indicated that Canada could no longer satisfy Canadian demand and export requirements.

1972 Imperial Oil Ltd. annual report stated, "our present energy reserves using present technology are sufficient for our requirements for several hundred years. Export markets will not wait on our convenience: . . . once lost, export markets cannot easily be regained—assuming they can be regained at all—and their loss would be a genuine economic setback for Canada."

1972 NDP holding balance of power in newly elected minority Liberal Government of Canada.

1973 Foreign Investment Review Agency established.

1973 (Feb) Federal government in its "Statement on the Export of Crude Oil" stated that restrictions on petroleum exporting are to be put in place.

1973 (Mar) Canadian Arctic Resources Committee issued report on Canada Land Regulations, stating that the Diefenbaker government of 1961 had given the oil industry carte blanche in instigating the kind of land regulations that were most beneficial to their own interests.

1973 Syncrude deal reached with Lougheed government of Alberta.

1973 (Apr) Saskatchewan government set up Saskoil Company to explore, produce, refine, market, transport, and trade oil and natural gas.

1973 (June) Ontario announced it would test the constitutionality of Alberta's threat to restrict the flow of gas to Ontario.

1973 (June) Federal government released energy policy document, "An Energy Policy for Canada, Phase 1."

1973 (Oct) Lougheed cabinet abandoned its new royalty plan and unilaterally pegged royalty payments to rises in the price of international oil.

1973 (Dec) Alberta announced new regulatory package to strengthen their constitutional control over their resources, including the pricing of these resources in interprovincial and international commerce. Package included: *Arbitration Amendment Act*; *Freehold Mineral Taxation Act*; *Mines and Minerals Amendment Act* (required all producers to sell their oil through marketing commission); *Alberta Petroleum Marketing Act* (set up Alberta Petroleum Marketing Commission to control sale of oil); and *Gas Resources Preservation Amendment Act*.

1973 (Dec) Trudeau announced abolition of National Oil Policy and the proposed establishment of Petro Canada.

1973 In cooperation with Alberta, the federal government made $40 million available for research and development on the oil sands.

1973 Alberta Energy Company created as a joint public/private venture (50/50).

1973 (Dec) Saskatchewan enacted Bill 42 to "rationalize" virtually all freehold oil and gas rights and to impose a "royalty surcharge" on all Crown oil production.

1974 (Jan) *Energy Supplies Emergency Act* enacted, establishing the Energy Supplies Allocation Board.

1974 (Jan) Federal–Provincial First Ministers Conference on Energy took place. Principle of uniform oil price across Canada adopted. Oil Import Compensation Program (OICP) started. Agreement reached to continue voluntary oil price restraint. Ottawa also announced policy to encourage energy interconnections between regions. This policy would give grants for feasibility studies of such interconnections and would give loans for 50 percent of the construction costs.

1974 (Feb) Canadian Industrial Gas and Oil Ltd. challenged Saskatchewan's Bill 42 as imposing an unconstitutional provincial tax on the oil industry. The federal government intervened to argue against provincial rights and the provincial governments of Québec, Manitoba and Alberta intervened on the side of Saskatchewan.

1974 (Mar) Alberta announced new royalty rates, effective April 1.

1974 (Mar) First Ministers agreed to finance higher cost of foreign oil imported into eastern Canada through revenues generated from exporting western oil.

1974 (Mar) Berger named to head the Mackenzie Valley Pipeline Inquiry Commission.

1974 (Mar) Lougheed and Trudeau agreed on a single-step oil price increase to $6.50/bbl effective April 1, 1974.

1974 Oil import compensation program procedures put in place.

1974 (May) John Turner, federal Minister of Finance, first announced non-deductibility of provincial royalties for federal tax purposes.

1974 (May) Minority Liberal government defeated, but on July 8th a majority Liberal government elected.

1974 (Sept) Darcy McKeough, Ontario's Minister of Energy, issued his

"Statement on Natural Gas" which argued against scarcity pricing of gas when there are potentially large domestic supplies available in Alberta. Ontario also argued that reduced tax and royalty payments are just as effective at increasing supply as price increases would be and at the same time would not aggravate inflationary pressures.

1974	*Alberta Energy Company Act* passed. AEC was to be a resource investment vehicle for public and an instrument for economic growth—part of Lougheed's 1971 election platform.
1974 (Fall)	New Syncrude partnership formed giving Ottawa a 15 percent share of renegotiated costs.
1974 (Sept)	Federal government announced new uranium export policy stressing domestic demand needs be met first. The Uranium Resources Appraisal Group established within EMR. First annual report released in summer of 1975.
1974 (Oct)	NEB warned that Canadian Oil supplies are inadequate to serve Canadian markets and recommended exports be phased out.
1974 (Nov)	Federal budget revised income tax regulation to disallow the deduction of provincial resource royalties in calculation of federal taxable income.
1974 (Dec)	Alberta implemented contingency plan (Petroleum Exploration Plan) which reduced royalties and introduced new drilling incentives for oil exporters.
1974 (Dec)	Federal government issued its policy on nuclear sales and safeguards.
1974	Alberta Oil Sands Technology and Research Authority (AOSTRA) set up in Edmonton to do energy research on tar sands and heavy oils.
1975 (Jan)	Federal government allowed border price of Canadian natural gas exports to begin increasing, thus providing stimulus for increased exploration and development in Western provinces and Canada Lands.
1975 (Feb)	Syncrude package renegotiated with Imperial Oil, Canada-Cities Service, Gulf Canada to allow governments of Alberta and Ontario and federal government to become equity partners.
1975 (Feb)	Energy, Mines and Resources Minister announced energy conservation program in order to lower rate of growth in consumption and enhance self sufficiency.
1975 (Apr)	NEB warned that Canadian Natural Gas supplies would soon be insufficient to meet total demand and existing exports. Canada no longer considered self-sufficient.
1975 (Apr)	First Ministers Conference held. Federal government decided to increase domestic price of oil to reduce net transfer of income from Canadians to oil exporting nations. Revenues from export

surcharge no longer adequate to cover compensation bill for imported oil for eastern Canada. Oil consuming provinces in opposition to this for fear of increasing their provinces' unemployment and inflation rates.

1975 (Apr)   *Petroleum Administration Act* adopted, giving federal cabinet ultimate authority over oil and gas pricing.

1975   Several consuming provinces introduced extended price freezes
(Summer)   on petroleum products.

1975 (May)   Nova Scotian Supreme Court case between Imperial Oil Limited and Nova Scotia Light and Power Co. Ltd. brought into the open: Imperial Oil's use of Bermudan dummy companies to evade Canadian taxes and to resell to Canada at higher price than necessary.

1975 (June) Federal government budget speech. Twenty-five percent resource allowance brought in as partial substitute for non-deductible royalties; federal corporate income tax rate lowered to 40 percent from 50 percent on resource income; price of natural gas increased to make its energy unit comparable to oil's as of November 1, 1975.

1975 (July) Petro-Canada established under *Petro-Canada Act.*

1975 (Sept) Federal and Alberta governments reached agreement on domestic natural gas pricing and on the flowback system to producers at extra revenues from gas exported at a higher price.

1975 (Sept) Federal government formed Advisory Committee on Industrial Benefits for National Resources Development with objective of encouraging growth of Canadian content in Canadian industry and special projects.

1975 (Oct)   Anti-Inflation Program launched.

1975   Federal government issued "New Principles for International Business," a set of voluntary guidelines for foreign subsidiaries stressing need for greater R&D in Canada; development of Canadian supplies; regular publication of financial information; opportunity for Canadians to buy shares in Canadian subsidiaries.

1975 (Late) Price of Natural gas fixed at 85 percent of oil price at Toronto city gate.

1975 (Dec)   Alberta Energy Company awarded Syncrude pipeline contract to unionized contractor, passing over lower bid by non-unionized contractor.

1976 (Feb)   Federal government announced intention to impose efficiency standards for automobiles, buildings and appliances.

1976 (Apr)   Federal government issued policy document, *An Energy Strategy for Canada.*

1976 (May)   Federal government issued its *Proposed Petroleum and Natural*

Gas Act, which gave more substance to the incentives offered in the policy document *An Energy Strategy for Canada*.

1976 (May) Green Paper on Canada Lands issued by federal government. Advocated abolishment of twenty-one-year leases and replaced them with provisional five-year leases.

1976 (May) Alberta established Heritage Savings and Trust Fund to mobilize capital to spur diversification of Alberta's economy, improve quality of life, and provide alternative revenue base.

1977 (Aug) Federal government issued "Hare Report" on the management of Canada's nuclear waste.

1977 (Sept) CHIP program of home insulation grants begun.

1977 (Nov) Federal government introduced Bill C-14, Nuclear Control and Administration Act. This proposed act was first major legislation in nuclear sector since the AECB created in 1946. The proposed act died on the Order Paper in 1978.

1977 (Nov) Supreme Court ruled ultra vires the royalty surcharge section of Saskatchewan's Bill 42 but upheld its nationalization actions.

1977 Alberta Gas Trunk Line defeated the eastern Canadian and foreign-controlled Arctic Gas consortium for the right to transport Arctic gas south.

1977 Renewable Energy Resource Branch formed within EMR.

1977 Federal government began continuous appraisal of Canada's coal reserves by publishing its first annual "Assessment of Canada's Coal Resources and Reserves" report.

1977 Federal government rejected Mackenzie Valley Pipeline and approved Alaska Highway Pipeline.

1978 (Apr) Northern Pipeline Agency established under *Northern Pipeline Act*. Became a statutory mechanism to ensure Canadian industrial benefits.

1978 (June) *Petroleum Corporations Monitoring Act* enacted. Required petroleum companies to disclose financial and other statistical data.

1978 (June) Federal government and Ontario came to initial agreement on the management of irradiated nuclear fuel.

1978 (July) Ottawa announced $380 million package of renewable energy programs for period 1979 to 1985.

1978 Federal government agreed in principle to give Devco $265 million for a five-year project to develop a new coal mine on Cape Breton, Nova Scotia.

1978 (Nov) Through joint ownership between federal government and Newfoundland, the lower Churchill Development Corporation was created.

1979 (Feb) Ottawa issued energy policy document, *Energy Futures for Canadians*.

1979 (Mar) Conservative government of Lougheed re-elected with large majority.

1979 (Mar) *Energy Supplies Emergency Act, 1979* enacted.

1979 (May) Minority Conservative government of Joe Clark elected. Platform included promise to privatize Petro-Canada.

1979 (June) At Tokyo Summit, Canada pledged to adhere to strict energy conservation program and adopted net oil import targets for 1979–1981.

1979 (Nov) At First Ministers Conference, federal and Alberta governments reached partial agreement on crude oil price increases; all synthetic crudes given international price; all conventional oil to be 75 percent of lower Chicago or international price until 1983, and 85% for 1984. Formula applied to all conventional crudes.

1979 (Dec) Ottawa established Energy Supplies Allocation Board under legislation enacted earlier in the year.

1979 (Dec) Parliamentary defeat of the Crosbie budget and its energy proposals, including the 18-cent increase in transportation fuels tax.

1980 (Jan) Trudeau made Halifax energy campaign speech; stressed seven points, including: a made-in-Canada blended price to keep price below world levels; strengthen and expand Petro-Canada; emphasize conservation and substitution; and ensure that Canada's oil and gas industry becomes more Canadian owned and controlled (50 percent by 1990).

1980 (Feb) Liberals returned to power with 86 percent of parliamentary support in Ontario and Québec.

1980 (Apr) Liberal Throne Speech reiterated election energy promises.

1980 (May) Québec Referendum.

1980 (July) Government approved prebuild of Alaska Highway Pipeline.

1980 (Aug) In face of failed negotiations, Alberta unilaterally increased price of oil $2 a barrel.

1980 (Aug) Petroleum Monitoring Agency Survey for first half of 1980 released.

1980 (Oct) Liberal government introduced National Energy Program.

1980 (Oct) Alberta announced retaliation to NEP. Included 180 thousand barrel per day cutback in oil production, to be implemented in steps at three-month intervals starting on March 1, 1981. Alberta also announced legal challenge to the excise tax on natural gas including exports, and withheld approval of Alsands tarsands and Cold Lake heavy oil projects.

1980 (Dec) Introduction of Bill C-48, *Canada Oil and Gas Act.* It introduced a new fiscal system for Canada Lands. COGLA brought into being to administer new regime.

1980 (Dec) "Petroleum Incentives Program: The Basic Rules—A Framework" released. Modification of proposed PIP rules followed in June 1981.

1980 (Dec) British Columbia announced that it will withhold money from the Federal government's natural gas excise tax.

1981 (Jan) Bill C-57, the legislation to provide for the petroleum and gas revenue tax (PGRT) and natural gas and gas liquids tax (NGGLT), introduced.

1981 (Feb) Petro-Canada acquired Petrofina, an integrated Belgian-owned company for $1.46 billion.

1981 (Mar) Federal government announced increases in oil prices to pay for additional oil imported to compensate for Alberta government production cutbacks. Known as Lougheed Levy.

1981 (Mar) *The State of Competition in the Canadian Petroleum Industry*, the Report of the Director of Investigation and Research, *Combines Investigation Act* released. Also known as the Bertrand Report, it charged that as a result of uncompetitive practices the major integrated firms overcharged Canadian consumers by $12 billion between 1958 and 1973. Based on evidence contained in the Report, the Restrictive Trade Practices Commission began an investigation.

1981 (Apr) Federal government announced that it would implement a special Canadian ownership charge beginning May 1 on sales of petroleum products and natural gas to cover the costs of Petro-Canada's acquisition of Petrofina.

1981 (May) Announcement of inauguration of the Canada Oil Substitution Program (COSP).

1981 (June) *Major Canadian Projects: Major Canadian Opportunities*, the Report of the Major Projects Task Force on Major Capital Projects in Canada to the Year 2000 (Blair-Carr) released.

1981 (July) Finance Minister Allan MacEachen asked Canadian banks to help slow down the rate of takeover by Canadian firms of U.S. firms by making loans less readily available.

1981 (Sept) Canada–Alberta energy agreement signed. Agreements followed with British Columbia (September 24) and Saskatchewan (October 26).

1981 (Fall) Canada Development Corporation acquired 75 percent of Aquitaine Company, a French firm, for $1.2 billion.

1981 (Fall) Cold Lake mega-project abandoned by Esso Resources.

1981 (Oct) Ontario government purchased 25 percent of shares of Suncor, a U.S. firm.

1981 (Nov) Presentation of federal budget and accompanying document, *Economic Development for Canada in the 1980s*.

1982 (Feb) Newfoundland–federal government negotiations on offshore resources broke down. Newfoundland government announced a reference to the Newfoundland Supreme Court concerning ownership of offshore resources, which it subsequently lost.

1982 (Feb) Bill C-94, the *Energy Security Act*, tabled in House of Commons. Resulted in "Bells Affair." Division bells rang from March 2 to March 17 as parties negotiated about what to do with the energy bill. Eventually broken down into eight bills.

1982 (Mar) Canada–Nova Scotia Offshore Oil and Gas Agreement announced.

1982 (Mar) Announcement of $30 million to be spent during fiscal 1982–83 to expand the natural gas distribution system to new market areas, through funds made available to utilities.

1982 (Mar) Announcement of changes to CHIP, making homes built between January 1, 1961 and January 1, 1971 eligible for federal grants to defray the cost of insulating.

1982 (Mar) Newfoundland government announced provincial election for April 6, which it won. On March 16 Newfoundland government released documents relating to negotiations with the federal government on the offshore.

1982 (Apr) Alberta announced a $5.4 billion program consisting of royalty reductions and special grants and credits with the objective of increasing revenue flows to the industry in 1982–83.

1982 (Apr) Despite extensive high-level negotiations between the two levels of government and the Alsands sponsors (Shell), including the provision of "very generous" taxation and fiscal incentives by the governments, the sponsors decided to cancel the $13 billion mega-project.

1982 (May) NEP Update published. Included $2 billion worth of federal tax concessions.

1982 (Fall) Petro-Canada acquired the refining and distribution assets of BP Canada for $347.6 million.

1982 (Fall) Federal government and Canadian banks announced a "bail out" equity package to prevent receivership of Dome Petroleum.

1983 (Mar) OPEC countries agreed, after two-week summit meeting, to reduce OPEC benchmark oil price to $29 (U.S.) per barrel, and set production quotas.

1983 (Mar) As a result of decrease in international price, Canadian old oil had already exceeded the ceiling of 75 percent of world price. Consequently, Ottawa and Edmonton agreed to cancel a price increase due for July 1983.

1983 (Apr) Federal government dropped uniform border price for natural gas from $4.95 (U.S.) to $4.40 per thousand cubic feet.

1983 (June) New eighteen-month Ottawa–Alberta agreement reached. Conventional old oil prices frozen at $29.75 (83 percent of world price). Gas prices to go up but kept at 65 percent of oil price. Ottawa to cushion gas consumers through reduction in gas excise tax. The NORP would be extended to include oil discovered after March 31, 1974, and from oil produced from wells drilled in gaps in existing oil fields.

1983 (Aug)   Ottawa announced measures to control PIP costs. Wells costing over $50 million to receive individual ministerial approval. Companies required to show that drilling costs are competitive.

1984 (Feb)   Federal budget postponed for further year the introduction of the Incremental Oil Revenue Tax. It announced also that revenues from the Canadian Ownership Account would be treated as general revenues, in part because funds for the Dome rescue would not likely be needed, and in part to make it possible to use the funds for more flexible energy purposes.

1984 (Feb)   U.S. Economic Regulatory Commission issued policy guidelines favouring market prices for imported natural gas.

1984 (Feb)   Ontario Energy Board endorsed principle of direct purchasing of gas by Ontario industry and/or by permitting industrial users to be involved in producing their own natural gas. A federal Task Force on the petrochemical industry also recommended reduced gas prices and gradual deregulation of gas pricing.

1984 (Mar)   The Supreme Court of Canada decided unanimously that the federal government has jurisdiction over offshore resources.

1984 (July)   The Mulroney Conservatives announced a pre-election energy policy platform that included: a non-retroactive "Canada share" provision to replace the 25 percent Crown interest; a replacement of PIP grants with transferable tax credits; the "replacement" of the Petroleum Gas Revenue Tax with a tax on profits; some form of protection for Canadians from sudden price increases; and "market sensitive" pricing for exported natural gas, but with the caveat that Canadians will always pay less than Americans for Canadian natural gas.

1984 (Sept)   Conservative government of Brian Mulroney elected.

ALBERTA'S 12-POINT AGENDA
(FEDERAL–PROVINCIAL CONFERENCE ON ENERGY)
(NOVEMBER, 1979)

Meet the Tokyo Declaration and move towards world prices for oil over a reasonably short period, or at least to a price slightly below a United States' composite price;

Co-operatively construct oil sands and heavy oil plants on an accelerated and agreed upon schedule;

Provide more incentives for producers to implement enhanced recovery techniques in our existing oil fields;

Assure oil and gas explorers and producers of improved cash flow and tax incentives to provide the much needed funds required to provide more expensive new oil supplies;

Substitute where practical Canadian natural gas for imported foreign crude oil and put in place the necessary transportation systems;

Permit export of surplus natural gas to the United States on appropriate terms. This will help provide funds to develop additional energy supplies, improve our balance of trade, and strengthen the Canadian dollar;

Encourage Newfoundland and Nova Scotia to develop their offshore oil and gas potential;

Continue to encourage frontier exploration in the North, with appropriate tax and other incentives;

Support a western electric grid based on Manitoba hydro-electric potential;

Replace imported United States coal with Canadian coal;

Concentrate our energy research and development policy on evaluating the best possible substitutes for crude oil;

Encourage consumer restraint or conservation through price increases and other national programs such as home insulation.

HIGHLIGHTS OF THE CANADA–ALBERTA
1981 ENERGY AGREEMENT

- A two tiered price system governs oil prices with one price schedule for conventionally produced oil from existing fields and another for production from new fields, oil sands, and frontier oil.
- Old oil went up by $2.50 a barrel on October 1, 1981, by $4.50 in 1982 and by $8 a barrel a year thereafter to reach $57.75 a barrel in mid-1986.
- New oil will be at or near world price and is slated to reach $77.48 to producers in 1986.
- The ceiling on old oil will be 75 percent of world price and on new oil it will be 100 percent of world price.
- Natural gas will go up by 25¢/mcf every six months starting February 1, 1982.
- The federal government withdrew its export tax on natural gas on October 1, 1981.
- The Petroleum Gas Revenue Tax (PGRT) doubled from 8 percent to 16 percent.
- The federal government imposed a 50 percent tax on incremental oil revenues after royalties were paid.
- Both sides will work to encourage immediate start-up of oil sands projects.
- Neither side will make tax changes that will significantly alter the revenue position of the other side or the industry during the life of the agreement.
- Alberta will maintain production at levels consistent with sound engineering practices.

SELECTED BIBLIOGRAPHY

Books and Chapters of Edited Books

Adelman, M.A., *The World Petroleum Market* (Baltimore: Johns Hopkins University Press, 1972).

Banting, Keith and Simeon, Richard (eds.), *And No One Cheered: Federalism, Democracy, and the Constitution Act* (Toronto: Methuen, 1983).

Blair, John M., *The Control of Oil* (New York: Vintage, 1978).

Blakeney, Allan, "Resources, The Constitution and Canadian Federalism," in J. Peter Meekison (ed.), *Canadian Federalism: Myth or Reality*, 3rd edit. (Toronto: Methuen, 1977).

Bothwell, Robert and Kilbourn, William, *C.D. Howe: A Biography* (Toronto: McClelland and Stewart, 1979).

Bothwell, Robert; Drummond, Ian; and English, John, *Canada Since 1945* (Toronto: University of Toronto Press, 1981).

Bregha, François, "Canada's Natural Gas Industry," in James Laxer and Anne Martin (eds.), *The Big Tough Expensive Job: Imperial Oil and the Canadian Economy* (Toronto: Press Porcépic, 1976).

————, *Bob Blair's Pipeline: The Business and Politics of Northern Energy Development Projects*, updated edit. (Toronto: Lorimer, 1980).

Broadway, Robin W. and Kitchen, Harry M., *Canadian Tax Policy* (Toronto: Canadian Tax Foundation, 1980).

Brooks, David B., *Zero Energy Growth for Canada* (Toronto: McClelland and Stewart, 1981).

Carmichael, Edward A. and Herrera, C., eds., *Canada's Energy Policy: 1985 and Beyond* (Toronto: C.D. Howe Institute, 1984).

Carmichael, Edward A. and Stewart, James K., *Lessons from the National Energy Program* (Toronto: C.D. Howe Institute, 1983).

Clarke, Harold D.; Jenson, J.; LeDuc, L.; and Pammett, J.H., *Absent Mandate* (Toronto: Gage, 1984).

Clarkson, Stephen, *Canada and the Reagan Challenge* (Toronto: Lorimer, 1982).

Crane, David, *Controlling Interest: The Canadian Oil and Gas Stakes* (Toronto: McClelland and Stewart, 1982).

Dacks, Gurston, *A Choice of Futures: Politics in the Canadian North* (Toronto: Methuen, 1981).

Davis, David H., *Energy Politics* (New York: St. Martins Press, 1974).

Davis, E.M., *Canada's Oil Industry* (Toronto: McGraw-Hill, 1969).

Debanné, J.G., "Oil and Canadian Policy," in E.W. Erickson and L. Waverman (eds.), *The Energy Question: An International Failure of Policy*, vol. 2: North America (Toronto: University of Toronto Press, 1974).

Doern, G. Bruce, "Energy, Mines and Resources, the Energy Ministry and the National Energy Program," in G. Bruce Doern (ed.), *How Ottawa Spends Your Tax Dollars* (Toronto: Lorimer, 1981).

————, *Government Intervention in the Nuclear Industry* (Montreal: Institute for Research on Public Policy, 1980).

————, "Spending Priorities: The Liberal View," in G. Bruce Doern (ed.), *How Ottawa Spends Your Tax Dollars: Federal Priorities 1981* (Toronto: Lorimer, 1981).

Doern, G. Bruce and Phidd, Richard W., *Canadian Public Policy: Ideas, Structure, Process* (Toronto: Methuen, 1983).

Dosman, Edgar, *The National Interest: The Politics of Northern Development 1968-1975* (Toronto: McClelland and Stewart, 1975).

Engler, R., *The Brotherhood of Oil* (Chicago: University of Chicago Press, 1977).

Evans, Douglas, *Western Energy Policy: The Case for Competition* (London: Macmillan, 1978).

Foster, Peter, *The Sorcerer's Apprentices: Canada's Super-Bureaucrats and the Energy Mess* (Toronto: Collins, 1982).

————, *Other Peoples' Money* (Toronto: Collins, 1983).

Gray, Earle, *The Impact of Oil: The Development of Canadian Oil Resources* (Toronto: Ryerson Press, 1969).

————, *The Great Canadian Oil Patch* (Toronto: Maclean-Hunter, 1970).

Hamilton, R.G., "Natural Gas and Canadian Policy," in E. Erickson and L. Waverman (eds.), *The Energy Question: An International Failure of Policy* (Toronto: University of Toronto Press, 1974).

Hanson, E.J., *Dynamic Decade: The Evolution and Effects of the Oil Industry In Alberta* (Toronto: McClelland and Stewart, 1958).

Helliwell, John, "Impact of a Mackenzie Pipeline on the National Economy," in Peter H. Pearse (ed.), *The Mackenzie Pipeline: Arctic Gas and Canadian Energy Policy* (Toronto: McClelland and Stewart, 1974).

Hilborn, James (ed.), *Dusters and Gushers: The Canadian Oil and Gas Industry* (Toronto: Pit Publishing Co., 1968).

Hodgins, Barbara, *Where the Economy and the Constituion Meet in Canada* (Montreal: C.D. Howe Institute, 1981).

Hooker, C.A.; MacDonald, R.; Van Hulst, R.; and Victor, P., *Energy and the Quality of Life* (Toronto: University of Toronto Press, 1980).

Hunt, A.D. and Toombs, R.B., "Canadian Energy Policy and Federalism—Background Paper," in Livia M. Thur (ed.), *Energy Policy and Federalism* (Toronto: The Institute of Public Administration of Canada, 1981).

Irving, J.A., *The Social Credit Movement in Alberta* (Toronto: University of Toronto Press, 1959).

Kilbourn, William, *Pipeline: Trans-Canada and the Great Debate, A History of Business and Politics* (Toronto: Clark Irwin, 1970).

Lantzke, Ulf, "Summary and Conclusions," in *World Energy Outlook* (Paris:

International Energy Agency, 1982).

Laxer, James, *The Energy Poker Game: The Politics of the Continental Resource Deal* (Toronto: New Press, 1970).

———, *Canada's Energy Crisis* (Toronto: Lorimer, 1975).

———, *Oil and Gas* (Toronto: Lorimer, 1983).

Lucas, A.R., "The National Energy Board," in G. Bruce Doern (ed.), *The Regulatory Process in Canada* (Toronto: Macmillan, 1978).

Lucas, A.R. and Bell, Trevor, "The National Energy Board: Policy Procedure and Practice. (Ottawa: Law Reform Commission of Canada, 1977).

Lyon, J., *Dome: The Rise and Fall of the House that Jack Built* (Toronto: Macmillan of Canada, 1983).

Macpherson, C.B., "After Strange Gods: Canadian Political Science in 1973," in T.N. Guinsberg and G.L. Reuber (eds.), *Perspectives on the Social Sciences in Canada* (Toronto: University of Toronto Press, 1974).

———, *Democracy in Alberta: Social Credit and the Party System*, 2nd edit. (Toronto: University of Toronto Press, 1959).

Mallory, J.R., *Social Credit and the Federal Power in Canada* (Toronto: University of Toronto Press, 1962).

Maslove, Allan, "The Other Side of Public Spending: Tax Expenditures in Canada," in G. Bruce Doern and Allan Maslove (eds.), *The Public Evaluation of Government Spending* (Montreal: Institute for Research on Public Policy, 1979).

———, "Tax Expenditures, Tax Credits, and Equity," in G. Bruce Doern (ed.), *How Ottawa Spends Your Tax Dollars* (Toronto: Lorimer, 1981).

McDougall, I.A., *Marketing Canada's Energy* (Toronto: Lorimer, 1983).

McDougall, John N., *Fuels and the National Policy* (Toronto: Butterworths, 1982).

———, "Regulation Versus Politics: The National Energy Board and the Mackenzie Valley Pipeline," in Andrew Axline et al. (eds.), *Continental Community: Independence and Integration in North America* (Toronto: McClelland and Stewart, 1974).

Morton, W.L., *The Progressive Party in Canada* (Toronto: University of Toronto Press, 1962).

Nelles, H.V., "Canadian Energy Policy 1945–1980: A Federalist Perspective," in R. Kenneth Carty and W. Peter Ward (eds.), *Entering the Eighties: Canada in Crisis* (Toronto: Oxford University Press, 1980).

———, *The Politics of Development: Forests, Mines and Hydro-Electric Power in Ontario* (Toronto: Macmillan, 1974).

Odell, Peter R., *Oil and World Power*, 7th edit. (London: Penguin, 1983).

Panitch, Leo, "The Role and Nature of the Canadian State," in Leo Panitch (ed.), *The Canadian State: Political Economy and Political Power* (Toronto: University of Toronto Press, 1977).

Pratt, Larry, *The Tar Sands: Syncrude and the Politics of Oil* (Edmonton: Hurtig, 1976).

_____, "Petro-Canada," in Allan Tupper and G. Bruce Doern (eds.), *Public Corporations and Public Policy in Canada* (Montreal: Institute for Research on Public Policy, 1981).

_____, "Petro-Canada: Tool for Energy Security or Instrument of Economic Development," in G. Bruce Doern (ed.), *How Ottawa Spends Your Tax Dollars: National Policy and Economic Development 1982* (Toronto: Lorimer, 1982).

Richards, John and Pratt, Larry, *Prairie Capitalism: Power and Influence in the New West* (Toronto: McClelland and Stewart, 1979).

Sampson Anthony, *The Seven Sisters* (London: Coronet, 1980).

Scott, Anthony, ed., *Natural Resource Revenues: A Test of Federalism* (Vancouver: University of British Columbia Press, 1976).

Shaffer, Ed, *Canada's Oil and the American Empire* (Edmonton: Hurtig, 1983).

Simpson, Jeffrey, *Discipline of Power* (Toronto: Personal Library, 1980).

Smiley, Donald, *Canada in Question: Federalism in the Eighties*, 3rd edit. (Toronto: McGraw-Hill, Ryerson, 1980).

Smith, David E., "Western Politics and National Unity," in David Jay Bercusson (ed.), *Canada and the Burden of Unity* (Toronto: Macmillan, 1977).

Smith, P., *The Treasure Seekers: The Men Who Built Home Oil* (Toronto: Macmillan, 1978).

Stevenson, D.W., "Energy Issues Facing Canada: Three Perspectives," in Livia M. Thur (ed.), *Energy Policy and Federalism* (Toronto: The Institute of Public Administration of Canada, 1981).

Stevenson, Garth, "Federalism and the Political Economy of the Canadian State," in Leo Panitch (ed.), *The Canadian State: Political Economy and Political Power* (Toronto: University of Toronto Press, 1977).

Toner, Glen, "Oil, Gas, and Integration: A Review of Five Major Energy Decisions," in Jon Pammett and Brian Tomlin (eds.), *The Integration Question: Political Economy and Public Policy in Canada and North America* (Toronto: Addison-Wesley, 1984).

Toner, Glen and Bregha, François, "The Political Economy of Energy," in M.S. Whittington and Glen Williams (eds.), *Canadian Politics in the 1980s*, 2nd edit. (Toronto: Methuen, 1984).

Voyer, Roger, *Offshore Oil.* (Toronto: Lorimer, 1983).

Waverman, L., "The Reluctant Bride: Canadian–American Energy Relations," in E. Erickson and L. Waverman (eds.), *The Energy Question: An International Failure of Policy*, vol. 2 (Toronto: University of Toronto Press, 1974).

Journal Articles and Papers

Adelman, M.A., "The International Context," in Edward A. Carmichael and C. Herrera, eds., *Canada's Energy Policy: 1985 and Beyond* (Toronto: C.D.

Howe Institute, 1984), pp. 17–37.

Baldwin, John R., "Federal Regulation and Public Policy in the Canadian Petroleum Industry: 1958–1975," *Journal of Business Administration*, 13:1–2, 1982, pp. 57–97.

Ballim, John B., "The Energy Crunch and Constitutional Reform," *The Canadian Bar Review*, vol. 57 (1979), pp. 740–756.

———, "Oil and Gas Under the New Constitution," Inaugural Lecture delivered to the official opening of the Canadian Institute of Resources Law, Calgary, Alberta, December 2, 1982.

Berry, G.R., "The Oil Lobby and the Energy Crisis," *Canadian Public Administration* 17:4, 1974, pp. 600–636.

Bregha, François, "Arctic Pilot Project: CARC's Memorandum to Cabinet," *Northern Perspectives*, 10:2, April–May 1982.

Clarke, Harold; Jenson, Jane; Leduc, Larry; and Pammett, Jon, "Voting Behavior and the Outcome of the 1979 Federal Election: the Impact of Leaders and Issues," *Canadian Journal of Political Science*, XV:3, September 1982, pp. 517–552.

Doern, G. Bruce, "The Mega-Project Episode and the Formulation of Canadian Economic Development Policy," *Canadian Public Administration*, 26:2. Summer 1983, pp. 219–238.

Douglas, G.W. and MacMillan, J.A., *Alsands Energy Ltd., Economic Impact Study* (Calgary: Canadian Energy Research Institute, June 1981).

Eglington, Peter, "Historical Notes on Canada's Energy Industries," Mimeo, Ottawa, 1982.

Eglinton, Peter and Ufflemann, Maris, *An Economic Analysis of Oilsands Policy in Canada–The Case of Alsands and Wolfe Lake*, Discusion paper no. 259 (Ottawa: Economic Council of Canada, 1984).

———, *An Economic Analysis of the Venture Development Project and Hibernia*, Discussion paper no. 261 (Ottawa: Economic Council of Canada, 1984).

Feick, John F., "Prospects for the Development of Mineable Oil Sands," *Canadian Public Policy*, IX:3, September 1983, pp. 297–303.

Helliwell, John, "Canadian Energy Policy," *Annual Review of Energy: 1979*, no. 4, pp. 175–229.

Helliwell, John and McRae, Robert N., "The National Energy Conflict," *Canadian Public Policy*, 7:1, 1981, pp. 14–23.

———, "Resolving the National Energy Conflict: From the National Energy Program to the Energy Agreements," *Canadian Public Policy*, 8:1, 1982, pp. 15–23.

———, "Arctic Pipelines in the Context of Canadian Energy Requirements," *Canadian Public Policy*, 3:3, 1977, pp. 344–354.

Helliwell, John; MacGregor, M.E.; and Plourde, A., "The National Energy Program Meets Falling World Oil Prices," *Canadian Public Policy*, IX:3, September 1983, p. 294.

Henbest, Bruce. "Making Energy Legislation: The Role of Political Parties, the Public Service and Interest Groups in the Parliamentary Stage of the Canadian Policy Making Process," Masters Thesis, Department of Political Science, Carleton University, Ottawa, 1983.

Horwich, George and Weimer, David, "The Next Oil Shock—Giving the Market a Chance?" *Regulation*, March–April 1984, pp. 16–24.

McDougall, Ian. "The Canadian National Energy Board: Economic 'Jurisprudence' in the National Interest or Symbolic Reassurance?" *Alberta Law Review*, 22, 1973, pp. 327–82.

McDougall, John N. "Prebuild Phase or Latest Phase? The United States Fuel Market and Canadian Energy Policy," *International Journal*, 36:1, 1981, pp. 117–138.

Murphy, Larry J., "Adapting Canadian Energy Policy to Changing World Energy Trends," *Canadian Business Review*, Spring 1983, pp. 32–39.

Pratt, Larry. "Energy: Roots of National Policy," *Studies in Political Economy*, 7, Winter 1982, pp. 27–60.

Richards, John. "Review of *Fuels and the National Policy*," *Canadian Journal of Political Science*, 16:3, September 1983, p. 20.

Robinson, John B., "Pendulum Policy: Natural Gas Forecasts and Canadian Energy Policy 1969–1981," *Canadian Journal of Political Science*, XVI:2, June 1983, pp. 299–320.

Scarfe, Brian, "The National Energy Program after Three Years: An Economic Perspective" (Edmonton: University of Alberta,1984).

Scarfe, Brian L. and Wilkinson, Bruce. "The New Energy Agreement: An Economic Perspective." Revised Edition of a Paper presented to the Ontario Economic Council Outlook and Issues Conference, October 28, 1981.

Steward, Gillian. "Southern Discomfort: How Canadian Oilmen Lost Their Shirts in the U.S.," *Energy*, October, 1983, pp. 73–74.

Tussing, Arlon R. "An OPEC Obituary," *The Public Interest*, no. 70, Winter 1983, pp. 3–21.

Warrack, Allan, *The Alberta Heritage Savings Trust Fund: An Historical Evaluation*, Paper prepared for the Economic Council of Canada, October 1982.

Government Documents

Alberta, *Energy Issues for the People of Alberta*, December 1980.

Alberta, *Harmony in Diversity: A New Federalism for Canada*, Position Paper on Constitutional Change, 1978.

Berger, Thomas, *Northern Frontier, Northern Homeland*, Report of the Mackenzie Valley Pipeline Inquiry, vol. 1 (Ottawa: Supply and Services, 1977).

Canada, Department of Energy, Mines and Resources, *Canadian Petroleum Industry: 1979 Monitoring Survey* (Ottawa: Supply and Services, 1980).

Canada, Department of Energy, Mines and Resources, "Do Governments Take Too Much? An Examiniation of Pre- and Post-NEP Fiscal Regimes" (Ottawa: EMR, 1983).

Canada, Department of Energy, Mines and Resources, *An Energy Policy for Canada—Phase 2*, vol. 1 "Analysis" (Ottawa: Information Canada, 1973).

Canada, Department of Energy, Mines and Resources, *An Energy Strategy for Canada: Politics for Self-Reliance* (Ottawa: Supply and Services, 1976).

Canada, Department of Energy, Mines and Resources, *The National Energy Program* (Ottawa: Supply and Services, October, 1980).

Canada, Department of Energy, Mines and Resources, *The National Energy Program: Update 1982* (Ottawa: Supply and Services, 1982).

Canada, Department of Finance, *Federal–Provincial Resource Taxation Review* (Ottawa: Department of Finance, 1978).

Canada, Director of Investigation and Research Branch, Combines Investigation Act, *The State of Competition in the Canadian Petroleum Industry*, vols. 1–7 (Ottawa: Supply and Services, 1981).

Canada, The Major Projects Task Force on Major Capital Projects in Canada to the Year 2000, *Major Canadian Projects: Major Canadian Opportunities* (Ottawa: Supply and Services, June 1981).

Canada, Ministry of State for Economic Development, *Economic Development for Canada in the 1980s* (Ottawa: Supply and Services, November 1981).

Canada, National Energy Board, *Reasons for Decision: Northern Pipeline* (Ottawa: Supply and Services, 1977).

Canada, Petroleum Monitoring Agency, *Canadian Petroleum Industry: 1980 Monitoring Survey* (Ottawa: Supply and Services, 1981).

Canada, Royal Commission on Canada's Economic Prospects, *Final Report* (Ottawa: Queen's Printer, 1957).

Canada, Royal Commission on Energy, *First and Second Reports* (Ottawa: Queen's Printer, 1958).

Economic Council of Canada, *Strategy for Energy Policy* (Ottawa: Supply and Services Canada, 1984).

Geological Survey of Canada, *Oil and Natural Gas Resources of Canada 1983* (Ottawa: Energy, Mines and Resources Canada, 1984), p. 1.

Report of the Petrochemical Industry Task Force, Report to the Minister of Regional and Industrial Expansion (Ottawa: Supply and Services Canada, February 1984).

Senate of Canada, *Marching to the Beat of the Same Drum: Transportation of Petroleum and Natural Gas North of 60°*, Report of the Special Committee on the Northern Pipeline (Ottawa: Supply and Services, March 1983).

INDEX